ISBN 978-1-5280-8420-8
PIBN 10144869

HISTORY OF

COINAGE AND CURRENCY

IN THE UNITED STATES

AND THE PERENNIAL

CONTEST FOR SOUND MONEY

BY

A. BARTON HEPBURN, LL.D.

EX-COMPTROLLER OF THE CURRENCY, EX-SUPERINTENDENT
OF BANKING DEPARTMENT OF THE STATE OF NEW
YORK, VICE-PRESIDENT CHASE NATIONAL BANK

New York

THE MACMILLAN COMPANY

LONDON: MACMILLAN & CO., LTD.

1903

This Volume is inscribed to the Memory of

ALEXANDER HAMILTON

*Patriot, Soldier, Financier, Statesman, Creative
Genius. In the dawn of our national life, without guiding precedent, he evolved principles and
developed systems of inestimable and lasting value*

PREFACE

"OF making many books there is no end," and yet this volume seems to possess features which justify its creation. The general subject of this history has, in its different phases, been treated by many authors; but I believe there is no one work of convenient size and popular character covering the history of the coinage and currency of the United States, with data and details in chronological order, available as a book of reference. The crucial questions relating to coinage and currency which have involved the material and political interests of the country so largely throughout its history, and especially for the past quarter of a century, and the honest difference which many people have experienced in reaching right conclusions, demonstrate the present need of such a work. Most important currency questions remain to be solved, and this volume seeks to furnish a busy public, in convenient form, the experience of the past to aid in such solution.

The aim has been to place before the reader original data, so as to enable him to examine the same and reach his own conclusions. A documentary history pure and simple would be so voluminous as to possess little value save to the student and economist. A narrative history would amount to a treatise embodying largely

·the opinions and conclusions of the author. This volume seeks to combine the two, and in the text recites events and gives dates and data with painstaking care, in order to make it convenient and available for purposes of reference, while the Appendix contains the laws of the United States relating to the subject and such documents as are of paramount importance. The chapter on bibliography aims to review the standard literature of the subject and indicate its character, thus enabling any one to pursue, easily and intelligently, any particular branch or feature to as great length as may be desired.

The tables and statistical matter with which this work is replete have been prepared by, or verified by, Maurice L. Muhleman, formerly connected with the Treasury Department at Washington, and for so many years Deputy Assistant Treasurer in the city of New York. Mr. Muhleman is one of the ablest statisticians in the country, and upon all matters relating to finance is an expert and recognized authority. I take pleasure in acknowledging my very great obligation to him in the preparation of this work.

CONTENTS

INTRODUCTORY

PART II

THE PERIOD FROM 1861 TO 1890

I. THE UNITED STATES LEGAL TENDER NOTES

CHAPTER VIII. 1861 TO 1865

CHAPTER IX. 1866 TO 1875

III. THE NATIONAL BANKING SYSTEM

CHAPTER XIV. 1861 TO 1875

CHAPTER XV. 1876 TO 1882

CHAPTER XVI. 1883 TO 1890

PART III

FROM 1891 TO THE PRESENT DAY

SILVER CONTEST OF 1896

CHAPTER XVII. 1891 TO 1896

NATIONAL SOUND MONEY LEAGUE

(*NON-PARTISAN*)

JOHN K. COWEN, Baltimore, *President*

A. B. HEPBURN, Vice-President Chase National Bank, 83 Cedar Street, New York, *Treasurer and General Secretary*

Executive Committee

Geo. Foster Peabody, New York, *Chairman.*

M. E. Ingalls, Cincinnati, Ohio.

J. Kennedy Tod, New York.

H. P. Robinson, Chicago, Ill.

John B. Jackson, Pittsburg, Pa.

J. K. Cowen, Baltimore, Md.

James L. Blair, St. Louis, Mo.

Louis R. Ehrich, Colorado Springs, Colo.

Alternates

J. C. Schmidlapp, Cincinnati, Ohio.

A. E. Willson, Louisville, Ky.

A. B. Kittredge, Sioux Falls, S.D.

E. P. Wells, Jamestown, N.D.

W. H. Dunwoody, Minneapolis, Minn.

F. C. Winkler, Milwaukee, Wis.

J. W. Norwood, Wilmington, N.C.

William F. Ladd, Galveston, Texas.

Henry Hentz, New York.

Vice-Presidents

R. H. Clarke, Mobile, Ala.

Morris M. Cohn, Little Rock, Ark.

Donald Y. Campbell, San Francisco, Cal.

Platt Rogers, Denver, Colo.

N. G. Osborn, New Haven, Conn.

H. S. DuPont, Winterthur, near Montchanin, Del.

Henry G. Turner, Quitman, Ga.

John V. Farwell, Jr., Chicago, Ill.

Lucius B. Swift, Indianapolis, Ind.

W. W. Witmer, Des Moines, Iowa.

E. N. Morrill, Hiawatha, Kansas.

J. C. Morris, New Orleans, La.

Charles F. Libby, Portland, Maine.

Henry A. Parr, Baltimore, Md.

Edward Atkinson, Boston, Mass.

Edwin F. Conely, Detroit, Mich.

Thomas Wilson, St. Paul, Minn.

Addison Croft, Holly Springs, Miss.

James L. Blair, St. Louis, Mo.

Wilbur F. Sanders, Helena, Mont.

J. Sterling Morton, Nebraska City, Neb.

F. C. Faulkner, Keene, N.H.

John Kean, Elizabeth, N.J.

William C. Cornwell, Buffalo, N.Y.

William A. Blair, Winston, N.C.

J. M. Devine, La Moure, N.D.

Virgil P. Kline, Cleveland, Ohio.

A. J. Seay, Kingfisher, Oklahoma.

M. C. George, Portland, Oregon.

John B. Jackson, Pittsburg, Pa.

William B. Weeden, Providence, R.I.

George B. Edwards, Charleston, S.C.

Joseph F. Campbell, Galveston, Tex.

Charles W. Woodhouse, Burlington, Vermont.

W. L. Royall, Richmond, Va.

L. S. Howlett, N. Yakima, Washington.

Alfred Caldwell, Wheeling, W.Va.

F. G. Bigelow, Milwaukee, Wis.

Joseph M. Carey, Cheyenne, Wyo.

THE present organization of the *N*ational Sound Money League sufficiently appears, so far as its officers and principal committee are concerned, upon the preceding page.

The principal and most pointed issue upon which the Republican and Democratic parties were decidedly at variance in the campaign of 1896 is comprehended in the one word " tariff." The Republican party intended that the presidential contest of that year should be fought out on the question of protection. William McKinley, the champion of protection, was the leading aspirant and, subsequently, received the Republican nomination for the Presidency. The money question, however, could not be side-tracked. The St. Louis Convention, in very guarded language, favored the gold standard. Many distinguished members of that party, characterized as Silver Republicans, thereupon withdrew from the convention. It became apparent immediately that the question of the gold or silver standard would predominate among the issues in the ensuing campaign. The luke-warm support of the Republican party, as represented by its public speakers and the party press, placed the sound money cause at a very great disadvantage in comparison with the militant, aggressive, and, we may say, brilliant advocacy of the cause of silver by the opposition. It was very apparent that a proper advocacy of the gold standard and a proper distribution of sound money literature would not emanate from the regular Republican organization. The silver element in the party was very strong, and political leaders were disposed to placate and conciliate, rather than combat their position. The silver propaganda had for a long time been flooding the country with data and documents in advocacy of their cause, the press of the country being largely utilized for this purpose. In order that the friends of the gold standard might triumph in the contest, it was necessary that a campaign of education be inaugurated and that periodicals and documents properly discussing and presenting the subject be placed within the reach of the voters, in order to enable them to reach a proper conclusion and exercise an intelligent judgment. This view presented itself very clearly to Mr. Henry Villard, and he was instrumental in effecting an association of prominent men, mainly Sound Money Democrats, for the purpose of reaching the general public with non-partisan literature. A very large proportion of the Democratic party were disposed to, and did, ignore party lines and voted for the Republican candidate, solely on account of the money issue, believing that question to be of such paramount importance that they could well afford, at least temporarily, to forego their opposition to certain tenets and principles of the Republican party to which they were opposed.

While the contest resulted in the election of William McKinley, his past record on the silver question was a source of great anxiety to the friends of sound money, and it was believed to be very important to surround him and his administration with the strongest possible influence in favor of the gold standard. It was believed to be very important to continue a campaign of education upon this subject. Therefore, what had been an association during the contest of 1896 was perfected into a permanent organization by the creation of the National Sound Money League, with a constitution, by-laws, etc. A meeting for such purpose was held in the rooms of the New York Chamber of Commerce on Friday, February 5, 1897. Among others present were, Charles S. Fairchild, A. B. Hepburn, Joseph Larocque, Isidor Straus, Henry Hentz, Spencer Trask, J. Kennedy Tod, Charles J. Canda, E. V. Smalley, Gustav H. Schwab, Henry Villard, Robert Maclay, Horace White, A. S. Heidelbach, L. J. Callanan, George Foster Peabody, George H. Putnam, Simon Stern, and W. J. Schieffelin. A letter was read from Mr. H. H. Hanna, endorsing the organization. Mr. Hentz was elected Chairman of the meeting. Mr. E. V. Smalley explained the object of the meeting, outlined the work that had been done in the past and what was proposed to be done in the future. The following committee on permanent organization was appointed : Alexander E. Orr, A. B. Hepburn, Gustav H. Schwab, J. Kennedy Tod, W. J. Schieffelin, Isidor Straus, and Henry Hentz. E. V. Smalley was appointed Secretary. The organization was fully perfected on February 24, 1897. Delegates were present from most of the states in the Union. Mr. George E. Leighton, St. Louis, was elected President; A. B. Hepburn, New York, Treasurer; and E. V. Smalley, St. Paul, Secretary. The objects of the League were declared to be "*the continuance of the efforts made during the presidential campaign of 1896 for national honor and sound money, and the education of the people to a realization of the necessity for maintaining the gold standard.*"

Fully realizing the prejudice in the popular mind against everything upon the money question which emanated from the vicinity of Wall Street, it was determined to open the main office of the League in Chicago, with a branch in New York. It was also " Resolved, that the General Secretary is hereby authorized to issue a monthly publication, in small newspaper form, from the headquarters of the League in Chicago, to be called the *N*ational Sound *M* oney League Bulletin, to be mailed regularly to all members of the League," the contents of the bulletin to be mainly original and selected articles on the money question. This bulletin was mailed to the country press generally in the hope that the data and articles it furnished would be made use of by them. It was also mailed to an extensive list of people throughout the country, whose names were furnished by the local officers and representatives of the League as men who would profit by its reception and make good use of the same. The League at frequent intervals issued addresses, which were a comprehensive review of the situation and which were distributed in the form of documents. An especial acknowledgment is due to the literary men of the country for the cheerfulness with which they responded to requests for original articles for publication and distribution. Among those not officially connected with the League may be mentioned Hon. George E. Roberts, of Iowa, now Director of the *M* int; William Dodsworth, editor of the New York *Journal of Commerce*; Horace White, editor of the New York *Evening Post*; and A. B. Stickney, of *M* innesota. The officers and the Executive Committee of the League were especially helpful in this respect.

On *M* arch 23, 1898, the Hon. J. Sterling *M* orton, of *N*ebraska, became President, succeeding George E. Leighton; A. B. Hepburn, New York, was reëlected Treasurer; C. L. Hutchinson, Chicago, Associate Treasurer; and E. V. Smalley, St. Paul, was reëlected Secretary. The following Executive Committee was elected: J. Kennedy Tod, of New York; H. P. Robinson, of Chicago; Edwin Burritt Smith, of Chicago; John B Jackson, of Pittsburg; J. K. Cowen, of Baltimore; *M*. E. Ingalls, of Cincinnati; James L. Blair, of St. Louis; and Louis R. Ehrich, of Colorado Springs.

The Secretary's report of *M* arch 28, 1899, among other things, says: —

"The formidable movement for opening the *M* int to the free coinage of silver, at the obsolete ratio of 16 to 1 with gold, has been steadily declining since its defeat at the presidential election of 1896. The state elections of last fall showed enormous changes on this question in the states where the movement for lowering the money standard had been most active and successful. The masses of voters who gave an enthusiastic support to the Chicago platform only three years ago, now show no interest in the silver question, and only in the South is there at present any demand in the public press that it be revived as a leading issue in the next presidential campaign. The League may fairly claim some credit for the remarkable change of opinion on the money question shown by returns of the elections of last year in the Western states. Our publications were widely distributed by local committees in all those states, and they furnished facts and arguments which were used by the sound money speakers. Our paper has proven a very effective means for disseminating sound money ideas. In October last a National Currency Convention was held at Omaha, Nebraska, on the grounds of the Trans-Mississippi Exposition, under a call issued by the League and under the management of the officers of the League. Advocates of all phases of opinion concerning the currency of the country attended the convention and took part in an open debate. The meetings occupied three days, and all were attended by large audiences. The debates were printed in the newspapers and stimulated thought and discussion on money problems all over the West, and the general effect was, no doubt, to make decisive the sound money victories won about a month later in the Western state elections."

There was no change in the officers of the League for the year 1899 save that George Foster Peabody was elected a member of the Executive Committee and M. E. Ingalls was made Chairman. Mr. Peabody later succeeded Mr. Ingalls as Chairman.

On March 29, 1900, J. K. Cowen, of Baltimore, was elected President, to succeed J. Sterling Morton; A. B. Hepburn was reëlected Treasurer and elected General Secretary, to succeed E. V. Smalley, deceased.

The men who organized this League easily foresaw that the issues involved in a controversy over the standard of value would extend over a period of years, and necessarily enter into the presidential campaign of 1900. With wise foresight, the managers of the League at that time secured agreements from prominent men and business firms to pay a certain amount per annum for the period of four years. This secured to the League an annual income of a very considerable amount, and enabled it to plan and execute its work intelligently and efficaciously and free from financial embarrassment.

The trend of events throughout the world has probably settled, in favor of gold. the question of the standard of values. The Act of March 14, 1900, a square declaration in favor of the gold standard in this country, was, and is, the occasion of much gratification and rejoicing to every believer in sound finance and every well-wisher of his country's prosperity. The Sound Money League may well congratulate the country upon the result, and at the same time congratulate themselves in having borne an honorable and efficient part in the accomplishment of this glorious result. Since the declared object of the League was the "education of the people to a realization of the necessity for maintaining the gold standard," it may fairly be said that the object being accomplished, there is no necessity for continuing the organization. It has seemed, therefore, that the labors of the organization could be rounded out and completed in no better or more satisfactory manner than by the expenditure of what money remains in the treasury in the distribution to public and collegiate libraries of a history of the sound money controversy in the United States from the organization of the government down to date. A history of this controversy, in its various phases, subsequent to the Continental currency of Colonial times, showing the evolution of our coinage and currency systems, with original documents and data which will enable a student or inquirer to make an examination of the facts and conditions upon which action was predicated, and reach his own conclusions thereupon, is believed to be most desirable. We regard this volume as such a history, and present it in the hope and belief that by so doing we contribute to the cause of sound money and good finance.

The declared purpose of the National Sound Money League was academic in its character. and its labors were educational. By adopting this course in bringing our labors to a close, we adhere to the spirit and purpose of our undertaking.

JOHN. K. COWEN,
President of the National Sound Money League.

GEORGE FOSTER PEABODY,
Chairman of the Executive Committee.

CONTEST FOR SOUND MONEY

INTRODUCTORY CHAPTER

OUR laws with reference to paper currency have
been largely influenced by the distribution of governmental authority peculiar to the United States, and
entirely separate and distinct interests have thereby
been brought in antagonism to the adoption of the
most desirable currency system.

For eighty-five years after the Declaration of Inde- Economic
pendence the United States as a nation was in a forma- problems at
Nation's
tive period. The thirteen colonies had organized a birth.
confederacy to resist oppression from abroad, but with
insufficient and ill-defined powers, and as soon as they
had fought to a successful issue and been recognized
as an independent nation, they began to be jealous and
distrustful of the powers which must necessarily be
given to the general government in order to form a permanent nation. Oppressive debt, disorganized business
and depreciated currency presented grave economic
problems for solution, at a time when the greater and
graver problem of creating a government, based upon
the consent of the governed, evidenced by popular suffrage, must first be solved, in order that it might in
turn bring order, credit and prosperity out of existing
chaos. The colonies were held together by the co-
hesive force of self-preservation in presence of the arms
of a powerful and aggressive foe. This pressure once
removed, the tendency toward separate action and asser-

B   ʳ

tion of individual interests on the part of the colonies became pronounced.

Local politi-cal jealousy.   Tenacious of their liberties, the people were greatly impressed with possible danger from an arbitrary exercise of power on the part of a central government, and in framing the Constitution, the powers of the several states were subordinated to the national government with halting jealousy and only where deemed indispensable. The Nation was thus started with a dual sovereignty. The citizens owed allegiance to the states in which they lived as well as to the Nation, and the respects in which each was paramount were as to many questions left in the realm of debate. Seven of the original thirteen states accompanied their ratification of the Constitution with proposed amendments, and many states seemed to regard its obligations lightly. Withdrawal from the Union was freely discussed as an alternative and by no means impossible remedy for unsatisfactory treatment.

The State Rights doctrine.   In 1798, Kentucky, roused by its opposition to the alien and sedition laws passed by Congress, adopted resolutions, among other things, reciting that the government was created by a compact among the states and " was not made the exclusive or final judge of the extent of the powers delegated to itself, but that, as in all other cases of compact among powers having no common judge, each party has an equal right to judge for itself as well of infraction as of the mode and measure of redress." Virginia passed similar resolutions in 1799. In other states similar doctrines were at times proclaimed.

If the House of Representatives, the Senate, and the President concur as to an act of legislation, it becomes a law. If any question as to its constitutionality arises, the theory of the Constitution is that such question is to be determined by the Supreme Court, thus making four separate parties whose concurrence is necessary before a law becomes final and binding beyond question. The Kentucky resolutions sought to introduce a fifth party and assert that each state as a party to the compact of federation may determine for itself the limitation of power which the general government possesses.

This doctrine, in all its refinement, culminated in the nullification ordinance adopted by South Carolina in November, 1832, in which it declared the United States tariff law "null and void, and no law, nor binding on this state, its officers, or citizens," and no duties were to be paid in that state and no appeal to the Supreme Court of the United States was to be permitted. The energetic determination of President Jackson to enforce the law, coupled with the "Clay Compromise," a modification of some of the law's most objectionable provisions, deferred but did not settle the constitutional issues involved. Nullificatior 1832.

The status of slavery in the Constitution was the occasion of prolonged controversy; and as finally settled, the importation of slaves could not be prohibited for twenty years, and three-fifths of the slave population was to be counted in determining the basis of representation of the several states in Congress and in the Electoral College. Each state was given two senators, and representatives were apportioned according to population. The number of votes to which each state is entitled in the Electoral College, which chooses the President and Vice-president, is equal to its congressional representation, that is, its senators and representatives combined. Allowing three-fifths of the slave population, while not enjoying the suffrage, to be counted in determining the representative population, gave to the white population of the slave-holding states a preponderating influence in national affairs which was Influence of slavery.

bound to provoke controversy. In laying the foundation of the Nation, the framers of the Constitution also
laid the foundation of an irrepressible conflict, and the
opposition to slavery which found expression in the
constitutional debates was continued with growing intensity, but as a moral rather than political question.
Its abolition in the northern states, owing very largely
to climatic conditions, as well as for ethical reasons,
made the question of slavery a sectional one.

Missouri Com-promise.

The first pronounced conflict arose over the admission
of Missouri as a state in 1818–1819. It was admitted in
1821 as a slave state, after the " Missouri Compromise "
(Act of March 2, 1820) had provided that slavery should
forever be excluded from all territory west of Missouri
and north of 36° 30' north latitude (the southern boundary of the state). In 1846 the " Wilmot Proviso," an
amendment to an act appropriating money with which
to purchase territory from the government of Mexico,
proposed to exclude slavery and involuntary servitude
forever from all territory so acquired. It was adopted
by the House, but later reconsidered and defeated. This
episode marked the formation of a political party, whose
avowed and direct purpose was to prevent the extension
of slavery in the territories of the United States. Their
propaganda was followed by a powerful and continuous
onslaught upon the institution of slavery upon moral
and religious grounds, and created a strong sentiment
in favor of its abolition, which ultimately became
effective.

Narrow con-struction of Constitution.

Slavery, involving enormous property interests, depended for protection upon the several state governments, and this fact all along gave to the doctrine of
state rights and " state sovereignty " its principal element of strength. The power given the general government under the Constitution was rigidly construed,

circumscribed within the narrowest limits, and any attempt at liberal construction or enlargement with reference to any subject was tenaciously fought by the champions of state rights. All efforts by the general government to regulate banking and currency, encountered this opposition in all its virulence as well as that of the state bank interests.

The preservation of the Union is traceable to the fact that the National or Federal party controlled the councils of government during its earlier years. In this connection too much praise cannot be bestowed upon the genius and statesmanship of Hamilton, the judicial wisdom and statesmanship of Marshall. It will appear in the following history that whenever national sentiment and national influence have moulded legislation and controlled the general government, enhanced prosperity ensued; witness the periods of the first and second United States banks and that of the national banking system. Whenever the disintegrating influence involved in the doctrine of "state sovereignty" has been paramount, adverse conditions have prevailed; witness the period following the expiration of the charter of the first United States Bank (1811) until the second bank was well under way, and the period between the expiration of the charter of the second bank (1836) and the creation of the national banking system (1863).

Nationalization and prosperity.

The right of secession and the doctrine of state sovereignty as it had been proclaimed, as well as slavery itself, were buried and the permanency of the Union, the paramountcy of the general government, proclaimed as the verdict of the Civil War (1861–1865). Spurred by "military necessity" and against its declared conviction as to its constitutional power, Congress asserted in 1862 the national sovereignty with reference to the currency question by issuing legal

Nationalism triumphs.

tender notes. In order to meet current liabilities Congress issued and used in paying such indebtedness, notes reading on the face " The United States will pay the bearer —— dollars," and on the back " This note is a legal tender at its face value for all debts public and private except duties on imports and interest on the public debt." These notes, in addition to paying the current indebtedness of the government, went into general circulation as money and have since formed an important portion of our circulating medium.

Confirmed by Supreme Court.

After having the question before it for the third time, by instalments, as it were, the Supreme Court decided that Congress had the power to issue full legal tender notes at any and all times in its discretion, and by inference decided that all sovereign powers pertaining to government were reposed in Congress except where specially prohibited. This decision was reached in 1884 after nearly a century of national existence.

Currency system still affected by antagonism.

The faults of our currency system after the establishment of the national banks and the assaults upon the principles of sound finance continuing in various forms up to the close of the presidential election in 1900, symbolize the same contending policies which had existed prior to the Civil War. It seems strange, while all recognized the desirability of having the coinage regulated by the central government, so much so that the power was given exclusively to Congress in the Constitution, thus insuring uniformity throughout the Nation, that there should not have been an equal desire to have the paper currency regulated by the same central authority and thus likewise made uniform and good throughout the length and breadth of the land. Such, indeed, was the design of Hamilton and Marshall; but the matter having been left in doubt in the organic law the contrary doctrine became ascendant when political exigencies involved the question, and the regulation of paper currency was for years left to the different states.

There is always difficulty in changing existing conditions when by so doing you disturb vested interests and interfere with established business. Precedent and habit are important factors in public as well as private affairs. But the failure earlier to appreciate and adopt a national system of paper currency can only be explained by the jealous desire on the part of the states to minimize the powers of the general government.

Whether it be a great university, a great industrial enterprise or a great nation, successful conduct and maximum development depend upon efficient, intelligent central control. The unity of the Nation, the paramount sovereign powers of the central government over all questions except as clearly limited by the Constitution, have been settled by force of arms, by public sentiment, by law and judicial interpretation.

Naught but a national currency will now be tolerated. Such a currency we have, and the problem is to improve the system upon lines requisite to give the greatest measure of utility possible and make the currency in fact what it is in theory, the handmaiden of commerce and the cornerstone of prosperity. The experience of the past yields present wisdom and future guidance. The experience of the colonies and the states presents the money question as affecting individuals and government in every conceivable phase. Sound principle and false theory are wrought out in the fierce fires of controversy and proved or disproved by the severe test of experience, and yield their lessons of value for all charged with the duty and responsibility of citizenship.

Sound money means money made of (or unquestionably redeemable in) a commodity which has a stable value in the markets of the world independent of fiat.

Nationalization indispensable.

What is
sound
money ?

Sound money as applied to coin means money wherein the commercial value of the bullion equals its coinage value. Sound money as applied to paper or token money of any kind means that which is redeemable in money wherein the commercial value of its bullion equals its coinage value.

The term " sound money " doubtless originated from the auricular test commonly applied to coins. The counter or other convenient surface offering an opportunity, the coin is dropped thereon, and its quality depends upon whether the resulting ring possesses the true sound or not.

The test of sound money varies with different periods, and is determined by varying conditions. It has, however, a general significance easily understood, is concise, cogent, and seems to have found a permanent place in our economic literature.

PART ONE

PERIOD PRECEDING THE CIVIL WAR

I. THE COINAGE SYSTEM

CHAPTER I

1776 TO 1789

THE American colonies, prior to the confederation in 1778, had almost as many systems of money as there were distinct colonies. Inasmuch as the majority of the inhabitants were of British birth and traded chiefly with the mother country and with each other, the monetary units were in some measure similar, although, as frequently occurs in colonies, the money of account imposed by the mother country differed from the money in actual use.

The colonies generally reckoned in pounds, shillings and pence, but in actual transactions other coins, chiefly the Spanish dollar and its subdivisions, constituted the medium of exchange. The gold coins in use other than British pieces were the French guinea and pistole, the Portuguese moidore and johannes or "joe," the Spanish doubloon and pistole. Silver coins in circulation other than British were the French crowns and livres and the Spanish pieces, the latter being, as before stated, most prevalent.[1]

The people were naturally compelled to find an equivalence between the money of account and that of exchange, and hence the practice of reckoning the dollar at so many shillings obtained. The valuation varied in

---

[1] MS. Reports, Committee on Finance, Continental Congress, Vol. 26; reprinted in International Monetary Conference, 1878, p. 422.

Rating of the dollar and "shillings." different colonies. In what is known as New England and in Virginia the dollar was six shillings; in New York and in North Carolina it was valued at eight shillings; in Georgia at five; in South Carolina at thirty-two and one-half; and in the remaining four colonies at seven and one-half.[1]

The "shillings" here referred to evidently differed in value and were not in fact the English shillings, for it is declared in a law of Massachusetts of 1750 (23d George II., Chapter V.)[2] that the value of the English shilling was equal to one and one-third of the Massachusetts shillings. The "shillings" of most of the other colonies must have been worth much less, therefore, in English coin. The established rate of exchange with London was four shillings and sixpence to the dollar.

Jefferson's Notes on the shilling. Jefferson stated that the tenth part of a Spanish dollar was known as the "bit,"[3] yet in states other than Virginia the term was applied to the eighth of a dollar, the same as the "York shilling," and to this day in the western and southwestern sections of the country the quarter-dollar is called "two bits."

The Continental Congress undertook the task of creating a uniform system out of this apparent chaos at a time when the actual currency in circulation was depreciated paper. It may be said to have fixed upon the *unit* finally adopted as early as 1775, when it authorized the issue of notes payable in "Spanish milled[4] *dollars*," but it was not finally specifically determined upon until several years later.

[1] Report of Robert Morris, Superintendent of Finance, Vol. I., p. 289.
[2] See Appendix.
[3] Jefferson's *Notes* ; Appendix.
[4] " Milled " money means coins struck in a mill or coining press as distinguished from those produced by a die by striking it with a hammer.

In April, 1776, the Congress appointed a committee of seven "to examine and ascertain the value of the several species of Gold and Silver coins, current in these colonies, and the proportions they ought to bear to Spanish milled dollars."[1]

The committee reported, in September following, a resolution fixing such values for the several kinds of coin in circulation, under which the English shilling was rated at two-ninths of a dollar, or about $22\frac{2}{9}$ cents, deduction being made for abraded coins. This resolution also fixed the value of gold bullion at $17 and of silver bullion at 1\frac{1}{9}$ per ounce Troy, thus attempting to establish a legal ratio between gold and silver of 15.3 to 1.[2]

Rating of other coins.

The Articles of Confederation which governed the colonies now known as the United States were adopted in 1778, and continued in force during the remainder of the Revolution and until 1789, when the present Constitution went into operation. Article IX. provided that

Under the Articles of Confederation.

"The United States in Congress assembled shall also have the sole and exclusive right and power of regulating the alloy and value of coin struck by their own authority or by that of the respective states."

Thus the states retained the power to coin money coördinately with the Confederation, but the power to regulate its value was given to Congress.

In August, 1778, after the adoption of the Articles of Confederation, Congress appointed a committee with Robert Morris as chairman, to consider the state of the money and finances of the United States. Morris was subsequently appointed Superintendent of Finance, but

---

[1] Journal Continental Congress ; reprinted in International Monetary Conference, 1878, p. 419.

[2] MS. Reports, Committee on Finance ; reprinted in International Monetary Conference, 1878, p. 422.

apparently no definite action was taken until January, 1782, when he was instructed to prepare for Congress a table of rates at which the various foreign coins should be received at the Treasury of the United States. On January 15 Morris submitted a comprehensive report[1] on a coinage system, in which he pointed out the need not only of a uniform system of coins, but of legal tender provisions as well.

Reports on coins and establishment of a mint.

After discussing the ratio of silver to gold and the fluctuations in the market value of the precious metals, he concluded that the money standard for the United States ought to be affixed to silver. He favored a coinage charge, urged that the money unit should be very small, and that the decimal system be established.

Robert Morris's plan.

After suggesting that the Spanish dollar had undergone the least change in intrinsic value, he recommended a money unit which would be the 1440th part of a dollar, or a quarter of a grain of pure silver. Such a unit agreed without a fraction with all the differing valuations of the dollar in the several states. Of these units he proposed that 100 constitute the lowest silver coin, to be called the cent, containing, therefore, 25 grains of silver, to which he proposed adding for alloy two grains of copper; five of these cents to constitute a piece to be called the quint; and ten, or one thousand of the original units, a piece to be called the mark. He favored a ratio between silver and gold of $14\frac{1}{2}$ to 1. He recommended the establishment of a mint and the coinage of the pieces suggested. Congress on February 21, 1782, approved this recommendation and directed Morris to report a plan therefor.[2] This was the first action toward establishing a federal mint.

[1] MS. Reports, Superintendent of Finance, Vol. I.; reprinted in International Monetary Conference, 1878, p. 425.

[2] Journal Continental Congress; International Monetary Conference, 1878, p. 432.

In December, 1782, Morris recommended to Congress a resolution fixing a valuation of foreign coins, measured in dollars, in order to prevent their exportation, thus denuding the country of specie. In April, 1783, he submitted to Congress specimens of coins prepared by him, and asked further consideration of his mint and coinage proposition. Both these matters were referred to a committee, which did not report for some time.

Meanwhile Jefferson had taken up Morris's plan for a coinage system and submitted a substitute.[1] He recommended the adoption of the Spanish dollar as the unit, as best answering all requirements, and easy of adoption because then practically in general use. His system comprised a gold coin of ten dollars, the unit or dollar of silver, the tenth of a dollar, also of silver, and the one hundredth of a dollar of copper, and supplemental thereto a half dollar, a double tenth (twenty cents), and a twentieth of a dollar. He criticised Morris's plan as less easy of adoption and more laborious in operation than the purely decimal system. *Jefferson's plan.*

As to the contents of the dollar, he recommended finding the average weight of pure silver in the dollars then in use and adopting the resulting weight, to be coined at a fineness of eleven-twelfths. He proposed fixing a proportion between gold and silver coinage at the average ratio of the nations trading with the United States, which would probably be 15 to 1; also that the coins provided be made lawful tender unless diminished in weight. *Jefferson on the ratio.*

Jefferson's paper was also referred to a committee, which did not, however, reach a conclusion until May, 1785. Morris had meanwhile retired from the Finance Department.

In general the committee approved Jefferson's plan, regarding Morris's proposed system as introducing coins

[1] In full in the Appendix.

altogether unknown, departing from the national mode of keeping accounts and preventing rather than promoting uniformity. The system recommended was as follows:

Ratio of the metals 15 to 1 ; a gold piece of five dollars ; a silver dollar or unit, containing 362 grains of pure silver; 50, 25, 10, and 5 cent pieces of silver; all gold and silver coins to be eleven-twelfths fine, with a coinage charge of 2 to 2¼ per cent ; two copper coins of one cent and one-half cent respectively.[1]

Action upon the report as a whole was postponed, but in July, 1785, the following resolutions, fixing upon three fundamental propositions, were adopted by Congress : —

The dollar unit adopted.

"That the money unit of the United States of America be one dollar."

"That the smallest coin be of copper, of which 200 shall pay for one dollar."

"That the several pieces shall increase in decimal ratio."[2]

In April, 1786, the Board of Treasury submitted to Congress three alternative propositions concerning the weight and fineness of the coinage proposed, as exhibited in the table below.

WEIGHT OF PURE METAL

	Silver Dollar	Gold Dollar	Ratio
	grains	grains	
I.	375.64	24.6268	15.253 to 1
II.	350.09	23.79	14.749 to 1
III.	521.73	34.782	15 to 1

Congress on August 8, 1786, passed a resolution[3] fixing the fineness of gold and silver coins at eleven-

[1] MS. Reports, Committee on Finance, Vol. 26; International Monetary Conference, 1878, p. 445.

[2] Journal Continental Congress ; International Monetary Conference, p. 448.   [3] In full in the Appendix.

twelfths, the dollar or unit to contain 375.64 grains of pure silver as in the first mentioned of the propositions above. It provided for mills, or 1000ths of a dollar, as the lowest money of account, and coins as follows : half cents and cents of copper ; dimes or tenths of a dollar, double dimes (20 cents), half dollars and dollars, of silver ; five dollars and ten dollars, of gold ; the latter being coined at 24.6268 grains pure metal to the dollar, thus giving the ratio 15.253 to 1 as above stated. The copper coinage was to be at the rate of 100 cents for $2\frac{1}{4}$ pounds Avoirdupois of copper.

Finally, pursuant to a report of the Board of Treasury of September 20, 1786, Congress on October 16 of that year passed the ordinance establishing the mint.[1] *The Mint Act of 1786.*

The mint price of standard gold, eleven-twelfths (or .916$\frac{2}{3}$) fine, was fixed at $209.77 and of standard silver, of the same fineness, at $13.777, for the pound Troy, with a coinage charge of 2 per cent, giving a ratio of 15.22 to 1. Deposits of gold or silver were to be paid for, 95 per cent in gold or silver and 5 per cent in copper coin.

The act never became fully operative. Only copper coins were actually struck under this law, and these were made receivable for taxes and public dues to the extent of 5 per cent in any payment, all other copper coins being excluded. After September 1, 1787, foreign copper coins were to cease to be current, and copper coins struck by the states were rated by weight at the value fixed by the coinage law of August 8, 1786, viz., 100 cents for $2\frac{1}{4}$ pounds.

The financial as well as the general economic condition of the country at this time was so unsettled, that it became obvious to most of the leading men in the colonies that a more stable form of government for the *The Federal Constitution.*

[1] The important parts of the act are given in the Appendix.

confederation was absolutely necessary.   A convention
of the states was called to meet in Annapolis, Md., in
1786.   Nothing came of this, and another convention
met in Philadelphia in 1787.   Although primarily
assembled to consider economic questions, the deliberations of the convention ultimately produced a new form
of government, the present Constitution (without the
amendments).

Respecting the coinage system that instrument
provides

The consti-
tutional pro-
visions.

ART. 1, SEC. 8.   " The Congress shall have Power . . .
" To coin Money, regulate the Value thereof, and of foreign
Coin."

SEC. 10.   " No State shall . . . coin Money;   make any
Thing but gold and silver Coin a Tender in Payment of Debts."

Thus the states surrendered the right to coin money,
the power over the standard becoming an exclusively
federal function.

STATISTICAL RÉSUMÉ

COMMERCIAL RATIO OF SILVER TO GOLD

Soetbeer's Estimate based on Hamburg Prices

1775 . . . 14.72	1779 . . . 14.80	1783 . . . 14.48	1787 . . . 14.92
1776 . . . 14.55	1780 . . . 14.72	1784 . . . 14.70	1788 . . . 14.65
1777 . . . 14.54	1781 . . . 14.78	1785 . . . 14.92	1789 . . . 14.75
1778 . . . 14.68	1782 . . . 14.42	1786 . . . 14.96	1790 . . . 15.04

PRODUCTION OF GOLD AND SILVER

The most reliable data respecting the world's production
of gold and silver toward the close of the eighteenth century
give the following *annual averages :* —

DECADE	GOLD	SILVER
1761–1780	$13,761,000	$27,133,000
1781–1800	11,823,000	36,540,000

No reliable data for annual periods are available, the above estimates being conclusions reached by Soetbeer after the most exhaustive study of the subject ever attempted.

The evidence all tends to verify the general conclusion that the production of gold diminished and that of silver increased, thus accounting for the fall in the market price of silver as indicated in the table of ratios.

The production of precious metals in the United States prior to 1800 was insignificant in amount.

CHAPTER II

1790 TO 1830

THE new form of government was nominally put into operation on March 4, 1789. Actually the transition was very deliberate. Washington was not inaugurated as President until April 30, and the Treasury Department was not provided for by law until the following September.

Hamilton's Mint report.

Alexander Hamilton was the first Secretary of the Treasury, and soon after organizing the Department set himself the task of establishing a comprehensive federal monetary system. He first took up the question of the public debt, then the establishment of a banking system, and on January 21, 1791, presented to Congress his justly celebrated report upon the establishment of a mint and a coinage system for the United States.[1]

He examined this comprehensive subject in all its aspects and ramifications, presenting the facts and arguments bearing upon both sides of each question, and after careful analysis reached the following conclusions:

The unit.

1. That the dollar, because it had been in actual use as the measure of values in practically all of the states, was the most suitable unit for the proposed system; that it was of the utmost importance to define as exactly as possible just what the dollar was, in order that neither debtors nor creditors might be injuriously affected. The dollars in existence varied considerably, Spain having degraded or changed the standard at different times. He therefore recommended a dollar containing 371.25

[1] In full in the Appendix.

grains of pure silver, as best expressing the actual average value of the coin in use.

2. That the decimal system was of demonstrated superiority over the duodecimal of Great Britain.

3. That inasmuch as the undervaluation of either metal would cause its exportation, thus shifting the standard to the other, which might result injuriously, and since it was very desirable to have coins of both metals in actual use, the ratio should conform as nearly The ratio. as possible to the commercial ratio, rather than follow any specific European precedent. He therefore recommended the ratio of 15 to 1.

4. That the silver dollar was the equivalent of 24.75 grains of gold, and therefore a gold dollar containing that quantity of metal be also provided for, in order that there might be a unit coin in each metal.

5. That the fineness of the coins should be eleven-twelfths or .916$\frac{2}{3}$, corresponding with the British standard of fineness for gold; the alloys being for gold coins, Alloy and silver and copper; for silver coins, copper only. mint charge.

6. That no mint charge should be imposed upon the bullion brought for coinage, the cost thereof being properly a general charge rather than one to be imposed upon specific individuals, and to impose a charge might influence prices in international relations, being in effect a reduction of the standard of the coin, as compared with bullion.

7. That foreign coins should be permitted to circulate for one year, that thereafter certain foreign pieces might be tolerated for another year or two; anticipating that the mint would be prepared to provide all the Foreign coin needed, he concluded that after three years the use coins. of foreign coins should be prohibited.

Hamilton's report was reviewed by Jefferson, who, in a short letter, expressed concurrence upon the bimetallic proposition and other features of Hamilton's plan.[1]

Congress gave Hamilton's recommendation attention and passed a resolution for the establishment of a mint on March 3, 1791, but it was not until April 2, 1792, after being spurred by President Washington, that the act establishing a coinage system was finally passed.

In general, Hamilton's recommendations were adopted, but Congress refused to provide for a gold dollar, thus partly destroying Hamilton's ideal of a bimetallic standard, and altered the fineness of the silver coins by substituting a fraction resulting in .892,43.[2] In all other particulars the law was practically an enactment of Hamilton's own language into a statute.

Coinage Act of 1792.

The act,[3] after providing for the organization of the mint directs, in Section 9, the coinage of the following pieces : —

DENOMINATIONS		WEIGHT IN GRAINS	
		Gross	Fine
Gold	Eagles, $10	270	$247\frac{1}{2}$
	Half Eagles, $5	135	$123\frac{6}{8}$
	Quarter Eagles, $2½	$67\frac{4}{8}$	$61\frac{7}{8}$
Silver	Dollars or Units	416	$371\frac{4}{16}$
	Half Dollars	208	$185\frac{10}{16}$
	Quarter Dollars	104	$92\frac{13}{16}$
	Dismes	$41\frac{3}{5}$	$37\frac{2}{16}$
	Half Dismes	$20\frac{4}{5}$	$18\frac{9}{16}$
Copper	Cents	264	264
	Half Cents	132	132

Section 10 provides for devices on coins.

Ratio 15 to 1.

Section 11 fixes the ratio at 15 to 1, the language being

[1] See Appendix.   [2] It is not clear why this was adopted.   [3] See Appendix.

which shall by law be current as money within the United States, shall be as 15 to 1, according to quantity in weight, of pure gold or pure silver ; that is to say, every 15 pounds' weight of pure silver shall be of equal value in all payments, with 1 pound weight of pure gold, and so in proportion as to any greater or less quantities of the respective metals."

Section 12 fixes the standard of fineness for the gold coins at eleven-twelfths, the British standard, equal to .916$\frac{2}{3}$, the alloy to be silver and copper, not to exceed one-half of the former metal.

The fineness of the silver coins was by Section 13 fixed at 1485 parts pure metal and 179 parts copper alloy, equal to .892,43.[1]

No charge was imposed for coining the bullion brought to the mint, unless the depositor preferred to have payment immediately, instead of awaiting the coinage of the bullion, in which case a deduction of one-half of one per cent was to be made. A strict provision against giving preference to depositors was included in Section 15.

Section 16 declared that the gold and silver coins provided for "shall be a lawful tender in all payments whatsoever," abraded coins to be legal tender for the relative weight thereof. ^{Legal tender.}

After prescribing directions for the officers and imposing the penalty of death for fraudulently debasing the coinage or embezzlement, on the part of such officers, the act concludes (Sec. 20) with the provision that "the money of account of the United States shall be expressed

---

[1] It appears that notwithstanding the statute, the first and second directors of the mint coined dollars at the fineness of .900, thus giving them 374.4 grains of pure metal. This appears to have been tacitly sanctioned by both Jefferson and Hamilton. The ratio was thus altered to 15$\frac{1}{4}$ to 1. See White's Report, No. 496, 22 Congress, 1st Sess., p. 17; quoted by Watson, Hist. of Amer. Coinage, p. 230.

in dollars, dismes or tenths, cents or hundredths, and milles or thousandths,' and the accounts of public officers were to be kept and proceedings of courts to be had accordingly.

When the act first passed the Senate it provided for an impression on the coins of the head of the President for the time being. in imitation of the coinage of most European countries. This proviso was stricken out in the House of Representatives, and after some discussion the Senate concurred.

Much to Hamilton's chagrin the business of the mint was attached to the Department of State, under Jefferson, and not until after Hamilton, when resigning, called attention to this anomaly, was it transferred to the Treasury Department.[1]

First bimetallic law.

This legislation based upon the report of Hamilton was the first attempt in the world to adopt *by law* a bimetallic standard with all the requisite features of free and unlimited coinage of both metals and giving full legal tender power to both.

Hamilton's conception of the proper ratio was not far out of the way, as is shown by the table giving the commercial ratio for the period. Hamilton was *not* aware that the relative production of silver was increasing, so that the commercial ratio would very soon be changed, and naturally when in 1803 France adopted a ratio of $15\frac{1}{2}$ to 1 the disappearance of gold from this country resulted. It was thus early in the history of the United States demonstrated that it was impossible to maintain *independently* a ratio between the metals differing materially from that fixed by the world's markets.

On May 8, 1792, Congress passed an act providing for the purchase of 150 tons of copper for the coinage

[1] Life of Hamilton, Vol. VI., p. 186.

of cents and half cents, and that when $50,000 of these pieces had been struck, public notice be given that after six months from that date no other copper pieces were to pass current, or be offered, paid, or received in payment for any debt, etc., under penalty of forfeiture and fine, recoverable by the informer.

The first coins were struck in October, 1792, being a small amount of half dimes, referred to in President Washington's address to Congress at. its following session : —

" There has also been a small beginning in the coinage of half-dismes, the want of small coins in circulation calling for the first attention to them."

The weight of the copper coins was reduced by the act of January 14, 1793, to 208 and 104 grains respectively. By the act of March 3, 1796, further reduction in weight by proclamation of the President was authorized.

Sundry other acts relating to the mint and coinage were passed prior to the general revision of 1834. It is necessary to note only the following : —

March 3, 1796, authorizing a charge upon bullion deposited for coinage if below the standard.

April 24, 1800, March 3, 1823, and May 19, 1825, further providing for charges upon bullion deposits not suitable for immediate coinage, whether above or below the standard.

It was not until February 9, 1793, that Congress modified the existing valuations of foreign coins.[1] From and after the first of July following the date of the act, British and Portuguese gold pieces were to pass current and be *legal tender* at the rate of 100 cents for every 27 grains' weight, French and Spanish gold pieces at 100 cents for $27\frac{2}{5}$ grains, the difference being due to the

[1] Fixed by tariff law of July 31, 1789.

greater fineness of the gold coin of the first-mentioned countries. Silver coins were rated as follows: the Spanish dollar if weighing 17 pennyweight 7 grains, at 100 cents, and proportionately for smaller coins; French crowns at 110 cents, if weighing 18 pennyweight 17 grains, and proportionately for parts of a crown.[1]

Their use limited.

It provided further, that after three years from the date of the beginning of the coinage of gold and silver at the mint (to be proclaimed by the President) no foreign coins *except the Spanish dollar and parts thereof*[2] were to be legal tender. Other foreign coins received by the United States thereafter were to be recoined into coins prescribed by the mint act.

The coinage of the mint was not sufficiently large, however, to provide for the country's needs, and accordingly the above-mentioned act giving legal tender power to foreign gold and silver coins was renewed without change by the acts of February 1, 1798, and April 10, 1806.[3]

Legal tender of foreign coins continued.

The act of April 29, 1816,[4] again continued the provision for three years, including the French five-franc pieces; this was again continued by the act of March 3, 1819, until November 1, 1819, for gold coins (after which date they were no longer legal tender) and until April 29, 1821, for the French silver coins. The act of March 3, 1821, continued the same provision as to the French pieces for two years more, and the act of March 3, 1823, for four years from that date. On the same day, foreign gold coins were made receivable in payment for public lands, in order to facilitate their sale to immigrants.

---

[1] See Appendix.

[2] Subsequent legislation did not alter this proviso; thus the Spanish dollar and its subdivisions continued legal tender until 1857.

[3] See Appendix.   [4] *Ibid.*

Notwithstanding this action favorable to foreign coin and notwithstanding a substantial supply of gold came from the Spanish and French traders in the southwest, enabling the mint to coin considerable sums annually, the exports of gold practically drained the country of that metal. During the third decade of the nineteenth century it disappeared from circulation. Gold exported.

This movement was stimulated, not only by the French coinage law of 1803, which fixed a ratio of $15\frac{1}{2}$ to 1, but also by the conditions during the War of 1812 and the adoption of the gold standard by England in 1816, with a subsidiary silver coinage at the ratio of 16 to 1.

During a considerable period after the refusal to renew the charter of the first bank of the United States, depreciated paper was the chief currency, — a condition not remedied until after the second bank was chartered in 1816.

Respecting silver, the country was not much more fortunate, for although the mint was turning out large amounts of the new coinage, the actual specie in use continued to be Spanish piastres (or dollars), and the subdivisions thereof, as a rule much cheapened by abrasion. Although somewhat less in weight than the Spanish pieces, the American dollars were accepted *by tale* throughout the West Indies and were exported for that reason. Spanish and Mexican pieces were imported, and those of full weight, or nearly so, were recoined into dollars at the mint, the depositors reaping the profit. Silver also exported.

President Jefferson undertook to check this business in 1806 by directing that the mint suspend the coinage of the dollar pieces. This suspension continued until after the legislation of 1834. A similar fate befell the fractional coins, which were equally valuable for export, Dollar coinage suspended.

and the result was that the Americans were coining for other people while actually using worn foreign coin.

The evils of the disordered metallic currency grew intolerable, and Congress became impressed with the necessity for action. In consequence, numerous reports were prepared and laid before that body, but, as will appear, no action was taken until 1834.

In 1817 the Senate requested John Quincy Adams, then Secretary of State, to prepare a report upon weights and measures, which was not, however, submitted until 1821.

J. Q. Adams's report.

In connection with the general subject Adams discussed the coinage system,[1] prefacing it with a criticism of the law fixing the par of exchange for the pound sterling at $4.44, when in fact the value of the pound was $4.56572 in gold, and, owing to the demonetization and lower rating of silver in England, $4.3489 when reckoning in the white metal. It is not necessary to follow and verify Adams's calculations; suffice it to say that this very low rating of the pound served to embarrass transactions involving international exchange.

Adams also pointed out that the ratings in the acts governing the valuations of foreign coins were inaccurate. He did not discuss the question of the ratio specifically, but provided those who desired to do so valuable and accurate material relative to the weights of coins. The inevitable deduction from the facts he presented and his reasoning based thereon is that he regarded the ratio very much at fault.

Although not free from errors, Adams's paper shows great labor and research upon a subject concerning which at that time very little material was available to the student.

In the meantime the House of Representatives had

[1] See International Monetary Conference, 1878, p. 490.

referred to a committee the question "whether it be expedient to make any amendment in the laws which regulate the coin of the United States and foreign coins respectively," which reported, January 26, 1819, a bill recommending that the gold coins be reduced in weight from 24.75 grains to 22.798 grains, that a seigniorage of 14.85 grains pure silver to the dollar be charged for coinage, and that the legal tender of silver coin below the dollar be limited to five dollars. This is the first suggestion that fractional silver be made subsidiary.

After discussing the various ratios prevailing, the report concludes as follows : —

Lack of specie.

"As the committee entertain no doubt that gold is estimated below its fair relative value, in comparison to silver, by the present regulations of the Mint ; and as it can scarcely be considered as having formed a material part of our money circulation for the last twenty-six years, they have no hesitation in recommending that its valuation shall be raised, so as to make it bear a juster proportion to its price in the commercial world. But the smallest change which is likely to secure this object (a just proportion of gold coins in our circulation) is that which the committee prefer, and they believe it sufficient to restore gold to its original valuation in this country, of 1 to 15 $\frac{6}{10}$." [1]

The coinage charge imposed by this bill would have made the ratio of the bullion actually 15 to 1. Congress, however, took no action.

On March 1, 1819, the House directed Crawford, Secretary of the Treasury, to report, among other matters, "such measures as, in his opinion, may be expedient to procure and retain a sufficient quantity of gold and silver coin in the United States."

A very able state paper was prepared by Crawford in response to this resolution and presented to the House in February, 1820. [2]

Crawford's report.

[1] Abridgment of Debates, Vol. 6, p. 273.
[2] See International Monetary Conference, 1878, p. 502.

He argued that the difference of 1 per cent between the Spanish and American dollar would have
retained the latter in circulation if the former had not
been made legal tender. In discussing the ratio he
correctly alleged that the derangement was due to the
appreciation of gold, and urged that no injustice would
result from a change in the ratio which would make it
correspond to the market value. He recommended the
ratio of 15.75 to 1 as best calculated to correct the disparity, as it would cause the importation and retention
of gold, and would not cause silver to go out unless the
state of the foreign trade warranted. Upon the other
hand he pointed out that the retention of a metallic currency was dependent upon the volume of paper currency
in use (a subject also discussed in his report), that in
fact the value of gold and silver had been materially
affected by the general use of paper in leading countries,
followed by the suspension of specie payments, and subsequently by efforts to resume.

Crawford's report was referred to a select committee
which in February, 1821, reported conclusions agreeing
with his. It was pointed out that a gold coinage
amounting to $6,000,000 had practically disappeared
from use, that this was unquestionably due to the ratio
of 15 to 1 under which the gold coins were more valuable for export than for home use, the difference being
about sixty cents upon every $15 or three half eagles.

Secretary Crawford, in a letter to a committee of the
House of Representatives in February, 1823, apparently
modified his view as to the ratio somewhat. He said : —

"In terminating this letter I feel it my duty to observe that
the relative current value of gold and silver differs materially
from that established by the laws of the United States. The
consequence has been that the gold coin of the United States
has always been exported whenever the rate of exchange be-

Change of
ratio dis-
cussed.

tween the United States and the commercial nations of Europe
has been in favor of the latter. If the gold coins of the United
States should be made equal in value to sixteen times the value
of silver coins of the same quantity of pure silver, they would
be exported only when the rate of exchange should be greatly
against the United States." [1]

In a report submitted to the House by a committee
having under consideration the valuation of foreign
coins, in 1823,[2] it is stated that the coinage of gold and
silver at the mint had been in excess of $20,000,000,
whereas the amount of specie in the country, inclusive
of foreign coin, was estimated at $16,000,000 (less by
$1,500,000 than in 1804), and by far the greater part of
the coin in the country consisted of French silver pieces,
which, it will be recalled, had full legal tender power.
It was upon the recommendation of this committee that
this power was continued until 1827.

Specie in the country.

In the Senate at about the same time (January, 1819)
the Finance Committee had reported upon a resolution
as to the "expediency of prohibiting by law the exportation of gold, silver, and copper coins," concluding that
it was *not* expedient. Three quotations from this report
are of interest: —

Prohibiting exports suggested.

"Of the inefficiency, if not entire impotence, of legislative
provisions to prevent the escape of the precious metals beyond
the territorial limits of the Government, the history of all
countries in which the power of legislation has been thus exercised, bears testimony. . . . Indeed, no error seems more
entirely renounced and exploded, if not by the practice of all
nations, at least in the disquisitions of political economists, than
that which supposed that an accumulation of the precious
metals could be produced in the dominions of one sovereign
by regulations prohibiting their exportation to those of any
other. . . . In short, it is the opinion of your committee,
that commerce is always destined to flourish most where it is

[1] Abridgment of Debates, Vol. 7, p. 429.   [2] *Ibid.*, p. 427.

permitted to pursue its own paths, marked out by itself, embarrassed as little as possible by legislative regulations or restrictions."[1]

For more than a decade this question had thus been before Congress without definite progress toward the adoption of a remedy. Meanwhile the opposition to the bank of the United States (described in a later chapter), had begun, and materially interfered with calm, deliberate action.

STATISTICAL RÉSUMÉ

COMMERCIAL RATIO OF SILVER TO GOLD

Soetbeer's Estimate based on Hamburg Prices

1793 . . . 15.00	1802 . . . 15.26	1812 . . . 16.11	1822 . . . 15.80
1794 . . . 15.37	1803 . . . 15.41	1813 . . . 16.25	1823 . . . 15.84
1795 . . . 15.55	1804 . . . 15.41	1814 . . . 15.04	1824 . . . 15.82
1796 . . . 15.65	1805 . . . 15.79	1815 . . . 15.26	1825 . . . 15.70
1797 . . . 15.41	1806 . . . 15.52	1816 . . . 15.28	1826 . . . 15.76
1798 . . . 15.59	1807 . . . 15.43	1817 . . . 15.11	1827 . . . 15.74
1799 . . . 15.74	1808 . . . 16.08	1818 . . . 15.35	1828 . . . 15.78
1800 . . . 15.68	1809 . . . 15.96	1819 . . . 15.33	1829 . . . 15.78
1801 . . . 15.46	1810 . . . 15.77	1820 . . . 15.62	1830 . . . 15.82
	1811 . . . 15.53	1821 . . . 15.95	

PRODUCTION OF GOLD AND SILVER

DECADE	WORLD		UNITED STATES	
	Gold	Silver	Gold	Silver
1801–1810 .	$118,152,000	$371,677,000	——	Insignificant
1811–1820 .	76,063,000	224,786,000	——	
1821–1830 .	94,479,000	191,444,000	$715,000	

---

[1] Abridgment of Debates, Vol. 6, p. 190.

COINAGE OF THE UNITED STATES

Years	Total Gold	Silver Dollars	Fractional Silver
1792–1795 . .	$ 71,485.00	$ 204,791.00	$ 165,892.80
1796–1800 . .	942,805.00	1,052,667.00	17,103.95
1801–1805 . .	1,533,267.50	182,059.00	287,889.00
1806–1810 . .	1,717,475.00		3,099,217.25
1811–1815 . .	1,345,925.00		2,622,316.50
1816–1820 . .	1,820,585.00		3,348,494.45
1821–1825 . .	600,315.00		5,844,178.95
1826–1830 . .	1,302,777.50		10,936,868.00

IMPORTS AND EXPORTS OF GOLD AND SILVER, UNITED STATES

Prior to 1821 the commercial movement of precious metals was not separately reported; nor were the exports and imports of silver correctly given separate from gold, until 1864.

Years	Imports	Exports
1821–1825	$ 31,062,367	$ 43,472,833
1826–1830	38,081,413	28,065,712

D

CHAPTER III

1830 TO 1860

Further efforts to adjust the double standard.

THE ratio existing during the period from 1820 to 1830, by consensus of opinion, undervalued gold. The only differences of opinion related to the proper ratio to be adopted and the correlated question whether gold or silver should be the standard.

On May 4, 1830, Secretary Ingham, of the Treasury, in response to a resolution of the Senate of December 20, 1828, requiring him to "ascertain, with as much accuracy as possible, the proportional value of gold and silver in relation to each other; and to state such alterations in the gold coins of the United States as may be necessary to conform those coins to the silver coins, in their true relative value," presented a report upon the subject containing the most thorough and exhaustive treatment it had received up to that date.

Ingham's report.

He insisted that the loss of gold by the country was by no means entirely due to the undervaluation in ratio. He adduced the fact that prior to 1821 the market value in the United States had not varied materially from the mint value, and contended that the introduction of bank paper had been the chief cause of the exportation of gold. He argued that the exportation of gold alone did not cause serious trouble, but that actual distress ensued when silver also went abroad, leaving the country inadequately supplied. He set forth with great force the futility of endeavoring to maintain a bimetallic standard, and urged the adoption of a single standard, and that

34

silver. He favored silver because contracts in the country had been for many years based upon the silver dollar, and also because no exact adjustment of the relation
of the two metals could be maintained with any degree
of permanence, and silver *could* be retained at home by
reducing the mint value of gold. The country could
not possibly get along without silver, whereas it could
without gold by the use of sound bank currency. As
to the ratio, he suggested that, since the market ratio
appeared to be about 15.8 to 1, and it was desirable
under his plan to have gold at a slight premium, the
coinage ratio should be 15.625 to 1.

Secretary Ingham addressed many persons familiar
with the subject, for information, and he thus obtained
much valuable material which was published with his
report.[1]

Gallatin, who had been Secretary of the Treasury
under Jefferson, contributed a lengthy letter and statistical information. He favored the adoption of the
French bimetallic system, ratio $15\frac{1}{2}$ to 1, with coins
.900 fine. He criticised the English single gold standard, with its " adulterated silver currency," but not with
his usual perspicacity. His general conclusion was that
the bimetallic standard should be adopted for the reason
that the fluctuations of gold and silver would be less
than that of one metal only. If a single standard were
selected, silver was preferable to gold because it was
then the existing standard metal, was more abundant,
requiring a greater premium before it could be exported,
and was the only means of suppressing small notes, the
worst form of paper currency.

Very valuable statistical and other data relative to
exchange, premium on gold, coins, etc., covering many
years, were furnished by Samuel Moore, Director of the

Gallatin's views.

---

[1] Printed in full in International Monetary Conference, 1878, p. 558.

Mint, and by John White, Cashier of the Bank of the United States.

The views of Alexander Baring, the famous banker of London, upon the single gold standard system of England, in which he expressed decided preference for the double standard at 15½ to 1 and voiced existing dissatisfaction with the new British system, were also reprinted in the report.

Ingham's report unquestionably influenced many of the leading men in Congress. To counteract the tendeney toward the single standard Senator Sanford of New York, in December, 1830, reported a bill for the continuation of the double standard at the ratio of 15.9 to 1, altering the weight of the gold coins only. The bill was ably supported in the committee's report[1] which formed the basis of two reports to the House of Representatives in 1831,[2] one on silver and the other on gold, by Representative C. P. White, also of New York. The latter made two further reports in March and June, 1832.[3] Together, these five reports constitute an encyclopedia of the then existing information on the subject. The House Committee opposed the double standard because of "the impossibility of maintaining both metals in concurrent, simultaneous, or promiscuous circulation," urged that the single standard is the nearest approach to stability precluding the need of further legislation with each change in relative commercial value, and asserted that if a metallic circulation was desired, notes of ten dollars and under must be prohibited.

White would not admit, as Sanford claimed, that injurious consequences would ensue if one of the metals

The Sanford and White reports.

---

[1] Senate Reports, 21st Congress, 2d Sess., No. 3.

[2] House Reports, 21st Congress, 2d Sess.

[3] House Reports, 22d Congress, 1st Sess., Nos. 278, 496.

were rejected. He recommended the adoption of the White for
silver
standard. ratio of 15.625 to 1 and .900 as the standard of fineness. As to this ratio, he regarded it the utmost limit to which the value of gold could be raised if silver was to be retained, and finally he stated that "the standard ought to be legally and exclusively, as it is practically, regulated by silver."

The influence which the large volume of small notes exercised in driving out coins was fully appreciated in the House Committee reports.

The discussion proceeded without action for two years longer. In February, 1834, White again reported upon the subject, repeating his former bill and recommendations.[1]

In May the banks of New York, under the lead of Gallatin, then president of one of them, sent a memorial to Congress asking for the enactment of a law to coin gold at the rate of 23.76 grains of pure and 25.92 grains standard metal to the dollar.[2] This would have continued the fineness of the coin at .916⅔ (or eleven-twelfths) and, since the silver dollar remained unchanged, would have resulted in a ratio of 15.625 to 1. They also asked that the silver dollars of the Latin-American states and the five-franc pieces of France be made legal tender as well as the Spanish dollars, at their proper mint values. These coins had in fact become the chief elements in the country's specie circulation, and some action was necessary to provide a sufficient volume of legal tender money.

Later in the session, when the desire for action be- White for
gold
standard. came pressing (and only one week before the act of 1834 actually passed), White completely changed his position and reported a bill which practically favored the gold instead of the silver standard, fixing a ratio of

---

[1] House Reports, 23d Congress.
[2] International Monetary Conference, 1878, p. 679.

about 16 to 1.   What the influences were which caused such a radical change does not clearly appear.   Many of his followers, for he had become the recognized leader on the subject in the House, severely criticised his course.

Benton's views.

From the speeches of Benton, the champion of gold in the Senate, it would appear that the policy of adopting a ratio that undervalued silver, according to the judgment of all expert economists, and thus cutting loose practically from both Great Britain and France, was influenced by the desire to place the country in position to draw, in competition with Spain, the precious metal product of Mexico, Central and South America. The Spanish ratio had for years been 16 to 1, and it was presumed that this caused the flow of gold from the Spanish-American countries to the former mother country, even after the separation of those colonies between 1820 and 1830.[1]

There is evidence that the action was in part influenced by the fact that gold had been found in North Carolina and Georgia.   The production there had been increasing until the annual output was nearly one million dollars, and indeed the people of that section of the country believed that the new Eldorado had been discovered.

Gold mines in Southern states.

(In 1835 mints were established at Dahlonega, Ga., and at Charlotte, N.C.)   The argument that prosperity, so long absent from the states, would be restored if this gold product could be kept at home, proved very captivating, and in order to make assurance doubly sure the ratio was made sufficiently advantageous to retain that gold beyond peradventure.

Benton said : —

"Gold goes where it finds its value, and that value is what the laws of great nations give it.   In Mexico and South Amer-

[1] Benton, Thirty Years' View, p. 436.

ica, the countries which produce gold, and from which the United States must derive their chief supply, the value of gold is 16 to 1 over silver; in the Island of Cuba it is 17 to 1; in Spain and Portugal it is 16 to 1; in the West Indies, generally, it is the same. It is not to be supposed that gold will come from these countries to the United States, if the importer is to Benton for gold. lose one dollar in every sixteen that he brings; or that our gold will remain with us, when an exporter can gain a dollar upon every fifteen that he carries out. Such results would be contrary to the laws of trade, and therefore we must place the same value upon gold that other nations do, if we wish to gain any part of theirs, or to regain any part of our own."

He made his acknowledgments "to the great apostle of American liberty" (Jefferson) for the wise, practical idea that the value of gold was a commercial question, to be settled by its value in other countries. He had seen that remark in the works of that great man, and treasured it up as teaching the plain and ready way to accomplish an apparently difficult object; and he fully concurred with the Senator from South Carolina (Mr. Calhoun) that gold in the United States ought to be the preferred metal; not that silver should be expelled, but both retained; the mistake, if any, to be in favor of gold, instead of being against it.[1] Looking to the actual and equal circulation of the two metals in different countries, he noted that this equality and actuality of circulation had existed for above three hundred years in the Spanish dominions of Mexico and South America, where the proportion was 16 to 1. White gave up the bill which he had first introduced and adopted the "Spanish ratio." John Q. Adams would vote for it, though he thought gold was overvalued, but if found to be so, the difference could be corrected thereafter.[2]

Speaking of the domestic supply of native gold, Benton

[1] Benton, Thirty Years' View, p. 443.
[2] *Ibid.*, p. 469.

Benton's
sanguine
hopes.

said that no mines had ever developed more rapidly or promised more abundantly than those in the Southern states In the year 1824 they were a spot in the state of North Carolina, they are now a region spreading into six states. In the year 1824 the product was $5000, in 1832 he claimed the product in coined gold was $868,000, in uncoined as much more, and the product of 1834 was computed at $2,000,000, with every prospect of continued and permanent increase. The probability was that these mines alone, in the lapse of a few years, would furnish an abundant supply of gold to establish a plentiful circulation of that metal if not expelled from the country by unwise laws.

It was on June 21, 1834, that the White substitute bill was introduced. In one week it became law, only thirty-six representatives and seven senators voting against it upon final passage. It is apparent that the action was taken from a desire to accomplish something quickly. Political exigency rather than careful deliberation caused the House to ignore the ratio of 15.625, which was held by White two years before to be the "utmost limit to which the value [of gold] could be raised," and favor 16 to 1, without regard to the commercial ratio.

The act of
1834.

The only change made by the act of June 28, 1834,[1] respecting the coinage, was to alter the weight of the gold coins, giving them 23.2 grains of pure gold and 25.8 standard to the dollar. This changed the fineness to nearly .900, instead of .916⅔. The resulting ratio was 16.002 to 1. Another act, passed the same day, provided that foreign gold coins were to be received and pass current at the new ratings which the preceding law established.

As the Spanish-American colonies were now separate states, their silver coinage was, by the act of June 25,

[1] See Appendix.

1834, made receivable the same as the "Spanish dollars" if of full weight. In fact, they superseded the Spanish coins which had been issued from the same mints. Few, if any, of the "Spanish milled dollars" that came to the United States were coined in Spain.

The legislation of 1834 left the silver dollar exactly as the act of 1792 had fixed it. When in 1836 it was found desirable to revise the laws regulating the mint, a bill containing thirty-eight sections was introduced, and several important changes in coins were included. This bill passed January 18, 1837.[1] Section 8 prescribes that the standard of fineness for both gold and silver coins shall be .900, thus avoiding the awkward fraction fixed by the law of 1792. The weight of pure silver in the dollar remained the same, 371.25 grains; the gross weight was altered from 416 to 412.5 grains, and fractional pieces were changed in proportion. The legal tender power of all silver pieces remained unchanged. The fineness of the gold coins was slightly increased to make it exactly .900. The eagle thus weighed 258 grains, of which 232.2 grains were pure gold. The ratio became 15.988 to 1, the same as it is to-day. The difference is so slight that the custom has become universal to characterize the present coinage ratio as "16 to 1," thereby ignoring the fractional difference of .012. The coinage of both metals was made free and unlimited, and in fact the coinage of silver dollars was resumed.

The above-mentioned ratio placed a valuation upon gold of 52 cents per ounce higher than that generally prevailing in Europe. It made the silver dollar worth $1.03 measured by the gold dollar. Ere long silver began to depart for Europe, where the ratio of $15\frac{1}{2}$ to 1 prevailed, and also to India, which had adopted the single silver standard in 1835 at the ratio of 15 to 1.

The act of 1837.

Ratio 16 to 1 Gold the standard.

Silver exported.

[1] See Appendix.

The commercial ratio of gold to silver did not equal our coinage ratio until 1874, silver all this time commanding a small premium. Although trade balances were for a number of years adverse, the placing of investments abroad proved more than an offset and the stock of gold in the country increased. Notwithstanding the continual export of United States silver coin, the influx of silver coins from Central and South America, which had been made legal tender, prevented any serious shortage of small coins for some time.

The rate for sterling exchange.

The legal rate of the pound sterling was $4.44⅛ as fixed by the revenue act of July 31, 1789 (prior to the first coinage law), under which imported wares from British sources were appraised. Adams tells us that this rating was in accord with the valuation of the silver dollar that had been adopted by the Continental Congress by the ordinance of 1786.

The customs rating was $4.44⅘, the actual rating $4.566, and thus the quotations of exchange at par prior to 1834 were in figures 102.7. No legal change was made after the alteration of the weight of the gold coin in 1834–1837, yet by that alteration the 113.001 grains of pure gold in the pound sterling, estimated in dollars of 23.22 grains pure gold, gave $4.86⅔. The difference between this last-mentioned equivalent and the one of 1789 amounts to 9½ per cent,[1] and hence from 1837 onward the par of exchange was expressed with a nominal premium figure, thus 109½, notwithstanding an act of 1842 which rated sterling at $4.84 in payments by and to the Treasury. This anomaly continued until 1873.[2]

Increase in gold product.

The gold fields of the South proved disappointing, but California, recently acquired from Mexico, proved

[1] Hunt, Merchant's Magazine, Vol. I. p. 536.
[2] See Chapter XII.

an Eldorado indeed, yielding $10,000,000 in 1848 and $40,000,000 in 1849. In the following decade the annual output continued large, the maximum being $65,000,000 in 1853. This enormous production dazzled the world at that time, attracted foreigners and foreign capital, and proved of the greatest value to our currency and credit. But the country was denuded of silver, only the abraded foreign coins remaining in circulation. The inconvenience suffered by the public for want of small change became a crying evil, and Congress was impressed with the necessity for action. Dearth of silver coin.

Thomas Corwin, Secretary of the Treasury, in an elaborate report early in 1852,[1] recommended the reduction of the amount of silver in coins as the only remedy, and suggested that the weight of all silver pieces, including the dollar, be reduced so as to give the ratio of 14.88 to 1.

Senator Hunter, in the same year, made a comprehensive report[2] in which he referred to the fears existing that the great gold production would unsettle values. This he believed would not result, in view of the great increase of wealth and capital, if natural laws were permitted to operate. But paper currency was interfering with natural laws. He favored a system of subsidiary silver coinage in place of bank-notes of smaller denominations than one dollar which had become prevalent. He added, "The great measure of readjusting the legal ratio between gold and silver cannot be safely attempted until some permanent relations between the market values of the two metals shall be established." Hunter's report. Remedies proposed.

The act of July 3, 1852, established the mint in San

---

[1] Special Report, Finance Report, 1852.
[2] Senate Reports, 32d Congress, 1st Sess., No. 104.

Francisco, to provide for the official handling of the large gold product of the Pacific slope.

Corwin, in January, 1853, again called attention to the general conditions, saying that no indication of relief was near, rather a prospect of reduced supplies of silver.   He added : —

Corwin on
scarcity of
silver.

" This state of things has banished almost entirely from circulation all silver coins of full weight, and what little remains in
the hands of the community consists principally of the worn
pieces of Spanish coinage of the fractional parts of a dollar,
all of which are of light weight, and many of them ten or
twenty per cent below their nominal value." [1]

He discussed the objection which had been seriously raised that the proposed silver currency could not, with- out a violation of contracts, be made a legal tender for the payment of debts, and that the gold thereafter would be the only legal tender.   He said : —

" It is true that heretofore the laws of the United States have
recognized the coin of either metal as a legal tender, and if it
was at the option of the creditor to select what he would receive
there would be a very serious objection to changing either the
weight or standard fineness of any portion of the coin. But
this is not the fact, as it rests with the debtor to say with which
description of coin he will pay his debts, and the natural and
inevitable consequences of the premium which silver now bears
have been to establish, practically, gold as the only legal
tender."

Subsidiary
coinage act,
1853.

These efforts finally resulted in the act of February 21, 1853,[2] which provided that after June 1, 1853, the weight of the half dollar or piece of fifty cents should be 192 grains, the quarter dollar, dime, and half dime respectively one-half, one-fifth, and one-tenth of the weight of the half dollar ; the fineness to continue at

[1] Finance Report, 1853.
[2] See Appendix.

.900; the silver coins thus ordered to be legal tender in payment of debts for all sums not over five dollars. The mint was authorized to purchase silver bullion for coinage, and further deposits for coinage into fractional silver pieces for private account was prohibited, but the deposit of gold and silver for casting into bars or ingots of either pure or standard metal at a charge of one-half of one per cent was permitted. The law also authorized the coinage of $3 gold pieces. The coinage of $20 gold pieces had been previously authorized in 1849.

The weight thus prescribed for the small silver coins, 384 grains of standard silver or 345.6 grains fine to the dollar, gave, as compared with gold, the ratio of 14.882 to 1, but as it proved, the question of the ratio of these coins was of no importance so long as it reduced their value below the export point. In a short time the country possessed a fairly adequate supply of small silver.

The act of 1853 did not disturb the coinage of silver dollars. It related solely to the establishment of a subsidiary currency of silver to take the place of fractional bank-notes and to establish a circulation of domestic coin in place of the light weight foreign coins. Yet speaking on the question in the House, Chairman Dunham of the Ways and Means Committee said:[1] —

Gold standard contemplated.

> " We propose, so far as these coins are concerned, to make silver subservient to the gold coin of the country. We intend to do what the best writers on political economy have approved, what experience, where the experiment has been tried, has demonstrated to be the best, and what the Committee believe to be necessary and proper, to make but one standard of currency and to make all others subservient to it. We mean to make gold the standard coin, and to make these new silver coins applicable and convenient, not for large but for small transactions."

[1] Congressional Globe, XXVI., p. 190.

Farther on in his speech he said : —

"Another objection urged against this proposed change is
that it gives us a standard of currency of gold only. . . . The
constant though sometimes slow change in the relative value of
the two metals has always resulted in great inconvenience and
frequently in great loss to the people. Wherever the experiment of a standard of a single metal has been tried it has
proved eminently successful. Indeed, it is utterly impossible
that you should long at a time maintain a double standard. The
one or the other will appreciate in value when compared to the
other. It will then command a premium when exchanged for
that other, when it ceases to be a currency and becomes merchandise. It ceases to circulate as money at its nominal value,
but it sells as a commodity at its market price. This was the
case with gold before the act of 1834, but it is now the case with
silver. Gentlemen talk about a double standard of gold and
silver as a thing that exists, and that we propose to change.
We have had but a single standard for the last three or four
years. That has been and now is, gold. We propose to let
it remain so and to adapt silver to it, to regulate it by it."

Despite this manifest purpose the silver dollar remained in the law, with full legal tender power equally
with gold.

The principal opponent of the bill was Andrew Johnson of Tennessee, later Vice-President and President.
The following extract from his remarks is of interest:

" I look upon this bill as the merest quackery — the veriest
charlatanism — so far as the currency of the country is concerned. The idea of Congress fixing the value of currency is
an absurdity, notwithstanding the *language* of the Constitution
— not the meaning of it. . . . If we can, by law, make $107
out of $100,[1] we can, by the same process, make it worth $150.
Why, Sir, of all the problems that have come up for solution,
from the time of the alchemists down to the present time, none

[1] The act of 1853 altered the value of the silver in the subsidiary coin
about 7 per cent.

can compare with that solved by this modern Congress. They alone have discovered that they can make money — that they can make $107 out of $100. If they can increase it to that extent they can go on and increase it to the infinity, and thus, by the operation of the mint, can the Government supply its own revenues. The great difficulty of mankind is solved, the idea that so much money is wanted all over the world is at length at an end." [1]

By an act of March 3, 1853,[2] the date fixed for the beginning of the subsidiary coinage was changed from June 1 to April 1, 1853, and the weight of the three-cent silver piece was changed to correspond with the new standard for subsidiary coin. Over $1,000,000 in these pieces had been coined at the lower fineness under the law of March, 1851, showing the great need for small coin, especially for postage, then three cents. *(Other legislation of 1853.)*

Another act of the same date [3] provided for the establishment of an assay office at New York and permitted the deposits therein of gold and silver bullion, dust or foreign coin, for manufacture into bars or coin at the will of the depositor and the issue of certificates of deposit for the kind of metal deposited, which certificates were made receivable in payment of customs dues at the port of New York, for sixty days from date thereof.

The estimates of specie in the country show an increase of $170,000,000 from 1841 to 1861. Of this increase $130,000,000 occurred subsequent to the year 1849. The principal cause was, of course, the domestic production of gold which was in large measure retained despite the exports due to adverse trade balances and the inflated condition of the paper currency from 1850 to 1860.[4] *(Great increase of specie.)*

[1] Congressional Globe, XXVI., p. 475.
[2] See Appendix.   [3] *Ibid.*
[4] Treasury Circular of Information, No. 113, 1900, pp. 61 and 62.

Australia as well as California had become a large producer of gold, and the commercial ratio of silver to gold continued to rise under the influence of this largely increased production. In 1853 the ratio rose above 15½ and did not again recede to that point until 1861. For the year 1859, 15.19 was recorded. The premium on the silver dollar was four to five per cent. No dollars could have circulated under these conditions, and hence but few were coined. The government actually coined less than 2,800,000 of these pieces from 1834 to 1861.

Foreign coin no longer a tender. The final act in the series to establish a currency of domestic coin, in place of the depreciated foreign pieces, became law February 21, 1857.[1] It repealed all statutes permitting the circulation of and giving legal tender power to foreign coins, excepting only the Spanish-American fractional silver pieces, which were to be received only at government offices at a greatly reduced rate and at once recoined. Changes were made in the minor coins, nickel being then first used in combination with copper. The coinage of the half cent was discontinued and the weight of the cent was reduced from 168 to 72 grains.

The act also transferred from the Secretary of the Treasury to the Director of the Mint the duty of annually reporting the values of foreign coins, and required the latter officer to make his reports to the Treasury instead of to the President.

General review. A review of the history of the coinage laws prior to 1861 shows that all the leaders in the government of the country were convinced of the imperative necessity of uniformity in the standard of value as represented by coin. Hence there was no contest over the provision in the Constitution which deprived the several states of the power to coin money and fix the value of coins. Nor

[1] See Appendix.

Australia as well as California had become a large producer of gold, and the commercial ratio of silver to gold continued to rise under the influence of this largely increased production.   In 1853 the ratio rose above $15\frac{1}{2}$ and did not again recede to that point until 1861.   For the year 1859, 15.19 was recorded.   The premium on the silver dollar was four to five per cent.   No dollars could have circulated under these conditions, and hence but few were coined.   The government actually coined less than 2,800,000 of these pieces from 1834 to 1861.

Foreign coin no longer a tender. The final act in the series to establish a currency of domestic coin, in place of the depreciated foreign pieces, became law February 21, 1857.[1]   It repealed all statutes permitting the circulation of and giving legal tender power to foreign coins, excepting only the Spanish-American fractional silver pieces, which were to be received only at government offices at a greatly reduced rate and at once recoined.   Changes were made in the minor coins, nickel being then first used in combination with copper.   The coinage of the half cent was discontinued and the weight of the cent was reduced from 168 to 72 grains.

The act also transferred from the Secretary of the Treasury to the Director of the Mint the duty of annually reporting the values of foreign coins, and required the latter officer to make his reports to the Treasury instead of to the President.

General review. A review of the history of the coinage laws prior to 1861 shows that all the leaders in the government of the country were convinced of the imperative necessity of uniformity in the standard of value as represented by coin.   Hence there was no contest over the provision in the Constitution which deprived the several states of the power to coin money and fix the value of coins.   Nor

[1] See Appendix.

made to foresee the eventual change in the commercial ratio, no provision was made for an alteration in the legal ratio.

Hesitating to depart from the bimetallic policy adopted under the inspiration of these men, the followers of both in Congress did not venture upon a radical change such as Great Britain had made, but endeavored first by the legislation of 1834 and 1837 to adjust the legal to the commercial ratio, the disparity in which had deprived the country of gold currency; and later, in 1853, by reducing the amount of silver in the fractional coins they sought to retain the same in circulation as the small change of everyday transactions by making the coins worth more as money than they were as bullion for export. For nearly half a century prior to 1853 the people had suffered from a dearth of coin and especially fractional parts of a dollar, with all the economic disturbances resulting therefrom.

Notwithstanding the declared purpose in 1853 to establish the single gold standard, the bimetallic law remained, and silver dollars, equally with gold, possessed full legal tender power. The failure of Congress to provide a sound coinage system with a single standard of value materially affected the paper currency system, which is now to be discussed, and left the seed from which was to grow the greatest monetary heresy of modern times, destined to threaten the welfare of the people for a quarter of a century.

WORLD'S PRODUCTION OF GOLD AND SILVER

(Amounts in millions of dollars)

PERIOD	ANNUAL AVERAGE		PER CENT BY VALUE	
	Gold	Silver	Gold	Silver
1831–1840 . . .	13.5	24.7	35.2	64.8
1841–1850 . . .	36.4	32.4	52.9	47.1
1851–1855 . . .	132.5	36.8	78.3	21.7
1856–1860 . . .	134.1	37.6	78.1	21.9

The great increase in production of gold, shown in the above table, accounts for the marked rise in the price of silver, as indicated by the fall in the commercial ratio.

COINAGE, UNITED STATES

YEARS	TOTAL GOLD	SILVER DOLLARS	FRACT. SILVER
1831–1835 . . .	$8,631,700	—	$15,371,605
1836–1840 . . .	10,146,100	$62,305	11,909,529.60
1841–1845 . . .	20,214,180	567,218	10,841,782
1846–1850 . . .	69,001,515	435,450	10,518,680
1851–1855 . . .	214,142,519.50	107,650	22,864,243
1856–1860 . . .	130,264,446	1,527,930	23,132,280

Exports and Imports, United States

Years	Exports		Imports	
	Gold	Silver	Gold	Silver
1831-1835	$7,963,900	$17,873,605	$8,351,935	$42,974,961
1836-1840	13,578,435	17,423,953	25,588,296	30,554,104
1841-1845	10,724,258	19,705,113	21,525,334	19,771,321
1846-1850	20,695,177	13,886,373	31,739,452	13,799,885
1851-1855	184,017,429	13,145,180	13,960,026	11,799,057
1856-1860	279,799,526	18,158,678	23,845,192	28,683,659

General Statistics, Precious Metals, United States
(Amounts in millions of dollars)

Year	Gold Exports	Gold Imports	Silver Exports	Silver Imports	Domestic Coin Exports	Production of Gold	Gold Coinage	Silver Coinage
1831 . . .	0.9	0.9	6.0	6.4	2.1	0.5	0.7	3.2
1832 . . .	0.6	0.7	3.6	5.2	1.4	0.7	0.8	2.6
1833 . . .	0.5	0.6	1.7	6.5	0.4	0.7	1.0	2.8
1834 . . .	0.3	3.8	1.4	14.1	0.4	0.9	4.0	3.4
1835 . . .	0.6	2.3	5.1	10.8	0.7	0.7	2.2	3.4
1836 . . .	0.3	7.2	3.7	6.2	0.3	0.7	4.1	3.6
1837 . . .	1.9	2.4	2.8	8.1	1.3	0.7	1.1	2.1
1838 . . .	0.7	11.7	2.3	6.1	0.5	0.6	1.8	2.3
1830 . . .	2.0	1.2	4.0	4.4	1.0	0.6	1.4	3.3

GENERAL STATISTICS, PRECIOUS METALS, UNITED STATES

YEAR	EXPORTS (GOLD)	IMPORTS (GOLD)	SILVER EXPORTS	SILVER IMPORTS	DOMESTIC COIN EXPORTS	PRODUCTION OF GOLD	GOLD COINAGE	SILVER COINAGE
1850	2.5	1.8	3.0	2.9	2.0	50.0	32.0	1.9
1851	4.8	3.6	6.6	1.9	18.1	55.0	62.6	0.8
1852	2.6	3.7	2.6	1.8	37.4	60.0	56.8	1.0
1853	1.9	2.4	2.0	1.8	23.5	65.0	39.4	9.1
1854	2.5	3.0	0.7	3.7	38.1	60.0	25.9	8.6
1855	1.2	1.1	1.1	2.6	54.0	55.0	29.4	3.5
1856	0.9	1.0	0.7	3.2	44.1	55.0	36.9	5.1
1857	5.2	6.7	3.9	5.8	60.1	55.0	32.2	5.5
1858	7.6	11.6	2.6	7.7	42.4	50.0	22.9	8.5
1859	3.6	2.1	2.8	5.3	57.5	50.0	14.8	3.3
1860	1.5	2.5	8.1	6.0	56.9	46.0	23.5	2.3

The production of silver in the United States was only $1,150,000.

The silver coinage included only 1,682,080 silver dollars.

Domestic coin exports included both gold and silver, but the Mint reports include them with the gold. The figures are presented as the best available, without claiming accuracy.

THE history of the United States shows that the people have experimented with every known description of paper currency. The history of the colonial paper issues would form a bulky volume.

Prior to 1775 every one of the colonies had at one time or another made use of note issues, generally under government authority, but in some cases emanating from private banking concerns. In most instances the issues were made to obviate raising revenue by taxation, but the volume was doubtless increased owing to the scarcity of coin, since notes of denominations as low as three-pence, issued during that period, are still in existence. Massachusetts appears to have taken the lead in this as well as in many other matters, and as early as 1690 issued "bills of credit" to pay soldiers.[1] No adequate provision for the redemption of the notes was made, and depreciation generally followed; and this proved equally true where the currency was given forced pay-ing power. Some of the earlier forms merely certified that the bearer was entitled to receive so many dollars, some promised interest, but later the form "This bill shall pass current for ——dollars" was quite generally adopted.

When an issue had depreciated to such an extent as

The colonial period.

Forced cur-rency.

[1] Knox, United States Notes, 1.

to be thoroughly discredited it would be redeemed at a percentage, and sometimes a very small percentage, of its par value, in a new issue put forth with solemn pledges for its redemption, which new issue underwent in turn a like depreciation. The losses suffered by New England on account of depreciated paper currency prior to the Revolution were much greater proportionately than the losses sustained by the other colonies. This section was more prolific in schemes with reference to currency.

Gouge reports that in 1748 the quotation for £100 in coin ranged from £120 in Virginia paper to £1100 in that of New England.[1] No definite record of the amounts of such currency is available, but that the values destroyed by depreciation were very great, considering the relative poverty of the colonies, is beyond doubt.

All the bitter experiences which must have resulted were, however, apparently forgotten during the days of the Revolution. As early as May, 1775, the movement *Continental* to emit bills of credit was begun. Both Massachusetts *currency.* and New York communicated to the Continental Congress a desire for the issue of paper, the former colony advising that body of an authority given to its receiver-general to borrow £100,000 "to support the forces," and asking Congress to assist in giving the notes "a currency through the continent."[2] The communication from New York urged Congress to issue notes, rather than have separate issues by the colonies, but events moved too rapidly, for we find that New York itself issued $112,500 in that year.[3]

---

[1] Gouge, Short History of Paper Money and Banking in the United States.

[2] Journal, Continental Congress.

[3] Schucker's, Finances of the Revolutionary War.

The Continental Congress was powerless to impose taxes, and hence unable to make loans; consequently, burdened with the duty of prosecuting a war, no other recourse than note-issuing seemed possible. Accordingly, on June 22, 1775, but not without considerable opposition, a first issue of what was afterwards known as Continental Currency was authorized, in denominations from $1 to $8 and of $20, to the amount of $2,000,000.[1]

The form adopted was simple. It read: "This bill entitles the bearer to receive —— Spanish milled dollars, or the value thereof in Gold or Silver, according to the resolution of the Congress, held at Philadelphia on the 10th day of May, A.D. 1775." The notes were numbered in ink and signed by two persons duly designated by Congress. While no terms of redemption were fixed, Congress pledged the faith of the colonies to such redemption.

Form of the notes.

A second issue of $1,000,000 was authorized in July, and at this time Congress apportioned the liability for the total issue to the several colonies in proportion to the estimated population.[2] Under this act the redemption of the currency was to be provided for in four instalments, beginning in 1779. In November a further issue of $3,000,000 was voted.

Further issues.

It will be observed that the currency bore no legal tender provision. The notes were generally received without objection for a time, but early in 1776 difficulties were encountered and a question arose as to the value of the coins in which the notes were payable. Congress thereupon adopted resolutions fixing the value of these coins. The following portions of the resolution show the status of the paper issues : —

---

[1] Journal, Continental Congress.   [2] *Ibid.*

"Whereas the holders of bills of credit emitted by authority of Congress will be entitled, at certain periods appointed for redemption thereof, to receive out of the treasury of the United Colonies the amount of the said bills in Spanish milled dollars, or the value thereof in gold or silver, and the value of such dollars, compared with other silver and gold coins, is estimated by different standards in different Colonies, whereby injustice may happen in some instances to the public, as well as to individuals, which ought to be remedied.

Redemption of currency discussed.

"And whereas the credit of the said bills as current money ought to be supported by the inhabitants of these Colonies, for whose benefit they were issued at the full value therein expressed, and who stand bound to redeem the same, according to the like value, and the pernicious artifices of the enemies of American liberty to impair the credit of the said bills by raising the nominal value of gold and silver ought to be guarded against and prevented, therefore . . .

"Resolved, That all bills of credit emitted by authority of Congress ought to pass current in all payments, trade and dealings in these Colonies, and be deemed equal in value to gold and silver, . . . and that whosoever shall offer, demand, or receive more in the said bills for any gold or silver coins, or bullion, than at the rates aforesaid, or more of the said bills for any lands, houses, goods, wares or merchandise than the nominal sums at which the same might be purchased of the same person with gold or silver, every such person ought to be deemed an enemy to the liberties of these Colonies, and treated accordingly, being duly convicted thereof before the committee of inspection of the city, county or district, or in case of an appeal from their decision, before the assembly convention council or committee of safety or before such other persons or courts as have or shall be authorized by the general assemblies or conventions of the Colonies respectively to hear and determine such offences."[1]

Drastic force laws contemplated.

An earlier pronouncement contained this language : —

" . . . that any person who shall hereafter be so lost to all virtue and regard for his country as to refuse to receive said bills

[1] Journal, Continental Congress.

in payment, or obstruct and discourage the currency or circulation thereof, and shall be duly convicted . . . shall be deemed, published and treated as an enemy of his country, and precluded from all trade or intercourse with the inhabitants of those colonies." [1]

In 1776 Congress authorized the issue of $19,000,000, in 1777, $13,000,000 more, making the total so far $38,000,000. The states had issued in the same period about $10,000,000, so that the total volume was about $16 per capita.[2] Accordingly, in the latter year depreciation began, and stringent legal tender laws were passed by all the states, in the vain hope of forcing the people to take these notes as the equivalent of coin. Congress recommended taxation by the states and attempted also to borrow money, but these efforts were fruitless. In 1778 further issues of $63,500,000 were made, and naturally further depreciation ensued. At the end of the year the ratio to coin was, as officially fixed by Congress, 100 to $13\frac{1}{2}$.[3] Actually the depreciation was greater, the rating by Congress having been too favorable to the paper currency. In 1779 the issue exceeded $140,000,000, thus making a total of over $241,500,000 (although a limit of $200,000,000 had been resolved upon),[4] to which must be added about $20,000,000 of local issues. Counterfeiting had become quite prevalent and accelerated depreciation so that at the end of 1779 the official rating to coin was about as 100 to $3\frac{1}{2}$.[5] Congress stopped further emission, but some of the states (notably Virginia and North Carolina) increased their issues, redeeming some of the old issues

Further expansion.

Rapid depreciation.

[1] Journal, Continental Congress.
[2] Schuckers, Finances of the Revolutionary War.
[3] Phillips, Continental Paper Money.
[4] Journal, Continental Congress.
[5] Phillips, Continental Paper Money.

at the depreciated value with the new ones. Some of these new issues were six-year interest-bearing notes indorsed by the United States. Such redemption practically repudiated thirty-nine fortieths of the notes, yet creditors were compelled to accept the old notes at face value under the legal tender laws.[1]

In 1780 the state issues amounted to over $37,000,000, of which Virginia had emitted over $30,000,000; in 1781 to upward of $116,000,000, of which Virginia had emitted $87,500,000 and North Carolina $26,250,000.[2]

Great distress.

The distress resulting was manifestly extreme. The paper currency had reached a volume averaging about $150 per capita. The continental notes in 1871 were quoted at the ratio of 225 to 1 of coin, later 500 to 1 is mentioned, and Pelatiah Webster states that its circulation "was never more brisk" than at that time.[3]

It should be noted that the Articles of Confederation adopted in 1781 gave Congress the power, coördinately with the states, "to borrow money, or emit bills on the credit of the United States," but accorded to it no power to levy taxes. A large loan from France at this time no doubt saved the embryo government from impending dissolution.

Legal tender again discussed.

At the behest of Congress the states revised and relaxed their legal tender laws so far as continental currency was concerned. Some of them continued extreme penalties for refusal to accept the local issues, although not without strenuous protests. In one of these protests appears the following: "That if public confidence was wanting tender laws could not replace it. . . . If the paper were of full value it would pass current without such aid; if it were not, then to compel persons to receive it at the nominal value would be an act of dis-

[1] Phillips, Continental Paper Money.
[2] *Ibid.*
[3] Political Essays.

honesty. That it was inconsistent with true principles to interfere in any manner with the free disposal of property." [1]

The craze practically passed with 1781. It is not very clear how much continental currency was actually issued during the period, but it was unquestionably in excess of $200,000,000. One account places the sum at $357,000,000, but this no doubt includes " re-issues," new notes substituted for old. That the limit attempted to be fixed by Congress was exceeded appears beyond question. [2]

In 1783 Congress considered the question of redeeming the notes, but no action was taken until after the adoption of the Constitution, when, in 1790, redemption at 100 to 1 was provided for, if notes were presented prior to September 30, 1791. [3] This time limit was extended by subsequent acts of Congress, finally until December 31, 1797. [4] Since continental notes were so depreciated in value as to be quoted, in 1781, at a ratio of 225 to 1 in coin (in other words, continental notes were worth in coin .0044+), it is probable that those who received the notes in the later years of the Revolution suffered no loss in having them redeemed in coin at the ratio of 100 to 1 or .01 of their face value. Nevertheless, it is a rather humiliating fact that the United States scaled down the obligations issued in prosecuting the war which achieved its independence as a nation, 99 per cent.

Redemption of continental currency.

Beside the French loan another important event in 1781 materially assisted in maintaining the credit of the country. Robert Morris persuaded Congress to authorize the establishment of the Bank of North America, [5] the

---

[1] Phillips, Continental Paper Money.
[2] Nourse, Register United States Treasury, in American Almanac, 1830.
[3] United States Statutes, Vol. I.   [4] *Ibid.*
[5] Clarke and Hall, Documentary History of Bank of United States, p. 9.

The first
corporate
bank
founded.
first incorporated bank in the country, still in existence in Philadelphia as a national bank.[1] The capital was $400,000, of which the government took $250,000, but sold its holdings in 1783, being induced to do so by extreme financial needs. The bank's charter was perpetual, and a number of the states granted it local charters. It rendered the government valuable assistance and commanded general confidence. Its note issues soon found their way into general use, circulating at par.

Other banks
established.
In 1784 the Bank of New York, in New York City, and the Massachusetts Bank, in Boston, were organized and are still doing a successful business. Alexander Hamilton was a controlling influence in the organization of the Bank of New York, and drew its charter, which, however, was not granted by the Legislature until 1791. These three institutions were the only ones which preceded the establishment of the Bank of the United States. Their notes gave the people an excellent paper currency which served as an educating influence against "fiat money" schemes, the disastrous effects of which led to the adoption of sounder principles in framing the Constitution in 1787. That instrument, which went into effect in 1789, provided as follows : —

The Constitution and
paper
money.
ART. I. Sec. 8. "The Congress shall have power . . . to borrow money on the credit of the United States, . . . to coin money, regulate the value thereof, and of foreign coin."

ART. I. Sec. 10. "No state shall . . . coin money, emit bills of credit, make anything but gold and silver coin a tender in payment of debts, pass any . . . law impairing the obligation of contracts."

Fresh from their experiences with continental paper currency, so disastrous to all, it would appear reasonable

[1] It was in a sense the successor of an informal banking association organized in Pennsylvania a few years earlier, to assist the Continental Congress.

to assume that the intention of the framers of the Constitution was to prohibit all issues of legal tender paper by Congress. George Bancroft contends, in antagonism to the Supreme Court, that the record of the proceedings of the convention leaves no doubt of such intention.

Upon the question whether the power to "emit bills of credit," as stated in the draft of the Constitution then under consideration, should be given the United States, Gouverneur Morris, in opposition, remarked that "if the United States have credit, such bills will be unnecessary ; if they have not, will be unjust and useless." He was vigorously supported by other delegates. Ellsworth said it was a favorable moment to "shut and bar the door against paper money." Wilson said that the striking out of the provision would "remove the possibility of paper money." Langdon preferred rejecting the whole plan rather than retain the three words " and emit bills." Madison, who hesitated to strike out the words, finally assented after having, as he said, satisfied himself that it would not disable the government from using its credit, but would cut off the pretext for a paper currency and particularly for making bills a tender either for public or private debts.[1]

Debate in convention.

The words were stricken out by a vote of four to one, and unquestionably the convention intended to withhold from the federal government the power to create paper money with legal tender attributes.

The foregoing comments are here briefly introduced in chronological order, but will again be referred to in discussing government paper currency issues in later years.

The course pursued by the "fathers" respecting bank paper currency under the Constitution will now be considered.

[1] Bancroft, A Plea for the Constitution, quoting Elliot's Debates of the Constitutional Convention.

Hamilton's report on a bank.

In reply to an order from Congress, to inform that body what further provisions he deemed necessary to establish the public credit, Alexander Hamilton, in December, 1790, submitted his plan for the establishment of a Bank of the United States, similar in its constitution to the Bank of England.[1] He regarded it necessary, owing to the lack of knowledge of the functions of banks, to devote a large portion of the report to that subject. He showed very lucidly how the system of discounts and credits and the use of checks, operated to supplement the stock of coin and foster trade and com-

Its great utility.

merce. He demonstrated that the organization of such a bank of issue would enable the country to obtain a manifold use of the volume of coin available, would aid the government in obtaining loans in sudden emergencies by having the capital concentrated, would facilitate the payment of taxes by extending credit and also furnish a convenient medium for remittance from place to place, which latter function would be further facilitated by the system of branches proposed. The bank would serve as the receiver and disburser of public funds, and the money derived from taxes would not be locked up awaiting the government's expenditures, but remain all the while in circulation. He thus anticipated the arguments against the present subtreasury system.

Objections answered.

He controverted the current charges that banks "serve to increase usury," that they "tend to prevent other kinds of lending," "furnish temptations to overtrading," "afford aid to ignorant adventurers," "give to bankrupt and fraudulent creditors fictitious credit," and "have a tendency to banish gold and silver from the country."

Upon the last point he remarked : —

"A nation that has no mines of its own must derive the precious metals from others ; generally speaking, in exchange for

[1] Appendix.

the products of its labor and industry. The quantity it will possess will, therefore, in the ordinary course of things, be regulated by the favorable or unfavorable balance of its trade ; that is, by the proportion between its abilities to supply foreigners, and its wants of them, between the amount of its exportations and that of its importations. Hence, the state of its agriculture and manufactures, the quantity and quality of its labor and industry, must, in the main, influence and determine the increase or decrease of its gold and silver. If this be true, the inference seems to be that well constituted banks favor the increase of the precious metals. It has been shown that they augment, in different ways, the active capital of a country. This it is which generates employment, which animates and expands labor and industry. Every addition which is made to it, by contributing to put in motion a greater quantity of both, tends to create a greater quantity of the products of both, and, by furnishing more materials for exportation, conduces to a favorable balance of trade, and consequently to the introduction and increase of gold and silver."

Currency volume increased by a bank.

These statements of rudimentary banking principles and defence of the character and purpose of banks sound very droll, read in the light of the wonderful development of modern banking, and yet the primitive conditions demanded such an exposition and such defence.

Comparing a government with a bank currency, he said : —

" Among other material differences between a paper currency issued by the mere authority of government and one issued by a bank, payable in coin, is this ; that in the first case there is no standard to which an appeal can be made as to the quantity which will only satisfy or which will surcharge the circulation ; in the last that standard results from the demand. If more should be issued than is necessary it will return upon the bank. Its emissions, as elsewhere intimated, must always be in a compound ratio to the fund and the demand, whence it is evident that there is a limitation in the nature of the thing ; while the discretion of the government is the only measure of the extent of the emissions by its own authority."

Advantage o bank over government currency.

State banks, he showed, could not serve the government, being unable to furnish adequate security for public moneys, and not amenable to Congress or federal authority. He would have favored the utilization of the Bank of North America under its perpetual charter from the Continental Congress had the bank not been handicapped by the acceptance of charters from several states. Even its original charter from Congress, in Hamilton's opinion, required material amendment to serve the purpose he had in view.

The constitutional objections.

The bank charter bill passed Congress substantially in the form presented by Hamilton, despite the objections of most of the adherents of Jefferson and Madison, who opposed it upon constitutional as well as other grounds.[1] The Cabinet of Washington was evenly divided upon the question, but the bill received Washington's approval on February 25, 1791. Before it was approved, Hamilton prepared a masterful argument upon the subject of its constitutionality, in reply to Jefferson and Edmund Randolph, who advised against approval on the ground that it was not authorized by the Constitution.[2]

This was practically the first important crossing of swords between the strict constructionists of the organic law and those who believed in broader lines of interpretation. In the final analysis the argument turned upon the question of the expressed and the implied

Hamilton's broad-gauge views.

powers of the federal government. While practically admitting that there was no express grant of power to Congress to create corporations, Hamilton urged that implied powers were equally authoritative — that the sole question was whether the end to be served came

[1] Clarke and Hall, Documentary History of Bank of United States.
[2] Ibid.

within the scope of the federal authority and needs —
"within the sphere of the specified powers." If this
were answered affirmatively, the means necessarily
employed to accomplish such end must be constitutional. For example, under the expressed power of
regulating commerce, lighthouses, etc., were provided
for, and the power thus implied to establish lighthouse
service was also a sovereign and unlimited power.

He then proceeded to show how the incorporation of
the bank was a means to the end of facilitating the
government's fiscal operations, as well as establishing
a broader and stronger credit and currency system for
the entire country, promoting uniformity in those important particulars, and hence the general welfare, functions which the state banks could not possibly exercise
to advantage.

A bank as a government auxiliary.

Replying to Jefferson's contention that while convenient this was not necessary, and that necessity constituted the only valid reason for exercising implied
powers, he maintained that to define that word so narrowly would lead to a restriction of the powers of the
federal government which would largely defeat the purpose of the Constitution. The following quotation contains the gist of his argument : —

"This general principle is inherent in the very definition of
government, and essential to every step of the progress to be
made by that of the United States ; namely, that every power
vested in the government is, in its nature, SOVEREIGN, and includes, by force of the term, a right to employ all the means
requisite and fairly applicable to the attainment of the ends of
such power and which are not precluded by restrictions and
exceptions specified in the Constitution, or not immoral, or not
contrary to the essential ends of political society."

Sovereign powers of federal gov-ernment.

The argument of Hamilton was adopted by Chief

Marshall
sustains
Hamilton.

Justice Marshall in sustaining the United States Bank charter, and later by the Supreme Court in upholding the legal tender power of United States notes. Hamilton's position was indorsed by Washington, and in several instances when amendatory acts were passed by Congress, Jefferson, when he became President, interposed no objection nor did the charter ever come for review before the Supreme Court. The charter of the second bank did, and since many of the points at issue in 1791 were then reviewed and determined, and since it was the first comprehensive exposition of the scope and principles of the Constitution, I insert here the syllabus and excerpts from the opinion by Chief Justice Marshall.

SYLLABUS

McCulloch *vs.* Maryland, 4 Wheaton 413

Supreme
Court on
bank
charter.

" Congress has power to incorporate a bank.

" The government of the Union is the government of the people ; it emanates from them ; its powers are granted by them, and are to be exercised directly on them and for their benefit.

" The government of the Union, though limited in its powers, is supreme within its sphere of action, and its laws, when made in pursuance of the Constitution, form the supreme law of the land.

" There is nothing in the Constitution of the United States, similar to the articles of confederation, which excludes incidental or implied powers.

Power of
Congress set
forth.

" If the end be legitimate and within the scope of the Constitution, all the means which are appropriate, which are plainly adapted to that end, and which are not prohibited, may constitutionally be employed to carry it into effect.

" The power of establishing a corporation is not a distinct sovereign power or end of government, but only the means of carrying into effect other powers which are sovereign. Whenever it becomes an appropriate means of exercising any of the powers given by the Constitution to the government of the Union, it may be exercised by that government.

"If a certain means to carry into effect any of the powers expressly given by the Constitution to the government of the Union, be an appropriate measure, not prohibited by the Constitution, the degree of its necessity is a question of legislative discretion, not of judicial cognizance. Implied powers.

"The act of 10th April, 1816, c. 44, to 'incorporate the subscribers to the Bank of the United States,' is a law made in pursuance of the Constitution. The Bank of the United States has, constitutionally, a right to establish its branches, or offices of discount and deposit, within any state.

"The state within which such branch may be established cannot, without violating the Constitution, tax that branch. States cannot tax bank.

"The state governments have no right to tax any of the constitutional means employed by the government of the Union to execute its constitutional powers.

"The states have no power, by taxation or otherwise, to retard, impede, burden, or in any manner control, the operations of the constitutional laws enacted by Congress, to carry into effect the powers vested in the national government.

"This principle does not extend to a tax paid by the real property of the Bank of the United States, in common with the other real property in a particular state, nor to a tax imposed on the proprietary interest which the citizens of that state may hold in this institution, in common with other property of the same description throughout the state."

*　　*　　*　　*　　*　　*　　*　　*　　*　　*

The Chief Justice said : —

"Although among the enumerated powers of government, we do not find the word 'bank' or 'incorporation,' we find the great powers to lay and collect taxes, to borrow money, to regulate commerce, to declare and conduct a war, and to raise and support armies and navies. . . . A government entrusted with such ample powers, on the due execution of which the happiness and prosperity of the nation so vitally depends, must also be entrusted with ample means for their execution. . . . Express powers imply others.

"The government which has a right to do an act and has imposed on it the duty of performing that act, must, according to the dictates of reason, be allowed to select the means, and those who contend that it may not select any appropriate means, that one particular mode of effecting the object is excepted, take upon themselves the burden of establishing that exception. . . .

Necessary means at discretion of Congress.

" But the Constitution of the United States has not left the right of Congress to employ the necessary means for the execution of the powers conferred on the government, to general reasoning. To its enumeration of powers is added that of making ' all laws which shall be necessary and proper for carrying into execution the foregoing powers, and all other powers vested by this Constitution in the government of the United States or in any department thereof.' . . .

"The word 'necessary' is considered (by counsel for the state) as controlling the whole sentence, and as limiting the right to pass laws for the execution of the granted powers, to such as are indispensable, and without which the power would be nugatory. That it excludes the choice of means and leaves to Congress in each case that only which is most direct and simple. Is it true that this is the sense in which the word ' necessary ' is always used ?

*　　*　　*　　*　　*　　*　　*　　*　　*　　*

" To employ the means necessary to an end is generally understood as employing any means calculated to produce the end, and not as being confined to those single means without which the end would be entirely unattainable.

*　　*　　*　　*　　*　　*　　*　　*　　*　　*

Necessity to be broadly construed.

" To have declared that the best means shall not be used, but those alone without which the power given would be nugatory, would have been to deprive the legislature of the capacity to avail itself of experience, to exercise its reason, and to accommodate its legislation to circumstances.

*　　*　　*　　*　　*　　*　　*　　*　　*　　*

Examples from other provisions.

"Take, for example, the power 'to establish post offices and post roads.' This power is executed by the single act of making the establishment. But, from this has been inferred the power and duty of carrying the mails along the post road, from one post office to another, and, from this implied power, has again been inferred the right to punish those who steal letters from the post office or rob the mail. It may be said, with some plausibility, that the right to carry the mail and to punish those who rob it is not indispensably necessary to the establishment of a post office and post road. This right is indeed essential to the beneficial exercise of the power but not indispensably necessary to its existence.

* * * * * * * * * *

" All admit the constitutionality of a territorial government, which is a corporate body.

" If a corporation may be employed indiscriminately with other means to carry into execution the powers of the government, no particular reason can be assigned for excluding the use of a bank, if required for its fiscal operations. To use one must be within the discretion of Congress, if it be an appropriate mode of executing the powers of government. That it is a convenient, a useful and essential instrument in the prosecution of its fiscal operations, is not now a subject of controversy. All those who have been concerned unite in representing its importance and necessity, and so strongly have they been felt that statesmen of the first class whose previous opinions against it had been confirmed by every circumstance which can fix the human judgment, have yielded those opinions to the exigencies of the nation. *If appropriate and not prohibited.*

* * * * * * * * * *

" It can scarcely be necessary to say that the existence of state banks can have no possible influence on the question. No trace is to be found in the Constitution of an intention to create a dependence of the government of the Union on those of the states for the execution of the powers assigned to it. Its means are adequate to its ends, and on those means alone was it expected to rely for the establishments of its ends. To impose on it the necessity of resorting to means which it cannot control, which another government may furnish or withhold, would render its course precarious, the result of its measures uncertain, and create a dependence on other governments which might disappoint its most important designs, and is incompatible with the language of the Constitution. But were it otherwise, the choice of means implies a right to choose a national bank in preference to state banks, and Congress alone can make the selection." *Choice of means in Congress.*

The first bank's charter.   The charter was an exclusive one for twenty years.[1] The capital was fixed at $10,000,000 divided into shares of $400 each, the government taking one-fifth. Small investors in the shares were protected by being given a relatively greater voting power, and no one was allowed to cast more than thirty votes ; foreign shareholders had no votes. Twenty-five directors were to govern the institution. The government's shares were to be paid for with money borrowed from the bank, repayable *Note issues.* in instalments. No specific authority to issue notes was conferred, this being apparently understood to exist without a special proviso, but other parts of the act referred to the notes to be issued, and the notes were to be included in the liabilities. The notes and other debts (exclusive of deposits) were not to exceed the capital of the bank, directors being liable for such excess. Furthermore, the notes while payable on demand in coin were to be "receivable in all payments *Branches.* to the United States." Branches were authorized to be opened at any place in the United States, and the Secretary of the Treasury was empowered to require reports and to inspect the *general* accounts upon which such reports were based. The bank was not allowed to hold real estate beyond that necessary for offices, etc., unless acquired in satisfaction of preëxisting debt. It was prohibited from loaning more than $100,000 to the United States or more than $50,000 to any state, or making any loans to a foreign prince or state, unless sanctioned by Congress. It was not permitted to deal in stocks and bonds (except to sell those it acquired at the outset), or, generally, in anything but bills of exchange and bullion, nor was it to charge more than 6 per cent upon loans or discounts. A very important provision was that three-fourths of the stock had to be

[1] See the act in Appendix.

paid for in 6 per cent bonds of the United States then being issued. Thus the government was to be materially assisted at the outset in floating its loans.

The stock of the bank was considerably oversubscribed in two hours after the books were opened.

The bank began business in Philadelphia, branches being eventually opened in New York, Boston, Baltimore, Washington, Norfolk, Charleston, Savannah, and New Orleans. The government almost immediately became a borrower from the bank, and ultimately it was compelled to realize upon its shares in the bank to repay part of the debt. In 1802 it ceased to be a shareholder, having, however, realized a net profit of nearly 57 per cent upon its investment. *Its operations.*

No reports of the bank's condition seem to have been required by the Treasury, and only two reports are known to exist, having been communicated to Congress by Secretary Gallatin in 1809 and 1811.[1] The rate of dividend paid (in excess of 8 per cent) indicates that it was a very successful enterprise, besides having been of incalculable benefit to the government in its most trying days during the period under review. From the reports in question it is gleaned that its circulation was $4,500,000 to $5,000,000, individual deposits $8,500,000 in 1809 and $5,900,000 in 1811, loans about $15,000,000, specie about $5,000,000. The latter of the two reports was for a date within a few months of the expiration of its charter. *Reports of condition.*

Aside from the service to the government which the bank performed admirably, as testified to by Gallatin, Jefferson's Secretary of the Treasury, it exercised a most salutary influence upon the currency. Its own issues were never very large compared with its specie reserve, it issued no notes under ten dollars, and it

[1] Gallatin's Reports, Finance Reports, Vol. I.

checked undue expansion on the part of the state banks, which now were increasing in number annually, by forcing redemption in specie when occasion warranted.[1]

Gallatin on the national bank.

Although the charter was not to expire until 1811, a petition from the bank for its renewal was presented to Congress early in 1808. It was referred to committees, and Gallatin was directed to submit his views on the subject. He favored a new charter rather than a renewal, but was unquestionably favorable to the use of such a bank, particularly for the collection, safe keeping, and transmission of public moneys, and as an aid to the government in respect to loans.[2] The strongest objection to the renewal was the fact that $7,200,000 of the $10,000,000 capital was owned abroad. He therefore recommended a national bank, capital $30,000,000, two-sixths to go to the shareholders of the existing bank, three-sixths to the United States and the states, and one-sixth to the public, both the federal and the state governments to have a voice in the direction ; the United States to receive interest on its deposits in excess of $3,000,000, and in emergencies to be accommodated with loans to the extent of $18,000,000 at 6 per cent.

In 1810 a committee reported a bill upon the lines indicated by Gallatin, simply grafting the new features on Hamilton's act of 1791.[3] Subsequently another bill

Efforts to renew charter.

was reported to renew the charter for twenty years with some such modifications as recommended by Gallatin, excluding the participation of the states. In January, 1811, Gallatin submitted the second of the reports of the condition of the bank, already referred to. Another bill for renewal was introduced and pressed. An extended debate ensued, in the course of which the entire question was thoroughly discussed. Much of the oppo-

[1] Gallatin's Reports, Finance Reports, Vol. I.   [2] *Ibid.*
[3] Clarke and Hall, History of Bank of United States.

sition was based on constitutional objections. In the
House the bill was defeated by the close vote of 65 to
64. In the Senate Crawford (afterwards Secretary of
the Treasury) favored the renewal, in a strong report,
believing, like Gallatin, in the great practical utility of
the bank. He obtained from Gallatin a forcible plea
for his bill, in which the inability of state banks to serve
the desired purpose was conclusively shown. Crawford
pointed out that despite the admitted usefulness of the
bank and its influences upon the country's prosperity,
the legislators were being carried away by the supposed
public sentiment against the bank. Henry Clay opposed
the bill upon constitutional grounds; he also appears to
have been afraid of foreign control. The vote in the
Senate was 17 to 17, and Vice-President George Clinton
gave the casting vote against the bill. So renewal was
defeated. A petition from the bank for a brief extension in order to wind up its affairs was likewise negatived. Clay in the Senate made the committee report
against the petition, saying that inasmuch as the original
act was unconstitutional, any extension would be equally
so. In the House the same reason was given for
refusal.[1]

The assets of the institution were acquired by Stephen
Girard, who continued the business in Philadelphia as
Girard's Bank, which still flourishes there under a
national charter.

In the final liquidation it paid $434 for each of its
$400 shares, after having paid dividends averaging $8\frac{1}{2}$
per cent.[2]

In 1784 there were but three state banks with a capital of $2,100,000. From the meagre reports available it
is gathered that the number increased by 1800 to 28

[1] Clarke and Hall, History of Bank of United States.
[2] Knox, History of Banking.

with $21,300,000 capital, in 1805 there were 75 with
over $40,000,000 of capital, and in 1811 there were 88
with nearly $43,000,000 of capital. Of these last men-
tioned 47 with $12,200,000 capital were in New Eng-
land, where the laws imposed wholesome regulation,
particularly in Massachusetts, which required public reports from 1803. Although the systems in other states
were with rare exceptions very carelessly supervised, or
not at all, and charters were granted as spoils of party
in some, the circulation issued relative to the specie
holdings was not excessive in volume until after 1811.[1]

Banks
owned by
states. In 1806 Vermont had organized a bank, with branches,
owned and operated exclusively by the state. Ken-
tucky in the same year, Delaware in 1807, and North
Carolina in 1810, each chartered a bank in which the
state took a substantial stock interest. That of Delaware is still in existence, under the old charter.[2]

Taken all together the period covered by the two dec-
ades during which the first United States Bank existed
was one of prosperity, perhaps without parallel in any
new country after an impoverishing war, and although
natural advantages and the energies of the people had
much to do with this prosperity, it is but just to give
credit to the fathers of the Republic for their foresight
in laying its foundations, and especially to the genius of
Hamilton, who at the age of 32 took charge of the Treasury Department, and for about six years had the almost
exclusive direction of the economic affairs of the
new nation. His four reports on the Public Credit, the
Establishment of a Coinage System, on the Bank, and
on Manufactures and Tariff, constitute a monument to
the incomparable ability of this greatest of all our financial ministers.

[1] See Crawford's Report of 1820, also Gallatin, Currency and Banking
System, 1831.   [2] Knox, History of Banking.

STATISTICAL RÉSUMÉ

ESTIMATES OF BANK CAPITAL AND CIRCULATION, AND THE MONEY IN
THE COUNTRY FOR VARIOUS DATES TO 1811

Compiled from Crawford's Reports and Elliot's Funding System

(In millions except in last column)

	BANKS (INCLUDING BANK OF UNITED STATES AFTER 1790)			MONEY VOLUME			
	Number	Capital	Circulation	Specie	Total	Population	Per Capita
1784	3	2.1	2.0	10.0	12.0	3.0	$4.00
1790	4	2.5	2.5	9.0	11.5	3.8	3.00
1795	24	21.0	16.0	19.0	35.0	4.5	7.77
1800	29	31.3	15.5	17.5	33.0	5.3	6.22
1805	76	50.5	26.0	17.5	43.5	6.2	7.00
1811	89	52.7	28.1	30.0	58.1	7.3	8.00

It is reported that in 1811 the banks held about $15,000,000 of specie. Statements purporting to give specie holdings prior to that date are misleading.

CHAPTER V

1812 TO 1836

State bank currency.

THE currency history of the country for the quarter-century following the expiration of the charter of the first Bank of the United States is divisible into three almost equal periods, — the disorganized condition of the currency during and following the War of 1812, and the struggle for its reformation, which extended to 1820; a period of sound currency under regulation by the second Bank of the United States followed and continued until 1829; then began the war upon the bank resulting in the failure to renew its charter and the downfall and breaking up of the system of which the bank had been the controlling influence.

Statistics relating to banking and currency from 1812 to 1834 are exceedingly meagre. Subsequent to 1834, pursuant to a resolution of Congress directing the collection and reporting of information, the Treasury reports contain fairly satisfactory data. Secretary Crawford,[1] and afterward ex-Secretary Gallatin,[2] undertook to give some comparative figures for certain years. For the period from 1821 to 1828, inclusive, the only available statistics are found in the reports of the Massachusetts banks (required by state law from 1803) and those of the second Bank of the United States, also required by law.

[1] Report of 1820, in full in International Monetary Conference, 1878, p. 502.
[2] Currency and Banking System, 1831.

The second war with Great Britain began in 1812. The government found it necessary to borrow money, and as predicted by Hamilton, Gallatin, and Crawford, the state banks proved unequal to the emergency. Instead of the anticipated contraction of banking facilities after the liquidation of the first bank, a rapid expansion had taken place, but much of the alleged bank capital was fictitious, a large number of banks having been organized upon capital represented by notes of hand of the subscribers.

State banks.

Crawford estimated that in the four years, 1811–1815, the number of banks increased from 88 to 208, the capital from less than $43,000,000 to over $88,000,000, and the circulation from $23,000,000 to $110,000,000. In 1816 there were 246 banks with $89,400,000 capital. For 1817 the number of banks is not given, but the capital is estimated at $125,700,000. In 1820 there were 307 banks, but the capital was only $102,100,000. Adequate legal restrictions were wanting in most of the states, and notes were issued with ease and without regard to capital or specie holdings. In order to increase the volume as much as possible, since note-issues were their principal means of making loans and discounts, a mass of small denominations, some as low as six cents, were issued. Adding to this the stress of war and the consequent hoarding of specie, suspension of coin payments naturally followed. Most of the banks outside of New England suspended in August, 1814. The depreciation of Southern and Western bank-notes was most severe. At Baltimore, where notes from Southern banks were found in greatest abundance, the discount on some issues reached 23 per cent. In New York and Philadelphia 16 per cent was the maximum discount. Boston and New England notes alone were quoted on a par with specie. The range of the dis-

Inflation and suspension.

counts by years was: 1814, 10 @ 20 per cent; 1851,
2 @ 21½ per cent; 1816, 1¾ @ 23 per cent; and 1817,
the year of resumption, 2½ @ 4½ per cent. Lack of
specific information prevented the public from exercising a wise discrimination, as between banks, and
hence they discriminated against localities. As late as
1823 discounts reaching a maximum of 75 per cent upon
notes of certain Kentucky banks are recorded.[1]

Treasury
notes and
loans.

The funds of the government were deposited in many
of these banks throughout the country, and when suspension took place amounted to $9,000,000. Congress,
in 1812, had been compelled to resort to an issue of
"Treasury Notes" (the first since 1781) to cover short
term loans. Five separate issues were authorized during
the war. At first all were interest-bearing, payable in
one year and in denominations of $100 only. Later
notes of $50, $20, and $5 were authorized; the $5 notes,
however, did not bear interest. They were not made
legal tenders, the proposition to do so having been
promptly defeated; but being receivable for all public
dues, and payable to public creditors, they circulated
freely. In all $60,500,000 were authorized, but less
than $37,000,000 were actually issued.[2] These notes
were all funded into bonds or paid, except a very few
which were probably destroyed or lost.

The government did not succeed in disposing of its
obligations at par. An official report shows that of the
$80,000,000 of bonds and notes placed during the War
of 1812, owing to the discounts thereon and the depreciated currency received in payment therefor, the
Treasury actually obtained only $34,000,000.[3] In other
words, had the Treasury been able to dispose of its

[1] Gouge, History of Paper Money.
[2] Bailey, National Loans.
[3] McDuffie's Report on Bank of United States, 21st Congress, 1st Sess.

notes and bonds at par in coin, and had its balances Loss through depreciated currency. in the various state banks been available, a loan of $34,000,000 properly financed would probably have covered the expenses of the war, for which, ultimately, the people paid $80,000,000 and interest. Gallatin, in reviewing the period, expressed the opinion unequivocally that, had the Bank of the United States been rechartered, suspension of specie payments would have been avoided and so this loss, enormous for that period, would not have been incurred.[1]

Many of those in Congress who had aided in defeating the renewal of the federal bank charter began to see the error of that policy. It will be recalled that a change of one vote in each House of Congress would have carried one of the measures proposed. Even Madison, now President, who in 1791 was the leader of the opposition to the first bank charter, modified his opinions. The "object lesson" had been an instructive one.

Jefferson advised Madison to propose the issue of government currency, $20,000,000 annually so long as needed, and appeal to the states to relinquish the right to establish banks of issue.[2] This appears to be the first important suggestion for a government note-issue.

Early in 1814 New York members in Congress presented a petition for the establishment of a national National bank proposed. bank with a capital of $30,000,000.[3] The House Committee reported adversely, upon constitutional grounds. Calhoun, then a representative from South Carolina, endeavored to have such a bank established in the District of Columbia, which, being under exclusive federal

[1] Gallatin, Currency and Banking System.
[2] Bolles, Financial History of United States.
[3] Clarke and Hall, Documentary History of Bank of United States.

jurisdiction, made the measure constitutional. A bill
for this purpose was reported in February, but was soon
dropped.   In October the Secretary of the Treasury,
A. J. Dallas, upon request from the House Committee
on Ways and Means to furnish suggestions for the
maintenance of the public credit, submitted a report[1]
strongly favoring a national bank.   Jeffersonian though
he was, and in the cabinet of Madison, Dallas said that
if after twenty years of tacit sanction of the old bank
charter the Constitution had not been amended upon
this question, he considered himself justified in regarding it settled in favor of the constitutionality of the
charter.   He regarded such an institution "the only
efficient remedy for the disordered condition of our cir-

Dallas's
plan.

culating medium."   He recommended a $50,000,000 bank,
two-fifths of the capital to be taken by the United States,
$6,000,000 to be paid in specie by outside subscribers,
$24,000,000 in the recent issues of public debt, and the
$20,000,000 taken by the United States to be also paid
for in such obligations ; the bank to loan the government $30,000,000, and the government to have five of
the fifteen directors and the right of inspection.

Calhoun proposed a substitute bill providing that all
the shares were to be open to public subscription, and
omitting the required loan to the government.   Another
bill, containing a clause permitting the bank to suspend
coin payments during the war, was introduced.   The
suspension clause was rejected by the casting vote of
Speaker Langdon Cheves (afterwards president of the
second bank).   Daniel Webster, with his accustomed
vigor and eloquence, also opposed the suspension clause.
Amended in various particulars the bill finally passed,
but since the capital was reduced to $30,000,000 and no
loan to the government was provided for, Dallas pro-

[1] Finance Reports, Vol. II. ; also Clarke and Hall's History.

nounced the measure inadequate and President Madison vetoed it on January 30, 1815.[1]

Among the objections urged by Madison was that the bank would be compelled to maintain coin payments, thus restricting note circulation and diminishing the bank's usefulness during the war period.[2]

The war came to an end soon thereafter, but the disordered condition of the currency required attention, and Madison, at the opening of the next Congress, December, 1815, gave special attention to the subject in his message.[3] He referred to the absence of specie and the need of a substitute; if state banks could not supply a uniform national currency, a national bank might; if neither could, it might "become necessary to ascertain the terms upon which the *notes of the Government* (no longer required as an instrument of credit) shall be issued, upon motives of general policy, as a common medium of circulation." The exigency must have been great indeed to produce such a change of views since the days when he sat in the Constitutional Convention.

Madison suggests national currency.

Dallas in his annual report for 1815 again discussed the subject, concluding that "the establishment of a national bank is regarded as the best, and perhaps the only adequate resource"; believing that such a bank would aid and lead the state banks in the work of restoring credit, public and private.[4] He recommended a capital of $35,000,000, three-fourths government bonds, one-fourth specie (the capital to be afterwards augmented to $50,000,000 by Congress, the additional

Dallas's revised bill.

---

[1] Clarke and Hall, History of Bank of United States. Messages of Presidents, Vol. I.

[2] Messages of Presidents, Vol. I.   [3] *Ibid.*

[4] Clarke and Hall, History of Bank of United States, also Finance Reports, Vol. II.

$15,000,000 to be taken by the states); the United States to take $7,000,000 of the capital and to have one-fifth of the directors; the bank to pay $1,500,000 for the charter out of its earnings. Suspension of coin payments was not permitted, branches were allowed, and the ordinary government business was to be transacted without charge.

Calhoun reported a bill to the House upon the lines suggested by Dallas. Webster desired to reduce the capital. Clay, now in the House, favored the bill, explaining that his former opposition in the Senate to a national bank was due to supposed instructions from the Kentucky legislature, to the supposed desire of his constituents, and to his conviction that the *necessity* for using an implied constitutional power did not exist; now the case was different; such a bank was indispensable to remedy existing evils. The bill passed the House March 14, 1816, by a vote of 80 to 71. It received the support of Calhoun, Clay, and Ingham (afterwards Secretary of the Treasury); Webster and most of the Whigs voted against it, objecting finally to the participation of the government in the bank. (The Jeffersonians were to have control.) The vote was by no means sectional. The Senate passed the bill in April, and it was approved by Madison on the 10th of that month.[1]

The second bank's charter was drawn largely upon the lines devised by Hamilton for that of the first bank. Numerous provisions repeat his language word for word.[2] The capital was fixed at $35,000,000, three and one-half times that of the first bank, with shares of $100 (instead of $400) each. The government took one-fifth of the stock, paying for it with its obligations in instalments, the last one being paid in 1831. Of the remain-

Margin notes: Congressional action. / The second bank's charter.

---

[1] Clarke and Hall, History of Bank of United States.
[2] See the Appendix.

ing $28,000,000, one-fourth was to be paid for in specie, the balance in specie or government bonds, in three equal half yearly instalments. No single subscription for more than three thousand shares was to be accepted unless the full amount was not taken on the date fixed. The restrictions upon voting shares which the first charter contained, were repeated. There were twenty-five directors, as in the first bank, but now the government had one-fifth of the board, to be appointed by the President.

In lieu of making a loan to the government, the bank paid a bonus of $1,500,000, and it was to act as the fiscal agent of the government, including the transfers of funds, without compensation. The deposit of public moneys was to be made in the bank and branches where they existed, unless otherwise directed by the Secretary of the Treasury, and when that officer gave such directions he was to report his reasons therefor to Congress. The bank was empowered to establish branches anywhere, with a local organization, and it had to have a branch in the District of Columbia and in every state where two thousand shares of its stock were held. Reports were to be made to the Secretary of the Treasury as often as required, and the bank was subject to his inspection and to that of a committee of Congress. *Relations to the government.*

The note-issuing function was more specifically provided for than in the first charter. Denominations under $5 were prohibited and all under $100 were to be payable to bearer on demand. The suspension of coin payments of notes and deposits was prohibited, subject to a penalty of 12 per cent per annum. As in the old charter the liabilities, other than for deposits (therefore including note-issues) were not to exceed the amount of the capital, unless authorized by Congress, and directors were personally liable for any excess. The *Note-issues regulated.*

notes of the bank were to be receivable in all payments to the United States.

The provisions relative to the holding of real estate, dealing in anything but exchange and bullion, and de-manding more than 6 per cent upon loans, were the same as in the old charter. The sale of the govern-ment bonds held by the bank was limited to $2,000,000 a year, and if sold in this country they were first to be offered to the government at current rates. Congress agreed further to incorporate no other banks, except in the District of Columbia, during the life of the charter.

The shares were not fully subscribed at once, and Stephen Girard ultimately took the remnant of 30,383 shares.

Opening of the second bank.

The bank opened for business on January 17, 1817. The second instalment of subscriptions to shares was then due, but neither this nor the third was paid in according to the charter. The bank received less than $2,000,000 (instead of $7,000,000) in specie, having accepted promissory notes and bank-notes in lieu of coin. Consequently the bank was compelled in 1818 to import specie. The officers permitted the transfer of the shares upon the books of the bank before they were fully paid for. A number of the officers and directors speculated in the stock of the bank, discounting their loans for the purpose at the bank or its branches. The first two years' operations showed losses, due largely to this speculation, of more than $3,500,000; nevertheless it paid dividends.[1]

Investigation of irregulari-ties.

On November 30, 1818, the House of Representatives appointed a committee to investigate the bank's affairs. In its report made by John C. Spencer, afterwards Secretary of the Treasury, in February following, the

---

[1] House Reports, 15th Congress, 2d Sess. See also Cheves's Report in Goddard's History of Banks, 1831, p. 106.

speculations and other derelictions above referred to were published.[1] The bank was nearly insolvent and had violated its charter, nevertheless the House refused to declare it forfeited, preferring that the shareholders correct the mismanagement. In March, 1819, Langdon Cheves became president, and under his able and conservative administration, covering four years, the evils were corrected and the bank became very prosperous. From 1823 to the expiration of the charter Nicholas Biddle was president of the institution.

Coin payments were not at once restored. Secretary Dallas had endeavored, but without success, to prepare the way in 1816, by urging the state banks to resume,[2] but the existing conditions were very profitable to them, and they were not inclined to do so. The greater their note-issues and the longer specie resumption was delayed, the larger would be their dividends. In October, 1816, Dallas was succeeded by Crawford, who continued the efforts for resumption and finally succeeded in having July 1, 1817, fixed as the date for its beginning. Crawford felt, however, that the bank's assistance was requisite, and accordingly influenced it to negotiate an agreement with the state banks in the principal cities, to resume on February 20 instead of July 1.

Resumption of specie payments.

This proved easier said than done. The country was unquestionably short of specie. The bank could not, as has been stated, obtain its required quota without importation, and there appears to have been a premium on foreign exchange the greater part of the years 1817 and 1818, so that the imported specie promptly returned abroad. This served to aid the state banks to continue redundant paper issues. The Spencer committee laid

Difficulties encountered

[1] House Reports, 15th Congress, 2d Sess.
[2] Finance Reports, Vol. II.

a large portion of the blame for this upon the bank, declaring that its measures were not sufficiently vigorous. The problem which confronted the bank was, however, a formidable one. The Treasury had turned over to it nearly $11,000,000 of "public deposits" from the state banks, consisting largely of depreciated paper. Specie resumption meant contraction of state bank circulation and serious curtailment of credits which they had extended. The United States Bank could not, owing to its lack of strength in specie, safely supply the credit thus curtailed, and at the same time maintain coin payments. A too rapid contraction necessarily tended to precipitate disaster. While the management of the bank in the first and second years of its existence was open to serious criticism (the speculative tendency of the time having unquestionably influenced many of those who had the business in charge), some of the subsequent currency difficulties might have been avoided if the bank's policy of compelling the *gradual* retirement of state banknotes had been continued.

Violent contraction of currency.

Nevertheless, in obedience to the desire of Congress, the bank acted more vigorously. The volume of notes in the country, which in 1815 stood at $110,000,000, and probably higher in 1816 and 1817, was reduced by the end of 1819 to $45,000,000.[1] The volume of specie was practically unchanged. Loans were violently contracted, prices necessarily fell seriously, "hard times" came upon the land and propositions to issue government paper, as is usual under such conditions, were numerous. Secretary Crawford, asked by the House of Representatives for his views upon this as well as the general subject of the currency, vigorously and suc-

[1] See Crawford's Report, in International Monetary Conference, 1878, p. 502.

cessfully opposed the propositions. Without discussing
the question of the constitutionality of such a measure,
which he assumed was not intended to be put before
him, he asserted that "as a measure of alleviation, it
will be more likely to do harm than good," pointing out,
as if he had lived through the later period when a similar policy prevailed (1862–1879), the effects of such
a paper currency upon practically all lines of human
activity.

Much of the disturbance during this period was no
doubt due to the great fluctuation in exchange between the states of the East, and those of the West
and South. The latter, owing largely to their limited
and widely distributed population, were continually at a
disadvantage, and this condition was largely responsible
for the unstable character of the banks in those sections
and the resulting discount on their notes. The government drew large sums from the people in those states in
payment for public lands, whereas the bulk of the disbursements were made in the East. The bank endeavored to alleviate this condition by redeeming its
notes, no matter where issued, at any of its branches at
par, thus affording a medium of exchange available
throughout the country. It was compelled to modify
this policy in 1818, when it found that the operation
caused embarrassment, serious enough to threaten
suspension.[1] Its notes thereupon depreciated somewhat excepting as to the three New England branches;
but the amount of depreciation was inconsiderable,
ranging from 1 per cent in the early years to $\frac{1}{2}$ and $\frac{1}{4}$
per cent later. All notes were redeemed at Phila-
delphia as well as at the places of issue; notes of five
dollars were redeemed at all offices, and at times all

Domestic exchanges.

Bank endeavors to regulate.

[1] Cheves's Report in Goddard's History of Banks.

notes were received at all the offices from individuals, but not from banks.

Branch drafts.

Another practice of the bank which led to criticism was the issue of "branch drafts" drawn for five dollars, ten dollars, and twenty dollars, by the branches upon the parent bank in Philadelphia, which practically circulated as notes of the bank and were treated as such in its reports. This was done at first (1826) to obviate the great labor of signing notes that the law imposed upon the president and cashier of the parent bank, a task which on account of the large volume of circulation they were physically unable to perform, and which Congress, notwithstanding repeated petitions, refused to alter.[1] The practice eventually became so general, and partook so much of the nature of "kiting," that it was regarded as unwise. At one time these drafts constituted one-third of the circulation.

Opposition to the bank.

The presentation of local bank-notes for redemption by the bank instead of paying them out in the regular course of business, aroused antagonism which many of the state banks fostered for their own advantage. In Kentucky, Ohio, Georgia, and Maryland particularly, the friction became serious. It was upon the question of taxing the bank in the last-mentioned state that the Supreme Court upon appeal finally settled the controversy, prohibiting state interference with the bank.[2]

Nevertheless in Ohio the bank was declared an outlaw for resisting exorbitant taxation, and the entire machinery of the state government was used against it for a time. In Georgia a law was passed virtually justifying creditors of the bank in refusing payment of their debts to it. Kentucky passed "stay" laws practically relieving debtors of their obligations. For pre-

[1] Clarke and Hall, Documentary History of Bank.
[2] McCulloch vs. Maryland ; see Chapter IV., ante.

senting notes of local banks for payment in specie, the
bank was regarded as a criminal; the people there
seemed to think it the duty of the bank to lend its
capital to the state banks without interest (by holding or
paying out their notes) although many of these local
banks were founded upon "moonshine."

As has been stated, the second bank began under
maladministration calculated to defeat the object of its
creation. Its circulation in 1818 had expanded to nearly
$10,000,000, an amount not warranted by the specie it
held. Cheves corrected this, and under his management the amount of the circulation exceeded $6,000,000
only in three monthly statements, the amount having
been as frequently under as over $5,000,000, and at
times it held more specie than the notes outstanding.
The discounts showed a conservative policy, absolutely
necessary in this critical period. In 1817 the deposits
were usually in excess of $12,000,000, continuing so
until near the end of 1818; during Cheves's term the
minimum was $4,700,000, the maximum $8,600,000. ·

Cheves
corrects
mismanage-
ment.

In September, 1819 the bank had eighteen branches,
of which only five were north of the parent office at
Philadelphia, showing the disposition to establish them
where they were most needed. The Baltimore branch
was the most important, and five others did a larger
business than the branch at New York.

The statistics of state banks prior to 1817, such as
they are, show conclusively that the general practice
was to organize banks mainly for the purpose of issuing
notes, and then exert political influence to obtain government deposits. The policy of having the states interested
as shareholders and participating in the profits operated
to prevent the use of restraining power, except in a very
few states.

State banks'
currency.

Not since the continental days had the country had

Depreciated paper. such a wretchedly bad circulating medium as from 1812 to 1819. It was composed of a relatively small amount of notes of sound banks, an almost equally large amount of counterfeits, and a mass of paper the value of which could rarely be known from one day to another. The location of many " banks " was practically unknown, and many of them had failed. Their notes were nevertheless in use; others deliberately repudiated their notes, still others pretended falsely to redeem upon demand. Other corporations and tradesmen issued "currency." Even barbers and bartenders competed with the banks in this respect. Altogether it appears marvellous that, when nearly every citizen regarded it his constitutional right to issue money, successful trade was possible at all.

The influence upon public men and Congress by individuals and corporations who were profiting by the demoralized condition of the currency is wonderful, almost incredible. Politics of the present time seem pure compared with those of that period.

Congress passed a resolution on April 26, 1816, declaring

Paper money and the revenue. "That the revenues of the United States ought to be collected and received in the legal currency of the United States, or in Treasury notes, or in the notes of the Bank of the United States, as by law provided and declared,"

and requiring the Secretary of the Treasury to adopt such measures as he deemed necessary, to cause, *as soon as may be*, all taxes to be so collected and paid, and that after the first day of February, 1817, no taxes, etc., "ought to be collected or received otherwise than in the legal currency of the United States, or Treasury notes, or notes of the Bank of the United States, as aforesaid."

Dallas's successor (Crawford) under the authority of

this resolution, gently but firmly brought about a reform, first by persuasion, ultimately by publishing the names of the banks whose notes were not to be received for public dues. The great care exercised by him in this enormous task of endeavoring to obtain for the Treasury the revenue to which it was entitled, without precipitating a crisis, is shown in a large volume of correspondence preserved in the annals of the government.[1] Every possible subterfuge to foist upon the Treasury depreciated and worthless paper was used. Notes passing current in one locality at par could be paid out by the government in another only at a considerable discount, and in places where local notes were really at par in specie depreciated paper imported from other points for the specific purpose was paid to the Treasury. These devices in a multitude of varying forms had to be met by Crawford and afterwards by the bank. Ultimately, however, they brought order out of chaos, but the losses were enormous.

The Treasury and state banks.

Gallatin, writing in 1831, gives a list of 165 banks that failed between 1811 and 1830, most of them undoubtedly "going to the wall" between 1817 and 1821.

Crawford states in his special report early in 1820 that the *worst* of the troubles resulting from the war and the inflation of the currency had then practically passed, and soon thereafter the monetary conditions, the industries of the people, and the finances of the government gradually improved. The reduction of the federal debt began, the antagonism to the bank disappeared, and it prospered so that its shares were at a premium of 20 to 25 per cent.

Sounder principles in local currency regulation began to be introduced. In a number of the states the business of banking was placed under supervision, the issue

Reformation begun.

[1] American State Papers, Vol. III.

of "currency" by persons or associations not authorized
to do banking business prohibited, and penalties for
non-redemption of notes were provided. The evil of
small note-issues was not materially checked, however.[1]

The policy of having the states more or less interested in the banks by the ownership of stock increased,
in most cases with disastrous results. The state bank
of South Carolina, owned entirely by the state, was
one of the few that made a satisfactory showing during
this period.[2]

That restraining force which legislation failed to provide was, in New England, supplied by the banks themselves. Profiting by the lesson taught by both Banks
of the United States, Boston banks undertook to regulate the currency by compulsory redemption. The
Suffolk Bank led in this movement, and the system
which developed was known by its name.[3] Practically
this bank, with the coöperation of six other Boston
banks, organized a clearing-house for notes of outside
institutions, by establishing a redemption fund in the
Suffolk Bank. The banks which entered the system
would have their notes received at par in Boston, the
financial centre, and would be called upon for redemption only at specified periods by the Suffolk, which
would receive in redemption, also at par, any notes
of banks in good standing in lieu of specie. Banks
which refused to enter the "system" were called upon
to redeem their notes in specie on demand. The result
of this system was that banks which had a redundant
circulation were compelled to contract to reasonable
limits. On the other hand, the Boston redemption gave
their notes a more extended circulation, and the people
were not subjected to the onerous discounts which

Suffolk system.

Its effect.

[1] Knox, History of Banking ; Sumner, History of Banking.
[2] *Ibid.*   [3] D. R. Whitney, The Suffolk Bank.

country bank-notes otherwise suffered in the money centres. This loss had been from 3 to 5 per cent. The New England Bank of Boston had reduced it to less than 1 per cent, the actual cost of sending notes for redemption, but the Suffolk reduced it even more, so that ultimately the cost was only 10 cents per $1000, and this was borne by the banks.[1]

These results were not accomplished without much opposition. The practice of making a bank keep its promise to pay specie when it did not provide for redemption at Boston was deemed arbitrary, but the communities securing a sound currency heartily approved, and almost all of the banks in New England found it to their interest to enter the system.

The "Safety Fund System" was adopted by statute in New York State in 1829,[2] when the legislature was considering the renewal of a large number of expiring charters. It required the banks so rechartered, and any others desiring to come under the system, to contribute to a joint fund for the redemption of notes and payment of deposits of any of their number which should be overtaken by disaster. The system was adopted by only a few of the existing banks, and, as will be seen later, was not a success.

Safety Fund System.

What the Suffolk system was doing for New England, the Bank of the United States was endeavoring to accomplish for the rest of the country, particularly for the South and West, although necessarily upon different lines. It had no redemption fund, but it was the government fiscal agent, and exercised the power of regulation by means thereof. Banks not in good standing found their notes rejected by government officers and specie redemption was required of them. Although firm in these requirements to maintain notes at or near

Regulation by the bank.

---

[1] Sound Currency, Vol. II.   [2] Knox, History of Banking.

par, the bank cultivated friendly relations with state banks wherever it could. It received their notes, when good, for government dues and paid the Treasury drafts with its own. Some of them acted as its agents at points where it had no branches. It continuously had large balances with them and carried their notes. In 1819 the amount due it from various state banks was over $2,600,000 on current accounts and nearly $1,900,-000 on account of their notes which it held. Its own circulation at the time amounted to $6,600,000. In later years the total of items due it by state banks at the periods of its annual reports was lowest in 1826 at $1,860,000 and highest in 1832 at $6,100,000, the average being about $3,500,000.[1]

The policy of Cheves to limit discounts and note-issues was generally adhered to by Biddle, but as the business of the country improved, that of the bank correspondingly increased. The statement at the end of the chapter, giving the condition of the bank annually is one of the most interesting exhibits in the monetary history of the United States.

Operations of the bank.

The average of deposits rose to $14,500,000 for the period 1823–1832, the annual average never falling below $10,000,000 and rising to nearly $23,000,000 in 1832. In that year the "Bank War" became active and the business of the institution diminished. The loans and discounts kept pace fairly with the deposits, the minimum being about $28,000,000, the maximum about $66,000,000 (in 1832). The holdings of bonds and stocks reached a maximum in 1825 of $18,400,000, and diminished to nothing as the government debt was paid off.[2]

The circulation of the bank, even when "branch drafts" were included, was never excessive. The maxi-

---

[1] See statement at end of chapter.   [2] *Ibid.*

mum prior to 1836 was $21,300,000 (1832), but up to 1824 it never exceeded $6,000,0co, and the specie holdings were frequently in excess of the notes until after that year. Even in the later years (prior to 1832) the specie never fell below 40 per cent of the notes outstanding, and was usually in excess of 50 per cent.

The evidence is conclusive that the bank was, after reorganization by Cheves, and particularly under Biddle's régime, a strong institution, a valuable auxiliary to the government, a bulwark against rotten bank-note issues, a most serviceable instrument to the trade of the country, and in its international relations a protection to American industry and commerce. In his annual report for 1828 [1] Secretary of the Treasury Rush, reviewing his administration, sets forth all these facts. He said : —

Secretary Rush on the bank.

" This capacity in the Treasury to apply the public funds at the proper moment in every part of a country of such wide extent, has been essentially augmented by the Bank of the United States. The department feels an obligation of duty to bear its testimony, founded on constant experience during the term in question, to the useful instrumentality of this institution in all the most important fiscal operations of the nation. . . . It receives the paper of the state banks paid on public account in the interior, as well as elsewhere, and by placing it to the credit of the United States as cash, renders it available wherever the public service may require. . . . Such, also, is the confidence reposed in the stock of the Bank of the United States, that it serves as a medium of remittance abroad in satisfaction of debts due from our citizens to those of other countries, which otherwise would make a call upon the specie of the country for their discharge. Nor are these all the uses of this institution in which the government participates. It is the preservation of a good currency that can alone impart stability to prosperity, and prevent those fluctuations in its value, hurtful alike to individual and to national wealth. This advantage

[1] Finance Reports, Vol. II.

Its great
usefulness.
the bank has secured to the community by confining within
prudent limits its issues of paper, whereby a restraint has been
imposed upon excessive importations, which are thus kept more
within the true wants and capacity of the country. Sometimes
judiciously varying its course, it enlarges its issues, to relieve
scarcity, as under the disastrous speculations of 1825. The
state banks following, or controlled by its general example,
have shaped their policy towards the same salutary ends, adding fresh demonstrations to the truth that, under the mixed
jurisdiction and powers of the state and national systems of
government, a national bank is the instrument alone by which
Congress can effectively regulate the currency of the nation.
. . . A paper currency too redundant, because without any
basis of coin, or other effective check, and of no value as a
medium of remittance or exchange beyond the jurisdiction of
the state whence it had been issued, a currency that not unfrequently imposed upon the Treasury the necessity of meeting,
by extravagant premiums, the mere act of transferring the revenue collected at one point to defray unavoidable expenditures
at another ; — this is the state of things which the Bank of the
Sound
currency
provided.
United States has superseded. In the financial operations of
the Nation, as in the pecuniary transactions between man and
man, confidence has succeeded to distrust, steadiness to fluctuation, and reasonable certainty to general confusion and risk.
The very millions of dollars not effective, of which the Treasury
for many years has been obliged to speak, is but a remnant of
the losses arising from the shattered currency, which the bank,
by a wise management of its affairs, has cured."

In December, 1827, a resolution to sell the shares to
profit by the premium (then $23\frac{1}{2}$ per cent) was defeated
in the House of Representatives, only 9 votes favoring,
174 opposing.[1] The hostility seemed to have entirely
disappeared under these conditions.[2] Gallatin wrote
that in 1829 the currency of the country was as sound
as could be expected under any system of paper money.[3]

[1] Abridgment of Debates.
[2] Parton, Life of Jackson. Vol. III., p. 256.
[3] Gallatin's Writings, Vol. III., p. 390.

It was therefore a surprise to the country that President Jackson as early as 1829, more than six years before the expiration of the bank's charter, announced his opposition to its renewal. The language he used in his message to Congress was as follows : — Jackson attacks the bank.

"The charter of the Bank of the United States expires in 1836, and its stockholders will most probably apply for a renewal of their privileges. In order to avoid the evils resulting from precipitancy in a measure involving such important principles and such deep pecuniary interests, I feel that I cannot, in justice to the parties interested, too soon present it to the deliberate consideration of the legislature and the people. Both the constitutionality and the expediency of the law creating this bank are well questioned by a large portion of our fellow-citizens and it must be admitted by all, that it has failed in the great end of establishing a uniform and sound currency.

"Under these circumstances, if such an institution is deemed essential to the fiscal operations of the government, I submit to the wisdom of the legislature whether a national one, founded upon the credit of the government and its revenues, might not be devised which would avoid all constitutional difficulties, and at the same time secure all the advantages to the government and country that were expected to result from the present bank." [1]

South Carolina's legislature immediately took up the suggestion of a *national* bank,[2] looking upon it as in line with its own state bank policy, and estimating the demand of the country for currency (and banking capital) at $1,000,000,000 it recommended that the United States issue that amount of currency pledging its faith to its redemption, apportion it as banking capital to the several states to be used by them or farmed out to corporations, the states to guarantee the federal government against any loss that might result and to pay 1 per cent South Carolina's plan.

---

[1] Messages of Presidents, Vol. II.
[2] Niles Register, 1830.

for its use. No official action appears to have been taken by other states.

Both houses of Congress referred the subject to committees. The report of that of the House (1830) was very voluminous,[1] and its chairman (McDuffie, S.C.), after a complete presentation of the facts, defended the federal bank policy. He reviewed the question of its constitutionality and utility, as well as the expediency of Jackson's recommendation of a "national bank" founded on the credit of the government. Upon the first point he recalled that most of the leading opponents, both in the legislative and in the executive departments of the government, taught by the "very brief but fatal experience" (1811–1816), yielded their views, and the judicial department had unanimously decided the question of the constitutionality of the charter. He argued that the power to regulate the value of money given by the Constitution to Congress unquestionably carried the power to establish efficient means to that end. He forcibly and conclusively controverted Jackson's assertion that the bank had failed to serve the purpose for which it was established, and demonstrated that the paper currency had been made uniform and sound.

Jackson's national bank plan was fairly "riddled." It was the general opinion that it would ultimately result in merely a government note-issue, and the impossibility of providing a satisfactory currency of this character, subject as it would be to partisan influences, was conclusively demonstrated.

In the Senate the suggestion of Jackson met a similar reception. The report (made by Smith of Maryland) maintained that a sound and uniform currency system

---

[1] House Reports, 21st Congress, 1st Sess. Also in Clarke and Hall, History of Bank of United States.

existed, provided by the Bank of the United States, and that there were "insuperable and fatal" objections to the scheme proposed by Jackson, which the committee pronounced impracticable. Both houses were favorable to the bank.

Notwithstanding this advice of his friends in Congress (for the committees were both controlled by Jacksonians), and notwithstanding the opinions of all but one member of his Cabinet, which included Ingham as Secretary of the Treasury, Jackson repeated his attack upon the bank in his message in 1830 and in a milder form in 1831. *Jackson renews attack.* It was well known to the leaders, as Adams showed in his report in 1832, although not fully understood by the public until later, that he was secretly influenced by a cabal of lesser politicians, generally known as the "Kitchen Cabinet" (with Amos Kendall, afterward Postmaster-general, at its head),[1] whose motives were anything but patriotic. They used Secretary Ingham to open an attack upon the management of the bank's branch in New Hampshire upon allegations which proved entirely unfounded. The cabal ultimately forced Ingham, who believed in the bank, out of the Cabinet.[2]

The question of rechartering soon became one on which the political parties divided. Clay, then the Whig candidate for the presidency, espoused the cause of the bank, and upon the advice of the leaders of that party, Biddle early in 1832 petitioned Congress for a *Petition for recharter.* renewal of the charter. Jackson and his partisans regarded this as a challenge to battle, and Benton assumed the leadership of the opposition.[3] In the House, Polk,

---

[1] Sumner, History of Banking in United States ; Horace White, Money and Banking, pp. 288–291 ; Niles Register ; Duane's Narrative.

[2] Niles Register.

[3] Benton, Thirty Years' View, Vol. I., p. 236.

afterwards President, was the anti-bank leader. Benton was in fact opposed to all bank currency, entertaining the opinion, which he aired upon every possible occasion, that the country would be more prosperous with a circulation composed of coin only.

Committee investigates the bank. In March, under the influence of Benton, a committee of the House of Representatives was appointed to examine the bank. The report[1] was in three parts, one adverse to the bank by the majority (including Clayton of Georgia, the chairman), the second favorable to the bank, by McDuffie, and the third by John Quincy Adams, also favorable, and giving special prominence to certain features. In many particulars the Clayton attack (openly fathered by Benton) was frivolous. Usury, the issue of " branch drafts " already referred to, selling foreign coin, domestic exchange and stocks, nonuser of charter by refusing to issue notes at certain branches, making donations for roads and canals, building and renting houses, were the principal criticisms, and were manifestly made in order to create political capital. Upon none of these charges would serious-minded individuals have justified a discontinuance of the bank. The criticisms applied to its administration rather than the bank itself. One charge that the bank purchased newspaper support by granting a loan was fully disproved, one of the members of the majority acquitting the bank of any such motives.[2] On the other hand, it developed that some members of the cabal had failed in their purpose to drag politics into the management of one of the branches, for their pecuniary benefit, which indicated the motive for their secret machinations. This evidence, as well as Biddle's

---

[1] House Reports, 22d Congress, 1st Sess.

[2] R. M. Johnston, who, however, admitted that he had not looked at a document.

masterly defence of the bank, was suppressed by Clayton but brought out by Adams.[1] The chief witness against the bank (Whitney) was subsequently proven guilty of perjury, nevertheless he was received into the "Kitchen Cabinet"[2] in good fellowship.

A bill for the extension of the charter was reported, in the Senate from a committee headed by G. M. Dallas (son of the former Secretary) and Webster, and in the House from McDuffie's committee (Ways and Means). Dallas thought the time inopportune, a presidential campaign being at hand, but he supported the measure heartily. The Senate bill passed. It provided for an extension of the charter for fifteen years, upon the payment of an annual bonus of $200,000. It also contained a provision (to which Dallas had objected) compelling the bank to accept its own notes from state banks no matter where issued or where tendered. "Branch drafts" were prohibited, but subordinate officers were permitted to sign notes, and Congress reserved the right to prohibit notes under $20. The vote on the bill in the upper house was 28 to 20, in the lower one 107 to 85. Jackson vetoed the measure (July 10, 1832), and it failed to command the necessary two-thirds to pass it over the veto.

Recharter bill.

Jackson's objections[3] were (1) that the recharter continued a practical monopoly, (2) benefited the shareholders by giving them a valuable gratuity, (3) foreigners held a large part of the shares, and in case of war the bank could be used by the enemy, (4) finally that it was unconstitutional. He waived aside the argument that the liquidation of so large a concern would cause disturbances, and held that neither he nor Congress was

Jackson's veto.

---

[1] House Reports, 22d Congress, 1st Sess.
[2] White, Sound Currency, Vol. IV., No. 18.
[4] Messages of Presidents, Vol. II.

bound by the decision of the Supreme Court that the charter was constitutional. Upon this last point Madison had just previously published a letter in which he radically disagreed with Jackson.[1]

The Supreme Court had passed upon the charter of the bank, and held it constitutional ten years prior to Jackson's attack in 1829. It seems strange therefore that he should make the principal ground for vetoing the renewal bill the unconstitutionality of the original charter. His position that his oath to support the Constitution bound him to support it as he construed it and not as interpreted by the Courts, was untenable. The President, of all persons, is bound by the Constitution and laws as interpreted by the Supreme Court. Jackson believed the bank was being used in opposition to him politically, and the subsequent virtual alliance between the Whig party and the bank would indicate that his belief may have been well founded. Be this true, he had wantonly begun the attack when he, as a statesman, should have sought to correct the management rather than destroy the bank. It seems strange that political fortune could induce men to attack with such vehemence an institution when the inevitable effect must be to jeopardize the national interests of the whole people. Our fathers had many virtues which it is well to emulate, but in respect to political rancor and partisan vindictiveness the present is certainly a great improvement upon the period under discussion.

It should be borne in mind that the constitutional objection which confronted every attempt to exercise any power not specially delegated to Congress was brought forward by representatives of the slave states. The agitation against slavery kept its champions constantly on the alert lest some precedent be established that

Jackson's views considered.

[1] Letters to C. J. Ingersoll, Clarke and Hall's History, p. 778.

might tend to provoke national interference with that institution. The less the power conceded to Congress, Effect of state rights doctrine. and the greater the power reposed in the states, the less likelihood there would be of outside interference either by law or by failure to suppress efforts constantly being made to aid slaves in escaping. Vermont and Kentucky were admitted as states at the same time, and when Maine applied for admission she was kept waiting pending the controversy over the question of slavery in Missouri. Nothing was permitted to be done which tended to impair the relative power of the slaveholding interests. This policy of minimizing the powers of the general government is largely responsible for the failure to provide a national currency free from the evils which seemed inseparable from a currency issued under the heterogenous laws of the states. In criticising Jackson for overthrowing the second bank it should be borne in mind that the Whig party under the leadership of Clay sought to gain power by forcing the renewal of the charter forward as a political issue.

Jackson's veto caused great excitement, and was used The veto a political issue. to aid him in his campaign for reëlection (1832). The friends of the bank were equally active, and public meetings were held at which Jackson was denounced in unmeasured terms.

Naturally the great majority of the business men of the day ranged themselves with the bank party, which gave Jackson's partisans an additional weapon, re-enforcing the cry of "monopoly" and "wealth" with which they were inciting the masses to believe that their liberties were in danger. Unfortunately for the bank Biddle took an active part in the contest, which soon became personal, although he insisted that he was merely defending the bank against the unwarranted attacks of the cabal. It thus gave some color to the charge that this powerful institution was using its untold millions, including the government's money on deposit with it, to defeat the popular idol, the hero of the War of 1812. In fact the total sum used by the bank for "literature" during the campaign did not amount to $50,000,[1] and no evidence that it used its power in business lines (by refusing discounts, etc., as was charged) was produced. Jackson was reëlected by a larger electoral vote than in 1828, although the popular vote was smaller.

Jackson reëlected.

In his message in December, 1832,[2] Jackson suggested to Congress that the government deposits be transferred, in whole or in part, from the bank to the state banks. He said: —

Public deposits in the bank.

"Such measures as are within the reach of the Secretary of the Treasury have been taken, to enable him to judge whether the public deposits in that institution may be regarded as entirely safe; but as his limited power may prove inadequate to this object, I recommend the subject to the attention of Congress, under the firm belief that it is worthy of their serious investigation. An inquiry into the transactions of the institution, embracing the branches as well as the principal bank, seems called for by the credit which is given throughout the country to many serious charges impeaching the character, and which if true, may justly excite the apprehension that it is no longer a safe depository of the money of the people."

He also recommended the sale of the government's shares in the bank.

Secretary McLane had stated in his report in 1831[3] that —

"It must be admitted, however, that the good management of the present bank, the accommodation it has given to the

---

[1] Report of Government Directors, Finance Reports, Vol. III., and Congressional Report of 1832.

[2] Messages of Presidents, Vol. II.

[3] Finance Reports, Vol. III., p. 222.

government, and the practical benefits it has rendered the McLane on the bank. community, whether it may or may not have accomplished all that was expected from it, and the advantages of its present condition, are circumstances in its favor entitled to great weight, and give it strong claims upon the consideration of Congress in any future legislation on the subject."

These considerations induced him to recommend a recharter with modifications, at the proper time. In 1832 he directed a special examination of the bank and its branches, which the "Kitchen Cabinet" expected would prove it to be insolvent. To their disgust the examiner reported that the bank had upward of $42,000,000 in excess of its liabilities, hence more than $7,000,000 in excess of its stock obligation.[1] The House of Representatives after an examination of the Special examination of bank. bank by the Committee on Ways and Means, by a vote of 109 to 46, declared by resolution that the public funds were absolutely safe in the bank, and by a vote of 102 to 91 opposed the sale of the shares. In the report by Verplanck of the committee it was shown that in sixteen years the transactions of the government had aggregated $440,000,000, and not one dollar had been lost. Polk in the minority report expressed serious doubts as to the safety of the public funds.[2]

Immediately after the adjournment of Congress, in March, 1833, Kendall and his associates began the work of utterly destroying the bank. Soon after the re-inauguration of Jackson, plans were devised to use the provision of law authorizing the Secretary of the Treasury to place the government moneys elsewhere Removal of deposits proposed. (provided he explained his reason to Congress), as the first measure in the renewed warfare. McLane refused to be a party to this transaction and was made

[1] Niles Register.
[2] House Reports, 22d Congress, 2d Sess., No. 121.

Secretary of State, W. J. Duane being appointed to the Treasury. State banks had been negotiated with by Kendall to be prepared. Jackson read to his cabinet in September a paper in which the plan was set forth. He felt that in reëlecting him the people had decided against a recharter. All the old charges were rehearsed. The bank had opposed his reëlection and should be punished. A majority of the cabinet, including McLane, Duane, and Cass, did not favor the step proposed. Duane, who was not favorable to the bank's recharter, particularly opposed it as unwise, arbitrary, uncalled for, a breach of faith, and dangerous because no other *safe* depository could be found. Duane stated that not only had he refused, when pestered by the "irresponsible cabal," to change the system, but had been promised by the President that he would be allowed to manage his department without interference, particularly upon this point. Upon being *ordered* to "remove the deposits" by Jackson, Duane flatly refused, declaring such action unconscionable and opposed to the express will of Congress, and denying the power of the President under the law to *order* the Secretary of the Treasury to do so.[1] Jackson promptly removed Duane and appointed in his stead Taney, then Attorney-general and afterwards Chief Justice of the Supreme Court, who at once signed the order for the removal of the deposits. Many of Jackson's friends condemned his policy in this respect.

At first the process adopted was not to *remove* the deposits from the bank, but to place the revenues as received in state banks, drawing on the bank for all disbursements. Later deposits were actually transferred.

Deprived speedily of one-half of the public money, and its total deposits shrinking to nearly $10,000,000,

Duane's position.

Removal of deposits by Taney.

---

[1] Duane's Narrative.

the bank was necessarily obliged to curtail its loans, which caused a stringency, for which it was again attacked. Actually, the curtailment was less than three-quarters of the loss of deposits. Biddle, knowing the unscrupulousness of the cabal, conducted the business most cautiously. Kendall showed his real object in a published letter, in which he said that the bank only continued to exist because of Taney's forbearance, and apparently gave it only a forty days' lease of life.[1] No measure was too contemptible for Kendall to employ. The invariable custom of advising the bank of Treasury drafts was at his instigation abrogated and secret drafts for over two and a quarter millions were issued, transferring deposits to pet state banks, with the hardly disguised purpose of causing a "run."[2]

When Congress met in December the President and Secretary Taney reported upon the subject.[3] The Senate, then anti-Jackson, refused to confirm Taney's nomination made during recess. In the House the Jacksonians controlled and voted 132 to 82 that the bank ought not to be rechartered, and 118 to 103 that the deposits should not be returned to the bank.[4] Levi Woodbury became Taney's successor in the Treasury.

Congress disagrees.

In the Senate Clay had a resolution passed (23 to 18) calling upon the President to say if the published paper purporting to be the one read to the cabinet in September was genuine, and asking that the Senate be furnished with a copy.[5] Jackson declined, standing upon his constitutional rights. Thereupon the Senate passed a resolution declaring that in his action relating to the public revenues the President had exceeded his powers, and

Jackson cen sured.

[1] White, Money and Banking.   [2] Niles Register.
[3] Finance Reports, Vol. III. Special Report on Removal.
[4] Williams, Statesman's Manual, Vol. II.
[5] Benton, Thirty Years' View.

another, supported by Webster, which pronounced the reasons given by Secretary Taney for removing the deposits "unsatisfactory and insufficient."[1]   Jackson sent in a message protesting against the first resolution. After long discussion the Senate by a vote of 27 to 16 refused to receive the message, regarding it as a breach of its privileges on the part of the President and deny-ing his right to protest to the Senate against any of its proceedings.[2]

Another con-
gressional
examination.

The House of Representatives again ordered an ex-amination of the bank, to which it did not, in the opinion of the majority of the committee (Jacksonian), submit gracefully. The minority, headed by Edward Everett, contended that the bank had shown every disposition to aid the examination of the affairs relating to the ques-tion of violation of the charter, which was the limit of the power of the committee and which the majority had endeavored to transcend.[3] The Senate also ordered an examination which was reported by Tyler (afterward President) and was favorable to the bank.[4] No specific action was taken, but the President felt called upon to send a special message to Congress criticising the bank's action at that time.[5] In the Senate Jackson's nominees for government directors of the bank were not con-firmed ; the vote stood 30 to 11. In December, 1834, in his annual message to Congress,[6] the bank is char-

Jackson's
further criti-
cism.

acterized as "the scourge of the people." All his former charges were repeated, and he recommended the sale of the government holdings of stock and the repeal of that part of the charter making the bank's notes receivable for public dues. He averred that events had proved that the bank was unnecessary, that

[1] Statesman's Manual.   [2] Ibid.   [3] Ibid.
[4] Senate, Doc. 17, 23d Congress, 2d Sess.
[5] Messages of Presidents, Vol. III.   [6] Ibid.

the state banks had been found fully adequate to serve the government, and would soon be in position to supply all the wants of the people, and that if the states reformed their systems, prohibiting small notes, the country would in a few years have as sound a currency as any.

In the interval the bank had obtained a charter from the state of Pennsylvania and continued business under it after March, 1836, when its federal charter expired. The government continued to hold the shares until liquidation.

The bank is chartered in Pennsylvania.

In December, 1836,[1] Jackson's last message complained that the bank had not yet settled its affairs and was doing a number of things which he disapproved.

He again referred to the state banks, representing that their services to the government were far greater than those rendered formerly by the bank. But he also showed that little progress had been made in retiring small notes, and that the state banks had entered into speculation in public lands and resorted to inflation in order to do so.

In his "farewell address" (March, 1837),[2] he launched his final bolt against the bank, including the entire paper currency system, banks generally, the "moneyed interests" and their encroachment, as dangerous to the liberties of the people.

Jackson on "moneyed interests."

Woodbury's report for 1836 was a confession that the state banks were using the public deposits both speculatively and to increase their note-issues, which had been expanded fully 50 per cent since 1833; nevertheless the public moneys were regarded safe.

With the destruction of the bank perished by far the best instrumentality for furnishing the people of the

---

[1] Messages of Presidents, Vol. III.   [2] *Ibid.*

United States a sound paper currency that could be devised under the circumstances and conditions then prevailing. It merited and received the commendation of a host of the ablest men of the country, who in other particulars differed radically from the political views of Hamilton, who may be fairly called the designer of the second as well as of the first United States Bank. That its *destruction* was planned, and not regulation or reformation of the defects which experience brought to light, is clearly shown by the evidence. The men behind the scenes endeavored to use the bank for their own ends, and failing, resolved to destroy it, and circumstances so shaped events that Clay, the inveterate opponent of Jackson, became its champion, thus involving it in the mælstrom of politics against its will.

The bank and its management were not perfect, but every defect which had manifested itself could have been easily remedied, and indeed most of them were provided for in the recharter bill.

Webster, in discussing another subject, after stating that the question of recharter was settled not to be reopened until the people called for it, expressed his judgment on the bank in the following words :[1] —

" The bank has been assailed by party, mainly, as I believe, because it would not yield itself to party objects. No cry was raised against its constitutionality, no doubt expressed on that point, till its directors had resisted suggestions, the effect of which would have been to render the bank a servile instrument in the hands of political men. In my judgment, those directors were entirely right, and the country, I think, should rejoice that they staked and risked the continuance of the charter on that point. They could easily have secured the renewal of their charter. A little compliance would have done the whole business. They were courted before they were denounced. If, in

---

[1] Webster's Works.

1829 and 1830, they would have consented to make a partnership with the Treasury, and to yield themselves to power, they would have been commended, extolled in many a message and report, and enabled to take their own time for a renewal. The bank has fallen in its independence, and by reason of its independence. It should be proud so to have fallen; and it is much better for the country that it should thus fall, than that it should purchase a prolonged existence by rendering itself a tool of party power.

"It is well known to be my opinion that direct injustice was done to the bank in the withdrawal of the deposits; and injustice has been done to it also, as I think, by the gross and unfounded imputations made upon its general management. The bank now, for many years, has accomplished every object intended by its establishment. It has reformed the currency, sustained it when reformed, and upheld a system of internal exchange, safe, cheap and of unprecedented and unparalleled facility. No country has seen the like; nor shall we see it soon again when the operations of the bank shall cease. The directors, of late years especially, have had a most difficult and undesirable duty to perform; but they have performed it, as I think, with entire uprightness and great ability. Every fair investigation has proved this, and the state of the bank itself, the best of all proofs, abundantly shows it. The time will come, I am sure, when justice will be done them, universally, as it is done them now by those who have sought for information, and have formed their judgments with candor and good sense." *Bank unjustly treated*

Ingham in 1832 (after his retirement from the Treasury) said:[1] —

"The bank has purified one of the worst currencies that ever infested any country or people. It consisted of mere paper, of no definite value, accompanied by worthless tickets issued from broken banks, petty incorporations and partnerships, in almost every village. Instead of this, the United States Bank has given us the best currency known among nations. It supplies a *Ingham's views on the bank.*

[1] Niles Register.

medium equal in value to gold and silver, in every part of the
union.   It preserves with a steady and unerring power a uniform
and equal value in the paper of the local banks ; gives stability
and certainty to the value of all property, and to the incalculable
benefits of internal commerce ; it maintains domestic exchanges,
at a less premium than it would cost to transport specie; and
enables the government to transmit its funds from one extremity
of the union to another, without cost, without risk, without pressure upon the section from which they are withdrawn, and with
a despatch which is more like magic than reality."

The political rancor and sordid motives which entered into this controversy over the renewal of the
charter are in sad contrast to the exalted patriotism
and statesmanlike qualities we usually ascribe to the
"fathers."

Salutary
influence of
the bank.
When it is borne in mind that the means of communication with the remote parts of the country were exceedingly primitive (no railways existed), the undisputed fact
that the bank raised the credit of the bank circulation
throughout the Union, made transfers at little or no cost,
and reduced the cost of exchange to a minimum, prove
its great value to the country.   McDuffie states that in
1830 only the banks in North Carolina were not specie-
paying.

Altogether it was a reactionary victory over the intel-
ligence of the day, and the people paid roundly for it.
Practically all those who by reason of their study and
experience had actual knowledge upon the subject
opposed the destruction of the bank as a positive
evil which would result in an unsound currency, just
as they opposed the violent alteration of the ratio of
coinage.

State bank
inflation.
As was generally foreseen, the removal of deposits
caused the organization of a large number of state banks.
The revenues were about to accumulate in the Treasury,

the public debt having been entirely paid, and holding public moneys by political favor became an important feature in banking. The number of banks increased from 1830 to the end of 1836, from 330 to 788[1] and the note-issues from under $49,000,000 to $149,000,000. Thus the circulation of the country which in 1829 was about $7 per capita and then regarded by Gallatin as "sound," was increased to $15 per capita, an amount equalled only in the days of continental currency.[2] The government had in 59 state banks nearly $50,000,000, before any law regulating the deposits became effective. Speculation in public lands, in payment for which the government accepted almost any form of paper, assumed tremendous proportions. Congress was asked to stop the speculation by restricting the funds receivable to specie, but the counter-influence was too great and the defective measure passed for that purpose did not receive Jackson's approval. Congress had adjourned and Jackson undertook by means of a Treasury circular to require specie for land purchases. This caused a violent collapse of the speculation and serious troubles generally, notably in the West.

Jackson's attempt to curb inflation.

The act of June 23, 1836,[3] regulating deposits, directed the Secretary of the Treasury to select in each state banks which in his judgment were in a satisfactory condition, in which to deposit the revenues subject to the Treasury drafts. The limit of deposit was 75 per cent of paid-up capital, the banks were required to report their condition periodically to the Secretary, to credit all deposits as specie and pay specie on demand for Treasury drafts, to make transfers and perform such other functions as the Bank of the United States was required to by its charter. The Secretary might also

Deposit act of 1836.

---

[1] Report on Banks, 1863.   [2] See table at end of chapter.

[3] See Appendix.

require further security from the banks if in his judgment it was requisite. He was required to report his selections or changes in depositories to Congress, to discontinue depositories that suspended specie payments, or issued notes under five dollars, and to receive for public dues no notes of banks issuing denominations under five dollars. He was given power to require depository banks to have a reasonable amount of specie on hand. For deposits in excess of one-fourth of the capital banks were to pay interest at 2 per cent per annum, and the banks were subject to examination. Transfers of deposits, excepting on account of public business, were especially prohibited. This was due to the alleged practice of making transfers to accommodate certain banks.

This law Jackson deemed onerous upon the banks.

Distribution of surplus.

The same act provided that the surplus in the Treasury in excess of $5,000,000 for a working balance be deposited with the states, in proportion to their representation in Congress, in four equal instalments, beginning January 1, 1837, provided the states authorized their treasurers to receive the money and pledge its return on demand of the Secretary of the Treasury. Although the act specifically provided that the funds were to be held as "deposits," the general opinion was that they were given to the states. This measure was finally passed after years of discussion on the subject and after a bill to donate the money to the states had been vetoed as unconstitutional. The amount finally transferred was $28,101,644.

. The prospect of the transfer of such a large sum from the depository banks to the states served to add to the general tendency to expansion, and the usual results followed.

This deposit act of 1836 was designed to accomplish several improvements in the currency which under other conditions would probably have been realized. It brought a considerable number of banks throughout the country under the supervision of the Treasury Department, and the importance given these institutions in their localities by being depositories, so regulated, could not have failed to exercise an influence upon others. It also contemplated in an indirect manner the ultimate elimination of small notes, instead of going directly at this evil by taxing them out of existence as Gallatin had proposed. It further undertook to compel maintenance of specie payments by making it profitable. But the act came too late : Jackson and Woodbury had repeatedly asked for it in vain, and when it came, the provision for distribution of the surplus and Jackson's specie circular deprived the country of whatever good results might have been expected from it.

The following data of the depository banks at about this period are of special interest.[1]

	In Millions		
	36 Banks April 1, 1836	36 Banks June 1, 1836	59 Banks Nov. 1, 1836
Capital	43.7	46.4	77.6
Circulation	28.8	28.0	41.5
Public deposits	36.8	41.0	49.4
Other deposits	15.5	16.0	26.6
Due banks	15.4	17.1	24.1
Other liabilities	12.6	13.8	24.6
Total	152.8	162.3	243.8
Loans and discounts . . .	101.6	108.5	164.0
Specie	10.9	10.5	15.5
Notes of other banks . . .	11.1	11.0	16.4
Due from other banks . .	15.9	17.9	26.6
Other resources	13.3	14.4	21.3

[1] Finance Reports, Vol. III.

Considering the circulation alone the specie fund was fairly satisfactory, but when public deposits are included the reserve was rather slender.

The government and the Bank of the United States.

For the purpose of winding up the business of the government with the Bank of the United States, several acts were passed: April 11, 1836, to discontinue the functions of the bank in connection with government loans ; June 15, 1836, repealing the section of the charter which made the notes of the bank receivable for public dues ; June 23, 1836, appointing the Secretary of the Treasury agent to settle for the government's shares in the bank.

The United States derived a profit of over $6,000,000 on its investment.[1] It will be recalled that its subscription was paid for with 5 per cent obligations. They amounted to

Principal	$ 7,000,000.00	
Interest	4,950,000.00	$ 11,950,000.00
The bank paid in settlement for the same	9,424,750.78	
The dividends paid amounted to .	7,118,416.29	16,543,167.07
Profit		4,593,167.07
Bonus paid by the bank for the charter		1,500,000.00
Making a total of		$ 6,093,167.07

Liquidation of the bank.

Although both Jackson and Benton charged that the bank was not getting ready to wind up its affairs, the fact is that prior to the determination to continue under a state charter, the bank took definite steps toward preparation for liquidation, disposing of its branches and converting its resources into short paper and increasing its cash, as the following table shows :[2] —

[1] Finance Report, 1876, p. 127.   [2] Niles Register.

ITEMS REPORTED AS OF APRIL 1, EACH YEAR, IN MILLIONS

	1831	1832	1833	1834	1835
Total loans	58.5	69.9	64.8	54.8	60.1
Bills of exchange . . .	14.7	21.5	22.7	18.7	22.9
Circulation	18.2	21.4	18.0	17.5	20.5
Specie	12.5	7.0	9.0	10.2	16.4

The public deposits at the last-mentioned date were about 1.5 millions.

The statistics of the banks of Massachusetts, the only state that furnished continuous returns from an early date (1803), afford an indication of the results which would have been possible in the whole country had anything like sound principles prevailed. The number of banks, their capital and circulation, grew almost normally and steadily during the entire period from 1803 to 1836. There was no great expansion when the first Bank of the United States expired, no suspension in 1814, hence no contraction necessary in 1819. During the existence of the second bank, the banks increased gradually and steadily. This was not accomplished without many sad experiences, but the people profited by these and remedied the evils in order to avert the greater ones which afflicted others. From 1784 to 1836 only ten banks suspended or discontinued business; the total losses to the shareholders and to the public were estimated at $300,000.[1] Gallatin's list of banks that failed between 1811 and 1830 includes only 6 of Massachusetts, but 16 of Pennsylvania and 18 of Kentucky.[2]

Massachusetts banks.

[1] Knox, Finance Report, 1876, p. 132.
[2] Gallatin, Currency and Banking System.

STATISTICAL RÉSUMÉ

(Amounts in millions of dollars)

BANK STATISTICS, 1812 TO 1837

State Banks

Estimates prior to 1834

YEAR	NUMBER	CAPITAL	DEPOSITS	CIRCULA-TION	SPECIE	LOANS
1813	—	65.0	—	62–70	28.0	117
1814	—	80.4	—	—	—	—
1815	208	88.1	—	90–110	16.5	150
1816	246	89.4	—	110	19.0	—
1817	—	125.7	—	—	—	—
1819	—	125.0	—	45–53	21.5	157
1820	307	102.1	31.2	40.6	16.7	—
1829	329	110.1	40.8	48.3	14.9	—
1830	330	110.0	39.0	48.4	13.5	160

No data available for 1812, 1818, and from 1821 to 1829. Figures given for 1820 and 1829 are Gallatin's; those prior to 1820, Crawford's; for 1830 the statement is composite, and probably erroneous. All are to a great extent based upon actual figures, supplemented by estimates.

Official Reports after 1834

JANUARY 1	NUMBER	CAPITAL	DEPOSITS	CIRCULA-TION	SPECIE	LOANS
1834	506	200	76	95	26	324
1835	704	231	83	104	44	365
1836	713	252	115	140	40	457

No returns in 1834 from Del., N.J., S.C., Ga., Fla., La., Ark., Ky., Ohio, Ind., Ill., Mich., Mo.

No returns in 1835 from Del., Md., N.C., Ark.

No returns in 1836 from N.J., R.I., Ark.

No returns in 1837 from Ark.

Incomplete returns in 1835 from S.C. and Ohio.

Massachusetts Banks

1803 to 1837

YEAR	NUM-BER	CAPITAL	DEPOSITS	LOANS	CIRCULA-TION	SPECIE	NOTES OF OTHER BANKS
1803 . .	7	2.2	1.5	3.9	1.6	1.1	0.4
1808 . .	16	6.0	2.5	7.4	1.0	1.0	0.5
1811 . .	15	6.7	3.4	10.1	2.4	1.5	0.3
1815 . .	25	11.5	4.1	13.7	2.7	3.5	0.4
1817 . .	26	9.3	3.5	12.6	2.5	1.6	0.7
1820 . .	28	10.6	3.2	13.5	2.6	1.3	0.9
1825 . .	41	14.5	2.7	22.0	4.1	1.0	0.7
1830 . .	63	19.3	3.6	28.0	5.1	1.3	1.4
1835 . .	105	30.4	12.9	48.3	9.4	1.1	2.1

Bank of the United States [1]

BEGINNING OF	DEPOSITS	LOANS	BONDS, ETC.	CIRCULA-TION	SPECIE	STATE BANK NOTES	DUE FROM BANKS	DUE TO BANKS
1817 . .	11.2	3.5	4.8	1.9	1.7	0.6	8.8	—
1818 . .	12.3	41.2	9.5	8.3	2.5	1.8	2.2	1.4
1819 . .	5.8	35.8	7.4	6.6	2.7	1.9	3.2	1.4
1820 . .	6.6	31.4	7.2	3.6	3.4	1.4	3.0	2.1
1821 . .	7.9	30.9	9.2	4.6	7.6	0.7	1.3	2.1
1822 . .	8.1	28.1	13.3	5.6	4.8	0.9	2.8	2.0
1823 . .	7.6	30.7	11.0	4.4	4.4	0.8	1.4	1.3
1824 . .	13.7	33.4	10.9	4.6	5.8	0.7	2.7	1.0
1825 . .	12.0	31.8	18.4	6.1	6.7	1.1	2.2	2.4
1826 . .	11.2	33.4	18.3	9.5	4.0	1.1	1.2	0.3
1827 . .	14.3	30.9	17.8	8.5	6.5	1.1	2.1	0.3
1828 . .	14.5	33.7	17.6	9.9	6.2	1.4	0.4	3.2
1829 . .	17.1	39.2	16.1	11.9	6.1	1.3	2.2	1.4
1830 . .	16.0	40.7	11.6	12.9	7.6	1.5	2.7	—
1831 . .	17.3	44.0	8.7	16.3	10.8	1.5	2.4	0.7
1832 . .	22.8	66.3	—	21.4	7.0	2.2	4.0	2.0
1833 . .	20.3	61.7	—	17.5	9.0	2.3	6.8	2.1
1834 . .	10.8	54.9	—	19.2	10.0	2.0	4.9	1.5
1835 . .	11.8	51.8	—	17.3	15.7	1.5	6.5	3.1
1836 . .	5.1	59.2	—	23.1	8.4	1.7	4.1	2.7

NOTE. — The government deposits have never reached $10,000,000, and were, in the earlier period, never more than $6,000,000. After 1827 the

[1] Finance Report, 1876, p. 193.

discounts included important amounts of domestic bills of exchange; in the last four years this item constituted from 25 to 40 per cent of the total. The item "due to banks" prior to 1828 was composed entirely of European credits, and that "due from banks" included large sums abroad in many of the years. Circulation is *net*, and includes "branch drafts."

CIRCULATION OF THE COUNTRY

YEAR	SPECIE	BANK NOTES		TREASURY NOTES	TOTAL	POPULA-TION	PER CAPITA
		State	U.S.				
1813	30	62	——	9	101	7.9	$12.78
1814	28	70	——	11	109	8.2	13.30
1815	25	75	——	24	124	8.5	14.58
1816	23	68	——	18	109	8.7	12.53
1817	22	75	1.9	5	104	8.9	11.68
1818	20	60	8.3	1	89	9.1	9.78
1819	20	45	6.6	——	72	9.3	7.74
1820	24	41	3.6	——	69	9.6	7.19
1821	23	40	4.6	——	68	9.9	6.87
1822	18	40	5.6	——	64	10.2	6.27
1823	17	41	4.4	——	62	10.5	5.90
1824	19	42	4.6	——	66	10.9	6.06
1825	18	43	6.1	——	67	11.2	6.00
1826	20	44	9.5	——	74	11.5	6.43
1827	21	46	8.5	——	76	11.8	6.44
1828	23	47	9.9	——	80	12.2	6.55
1829	26	48	11.9	·——	86	12.5	6.88
1830	32	48	12 9	——	93	12.8	7.26
1831	32	61	16.3	——	109	13.2	8.26
1832	30	70	21.3	——	121	13.6	8.90
1833	31	73	17.5	——	121	14.0	8.64
1834	41	95	19.2	——	155	14.4	10.76
1835	51	104	17.3	——	172	14.8	11.62
1836	65	140	23.7	——	229	15.2	15.06

NOTE. — In this table the specie is given for 1820 and 1830–1836 as usually accepted, although the movement abroad, as shown in the next table, does not warrant the conclusions. It should be borne in mind that from 1814 to 1817 specie was hoarded, hence not actually in use.

The notes of state banks are based on Gallatin's and Crawford's estimates, the latter appearing to have been excessive, the former, too conservative.

Specie and Trade Movement and Exchange

Net Import, +. Export, −.

Year	Specie	Merchandise	Exchange on London
1821	− 2.4	− 0.1	3¾ @ 12½ premium
1822	− 7.4	+ 18.5	8½ @ 13 "
1823	− 1.3	+ 4.2	5 @ 12½ "
1824	+ 1.4	+ 3.2	7½ @ 11¼ "
1825	− 2.6	− 0.5	5 @ 10½ "
1826	+ 2.2	+ 5.2	7¾ @ 12¼ "
1827	+ 0.1	− 3.0	10 @ 11½ "
1828	− 0.8	+ 17.0	9½ @ 11 "
1829	+ 2.5	− 0.3	8½ @ 10 "
1830	+ 6.0	− 8.9	6 @ 9¾ "
1831	− 1.7	+ 23.6	6 @ 10¾ "
1832	+ 0.3	+ 13.6	7 @ 11 "
1833	+ 4.5	+ 13.5	5 @ 9 "
1834	+ 15.8	+ 6.3	− 2 @ 8 "
1835	+ 6.7	+ 21.5	7½ @ 10 "
1836	+ 9.1	+ 52.2	7 @ 10½ "

It is quite evident from the above table that a·considerable amount of foreign capital came to the country after 1830. It was estimated that the debt abroad probably exceeded two hundred millions in 1835. At that time (no United States bonds being outstanding), the bonds of the states of New York, Pennsylvania, Ohio, Louisiana, Mississippi, Alabama, Florida, and Indiana were quoted in London; also certain bank shares and canal company bonds.

Conditions
in 1837.

BRIEFLY recapitulated the conditions affecting the currency early in 1837 were as follows: the Bank of the United States had acted as regulator of the circulation of state banks by refusing the notes of doubtful concerns and requiring the redemption of others; now, since its federal charter had expired and it was operating under a charter from the state of Pennsylvania, it necessarily ceased to perform that function and was merely a very largely capitalized state institution. This check upon the state bank issues having been removed and the enticing prospect of obtaining public deposits being held out by the Jackson administration resulted, as it did in 1811–1817, in a large increase in the number of state banks and an inordinate inflation of both notes and discounts. Many banks were conducting business without a dollar of actual capital paid in, and a majority were subject to no legal restriction. The distribution to the states of the surplus in the Treasury caused a number of the states to create "fiscal banks," and the others selected state banks as public depositories; thus this large sum was transferred from " pet " federal to " pet " state depositories. These transfers naturally necessitated the calling of loans, for the federal depositories had loaned the funds, and a general curtailment of credits ensued, thereby involving domestic exchange in more or less confusion.

The states had undertaken various enterprises to employ the surplus, the first instalment of which was paid in January, 1837, and an era of unbounded speculation set in.

The states'
and the
surplus.

122

The federal government under the existing regulation (the "specie circular") required payments to it for public lands (a large source of revenue) to be made in specie, and other taxes were to be collected in the notes of specie-paying banks. Congress received at this time, and ignored, a petition from the Board of Trade in New York, which, foreseeing trouble, asked for a reëstablishment of a national bank for the regulation of the disordered currency and exchanges.

Van Buren, who became President in March, 1837, continued Woodbury as Secretary of the Treasury and adhered to Jackson's policy.

After the second instalment of surplus had been paid to the states in April, the serious nature of the financial and commercial situation became very apparent. A public meeting in New York in that month appointed a committee of fifty, with Gallatin at its head, to appeal to the administration to abandon a policy which threatened destruction of the material interests of the nation. Over two hundred and fifty failures had already occurred.[1]

In May specie payments were suspended and the people were compelled to take irredeemable bank-notes, as well as "shin-plasters" of all sorts, in order to carry on the necessary transactions of each day. On May 15 Van Buren called Congress to meet in special session the following September. Notwithstanding the fact that the depository banks had suspended and the Treasury funds were running low or becoming unavailable by reason of the inability of the state depositories to make payment when required, Woodbury in July paid the third instalment of the surplus to the states (over $9,300,000), and in so doing barely escaped defaulting in his own payments.[2]

Suspension of specie payments.

[1] Sumner, History of Banking.   [2] Finance Reports, Vol. III.

Van Buren's message. When Congress met, Van Buren in his message, a most discursive document of twenty-four pages, recounted the events and cast upon the banks, depositories included, the blame for the deranged business conditions. These institutions, which but nine months before had been declared by Jackson to be satisfactorily performing their functions, and thereby demonstrating that a national bank was unnecessary, were now denounced as unfaithful to their trusts. Regarding banks as a necessary evil, he believed that the government should entirely sever all connections with them and keep its own revenues, to be collected only in specie, until needed for disbursements.[1]

Subtreasury suggested.

Secretary Woodbury reported that funds in but six out of the eighty-six depository banks were available. Five others had in a measure been able to meet the demands of the Treasury. His nominal balance was $34,000,000, but of this $28,101,644 was on deposit with the states, and over $5,000,000 was in suspended banks, leaving him actually but $700,000. He had arranged to have the revenues retained by the collectors and receivers subject to Treasury drafts, instead of depositing the same in banks as formerly.

Treasury notes. To meet the pressing obligations Congress did not call upon the states to repay the deposits recently made with them, but an act of October 2 postponed the payment of the fourth instalment until January 1, 1839, at which time there proved to be no surplus to divide. On October 12 an act was passed providing for an issue of $10,000,000 of one year Treasury notes, receivable for public dues and bearing not to exceed 6 per cent interest, and also an act postponing the payment of customs bonds. On October 16 Congress took away from the Secretary of the Treasury the power to recall the deposits with the states, reserving the right to itself.

[1] Messages of Presidents, Vol. III.

The amount which had been paid in the three instalments, as given above, it may be remarked, remains "on deposit" to this day, and is carried on the books of the Treasury as "unavailable."[1] Its recall has on several occasions been suggested. On the other hand, a number of the states have, even in recent years, asked for the fourth instalment, which, however, has never been distributed.

Van Buren's recommendations for an independent treasury were formulated into a bill, reported by Silas Wright (N.Y.) in the Senate, where it passed over Clay's vigorous opposition by a vote of 26 to 20; in the House, however, a contingent of Jacksonians who favored banks refused to act with their party, and the measure was defeated 107 to 120. _{Subtreasury bill defeated.}

The Whigs, under the lead of Clay and Webster, insisted that a national bank was the only adequate remedy for the existing evils. The chief need was a uniform currency system with a proper regulation of the issues of the local banks, which only a central bank could enforce. Van Buren's supporters, under the lead of Wright and Benton declared (in the face of the facts) that the Bank of the United States had been unable to prevent over-issues, that it was no part of the government's duty to regulate exchange, that the people wanted a separate establishment, that the public money would be more secure in subtreasuries than in banks, that by this system the use of specie would be encouraged and the depreciated bank-notes rejected, thus leading to a uniform currency.

Webster declared the subtreasury plan a conception belonging to barbarous times, leading to the hoarding of money, keeping from general use the sums which the government should receive to-day only to pay out again *Webster on subtreasury plan.*

[1] Finance Report, 1902, p. 183.

to-morrow. Other Whigs and some conservative Democrats regarded the scheme as an attack on the whole
credit system, sure to lead to contraction of the currency, besides increasing the presidential patronage and
power.

Calhoun, now again with the administration, admitted
that a central bank was the true remedy, but as he believed it unconstitutional, he supported the subtreasury
plan in part, although finally voting against it.

In his message in the following December, Van
Buren, reverting to his subtreasury plan, thought he
saw popular demonstration in its favor in a few local
elections which had taken place, and hoped Congress
would yield respect to this expression of the public
voice. Congress again considered the subtreasury
measure. The opposition received encouragement from
the resolutions of the legislatures of Tennessee, Pennsylvania, and New Jersey, instructing their senators to
vote against it. One New Jersey senator refused to
obey his instructions, and the bill passed the Senate in
March, 1838, by a vote of 27 to 25; the House again
rejected it by a majority of 14.

*Subtreas-
ury bill again
defeated.*

The opposition developed the argument that the
scheme was but a continuation of the suggestion of
Jackson's message of 1829 for the ultimate establishment of a treasury bank with enormous patronage, the
plan of Jackson's " Kitchen Cabinet" for perpetuating
the party in power. The great bank had been destroyed,
and it was now the turn of the lesser ones to go, and
the subtreasury plan would develop into the institution
desired by the party managers. Thus the President
would have the supreme control of the Nation's purse
and patronage.

These arguments were combated with ability by the
Democrats, who maintained that they were for a consti-

tutional treasury system and were not attacking the
banks; that the remedy against hoarding, as alleged,
was to have no surplus to hoard; that it was much
better for the people to have the government look after
its own finances and not be meddling with the banks;
that the Whigs themselves admitted that most of the
local banks were unsafe depositories.

The Treasury funds ran very low in May, 1838, due
to the fact that Congress had not provided for the reissue of the Treasury notes that were received for taxes.
The balance was down to $216,000 at one time, and Van
Buren sent a special message to Congress in May asking for relief. Accordingly Congress at once passed an
act permitting the reissue of the $10,000,000 authorized
in 1837. In July it passed an act amending the provision of the law of 1836, which prohibited the receipt
of notes of banks issuing denominations under $5, so
the same should not take effect until October 1, 1838;
another prohibiting the United States Bank (of Pennsylvania) from reissuing the old bank's notes, issued
while it was doing business under its federal charter;
and another act prohibiting notes under $5 in the Dis-
trict of Columbia. Congress also abrogated the "specie
circular," issued by order of President Jackson.

Van Buren repeated his recommendations in December, 1838, arguing that giving the banks public deposits
merely induced expansion of an unhealthful kind. As
to the national bank plan, he was gratified that Congress
did not, as in 1816, permit the suspension of coin payments to lead to a reëstablishment of so dangerous an
institution. The policy of depositing public money in
banks he regarded as a scheme for the benefit of the
few against the rights of the community at large.[1]

In the canvass of 1838 for the election of representa-

Government balance low.

Van Buren on public deposits.

[1] Messages of Presidents, Vol. III.

tives in Congress the subtreasury plan received much
attention. The result was almost a defeat for the adherents of Van Buren, the control of the House turning
upon the contested election of five Whigs from New
Jersey. The Democrats were seated.

Van Buren
on banks.

In his message in December, 1839, Van Buren made
his final effort to have his pet scheme become law.
He said that the existing embryonic subtreasury system had worked well and economically; the second suspension of coin payments in 1839 emphasized the need
of becoming absolutely independent of the banks;
speculation was too large a part of the business of
banks; the dependence of banks upon each other, subjecting the country institutions to those of the cities,
and the latter to those of London, practically placed
the business of every hamlet in the country under the
influence of the money power of Great Britain. Every
new debt contracted in England affected the currency
throughout this land, thus subjecting the interests of
our people to whatever measures of policy, necessity,
or caprice were resorted to by those who control credits
in England. The impropriety of using institutions thus
affected as public depositories was obvious — the independence of the government would be impaired by thus
placing its fiscal affairs in the control of foreign moneyed
interests.

Holding public deposits induced banks to favor heavy
taxes, large appropriations, and a surplus. The same
objection applied to the use of bank-notes for revenue
payments. He insisted upon payment in specie, instead
of letting the banks hold the specie and the government
take their promises to pay. The supposed danger of
confining the payments to specie did not really exist;
only four to five millions would be necessary, the government's drafts being used in large measure in lieu of

the actual coin. Moreover, the use of coin would tend to bring more into the country to meet the demand.

The argument against banks applied equally against one central bank; the difference was only in degree. He believed that the states would remedy the evils of the depreciated currency by legislation. Legislation and inflexible execution of the laws were necessary, and the federal government should coöperate on the lines he suggested to bring about the reform.[1]

Congress had again authorized the reissue of the Treasury notes of 1837 and practically extended the limit to $15,000,000. The issues and reissues amounted to over $31,000,000, but the limit was never exceeded. These notes were not authorized without much opposition on constitutional grounds. Benton particularly opposed the small denominations; Clay and Webster also opposed small notes.

Treasury note issues.

The interest ran from 1 per mille to 6 per cent, the former rate on the smaller notes, which prevented their remaining out. The notes were for a time below par, but at other times commanded a premium of 5 per cent.

Congress also took up the subtreasury bill. It was debated even more fully than before, but practically few new arguments were adduced on either side and the discussion was largely political. The bill passed the Senate by a vote of 24 to 18 and the House by 124 to 107, was signed by the President July 4, 1840, and at once put in operation.

Subtreasury bill passed.

The act provided for the collection, safe-keeping, transfer, and disbursement of public moneys by the Treasury through treasurers and receivers-general, of whom a definite number were to be appointed for the purpose; public money was not to be loaned or de-

[1] Messages of Presidents, Vol. III.

K

posited in bank, under severe penalties, except that when a large surplus was on hand it might be specially deposited in banks designated by the Secretary, but could not be loaned by the banks; the banks so used were to receive $\frac{1}{8}$ per cent commission; officers handling the funds were to be bonded; vaults were to be built, etc. The specie clause, an important feature which nearly killed the bill, was modified so as to have all public dues paid one-fourth in specie for the first year and an additional fourth each succeeding year until the whole was so payable.

Under the lead of the safety fund banks of New York, whose period of suspension had been limited by law to a year, resumption of coin payments began in May, 1838, but general resumption was not brought about until February, 1839, after several sessions of a convention of bankers in Philadelphia. It proved to be short-lived. The total note-issues had, it is true, been contracted, apparently by $33,000,000, but in many sections coin payment was merely nominal, and thus the conservative banks, which actually paid out coin, at the same time receiving notes of other banks, were the sufferers, being loaded up with notes that were practically irredeemable. The contraction and general liquidation had not been sufficient. Biddle's bank particularly failed to serve as a regulator; on the contrary, from its preponderating size it was the greatest source of embarrassment. Suspension again took place in November, 1839, and continued until 1842.

The question of the constitutionality of note-issues of banks owned or controlled by states, came before the Supreme Court of the United States from Georgia and Kentucky in 1824 and 1829; the question was finally decided early in 1837. It was argued that as a state could not emit "bills of credit," it could not authorize such emissions through a bank which it owned in whole or part. The decision (Briscoe *vs.* Bank of the Commonwealth of Kentucky, 11 Peters) held that in order to give notes the character of "bills of credit" they must be issued by the state on the faith of the state, and be binding on the state. The notes of the bank named were not such, but ordinary bank-notes, and hence constitutional issues. Justice Story dissented. In the case of Craig *vs.* Missouri, in 1830 (4 Peters 140) it was decided that certificates issued by a state, made receivable for taxes and salaries, were bills of credit and prohibited by the Constitution.

The notes of state banks were quoted at varying rates of discount. Thirty-five per cent discount on Mississippi notes is the lowest quoted during 1838 for notes that actually passed at all. During suspension of coin payments domestic exchange fluctuated violently; bills on Southern points were quoted from 5 to 25 per cent discount. The brief resumption in 1839 restored rates to normal conditions, the maximum being $4\frac{1}{2}$ per cent. The second suspension again brought about heavy discounts, continuing until 1842, the greatest being 17 per cent on Mobile; Cincinnati and Nashville falling at times to 16. The lowest rate of discount at New Orleans was 10.[1]

Discount on bank-notes.

All interests suffered greatly from the unsettled policy of the government. The continuing controversy between the supporters of a United States bank as against utilizing the state banks, and the controversy between the advocates of an independent treasury and those who insisted that banks in some form must be used in order to keep current funds in current use, rendered the policy of the government dependent upon whichever interest happened to be in power. That

[1] Finance Report, 1876, pp. 197, 198.

these political agitations served to delay resumption is unquestionable.

The United States Bank (of Pennsylvania).

The United States Bank, as we have seen, was continued with its $35,000,000 capital under a Pennsylvania charter and continued to exercise a very extensive influence both at home and abroad. Biddle had purchased the shares of the old bank from the government at about $115\frac{1}{2}$ and disposed of the new ones abroad at 120 to 126. Through his influence millions of dollars were brought from Europe and invested in the South and West. No one better than he understood the *whole* situation. When suspension of coin payments came in May, 1837, his bank also suspended. In his opinion liquidation was unavoidable, but at the same time he employed his credit abroad to bring about indulgence to debtors here, and in view of the fact that the debt held abroad was then about $200,000,000, this service was of great value.

Its final liquidation.

However, he became involved in a gigantic cotton speculation (that staple having become the principal export commodity), which resulted in heavy losses: his personal prestige suffered greatly from continued and virulent political attacks, and altogether his position was rendered untenable. He resigned from the bank in 1839, leaving it, as he claimed, prosperous; but after three assignments and two attempts at resumption, all in 1841, the institution succumbed, due no doubt to its having undertaken too great a load under the unfavorable business conditions. Its notes and deposits were paid in full, but the stockholders lost all, and Biddle was impoverished by the catastrophe.[1]

The statements of the bank during its existence as a state institution show (in millions of dollars): —

---

[1] Sumner, History of Banking in United States.

UNITED STATES BANK OF PENNSYLVANIA [1]

Year	Loans	Stocks and Bonds	Specie	Deposits	Net from State Banks	Circulation	Due Abroad	Other Liabilities
1837 . .	57.4	——	2.6	2.3	1.2	11.4	6.9	——
1838 . .	45.3	14.9	3.8	2.6	——	6.8	12.5	8.0
1839 . .	41.6	18.0	4.2	6.8	4.6	6.0	12.8	9.3
1840 . .	36.8	16.3	1.5	3.3	4.7	6.7	5.0	8.1

These figures indicate the great efforts which were made to maintain the bank in a dominating position and yet conserve its strength ; there was no undue expansion of its circulation and a fair reserve of specie; but doubtless the items of loans and securities included a large amount of paper made worthless by the disasters of 1837; the losses must have been enormous to entirely dissipate the capital.

Had Biddle avoided speculation, pursued a conservative course, and maintained specie payments instead of suspending (which he professed he was able to do), the Treasury would, as Gouge pointed out, have been morally compelled, under the law of 1836, to use his bank as one of the very few specie-paying banks, and the effect of this would have so influenced Congress as to cause the defeat of the subtreasury plan.

A comparison of the condition of the state banks generally is rendered impracticable by reason of the imperfect returns for 1834, the first year for which a compilation appears in the Treasury reports. That the expansion was quite general appears certain, and that it was greatest in the South and West is also demonstrable. From the most complete unofficial statement published the following is abstracted (amounts in millions): —

Condition of state banks.

[1] Finance Report, 1876, p. 193.

All Banks	1834	1837	Increase
Capital	200	291	91
Circulation	95	149	54
Deposits	76	127	51
Loans	324	525	201

Comparing 1837 with 1835, the following data are presented from the official sources, the same states being used in each case : —

	Capital	Circula- tion	Deposits	Specie	Loans
5 New England States :					
1835	53	17	18	2	79
1837	65	19	20	3	97
4 Middle States :					
1835	51	24	30	11	94
1837	67	41	47	10	135
9 Southern States :					
1835	57	26	17	8	87
1837	98	54	39	14	180
5 Western States :					
1835	8	6	4	3	12
1837	14	13	16	6	29

The expansion.

Circulation increased in the eastern group $19,000,000, and loans $59,000,000, whereas in the much more sparsely populated states of the South and West the note-issues increased $35,000,000 and loans $110,000,000.

Deprived of the steadying force and conservative influence of a national bank, and taught by the disastrous experiences of the several years following the expiration of the charter of the second United States Bank, some of the states seemed to realize an added sense of responsibility, and these enacted laws based upon sound and conservative principles and provided for intelligent and adequate supervision. In Massachusetts, where thirty-two banks had discontinued, the new law provided for examinations by state commissioners annually, and specially if found desirable. The Suffolk Bank system continued, with some improvements, and doubtless served to avert greater disaster to New England banks. Rhode Island restricted loans and circulation of banks. Its banks, as well as those of Connecticut, weathered the storm of 1837–1840 without a failure.

In New York the safety fund, apparently through inadvertence in legislation, was made applicable to all the indebtedness of the banks, and proved altogether inadequate. · The principle established was correct, and had the law providing for the same been drawn with sufficient detail and with sufficient solicitude for its enforcement, its practical working would have vindicated the principle. A careful analysis shows that slight changes would have achieved well-recognized success instead of failure. The principle made the banks mutually insure the redemption of the notes of all by contributing to a safety fund an amount annually which any bank could well afford to pay for the privilege of note-issue. Each bank contributed annually an amount equal to $\frac{1}{2}$ per cent of its capital until the same equalled 3 per cent of the total bank capital. The tax should have been predicated upon the volume of note-issues. Had care been taken to prevent over-issues, and had the fund been limited in its application to the circulation of the banks, it would have been sufficient to protect all note holders from loss, as shown by Millard Fillmore in his report as Comptroller of the state of New York (1848). The legislature felt impelled to waive the penalty of forfeiture of charters, on account

Safety fund system fails.

of suspension of coin payments, which the law provided, because of adverse business conditions, but more especially because suspension had been very general throughout the country. Prior to this period all bank charters had been granted by special act of the legislature, and were regarded as patronage to be extended to political favorites.[1] To avoid the scandals growing out of this practice and to avoid the just charge of monopoly, a "free banking" law was passed in 1838.

First free
banking law.

As finally adjusted, the law provided that one or several persons might qualify and enjoy the right of issuing notes to circulate as money. By depositing with the state comptroller stocks of the United States, of the state of New York, or of any other state approved by the comptroller and by valuation made equal to a 5 per cent stock of the state of New York; or by depositing bonds bearing not less than 6 per cent secured by mortgage on productive, unencumbered real estate worth double the amount of the mortgage; the right to receive circulating notes for an equal amount was established. In case of default these securities were to be sold and the notes redeemed with the proceeds. Interest on the securities deposited was paid to the party depositing the same, so long as there was no failure to redeem notes and the security was deemed adequate. Provision was made for the surrender of notes and the return of securities. The state in no wise guaranteed the notes. A reserve of at least 12½ per cent in specie was required, and refusal to redeem notes brought a penalty of 14 per cent.

Bond
deposit plan
considered.

Under this system the number of banks at once increased rapidly. Individuals in need supplied mortgages to be deposited as a basis for circulation upon condition of obtaining accommodations. Very many if

[1] Fillmore, Report Comptroller, New York, 1848.

not most of the banks organized under this law were
started for the sole purpose of issuing notes, and were
not banks of discount and deposit. They simply converted the securities which they deposited with the state
authorities into bank bills. Had the note-issues been
merely an incident or adjunct to a regular banking business the system would have had a fairer test. It was not,
however, comparable to the safety fund system, since no
bond-secured circulation can possess elasticity. The
first case of failure occurred in 1840, and the bank's
securities realized sixty-eight cents on the dollar of its
note-issues. Mortgages were not convertible, and the
legislature in 1843 limited securities which might be
deposited to stocks of the state of New York. Later
the act was amended so as to include United States
bonds. In order to prevent individuals residing in one
place from issuing notes payable in another, a law was
passed requiring all interior banks to redeem their notes
either in New York or Albany at not exceeding 1 per
cent discount (subsequently made ¼ per cent), and
later that no one should transact the business of a
banker except at his place of residence, and still later
all banks were required to be banks of discount and
deposit as well as of circulation. In 1846 the new
constitution prohibited organization of banks except
under the general law, prohibited the legislature from
authorizing the suspension of specie payments, imposed
the double liability of shareholders, and made note
holders preferred creditors.

The legislature seemed disposed to correct the faults of
the system, and had not the Civil War intervened it is
fair to assume the New York bank system would have
been perfected. From the passage of the free banking
act up to 1850, thirty-two banks failed, entailing a loss
upon note holders of $325,487, some paying as low a

Results in
New York.

percentage as thirty cents on the dollar. From 1850 to 1861, twenty-five failures entailed a loss upon note holders of only $72,849.[1] In view of the crisis in 1857 these statistics show an improving condition.

The free banking system with bond-secured circulation was adopted in many other states, notably Illinois, Indiana, and Wisconsin. In many it met with unfortunate results, in some with indifferent success. The first effect was inflation of note-issues. Note-issues were the one certain resource for obtaining credit, and public sentiment would not apply wholesome restraint and enforce conservative management. The system in our principal states was rapidly improving, however, when the crisis of the Civil War overtook the country, and that resulted in substituting what every interest and every industry required — a national system of currency.

The condition of Michigan banks during this period gave the name " red dog " and " wild cat " currency to the notes of the mushroom banks generally. A dog in red color and the wild cat were common imprints upon their current bills. Michigan had (1839) endeavored to imitate Indiana with a state bank and branches, but while the plan was the same, the management was radically different, to the cost of the note holders. Two of these Michigan banks held $1,800,000 public moneys when their capital as reported was less than $600,000 and specie $122,000.[2]

In many of the states the suspension of coin payments for a limited time was legalized, and stay laws[3] again appeared upon the statute books.

The banks of states (*i.e.* banks in which states were interested as owners of stock) proved in most instances costly experiments. Political influences entered into the

---

[1] White, Money and Banking.   [2] Finance Report, 1876, p. 200.

[3] Sumner, History of Banking in United States.

management and control in many commonwealths to the great detriment of their business interests, and where states had issued bonds to capitalize such banks, the people had them to pay by means of taxation. There were, however, notable exceptions. As before stated, Delaware and South Carolina had very successful state banks.

The Indiana state bank was phenomenally successful. It consisted of ten branches, each with a capital of $160,000, the parent bank located at ·Indianapolis being practically a board of control, and exercising its banking functions through its branches. The bank was chartered for a period of twenty-five years immediately after Jackson's veto of the renewal charter of the second United States Bank, and was exclusive in character. The state owned one-half the stock, and individuals one-half, all of which was paid in in specie. The state issued bonds with which to raise funds for its part of the capital, and also advanced to individuals $62\frac{1}{2}$ per cent of their subscriptions, taking a lien upon their shares, and also real estate security as collateral to such advances. The president and four directors of the parent bank were chosen by the legislature, and one director by the private stockholders of each branch. The assets of each branch belonged to its shareholders exclusively, and the branch was managed by the local shareholders subject to the parent board at Indianapolis, which alone could declare dividends. In this manner each branch reaped the benefit of superior management and greater earnings, and had every incentive to energy and conservatism.

Each branch was liable for the debts of every other branch, and in case of insolvency its indebtedness must be liquidated within one year. This induced an interested if not a jealous watchfulness of each other, and a

State bank of Indiana.

Its organization and branches.

most intelligent and vigorous system of examinations and supervision on the part of the central board. Loans exceeding $500 could only be made by a five-sevenths majority of the board, the vote and the names to be entered on the minutes, and officers and directors could not vote upon a proposition in which they were financially interested. Directors were individually liable for any loss resulting from loans made in violation of the law unless they could prove they voted in opposition. Favoritism in loans to officers and directors was forbidden. The insolvency of any branch was presumptively fraudulent, and unless the fraud was disproved, the directors were liable without limit for the debts. After their estates were exhausted the other stockholders were liable for an amount equal to the par of their stock. Any director in order to protect his estate must be prepared to prove good faith, and this insured a high degree of efficiency and conservatism. Loans upon their own stock were forbidden. (See statement p. 154.)

Internal regulation. The debts to or from any branch except on account of deposits could not exceed twice the capital stock. The intended and actual effect of this provision was to limit the circulating notes to twice the capital. Rediscounts or loans by banks at that time were very uncommon. No bank would borrow from another and pay interest thereon when it could issue its circulating notes without interest. Each branch redeemed its notes in specie on demand and was compelled to receive the notes of all other branches. The notes were signed by the president and issued to the branches by the parent bank. Discounts could not exceed two and one-half times the capital. Restriction upon voting the shares prevented monopolization.

The bank was liquidated at the expiration of its charter, netting stockholders $153.70 in addition to good dividends, which it paid regularly. The state realized, after the payment of principal and interest of the bonds issued in capitalizing the same, $3,500,000 net profit.[1]

This was a model bank in every respect. With independent ownership of assets and joint liability for debts, the greatest degree of efficiency and watchfulness was secured in the separate branches, and though widely separated, they were for all essential purposes closely woven together as one harmonious whole. It is an exemplary illustration of the efficacy of branch banking as a system. It is an equally potent illustration of the safety and efficiency of credit or asset currency when administered by a good system with competent management. It also presents supervision and examination in its ideal form. Examination by a government examiner, compensated by a lump sum without regard to the time expended or labor involved, is very valuable; but examination by an expert banker, an accountant, a judge of credits who inventories both assets and liabilities, knows the symmetry and proportion of banking in that particular locality, and can judge intuitively whether in any department or in any respect the rules of prudence have been infringed; who, in short, sees all and judges all through the eye of a stockholder and from the standpoint of dividends — such examinations are effective, are ideal.

A model institution.

To-day deposits are the main instrumentality which enables banks to extend loans and discounts to their patrons. Capital and surplus are the margin of safety that commands public confidence. Circulating notes are a trivial factor at best, and really do not count at all, since more money is invested in bonds as security than is received in return in notes. At that time deposits were a meagre factor and circulating notes counted twice as much as capital stock, even in this strong and

[1] White, Money and Banking.

conservative bank. Circulating notes counted in much greater ratio in less conservative banks, and were practically the only resource in many. This explains why the people clung to and supported the note-issuing function of banks when security was so meagre and inevitable losses so great. There was practically no other resource for extending to them loans. Bank-notes were the most convenient means of utilizing loans in the circumscribed limits of trade at that time. Credit on the books of the banks to be utilized by checks and drafts were little used.

The severe strictures upon the banks owned and conducted by states are as a general proposition wholly justified. There were, however, exceptions, whose organization and management would prove safe models at the present time with all our added experience and with all our wonderfully increased facilities for the transmission of credit and exchange of values. Such an one is the state bank of Indiana. It maintained the highest credit at all times and supplied the needs of the commercial public. Its notes were at all times redeemed in specie, even in the panic of 1857, when all the banks in the Eastern states and in New York (except the Chemical) were forced to suspend.

's   The state of Louisiana in 1842 enacted a general banking law which embodied the sound principles of banking which experience with state and United States banks had demonstrated. It also contained some restrictions, which, however practical then, would interfere with legitimate business now. No bank could have less than fifty shareholders owning not less than thirty shares of stock each, hence minimum capital of $150,000. Specie reserve against all liabilities of 33⅓ per cent was required; all banks were to be examined by a board of state officers quarterly or oftener; directors were personally liable for all loans approved by them and which were made in

violation of law ; no bank could pay out any notes but
its own ; all banks were required to pay their balances
to each other every Saturday under penalty of being put
in liquidation. The above requirements were wholesome
and in the interest of good banking, and afford the first
instance of a legal requirement of a definite reserve.
Some other requirements that seem to reflect somewhat
upon the standard of commercial honor at that time were
as follows : no commercial paper having more than ninety
days to run could be discounted or purchased, and none
could be renewed ; if any paper was not paid at maturity
or a request for its renewal made, the account of the
party was to be closed and his name posted as a delinquent and other banks advised ; any director being
absent from the state for more than thirty days or failing to attend five successive meetings was deemed to
have resigned and the vacancy filled at once. This law
was in successful operation until interrupted by the
events of the Civil War in 1862.

The state bank of Ohio (organized in 1845) was
similar to the state bank of Indiana. Any number of
banks not less than seven might compose its branches.
These might be existing banks or those organized for
the purpose. It started with a capital of $3,300,000.
The branches could issue notes in a ratio graduated to
their capital; for the first $100,000 of capital, $200,000
of notes ; for $200,000 capital, $350,000 notes, the amount
of notes diminishing as the capital increased. The
branches were required to maintain a reserve fund with
the central board of control equal to 10 per cent of their
circulating notes. The central board of control could
invest this in bonds of Ohio or the United States or in
real estate mortgages, the interest inuring to the respective branches. All branches were jointly liable for the
notes of each, but not for its general debts. In case of

The Ohio system.

failure of any branch to redeem its notes, the board of control immediately assessed the branches pro rata and raised sufficient funds to redeem such notes, and then reimbursed the branches as soon as the assets in the safety fund could be reduced to cash for that purpose, and in turn reimbursed the safety fund from the assets of the failed branch, the claim for such reimbursement having a prior lien. The bank ceased to exist with the expiration of its charter in 1866, the national bank system having rendered state banks less desirable. It had thirty-six branches, and was well managed and successful.[1]

Harrison elected.

Van Buren's victory in establishing the subtreasury system was short-lived. In the presidential contest of 1840, the subtreasury question being at issue, the Whigs elected Harrison and a congress (both houses) by large majorities. Van Buren, in his last message (December, 1840), insisted that the subtreasury system was working satisfactorily; nevertheless, its abolition had apparently been decreed by the popular vote. Harrison called Congress to meet in extra session on May 31, but he died in April, and the Whig leaders who had nominated and elected Tyler as Vice-President because of his views against the subtreasury act, found, when he succeeded to the presidency, that he did not agree with Clay, the actual leader of the party. The act repealing the sub-

Repeal of subtreasury act.

treasury law passed by a vote of 29 to 18 in the Senate and 134 to 87 in the House, and became a law August 9. The repeal of the deposit act of 1836 was also speedily accomplished. Meanwhile Tyler's Secretary of the Treasury, Thomas Ewing, had, by request of Congress, prepared the President's plan for a "fiscal bank," to be located in the District of Columbia: capital $30,000,000, of which the United States was to take two-tenths, the states three-tenths, to be paid for by the United States

[1] White, Money and Banking.

in place of the "fourth instalment of surplus," not yet A central bank bill. distributed, and to which the states seemed to think they had a claim; with branches to be located in the states *only after their assent.* The latter proviso was the chief point of controversy. Under the influence of Clay this feature of the bill was remodelled so as to provide that unless the legislatures actually dissented at once it was to be presumed that they had no objection. The Senate passed it 26 to 23, the House 128 to 97. Tyler vetoed this bill in August, 1841.

The special features of the bill were : that the parent bank was to make no loans except to the government in accordance with law; dividends were limited to 7 per cent, any surplus earnings to go to the government; the debts were limited to $1\frac{3}{4}$ times the capital and $25,000,000 in excess of deposits; loans were not to be renewable and were to cease when circulation reached more than thrice the specie on hand; dealing in stocks and commodities was prohibited. The objection of Tyler (a Virginian and strict constructionist) was chiefly Tyler's veto. that it was unconstitutional to authorize branches in the states without their consent, but he also objected to giving the bank the discounting privilege.[1]

The actual difference between the bill drafted by Ewing for the President, and that reported by Clay and passed was very slight.

The will of the people as expressed at the polls was ignored, the establishment of a central bank and thereby a uniform system of paper currency, national in character, was also defeated by this hair-splitting construction of the Constitution, extreme assertion of state sovereignty, and jealous determination to minimize the powers of the federal government.

The Whigs were angered by the veto upon such a

[1] Messages of Presidents, Vol. IV.

slender pretext. Webster, who was Secretary of State, counselled yielding, since the end was to obtain a means of regulating the currency, equalizing exchanges, and taking care of public moneys. It was reported that Tyler had agreed to sign the Ewing bill. He outlined in his veto message the kind of a bill he would sign; accordingly such a bill was drawn and approved by Webster, who took it to Tyler, who also approved it, whereupon Congress passed it September 3. In the meantime John Minor Botts, representative from Virginia, had written a violent letter in which Tyler was charged with currying favor with the Democrats. The letter was published, and naturally Tyler was offended. He then desired, as Ewing says, to have the bill postponed, which did not, however, suit the Whigs, and the legislation was hurried through as stated. Tyler vetoed the bill on September 9, and the Whigs could not pass it over the veto. The entire cabinet thereupon resigned, excepting Webster, who remained for some time in order to complete with dignity certain important negotiations with foreign countries.[1]

The second bill and Veto.

Ewing in his letter of resignation pointed out the inexplicable inconsistencies of Tyler's second veto, declaring unequivocally that the very features objected to were approved by Tyler before the bill was introduced, and some of them included upon his own suggestion. He properly resented Tyler's action in having him (Ewing) prepare a bill upon lines to satisfy the earlier objections, and then vetoing it without consulting him. These statements of Ewing's were publicly confirmed by at least two other members of the cabinet, showing such a breach of faith toward the Secretary of the Treasury as made his remaining in office impossible.[2]

From the evidence it was clear (1) that Tyler was

[1] Statesman's Manual, Vol. II.　　　　[2] *Ibid.*

desirous of establishing some form of fiscal corporation to perform the functions set forth above, (2) that he was hypercritical and hair-splitting on the constitutional point, (3) that in view of the Botts letter the Whigs should have postponed action as Webster said, (4) that notwithstanding the Botts letter, which did not alter the facts, Tyler was not justified in vetoing the bill which he had previously approved; by so doing he placed his personal feelings above his public duty respecting a great public measure.

Webster's view that Tyler was sincerely trying to adjust his constitutional views to the occasion, appear to be borne out by the second veto message in which Tyler literally implored Congress not to press the differences on this measure to a rupture of harmony. Postponement for more deliberation was asked, in terms which showed anxiety.

The Democrats could not resist exulting, and the Whig leaders denounced Tyler, declaring political coöperation with him at an end. But many, like Webster, believed in waiting. The new cabinet included a number of distinguished Whigs, Walter Forward becoming Secretary of the Treasury.

With both the subtreasury act and the deposit law of 1836 repealed the Treasury fell back upon the system in use prior to the establishment of the first Bank of the United States, a sort of half independent treasury, half bank-deposit system. The Treasury was at this time still borrowing money.

The congressional election of 1842 was won by the Democrats, the Senate remaining Whig, and legislation was therefore blocked.

Interest-bearing Treasury notes were issued quite extensively during these years, in the usual form. Early in 1843 it was necessary to ask for authority to reissue redeemed notes. In all $43,000,000 Treasury notes were used.[1] Forward was succeeded in the Treasury by John C. Spencer.

In 1844 the Whigs with Clay as candidate for the presidency suffered severe defeat. Polk, formerly Speaker, was chosen.

Tyler had continued in his messages to urge his plan upon Congress, but without avail. He referred to the use by the people of the Treasury notes as evidence that his plan of using such notes secured by a specie reserve would have proved satisfactory.

Polk had continually been opposed to the national bank. In his message, December, 1845, he also opposed the use of state banks, not only because they had proved faithless, but upon constitutional grounds, pointing out that as there were only four banks in the country when the Constitution was adopted, it could not have been contemplated holding public money anywhere but in a national treasury. He therefore urged the establishment of a "constitutional treasury," a more elaborate measure than that of Van Buren, to absolutely divorce the government from the banks, and prevent the latter from using the public moneys for private gain.[2] He was ably supported by his Secretary of the Treasury, Robert J. Walker (Mississippi), who took the extreme view that it was necessary to exclude bank-notes from the revenues entirely, because it would be useless to have an independent treasury receiving and disbursing bank paper.

Polk's sub-treasury plan.

The advocates of a national bank, as the proper solution of the currency difficulties and the best instrumentality through which the government could transact its fiscal affairs, failed to establish such an institution owing to the successive vetoes of Tyler. If

[1] Knox, United States Notes.   [2] Messages of Presidents, Vol. IV.

with both branches of Congress in political accord and favorable they failed to establish a national bank, one was not likely to be established under any circumstances, and public sentiment turned in other directions. The evidence was cumulative and clear that the state banks could not be relied upon, and under the circumstances no doubt public opinion favored the subtreasury measure. The act was clearly a device to protect the government's money and at the same time avoid any regulation of the currency by the federal government, under the plea that Congress had no constitutional power over the same. If Congress were conceded the undelegated power to regulate paper currency, other similar powers might be assumed, for instance the power to interfere with slavery. *Its object.*

Congress took up the subject at once, and after long debate passed Polk's measure, in the House by 123 to 67, in the Senate by 28 to 24. It was approved by the President August 6, 1846.

Thus in a government for the people and controlled by them, it was claimed by the leaders in public life of that day that no matter how imperfect, unsafe, or disgraceful, even, the existing paper currency systems might be, there was no remedy which could provide a safe, sound, and uniform paper medium. So the makeshift to provide only for the safety of the government revenues was enacted, supported solidly by those who, under Benton's lead, insisted that the country's business could be done by the use of specie only, arguing that the example of the government would be followed by all.

The chief features of the act were the prohibition against depositing public moneys in banks, or disposing of them in any manner other than in payments of Treasury drafts or transfer orders. The officers of the *The subtreasury act of 1846.*

government were required to hold the funds "safely" in the meantime; revenues were after January 1, 1847, all to be paid in specie or Treasury notes, and severe penalties for disregard of the act were imposed.[1]

Years elapsed before the officers of the government were provided with proper facilities for safely handling funds. Gouge, the official examiner of subtreasuries, reported in 1854 that Western depositories were inadequately protected. He found, for example, the subtreasury at Jeffersonville, Indiana, in a tavern adjoining the bar-room, with which it was connected by a door with glass lights, so that the subtreasurer might, when in the bar-room, see into his office. The entrance for the public was through a back passage under a stairway. The office was divided into two rooms by a temporary partition, lighted by a single window defended by iron grates. The silver was kept in wooden boxes, the gold in an iron safe. The subtreasurer slept in one of the rooms with his weapons.[2]

The requirement that all payments be made in specie was not rigidly carried out. It was indeed practically impossible at post-offices, etc., but in the main, Walker was gratified with the result.

Mexican War. The war with Mexico occurred at this period (1846), and the government being constrained to borrow made use of its notes to the extent of $20,000,000, which paid current expenditures and went into general circulation as money. Bond issues were also resorted to, and were in part used to fund the notes above mentioned.

Both Polk and Walker pointed with pride to the "constitutional treasury" which had by preventing inflation and suspension during the war period enabled the government to issue its notes freely and sell its bonds at a premium. Such were the facts. True, the

[1] See Appendix.   [2] Finance Report, 1854.

war was a short one, and not nearly so expensive as that of 1812; furthermore, the existing banks had but recently passed through a period of liquidation and contraction, bringing about sounder conditions, all of which served to aid the Treasury. Polk maintained that the country was saved from the effect of the crisis of 1847 in Great Britain by the check both upon bank-note inflation and the resulting speculation.[1]

The execution of the law showed many defects which both Polk and Walker asked Congress in vain to remedy. The war and the tariff occupied the legislators' attention. The issues growing out of the tariff caused the defeat of Polk and the success of the Whigs with Taylor in the presidential contest of 1848.

Whenever specie payments were suspended there occurred a marked increase in the number of banks, because the profit upon circulation was large, and under meagre laws and lax supervision the liability almost insignificant. From 1837 to 1840 the number of banks increased 113, the nominal capital $68,000,000; by 1843 the resumption of coin payments had become quite general and the number had diminished 210, the capital $130,000,000. Note-issues, which it will be recalled aggregated $149,000,000 in 1837, now amounted to less than $59,000,000. The liquidation had reduced the money supply per capita from $13.87 to $6.87; needless to add that the number of failures was without precedent in the country's history. The estimate of losses during the period was nearly $800,000,000.

The banks which were founded upon a flimsy basis were of course the first to go to the wall, but many which had been properly organized also suffered extinction. The catastrophe was so general and wide- spread that the subject of banking reform was taken up

[1] Messages of Presidents, Vol. IV.

seriously, as we have seen.   In sixteen of the states the New York plan of free banking with bond deposit to cover circulation and the double liability of shareholders was copied.   Quite a number of states experimented with banking laws that had been tried elsewhere and found wanting and with schemes which had never been tried.

Review of the period.   Regarding only the safety of the federal revenues, in view of the condition of the banks and their currency, the subtreasury act was a proper measure.   It served its purpose so well during this period only because conditions were exceptionally favorable.   Secretary Walker claimed for it the credit of having caused the $22,000,000 net import of specie in 1847 to be put into circulation instead of being used by the banks, as formerly, to inflate their note-issues.[1]   In fact, however, when the bank reports were published later, it appeared that the banks had absorbed fully one-half of this coin and increased their circulation by $23,000,000.   Indeed, the financial transactions of the government for a number of years after 1846 were relatively so insignificant in volume that the question whether upon the whole the "constitutional treasury" was detrimental or not was subjected to no real test.   President Taylor in his first message (1849) gave the subject only three lines, leaving it to the wisdom of Congress to retain or repeal the law, and Congress took no action.

It is worthy of note that Congress had devised no method of ridding the people of depreciated paper; not even the small bills (under $5) against which so much had been said were done away with.

Banking power by sections.   Reference has been made in previous chapters to the dissatisfaction of the Southern and Western states due to the disadvantage under which they labored owing to inadequate banking facilities.   The following table gives

[1] Finance Report, 1847.

for the several sections the banking power, composed
of capital, circulation, and deposits of reporting institutions, and the relative amount per capita (excluding
slaves in the Southern states).

	Banking Power (In Millions)			Per Capita		
	1830	1840	1850	1830	1840	1850
New England . . .	54	89	114	$ 27.66	$ 39.98	$ 41.89
Middle	107	131	185	25.87	25.64	27.95
Southern	80	196	117	15.54	48.75	22.28
Western	7	38	35	4.47	11.29	6.35
Total	248	454	451	19.33	26.64	19.47

Note. — For 1830 the figures include the Bank of the United States distributed according to branches, but omitting $14,000,000 of capital invested
in United States bonds.

The table illustrates not only the disparity referred
to, particularly in the Western states, but also the location of the enormous expansion in 1840.

STATISTICAL RÉSUMÉ

(Amounts in millions of dollars)

Condition of Banks, 1837 to 1849

Year	No.	Capital	Circulation	Deposits	Specie	Loans
1837	788	291	149	127	38	525
1838	829	318	116	85	35	486
1839	840	327	135	90	45	492
1840	901	358	107	76	33	463
1841	784	314	107	65	35	386
1842	692	260	84	62	28	324
1843	691	229	59	56	34	255
1844	696	211	75	85	50	265
1845	707	206	90	88	44	289
1846	707	197	106	97	42	312
1847	715	203	106	92	35	310
1848	751	205	129	103	46	344
1849	782	207	115	91	44	332

THE STATE BANK OF INDIANA

YEAR	LOANS	SPECIE	OTHER ASSETS	NOTES	DEPOSITS	CAPITAL	SURPLUS
1835	1.8	0.8	1.9	1.5	0.4	1.2	—
1838	4.2	1.3	1.1	3.0	0.4	2.2	0.3
1841	4.7	1.1	1.0	3.1	0.3	2.7	0.3
1844	3.5	1.1	1.4	3.1	0.3	2.1	0.3
1847	3.8	1.1	2.1	3.6	0.6	2.1	0.5
1850	4.4	1.2	1.5	3.4	0.6	2.1	0.8
1853	5.1	1.3	1.5	3.8	0.7	2.1	1.0
1856	5.0	1.1	1.9	3.4	0.6	2.1	1.3

Loans include advances to the state and bonds.

CIRCULATION 1837 TO 1849

YEAR	BANK-NOTES OUTSTANDING	SPECIE IN U.S.	TOTAL MONEY IN U.S.	SPECIE IN TREASURY	MONEY IN CIRCULATION	POPULATION	PER CAPITA
1837	149	73	222	5	217	15.7	$13.87
1838	116	88	204	5	199	16.1	12.33
1839	135	87	222	2	220	16.6	13.26
1840	107	83	190	4	186	17.1	10.91
1841	107	80	187	1	186	17.6	10.59
1842	84	80	164	—	164	18.1	9.02
1843	59	90	149	1	147	18.7	7.87
1844	75	100	175	8	167	19.3	8.68
1845	90	96	186	8	178	19.9	8.95
1846	106	97	203	9	193	20.5	9.43
1847	106	120	226	2	224	21.1	10.59
1848	129	112	241	8	232	21.8	10.66
1849	115	120	235	2	233	22.5	10.34

CHAPTER VII

1850 TO 1861

THE element of federal politics incident to the competition for public deposits having now been definitely eliminated from the banking business, commercial banking developed in a greater degree than ever before. Issuing currency, instead of being the primary object of banking, began to be regarded as of less importance in most of the older sections of the country.

The distressing experiences already described produced a revulsion of sentiment in some of the states which led to the severest restrictions upon all banks by legislation and in a few by constitutional amendment. Nine states had no banks in 1852.[1] After a few years this rigidity relaxed and local bank-note issues were again reported from nearly all of the states. The scarcity of silver coin, discussed in another chapter, had caused a large increase in small note-issues.

Improvement in state banks.

Many states adopted the New York free banking and bond deposit plan, but not without modifications that operated more or less to neutralize its beneficial features. Bonds of states that afterwards depreciated, railway bonds some of which proved of little value, and miscellaneous securities, were permitted to be used, entailing losses upon the note holders. Many banks reported no deposits and no specie, the bonds deposited to secure circulation being all the protection note holders could expect.

[1] Sumner, History of Banking in United States.

The publication of reports of condition, now required by law in many states, no doubt assisted in correcting many evils and removed much of the mystery which had surrounded the business.

In New England compulsory specie reserve laws were enacted, and the Suffolk system, supplemented by other wise legislation, served to maintain prompt redemption and a safe bank currency, acceptable almost everywhere in the Union. In 1858 the Suffolk Bank made over that special business to the Bank of Mutual Redemption, organized for the purpose by country banks. In 1856 the Boston Clearing-house was established, following the lead of New York City, where a similar institution was organized three years earlier.

The New York State Banking Department was established in 1851. The Metropolitan Bank of New York City was established to act as a central redemption bank (like the Suffolk) in the same year. These circumstances and the establishment of the clearing-house in New York City in 1853 brought about a much more stable and secure system of paper currency.

In the metropolis weekly reports were required to be made to the clearing-house by the associated banks, and in 1858 a fixed ratio of cash reserve to be held against deposit liabilities was agreed upon. The clearing of checks obviated the use of currency to a considerable extent, and in other particulars the association of the banks of the city, voluntarily imposing restrictions upon their business, contributed greatly to make them strong and influential.

There is one fundamental principle underlying the clearing-house system. Each bank settles its daily business with all the other banks of the city precisely as it would if there were but one other bank in the city. For instance, the First National Bank delivers to the clearing-house at ten o'clock A.M. every day all the Its opera-tion. debit items it holds against all the other banks and receives credit for the amount by the clearing-house. The clearing-house in turn, having received the same from the other banks, delivers to the First National all the items which all the other banks of the city hold against it and debits the First National with the amount. The First National is either debit or credit according to whether the amount of checks, etc., it brought to the clearing-house exceeds or is exceeded by the amount of checks, etc., which the other banks brought against it, and pays or receives the difference or balance in cash, as the case may be. The average daily exchanges of the New York banks for the year 1902 were $245,898,649 and the average cash balances were $11,110,210. The average daily use of money was lessened by the clearing-house system of exchanges $234,788,439, being the difference between the cash actually used and the amount of the checks exchanged. The system not only minimized the use of actual cash, but removed the risk involved in sending so much cash about the streets and greatly reduced the expense involved in messengers, runners, and bookkeeping.

The making of the settlement at the clearing-house involves only about forty-five minutes on the average. The payment of debit balances is made at a bank's convenience any time prior to 1.30 P.M., at which time all credit balances are paid.

The clearing-house fixed a cash reserve and bound Reserves required. each member to maintain the same ; took the public into its confidence by publishing weekly reports of condition showing the standing of each bank. This action, more than any legislation, more than anything else, aided in building up a sense of moral responsibility to the public on the part of banks throughout the country, in restraining the undue expansion of note-issues and the many other reprehensible practices which characterized the banking of that period.

Philadelphia banks organized a clearing-house in 1858. Pennsylvania enacted a redemption law similar to that of New York and also prohibited notes under Action in other states. $5. The latter provision was likewise embodied in the laws of Maryland, Virginia, Alabama, Arkansas, Louisiana, Kansas, and Missouri,[1] one of the objects being to enforce the use of silver and gold in the smaller transactions of daily barter. It failed for want of coöperation among the states. A similar effort failed many years later, when the Treasury tried to enforce the general circulation of the silver dollars coined under the act of 1878. The people demanded small notes.

Notwithstanding the strength of the state bank of Indiana, the state itself was for a time the favorite place for incubating note-issuing "banks" without capital, banking offices, or furniture. A circular letter issued offering aid to any one desiring to start such a bank stated that the sole cost necessarily incurred in starting a $100,000 "bank" would be $5000 for plates to print the notes and expenses, including compensation to the promoter, and $5000 as margin to carry the necessary bonds to be deposited.[2] The owner of the "bank" could as well reside in New York as Indiana.

A notable instance of the opposite extreme was "George Smith's money." These notes were issued by the Wisconsin Marine and Fire Insurance Company, which was controlled by George Smith. The company clearly had no right to issue circulating notes, but the notes were convertible into specie at all times with such absolute certainty that they passed at par everywhere,

---

[1] Sumner, History of Banking in United States.
[2] Hunt's Merchant's Magazine, Vol. XXXVIII., p. 261.

and for years constituted the best currency in the Northwest.[1]

It was necessary to exercise great discrimination as to the notes of certain sections and certain banks, which were at a discount of from one to fifty per cent. In order to feel assured that a note when tendered was good, one of the numerous "bank-note detectors" had to be consulted, and it was exceedingly difficult for those weekly publications to keep pace with the brisk "bank starter" and "note issuer." Says Sumner in his History of Banking : —

Bank-note detectors.

"The bank-note detector did not become divested of its useful but contemptible function until the national bank system was founded. It is difficult for the modern student to realize that there were hundreds of banks whose notes circulated in any given community. The bank-notes were bits of paper recognizable as a species by shape, color, size and engraved work. Any piece of paper which had these came with the prestige of money ; the only thing in the shape of money to which the people were accustomed. The person to whom one of them was offered, if unskilled in trade and banking, had little choice but to take it. A merchant turned to his "detector." He scrutinized the worn and dirty scrap for two or three minutes, regarding it as more probably "good" if it was worn and dirty than if it was clean, because those features were proof of long and successful circulation. He turned it up to the light and looked through it, because it was the custom of the banks to file the notes on slender pins which made holes through them. If there were many such holes the note had been often in bank and its genuineness was ratified. All the delay and trouble of these operations were so much deduction from the character of the notes as current cash. A community forced to do its business in that way had no money. It was deprived of the advantages of money. We would expect that a free, self-governing, and, at times, obstreperous, people would have refused and rejected these notes with scorn, and would have

Disreputable condition currency.

[1] White, Money and Banking.

made their circulation impossible, but the American people did not. They treated the system with toleration and respect. A parallel to the state of things which existed, even in New England, will be sought in vain in the history of currency."

The following statement illustrates the condition of the currency from the detector's point of view : —

	1856	1862
Number of banks reported	1409	1500
Number whose notes were not counterfeited . .	463	253
Number of kinds of imitations	1462	1861
Number of kinds of alterations	1119	3039
Number of kinds of spurious	224	1685

This does not include notes in circulation of suspended banks, whose value was so doubtful pending liquidation that the discounts thereon were always heavy.

General condition of banks.

An examination of the reports of the banks indicates that upon the whole the general business was regulated in greater measure by the demands of trade and less by speculative ventures than in any previous period. The circulation bore a fair relation to the specie, and deposits constituted an increasing portion of the amounts loaned.

The great weakness of the banks of the Western states was their investments in " stocks" (securities generally); fully one-half of their capital was so invested, whereas New England and Middle state banks showed but 2 per cent.

Owing to the non-enforcement of laws requiring redemption of notes, it had become the habit of bank officers and others to regard the presentation of notes for *redemption* in specie as an act to be reprobated, manifesting a desire to injure the bank and through it the community where it was located.

As has been stated, the operation of the subtreasury act exerted little influence upon the currency so long as the federal revenues were not largely in excess of expenditures. Repeatedly the secretaries of the Treasury reported that no disturbance had been experienced — indicating that the fear that such an event might occur was lurking in their minds.

In 1853–1854 the surplus revenue assumed considerable proportions, and Secretary Guthrie found it advisable to use it to relieve stringencies in the money market by the purchase of bonds at extraordinary premiums.[1] On one occasion he paid as high as 21 per cent premium. He did not hesitate to say that he regarded it necessary to avert a panic, and he repeated the operation on several other occasions for the same reason.

Guthrie gave the subject of the currency much attention during his administration of the Treasury (1853–1857).

In 1855[2] he reviewed the history of banks from 1790. He expressed himself in no uncertain language upon the laxity of the state governments in failing to properly regulate the note-issues, and especially, to abrogate the use of small denominations. Like his predecessors of the Jackson school, however, he saw no way to coerce the states or the banks : several judicial decisions (the Briscoe case already referred to and the case of Darrington *vs.* Bank of Alabama, 13 How. 12) had settled the question of the constitutionality of state bank issues, and he regarded it too late then (1855) to have the courts retrace their steps, nor could he hope for the coöperation of the states, influenced as they were by local interests. He said, however, that if the states continued this policy Congress would be justified in levying a tax on the notes that would in effect abrogate the power.

Influence of subtreasury.

Guthrie's views.

[1] Finance Reports, 1853 and 1854.
[2] Finance Report, 1855.

M

In his last report (1856), however, Guthrie confessed that a purely specie currency was out of the question; he estimated the volume of small notes ($5 and under) at $50,000,000, but regarded it premature to tax them out of existence, recommending a constitutional amendment giving Congress the power to regulate these issues. He added : —

"At present, an attempt to prohibit and restrain the issue and circulation of small notes, by a resort to taxation, or by applying bankrupt laws to these corporations, would be premature. In my former reports the subject has been brought to the attention of Congress, with a view to the full consideration of the evil and danger to our currency, from their continued use, under the hope that Congress or the states authorizing their issues, would take action, to extend the restriction and make it general.

"If the small notes are withdrawn and prohibited, it is believed the operations of the Treasury, in the collection and disbursement of the national revenue, would be as salutary a restraint upon the banks and upon commercial transactions as could be interposed, *and all-sufficient to secure as sound, healthy, and uniform a currency as it is practicable to have.*"

The Treasury at this time held $30,000,000, in coin, surplus.

In order to save the expense of transferring specie from depositories where it accumulated beyond the local needs, the Treasury entered upon the business of selling drafts, thus assuming the function of dealing in domestic exchange, which had been regarded so pernicious when done by the Bank of the United States.

Disbursing officers of the government, to whom large sums were from time to time advanced, continued to deposit these funds in the banks until an act of 1857 (repeatedly asked for by every Secretary of the Treasury since 1846) compelled the deposit in the subtreasuries, the payment to be made by checks instead of by cash, — another departure from the original plan.

The banks had during the period prior to 1857 become heavily interested in railway construction which at this time assumed very extensive proportions. So large a part of their means was tied up in this relatively permanent form of investment, that they felt it impossible in the summer and fall of 1857 to satisfy the demand for commercial discounts. Rates of interest became exorbitant. The troubles began in August and became quite general by October, when the New York City banks, except the Chemical, suspended specie payments, followed generally by all the banks in the country excepting South Carolina, Louisiana, the state banks of Ohio and Indiana, and a few others.

Inflation of securities.

Suspension of 1857.

New York City was and had been for years the actual monetary centre of the country; its banking capital had steadily grown from $20,000,000 in 1840 to $25,400,000 in 1849, $35,500,000 in 1852, $55,000,000 in 1856, and $65,000,000 in 1857. The associated banks of the metropolis were looked to for leadership.

It is therefore of special interest to note their condition during the year of the crisis. The specie in the New York subtreasury is also given in the following table[1] (in millions of dollars): —

New York City banks in 1857.

Date	Capital	Loans	Specie	Circu- lation	Deposits	Sub- treasury
Jan. 3 .	55.2	109.1	11.2	8.6	95.8	11.4
April 11 .	59.5	115.4	10.9	8.8	96.5	15.2
Aug. 1 .	64.6	120.6	12.9	8.7	94.6	12.2
Oct. 3 .	65.0	105.9	11.4	7.9	68.0	7.7
Dec. 5 .	63.5	96.3	26.1	6.6	78.5	4.0

[1] Compiled from Hunt's Merchant's Magazine.

The loans had reached a minimum of $95,000,000 on November 28, the deposits of $53,000,000 and specie $7,800,000 on October 17.

The tremendous increase in railway construction, especially in the Central and Western states, was the most important factor in bringing about the stringency of 1854 and finally the crisis of 1857. In 1850 there were 9021 miles of railway in operation, in 1854, 16,726; in 1857 the number was 24,503; this represented an increase of railway securities of nearly $600,000,000, more than half of which was issued in 1854–1857.

For the seven years the country's imports exceeded the exports over $300,000,000, and all but $50,000,000 of this sum was covered by net exports of specie. The foreign holdings of our securities, estimated at $261,000,-000 in 1852, were in 1857 placed at $400,000,000.

Expansion of circulation.
With but an indifferent foreign market for the large mass of securities and a home market incapable of absorbing all of it, the banks of the country were compelled to carry them to the detriment of the mercantile community. So in 1854 the total circulation of the banks of the country expanded until the money per capita was over $16; in the two following years contraction took place, but in 1857 the general expansion was in even greater proportion. (See table at end of chapter.)

The New York City banks were subjected to a steady drain of specie by the subtreasury (which was, owing to the large importations, collecting heavy revenues) and pressed for loans. They had expanded their credits until they thought they had reached the limit of prudence in August, and began to contract existing loans at a rapid rate and refused all applications for new ones, endeavoring in this way to avoid suspension which was prohibited by the state constitution.[1]

[1] Sumner, History of Banking.

A desperate struggle ensued. Notes of country banks were rushed for redemption, and failure to redeem promptly caused reports of failures of such banks. The telegraph, then lately come into general use, spread the news and was named as one of the "causes of the crisis." Bank shares which had been at par sold under 40, stocks fell from 10 to 40 per cent, and foreign exchange broke more than 10 per cent without bringing in specie.[1] The Treasury had begun early in the year to buy government bonds in small amounts, and the banks were disposed to look to it for further help. Secretary Howell Cobb increased his purchases, but the withdrawal of deposit accounts which were reduced over $40,000,000 in ten weeks, thereby greatly diminishing the specie fund, finally caused suspension of the banks October 14.

"Treasury relief."

It should be noted that the courts decided that the constitutional provision against suspension was not applicable so long as a bank was not actually insolvent.[1] The suspension was only for a short time against the notes of the banks. They had suspended paying deposits and making loans. There was no premium on gold. Speaking of the great withdrawal of deposits the Superintendent of the Bank Department of New York said:

"The great concentrated call loan was demanded, and in such amounts that a single day's struggle ended the battle ; and the banks went down before a storm they could not postpone or resist. . . . The most sagacious banker, in his most apprehensive mood, never for a moment deemed it possible to have a general suspension in this state from a home demand for coin, while coin itself was at little or no premium with the brokers."[2]

The banks in the Central and Western states being the largest holders of railway securities suffered more than those of the South. Indeed, in some parts of the South the crisis was hardly felt.

[1] Hunt's Merchant's Magazine, Vol. XXXVII.   [2] Report, 1857.

Resumption.   After suspension in New York the Treasury continued to buy bonds, gold arrived from California and from abroad, and on the 12th of December the banks were able to resume. Other Eastern banks did so early in 1858, Western and Southern banks delayed much longer.

Over 5100 failures with liabilities of nearly $300,000,-000 were recorded. Prices of stocks, breadstuffs, and other commodities fell ruinously, imports diminished immediately, many cargoes being returned without landing. The exchanges at the New York clearing-house diminished 43 per cent.

Says Sumner:—

"The suspension was preceded by a desperate struggle between all the banks themselves, and distrust and fear of currency was more apparent among them than with the public generally. The banks began a savage contraction, being in no position whatever to meet the crisis by bold loans to solvent borrowers. It was afterwards said, with great good reason, that the panic was entirely unnecessary and need not have occurred, but the banks put all the pressure on their loans to merchants because they could not recall those to the railroads."[1]

Buchanan attacks state banks.   President Buchanan and Secretary Cobb were most severe in their denunciation of the banks. The former in his message[2] said that such revulsions must occur when 1400 irresponsible institutions are permitted to usurp the power of providing currency, thus affecting the value of the property of every citizen; this power should never have been disseevered from the money-coining power exclusively conferred upon the federal government. Unfortunately, as it was, nothing could be done; a national bank, even if constitutional, would not serve, as was shown by the history of the second bank. Referring to the existing systems he pointed out that only in one state, Louisiana, were banks re-

[1] History of Banking in United States.
[2] Messages of Presidents, Vol. V.

quired to keep adequate specie reserves; according to the standard adopted by Louisiana, the banks should have had one dollar in three against notes and deposits, whereas they had only $58,000,000 of specie against $445,000,000 of those obligations, considerably less than one in seven. Slight pressure for cash thus inevitably brought failure. He favored a compulsory bankrupt law for banks failing to meet their obligations, and even suggested depriving banks of the note-issuing power altogether.

Cobb insisted that the disbursements of specie by the subtreasuries had aided in restoring coin payments, and contrasted the conditions with those of 1837. He thought so well of the independent treasury that he urged the several states to adopt the same system for their own affairs.[1] Ohio actually did so in 1858.

The Treasury suffered in its revenue by the diminished imports, and the act of December 23, 1857, authorized covering the deficit by the issue of $20,000,000 in 6 per cent one-year Treasury notes. In June, 1858, the Treasury was authorized to issue a fifteen-year 5 per cent loan for $20,000,000. In 1859 authority was given to reissue the Treasury notes of 1857, and the amount used, including reissues, was $52,778,900. Most of them actually remained out until 1860. Thus the people suffered from taxation in addition to their losses on account of the ill-regulated currency system.

The aggregate bank returns for 1858 showed a contraction of deposits and circulation from $445,000,000 to $340,000,000 and an increase of specie to $74,000,000. Loans were diminished fully $100,000,000, of which $43,000,000 occurred in the banks of New York State alone. The banks of the latter state were also credited with almost the entire specie increase for that year.

Treasury notes.

[1] Finance Report, 1857.

At the end of this period (1861) the number of banks had increased to 1601, their capital to $697,000,000; circulation had again gone beyond the $200,000,000 point, and deposits to $257,000,000. Against the total of these obligations of $460,000,000 they had nearly $88,000,000 specie, or nearly one dollar in five.

Bank statistics 1861.

The following table shows the distribution by sections and for certain states, of the deposits, circulation, and specie in millions, and the relation of specie holdings to circulation and deposits, in 1861 : —

States	Deposits	Circula-tion	Specie	Specie to Notes. Per Cent	Specie to Both. Per Cent
New England .	41.9	33.1	10.4	31.4	13.8
Massachusetts .	34.0	19.5	8.8	45.1	16.4
Middle	152.0	53.4	39.0	73.0	18.9
New York . . .	114.8	28.2	26.4	93.6	27.2
Southern . . .	42.5	61.9	30.2	48.8	29.0
Louisiana . . .	17.1	6.9	13.7	198.5	57.0
Western . . .	15.8	38.2	9.6	25.0	17.7
United States .	257.2	202.0	87.7	43.8	19.2

The Louisiana system thus appeared in the front rank as far as security was concerned. New York and the Middle states, as well as the Southern states, reported conditions superior to those of New England. Indeed it was only after the crisis that the banks in the latter section were led to increase their specie. In prior years the specie of New England banks was usually less than 13 per cent on their circulation.

More Treasury notes.

In 1860 and early in 1861 the deficits in the revenue again compelled the Treasury to resort to loans and Treasury notes which were negotiated at a discount. This latter circumstance was due to the impending civil war and not to currency conditions. The amount authorized was $20,000,000; including reissues the amount used was $45,364,450.   .

The sectional disparity in banking and currency facilities largely disappeared during this period, the Southern states having been fairly well supplied, as the following table shows. (As before, the slave population is excluded in reaching a per capita.)

STATES	BANKING POWER (IN MILLIONS)		PER CAPITA	
	1850	1860	1850	1860
Eastern . .	114	209	$41.39	$66.89
Middle . . .	185	371	27.95	44.35
Southern . .	117	223	22.28	33.69
Western . .	35	83	6.35	8.52
United States	452	886	19.47	27.98

Banking power by sections.

The conditions existing from 1850 to 1861 were truly anomalous. The currency systems of the several states were as a rule based upon laws which on their face were fairly complete and conservative. In the aggregate, so far as the reports enable one to determine, the conditions were not radically unsound, and yet, owing to want of supervision and non-enforcement of the laws, they furnished the country a paper currency in large part so disreputable as to cause amazement that the people tolerated the same and endured the robbery which was thereby imposed upon them. Refusal to redeem notes was in most states an infraction of the law, to be followed by the forfeiture of the charter of the offending bank, and yet the law was habitually disregarded.

Banking conditions for the whole period of national existence prior to the Civil War may be classified as follows : — *General review.*

1. First United States Bank (1791–1811). Sound bank currency.

2. Interval (1812–1816). State bank currency inflation, suspension, disasters involving enormous losses.

3. Second United States Bank (1817–1836). At first unsettled conditions as to currency and business, then sound paper currency by reason of United States Bank enforcing redemption of state bank-notes and formulating a standard of credit to which the state banks in competition were obliged to conform; then during last years of its existence unsettled conditions owing to political power exerted to prevent renewal of bank's charter.

4. 1837–1846. Inordinate inflation, suspension, and losses measured by the hundred millions, withdrawal of government funds from the banks, with the declared hope of preventing undue expansion of bank-note issues by so doing.

5. 1847–1860. Banking becoming more conservative; deposits counting more and note-issues less as a means of extending credit; note-issues, however, unrestrained and entailing enormous losses upon the people; failure of subtreasury to restrain or control banking methods, but disastrously interfering with business by withdrawing from the channels of trade, and locking up, funds which should be current.

Central bank and subtreasury systems compared.

It is notable that only during the existence of a central bank did the country enjoy for extended periods a currency that could be regarded as sound, with domestic exchange reasonably well regulated, and discount rates fairly equitable in different sections. So long as the bank was limited in its charge for discounts by its charter, local banks were necessarily influenced in adjusting their rates; so long as the bank through its branches furnished exchange at rates which were not an exorbitant tax upon trade, other banks had to do the same; and so long as the bank enforced redemption of notes and accepted only those convertible into specie for payments to the Treasury, the local banks could not inflate their issues and found it profitable to maintain convertibility.

The Jacksonian Democrats, in contradistinction from Gallatin, Dallas, Crawford, and others, having taken position against the central bank system, and having by fortuitous circumstances maintained control of legislation for a long period, conceived the idea that currency and business evils could be regulated by the subtreasury system. Although they suffered defeat at the polls in 1840, their plans were materially aided by Tyler's weakness and virtual desertion of his party and the consequent failure to establish a central bank. In the meantime the judicial department of the government had declared that the state bank issues were constitutional. Thus the subtreasury act came into popular favor and became law. At its best it was only a partial remedy.

It may be of interest to insert here a criticism of the subtreasury system in 1902, after fifty years' experience, by ex-Comptroller of the Currency James H. Eckels:—

" The government in its Treasury Department by force of law undertakes to be a bank, but the futility of the undertaking becomes manifest when it is known that it is founded upon no banking principles and conducted in accordance with no recognized banking rules. In its subtreasury system it is the bank of the mere safety deposit vault or the stocking of the ignorant and suspicious citizen, who needs must have within his grasp always the actual money, who has no faith in credit and who refuses to contribute anything to maintaining the affairs of a business world carried on and enlarged by the instruments of credit. Into this government safety box each day are being lodged vast sums of money taken out of the channels of trade and commerce at a time when most needed, there to lie in wasteful idleness to the profit of none but to the loss of all. By such a system every business man is made to pause daily to consider how far he may expand, to what extent he must retrench, for all his dealings ultimately are so affected by the amount of money the government is withdrawing from the needs of the business world ; and thus whether he wills or

Eckels on the subtreasury.

not, the government is his partner and the government's acts control his own.

Based on false theories. "There can be no Secretary of the Treasury, no matter how wide his experience or acute his financial perception, who can accomplish more than a temporary makeshift for relief with the half-created banking system which makes up the subtreasury — an institution based upon false theories in economics and which in every part violates correct banking methods and principles. If the safety deposit theory of banking as exemplified in the subtreasury is the true one as applicable to national government fiscal affairs, it should prove equally essential in the governmental finance of states, counties, cities, and villages, and these all should go outside the banks and each establish its own respective strong box and withdraw still more of the country's currency from daily business life. So, too, the individual business man should do the same, for there can be no correct rule for one which is not applicable to all who are engaged in any business which requires the management of money and credits, whether it be a corporation or an individual. If all in business received deposits only to hoard them, soon interchange of commodities would cease, manufacturing come to a standstill, agricultural interests languish and transportation lines grow idle. That which no business man accepts as a correct principle in his own undertakings his government enforces to the wasting of his own and his fellows' substance."

Derelict state policy. The states which endeavored by the enactment of the bond deposit plan to remedy the currency evil imagined that they had done all that was requisite, but in the absence of compulsory provision for reserves and redemption, and the lax enforcement of the laws which existed, undue expansion was not prevented and illegitimate evasions went unpunished. Van Buren, Tyler, and Buchanan, as well as secretaries of the Treasury during the period after 1837, saw clearly wherein the states were derelict and appreciated fully the extent of the legalized misappropriation of the people's property resulting therefrom. Their narrow political tenets, however, rendered them blind to the fact that Congress had the power by taxation to extirpate the evil and afford the people protection. Their shuffling policies are well illustrated by the historic enunciation of Buchanan in another instance when he declared that the states had no right to secede, but that there was no power in the Constitution to coerce a sovereign state. To paraphrase, the state bank systems of currency were almost criminally wrong and unjust, but there was no power in the Constitution, ordained though it was "to establish justice," to prevent the wholesale fraud upon the people which the lax curreney systems of the states engendered. The Civil War resulted in enfranchising the slaves. It also liberated the whole people from evils of state bank currency.

Respecting the several issues of Treasury notes prior to the Civil War, it is interesting to note that the first emission of this form of "bills of credit" (1812) was made during the administration of Madison, and although a question as to the constitutionality arose, it was determined in favor of the issue both by Congress and the President. It was, however, held beyond the power of Congress to give the notes the legal tender function, but they were made receivable for all public dues. Later issues were authorized in the administration of Van Buren, Tyler, Polk, and Buchanan, all of them "strict constructionists." Both Jefferson and Tyler favored the use of these notes as currency, and when they were issued in small denominations, they actually became for short periods a part of the circulation of the country.

Hamilton's views on the subject were expressed in his report on the bank plan, as follows: "The emitting of paper money by authority of government is wisely prohibited to the individual states by the Constitution, and the spirit of that prohibition ought not to be disregarded by the government of the United States."

STATISTICAL RÉSUMÉ
(Amounts in millions unless otherwise indicated)
CIRCULATION, ETC.

Year	Estimated Bank-notes Outstanding	Estimated Specie in United States	Total Money in United States	Specie in Treasury	Money in Circulation	Population	Per Capita	New York Clearing-House Transactions
1850	131	154	285	7	278	23	$12.02	——
1851	155	186	341	11	330	24	13.76	——
1852	172	204	376	15	361	25	14.63	——
1853	188	236	424	22	402	26	15.80	——
1854	205	241	446	20	426	26	16.10	5750
1855	187	250	437	19	418	27	15.34	5363
1856	196	250	446	20	426	28	15.16	6906
1857	215	260	475	18	457	29	15.81	8333
1858	155	260	415	6	409	30	13.78	4757
1859	193	250	443	4	439	31	14.35	6448
1860	207	253	442	7	435	31	13.85	7231

BANK STATISTICS

Year	State Banks							Savings Banks		
	Number	Capital	Circulation	Deposits	Specie	Loans	Stocks	Deposits	Number Depositors (000's)	Average Deposit
1850	824	217	131	110	45	364	21	43	251	$173
1851	879	228	155	129	49	414	22	50	277	182
1852	——		——				—	59	309	193
1853	750	208	146	146	47	409	22	72	366	198
1854	1208	301	205	188	59	557	44	78	396	196
1855	1307	332	187	190	54	576	53	84	432	195
1856	1398	344	196	213	59	634	49	96	488	196
1857	1416	371	215	230	58	684	59	99	490	201
1858	1422	395	155	186	74	583	60	108	539	201
1859	1476	402	193	260	105	657	64	129	623	207
1860	1562	422	207	254	84	692	70	149	694	215

No returns for 1852. 1853 very imperfect.

PART TWO

PERIOD FROM 1861 TO 1890

I. THE UNITED STATES LEGAL TENDER NOTES

CHAPTER VIII

1861 TO 1865

THE financial and monetary conditions which con- fronted the administration of Lincoln in 1861 were such as would have severely taxed a finance minister with the genius of Hamilton and the wide experience of Gallatin. The Nation was at the brink of civil war, the outcome of which could not be foreseen. Its debt of about $76,000,000 was greater than at any time since the period following the War of 1812, and most of this debt had been created during years of peace. The Nation's credit was poor, its securities having been sold at more than 10 per cent below par by the outgoing Secretary of the Treasury.

The currency consisted of about $250,000,000 of specie and $200,000,000 of bank-notes, and whilst the 1600 banks, as a whole, possessed a fair quantity of specie (probably 45 per cent of their note-issues), most of it was held by the banks in the money centres. The condition of the paper circulation was very far from satisfactory. Great dissimilarity in the laws governing banks in the several states precluded uniformity, security, or safety. There was no central place of redemption, hence most notes were at a discount, varying with the distance from the bank of issue. It was estimated that there were 7000 kinds and denominations of notes, and fully 4000 spurious or altered varieties were reported.

The government's funds were held in the sub-treasuries and mints, in specie, but the amount was small, the revenues having been for some time insufficient to meet the expenses. The tariff law passed on March 2, 1861, had not yet become effective. The Treasury possessed power to issue bonds and Treasury notes, granted by the Congress which had just expired. As the bonds would not bring par (some selling at 94, others as low as 86), Treasury notes were issued, since, being receivable for duties, they were approximately worth par.

Chase's first report. Government needs became more pressing as the impending war developed, and Congress was called in extra session July 4, 1861. Secretary Chase, in his report to Congress,[1] estimated the sum required at $318,000,000 and recommended both taxation and loans. His plan embraced taxation sufficient to cover the ordinary expenses of the government, interest on the debt, and provision for the sinking fund, the extraordinary expenses to be covered by loans. His scheme for borrowing included non-interest-bearing notes payable on demand, interest-bearing notes for short terms, and bonds for long terms ; the first to be convertible into the second, and the second into the third, form of obligation. Thus he expected to avert the evil which many of his predecessors experienced, of being compelled to receive for payments to the Treasury the notes of state banks, most of which were fluctuating in value, and might even become valueless on his hands. He hoped that $100,000,000 of the loan might be placed abroad, but this hope was not realized. While thus suggesting notes to circulate as money, he urged great care " to prevent the degradation of such issues into an irredeemable paper currency, than which no more certainly fatal ex-

[1] Finance Report, July, 1861.

pedient for impoverishing the masses and discrediting the government of any country can well be devised."

Congress adopted Chase's plan in the act of July 17, 1861,[1] which authorized the borrowing of $250,000,000, either in 6 per cent twenty-year bonds, or 7.30 per cent three-year Treasury notes in denominations not less than $50, or in one-year 3.65 per cent notes, or non-interest-bearing notes of less than $50, redeemable on demand. Notes under $10 were prohibited, and the demand notes were not to exceed $50,000,000. These might also be issued to pay public creditors and be redeemed in 7.30's, and when redeemed they might be reissued at any time prior to December 31, 1862, provided the total limit of the loan was not exceeded. The amending act of August 5, 1861, provided for the exchange of the 7.30 notes into bonds, the limit of the loan ($250,000,000) not to be exceeded; for the issue of "demand" notes of $5; directed that the latter class be receivable for all public dues; furthermore, suspended the subtreasury act of 1846, so far as to permit the moneys received from loans to be deposited in "solvent, specie-paying banks" and drawn upon for payments. It will be observed that the demand notes were not made specifically payable in coin, but were universally regarded as coin notes, since no other legal tender money existed at the time.

Demand and 7.30 notes.

In his report in December, 1861, Chase, still hopeful of an early cessation of the war, discussed two plans for the currency. He pointed out that the banks in the states in rebellion had about one-fourth of the estimated circulation for the whole country, and that of the remaining $150,000,000 a very considerable part was of doubtful value in emergency. He ventured the opinion that the issue of state bank-notes was not constitutional, and proposed that the large amount thus practically

Chase's second report.

[1] See Appendix.

borrowed, without interest, from the people by state banks, should, by legislation, be made to inure to the advantage of the general government.   An issue of government notes would, in his opinion, serve the purpose of furnishing a uniform circulating medium, and at the same time aid the government in its emergency; but the dangers of overissue, inadequate provision for redemption, and consequent depreciation were, he thought, so great as to outweigh the advantages.   He

National currency recommended.

therefore recommended a national bank currency secured by bonds, which would yield all that a government issue could, and not be open to the same criticism.

The Treasury had met its immediate needs up to this time with demand and 7.30 notes, a sale of two lots of $50,000,000 each of the latter having been "underwritten" and "placed" by the banks of New York, Philadelphia, and Boston.   Chase had arranged with the banks for a further placing of $50,000,000 in 6 per cent bonds on a 7 per cent basis, and there was an understanding that still another $50,000,000 would be taken in January, 1862.   He also issued the Treasury notes authorized by the laws of the previous Congress.

War estimates increased.

At the special session of Congress in July, Chase had estimated the government's expenditures for the fiscal year at $318,000,000.   In his December report [1] the estimate was increased over $200,000,000, and at the same time he showed that the revenue would fall far below the amount he had expected. . Figures of such unusual magnitude at that time were appalling, and had a most depressing effect.   An international complication arose at this time which had a far-reaching influence upon the finances of our country.   The confederate government sought to send representatives abroad, presumably to negotiate for the recognition of the Confederacy by

[1] Finance Report, December, 1861.

European nations, and also to negotiate for loans. Captain Wilkes, commanding the *San Jacinto*, forcibly took from the British steamer *Trent*, plying between Havana and Southampton, two commissioners of the Confederacy, Messrs. Mason and Slidell. There was great rejoicing over this capture throughout the country, and Captain Wilkes was thanked by Congress. When the news of the capture reached England, the greatest indignation was aroused over what was deemed a wanton insult to the British flag. The surrender of the prisoners and an apology were demanded, coupled with instructions to the British Minister in Washington to ask for his passports in case the demands were not complied with. The patriotic fervor with which the capture had been received and applauded made it exceedingly difficult and certainly distasteful for the administration to comply with the British demands, and yet the alternative seemed war with a great and powerful nation, in addition to the struggle with the Confederacy. Calm consideration showed the British position to be well taken, and the demands were therefore complied with. The news of the British demand was received in New York December 16, and precipitated a *quasi* panic.[1]

The *Trent* affair.

Chase, as authorized in placing his loans with the banks and through them, had utilized the banks as temporary depositories of the proceeds of the loans. They rightfully expected these funds to remain on deposit and be checked out to meet the government's needs as they arose. Chase, however, construed the subtreasury act rigidly and required the transfer of the funds in specie to the Treasury. This at once deprived the banks of a large part of their reserve, created a money stringency, and coupled with the appalling expenditures of the government and the *Trent* affair resulted in suspension of

Chase and the banks.

---

[1] White, Money and Banking.

specie payments near the close of December, 1861. The banks had at the time, according to their reports, $102,-000,000 of specie against $184,000,000 of notes. The Treasury was compelled to suspend specie payments also, and the Secretary was forced to readjust his plans.

He still urged his bank-note measure, and a comprehensive bill for the purpose was introduced in Congress. A bill to issue more government notes was also prepared, which being shorter and less complex in its nature, appealed to Congress and was given precedence. Chase, harassed by inability to place bonds or 7.30 notes, with demands upon him amounting to a million and a quarter dollars daily, not only assented to the latter measure, but urged its speedy adoption. As demand notes at the time were not redeemed in coin "on demand," the Treasury found it difficult to pay them out. Banks and others were refusing them. It was therefore proposed to make the new issue legal tender, which Chase also urged upon Congress very reluctantly and under the plea of necessity.

Unlike Hamilton, he failed to grasp the principles of finance as applied to government. Instead of seeking the best way he seems to have sought the easiest. The most easily available resource which the government had was the issuance of United States notes with legal tender power. These were immediately available for the payment of the government's obligations. Whenever bonds were issued the element of time necessarily entered in order to negotiate their sale. Secretary Chase made a great mistake in not asking for largely increased taxation immediately at the outbreak of the war. The patriotic spirit of the country would undoubtedly have insured compliance with his request, thereby avoiding the occasion for issuing so great a volume of legal tender notes. Adams, in Public Debts, lays down the governing principle in such emergencies as follows : —

"It is a recognized fact that self-governing peoples are stronger for tax purposes than the subjects of a monarchical state, for their will lies more closely to the heart of the state. But the administration of a self-governing people should never undertake a war in favor of which there is no strong sentiment. As things go, then, in democratic countries, it does not appear that loans to the full extent of extraordinary demands are necessary, and there is no question as to the superiority of taxes over loans when their use will not curtail industrial energy. The measure of this first money-tax should be the popular enthusiasm for the war."

Taught by experience, Chase recognized this principle later. He said to Congress in 1863 that it was not too much, and perhaps hardly enough, to say that every dollar raised by taxation for extraordinary purposes or reduction of debt is worth two in the increased value of national securities. He excused his failure to ask for additional taxation immediately because of the impossibility of realizing in advance the long continuance and enormous expenditure involved in the war.[1]

Pending the discussion of the measure, Congress on February 11 authorized the issue of $10,000,000 more "demand notes." The legal tender act of February 25, 1862, provided for the issue of $150,000,000 United States notes (of which $60,000,000 were to redeem the demand notes) to be "lawful money" and legal tender for all debts, public and private, except customs duties and interest on the public debt, both of which were to be payable in coin. No denominations less than $5 were to be issued. They were made convertible into 6 per cent, five–twenty year bonds, and receivable at par the same as coin for all loans to the government, and when received by the Treasury might be reissued. The act further provided for the issue of $500,000,000 of the bonds mentioned above, to fund the notes, or to

Legal tender act passed.

5-20 bonds.

[1] Finance Report, 1863.

be sold at the market value for coin, or for any Treasury notes authorized to be issued. The coin from customs revenues was pledged for the interest on the debt and the creation of a sinking fund. The Treasury was further empowered to issue, in exchange for notes, temporary loan certificates in sums not less than $100, running not less than thirty days, with interest not more than 5 per cent, the amount not to exceed $25,000,000. The act also exempted securities of the United States from state and municipal taxation.

This measure caused much discussion, both in and out of Congress. There was no precedent for, and apparently every reason against, constituting the notes money and making them legal tender. Lincoln and Chase very reluctantly accepted it as a necessary evil. The Committee on Ways and Means was evenly divided on the question of favorably reporting the bill. Thaddeus Stevens (the Republican leader in the House), Spaulding, and others of the dominant party, declared the measure warranted only by the necessities of the war, *the saving of the Union*. Nevertheless such Republicans as Morrill, of Vermont, and Conkling, and nearly all the Democratic representatives, led by Pendleton and Vallandigham, opposed it as unnecessary, inexpedient, and unconstitutional. In the Senate Fessenden, Sherman, and Sumner gave reluctant assent, the first named opposing and voting in favor of omitting the legal tender clause. Among those afterwards prominent in curreney legislation who favored the bill were Windom, Kelley, Hooper, Morrill (Me.); and among the opponents, Morrill (Vt.), Cox, and Holman. The bill passed the House by a vote of 93 to 59; in the Senate the legal tender clause was retained by a vote of 22 to 17, and the bill passed by 30 to 7, only 3 Republicans voting nay.

Public opinion on legal tender law.

Opinion in banking and business circles was divided, but leading Chambers of Commerce passed resolutions urging the adoption of the measure, and popular opinion was generally favorable.

Chase in his letter to the House Committee said that he felt — Chase.

"a great aversion to making anything but coin a legal tender in payment of debts. It has been my anxious wish to avoid the necessity of such legislation. It is, however, at present impossible, in consequence of the large expenditures entailed by the war, and the suspension of the banks, to procure sufficient coin for disbursements, and it has, therefore, become indispensably necessary that we should resort to the issue of United States notes." [1]

He urged such legislation as would "divest the legal tender clause of the bill of injurious tendencies, and secure the earliest possible return to a sound currency of coin and promptly convertible notes." [1]

Spaulding said : — Spaulding.

"The bill before us is a war measure, a measure of *necessity*, and not of choice. . . . These are extraordinary times, and extraordinary measures must be resorted to in order to save our government, and preserve our nationality."

The tax and banking measure proposed would operate too slowly to provide means to continue the war.

Stevens said : — Stevens.

"No one would willingly issue paper currency not redeemable on demand and make it a legal tender. . . . I look upon the immediate passage of the bill as essential to the very existence of the government. Reject it, and financial credit, not only of the government, but of all the great interests of the country, will be prostrated."

Pendleton, opposing, said, as to the constitutionality : — Pendleton.

"I find no grant of this power in direct terms, or, as I think, by fair implication. It is not an accidental omission ; it is not

[1] Schuckers, Life of Chase.

an omission through inadvertency; it was intentionally left out of the Constitution, because it was designed that the power should not reside in the federal government."

Conkling.   Conkling on the same subject said : —

"Had such a power lurked in the Constitution, as construed by those who ordained and administered it, we should find it so recorded." The "universal judgment of statesmen, jurists, and lawyers has denied the constitutional right of Congress to make paper a legal tender for debts to any extent whatever."

Morrill.   Morrill of Vermont spoke of it as "a measure not blessed by one sound precedent, and damned by all!" He characterized it as of doubtful constitutionality, immoral, a breach of the public faith. He predicted that it would increase the cost of the war, banish all specie from circulation, degrade us in the estimation of other nations, cripple American labor, and throw larger wealth into the hands of the rich ; that there was no necessity for so desperate a remedy.

Fessenden.   In the Senate Fessenden said : —

"The . . . clause making these notes a legal tender is put upon the ground of absolute, overwhelming necessity ; . . . the question then is, does the necessity exist? . . ."

He would

"take the money of any citizen against his will to sustain the government, if nothing else was left, and bid him wait until the government could pay him. It is a contribution which every man is bound to make under the circumstances. We can take all the property of any citizen. That is what is called a forced contribution. . . . The question after all returns: Is this measure absolutely indispensable to procure means? If so, as I said before, necessity knows no law. . . . Say what you will, nobody can deny that it is bad faith. If it be necessary for the salvation of the government, all considerations of this kind must yield ; but to make the best of it, it is bad faith, and encourages bad morality, both in public and private. Going to the extent that it does, to say that notes thus issued shall be receivable in payment of all private obligations, however contracted, is in its very essence a wrong, for it compels one man to take from his neighbor, in payment of a debt, that which he would not otherwise receive, or be obliged to receive, and what is probably not full payment."

Collamer said that the men of the period of the adoption of the Constitution always

Collamer.

"entertained the opinion that the United States could have nothing else a tender but coin. While they lived there never was such a thing thought of as attempting to make the evidences of the debt of the government a legal tender, let their form be what they might."

There were two modes of replenishing the Treasury; one was by taxation, and the other was by borrowing. To borrow money there must be a lender and a borrower, and both should act voluntarily, and not compel the lender to part with his money without an inducement. "The operation of this bill is not anything like as honorable or honest as a forced loan."

Sherman said that the legal tender clause was necessary to make the notes acceptable; it was after all a mere temporary expedient necessary to save the government.

Sherman.

"I am constrained to assume the power, and refer our authority to exercise it to the courts. I have shown . . . that we must no longer hesitate as to the necessity of this measure. That necessity does exist, and now presses upon us."

He thought himself required to vote for all laws necessary and proper for executing the powers given to uphold the government.

"This is not the time when I would limit these powers. Rather than yield to revolutionary force, I would use revolutionary force."

Howe said : —

Howe.

"Those who deny the constitutional authority to pass this bill must deny its necessity or its propriety, . . . ought to show us some plan for avoiding it, some measure adequate to the emergency, and more proper than the one proposed by this bill. . . . It is evident that no substitute can be provided except it be taxation or direct loans."

Taxation alone could not provide the vast sums required, and direct loans were equally impracticable.

Bayard.

J. A. Bayard said : —

" No one can deny the fact that in contracts between man and man, and in government contracts to pay money, the obligation is to pay intrinsic value. If you violate that by this bill, which you certainly do, how can you expect that the faith of the community will be given to the law which you now pass, in which you say that you will pay hereafter the interest on your debt in coin? Why should they give credit to that declaration? If you can violate the Constitution of the United States in the face of your oaths, in the face of its palpable provision, what security do you offer to the lender of the money?"

Sumner.

Sumner said : —

" Surely we must all be against paper money, we must all insist upon maintaining the integrity of the government; and we must all set our faces against any proposition like the present, except as a temporary expedient, rendered imperative by the exigency of the hour."

Lincoln, engrossed with a multitude of onerous duties, approved the act without comment.

Much opposition was caused by the clause inserted by the Senate, which provided for payment of interest on bonds in coin, which practically meant a discrimination in favor of one class of creditors, and, as Stevens said, depreciated at once the money which the bill created.

Reasons for legal tender proviso.

It is obvious that few of the men charged with affairs believed the legal tender act constitutional. It was considered warranted only by extreme necessity, as a temporary measure, to save the Union and hence the Constitution itself. Had the banks been able to maintain specie payments and aid the Treasury in greater measure, and had the banks and the people accepted the demand notes, the legal tender provision would have been unnecessary.

It will be observed that the act did not specify how or when the notes were payable, nor was any other provision, except the convertibility into bonds, made for their eventual retirement. The power to reissue them when received into the Treasury contemplated their continuous circulation until Congress directed otherwise. The faces of the notes bore the simple statement that "The United States will pay the bearer —— dollars."

Congress passed additional tax laws, but these did not produce funds at once. An act of March 1, 1862, adopted Chase's recommendation that certificates of indebtedness, to run one year, at 6 per cent, be issued to public creditors who would receive them, and one of March 17, authorizing him to purchase coin with any securities authorized to be issued upon terms which appeared to him advantageous; increased the limit of temporary loan certificates to $50,000,000; and made the demand notes legal tender. It also permitted the issue of new for worn notes. *Temporary loans.*

The effect of the act of February 25 upon the general status of the currency was at first not specially marked. The premium on coin, which had earlier in the month reached $4\frac{3}{4}$, was at the end of it only $2\frac{1}{4}$ per cent, and in March and April ranged from two and a fraction down to one. Demand notes, being receivable for customs, were approximately equal to coin. The new notes literally took the place of the coin in circulation and were rapidly absorbed, few being presented for conversion into the 6 per cent bonds waiting for them at the Treasury. In May the premium on specie *Premium on coin.*

advanced beyond 4, and in June rose to $9\frac{1}{4}$. One hundred and forty-seven million dollars of both kinds of notes were in use, but did not return to the Treasury in sufficient volume to enable it to maintain payments.

More legal tenders.

Chase accordingly asked in June for authority to issue an additional $150,000,000 of legal tender notes. Congress gave the required authority by the act of July 11, 1862, reserving, however, $50,000,000 of the notes for the redemption of temporary loan certificates, which the act permitted the Secretary to expand to a total of $100,000,000. Congress also adopted Chase's recommendation that $35,000,000 of the notes to be issued be in denominations less than five dollars.

Fractional currency.

The total disappearance of specie had caused intolerable trouble in providing small change. The people had resorted to a variety of substitutes, including postage stamps, which suggested the authorization by the act of July 17, 1862, of an issue of stamps, and later currency, for fractional parts of a dollar, at first in the form of postal stamps engraved on the notes, subsequently in other forms. This currency was made "receivable," at first for all dues, later for all except customs, in sums not over five dollars, and was exchangeable for legal tender notes in like sums. The amount was not limited by this act. The issue of tokens or currency under one dollar by others was strictly prohibited.

Chase's third report.

In his report for December, 1862, Chase estimated that he would have to borrow nearly $300,000,000 for the remainder of the fiscal year (to June 30, 1863) and $600,000,000 for the following year, unless the war happily came to an end. In the discussion of the manner of borrowing he treated the currency question at great length, pointing out that the state banks had increased their note-issues by $37,000,000, deposits by $80,000,000, and discounts, $70,000,000. He argued that this expansion, and not the issue of legal tender notes, had caused the exports of, and the premium on, coin (now 34 per cent), since the government notes outstanding amounted to $210,000,000, only a trifle more than the coin in circulation in 1861, at the time of suspension. While admitting that the issue of more notes was an easy way for the government to pay the expenses, to do so to any material extent would prove calamitous, a "disastrous defeat of the very purposes sought to be obtained by it." A small addition to the volume might, however, not be unsafe. But he much preferred the adoption of the pending measure for a national bank currency, which would enable him to dispose of bonds, then not readily salable. He recommended taxing the state bank-notes so as to limit and reduce the volume and permit United States notes to fill the need for increased currency until the national bank system should supply the demand. In this way he suggested that $50,000,000 more of legal tender notes might be useful within the year, and a like amount the following year.

National bank currency urged.

President Lincoln in his message at this time (December, 1862) referred to the currency as follows : [1] —

Lincoln on legal tenders.

"The suspension of specie payments by the banks, soon after the commencement of your last session, made large issues of United States notes unavoidable. In no other way could the payment of the troops, and the satisfaction of other just demands, be so economically or so well provided for. The judicious legislation of Congress, securing the receivability of these notes for loans and internal duties, and making them a legal tender for other debts, has made them a universal currency ; and has satisfied, partially, at least, and for the time, the long-felt want of an uniform circulating medium, saving thereby to the people immense sums in discounts and exchanges.

"A return to specie payments, however, at the earliest period

[1] Messages of Presidents, Vol. VI.

Fluctuating
currency
injurious.
compatible with due regard to all interests concerned, should
ever be kept in view.   Fluctuations in the value of currency are
always injurious, and to reduce these fluctuations to the lowest
possible point will always be a leading purpose in wise legislation.
Convertibility, prompt and certain convertibility into coin, is
generally acknowledged to be the best and surest safeguard
against them ; and it is extremely doubtful whether a circulation
of United States notes, payable in coin, and sufficiently large
for the wants of the people, can be permanently, usefully, and
safely maintained.

" Is there, then, any other mode in which the necessary provision for the public wants can be made, and the great advantages of a safe and uniform currency secured?

Recom-
mends
national
banks.
" I know of none which promises so certain results, and is, at
the same time, so unobjectionable, as the organization of banking associations, under a general act of Congress, well guarded
in its provisions.   To such associations the government might
furnish circulating notes, on the security of United States bonds
deposited in the Treasury.   These notes, prepared under the
supervision of proper officers, being uniform in appearance and
security, and convertible always into coin, would at once pro-
teet labor against the evils of a vicious currency, and facilitate
commerce by cheap and safe exchanges.

" A moderate reservation from the interest on the bonds
would compensate the United States for the preparation and
distribution of the notes, and a general supervision of the system,
and would lighten the burden of that part of the public debt
employed as securities.   The public credit, moreover, would be
greatly improved, and the negotiation of new loans greatly
facilitated by the steady market demand for government bonds
which the adoption of the proposed system would create.

" It is an additional recommendation of the measure, of considerable weight, in my judgment, that it would reconcile, as
far as possible, all existing interests, by the opportunity offered to
existing institutions to reorganize under the act, substituting only
the secured uniform national circulation for the local and various
circulation, secured and unsecured, now issued by them."

State bank-
notes.
The report on state banks for January 1, 1863
(the last published by the Treasury), showed that

their circulation was nearly $239,000,000 and specie $101,000,000.

The army being unpaid and Chase being, as he stated, unable to sell bonds "at the market price," a joint resolution, authorizing the immediate issue of $100,000,000 of legal tender notes, was passed on the 17th of January, 1863. "Inability to sell bonds at the market price" meant that offering any large quantity would break the market price and force a lower quotation.

In approving this resolution Lincoln sent a message to Congress cautioning against further note-issues.

The act of March 3, 1863, authorized borrowing $300,000,000 for the current fiscal year (to June 30), and $600,000,000 for the next. As to the *forms* of the obligations, the Secretary was given wide discretion, as the circumstances required; first, bonds, payable in not less then ten nor more than forty years, the interest payable in coin, not to exceed 6 per cent, issuable in exchange for notes or other evidences of debt; second, notes payable in not exceeding three years, at interest not to exceed 6 per cent, in amount not to exceed $400,000,000; these notes might be made legal tender for their face, and be exchanged into the ordinary legal tender notes, for which purpose, *exclusively*, *another* $150,000,000 of the latter was provided for (this last-mentioned authority was not, however, used by Chase); third, legal tender notes in amount $150,000,000 for ordinary purposes of the government; fourth, fractional currency to the limit of $50,000,000; fifth, the issue of gold certificates for coin and bullion, and to an amount equal to 20 per cent, in excess of the actual deposit of gold. The act also provided for a tax of 2 per cent upon state bank-notes and for a prohibitive tax of 10 per cent upon fractional note-issues, and permitted

More legal tenders.

Tax on state bank-notes.

()

sales of bonds *below* the market value, for which Chase asked.

But the most important feature, after the first section, was the proviso that after July 1, 1863, the legal tenders could no longer be exchanged for bonds, practically repudiating the pledge made in 1862, thus diminishing the value of the notes and conducing to their remaining in circulation when not needed for that purpose. This proviso, which had also been asked for by Chase to aid in disposing of bonds, was regarded by the majority in Congress as in the nature of a limitation, and not a breach of the contract. Shortly before adjourning Congress passed the national currency act, for which Chase had striven so assiduously in his attempt to give the country a safe and uniform paper medium. (This is fully discussed in another chapter.)

The premium on coin had advanced to 60 in January and to 72½ in February; in March it receded, falling as low as 39. The Treasury was, however, still unable to float bonds in sufficient volume, and was compelled to use its note-issuing powers. By end of June $90,000,000 more of the new legal tenders had been put out, making a total of over $367,000,000 in circulation on that date.

Before presenting his annual report to Congress in December, 1863, Chase had begun the issue of one and two year interest-bearing notes, and under his discretionary power he made them legal tenders. In his report he showed that the tax laws produced much less than had been expected, and estimated an increase of the debt to June 30, 1864 (over the same date in 1863), of nearly $685,000,000, and for the following year $545,000,000. He entertained the hope, however, that internal revenue receipts would thenceforward increase and the war expenses diminish. Discussing the currency, he recommended that no further legal tender note-issues be made, as the increase beyond the $400,000,000 authorized (besides $50,000,000 for reserves) would certainly cause great depreciation. The country could not absorb more. He expected good results from the national banking law, under which bonds would be taken and a sound note-issue take the place of the state bank currency.

Congress authorized further issues of bonds, the prepayment of interest on the debt for a period of one year if the Secretary deemed it wise, and by the act of June 30, 1864, authorized the further issue of interest-bearing notes to run not more than three years, at interest not to exceed 7.30 per cent. These notes might be made legal tender for their face value, but were not to be in denominations under $10. The act also gave the Secretary authority to exchange notes of all kinds provided the limits fixed by law were not exceeded, and definitely provided that the issue of non-interest-bearing legal tender notes, which had become distinguished from other Treasury notes by the title "United States Notes" (and colloquially by the term "greenbacks"), should never exceed $400,000,000, besides $50,000,000 to be used as a reserve for the temporary loan certificates. The limit of issue of these last-named obligations was extended to $150,000,000, the limit of interest raised to 6 per cent, and the newly created national bank-notes were made receivable for such loans. The same act provided that the interest-bearing notes authorized were not to be legal tender for redemption of notes of banks. The national bank act was on June 3, 1864, amended in very important particulars.

The sales of bonds were for a time quite active, but Chase's attempt to float 5 per cents proved abortive, and such were the demands upon the Treasury for war expenses that he found it necessary to increase the

Increased loans.

Interest-bearing notes.

issue of the one and two year 5 per cent notes already referred to, to $211,000,000, and begin the issue of three year notes just authorized, making them 6 per cent compound interest, instead of 7.30 per cent. They were also made legal tenders for their face value. Such extreme use of the legal tender power shows to what extent the credit of the government under such enormous borrowing had become impaired. By June 30, 1864, there were in round numbers about $650,000,000 of legal tender notes of all kinds in existence. The interest-bearing varieties were not all in active circulation, but were used in reserves of banks, thus performing some of the money functions.

From December, 1863, the premium on gold rose steadily until it reached 86 in May. In order to check speculation Congress authorized the Secretary to sell coin accumulated in the Treasury beyond its needs; and on June 17, 1864, passed an act forbidding all sales of gold and foreign exchange on "time" contracts, and prohibited brokers from selling gold anywhere except at their offices, thereby hoping to break up the "gold exchange." This resulted in a rise in the premium to 185. The act was repealed on July 6, 1864. This short period sufficed to convince Congress of the futility of attempting to regulate the premium upon gold by legislation. On the first of July it became known that Chase had resigned, and the gold premium fluctuated between 122 and 150. Fessenden, who as Chairman of the Senate Finance Committee was fully conversant with all fiscal measures, became his successor.

Legal regulation of coin sales.

Compound interest notes.

Fessenden, adhering to Chase's policy in general, continued the issue of compound interest notes, with which he retired the short term 5 per cent notes and issued in addition some $55,000,000 more than was necessary for such retirement (the total issue having been

$266,000,000). Experiencing difficulty in placing bonds, he also made use of 7.30 notes, but without the legal tender power, to which, as has been shown, he seriously objected.

The expansion of the currency occasioned by the continued use of United States notes was at this time increased by national bank issues, which began to appear in considerable volume. On the other hand, the expansion was modified considerably by the very rapid disappearance of state bank circulation. Fessenden estimated that in November, 1864, the amount of the latter was $126,000,000. National bank notes at the time amounted to $65,000,000, the legal tender issues of all classes to $675,000,000, thus giving an aggregate of $866,000,000.[1] The gold premium fluctuated quite violently, ranging in March, 1865, between $48\frac{1}{3}$ and 101, but diminished after July.

In the act of March 3, 1865, complying with Fessenden's recommendations, $600,000,000 were provided for in bonds or Treasury notes convertible into bonds, interest on the former not to exceed 6 per cent, on the latter 7.30 per cent, and none were to be made legal tenders. Practically all the remaining needs of the government growing out of the war were supplied by means of this new issue of 7.30's (of 1864–65) of which approximately $830,000,000 were used. The interest as well as the principal was made payable in currency, and they were known as currency bonds. In the revenue act of March 3, 1865, Congress laid such a tax upon state bank notes (10 per cent) as to practically prohibit their use, and they gradually disappeared.

Currency bonds.

The provisions of the national bank act of June 3, 1864, constrained the banks to become large owners of legal tender notes as well as of United States bonds.

Legal tenders in bank reserves.

[1] Finance Report, 1864.

The banks were required to provide for the redemption of their notes in "lawful money," and to maintain reserves of such money for this purpose as well as against deposits. Many of these legal tender notes bore interest and hence were a profitable form of reserve. The non-interest-bearing ones were needed for current use. These wants necessarily employed a substantial amount of the several forms of legal tender notes. The act also provided that national banks might be designated as depositories of public money, upon giving security to the satisfaction of the Secretary in "government bonds and otherwise."

Before the close of the fiscal year 1865 (in April), the war ceased and the restoration of the finances to a peace basis could be considered. Fessenden returned to the Senate and was succeeded (March 4) by Hugh McCulloch, whose long experience with the state bank of Indiana and as the first Comptroller of the Currency under the national banking law, peculiarly fitted him for the great work.

Review of the period.

A brief review and correlation of the portentous events crowded into this short space of four years is requisite. Chase was the guiding spirit of the fiscal affairs of the Nation. Never before nor since had a finance minister wielded such power as was placed in his hands. In reviewing the manner in which the power was used due consideration must be given to the unprecedented conditions with which he had to contend. Without experience as a financier, he was required to provide for the expense of a gigantic war rendered extravagantly costly by inexperience, want of preparation, and failure to even approximately foresee its magnitude and duration. The cost averaged over $2,000,000 a day for the entire period, and at its maximum called for a daily expenditure of nearly $3,000,000.

He had a Treasury without funds, a shattered public credit, an insufficient revenue, and a heterogeneous state bank currency of fluctuating and uncertain value. He adopted at the outset a policy of providing a homogeneous circulating medium which would be safe alike for government and individual, and issued notes fundable into interest-bearing bonds. Believing that the volume of specie in the country, under the influence of adverse foreign trade balances and other demands, was totally inadequate to maintain coin payments for the enormous volume of transactions which would become necessary, unless an auxiliary were provided, he preferred risking the danger involved in the issue of the demand notes of the government rather than that certain to follow from the acceptance of state bank-notes. Chase's difficulties.

While Chase's distrust of state banks was extreme, and he was too rigid in his requirements in connection with the execution of the law authorizing him to deposit public moneys with them (a course which contributed materially to force suspension of coin payments), it is nevertheless true that the banks as a whole were unable to finance the extraordinary needs of the government, and it would have been unwise to rely upon them. The people were not prepared to absorb the enormous loans which the government had to make, and the banks could not invest all their funds in such loans. No loans could be placed abroad. The issue of United States notes, to circulate as money, under the circumstances seems to have been unavoidable and hence justifiable. It has been fully shown that both Lincoln and Chase, as well as Congress, believed it imperatively necessary a little later to give these notes legal tender power. Viewed in retrospection it seems to have been quite unnecessary. It is by no means fair, however, to judge the acts of men who could only conjecture the Chase's policy considered.

future by the standard of events as they afterwards transpired. The country was rudely awakened from a long period of profound peace. It was quite accustomed to the issue of "state sovereignty" and "popular sovereignty." Nullification by South Carolina in Jackson's time was recalled. The "Missouri Compromise,' Kansas-Nebraska controversy, and other important incidents had familiarized the North with the contention of the slave states. The North did not believe, let alone realize, that the South was determined to put the issue to the exhaustive test of final arbitrament by the sword. The best evidence of this is Lincoln's first proclamation calling for troops. Seventy-five thousand was the number asked for, and ninety days the period of enlistment.

Taxing policy wrong.

Nations, like individuals, should live within their income, and current taxes should always equal current expenses, including, of course, interest on any indebtedness. According to principles laid down by publicists and economists, extraordinary expenses, as in case of war, should be met by a judicious apportionment of increased taxation and loans. It is deemed just that a portion of extraordinary expenditure, whether incurred in war or for public utility or permanent improvement, be devolved upon the succeeding generation, which is profited thereby, by means of loans payable at a future date. Had Chase applied this principle in his demands from Congress in July, 1861, it would have stood him in good stead. Congress, beyond question, would have complied, and much embarrassment on account of loans and full tender notes would have been avoided. In saying this I do not forget that Lincoln's administration felt the necessity of winning victories at the polls as well as in the field, and cherished a wholesome and proper dread of the effect upon the public of largely increased taxation.

The one fixed purpose of Secretary Chase was to supplant the onerous, costly, and insecure state bank circulation by a safe, efficient national bank circulation secured by government bonds and further protected by a lawful money reserve against both circulation and deposits. In this way he expected to find a large demand and permanent use for both bonds and legal tender notes. Had Congress promptly created the national banking system instead of waiting until 1863, the Secretary's hopes would undoubtedly have been largely realized, and the volume of legal tender notes issued would have been very much less. The power of the state banks was enormous, and they looked upon the idea of converting into national banks under the proposed law with conservative fear. The treatment of the two United States banks at the hands of Congress was not at all reassuring. It is not surprising, however regrettable, that their influence should have so long defeated the national system and left the Secretary to meet his responsibilities by means of Treasury note-issues.

It would seem that a suspension of coin payments was inevitable, even had it not been precipitated by the events heretofore recounted. The great expansion of trade, caused primarily by the enormous government purchases, required a larger volume of money. Without credit for its securities abroad and with an adverse foreign trade balance, the country could not retain its specie, much less draw from abroad. Expansion of paper currency under either state or national authority was sure to follow. Had Chase adhered to state banks the reserves would have proved inadequate to maintain coin payments, and the country would have been

Currency policy sound.

Suspension probably inevitable.

flooded, as before, with an irredeemable currency varying in value from good to worthless. United States
notes and national bank-notes would at least be uniform and ultimately redeemed, and the advantages of
such circulation, instead of swelling private profits,
would inure to the benefit of the government and be
applied to the saving of the Union. Chase could not
but choose the latter. Fully appreciating the danger
of a redundant issue of government notes, he endeavored to limit the volume, but conditions forced
him to issue more and more, in the face of depreciation. He did so, doubting their legality, and hoping
and believing that the national bank circulation when
created would take their place and admit of their
retirement. In a formal communication to Congress
he later condemned his own policy in issuing so many
notes in lieu of imposing greater taxation. As Chief
Justice he pronounced the legal tender notes he had
issued unconstitutional — a most unique commentary
upon his own administration, and one that is surely
without parallel.

Recapitula-
tion of
events.   The chain of causes and effects may be recapitulated
as follows: Utter failure to foresee the probable length
and magnitude of the war, hence failure to provide
largely increased taxation, always unpalatable to short-
sighted legislators; first resort to note-issues rendered
necessary by the absence of a reputable currency system
and of credit abroad through which specie could be
drawn; the vain desire not to sell bonds at a discount,
and consequent inability to sell them as rapidly as needs
arose; wretched military administration and waste in
innumerable ways; suspension of coin payments precipitated by unwise management and foreign complica-
tions; forced legal tender currency loans and expansion
of prices, checking commodity exports and increasing

expenses ; heavy exports of specie naturally following ; more legal tender currency, with further rise in prices and increase in expenses ; repudiation of right to fund legal tender notes into bonds ; wild speculation in specie which extended into all lines of business, enriching the shrewd few at the expense of the many. Net result, — ultimate cost to the people very much more than it would have been had they been taxed more heavily at the outset.

As Franklin had pointed out in the days of continental currency, the people actually paid exorbitant sums *indirectly* because they did not pay the lesser amounts *directly*. It has been said that the " greenbacks " saved the Union. Be this as it may, it is certain that had a great national bank or a system of national banks existed, and had a proper scheme of taxation been adopted, the same result would have been accomplished at far less cost; and while suspension of coin payments would probably have been inevitable, the premium upon gold would have been controllable and prices kept within limits.[1]

STATISTICAL RÉSUMÉ

NATIONAL FINANCES (in millions of dollars)

(The government fiscal year ends June 30.)

FISCAL YEAR	REVENUE			EXPENSES			DEFICIT	DEBT	
	Customs	Other	Total	Ordinary	Interest	Total		Outstanding	Increase
1861	40	2	42	63	4	67	25	91	26
1862	49	3	52	456	13	469	417	524	433
1863	69	43	112	694	25	719	607	1120	596
1864	102	141	243	811	54	865	622	1816	696
1865	85	237	322	1218	77	1295	973	2681	865

[1] See Mitchell, Sound Currency, Vol. IV., No. 8.

CIRCULATION (in millions, except last column)

FISCAL YEAR	SPECIE	U.S. NOTES	BANK NOTES		FRACTIONAL CURRENCY	TOTAL	IN TREASURY	IN CIRCULATION	POPULATION	PER CAPITA
			State	National						
1861	250	—	202	—	—	452	4	448	32	$14.00
1862	25	150	184	—	—	359	24	335	25	13.40
1863	25	391	239	—	20	675	79	596	26	22.66
1864	25	447	179	31	23	705	36	670	27	24.81
1865	25	431	143	146	25	770	55	715	30	23.83

Specie includes after 1861 only the amount estimated in use on Pacific Slope. Population reduced by that of states in rebellion.

EXPORTS AND IMPORTS (in millions of dollars)

FISCAL YEAR	MERCHANDISE		EXCESS	SPECIE		EXCESS
	Exports	Imports	+ Import − Export	Exports	Imports	+ Import − Export
1861 . .	220	289	+ 69	30	46	+ 16
1862 . .	191	189	− 2	37	16	− 21
1863 . .	204	243	+ 39	64	10	− 54
1864 . .	159	316	+ 157	105	13	− 92
1865 . .	166	239	+ 73	68	10	− 58

THE GOLD PREMIUM AND PRICES

(See Sound Currency, Vol. III., No. 17.)

CALENDAR YEAR	PREMIUM ON GOLD			GOLD VALUE OF PAPER			GOLD PRICES U. S.	WAGES IN GOLD	PURCHASING POWER OF WAGES	COST OF GOLD IN LABOR
	High	Low	Average	High	Low	Average				
1860	—	—	—	—	—	100	100.0	100.0	1.000	1.000
1861	—	—	—	—	—	100	94.1	100.7	1.050	.993
1862	34.0	1.1	13.3	98.5	75.6	88.3	101.6	101.2	1.009	.988
1863	72.5	22.1	45.2	79.5	62.3	68.9	91.1	81.9	9.73	1.221
1864	185.0	51.5	103.3	64.3	38.7	49.2	110.7	66.6	9.00	1.500
1865	134.4	28.5	57.3	73.7	46.3	63.6	107.4	94.5	7.80	1.057

CHAPTER IX

1866 TO 1875

McCulloch's administration.

THE expenses of the government did not become normal at once after the close of the war. A great army had to be disbanded and many obligations remained to be paid. McCulloch reported (December, 1865) that the debt had increased during the fiscal year nearly $942,000,000; he estimated a deficit in the revenue for 1866 of $112,000,000, but a surplus in 1867 of almost the same amount. The total debt at its maximum, in August, 1865, stood at $2,845,900,000. It was expected that it would reach $3,000,000,000, but by this time the revenues increased and expenditures diminished. The fiscal year 1866 showed $290,000,000 surplus instead of the $112,000,000 deficit as estimated. Provision had been made for funding the floating debt, and this process, as well as the reduction, began in the fall of 1866. The debt in August, 1865, was composed of

The public debt.

Bonds	$1,109,600,000
Interest-bearing legal tenders	250,900,000
Non-interest-bearing legal tenders	433,200,000
7.30's	830,000,000
Temporary debt and other forms	222,200,000
The annual interest charge was in excess of . . .	150,000,000

McCulloch directed special attention to the currency portion of the debt, urging preparation for resumption of specie payments and ultimate repeal of legal tender acts. But a new idea had become prevalent. The United States notes, popularly called "greenbacks,"[1]

[1] The word "greenback," applied to the first legal tender notes issued by the government in 1862 because of the prevailing color of the back of

were a convenient form of money and a non-interest-bearing loan, hence their retention was urged on the double ground of convenience and economy. To these the Secretary opposed, first, the extra-constitutional exercise of power warranted only by war ; second, the breach of faith involved in failure to redeem ; third, the evil effects which would follow the continuance of the inflated currency. He recommended that the legal tender power of the interest-bearing notes be discontinned after maturity, and that he be authorized to sell bonds to retire these as well as the non-interest-bearing notes (greenbacks). He warned Congress against a continuance of the policy of an inconvertible currency, predicting that, unless remedied, the question would become a political one, and few less disturbing to the welfare of the country could be imagined.

Contraction of currency.

McCulloch estimated the amount of currency on October 31, 1865, at $704,000,000, not including $205,000,000 of interest-bearing legal tenders (nor the 7.30's); of the interest-bearing notes about $30,000,000 and some of the smaller 7.30's were circulating as money. The bank-notes included in the above total he placed at $250,000,000, of which $65,000,000 were state bank-notes, the remainder national bank issues ; of the latter class $115,000,000 might still be issued within the legal limit, some of which would, however, replace the state bank issues. The premium on coin which in the early months of the year stood at over 100 (reaching $133\frac{3}{4}$), fell as low as $28\frac{2}{3}$, closing in December at $45\frac{1}{2}$.

Volume of currency.

President Johnson supported the recommendations of McCulloch in his message. He said : —

the notes, is generally used as a comprehensive term including all legal tender notes issued prior to the law of 1890. It is used interchangeably with the term " United States notes," but colloquially is much more popular.

"It is our first duty to prepare in earnest for our recovery from the ever-increasing evils of an irredeemable currency, without a sudden revulsion and yet without untimely procrastination."[1]

A considerable number of public men were inclined to regard the war debt as only partially obligatory upon the Nation, owing to the fact that depreciated currency had been received for the greater part of it, and urged that payment in coin commanding a high premium ought not to be insisted upon. This led to the adoption, on motion of Representative Randall (Dem., Pa.), afterwards Speaker, of the following declaratory resolution in the House on December 5, 1865, with but one dissenting vote : — Debt repudiation rejected.

"RESOLVED, That, as the sense of this House, the public debt created during the late rebellion was contracted upon the faith and honor of the Nation ; that it is sacred and inviolate and must and ought to be paid, principal and interest ; that any attempt to repudiate or in any manner to impair or scale the said debt shall be universally discountenanced, and promptly rejected by Congress if proposed."

McCulloch had actually begun the retirement of greenbacks out of the surplus revenues. The House of Representatives on December 18, 1865, indorsed his policy by almost unanimous vote, and the act of April 12, 1866, authorized him to fund all notes into bonds or sell bonds to retire notes, provided the total debt was not increased. The act contained the limitation that not more than $10,000,000 of the "greenbacks" be retired in the ensuing six months, and $4,000,000 monthly thereafter. Other acts provided for nickel coins of three and five cents to retire those denominations of the fractional paper currency. McCulloch's policy indorsed.

This salutary legislation was not secured without opposition from those who might have been expected to

[1] Messages of Presidents, Vol. VI.

Some
opposition.

favor it. Stevens, who had proclaimed in 1862 that the "greenbacks" were only a temporary expedient, was content to continue them as a debt not bearing interest. Boutwell (afterwards Secretary) appeared to believe that Congress should not interfere with events which would bring about resumption of coin payments automatically. Senator Sherman (also later Secretary) believed that if the Treasury simply met current obligations, no power could delay resumption beyond a year and a half.

Gold certifi-
cates.

The authority conferred by the act of March 3, 1863, to issue gold certificates was first made use of by McCulloch on November 13, 1865. The act of July 13, 1866, amended the act imposing a tax of 10 per cent on state bank circulation, making it apply to individuals as well as to banks. This effectually prohibited their further use. The premium on coin fluctuated during the calendar year 1866 between $67\frac{3}{4}$ and $25\frac{1}{2}$ per cent, averaging $40\frac{9}{10}$, making the average value of the notes about 71 per cent.

In his report for 1866 McCulloch showed that he had reduced the debt from August, 1865, $164,000,000, and had a larger cash balance by $42,000,000. The funding had progressed satisfactorily. Nearly $100,000,000 of the interest-bearing legal tenders were out of the way, and "greenbacks" had been reduced by nearly $43,000,000, standing at $390,195,785. The financial operations were no doubt greatly facilitated by the increased investment of foreigners in our securities, thus enabling the country to retain a substantial part of its gold product.

Debt held
abroad.

McCulloch estimated in 1866 that $600,000,000 of such securities ($350,000,000 in United States bonds) were held abroad. The amount of specie in the country, estimated at $66,000,000 in 1865, was in 1867 given as $139,000,000.

Criticised for holding so large a balance in the Treasury which might have been used in great measure to save interest, he pointed out the necessity for keeping the Treasury strong in order to maintain the stability of the irredeemable currency, regarding this end much more important to the people than saving some interest. His purpose was to hold a reserve against these issues precisely as a bank would, selling gold when in his judgment advisable to reduce the premium, to limit depreciation of the notes. To correct the evils which would unquestionably enrich the few at the expense of the many, he recommended contraction, tariff revision, and refunding the debt; and also an amendment of the national banking law to compel banks to redeem their notes at the Atlantic cities as well as at their counters. McCulloch's gold reserve.

The act of March 2, 1867, authorized 3 per cent temporary loan certificates to take up a part of the 6 per cent compound interest legal tender notes, thus substituting a form of obligation not legal tender. The certificates were, however, made available for bank reserves, and thus served as a substitute for "lawful money." The issue was limited to $50,000,000. Three per cent certificates.

A very substantial sentiment had by 1867 manifested itself against the retirement of legal tender notes, against the national banks, and favorable to paying the public debt in greenbacks. The word "contraction" was made to appear to the masses as signifying a monstrous power which would not unlikely rob them of their daily bread. The greenbacks outstanding had been reduced to $356,000,000, and the average gold premium in 1867 was 38.2 per cent. Opposition to contraction.

President Johnson's message for 1867 showed that he had not escaped the political influence of the day. He favored measures looking to resumption of coin payments, but, he added, a "reduction of our paper circulating medium need not necessarily follow." He declared it was unjust to pay bondholders in coin and other creditors in depreciated paper. He was endeavoring to obtain the support of the "greenback" element for a renomination. A wave of economic heresy had struck the people, especially in the West. Crop failures, high prices, speculation, and resulting business troubles gave strength and numbers to the movement. The greenbacks were regarded as the means of curing the evils which in fact they caused. The Democratic party, which had opposed the legal tender acts as unconstitutional, now became their especial advocate. Pendleton, who in 1862 vigorously denounced the first act, now aiming for the presidency in 1868, led the movement in favor of perpetuating the greenbacks.

Greenback heresy.

Many of the Republican leaders, anticipating defeat unless their sentiments were modified, yielded to the storm. Senator Sherman, who had predicted resumption before 1868, and who had expressed the opinion that the paper currency was not redundant at a time when the premium on coin was nearly 50 per cent, now believed it proper to pay the bonds in greenbacks, and in deference to public opinion proposed to stop contraction. Senator Morton, of Indiana, favored more note-issues. Thus a Republican Congress, which had in December, 1865, "pledged coöperative action" toward resumption by retirement of the notes, and early in 1866 had passed a law authorizing contraction, in February, 1868, passed an act suspending the authority and prohibiting further reduction of the currency by retiring notes. President Johnson, then at odds with Congress, and uncertain as to the best policy, did not approve the act, nor did he veto it, but allowed it to become law without his approval.

Contraction suspended.

The act of June 25, 1868, authorized the increase of 3 per cent certificates to the amount of $75,000,000 to retire the remaining compound interest notes. A bill passed both houses of Congress on July 27, 1868, providing for refunding the debt at lower interest rates, but Johnson failed to approve the measure, and it lapsed by the adjournment of Congress.

The national conventions of 1868 adopted the following platform resolutions respecting the debt and the currency question : —

Republican Platform, at Chicago, May.

"We denounce all forms of repudiation as a national crime, and the national honor requires the payment of the public indebtedness in the utmost good faith to all creditors at home and abroad, not only according to the letter, but the spirit of the laws under which it was contracted. The national debt, contracted as it has been for the preservation of the Union for all time to come, should be extended over a fair period for redemption. It is the duty of Congress to reduce the rate of interest thereon whenever it can honestly be done.

"That the best policy to diminish our burden of debt is to so improve our credit that capitalists will seek to loan us money at lower rates of interest than we now pay, and must continue to pay so long as repudiation, partial or total, open or covert, is threatened or suspected."

Repudiation denounced.

Democratic, at New York, July.

"Payment of the public debt of the United States as rapidly as practicable ; all moneys drawn from the people by taxation, except so much as is requisite for the necessities of the Government, economically administered, being honestly applied to such payment, and where the obligations of the Government do not expressly state upon their face, or the law under which they were issued does not provide that they shall be paid in coin, they ought in right and in justice, to be paid in the lawful money of the United States.

"Equal taxation of every species of property according to its real value, including Government bonds and other public securities.

Payments of bonds in greenbacks.

"One currency for the Government and the people, the laborer and the office-holder, the pensioner and the soldier, the producer and the bondholder."

The sound element in the Republican party having thus been able to stem within its ranks the tide of repudiation, and having nominated Grant, whose popularity as a hero of the war unquestionably assisted them materially, the greenback movement received a check at the polls.

Although discouraged by the reactionary legislation of Congress, McCulloch nevertheless continued, in his report in December, 1868, to urge upon that body the need of bringing the currency to a coin basis.

He estimated the amount of American bonds held abroad at $850,000,000, of which $600,000,000 were in "governments."

In his message of December, 1868, Johnson repeated his views on the currency of the previous year, and came out more broadly in favor of "scaling" the public debt, which brought forth the following resolution in the Senate : —

"RESOLVED, That the Senate, properly cherishing and upholding the good faith and honor of the nation, do hereby utterly disapprove of and condemn the sentiments and propositions contained in so much of the late annual message of the President of the United States as reads as follows:

"'It may be assumed that the holders of our securities have already received upon their bonds a larger amount than their original investment, measured by a gold standard. Upon this statement of facts, it would seem but just and equitable that the six per cent. interest now paid by the Government should be applied to the reduction of the principal in semi-annual installments, which in sixteen years and eight months would liquidate the entire national debt. Six per cent. in gold would at present rates be equal to nine per cent. in currency, and equivalent to the payment of the debt one and a half times in a fraction less than seventeen years. This, in connection with all the other advantages derived from their investment, would afford to the public creditors a fair and liberal compensation for the use of their capital, and with this they should be satisfied. The lessons of the past admonish the lender that it is not well to be over anxious in exacting from the borrower rigid compliance with the letter of the bond.' "

The hard fight that the friends of sound money had to make can well be imagined when the President, the official representative of the nation, in his message to Congress, urged such repudiation.

The Senate resolution was passed by a strict party vote of 43 to 6; and in the House a similar resolution was passed by 155 to 6; not voting 60.

Repudiation finally defeated.

Subsequently a section in the fourteenth amendment to the Constitution settled the question in the following terms : —

"The validity of the public debt of the United States, authorized by law, including debts incurred for payment of pensions and bounties for services in suppressing insurrection or rebellion, shall not be questioned. But neither the United States nor any State shall assume or pay any debt or obligation incurred in aid of insurrection or rebellion against the United States, or any claim for the loss or emancipation of any slave ; but all such debts, obligations, and claims shall be illegal and void."

On February 19, 1869, Congress passed an act prohibiting national banks making loans on collaterals of United States notes or national bank-notes, a practice which might obviously be used to cause a considerable contraction of the currency.

A bill was also passed on March 3, 1869, to strengthen the public credit by a declaration of the purpose of the government to pay bonds in coin, and legalizing coin contracts, as recommended by McCulloch; but Johnson refused to approve it, and Congress having adjourned the same day, it failed to become law.

Public credit act.

In his inaugural address, on March 4, 1869, President Grant said : —

> "A great debt has been contracted in securing to us and our posterity the Union. The payment of this, principal and interest, as well as the return to a specie basis, as soon as it can be accomplished without material detriment to the debtor class or to the country at large, must be provided for. To protect the national honor every dollar of government indebtedness should be paid in gold, unless otherwise expressly stipulated in the contract. Let it be understood that no repudiator of one farthing of our public debt will be trusted in public place, and it will go far toward strengthening a credit which ought to be the best in the world, and will ultimately enable us to replace the debt with bonds bearing less interest than we now pay."

Boutwell's administration.

George S. Boutwell succeeded McCulloch as Secretary of the Treasury in March.

Congress was called in extra session by Grant at once, and on the 18th of March the act to strengthen the public credit, already referred to, became law, but without the coin contract clause. It declared the purpose of the United States to pay its notes and bonds in coin or the equivalent, solemnly pledging the faith of the nation to such payment, and "to make provision at the earliest practical period for redemption of United States notes in coin"; another declaration was that no bonds would be paid before maturity unless greenbacks were convertible into coin at the option of the holder or unless at such time bonds bearing a lower rate of interest could be sold for par in coin.

The coin contract clause was stricken out by a vote of 82 to 56 in the House and 28 to 15 in the Senate; the bill passed by 97 to 47, and 42 to 13 respectively.

It should be borne in mind with reference to the word "coin" as used in the several statutes that the silver dollar was at this time worth in the market about 4 per cent more than the gold dollar.

This declaration no doubt served its purpose but, as will be seen, it was not acted upon, so far as notes were concerned, for nearly six years, and not actually made effective until nearly ten years thereafter. Bonds were in fact almost immediately "paid before maturity," although the sale of lower rate bonds at par for coin did not begin until 1871. The volume of greenbacks remained practically undisturbed at $356,000,000 for nearly five years, and then the amount was not reduced but *increased*. This was the interpretation given the declaration "earliest practical period" to which the faith of the nation was pledged.

Public credit act ignored.

The Democratic state platforms still opposed the policy above outlined; that of the Ohio convention of July 7, 1869, contained the following : —

Opposition develops.

" RESOLVED, That exemption from tax of over $2,500,000,000 Government bonds and securities is unjust to the people, and ought not to be tolerated, and that we are opposed to any appropriation for the payment of the interest on the public bonds until they are made subject to taxation.

"That the claim of the bondholders that the bonds which were bought with greenbacks, and the principal of which is by law payable in currency, should, nevertheless, be paid in gold, is unjust and extortionate, and if persisted in will force upon the people the question of repudiation.

"That we denounce the national banking system as one of the worst out-growths of the bonded debt, which unnecessarily increases the burden of the people $30,000,000 annually, and that we demand its immediate repeal."

That of Iowa, a week later, the following : —

"That we favor a reform in the national banking system looking to an ultimate abolishment of that pernicious plan for the aggrandizement of a few at the expense of the many."

Boutwell's
policy.

It soon became obvious that the plan of the new administration differed from that of McCulloch although officially announcing the same end in view, resumption. For while both Grant and Boutwell urged consideration of the subject and early legislation (but with due regard for the "debtor class"), the policy carried out in the absence of legislation was to reduce the debt, under the sinking fund law of 1862, thus raising the national credit, and cause a change in the trade conditions which would bring specie into the country, or at least enable the country to hold part of its own product. In this manner it was expected that coin and paper would come to a parity. The result was apparently favorable, as the net exports of specie fell off more than 50 per cent. The country's stock of coin was increased, and although the maximum premium for coin was higher than in the previous year, reaching $62\frac{1}{2}$ per cent, the minimum was much lower, $19\frac{1}{2}$, and the average for the year was only 33 against $39\frac{7}{10}$ the year before. The average value of greenbacks in coin thus rose to 75.2 per cent. Boutwell redeemed over $75,000,000 of bonds in nine months, paying for them in coin, thus retiring them at a little over 88 per cent.

President Grant in his message, December, 1869, said : —

Grant on the
currency.

"Among the evils growing out of the rebellion and not yet referred to, is that of an irredeemable currency. It is an evil which I hope will receive your most earnest attention. It is a duty, and one of the highest duties, of government to secure to the citizen a medium of exchange of fixed, unvarying value. This implies a return to a specie basis, and no substitute for it can be devised. It should be commenced now, and reached at the earliest practical moment consistent with a fair regard to the interests of the debtor class. Immediate resumption, if practicable, would not be desirable. It would compel the debtor class to pay, beyond their contracts, the premium on gold at the date of their purchase, and would bring bankruptcy and ruin to thousands. Fluctuation, however, in the paper value of the measure of all values (gold) is detrimental to the interests of trade. It makes the man of business an involuntary gambler, for, in all sales where future payment is to be made, both parties speculate as to what will be the value of the currency to be paid and received. I earnestly recommend to you, then, such legislation as will assure a gradual return to specie payments, and put an immediate stop to fluctuations in the value of currency.

"The methods to secure the former of these results are as numerous as are the speculators on political economy. To secure the latter I see but one way, and that is, to authorize the Treasury to redeem its own paper, at a fixed price, whenever presented, and to withhold from circulation all currency so redeemed until sold again for gold."

The legal tender notes were treated as if they had "come to stay," their ultimate retirement *in toto* was no longer considered, and the newly given pledge of Congress to make the notes convertible into coin before paying off bonds not due and payable was not referred to.

One circumstance remains to be noted. Although the act of 1866 provided that greenbacks were to be retired and cancelled and there had been destroyed some $77,000,000, reducing the volume to $356,000,000, it was urged that since the maximum issue authorized by the act of June 30, 1864, had been fixed at $400,000,000, and the act not repealed, the difference between that sum and the existing amount, viz. $44,000,000, was a "reserve" available to the Treasury. Under this supposed authority Boutwell had issued in 1869 $1,500,000 of notes from the "reserve," but had retired them again soon thereafter. This remarkable construction of the status of cancelled and retired notes subsequently led to actions which for a time threatened serious results.

The greenback "reserve."

Speculation in gold was very active during the year, at one time in midsummer reaching unprecedented proportions. Unscrupulous speculators, believing that the Treasury policy of not selling its specie would render such an operation easy, undertook to "corner" gold, causing serious disaster to those compelled to use it; but the Treasury did sell gold in time to avert a general panic. Congress ordered an investigation, which disclosed a thoroughgoing conspiracy in which several persons supposed to be close to the administration were implicated.

Currency resolutions in Congress.

Congress on July 14, 1870, authorized the refunding of the 6 per cent bonds into 5, 4½, and 4 per cents. Amendments for funding the greenbacks into bonds and for retiring them before unmatured bonds were paid, were defeated, and also one to scale the debt. On February 14, 1870, the House of Representatives voted that the business interests of the country required "an increase in the volume of circulating currency," and favored a bill "increasing the currency" to the amount of at least $50,000,000; and on March 21 that the interest-bearing debt "should not be increased by causing a surrender of any part of our present circulating medium not bearing interest, and the substitution therefor of interest-bearing bonds."

In the Senate on February 24, 1870, the following was agreed to : —

"RESOLVED, That to add to the present irredeemable paper currency of the country would be to render more difficult and remote the resumption of specie payments, to encourage and foster the spirit of speculation, to aggravate the evils produced by frequent and sudden fluctuations of values, to depreciate the credit of the nation, and to check the healthful tendency of legitimate business to settle down upon a safe and permanent basis, and therefore, in the opinion of the Senate, the existing volume of such currency ought not to be increased."

But no further action was taken.

On July 12, 1870, an act was passed to retire the 3 per cent certificates and issue $54,000,000 additional national bank-notes, an amendment to retire green-backs as bank-notes were increased being voted down.

While this measure was under discussion the antici- Legal tender
decision. pated decision of the Supreme Court that the legal tender acts as applied to preëxisting contracts were unconstitutional, was published.

No effort was made by Congress or the administration to conform to this decision; on the contrary, steps were taken to secure its reversal.

In order to enable banks to have a form of money in large denominations, available as reserves and convenient in paying large sums, Congress, June 8, 1872, authorized the issue of certificates, bearing no interest, for deposits of greenbacks, in denominations of $5000 and $10,000. These were issued only to national banks, were payable to order, were counted as reserve, and intended to be used in settling balances at clearing-houses.

The currency question played a subordinate part in Currency in
politics, 1872. the presidential contest of 1872 (Grant-Greeley). The platforms of the two parties were practically identical. That of the Republicans contained the following : —

" We denounce repudiation of the public debt, in any form or disguise, as a national crime. We witness with pride the reduction of the principal of the debt, and of the rates of interest upon the balance, and confidently expect that our excellent national currency will be perfected by a speedy resumption of specie payment."

The Democratic-Liberal-Republican platform contained the following : —

" The public credit must be sacredly maintained, and we denounce repudiation in every form and guise. A speedy return to specie payment is demanded alike by the highest considerations of commercial morality and honest government."

By 1872 there had been a large increase in national bank-notes, and a slight increase in the average gold premium, due to the inflation, had appeared. Boutwell held that Congress and the country were opposed to contraction, so that the only alternative to bring about resumption was to await the increased need for circulation by the natural growth of population and business. Both Grant and his Secretary occupied an "opportunist" attitude toward the currency during his first term, in strong contrast to the vigorous sound money attitude of McCulloch.

Second legal tender decision.
The second decision of the Supreme Court (reversing the former decision), published early in the year, had declared the legal tender notes constitutional. The Court, however, seemed to base its approval of the act upon the necessities growing out of the war. It left a doubt as to whether they could be issued in time of peace and in the absence of some crucial necessity.

Boutwell had again in 1872 issued a small amount of his so-called "reserve" of greenbacks. This led to an examination of the question by the Finance Committee of the Senate early in 1873. Boutwell justified the issue, but Sherman, speaking for the committee, disagreed with him, stating that greenbacks once "retired and cancelled," as provided by the act of 1866, could no more be reissued than the bonds and interest-bearing notes retired and cancelled under the same law. No legislation in relation to the matter resulted.

On February 12, 1873, the act revising the coinage laws, which eliminated the silver dollar and made the gold dollar the unit of value, was passed. This is fully discussed in another chapter.

Sherman in vain endeavored during the winter of

1872–1873 to obtain consideration of a bill providing for resumption by January 1, 1874, and for "free banking."

In his inaugural address in March Grant, in pledging himself to a programme for his second administration, included as one feature "the restoration of our currency to a fixed value as compared with the world's standard — gold, and if possible to a par with it." Economic conditions had now reached a climax. The long-continued period of speculation and inflation had reached a limit. Early in 1873 the coin value of the greenbacks, which had in January, 1872, risen to nearly 92, fell below 85. When the crop-moving period came, a sharp stringency in money manifested itself, a severe panic involving a large number of important concerns and spreading over the entire country followed, and since the government was the creator and regulator of the country's currency, the Treasury was naturally appealed to for relief.

William A. Richardson, then Secretary, with the full approval of the President, purchased bonds with a large part of the so-called greenback reserve. By the end of December he had added $22,000,000 to the outstanding greenbacks by issuing part of those which had been "retired and cancelled" by McCulloch under the act of 1866, and he continued the policy until the amount so added was nearly $29,000,000. In his report, rendered early in December, no mention is made of this issue, but the purpose to make use of the "reserve" in the absence of congressional action was declared. Richardson pointed out the total absence of flexibility in the currency as an evil which should be remedied, and suggested a restricted reserve of greenbacks to be used in emergencies and legislation which would prohibit, or at least restrict, the payment of interest on deposits by the banks.

Grant's second term.

Inflation of 1873.

    The President gave the currency considerable space
in his message.   He regarded the accumulation of gold,
by increasing our commodity exports, as essential, and
for this purpose the industries must be encouraged by
sufficient currency; not inflation, but "just enough,"
combined with elasticity.   "The exact medium is specie.
. . . That obtained, we shall have a currency of an exact
degree of elasticity."   He thought the panic proved the
greenbacks to be the best currency "that has ever been
devised," because during the panic they were hoarded
like gold.   In his opinion the currency was not redundant.

    Whatever else may be said of the discussions of the
President and Secretary, it must be admitted that these
and the panic stirred Congress to action.   The House
began in January, 1874, consideration of measures,
amending the currency acts, and providing for free banking.   The latter feature will be considered in another
chapter; those relating to greenbacks were numerous : —

    1. To issue notes, payable in gold in two years from date,
at the rate of $4,000,000 monthly, in lieu of the greenbacks.
    2. To apply the sinking fund solely to the extinction of the
greenback debt.
    3. As national bank-note issues increase cancel a like amount
of greenbacks, down to $300,000,000.
    4. To issue notes and 3.65 bonds interconvertibly, limit of
notes otherwise to be $400,000,000.
    5. Substitute greenbacks for national bank-notes, redeeming
the 5.20 bonds on deposit to secure the same, in such notes.
    6. Repeal the legal tender act, to go into effect July 1, 1876,
notes to be funded into bonds.

    The Senate was engaged with measures of similar
scope and import.   A bill finally passed in April fixing
the maximum amount of greenbacks at $400,000,000,
and national bank-notes at the same amount.   The vote
was 29 to 24 (19 not voting) in the Senate, 140 to 102

(48 not voting) in the House. Congress practically divided geographically, the Eastern members being arrayed against the bill, with Ohio as the dividing line. The measure was known as the " inflation bill," and public meetings were at once held to denounce it, and to influence Grant to use the veto power, it having been reported upon good authority that he might approve the bill. The movement was successful, and the veto came April 22. In his veto message, Grant questioned whether the bill would actually increase the currency, but if it did, it must be regarded a departure from true principles of finance and the pledges made by Congress and the Executive. Until the government notes were Inflation defeated. convertible into coin, free banking would not be safe, and in order to provide for such convertibility, the revenues would have to be increased.

A second bill was passed June 20, 1874, limiting the maximum of greenbacks to $382,000,000, and providing for the redistribution of bank issues and the substitution for the reserve required on circulation of a 5 per cent redemption fund to be maintained in the Treasury. It also authorized the retirement of circulation by deposits of legal tenders with the Treasury. The Treasurer was thereafter required to redeem all national bank-notes upon presentation.

The congressional elections in 1874 changed a Republican majority of 110 into a minority of 71. No doubt this was due largely to " hard times," following the panic. It certainly roused the Republicans and inspired them to redeem their long-neglected pledges.

Benjamin H. Bristow followed Richardson as Secretary Bristow's administration. of the Treasury in June, and proved a worthy successor of McCulloch as a vigorous champion of sound finance. He regarded the failure to provide for resumption a breach of the Nation's pledges. The United States notes were merely a temporary expedient, warranted only by the exigency of the war. Resumption was essential to the honor of the government and the general welfare. To accomplish this, contraction was necessary, and he recommended legislation which would fix a day in the near future when the notes would cease to be legal tender as to contracts thereafter made, also the conversion of the notes into bonds or their redemption in coin, for the acquisition of which sales of bonds should be authorized.

Grant also adopted stronger language. The failure to make the notes equal to gold was not honorable, and it should be no longer delayed; the duty to act rested with Congress; no real prosperity could be expected unless this first duty was attended to. He recommended a measure removing the limitation upon the volume of national bank-notes, popularly termed "free banking." The premium on gold fluctuated during the year between $14\frac{3}{8}$ and 9 per cent, averaging $11\frac{2}{16}$, and giving an average value to the greenbacks of 89.9.

Resumption act. The Republicans still having control of Congress for the short session ending March 3, 1875, Sherman immediately prepared a bill which, while by no means as satisfactory as might have been expected, was all that in his opinion Congress would assent to. It provided for the retirement of the fractional currency with subsidiary silver coin; the repeal of the gold coinage charge; free banking and the retirement of greenbacks to the extent of 80 per cent of new bank-note issues, until the amount of the former was reduced to $300,000,000; the redemption of greenbacks in coin on and after January 1, 1879; authorized the use of the surplus coin in the Treasury for this purpose and the sale of bonds without limit to provide such further coin as might be needed. The bill was reported from the Finance Committee December 21; passed the Senate December 22 by a vote of

32 to 14 (27 not voting); passed the House January 7, 1875, 136 to 98 (54 not voting). Not one Democratic vote was cast in favor of the measure, and a number of the extreme sound money Republicans in the House voted against it, as not sufficiently strong. Grant approved the bill January 14.[1]

Thus the authors of the legal tender acts, nearly a decade after the disappearance of the only justification for these acts, and after repeated violation of pledges, finally provided for convertibility of notes into coin at a fixed date. The resumption act did not permit the retirement of the greenbacks below $300,000,000, and was cleverly silent upon the question of reissue within the limit, but, obviously, the intention was to retain the currency in use. It gave the Secretary of the Treasury as great, if not greater, powers than the act of 1866, against which Sherman and other majority leaders had protested. Conditions made this necessary, but no more in 1875 than in 1866. On the day the act was signed gold closed at $12\frac{1}{2}$ per cent premium.

The history of this decade is but a repetition of the experience of every nation with fiat money. The first step taken, the rest follows easily — inflation, delusion of the people, breach of faith, disaster. Had the Nation been actually impoverished so that recuperation was long and tedious, some excuse might be found in such conditions. But the Nation was rich enough to reduce its debt during the period by $650,000,000. The use of one-third of that amount in retiring the legal tender debt would probably have brought about specie payments by 1870, and the application of two-thirds would have extinguished it altogether. This would have given the country a stable currency, would have raised the credit of the Nation much more rapidly, and would have

Review of the period.

[1] See Appendix.

saved the people great losses due to depreciation arising from the subsequent troubles.

Unsound currency ideas dominated.

The political leaders were "opportunists," bent upon retention of power, and willing in order to accomplish this purpose to delude the people with the false notions of wealth engendered by such a currency. Wittingly or unwittingly, these leaders helped to engraft upon the public mind, as a sound economic proposition, the absurdity that a currency which fluctuated daily and on some single days lost a tenth of its purchasing power, was the "best that could be devised." It is interesting to note that the surplus gold received from customs which was sold by the government at a premium from 1866 to 1876 exceeded $500,000,000.

The strength of the opposition to resumption and retirement of the greenbacks was located south of the Potomac and west of the Alleghanies, and the reason for this was the same which, as far back as the Jackson days, operated as an obstacle to sound currency legislation, viz. a lack of adequate banking facilities, adverse exchange conditions, and much higher interest rates. This great and growing agricultural section was suffering from conditions which were absent in the eastern sections, and blindly casting about for a remedy, advo-

Demand for "more money."

cated "more paper money." They thought they wanted more currency; what they needed was more capital. The leaders seemed incapable of meeting and solving the problem thus presented, and it was much easier to placate the people with more or less inflation than to devise legislation which would actually bring relief.

Having in mind continually the facts that the legal tender notes were of doubtful constitutionality, were to be but a temporary expedient, were at a fluctuating discount and hence a delusive measure of values, the lack of wisdom in the legislative halls is illustrated in this brief chronological record : —

1862, February	$150,000,000 legal tender notes. Temporary issue, fundable into bonds.
July	$150,000,000 more.
1863, March	$150,000,000 more. Funding right repealed.
1864, June	Limit of notes $400,000,000, and $50,000,000 more for reserve.
1865, December	Almost unanimous declaration of representatives for contraction looking toward retirement.
1866, April	Law providing for contraction, to promote specie payments.
1868, January	Contraction suspended. Volume of notes, $356,000,000.
1869, March	Public Credit Act. Notes payable in coin and to be made so before bonds are redeemed.
1869–1873	Hundreds of millions of bonds redeemed. Notes still at a discount.
1873, December	Reissue of so-called reserve. Increasing notes to $382,000,000. No objection from Congress. Resumption bill defeated.
1874	Inflation bill passed and vetoed. Act fixing maximum of notes at $382,000,000.
1875	Resumption act passed. Specie payments by 1879. Volume of notes to be reduced to $300,000,000.

Note in margin: Chronology of green-backs.

STATISTICAL RÉSUMÉ

NATIONAL FINANCES (in millions of dollars)

FISCAL YEAR	REVENUES			EXPENSES			—Deficit +Surplus	DEBT	
	Customs	Other	Total	Ordinary	Interest	Total		Outstanding	+Inc. −Dec.
1866	179	341	520	386	133	519	+1	2762	+81
1867	176	287	463	203	144	347	+116	2659	−103
1868	164	212	376	230	140	370	+6	2594	−65
1869	180	177	357	190	131	321	+36	2541	−53
1870	195	201	396	164	129	293	+103	2432	−109
1871	206	168	374	158	126	284	+90	2319	−113
1872	216	149	365	153	117	270	+95	2207	−112
1873	188	134	322	180	105	285	+37	2149	−58
1874	163	137	300	194	107	301	−1	2156	+7
1875	157	127	284	172	103	275	+9	2138	−18

CIRCULATION

(In millions of dollars, except last column)

Fiscal Year	Specie	U.S Notes	Bank-Notes		Fractional Currency	Total	In Treasury (Paper only)	In Circulation	Population	Per Capita
			Nat'l	State						
1866	25	401	281	20	27	754	81	673	35.5	$18.99
1867	25	372	299	4	28	728	66	662	36.2	18.28
1868	25	356	300	3	33	717	36	681	37.0	18.39
1869	25	356	300	3	32	716	51	665	37.8	17.60
1870	25	356	300	2	40	723	48	675	38.6	17.50
1871	25	356	318	2	41	742	26	716	39.6	18.10
1872	25	356	338	2	41	762	24	738	40.6	18.19
1873	25	356	347	1	45	774	23	751	41.7	18.04
1874	25	382	352	1	46	806	30	776	42.8	18.13
1875	25	376	354	1	42	798	44	754	44.0	17.16

The Treasury held substantial amounts of gold and the banks some, but this was not used except for special purposes. The amount of interest-bearing notes, not included, which probably circulated during the earlier years (1866–1868), did not exceed $25,000,000 to $35,000,000.

EXPORTS AND IMPORTS

(In millions of dollars)

Fiscal Year	Merchandise			Specie		
	Exports	Imports	Excess + Imports − Exports	Exports	Imports	Excess of Exports
1866 . . .	349	435	+86	86	11	75
1867 . . .	295	396	+101	61	22	39
1868 . . .	282	357	+75	94	14	80
1869 . . .	286	417	+131	57	20	37
1870 . . .	393	436	+43	58	26	32
1871 . . .	443	520	+77	98	21	77
1872 . . .	444	626	+182	80	14	66
1873 . . .	522	642	+120	84	21	63
1874 . . .	586	567	−19	66	28	38
1875 . . .	513	533	+20	92	21	71

The Gold Premium and Prices

Year	Premium on Gold			Gold Value of Paper			Gold [1] Prices U. S.	Wages [1] in Gold	Purchasing Power of Wages	Cost of Gold in Labor
	High	Low	Average	High	Low	Average				
1866 . .	67.8	25.5	40.9	78.6	66.0	71.0	134.0	111.1	.971	.900
1867 . .	46.4	32.0	38.2	74.3	69.7	72.4	123.2	121.8	1.129	.821
1868 . .	50.0	32.1	39.7	74.4	68.7	71.6	125.6	119.1	1.094	.839
1869 . .	62.5	19.5	33.0	82.3	71.8	75.2	112.3	123.5	1.232	.809
1870 . .	23.3	10.0	14.9	90.3	82.4	87.0	119.0	136.9	1.281	.730
1871 . .	15.4	8.4	11.7	91.5	87.3	89.5	122.9	150.3	1.333	.664
1872 . .	15.4	8.5	12.4	91.7	87.4	89.0	121.4	153.2	1.367	.652
1873 . .	19.1	6.1	13.8	92.1	84.9	87.9	114.5	147.4	1.385	.678
1874 . .	14.4	9.0	11.2	91.2	89.1	89.9	116.6	145.9	1.348	.685
1875 . .	17.6	11.8	14.9	88.9	85.4	87.0	114.6	140.4	1.318	.712

[1] Basis of 100 for 1860.

Sales of Gold by the Treasury

(Amounts in millions)

Year	Amount	Premium	Average Rate	Year	Amount	Premium	Average Rate
1867 . . .	38.4	14.2	37 %	1872 . .	77.6	9.4	12 %
1868 . . .	54.2	21.9	41	1873 . .	77.0	11.6	15
1869 . . .	32.0	12.4	39	1874 . .	38.0	5.0	13
1870 . . .	65.1	15.3	24	1875 . .	33.4	4.0	12
1871 . . .	72.4	8.9	11	1876 . .	26.2	3.8	14
				Total . .	514.3	106.5	21 %

CHAPTER X

1876 TO 1890

Resumption
act threat-
ened.

RESU м PTION of specie payments had been decreed by
the act of 1875, but Western Democrats soon began
to talk of repealing the act. The House of Representatives would presently be organized by their party for the
first time since the outbreak of the war. It proved,
however, that almost all of the Eastern members of that
party opposed repeal, while a substantial number of
Western Republicans favored it. The premium on gold
rose considerably on account of these manifestations.
It reached a maximum of $17\frac{5}{8}$, and the average for the
year was $14\frac{9}{10}$ per cent, lowering the average value of
the greenback to 87 compared with 89.9 the previous
year.

Bristow, in December, 1875, reported the redemption
of nearly $9,000,000 of legal tender notes under the
resumption law, but insufficient internal revenues compelled him to sell gold derived from customs, thus preventing its accumulation preparatory to resumption.
The national banks had made use of the privilege under
the recent law of depositing "lawful money" with the
United States Treasurer to retire their circulation, to
the extent of over $37,500,000, so that there was an
actual contraction going on. The policy of paying and
retiring the government's interest-bearing debt was continued during the year, over $30,000,000 of the revenue
being so applied.

Repeal
attempted.

A number of bills to nullify or repeal the resumption
law were presented in the House and considered by the
Banking and Currency Committee, but the presidential

230

contest (of 1876) was at hand, and the Democratic leaders were cautious. Repeated attempts to have the measures brought before the House were defeated until August, when Cox (New York) reported a bill to repeal the clause in the act providing for redemption of United States notes in coin on January 1, 1879, which passed, 106 to 86 (93 not voting). Only 11 Republicans voted aye, while 28 Democrats voted nay. Upon the question of repealing the entire act the vote was 111 to 158 (not voting 20), only 9 Republicans voting aye and 61 Democrats nay. Upon the proposition that the Constitution did not confer on Congress the power to make notes legal tender in time of peace, the vote was 97 to 146 (46 not voting); only 9 Democrats favored and 11 Republicans opposed. *Repeal defeated.*

A Democratic caucus measure proposed, in lieu of the resumption law of 1875, an accumulation in the course of ten years of a coin reserve by the government and banks equal to 30 per cent of the notes of each. It failed to pass in the House, the vote being 81 for, 157 against.

The Republican national platform of 1876 indorsed the policy of resumption. The Democrats, Tilden being their candidate, denounced the Republicans for the delay in bringing about resumption of which they had been guilty, and declared the redemption clause of the act of 1875 a hindrance to resumption.

This year is marked by the separation of the extreme paper money advocates from the two main parties and the organization of the "Greenback" party as a political force. It nominated Peter Cooper for the presideney, demanded the repeal of the resumption act, favored the issue of legal tender notes interconvertible to and for 3.65 per cent bonds, the abolition of bank currency, and the continuation of the fractional currency. *The "Greenback" party.*

The results of the election showed that the people had lost confidence in the Republican party. Their policy lacked the vigor of sincerity in dealing with monetary affairs. They had for fifteen years controlled the government in all its branches, and yet had failed to redeem their pledges. Their reconstruction policy in the South evinced a desire seemingly to build up and develop a political force rather than build up and develop the country so lately devastated by war. The result of the election was close, and the final ascertainment and counting of the deciding votes subjected our institutions and our electoral machinery to a severe strain. Congress and the whole country as well were absorbed in the controversy, and no legislation of a general nature was attempted.

Under the process of redemption under the act of 1875, the volume of legal tenders had been reduced to $367,500,000. New bank circulation amounting to $18,000,000 had been issued, but the banks had at the same time retired circulation to the net amount of $29,100,000. The premium on gold averaged 11½ per cent for the year. The relative commercial value of

Silver agitation begins.

gold and silver was gradually changing. In 1873 the market value of the silver dollar was about 3 per cent greater than the gold dollar, and this fact explains the ease with which the demonetization law passed Congress.[1] Gold was the cheaper metal, and legislators seem prone to favor the standard which tends toward the greater volume of money. The greater relative production of silver had changed the relative price, and the privilege of free coinage of silver would furnish silver producers a steady market for their product at a price much in advance of its commercial value. Their keen sagacity lost no time in seeking through Congress

[1] See Chapter XII.

to remonetize the silver dollar. The proposition was well received by the general public, who had since 1834 known silver as an appreciated and not a depreciated metal. The lower House voted to remonetize silver 167 to 53, and from this Congress dates the birth of the silver party, destined to play such an important part in fiscal and monetary affairs during the ensuing quarter of a century.

President Hayes in his inaugural, March 4, 1877, briefly but firmly supported resumption. He appointed John Sherman Secretary of the Treasury, and plans were at once matured to insure the successful execution of the resumption law. In Congress the House was again Democratic, although by a smaller majority,—20. In the Senate the Republicans had only 38 votes to 37 Democrats and 1 independent, David Davis (Ill.), heretofore a member of the Supreme Court.

Ewing (Dem., O.) at once introduced in the House a bill to repeal the resumption clause of the act of 1875, and reported it favorably from the Banking and Currency Committee October 31. Fort (Rep., Ill.) presented a measure for the same purpose differently worded, which latter measure passed November 23, by a vote of 133 to 120, 27 Republicans (practically all Western men) voting for it and as many Democrats, from the East, against it. Among the Democrats favoring the measure was Carlisle, afterwards Secretary of the Treasury ; voting against it was Foster, also later Secretary. The bill went to the Senate, but remained in the Finance Committee until April 17, 1878. *Resumption act again attacked.*

In December Sherman reported favorable progress in refunding the debt and the sale of bonds to procure gold for resumption purposes. The premium on gold had fallen so that notes were worth 97⅜ per cent. The outstanding legal tenders had been reduced to *Sherman's administration.*

$351,300,000. The trade balance continued favorable, helping him to secure gold. He urged a firm maintenance of the resumption policy — to reverse it would impair the public credit. It will be remembered that under the act of 1875, as new national bank circulation was taken out United States notes were to be retired to the extent of 80 per cent of such amount. He anticipated that bank-notes would not be taken out in sufficient volume to reduce the United States notes under the 80 per cent proviso to the minimum of $300,000,000, hence he recommended funding the excess into bonds, or if the silver dollars were remonetized, these might be used for that purpose.

He said that the act of 1875 did not clearly state whether the notes redeemed after 1879 might be reissued, but he thought they might be. "A note redeemed in coin is in the Treasury, and subject to the same law as if received for taxes or as a bank-note when redeemed by the corporation issuing it." He thought it well to settle the question by legislation, as his views were controverted. This would involve the question of making the notes permanent currency, and he used all the old arguments in favor of doing so with or without the legal tender quality.

He remarked : —

Sherman on greenbacks.

"The Secretary ventures to express the opinion that the best currency for the people of the United States would be a carefully limited amount of United States notes, promptly redeemable on presentation in coin, and supported by ample reserves of coin, and supplemented by a system of national banks, organized under general laws, free and open to all, with power to issue circulating notes secured by United States bonds deposited with the government, and redeemable on demand in United States notes or coin. Such a system will secure to the people a safe currency of equal value in all parts of the country, receivable for all dues, and easily convertible into coin.

Interest can thus be saved on so much of the public debt as can be conveniently maintained in permanent circulation, leaving to national banks the proper business of such corporations, of providing currency for the varying changes, the ebb and flow of trade."

National bank-note issues had diminished in volume, and the fractional currency had been practically replaced by silver coin. The economic conditions of the country were still unsettled, and as usual this was charged to the policy of currency contraction, the resumption law being especially attacked.

We have seen that by the aid of a few Republican votes the bill to repeal the resumption act passed the House. In the Senate, on April 17, 1878, it was reported by Ferry (Rep., Mich.) with a substitute making United States notes receivable in payment or redemption of bonds, and after October 1, 1878, for customs, and providing that the volume in existence at that date was to be the permanent volume and reissuable. By a vote of 30 to 29 this was substituted for the House bill, and then passed by the Senate by 45 to 15. Ten Democrats voted against the House bill and 9 Republicans voted for it.

Repeal defeated.

The House had tired of waiting for the Senate, and on April 29 passed a bill introduced by Fort (Rep., Ill.) to suspend the cancellation of redeemed United States notes, and directing their reissue. The vote stood 177 to 35, the negative vote including only 7 Democrats. Only the strongest representatives could resist the tide ; Foster and McKinley voted for it and Garfield against it. The Senate passed this bill May 28 by a vote of 41 to 18, having first rejected Bayard's amendment that such reissued notes were not to be legal tenders. The affirmative vote included Blaine, Davis, and Windom ; the negative Bayard, Conkling, Hoar, and Morrill.

Contraction suspended.

Generally speaking, the negative vote was from the Eastern states. Sherman favored the measure, and hence Hayes approved it on May 31 without a protest. The volume of notes then, as to-day, was $346,681,016.

Thus Republican votes assisted the Democrats in emasculating the measure to which the former had "pointed with pride," in the previous campaign platform. A veto by Hayes, in the face of the overwhelming votes in both houses of Congress, would very likely have been overridden. It is obvious that the approval of this act was contrary to his convictions, and that but for Sherman's leanings to the policy of continuing the United States notes as a permanent part of our currency, our financial history might have been altered by a vigorous veto of this reactionary measure.

Congress on February 28, 1878, passed the act re-monetizing the silver dollar over the veto of the President. (Discussed in another chapter.) Silver certificates were also provided for in this act. The silver movement developed rapidly in both parties during 1877-1878. The "Greenback ' party had conventions in many of the states and controlled a substantial vote. It had become a force in certain sections, and each of the old parties shaped platforms to gain its support, as well as that of the silver advocates. The election of 1878 gave the Democrats the House by a majority of 19, and the coöperation of 16 Greenbackers. The Senate became Democratic by 12 majority.

Silver certificates.

Despite all these political machinations against the gold standard and resumption, gold, which in January stood at 102, fell below 101 in April, and never thereafter reached that figure. In December it was but $\frac{1}{10}$ of 1 per cent premium, and resumption, so far as equality of notes and gold was concerned, was practically accomplished. Many there were, even astute

Resumption effected.

bankers, who believed even in December, 1878, that resumption would fail; but Sherman had made adequate preparation, and the economic conditions had grown month by month more favorable to his plans. As stated officially in his report in December, 1878, Sherman had Sherman's report.
acquired a gold fund of over $133,000,000, of which $96,000,000 had been derived from bond sales, the balance from surplus revenues, the income of the government having improved as "hard times" passed. He had suspended the issue of gold certificates; had arranged that the Treasury use the New York clearing-house to facilitate and cheapen the collection and payment of checks and drafts, with only partial use of cash, at the point where three-fourths of his payments were made; had concentrated his coin in New York, where alone under the act of 1875, notes could be presented for redemption, and had resolved to receive the legal tender notes for customs without legislation — a privilege he could in the absence of law revoke at any time. He feared that a law making United States notes receivable for customs would deprive the government of the power to exact coin, and might prove embarrassing if an emergency arose. He expressed the view that the act of 1878 prohibiting further cancellation of notes was wise, and stated his purpose to pay either gold or silver in redemption of notes, as preferred by the holder, but reserving to the government the right, which it had under the law, to pay in either.

In his message Hayes recommended that no financial legislation be undertaken to disturb the " healing influences " then at work. The House, notwithstanding, took up the amended repeal bill of the previous session, but on Garfield's motion it was " laid on the table," 141 to 110. Only 5 Republicans voted favorably to the measure, 27 Democrats against it. Thus the reactionary policy was definitely checked. At this time the fractional silver coin had become redundant, and by the act of January 9, 1879, its redemption in " lawful money " was provided for.

Sherman's
policy.
Sherman had to use the same means for resumption proposed by McCulloch, but did so only after much shifting, and in a manner which after all left much of the evil unremedied. While his remarkable changes of policy served to delay resumption, it should be borne in mind that he had much opposition within as well as without his party. He probably went as far in support of sound finance as he could without suffering political defeat. An uncompromising position by the Republican party in favor of retiring the greenbacks, or redeeming them in coin at an earlier day, would doubtless have resulted in placing the opposition in control. In view of that party's attitude, it leaves room for doubt whether after all the halting and vacillating course of the Republican party, typified by Sherman, did not eventuate in the greater good to the country.

No disturbance of currency conditions appeared for some time after resumption. Abundant crops, a large, favorable trade balance, larger investments by foreigners in our securities, caused an enormous inflow of gold. The refunding of the debt proceeded rapidly. Sherman contracted in one day for the placing of nearly $150,000,000 of bonds. Even the issue of the silver dollars and the fall in their commercial value could not affect the progress to solid prosperity, and the Republicans naturally took credit for the " good times " which resulted.

Silver
bullion
notes.
A bill for the free coinage of silver passed the House in May, 1879, but was defeated in the Senate. The reason for referring to it here is to recall one section (introduced by Ewing, Dem., O.), proposing that the

government buy bullion at market price, issue certificates against the same, and retain only 40 per cent of the dollar coined from the bullion as a reserve for their redemption. This passed 106 to 105, Speaker Randall voting aye; only 2 Republicans voted for, and 12 Democrats against, it. A subsequent vote eliminated the section from the bill.

Political conventions of the opposition still declared resumption a failure, in the local campaigns of 1879. Ewing, the author of the repeal bill, candidate for governor of Ohio, was badly beaten by Foster, and the Democratic-Greenback fusion in other states met a similar fate.

Sherman reported in December, 1879, that only about $11,000,000 of notes had been presented for redemption in coin, and the Treasury gold stock had increased nearly $20,000,000. He recommended that the legal tender proviso as to greenbacks be repealed as to future contracts, letting the notes sustain themselves by their convertibility into coin and their receivability for public dues. Thus the question of the constitutionality of making the reissued notes legal tender in time of peace, now before the courts, would be finally determined.

Sherman on legal tender.

The free banking law had not added materially to the volume of bank-notes, which, as Sherman reported, stood at $337,000,000. Thus with $305,800,000 estimated gold, $121,400,000 silver, and $346,600,000 greenbacks, the supply of money was $1,110,000,000. Of this amount, averaging nearly $23 per capita, $260,000,000 was in the Treasury, leaving for general use about $17 per capita.

In his message Hayes congratulated Congress on the successful execution of the resumption act. He urged action, however, to retire the greenbacks, it being his

Hayes on greenbacks.

conviction that the issue of the notes was, except in extreme emergency, "without warrant of the Constitution and a violation of sound principles."

The Greenbackers' platform.

In the House, in April, 1880, Weaver, the Greenback leader, introduced a resolution declaring against bank-notes and favoring the substitution of legal tenders, which was voted down 85 to 117 (not voting 90). Only one member classed as Republican voted for, and 29 Democrats against, it. The resolution also favored the coinage of more silver dollars, and their use in redeeming bonds.

In the presidential contest of 1880 Sherman's chance for the Republican nomination was clearly destroyed by his unstable record on the money question prior to 1877, but the dominating influence of Ohio was so great that Garfield obtained the nomination. The Republicans in their national platform made no promises for the future as to the currency, and seemed content to rest upon their laurels. The Democrats declared for "honest money, — gold, silver, and paper convertible into coin on demand," and the strict maintenance of public faith. Tilden, the logical nominee, was apparently undecided as to acceptance, owing to delicate health, and General Hancock became the nominee. The Greenback party nominated Weaver as its candidate, upon the platform which embodied his resolutions above referred to.

Election of Garfield.

Garfield won by a small plurality of the popular vote, but a large majority in the electoral college. Weaver received over 300,000 votes, against 81,000 for Cooper in 1884. The House of Representatives elected comprised, Republicans 150, Democrats 137, Greenbackers 10. The Senate was again evenly divided, counting Davis of Illinois against the Republicans.

Sherman in December, 1880, reported that only $706,658 notes had been presented for redemption in coin during the year, and his available coin was over $141,000,000, a portion being silver. He regarded the notes in form, security, and convenience the best circulating medium known — a burdenless debt. He concluded that the legal tender quality was not necessary to make them useful, and even if deprived of that, they would be the "favorite money of the people." Indeed be regarded the currency system of the United States the best ever devised. This happy but short-sighted optimism reads strangely in the light of the calamity which the Nation suffered during Cleveland's second administration on account of this "favorite money of the people." Sherman on greenbacks.

On the other hand, Hayes, in his last message, reiterated that the notes should be retired. As a war measure they served their purpose, but their indefinite employment was not warranted. They were a debt and, like any other debt, should be paid and cancelled; their retirement was a step to be taken toward a safe and stable currency. How statesmanlike this reads in contrast with the sentiments of his shifty Secretary!

The greenback agitation had given way to that for silver, in which the advocates of inflation found an easier field for their work. The silver law had increased the "stock of money" by nearly $73,000,000, but only $45,500,000 in dollars and certificates were in circulation, the remainder being in the Treasury, a useless asset. Sherman had indeed, under the law providing for free transportation of coin, effected a larger distribution by offering silver payable in Western and Southern points at par in exchange for gold in New York. The continual issue of silver already threatened the Treasury's reserves. Silver inflation.

Congress, during the short session after the election, passed a bill to refund the 5 per cent and 6 per cent

ᴅ

bonds maturing in 1881 into 3 per cents. The Republicans solidly opposed this measure because the new bonds were limited in amount to $400,000,000, and one section of the bill required national banks to use them exclusively as security for circulation. The bill also authorized the temporary use of the coin reserve in redemption of bonds. Hayes vetoed it upon the first-mentioned ground on the last day of the session.

Refunding
the debt.

This was the condition when William Windom succeeded Sherman in March, 1881, in the cabinet of Garfield, whose untimely death prevented him from impressing his views upon the legislation of that period. Windom remained in the Arthur cabinet for a time, and during the summer, when the 6 per cent and 5 per cent bonds matured, was able, by reason of the general prosperity, to extend the most of them at $3\frac{1}{2}$ per cent, the principal payable at the pleasure of the government, which proved to be one of the most brilliant operations in our financial history. The amount of bonds maturing at that time was $671,500,000, of which $597,800,000 were "continued," the remainder redeemed. The saving of interest was on the basis of nearly $10,500,000 annually, and the cost of the operation was not quite $10,500.

Windom returned to the Senate in November, and his place was taken by Charles J. Folger, of New York, who had in former years been Assistant Treasurer in New York City.

In Congress two measures, separately introduced, finally became law in one act, — the extension of charters of national banks, many of which would soon expire, and the 3 per cent refunding bill. The opposition to the former measure was pronounced, but unavailing. This is known as the act of July 12, 1882, and beside the chief features named above, provided for

Act of 1882.

the issue of gold certificates, making them receivable for all public dues ; both these and the silver certificates were made available for bank reserves, and national banks were forbidden to be members of any clearing-house where silver certificates were refused in payment of balances (which latter proviso was particularly directed against the New York clearing-house). It further pro- Gold reserve vided that the issue of gold certificates be suspended whenever the gold reserved for the redemption of notes fell below $100,000,000, the first legal recognition of the necessity of the " reserve."

At this time it was estimated that the stock of money in the country amounted to over $1,409,000,000, of which the Treasury had $235,000,000. The stock was composed of $506,700,000 gold, $197,000,000 silver, the fixed amount of greenbacks ($346,681,000), and nearly $359,000,000 of national bank-notes. The Treasury had over $35,000,000 in silver dollars in excess of certificates (hence absolutely unavailable) and was coining more.

The era of great prosperity was on the wane, but so long as the tide was favorable, the silver inflation at the rate of nearly $28,000,000 annually was not generally marked. A combination of circumstances again gave the Democrats the control of the House of Representatives, this time by a plurality of seventy-seven. Many states that had been strongly Republican reversed their votes, Massachusetts electing General Butler, now a Greenback-Democrat, governor, by a handsome plurality.

In the year 1883 little occurred directly affecting the legal tender notes, but the continued increase of silver and silver certificates began to show serious results. The national bank currency diminished, and greenbacks being preferred to silver were held back from the Treasury in payments. The government had to use its gold or force out silver only to have it return after a very brief circulation. The growing fear that the continued purchase and coining of silver would eventually disturb the basis of values was accentuated by reactionary business conditions, which, growing in intensity, resulted in a sharp stringency in the money market in May, 1884, — a virtual panic. It was not of long duration, in its intensity, but had a pronounced effect upon business and a very potential influence in the ensuing presidential campaign. During the panicky period the New York City banks, owing to the contraction of their cash reserves, due to hoarding money, as well as the general drain upon their resources, used a device which had been resorted to before on several occasions, to provide an "inter-bank" currency for the purpose of settling debit balances at the clearing-house. Loan certificates were issued by the clearing-house upon deposits of securities by banks amounting in the aggregate to $24,915,000. The first certificates issued bore date May 15.

Crisis of 1884.

Clearing-house certificates.

It was at this time that the Supreme Court decided, with but one dissenting voice, that the power to issue legal tender notes in time of peace as well as in time of war was accorded by the Constitution. In consequence, amendments to the Constitution prohibiting making aught but gold and silver legal tender were proposed, but not acted upon.

Campaign of 1884.

The presidential campaign (Blaine-Cleveland) was conducted upon lines other than the money question. Both parties wished to appear favorable to silver, and both protested that they favored sound money, the Republicans calling for "the best money," the Democrats for "honest money." The Greenback party, nominating General Butler for the presidency, claimed that the Supreme Court had upheld their chief tenet, demanded the substitution of greenbacks for bank-notes, and took special credit for forcing remonetization of silver and suspension of greenback retirement, the two unsound measures of 1878.

The people not only chose Cleveland President, but a House of Representatives strongly Democratic. The Senate continued Republican. The Greenbackers polled 133,000 votes, less than one-half as many as in 1880, and thereafter the party as such disappeared.

Folger died early in 1884, was succeeded by Gresham, previously Postmaster-general, who, however, remained but a few months at the head of the Treasury, resigning to become Circuit Judge. Arthur then turned to Hugh McCulloch and prevailed upon him again to take charge of the Treasury Department for the short period remaining of his administration. With a gold reserve rapidly diminishing, silver payments appeared at several times almost inevitable. The supply of money in circulation was estimated at $1,244,000,000, giving a per capita of $22.65, nearly $6 more than in 1879.

In his report for 1884 McCulloch asserted that, so long as the government issued notes, a reserve must be maintained, and correctly forecast the future in these words : " Many persons regard legal tender notes as being money, and hold that no means should be provided for their redemption. That this is a delusion will be proven whenever there is a large demand for gold for export. They are not money, but merely promises to pay it, and the government must be prepared to redeem all that may be presented, or forfeit its character for solvency." McCulloch's short term.

Silver dollars alone were really available in substantial amounts, but for these there was no demand. From January 1 to August 12 the gold had diminished $39,000,000, and the silver had increased by more than $21,000,000. McCulloch recommended the retirement of all notes under $10 to increase the use for silver and the suspension of coinage of the "white metal."

Early in 1885 McCulloch, with a shrinking gold reserve and only a small balance of greenbacks, actually paid the clearing-house at New York silver certificates. That body had revoked its resolution not to use silver in its transactions; but, by tacit understanding, no member had ever tendered silver up to this time. Prompted by a request not to embarrass the incoming administration, McCulloch did not persist in this policy.

Manning's administration. Daniel Manning became Secretary of the Treasury in the Cleveland administration in March, 1885. The uselessness of calling Congress in extra session was understood, and measures to tide over the dangers from inflation were undertaken by the executive alone. In order to conserve the gold balance, soon reduced to $115,000,000, bond purchases were for a time suspended, and extraordinary efforts were made to put silver into circulation. Under his discretionary power the Secretary discontinued the issue of $1 and $2 greenbacks (silver certificates were then limited to $10 and upwards), and the silver dollar surplus of $71,000,000 was somewhat reduced. The New York City banks exchanged with the Treasury nearly $6,000,000 in gold for subsidiary silver coin.

Treasury conditions. By the time Congress assembled in December, 1885, the Treasury was in much better condition, but still unsafe so long as the laws remained unchanged. Manning, in his report, emphatically attributed the danger to two laws, — the silver purchase act of February, 1878, and the act of May, 1878, suspending the retirement of greenbacks, which, he said, indefinitely postponed fulfilment of the solemn pledge of the public credit act of 1869. He earnestly recommended the repeal of both of these acts, but his argument was directed particularly against the silver law.

Cleveland, in his message, devoted special attention The silver danger. to the evil of the silver purchase and coinage law, by which the Treasury was compelled to pay out $27,000,000 of gold annually for silver, a policy which would soon bring about the single silver standard. Congress was deaf to admonition. A provision was, however, inserted in one of the appropriation acts (August 4, 1886), authorizing the issue of silver certificates in denominations of $1, $2, and $5, which put a substantial amount of silver into use, thereby relieving the Treasury. The country was also recovering rapidly from the effects of the depression following the panic of May, 1884. Revenues increased, and so did the surplus, and the gold reserve was replenished.

In the House Morrison (Dem., Ill.) introduced on July 14 a resolution directing the use of the money in the Treasury in excess of $100,000,000 (including the Treasury surplus. gold reserve) in buying bonds at the rate of $10,000,000 per month. McKinley (Rep., O.) proposed an amendment providing that the $100,000,000 gold, having been accumulated under the resumption act as a reserve fund for the redemption of greenbacks, be maintained for that purpose, and not otherwise used. This was defeated by a vote of 119 to 154. Only five Republicans voted against the amendment, and 13 Democrats, chiefly New York members, voted for it. Morrison's measure passed 207 to 67. The 13 Democrats again voted against it, but over 50 Republicans voted for the resolution. Manning, to whom the resolution had been referred for his opinion, expressed himself vigorously against it.

The Senate amended the resolution so as to give the Treasury a working balance of $20,000,000, and authorized the President to suspend the operation of the measure in case of exigency. The vote was 42 to 20. The negative vote included Beck, Ingalls, Plumb, Voorhees,

Wilson of Iowa, and others favorable to the "more money" policy. The House agreed to the amendments August 4; but as Congress adjourned that day, and the President declined to sign it, the measure failed.

Retirement of notes advocated. In his report for 1886 Manning recommended the application of the large and growing Treasury surplus to the redemption of the legal tender notes, gradually substituting the silver certificates for the notes, thus accomplishing the extinction of a debt actually due without contracting the currency, and at the same time aiding the Treasury in putting its silver funds in circulation. Discussing the decision of the Supreme Court, he urged that the power of making the notes legal tender was not exercised "in relation to any power to borrow money," for money is the standard and measure of the wealth borrowed. Changing the standard in the act of borrowing was "cheating or enriching the lender. Such proceedings found no defender among the lawyers, statesmen, or people. . . . Not until after 1861, when a great danger had beclouded most men's perceptions of financial as well as constitutional law, was a legal tender money made out of the debts of the United States. Not until the infection spread was it ever deliberately argued that any representative of the unit of value could justly be suffered to be made, or to abide, in permanent depreciation and disparity therewith."

Legal tender proviso denounced. He further urged that whether lawful or not to issue such notes after redemption and twenty-one years after the exigency which called them into existence had passed, every argument now forbade the continuance of the "legalized injustice." If the power had been conferred upon Congress by the Constitution, it should now be abrogated. "No executive and no legislature is fit to be trusted with the control it involves over the earnings and the savings of the people."

How unfortunate that Manning's recommendations were not adopted. The first and perhaps the greatest error committed in our financial legislation, after the issue of the legal tender notes, was the repeal of the law permitting them to be funded into government bonds. This closed the door to their retirement and, in the absence of affirmative legislation, left them as a permanent feature of our currency system.

In July, 1886, the silver funds in the Treasury amounted to over $96,000,000, the gold fund had reached $160,000,000, and the outstanding volume of national bank circulation was $311,000,000. The per capita circulation was about $22. Taxation was by no means burdensome, and yet the surplus over expenditure was constantly accumulating in the Treasury. The people were content with the tax budget, and certainly no more fitting or desirable conditions for retiring the legal tender notes could be hoped for. The sin of omission on the part of Congress at this time was most grievous.

Manning was succeeded by Charles S. Fairchild in 1887. The growing surplus in the Treasury had absorbed money from the channels of circulation to such an extent as to embarrass business and occasion uneasiness. Fairchild met the situation and established the policy of depositing receipts from internal revenue with designated national bank depositories, properly secured by United States bonds. About $40,000,000 of the internal revenue was thus placed instead of locking up the money in the subtreasuries.

The year's changes in the Treasury's cash are interesting. Nearly $17,000,000 silver funds had gone into circulation, in addition to the amount coined from monthly purchases of silver bullion, the minimum of which was fixed at $2,000,000. The gold fund was over $200,000,000. The outstanding national bank circula-

Fairchild's administration.

tion was reduced to $279,000,000. The reduction of bank circulation was effected chiefly by the deposit of " lawful money " with the Treasury under the act of June 20, 1874. This fund in the Treasury had gradually grown so that now it amounted to over $100,000,000, awaiting the presentation of bank-notes for redemption.

Cleveland made the surplus the paramount subject of discussion in his message to Congress. Instead, however, of urging retirement of greenbacks with the unused and unnecessary funds in the Treasury, he proposed revision and reduction of the tariff and thereby gave to the Republicans an issue which encompassed Cleveland's defeat in the ensuing presidential campaign.

The surplus again.

A resolution to use the surplus in excess of $100,000,000 again passed the House, without a division. The form was modified from that of the previous years by the insertion of the words " not otherwise specially reserved.' In the Senate it came up early in 1888 and Plumb (Rep., Kan.) proposed an amendment to issue in lieu of national bank-notes retired, Treasury notes redeemable in coin, to be legal tender for all debts public and private. The redemption fund was to be increased pro rata and not to be less than 25 nor more than 30 per cent of the outstanding notes of both kinds. Morrill (Vt.) moved to table the amendment, which was agreed to by a vote of 23 to 22. A little later Plumb offered the same proposition, omitting the words " public and private." Morrill again moved that it lie on the table, which was defeated, 24 to 24, and the Plumb amendment as modified then passed, 28 to 21. Beck (Dem., Ky.) proposed an amendment directing the purchase of silver bullion to the amount of national bank-notes retired, in addition to the purchases under the Bland act, the bullion to be coined and certificates issued, as provided by the act of 1878, which was carried by a vote of 38 to 13, March 26, 1888.   Allison, Cameron, Cullom, and thirteen other Republicans voted for it.   The bill failed in the House.   These proposed amendments to the law and the votes thereon are interesting as showing at a very recent date the attitude of the two great parties and prominent men in relation to greenbacks, silver, and national bank circulation.   Cleveland's pronounced and somewhat extreme anti-protection attitude upon the tariff precipitated many speeches in Congress made for general distribution and general effect, and roused the Republicans to press forward the policy of protection as the cardinal issue before the people.

For the time being the money question again took subordinate position in the campaign.   The platform of the Republicans indeed declared for " sound money," both gold and silver, and *denounced the attempt of the Democrats to demonetize silver*.   The efforts of both parties in turn to convince the silver advocates that " Codlin, not Short " was their friend, is rather amusing.   The Democrats, seriously divided between the sound views of the eastern wing, which was in position to dictate the nominee (Cleveland), and those of the western wing, which was for " more money " of any kind, — paper or silver, — were obviously in no condition to make a decisive declaration.   Thus the tariff became the general issue. *Political campaign of 1888.*

The Greenbackers had returned to their respective affiliations, but there were evidences that a third party, formed by separation of dissatisfied elements from both parties, chiefly in the agricultural sections, would at an early day bring the money question to the front. Cleveland received a plurality of the popular vote in November, but the electoral vote went to Harrison, the House also becoming Republican.   The Senate continued Republican by two majority. *Harrison elected.*

Fairchild's second report was an able presentation of the financial situation. He urged reduction in taxation and relief from the danger involved in the continual purchase and coinage of silver. Congress had granted authority asked for to purchase unmatured bonds at a premium with the surplus, and this resulted in a material reduction of the debt, although by expensive means.

The net silver in the Treasury had been reduced to $54,000,000, the net gold remained about $200,000,000, and public deposits in national banks amounted to $50,000,000. The "lawful money" fund deposited with the United States Treasury by national banks for the purpose of retiring their notes stood at $86,000,000.

Windom's second term. Again in power March 4, 1889, in both houses of Congress and the Executive Department, the Republicans were bent upon aggressive legislation. Windom was appointed Secretary of the Treasury. He continued the policy of reducing the debt by bond purchases, diminishing the gold fund somewhat, but the silver funds even more, bringing the latter down to $32,000,000. Under the pressure of these issues national bank-notes were retired from circulation so rapidly that the volume fell below $200,000,000. The silver question received Windom's special attention. The party leaders were convinced that something had to be done, but since Cleveland had favored the suspension of purchases and coinage of silver, this was His silver policy. not the policy to be adopted. With the desire to satisfy both the agricultural sections, again clamorous for "more money," and the mercantile communities, who urged the suspension, Windom, after an elaborate discussion, recommended a silver measure, which, because its result was a large addition to the volume of legal tender paper, will be outlined here.

He proposed to "issue Treasury notes against de- Treasury note inflation. posits of silver bullion at the market price of silver when deposited, payable on demand in such quantities of silver bullion as will equal in value, at the date of presentation, the number of dollars expressed on the face of the notes at the market price of silver, or in gold, at the option of the government, or in silver dollars at the option of the holder"; and to repeal the compulsory feature of the coinage act of 1878. These notes to be receivable for all public dues the same as the silver certificates. He urged that this would give the country a " paper currency not subject to undue or arbitrary inflation or contraction, nor to fluctuating values," "as good as gold," "an absolutely sound and perfectly convenient currency . . . to take the place of retired national bank-notes . . . meet the wants of those who desire a larger volume of circulation . . . and not encounter the opposition of those who deprecate inflation." He was convinced that the public sentiment demanded the continued use of silver in some form, and he regarded the proposed plan as the least dangerous form of so doing.

Windom's course in the Senate showed that he Windom's was a follower of Sherman, classifiable as a moderate attitude. paper money man, as distinguished from the inflationists like Morton, Logan, and Ferry. He would no doubt have favored the soundest system of money had it been politic to do so, but it was not, in his judgment, wise to fly in the face of the people. Few men could have so skilfully devised a plan calculated to satisfy the silver advocates, the Greenbackers, the gold men, and the inflationists, as well as those who favored contraction.

The plan was hailed by a majority in Congress as a solution of a troublesome problem which the legislators feared to undertake. Nevertheless they were not satis-

The law of 1890.

fled to adopt Windom's plan without tinkering, as the law, which is known as the act of July 14, 1890, shows. Congress insisted upon making the notes legal tender, fixed the amount of silver to be purchased monthly, and in other particulars changed the plan.   In addition, the national bank-note redemption fund, now amounting to $54,000,000, was "covered into the Treasury," to be used as an asset, the obligation to redeem the bank-notes being assumed as a part of the public debt.   The ultra silver element in the two parties was sufficiently strong, if united, to pass a free coinage bill had this measure been defeated.   Indeed the Senate had passed such a bill by a vote of 42 to 25, and the Democrats in the House favored it, but they failed to obtain the support of the silver Republican representatives.

This law, popularly called the Sherman Act, and fully set forth in the discussion of silver legislation in another chapter, caused inflation of the currency by about $50,000,000 in legal tender notes annually, without increasing the gold reserve fund.   At the same session acts were passed under which the revenues were reduced by over $50,000,000, largely by removing the duty on sugar, and the pension disbursements increased by about the same amount, a remarkable trio of laws, after a long period of inactivity on the part of Congress.

Review of the period.

The popular demand for "more money," which during this period influenced political leaders, was based upon false premises.   It came from the large agricultural sections and less developed portions of the country. Noting these vast undeveloped resources, and foreseeing the fortunes which could be speedily made by their rapid development, they exerted their political energies to increase the volume of currency, seemingly expecting that in some undefined way the increase would inure to their benefit.   They seemed oblivious to the fact that however great the volume of currency, no one could receive any portion of it except by giving something of value in exchange, either labor or property. As before stated, these sections needed more capital, not more currency.

That the alleged need for " more money " was fictitious or greatly exaggerated, is demonstrated by the fact that the national bank circulation diminished during the decade (1880–1890) from $359,000,000 to $186,000,000. This was the only form of paper money which was to an appreciable degree affected as to volume by the demands of trade, and the evidence is conclusive that it diminished chiefly because there was no legitimate demand for the continued large volume. The reported gold stock showed an increase of $343,000,000, and the silver supply was augmented $310,000,000; a growth of available money much greater than the increment in population and trade, for the amount per capita of money outside the Treasury, was in 1880 $19.41, in 1890 $22.82.

Volume of money.

STATISTICAL RÉSUMÉ

(Amounts in millions)

NATIONAL FINANCES

FISCAL YEAR	REVENUE			EXPENSES			SUR-PLUS	DEBT	
	Customs	Other	Total	Ordi-nary	Interest	Total		Out-standing	+ Inc. - Dec.
1876	148	142	290	165	100	265	25	2105	− 33
1877	131	150	281	144	97	241	40	2095	− 10
1878	130	127	257	134	103	237	20	2150	+ 55
1879	137	135	272	162	105	267	5	2183	+ 33
1880	187	147	334	169	96	265	69	2072	− 111
1881	198	163	361	177	83	260	101	1986	− 86
1882	220	184	404	187	71	258	146	1820	− 166
1883	215	183	398	206	59	265	133	1686	− 134
1884	195	154	349	190	55	245	104	1586	− 100
1885	181	143	324	209	51	260	64	1540	− 46
1886	193	143	336	192	51	243	93	1495	− 45
1887	217	154	371	220	48	268	103	1367	− 128
1888	219	160	379	215	45	260	119	1293	− 74
1889	224	163	387	241	41	282	105	1171	− 122
1890	230	173	403	262	36	298	105	1067	− 104

CIRCULATION

FISCAL YEAR	SPECIE	SUBSIDIARY SILVER	N. B. NOTES	U. S. NOTES	FRACTIONAL CURRENCY	TOTAL	IN TREASURY	IN CIRCULATION	POPULATION	PER CAPITA
1876	25	27	333	370	34	790	63	727	45	$16.12
1877	25	41	317	360	20	763	41	722	46	15.58
1878	41	61	324	347	17	790	61	729	48	15.32

CIRCULATION — (*Continued*)

Fiscal Year	Gold and Gold Certificates	Silver Dollars and Certificates	Subsidiary Silver	U. S. Notes	N. B. Notes	Total	In Treasury	In Circulation	Population	Per Capita
1879	246	41	70	347	330	1034	215	819	49	$16.75
1880	352	70	73	347	344	1186	212	974	50	19.41
1881	478	95	74	347	355	1349	235	1114	51	21.71
1882	506	123	74	347	359	1409	235	1174	52	22.37
1883	542	152	75	347	356	1472	242	1230	54	22.91
1884	546	180	75	347	339	1487	243	1244	55	22.65
1885	588	208	75	347	319	1537	245	1292	56	23.02
1886	591	237	75	347	311	1561	309	1252	57	21.82
1887	654	277	76	347	279	1633	316	1317	59	22.45
1888	706	310	76	347	252	1691	319	1372	60	22.88
1889	680	344	77	347	211	1659	278	1381	61	22.52
1890	695	380	77	347	186	1685	256	1429	63	22.82

EXPORTS AND IMPORTS

Fiscal Year	Merchandise			Specie		
	Exports	Imports	Excess + Imp. − Exp.	Exports	Imports	Excess + Imp. − Exp.
1876	540	461	− 79	57	16	− 41
1877	602	451	− 151	56	41	− 15
1878	695	437	− 258	34	30	− 4
1879	710	446	− 264	25	20	− 5
1880	836	668	− 168	17	93	+ 76
1881	902	643	− 259	19	110	+ 91
1882	751	725	− 26	49	42	− 7
1883	824	723	− 101	32	28	− 4
1884	741	668	− 73	67	37	− 30
1885	742	578	− 164	42	43	+ 1
1886	679	635	− 44	72	39	− 33
1887	716	692	− 24	36	60	+ 24
1888	696	724	+ 28	46	59	+ 13
1889	742	745	+ 3	97	29	− 68
1890	858	789	− 69	52	34	− 18

THE GOLD PREMIUM AND PRICES

Year	Premium on Gold			Gold Val. of Paper			Gold Prices U.S.	Wages Gold	Purchasing Power of Wages	Cost of Gold in Labor
	High	Low	Average	High	Low	Average				
1876	15.0	07.0	11.5	92.5	87.4	89.6	108.7	134.2	1.310	.745
1877	07.9	02.5	04.8	97.3	93.9	95.5	107.0	135.4	1.314	.738
1878	02.9	00.0	00.8	99.9	97.5	98.6	103.2	139.0	1.366	.719
1879	—	—	—	—	—	—	95.0	139.4	1.443	.717
1880	—	—	—	—	—	—	104.9	143.0	1.383	.699
1881	—	—	—	—	—	—	108.4	150.7	1.424	.663
1882	—	—	—	—	—	—	109.1	152.9	1.438	.654
1883	—	—	—	—	—	—	106.6	159.2	1.523	.628
1884	—	—	—	—	—	—	102.6	155.1	1.523	.644
1885	—	—	—	—	—	—	93.3	155.9	1.634	.642
1886	—	—	—	—	—	—	93.4	155.8	1.631	.642
1887	—	—	—	—	—	—	94.5	156.6	1.627	.638
1888	—	—	—	—	—	—	96.2	157.9	1.621	.633
1889	—	—	—	—	—	—	98.5	162.9	1.645	.614
1890	—	—	—	—	—	—	93.7	168.2	1.757	.594

CHAPTER XI

The Legal Tender Cases in the Supreme Court

THE question of taxing certificates of indebtedness and legal tender notes came before the Supreme Court for review on writs of error and was decided in 1868. The first-named form of security was declared not subject to municipal taxation in the case of Bank of New York *vs.* The Comptroller of New York City (7 Wall. 16) and the tax was declared unconstitutional. In another case, Bank of New York *vs.* Supervisors (7 Wall. 26), it was held that although the greenbacks circulated as money, they were also obligations of the United States, and hence not taxable. Legal status of green-backs.

Respecting legal tender, it was held in The County of Lane *vs.* The State of Oregon (7 Wall. 71) that taxes laid by a state were not "debts ' within the meaning of the legal tender act. In Bronson *vs.* Rodes (7 Wall. 229) it was held that an express contract to pay coin was not dischargeable with legal tender notes, one justice (Miller) dissenting from the decision.

As to the validity of the act of Congress taxing state bank-notes 10 per cent, it was held in Veazie Bank *vs.* Fenno (8 Wall..533) that the act was constitutional, the federal government having the power to tax out of existence such form of currency in order to make room for another form if national in character. Two justices, Nelson and Davis, dissented. State bank-note tax.

It was also held that the shares of stock in a national bank were subject to state tax even though the entire capital of the bank were invested in United States bonds.

The tax was held to be in the nature of a franchise tax or license to do business, and hence within the power of the state to impose.

Historical. The main question, whether the legal tender acts themselves were constitutional, did not come before the Supreme Court until 1867, and the decision was not published until February 7, 1870. (Hepburn *vs.* Griswold, 8 Wall. 603.) Circumstances attending this decision and its subsequent reversal (Legal Tender Cases, 1871, 12 Wall. 457) caused so much comment at the time that they will be given place here.

The Court in 1867 consisted of eight members, as follows: Chief Justice Chase, formerly Secretary of the Treasury, whom Lincoln appointed in 1864 upon the death of Chief Justice Taney, and who had for some time been regarded as more of a Democrat than a Republican; Justices Grier, Nelson, Clifford, and Field, looked upon as Democrats; and Justices Miller, Davis, Composition and Swayne, regarded as Republicans. An act of Congress of July 23, 1866, provided that the Court be reduced to seven members, the reduction to be effected by not filling the next vacancy caused either by death or retirement. While the first legal tender case was pending, a decision against the validity of the act was anticipated, and an act was passed in April, 1869, to take effect December 1, 1869, restoring to the Supreme Court the previous membership of nine. It was expected that Justice Grier would soon retire, thus enabling the appointment of two justices with Republican antecedents and favorable to the view of that party — that the greenbacks were, and should remain, lawful money.[1]

The case, as stated, came before the Court in 1867, but owing to its importance was held for reargument until 1868, and was actually decided November, 1869,

[1] Schuckers, Life of Chase.

by the expected vote, 5 to 3. The form of the opinion was, as is the custom, submitted to conference and adopted January 29, 1870, and would have been published two days later, but a week was given to the dissenting justices (Miller, Davis, and Swayne) to prepare their views.[1] On February 1, 1870, Justice Grier retired, and on the 14th of that month William Strong of Pennsylvania was appointed in his stead by President Grant. In March following Joseph P. Bradley of New Jersey was appointed to fill the place which the act of April, 1869, had "revived." Both of these appointees were known to favor the legal tender act, Justice Strong, when on the bench in his own state, having written an elaborate opinion declaring it constitutional.

The decision in Hepburn *vs.* Griswold was written by Chief Justice Chase, who thus passed upon the validity of his own acts as Secretary of the Treasury. The debt in this case had been contracted in 1860 and fell due February 20, 1862 (five days prior to the approval of the legal tender act). It was not paid, nor was payment tendered until March, 1864.

Hepburn vs. Griswold.

The opinion held that the act by its terms was manifestly intended to apply to all debts, those contracted before as well as those incurred after the act (from this there was no dissent); that therefore the act impaired the obligation of contract, compelling a creditor to receive $1000 in paper, in lieu of coin, when in fact $1000 in coin was at the time equal to $2000 or more in paper, and thus an arbitrary injustice would be done. The power to do this was not granted by the Constitution either expressly or impliedly. The power of Congress is limited by the fundamental law. Not only specifically expressed powers may be exercised, but it was within the power of Congress by implication to

Chief Justice Chase's opinion.

[1] Chase in the dissent, 12 Wall.

employ such means, not prohibited by nor repugnant to the Constitution, as were necessary and appropriate to execute any of the express powers. The power to determine what shall be legal tender is a governmental one, and in the United States vested in Congress so far as relates to *coins ;* but this grant of power does not carry with it that of clothing paper with the same quality. The emission of Treasury notes was, as a form of borrowing, held to be valid, but this did not carry with it the power to make them legal tender. Manifestly, if Congress were clothed with power to adopt any and all means it saw fit in executing the express powers granted by the Constitution, it had absolute power, which was not consistent with American ideas of government.

It was denied that giving the notes legal tender power was "appropriate" or "plainly adapted" to the purpose in view. It did not save them from depreciation but added to the long train of evils which irredeemable currency always brings, and since the result necessarily was an impairment of existing contracts and also the taking of private property (so large a portion of which consisted of contracts) without due process of law, the act was inconsistent with and prohibited by the Constitution.

In dissenting, Justice Miller urged that under the express power to declare war, support an army and navy, borrow money and pay national debts, provide for the common defence and general welfare, Congress had, in the emergency, no other recourse to save the government and the Constitution. The legal tender act furnished the means, the ordinary use of the government's credit having failed. It was passed reluctantly only after it had become imperative. That if, as the Court had just previously ruled (Veazie Bank case), in order to provide a national currency either by means of government notes or national bank-notes, Congress could place a prohibi-

Power of Congress.

Dissenting views.

tive tax on state bank-notes, how much more appropriate and effectual for the purpose it was to give the government notes legal tender power. Undoubtedly contracts were impaired, but the states, not Congress, were prohibited by the Constitution from enacting laws impairing the validity of contracts. National bankruptcy laws are constitutional although they clearly impair contracts. As to taking property without due process of law, the legal tender act does so indirectly, but so do other acts for great national purposes — the tariff laws, a declaration of war, additional bond issues depreciating those already out. Moreover, by declaring the act void all business would be disturbed, millions of dollars sacrificed, and thus great injustice done. In conclusion, the choice of means, the degree of necessity, lay with Congress, and were not questions for the Court to determine.

Broad construction.

So the legal tender act was declared unconstitutional. It was currently reported at the time that Chase, Nelson, and Clifford held that the act was void for all purposes; Grier and Field only as to preëxisting contracts. The decision occasioned no surprise and made no disturbance, as it was confidently believed that the Court, enlarged by the new appointees, would reverse the decision when occasion arose. The occasion was not long delayed. In the December term of 1870 several cases came up and were decided in May, 1871, the decision being published in January, 1872. The public expectation was realized, and the former decision reversed by a vote of 5 to 4.

The reversal of 1871-1872.

The opinion of the Court was written by Justice Strong, a concurring opinion by Justice Bradley, and dissenting opinions were filed by the Chief Justice, Justice Clifford, and Justice Field. The manner in which this' important decision was brought about was severely criticised as a radical departure from the settled practice of the Court, and it was reported that, for the first time in its history, heated arguments and recriminations were heard at its sessions.[1]

Justice Strong gave as a reason for reopening the question, the plea that the Court had not been full when Hepburn *vs.* Griswold was decided. To this Chase replied by pointing to the dates (heretofore stated), from which it is apparent that until the act of April, 1869, took effect (December, 1869), the Court was full, with a membership of eight, and would have been full if there had been but seven, so a full Court *heard* and decided the case. The form of the opinion was not agreed upon until after December, 1869, but the Court might then have been full had the President made an appointment, which he delayed until 1870, obviously because the vote would still have been against the validity of the act, and Justice Grier would not accommodate the President by retiring prior to the filing of the opinion.

Justice Strong's opinion. The revised opinion of the Court stated that if the United States could not *in any emergency* make Treasury notes legal tender, as other sovereignties did, the government was without the means of self-preservation. If the legal tender acts were held invalid, great business derangement, distress, and rankest injustice would be caused, since almost all contracts made since 1862 were made with the intent to discharge them in legal tender notes which have become the universal *measure of values.* Debtors would have a large percentage added to their obligations. No distinction could be made as to debts preëxisting. The act affected all obligations.

The incompatibility of laws with the Constitution must be plain before they can be declared invalid, for the presumption was in favor of laws of Congress being constitutional. The general purpose of the Constitu-

[1] Schuckers, Life of Chase.

tion must be considered and the intent of the framers discovered. It could not name specifically every power to be exercised, and the manifest object being to establish a sovereign government, every means not prohibited could be employed, *especially for its preservation.* The "general welfare" clause (Article I, Section 8) provides for that. The reasons for the first ten amendments to the Constitution were clearly to prohibit certain powers supposed to be deducible from the original document. If then the object were one for which the government was framed, the means conducive to the end were to be determined by Congress, if necessary, appropriate and not prohibited, nor could the degree of necessity be reviewed by the Court. It must therefore be clearly shown that the means were *not* appropriate, and due weight must be given to the exigencies of the case.

Preservation of government imperative.

At the time of the passage of the acts the Treasury was empty, the credit exhausted, the army unpaid, and the existence of the government at stake. The legal tender notes saved the country from disaster. If nothing else *could* have saved it, no one would question the power of Congress to take the course it did. Even if other means might have been employed, the Court could not therefore interfere, as the choice lay with Congress. But there were no other means. The then head of the Treasury Department (Chase) had seen no way to avoid the necessity.

Congress to determine means.

The legal tender notes having proved effective, the act must have been appropriate to the purpose. And if, as had been admitted in the Veazie Bank case, Congress could tax state bank currency to enable a national currency to circulate, it could certainly choose the more direct means of making the latter legal tender.

To the objection that the clause authorizing the coinage of money and fixing the value thereof by implication excluded the power to make paper legal tender, it was maintained that such a rule of construction was out of harmony with the entire history of the court; indeed it might more logically be held that as the states were prohibited from making aught but coin legal tender, it was intended that the federal government should have that power as other governments had. Whatever power over the currency existed was vested in Congress. If the power to declare what is and shall be money is not vested in Congress, it is annihilated. If this was intended, would it not, as in other cases where governmental powers were *prohibited*, have been definitely stated? In the absence of such a prohibition, is it not reasonable to say that it was intended to be used under the grant of the power to regulate the value of money?

Intent of Constitution.

As to the impairment of contract obligations by the acts, it has been held repeatedly that contracts to pay money generally are obligations to pay that which is money when payment is to be made. The coinage law of 1834 changed the weight of gold coins, and certainly could not be held unconstitutional. It was denied therefore that the acts did impair the obligation of contracts, since every contract to pay money is subject to the constitutional right of Congress over money. Congress is not prohibited from passing such a law; both expressly and by implication is the power given, as in bankrupt laws, declaration of war, embargo laws, tariff laws, and laws changing the coinage. All take from the worth of contracts and indirectly take private property, but they are part of the legitimate governmental functions which private contracts cannot defeat. However harsh or unjust, these considerations alone do not make them unconstitutional.

Power of Congress over money.

As to the alteration of the standard of value, the acts do not make paper a standard of value. It is not claimed that this power to issue rests on the power to coin money or regulate its value. It is not asserted that Congress can make anything which has *no value* money. But Congress has the power to enact that the government's promise to pay money shall be money *for the time being*, equivalent in value to the representative of value determined by the coinage acts. The legal tender acts fix no standard of value, nor do they make money of that which has no intrinsic value.

In dissenting, Chief Justice Chase asserted that it was the plain duty of the Court to declare unconstitutional any act of Congress not made in the exercise of express power, or coming within Marshall's rule that it is "necessary and proper," if under an implied power. Congress may not adopt any means it may deem fit, even to carry out an express power. The means must be "necessary and proper," and the Court is to determine the question. The necessity, however, need not be absolute. The power to tax state bank-notes was exercised under the express grant to regulate the value of money. *Chase's dissenting views.*

The occurrences of the war did not make the acts necessary. The notes would have circulated without the legal tender power, to which he had reluctantly assented as Secretary of the Treasury, only because he could not otherwise get authority to issue notes that were necessary. The legislation he favored contemplated notes receivable for public dues, which function would have fully served the purpose. Giving them compulsory circulation by the acts in question was an element of depreciation, a declaration that the government was insolvent. Every honest purpose would have been served without making them legal tender. The acts were really harmful, and largely increased the debt by the inflation consequent upon the great depreciation which these notes suffered. Not only were they not necessary, but they directly violated the express pro- *Legal tender quality unnecessary.*

visions of the Constitution.   To be warranted, laws must be not only not prohibited by, but also consistent with, the Constitution in letter and spirit, as Marshall stated.

The powers cited under which Congress may impair contracts or take private property are undisputed express powers.   Bankrupt laws are the only ones which Congress may pass directly affecting contracts; implied powers require different construction.

Congress no doubt had the power to issue notes, and it was also its duty to establish a standard of value, in order to measure values, but *every presumption* is against the interpretation that aught but gold and silver could be adopted for the purpose.   All legislation contemporaneous with and subsequent to the adoption of the Constitution and all judicial decisions until 1862, as well as all the facts in our history, sustain this view.   The published discussions of the framers of the Constitution, from which their intent must be deduced, show that they intended to cut off every pretext for making paper legal tender.   Webster's opinion was unequivocal that Congress had no power to make paper legal tender, and the Court had frequently held that coin alone constituted a legal tender under the Constitution.

Review of decisions.

It cannot be disguised that an exigency, not entirely free from a political coloring, influenced the rehearing and the decision of 1872.   Tried by the cold facts of history, the conclusion that the framers of the Constitution intended to absolutely prohibit the issue of paper as money with legal tender power seems unavoidable.   That the majority opinion was somewhat influenced by its probable effect is shown by the two opening paragraphs, in which the great distress likely to follow an affirmation of the decision in Hepburn *vs.* Griswold was set forth. The "debtor class," a phrase then very much in vogue among politicians, was referred to in sympathetic terms.

It is difficult to see how the *legal* status of the measure could be affected by the question whether debtors or creditors were upon the whole more numerous, or whether debtors were suffering more at the moment than creditors suffered when they were compelled to accept depreciated paper on anterior contracts. Moreover, the Court seemed to lose sight of the fact that its decision continued a depreciated currency, from which the masses always suffer most and the shrewd minority profit most.

Depreciated currency continued.

The evidence, however, is all but conclusive that the war could not have been carried on and the Union saved without a United States note-issue, and that the note-issue would not have been successful without the forced currency feature was evidently the opinion, at the time of Lincoln, Chase, and the leaders in Congress.

Justice Strong, despite the sweeping character of his opinion, qualified the power of Congress over the legal tender feature by the phrase "for the time being." Granted that the exercise of power was necessary, it was the almost unanimous opinion of those in Congress who voted for the act that it was but a temporary expedient; as such it was a necessary and proper public policy; although an evil, the remedy was to be speedily applied when the emergency passed. Virtuously indignant at the suggestion that they were about to create paper money, the leaders pledged a retracing of steps when the object was accomplished. They broke their pledges, for practically the same men were at the helm in 1865 and in 1868.

"Temporary expedient" made permanent.

The Court incidentally pointed out the underlying purpose of the first and second legal tender acts, which was that the notes should be funded at the option of the holder. The provision in the act of March 3, 1863, which repealed the funding pledge, is responsible for the trouble incident to the legal tender notes. Had that privilege been continued, these notes would have largely disappeared and national bank-notes have taken their place. The maintenance of a necessary volume of currency would doubtless have brought about free banking at an earlier date, and the trials and tribulations which this "temporary' currency in the forty years of its existence has brought the nation would have been in large measure avoided.

The Court had settled the right of Congress to issue legal tender notes in an emergency, but could these notes be reissued in time of peace? Had Congress the power to issue, at any time in its discretion, legal tender notes? This question was brought before the Court in the case of Juilliard vs. Greenman (110 U. S. 404, 1884) and argued by General Benjamin F. Butler and Senator George F. Edmunds respectively for and against the unlimited power of Congress to issue such notes.

Decision of 1884.

The majority of the Court (Justice Field alone dissenting) held that the Constitution created a national sovereignty, quoting the grants of express powers to lay taxes, to borrow money, to regulate commerce, to coin money and regulate its value, and the power to make all laws necessary and proper to carry into effect these and all other powers vested in it by the Constitution. It was repeated from previous decisions that the necessity need not be absolute and indispensable, and the power might include all means appropriate in the judgment of Congress. Expressly prohibited from making anything but gold and silver a tender, or passing laws impairing the obligation of contracts, the states could not exercise these powers. The question whether the framers intended to likewise prohibit the federal government from issuing paper money and making it a legal tender for private debts, in view of the silence of the Constitution, was answered in the negative; the power to borrow and

emit evidences of debt (*i.e.* bills of credit) was not con-
tested; the power to create banks for the issue of notes
was likewise conceded: as a logical consequence Congress has the power to issue its own bills of credit in
such form and with such qualities as currency as accord
with the usage of sovereign governments. The authority
to confer the legal tender quality is incident to the powers
referred to and universally understood to belong to other
sovereignties, and not being prohibited, it was within the
power of Congress. The power is as broad as that of
coining money and regulating commerce, nor is it restricted by the fact that the value of contracts may be
affected. And the question whether the issue is to be
made in times of special exigency, such as war, or generally in times of peace, is one solely for Congress to
determine.

Justice Field, dissenting, maintained that the history
of the events preceding the adoption of the Constitution
left no room for doubt as to the intent of those who
framed the instrument, respecting legal tender paper
and impairment of contracts. The analogy of power
exercised by other sovereignties was not pertinent, since
the organic law clearly limited the powers of Congress.
Neither the needs of the government nor the fact that
the Constitution was silent on the subject could give the
power. The power to borrow money did not include
the power to make the notes issued legal tender as
to private contracts, thus giving the debtor special privileges to pay his creditor less value than he agreed.
Such a power would enable the government to interfere
with all property rights. Nor was the power incident
to that of coining money, which did not mean coining
anything but metals. To claim such power was logically
claiming the power to debase the coinage, acknowledged
by all to be monstrous iniquity.

Strict con-
struction of
implied
powers.
Manifestly, if the power is not granted it is withheld, and to construe it as impliedly granted it must not only be appropriate, not prohibited, but, as Marshall also said, consistent with the letter and spirit of the Constitution. Since the United States notes had been greatly depreciated and might again be so, oppression and injustice resulted, and a law promoting either of these conditions was not consistent with the Constitution. He reminded the majority that upon the subject of laws impairing the obligation of contracts Marshall had also said, "It is against all reason and justice for a people to intrust a legislature with such powers, and therefore it cannot be presumed that they have done so" (3 Dall. 388).

If Congress has the power claimed by the majority, it may issue such notes indefinitely and pay its bonds with them, no matter how depreciated. Why then should the government continue paying interest on the bonds when the principal might be paid in a day?

Bancroft on
the decision.
The historian George Bancroft, already referred to, maintained, in reviewing the decision,[1] that the evidence was complete that it was the unalterable purpose of the framers of the Constitution to prohibit legal tender paper. He declared the dictum that the federal government had sovereign powers to be revolutionary. Its powers were clearly *limited*. It had no inherent sovereignty, but only that delegated to it by the Constitution. European sovereignties had *not* the power of making notes legal tender. The attitude of Bancroft illustrates the frame of mind in which the decision was received by many of our strongest and best men.

General
comment.
When the federal Constitution was created and adopted the people were in a revulsion of feeling over the suffering caused by the great depreciation of the Continental currency. It depreciated on every one's

[1] Bancroft, A Plea for the Constitution.

hands. The Continental Congress redeemed some of
its issues at an enormous discount in new issues that in
turn suffered a great depreciation. There is no doubt
that the framers of the Constitution intended, and thought
they had succeeded in, prohibiting Congress from issuing
an irredeemable currency and making the same a tender
for debt. The federal government was a compromise
in which the states sought by united strength to command respect and achieve consequence in the sisterhood
of nations, at the same time jealously retaining their
local sovereignties in order to avoid the dangers which
experience had taught them to apprehend from a strong
central government. In respect to intercommunication
they were remote from each other with the means of
travel existing at the time, and naturally wished their
local governments interfered with as little as possible.
The adoption of the federal Constitution gave to the
people two sovereigns — a double allegiance. The question which was paramount, state or national, was an
active issue until settled by the sword and sealed in
favor of the Nation, by the surrender at Appomattox.
A strengthening of the central government inevitably
ensued. State sovereignty ceased to be an influence,
and the courts were left free to discriminate between
what the framers of the Constitution had done and
what they thought they had done.

State sovereignty the issue.

Above all things the framers of the Constitution intended to create a perpetual government, and when the
life of the government was at issue the technical reading of the Constitution yielded perforce to broader lines
gauged by the civic and economic changes which a
century had wrought. The law of self-preservation construed the Constitution broadly as to the power of Congress over currency, in the interest of preserving the
government.

Nationalism dominated.

II. THE SILVER QUESTION

CHAPTER XII

1861 TO 1878

Capital and currency distinguished.

"CAPITAL is that portion of all the previous product of a nation which at any given time is available for new production. This will be a certain amount of tilled land, houses, buildings, stock, tools, food, clothing, roads, bridges, etc., which have been made and are ready for use in producing, transporting, and exchanging new products. These things are all the product of labor, and require time for their production. Nothing but labor spent upon them can produce others, and time is required for this labor to issue in new and increased possessions. Currency only serves to distribute this capital into the proper hands for its most efficient application to new production. Banks, it must be repeated, only facilitate the transfer of capital from hands where it is idle into hands by which it will be usefully employed. Currency, therefore, is not capital, any more than ships are freight; it is only a labor-saving machine for making easy transfers. Banks do not create wealth, they only facilitate its creation by distributing capital in the most advantageous manner. If, therefore, currency is multiplied, it is a delusion to suppose that capital is multiplied, or, if ' money is plenty,' by artificial increase of its representatives, it is only like increasing the number of tickets which give a claim on a specific stock of goods — the ticket-holders would be deceived and could, in the end, only get a proportional dividend out of the stock." — SUMNER, *A History of American Currency*.

Erroneous views.

For a quarter of a century the standard of value was imperiled, business disturbed, and the value of all property subjected to uncertainty by a propaganda on the part of a large portion of our people laboring under the conviction that *currency was capital* and that the free coinage of the silver product of our mines, at the behest of any one choosing to present the same at the mints, would add that vast sum to the capital of the country in form adapted to current use. The fiat of the government can impart legal tender quality to currency, either coin or paper, but its value as expressed in articles of commerce — what it will buy — is determined by its commercial value or by its convertibility into money whose commercial value is equal to its nominal currency value.

During the Civil War the coins of the United States disappeared from circulation owing to the premium thereon following suspension of coin payments in December, 1861. The only exception was in the country west of the Rocky Mountains, where the gold product of California assisted the people there, so far away from the seat of war and possessing but indifferent means of communication with the rest of the country, to maintain the coin standard. The specie in the rest of the country was in the Treasury, in banks or in private hoards, there being no substantial amount of coin in circulation outside the Treasury after 1863–1864.

Disappearance of specie.

The country exported the greater part of its estimated stock of $250,000,000 (1861) and its annual product besides.

No coinage laws whatever were passed from 1861 to 1865, and then only minor coins were provided for. Secretary Chase indeed recommended (1862) that the five-dollar gold piece be made equal to the British sovereign, but nothing came of it.

The mints turned out from 1861 to 1867 the following amounts : —

Gold coin	$230,358,000
Silver dollars	306,000
Subsidiary coin	8,731,000
Minor coin	5,638,000

The commercial ratio of silver to gold fluctuated between 15.35 and 15.57 to 1, indicating a value for the silver dollar of from $1.04 to $1.02½.

First monetary conference.

In 1867 an international monetary conference met in Paris at which this country was represented. This body among other things recommended the adoption of the single gold standard and an international coin. The latter proposition was favorably received. The Senate Finance Committee (June 9, 1868) made a report recommending the coinage of a dollar 3½ cents less in value than the existing one, thus making it equal to 5 francs. It was expected also that the British sovereign would be so modified as to make it exactly 25 francs or five of the proposed dollars. Nothing further was done in the matter.

Silver product increased.

The production of silver in the United States, which in 1861 was estimated at $2,000,000, steadily increased, chiefly due to the rich discoveries in Nevada; by 1868 the product was $12,000,000, in 1872 $28,750,000. The coinage of silver dollars increased at once, and from 1868 to 1872 over 3,200,000 of them were struck, and practically all were exported.

Germany's action.

The Franco-German War at this time (1870–1871) had a most important and far-reaching effect upon the monetary standards of the world. The brilliancy of the German campaign and the triumph of her arms placed the new empire in the front rank of military powers. She received an enormous war indemnity from France, 5,000,000,000 francs ($965,000,000), all of which was paid in a comparatively short time after the conclusion of peace. The prestige of her arms and the condition of her treasury greatly facilitated the work of welding together the separate states, commercially as well as politically, into one harmonious whole. The dream of the Hohenzollern was realized and a unified Germany was the result. The commercial aspirations of the German Empire proved equal to its military ambition, and turning to Great Britain, the chief commercial nation, as an exemplar, its banking system was copied largely and the gold standard adopted. The coinage of the country, which differed in the separate states, was unified, and the sale of the greater part of the old silver pieces was determined upon. France, in order not to be swamped with the white metal at its open mints, suspended silver coinage for the public, and the other nations belonging to the Latin Union followed her example.[1] The action of these nations in suspending the free coinage of silver has been held by many to be the principal cause of the fall in its commercial value.

Latin Union suspends silver coinage.

Contemporaneously with these events Congress was at work upon the revision of the mint laws, and its labors resulted in what is known as the coinage law of 1873. This revision was the result of several years of work and discussion, begun in 1869 by John Jay Knox under the direction of Secretary Boutwell.

United States coinage laws revised.

The report and draft of the bill were transmitted to the Senate early in 1870, referred to its Finance Committee, and ordered printed. The House received the documents in June, 1870.

The original bill made the gold dollar the unit of value, discontinued the coinage of the silver dollar, the half dime and three-cent piece, and the report not only called attention to the proposed discontinuance, but discussed the reasons for doing so. It had been proposed to have a dollar, subsidiary in character, of 384 instead of $412\frac{1}{2}$ grains, with legal tender power the same as subsidiary pieces, but this was finally eliminated from the bill. Obviously the reason for recommending the dis-

Gold dollar unit.

---

[1] The Latin Union consists of France, Italy, Switzerland, Belgium, and Greece.

continuance of the old dollar of 412½ grains was that its value (some 7½ per cent greater than that of the subsidiary silver) was then $1.02 in the world's markets. It was not provided for in any draft of the bill from the first to the passage thereof in 1873. The section omitting it (15th, afterward 16th) never mentioned it at any stage.

History of the act of 1873.

The bill was reported, with amendments, to the Senate December, 1870, debated and passed by a vote of 36 to 14 on January 10, 1871. Senator Sherman voted against, and Senator Stewart of Nevada for, the bill, but there was no division on the question of omitting the silver dollar and no amendment was offered to restore the same.

The bill reached the House January 13 and went to the Coinage Committee. It was not acted upon in that Congress, however, and in the next Representative Kelley (Rep., Pa.) reported the same bill from the committee after it had, as he said, "received as careful attention as I have ever known a committee to bestow on any measure." Subsequently it was amended to include a 384-grain dollar; on April 9, 1872, it was debated and every section discussed. The fact that the bill made gold the sole standard was also debated, Kelley stating that it was "impossible to retain the double standard." He called attention to the fact that the old silver 'dollar was worth more than the gold dollar, remarking also that "every coin that is not gold is subsidiary." On May 27, 1872, it passed by a vote of 110 to 13; the negative vote was not due to the omission of the silver dollar.

Trade dollar provided for.

The Senate amended the bill January 17, 1873, with a provision for the unlimited coinage of a "trade dollar" of 420 grains, commercially worth more than the Mexican dollar, to compete with the latter in the Oriental trade. Thus amended it became a law on February 12,

1873.[1] It was therefore before Congress nearly three
years, printed at least ten times, debated on several
occasions, and attention was directed to the omission of
the old silver dollar.   Nevertheless Kelley, a few years
later, said that he "did not know that the bill omitted
the silver dollar," and Stewart with others declared that
the bill was passed surreptitiously, denouncing the legislation as the "crime of 1873."   Yet in 1874 (February 11)
Senator Stewart in a speech in the Senate on another
measure had said, "I want the standard GOLD."   Later
he asserted that he was not aware until 1875 that the
dollar had been omitted from the bill of 1873.   Kelley,
who stated, when reporting the bill, that it had been
studied by the Coinage Committee line for line and
word for word, and had announced that the bill contemplated establishing the single gold standard, declared in
1877 that the demonetization was an unexplained mystery to him.

It is proper to pause to consider how far men are to
be intrusted with the great duty of legislating upon subjects affecting the interests of every citizen, if so glaring a neglect of duty is confessed.   It is unnecessary
to say that it was the *duty* of Kelley, Stewart, and all
the others then in Congress to *know* what they were
legislating upon.   If, therefore, the act was wrong, they
are themselves guilty of wrong, and their professed
ignorance (in Kelley's case disproved by the facts) is
merely an aggravation of the offence.   The truth is that
the growing political strength of the silver advocates
alarmed many men who voted for the law of 1873, and
they thought it better politics to explain their vote as an
unwitting act rather than justify it.

Marginal notes: "Crime of 1873." — Silver advocates professed ignorance.

---

[1] History of the coinage act of 1873, being a complete record of all
documents issued and all legislative proceedings concerning the act.
Public document printed in 1900.

The act of 1873 altered the coinage laws in several other particulars. The charge on gold coinage was reduced to one-fifth of 1 per cent; a three-dollar piece of gold was provided for; the subsidiary coinage was modelled after that of France as to weight, giving 25 grammes (185.8 grains) to the dollar in such coins instead of 184 grains; and these coins were continued legal tender to the amount of $5. Trade dollars were to be coined for the public, but subsidiary pieces only on government account.

The par of sterling exchange.

An act of March 2, 1873, reformed the absurd method of quoting the par of exchange with Great Britain, which continued as a relic from the old act of 1789, at the ancient rate of 4.44\frac{4}{9}$ to the pound sterling, notwithstanding the act of 1842, wherein $4.84 had been adopted as the par for payments by or to the Treasury. Thereafter the pound was to be rated at $4.8665, its actual value.

The law of January 14, 1875 (resumption act), repealed the coinage charge for the purpose of attracting gold to the mints, and provided for the issue of subsidiary silver to redeem the fractional currency, and the act of March 3, 1875, provided for the coinage of a twenty-cent piece in exact proportion to the other subsidiary coins.

The fractional currency was presented for redemption slowly, wherefore the act of April 17, 1876, provided for the issue of subsidiary coin in other payments, and the joint resolution of July 22, 1876, extended the limit of issue of such coin to $50,000,000.

Trade dollar coinage suspended.

The same enactment revoked the legal tender power of the trade dollar, inadvertently given it the same as to subsidiary pieces, by the act of 1873. It further provided that the Secretary of the Treasury might suspend its coinage when satisfied that there was no export demand, and inasmuch as these dollars had made their appearance in the country's circulation, it seemed that the coinage of $36,000,000 was in excess of the demand.

Returning now to the silver dollar. Although the act of 1873 omitted it from the coins provided for, and prohibited its coinage, it did not revoke the legal tender function of the dollars then in existence; but on June 22, 1874, Congress adopted a revision of the statutes then in force, and Section 3586, purporting to represent the law as it then stood, provided that "the silver coins of the United States shall be a legal tender at their nominal value for any amount not exceeding five dollars in any one payment." It was contended that this abrogated the full legal tender power of the existing dollars; on the other hand, it was held that a mere revision could not repeal the statute. No occasion then arose for determining this question. *Legal tender power of silver dollars.*

How and when the agitation to restore silver to free coinage actually began, seems in doubt, but the increased production in the far Western states, now averaging $40,000,000 annually, and the fall in price under the influence of diminished demand, unquestionably were the causes. The greater demand for gold coincident with the diminution of product, brought the commercial ratio of the metals to 17.5 to 1.

In March, 1876, a bill making certain appropriations was under consideration in the House, to which was appended a proviso for the redemption of fractional currency in silver coin. Reagan (Dem., Tex.) proposed an amendment making the silver dollar a legal tender up to $50, but not providing for coinage; this was adopted 124 to 94. In the Senate Sherman reported this bill from the Committee on Finance in April, modifying the legal tender power to $20, and providing for the coinage, *on government account*, of a dollar of 412.8 *Remonetization of dollars proposed.*

grains (giving a ratio of exactly 16 to 1), these dollars to be legal tender for all purposes except customs and interest on the public debt.   But subsequently the whole proviso was, upon Sherman's own motion, stricken out, together with the Reagan amendment.   Bogy (Dem., Mo.) in the course of the debate favored the free and unlimited coinage of the silver dollars with full legal tender power.

On July 19, Bland (Dem., Mo.) reported a bill in the House which provided for coin notes to pay for unlimited deposits of gold or silver, repayable on demand *in kind* (bars or coin), and for the coinage of a 412.8-grain silver dollar; the notes to be receivable for all public dues and the coins to be full legal tender.   As a substitute for this, on July 24, Kelley endeavored to pass a free coinage bill (previously introduced by him) under suspension of the rules (requiring a two-thirds vote).   The motion was defeated 119 to 66 (99 not voting), 32 Republicans voting favorably, 27 Democrats against.   Bland later made a similar attempt, which was also defeated.   The votes, however, demonstrated the ability of the silver men to pass such a bill.   A compromise measure was therefore introduced, and passed August 15, 1876, to appoint a commission to inquire into the whole subject and report to Congress.

The commission was to consist of three senators, three representatives, and not to exceed three experts, who were to inquire : —

First.   Into the change which has taken place in the relative value of gold and silver; the causes thereof, whether permanent or otherwise ; the effects thereof upon trade, commerce, finance, and the productive interests of the country, and upon the standard of value in this and foreign countries.

Second.   Into the policy of restoration of the double

standard in this country ; and if restored, what the legal relation between silver and gold should be.

Third. Into the policy of continuing legal tender notes concurrently with the metallic standards, and the effects thereof upon the labor, industries, and wealth of the country ; and

Fourth. Into the best means for providing for facilitating the resumption of specie payments.

The commission consisted of Senators Jones (Rep., Nev.), Bogy (Dem., Mo.), and ex-Secretary Boutwell ; Representatives Gibson (Dem., La.), Willard (Rep., Mich.), and Bland (Dem., Mo.), W. S. Groesbeck, of Ohio, Francis Bowen, of Massachusetts, professor in Harvard; and George M. Weston of Maine as secretary. It gave the matter undivided attention and presented a voluminous report March 2, 1877[1] (discussed below).

The political platforms in 1876 were silent on the subject; it had not developed sufficiently to permit declaration.

Bland could not await the report of the commission (of which he was a member). In December, 1876, he again pushed his bill, but ultimately preferred the Kelley substitute, which on the 13th of the month passed the House by a vote of 167 to 53. *Free coinage bill passed the House.*

In the Senate the Finance Committee reported it back without recommendation, desiring to await the report of the commission.

The report of the majority of the Silver Commission (an exhaustive document), favoring remonetization, was written by Senator Jones. Bogy, Willard, Bland, and Groesbeck concurred. Separate reports (minority) were presented by Boutwell and Bowen, Gibson concurring in the latter. Of the majority, Jones, Bogy, and Willard favored the coinage at the ratio of $15\frac{1}{2}$ to 1 (like that of

---

[1] Senate Report, No. 703, 44th Congress, 2d Sess.

France and the Latin Union); Groesbeck and Bland preferred the existing 16 to 1.

The majority contended that the fall in price of silver had not been due to increased production but to practical demonetization in so many countries at the same time; that there was an exaggerated idea of the volume of the silver product, whereas the gold product was actually diminishing, and by the stimulation of its use by the adoption of the single gold standard the price of silver was further depressed. The double standard was advocated as having a compensatory influence, so that prices would not be violently depressed, as was sure to follow if the demonetization were persisted in. There were no new circumstances warranting the change from bimetallism. Open mints in France and the United States would overcome the effects of fluctuation. The entire volume of coin money governed prices, and to reduce the volume would be an unjust interference with the course of prices. Decreasing volume and the resulting fall in prices were more disastrous than war, pestilence, or famine, as history showed.

Respecting the duty of the United States, they urged that with an enormous debt which was payable by the terms of the law and equitably as well in silver dollars, the proposition to make it payable in gold alone was to impose onerous and oppressive obligations upon the people. The existing economic troubles in the entire commercial world were due to a diminishing money supply.

They did not hesitate to insinuate that an international conspiracy was afoot to establish the gold standard and thus lay burdens upon the masses, pointing as evidence to the international conference of 1867 and Sherman's bill to make gold the sole standard thereafter, and also the act of 1873.

The questions propounded were substantially answered
as follows : —

That the change in the relative value of the metals
would not be permanent unless general demonetization
took place, in which case the most serious consequences,
social, industrial, political, and economical would follow.

That the double standard should be restored in order
to avert the danger threatening the entire world.

That paper could not be maintained concurrently with
coin unless its market value was made equal to coin by
convertibility.

That convertibility by means of resumption, extremely
difficult with coinage of both metals, would be impracticable with gold alone.

As stated, three of the majority members favored the
ratio $15\frac{1}{2}$ to 1 ; this in order to bring about concurrent
action with France and the Latin States.

Boutwell opposed the remonetization unless by international agreement.   Otherwise in his opinion silver
would flow to this country in such quantities that it
would be reduced to a silver, hence depreciated, standard.   He admitted that demonetizing one metal increased the purchasing power of the other, reduced
prices and increased debts ; the use of both metals furnished a more stable standard ; but the remonetization by
the United States alone would prove the worse for them ;
that it appeared public sentiment in Europe now favored
remonetization, so that coöperation could probably be
secured ; until then action should be delayed.

Professor Bowen's view, concurred in by Gibson, was
that the change in relative values was due to the fluctuation of silver, which was caused by increased product and
diminished use, proof of its unfitness as a money metal ;
whether permanent or not, was impossible to determine.
He regarded the double standard an illusion ; silver was

further unfitted except for subsidiary purposes by reason
of bulk; the concurrent use of government paper would
be unjust, since its redemption had been pledged; resumption was indeed practically at hand. He recommended a subsidiary dollar 345.6 grains pure silver
(380.16 grains standard) to be issued in exchange for
$1, $2, and $5 notes to be cancelled; the coin to be
legal tender to $20, but receivable in any amount for
public dues other than customs; small notes not to be
legal tender after 1878; gold to be coined at the rate of
22.6 grains pure to the dollar, so that the half eagle
would be practically equal to the pound sterling; legal
tenders to be retired at the rate of $3,000,000 monthly;
resulting deficits to be made up by sale of bonds.

Great fall in silver.
During 1876 silver had fallen so that at its lowest the
ratio was 20 to 1.

In 1877 Western Republican platforms called loudly
for remonetization, Iowa and Ohio taking the lead.
Even Pennsylvania joined in. The Democrats denounced the demonetization as a "Republican outrage,"
although Democrats had voted for the bill of 1873 quite
as solidly.

The Hayes administration with Sherman as Secretary
of the Treasury began March 4, 1877. In negotiating
a new contract for the sale of bonds the question arose
whether the new obligations would be payable in gold.

Payment of bonds in silver.
The refunding act of 1870 provided that the obligations
were to be payable in "coin of the *present* standard
value.' Inasmuch as the legal tender power of the
silver dollar was apparently not affected by the act of
1873, and certainly was an existing power in 1870, the
question was pertinent. Sherman answered that the
bonds would be payable "in coin" as required by
the law, but that they would bear date as issued (1877)
"when only one kind of coin is a legal tender for all

debts." After some discussion the matter was referred to Attorney-general Devens, who ruled that the bonds could not be made payable "in gold coin"; that under the statute of 1870 they were unquestionably redeemable in " coin of the standard value as it existed at the date of the act "; and that all the bonds would stand alike, no matter when issued, unless the law was altered.[1]

"Coin" not gold only.

Obviously the bonds authorized to be sold for resumption purposes (act of 1875) fell within the same category; and the legal tender notes were to be redeemed in *coin;* gold was not specified. Upon the other hand, in 1875 gold was, by the act of 1873, the unit of value; and according to the Revised Statutes (1874, already quoted), the silver coins were not legal tender above $5. The point could have been determined by reference to Congress, but that body was for silver by a large majority. It consisted of 156 Democrats and 136 Republicans in the House; the Senate was evenly divided, counting Davis of Illinois against the Republicans.

Bland again introduced his free coinage bill, and it passed under a suspension of the rules November 5, 1877. The vote, 163 to 34 (not voting 92), indicates that many representatives dodged the question; the negative vote included only 10 Democrats, Hewitt among these; on the Republican side, Frye and Reed; the affirmative, such Democrats as Carlisle, Cox, Ewing, Morrison, and Republicans, Foster, McKinley, Cannon, Kelley, and Keifer.

Another free coinage bill.

The bill was as follows : —

"That there shall be coined, at the several mints of the United States, silver dollars of the weight of 412½ grains troy of standard silver, as provided in the act of January 18, 1837, on which shall be the devices and superscriptions provided by said act; which coins, together with all silver dollars hereto-

[1] Specie Resumption, etc., Ex. Doc., No. 9, 46th Congress, 2d Sess.

fore coined by the United States, of like weight and fineness, shall be a legal tender at their nominal value, for all debts and dues, public and private, except when otherwise provided by contract; and any owner of silver bullion may deposit the same at any United States mint or assay office, to be coined into such dollars for his benefit upon the same terms and conditions as gold bullion is deposited for coinage under existing laws.

"All acts and parts of acts inconsistent with the provisions of this act are repealed."

In the Senate Allison reported the bill November 21, with an amendment proposing, in lieu of free coinage, the government purchase of a limited amount (not less than $2,000,000 nor more than $4,000,000 monthly) of bullion and coinage on its own account, leaving the dollars full legal tender, which was adopted by 49 to 22; the opponents were of course the extreme advocates of free coinage.

Meanwhile President Hayes in his first message in December took up the subject, earnestly urging Congress to consider the implied breach of faith involved in the proposed silver measure respecting the public debt, and the interference with the pending reduction of the interest rate; this involved a loss greater than the supposed gain of paying in a cheaper dollar. While opposed to the disparagement of silver, he recognized that equality with the commercial ratio was not attainable, hence the cheaper coin would drive the better abroad; and recommended a dollar that would approach nearer the commercial value of silver with only limited legal tender power. Without this, only mischief and misfortune would flow from silver coinage. The expectation of monetary ease from free coinage he regarded as a delusion.

Secretary Sherman in his report[1] practically stated

[1] Finance Report, 1877.

the same points in another form. He asked that the Sherman on silver.
bonds issued from 1873 to date, amounting to nearly
$593,000,000, be exempted from the operation of the
proposed silver law, having been paid for in gold ; but he
also favored the pledge of gold payments for all bonds.

He insisted that to coin a dollar worth 9 per cent
less than gold would drive out gold, just as it was driven
out under the act of 1792, and the same as silver was
driven out under the rating in 1834 ; that a dollar subsidiary in character, with limited legal tender power,
would be a great public advantage, unlimited coinage
a great public injury.

When the Senate resumed consideration of the Bland
Bill amendments to coin a heavier dollar, to accord
more nearly with the commercial ratio, were defeated
(49 to 18) by the combination of the extreme and the
moderate silver advocates ; the latter included Allison,
Windom, Davis, Matthews, and Blaine ; the anti-silver
vote included Morrill (Vt.), Conkling, Hoar, Dawes, and
Bayard. An amendment to make the dollars redeem- Amend-ments pro-posed.
able in gold, and one which made the dollars *not* a tender for customs or interest on the public debt, were
defeated.   An amendment by Booth (Cal.) (nominally
a Republican, but actually a Greenbacker, having been
candidate for Vice-President with Peter Cooper), providing for the issue of silver certificates on deposits of
dollars in the Treasury, and making such certificates receivable for all public dues and reissuable, was adopted ;
also an amendment calling for an international conference on silver, one providing that the dollars were to
be tenders only when not otherwise expressly stipulated
and not at all for redemption of gold certificates. The
final vote on the bill, February 15, 1878, was 48 to 21 ;
Blaine on this vote was on the negative side.

The House passed it, February 21, as amended by

Limited
coinage act
passed.

the Senate, 203 to 72; Hayes vetoed the bill on the 28th, and it was promptly passed over the veto on the same day; House 196 to 73, Senate 46 to 19. Among the Republicans voting to override the veto were Representatives Butler, Charles Foster, William McKinley, and Kelley; Senators Allison, Matthews, and Windom. Supporting Hayes were Representatives Hale, Reed, Garfield, and Frye; Senators Blaine, Conkling, Dawes, Hoar, and Morrill (Vt.).

The vote in both houses was sectional rather than partisan, only a few members of Congress, except from the East, opposing the measure.

Hayes's Veto.

Hayes's reasons for his veto were chiefly that making the dollars and certificates receivable for customs would soon deprive the country of its gold revenues; that the public credit was affected by making the debt payable in silver, thus practically scaling it 8 to 10 per cent, which represented the lower value of the silver dollar in the market at that time. Over $580,000,000 of the bonds had been issued since the act of 1873; gold was received for them, and the subscribers were practically assured that they would be paid in gold; the government received the benefit of a lower interest rate by such assurance. While some measures should be adopted to retain the use of silver as money of the country, this measure violated the obligation of the Nation, the keeping of which "transcends all questions of profit or public advantage."

"It is my firm conviction that if the country is to be benefited by a silver coinage, it can be done only by the issue of silver dollars of full value, which shall defraud no man. A currency worth less than it purports to be worth will in the end defraud not only creditors, but all who are engaged in legitimate business, and none more surely than those who are dependent on their daily labor for their daily bread."

Senator Matthews (Rep., O.) on January 16, 1878, in- troduced a *concurrent* resolution (not requiring the Presi- dent's approval and hence only declaratory) with long preambles, declaring that the bonds of the United States were payable in silver dollars, and making such dollars legal tender in payment of public debt was not a viola- tion of the public faith nor in derogation of rights of public creditors. The preamble argued that the act of 1869 made the obligations payable in *coin ;* all bonds issued under the funding acts of 1870 and 1871 were payable in coin of the then standard, which (being prior to 1873) included the silver dollar. The resolu- tion was adopted 43 to 22. All amendments were voted down, and one to the preamble reciting that only some 8,000,000 silver dollars had been coined from 1792 to date, that the coin was obsolete and had no existence when the bonds were authorized, that the coinage act of 1873 had made gold the standard, that creditors had a right to expect gold, that the government ought not to take advantage of obsolete laws, and that the dollar was worth only 92 cents, received only 17 affirmative votes, 13 being Republican. Only the strong sound money men supported the amendment.

In the House the resolution passed January 29 by 189 to 79, the vote being practically the same as the subsequent vote on the silver law.

The legislature of Illinois had, in May, 1877, passed an act to make all silver coins, the standard of which had been declared by Congress, a legal tender. Gov- ernor Cullom vetoed the act.

A new form of currency inflation was thus found in this use of silver. That the intent was to raise the price of silver is evident. The production of the white metal was increasing not only in this country but else- where. Whether free coinage would have raised the price except temporarily, is doubtful.   The compromise measure fathered by Senator Allison was not likely to " restore the value ' of silver, hence Bland's persistence in pushing the free coinage measure after the compromise had passed.

In accordance with the second section of the act of 1878, the chief commercial nations were invited by the President to send delegates to a conference to meet in Paris in August, to consider the adoption of

The international conference of 1878

" a common ratio between gold and silver, for the purpose of establishing, internationally, the use of bimetallic money, and securing fixity of relative value between those metals ; such conference to be held at such place, in Europe or in the United States, at such time within six months, as may be mutually agreed upon by the executives of the governments joining in the same whenever the governments, so invited, or any three of them, shall have signified their willingness to unite in the same."

Eleven countries replied favorably and were represented ; the United States by ex-Senator Fenton (N.Y.), Groesbeck (O.), Francis A. Walker (Mass.), with S. Dana Horton as secretary.

At the conference the American delegates found the representatives of European countries well informed, and many well disposed toward international bimetallism.   Others, however, were content to let the United States solve its problem alone.

The several propositions from the Americans, looking to the general reopening of the mints to coinage upon an agreed ratio which could be maintained, were thoroughly discussed and a mass of valuable material was laid before the body ; but the conference finally dissolved on August 29 without results.   The propositions were as follows : —

Propositions considered.

" I. It is the opinion of this assembly that it is not to be desired that Silver should be excluded from free Coinage in

Europe and in the United States of America. On the contrary, the assembly believe that it is desirable that the unrestricted Coinage of Silver, and its use as Money of unlimited Legal Tender, should be retained where they exist, and, as far as practicable, restored where they have ceased to exist.

"II. The use of both Gold and Silver as unlimited Legal-Tender Money may be safely adopted ; first, by equalizing. them at a relation to be fixed by international agreement ; and, secondly, by granting to each metal at the relation fixed equal terms of Coinage, making no discrimination between them."

The European delegates replied that they recognized :

"I. That it is necessary to maintain in the world the monetary functions of Silver as well as those of Gold, but that the selection for use of one or the other of the two metals, or of both simultaneously, should be governed by the special position of each State or group of States.

"II. That the question of the restriction of the Coinage of Silver should equally be left to the discretion of each State or group of States, according to the particular circumstances in which they may find themselves placed ; and the more so, in that the disturbance produced during the recent years in the Silver market has variously affected the monetary situation of the several countries.

"III. That the differences of opinion which have appeared, and the fact that even some of the States, which have the Double Standard find it impossible to enter into a mutual engagement with regard to the free Coinage of Silver, exclude the discussion of the adoption of a common ratio between the two metals." [1]

France, which had been expected to lead in support of the bimetallic proposition, while favoring it in theory, felt it impracticable to agree at the time, and certainly could not at any ratio other than her own, $15\frac{1}{2}$ to 1; Great Britain had sent delegates without power to commit the government, and these delegates (having had

Reply of European delegates.

[1] International Monetary Conference, 1878, Senate Ex. Doc., No. 58, 45th Congress, 3d Sess.

Conference ineffective.

the benefit of the report of a British silver commission in 1876–1877), while believing a general gold standard utopian, and while desiring the continued use of silver as money on account of India, could not favor the double standard ; Germany had refused to send delegates, being satisfied with her newly adopted gold standard; Russia and Austria, silver standard countries with actually depreciated paper currencies, might be favorable at some time ; Belgium and the Scandinavian states, as also Switzerland, favored gold; Italy alone, also suffering from depreciated paper, favored immediate adoption of the American proposal.

Bimetallists.

Consequent upon the publication of the deliberations of the conference there arose in the United States a distinct body of conservative silver advocates, logically favoring bimetallism, but insisting that the policy was proper only in the event of international action embracing practically all of the commercial nations. They cultivated relations with similar bodies abroad, and were sufficient in number when acting with the gold standard advocates in the two leading parties to thwart the efforts of those who agitated for free coinage by the United States alone. These bimetallists naturally labored for and fully expected another conference, basing the expectation upon the constantly diminishing gold product, which they concluded would not suffice for the world's needs.

STATISTICAL RÉSUMÉ

(Amounts in millions)

PRODUCTION OF GOLD AND SILVER, RATIO, ETC.

YEAR	WORLD			UNITED STATES			RATIO	BULLION VALUE OF SILVER DOLLAR	PRICE OF OUNCE OF SILVER
	Gold	*Silver*		Gold	*Silver*				
		Commercial Value	Coining Value		Commercial Value	Coining Value			
1861 . .	123	46	46	43	2	2	15.50	$ 1.031	$ 1.333
1862 . .	123	48	46	39	5	5	15.35	1.041	1.346
1863 . .	123	48	46	40	9	9	15.37	1.040	1.345
1864 . .	123	48	46	46	11	11	15.37	1.040	1.345
1865 . .	123	47	46	53	12	11	15.44	1.035	1.338
1866 . .	130	58	56	54	10	10	15.43	1.036	1.339
1867 . .	130	57	56	52	14	14	15.57	1.027	1.328
1868 . .	130	57	56	48	12	12	15.59	1.025	1.326
1869 . .	130	57	56	50	12	12	15.60	1.024	1.325
1870 . .	130	57	56	50	17	16	15.57	1.027	1.328
1871 . .	116	84	82	44	24	23	15.57	1.025	1.326
1872 . .	116	84	82	36	29	29	15.63	1.022	1.332
1873 .	96	82	82	36	36	36	15.93	1.004	1.298
1874 . .	91	71	72	34	37	37	16.16	.989	1.279
1875 . .	98	78	81	33	31	32	16.64	.961	1.242
1876 . .	104	78	88	40	35	39	17.75	.900	1.164
1877 . .	114	75	81	47	37	40	17.20	.930	1.202
1878 . .	119	85	95	51	40	45	17.12	.932	1.154

EXPORTS AND IMPORTS OF SPECIE, AND COINAGE

FISCAL YEAR	GOLD			SILVER			COINAGE OF	
	Exports	Imports	Excess +Imp. −Exp.	Exports	Imports	Excess +Imp. −Exp.	Gold	Silver[1]
1861 . .	27	42	+ 15	2	4	+ 2	83	4
1862 . .	35	14	− 21	1	3	+ 2	21	1
1863 . .	62	6	− 56	2	4	+ 2	22	1
1864 . .	101	11	− 90	5	2	− 3	20	1
1865 . .	58	6	− 52	9	3	− 6	28	1
1866 . .	71	8	− 63	15	3	− 12	31	1
1867 . .	39	17	− 22	22	5	− 17	24	1
1868 . .	73	9	− 64	21	5	− 16	19	1
1869 . .	36	14	− 22	21	6	− 15	18	1
1870 . .	34	12	− 22	25	14	− 11	23	1
1871 . .	67	7	− 60	32	14	− 18	21	3
1872 . .	50	9	− 41	30	5	− 25	22	3
1873 . .	45	9	− 36	40	13	− 27	57	4
1874 . .	34	20	− 14	33	9	− 24	35	7
1875 . .	67	14	− 53	25	7	− 18	33	15
1876 . .	31	8	− 23	25	8	− 17	47	25
1877 . .	26	26	− 0	30	15	− 15	44	28
1878 . .	9	13	+ 4	25	16	− 9	50	29

[1] Coinage of dollars prior to 1878 amounted to 3,900,000, of which 2,500,000 were coined from 1871 to 1873.

CHAPTER XIII

1879 TO 1890

THE silver men in Congress were by no means satis- Silver agitation continues. fied with the Bland-Allison law, and during the summer of 1878 the subject was agitated in the political field. The Republican platforms favored "both gold and silver," but Western Democrats declared persistently for free coinage, as did the "Greenbackers." The congressional elections resulted rather favorably to the silver advocates, but they were unable to count fully on their forces.

When Hayes sent in his second message (December, Hayes opposes free silver. 1878), resumption was practically at hand. He said that, with views unchanged, he had had the silver law of 1878 carried out faithfully, to afford it a fair trial. He recommended therefore that Congress abstain from disturbing business by legislation or attempts thereat, letting the people have an opportunity to bring about an enduring prosperity. Sherman's report, however, Sherman's report, 1878. recommended legislation limiting the coinage of silver or altering the ratio to make the silver dollar worth more. He assumed that Congress had not intended by the act of 1878 to adopt the silver standard, but as far as practicable a bimetallic system, with limited coinage. When the volume of dollars more than supplied the needs for such coin, he thought they would depreciate. The facts shown by the market quotations warranted a change in the ratio. To ignore this would mean the absorption of the surplus silver of Europe. He believed in fixing a ratio that would secure the largest use of both metals without displacing either. Therefore the coinage of dollars at 16 to 1 should be limited (say to $50,000,000) until the price of silver assumed a *definite ratio to gold*, and then that ratio should be adopted.

While maintaining that the resumption act contemplated redemption of notes in *gold*, he would use either metal, as holders of notes might demand, reserving the legal option, however, to pay in either.

Price of silver. At this time the ratio of silver to gold was (average) 17.92, and the bullion value of the silver dollar 93.2 cents.

In February a bill to make gold and silver coin interchangeable was defeated in the House, 101 to 136; one to pay out legal tender notes for any coin brought to the subtreasury in New York, by 105 to 129; bills to redeem trade dollars and recoin them into standard dollars were also defeated.

House favors silver. In the following Congress, the first session of which assembled in March, a free coinage measure, reported by A. J. Warner, (Dem., O.), passed the House by 114 to 97, 6 Republicans favoring and 8 Democrats opposing it. An attempt to limit the coinage to domestic product was defeated by 105 to 130, and one to provide for a 460-grain dollar by 52 to 176. A proposition to make gold and silver certificates legal tender was negatived by 73 to 135.

Senate against silver. In the Senate the free coinage bill was sent to the Finance Committee, from which it was reported adversely by Senator Bayard at the following session, and a resolution by Senator Vest (Dem., Mo.), declaring free coinage necessary to supply the needed volume of money, was sent to the same committee, for burial, by a vote of 23 to 22, 4 Eastern Democrats voting with the majority.

The House passed a resolution, with considerable support from the Republican side, directing the Secretary of the Treasury to pay out the silver dollars in the Treasury the same as gold; the vote was 143 to 75.

A bill was passed at this session (June 9, 1879), for the redemption of subsidiary coin in lawful money and for its issue for lawful money in sums or multiples of $20. This action was due to the existence of a troublesome surplus of such coin caused, not by excessive coinage, but by the return from abroad of pieces of the old coinage banished during the war period.

At this time a bill proposing a solution of the silver question by the minting of a "goloid" dollar containing both metals, was favored by Stephens (Dem., Ga.), formerly Vice-President of the Southern Confederacy. It proposed, also, to adopt the system for international use by coining a four-dollar piece. The measure never got beyond the committee stage.

In his report for 1879 Secretary Sherman repeated his recommendations of the previous year. No effort had been spared to put silver into circulation, but only 13,000,000 of the dollars were then in use out of a coinage of 45,000,000. The coin could be maintained at par only by holding a great part of it in the vaults of the Treasury. He urged limitation of the coinage to preserve the parity with gold. Sherman's report, 187ç

President Hayes recommended that the Treasury be authorized to suspend coinage of silver when parity was endangered. He expressed the belief that international agreement upon a ratio was possible, and hoped no legislation other than that recommended be undertaken, in order to avoid disturbances.

Congress, in appropriation acts now, and annually thereafter, provided for the distribution, free of expense, of silver dollars from mints and Treasury offices, the Free distribution of dollars.

cost to be charged against the "silver profit fund"; *i.e.* the amount representing the difference between the cost of the bullion and the nominal value of the dollars coined therefrom, sometimes also called "seigniorage."

The Senate, also Democratic, nevertheless contained a sufficient number of anti-silver Democrats from the East to defeat any free silver measure, hence no further attempts were made to press such bills. But Representative Weaver of Iowa, later Greenback candidate for the presidency, offered in the House a proposition to redeem bonds in silver, opening the mints to the free coinage of silver to provide means. This was defeated 85 to 117. The substance thereof became one of the cardinal principles announced in the platform of that party in the summer of 1880.

Greenback-silver alliance.

The principal parties omitted silver from their platforms in the presidential contest of 1880. It was an important and exciting issue, however, in very many congressional districts. Garfield, conspicuous for sound money views, was elected President, and with him a Republican Congress.

Continued inflation.

In his report for 1880, Secretary Sherman stated that the amount of silver was already in excess of the demand. Popular objection to the dollars arose from their bulk and their known deficiency in value. Less than $26,000,000 were in use out of nearly $73,000,000 coined, and less than $20,000,000 were floated by representative certificates, thus leaving $27,000,000 idle in the Treasury — almost the year's coinage. The average bullion value of the dollars was about 88½ cents. Sherman had adopted a policy of furnishing silver certificates, free of exchange charge, at Southern and Western points, for deposits of gold at New York.

President Hayes forcibly urged suspension of coinage in his message for 1880. It was demonstrated that the

coinage law of 1878 would not raise the commercial value
of silver, indeed its price had fallen. He also recommended increasing the amount of silver in the dollar.

With the silver situation thus remaining undetermined, Silver agitation abroad.
and the conditions in France, Italy, India, and other countries becoming more serious owing to the steadily diminishing supply of gold and the steadily falling price of
silver, opinion in both England and Germany underwent
a change. Leading advocates of the single gold standard
altered their views. France now consented to join this
country in an invitation to another conference to devise
a "system for the establishment by means of an international agreement of the use of gold and silver as bimetallic money, according to a settled relative value between
these two metals." (The ratio was now about 18 to 1.)

The conference met at Paris in April, 1881.[1] International
conference
of 1881.
England, on account of India, was seriously interested,
and Germany was also represented. In all, eighteen
countries sent delegates, our own being ex-Secretary of
State William M. Evarts (N.Y.), ex-Senators Allen G.
Thurman (O.) and Timothy O. Howe (Wis.), with S.
Dana Horton as expert. The membership of the conference in general was more favorable to bimetallism
than the previous one.

The questions considered were concisely these : —

Has the fall of silver been hurtful to prosperity ; is it
desirable that the relation be made more stable ?

Has the fall been due to increased product or to legislation ?

Can stability be restored if a large group of states
remonetize silver under unlimited coinage of full legal
tender pieces ?

If so, what measures should be taken to reduce fluctuation of the ratio to a minimum ?

[1] International Monetary Conference, 1881, House Misc. Doc., No. 396,
49th Congress, 1st Sess.

It was apparent that, as before, most of the Europeans imagined the United States interested because she was a great producer of silver. Germany at this time still had a very large stock of its old coins unsold. Great Britain, on account of India, showed a desire to have all others extend the use of silver in order to raise the price.

Long intervening recesses prolonged the conference until July. France and the United States finally joined in a declaration answering the questions practically thus : —

Declaration of the pro- silver dele- gates.

That the fall of silver was injurious and establishing a fixed ratio would be beneficial ; international agreement for free and unlimited coinage of both metals at a fixed ratio would cause and maintain stability ; the ratio of $15\frac{1}{2}$ to 1 was most suitable ; England, France, Germany, and the United States, with the concurrence of others, could by convention secure and maintain the stability of the ratio adopted.

Germany and England declined to enter into such a compact. The conference adjourned for politeness' sake to April 12, 1882 — to enable France and this country to work out a plan. Actually as it proved the adjournment was *sine die*.

Suspension of coinage urged.

Opinion here now took in large measure the view, as Secretary Folger expressed it in his report for 1881, that Europe was in fact more deeply interested in the solution of the silver question than the United States, that therefore the suspension of all coinage by us would tend toward the adoption of the bimetallic policy. Folger urgently recommended such action, since the supply of dollars was now in excess of the home demand, and further coinage would bring us to the single standard. He had been able to increase the dollars in use to $34,000,000, the certificates to $59,000,000, leaving in the Treasury some $11,000,000 net of silver funds.

In January, 1882, Congress called for a report upon Statistical. silver purchases, which when furnished showed that 92,550,000 fine ounces had been acquired at a cost of $95,119,000, producing 105,380,000 silver dollars. The Treasury had in the forty-six months bought only the minimum amount fixed by the law.

In the House an attempt was made under the lead of Dingley (Rep., Me.), to suspend coinage of silver and the issue of silver certificates, but it failed.

The act of July 12, 1882, authorized the issue of gold certificates, and made these as well as silver certificates available for bank reserves. It also prohibited any national bank from being a member of any clearing-house where silver certificates were refused in settlement of balances.

In 1882 Folger had been able to put into circulation only about 1,000,000 silver dollars, and the silver certifi-cates in use were less than the year before, so that practically the entire purchase of silver for the year, some $27,000,000, was idle in the Treasury, having dis-placed gold or legal tenders to that extent.

Further circulation of silver impos-sible.

The well-known opposition of President Arthur made further efforts to pass a free coinage measure useless, and no attempt was for a time made in that direction ; but the silver advocates tried to enact a law for the re-demption of trade dollars and their recoinage into the ordinary form. The bill failed in the Senate.

McCulloch became Secretary near the end of 1884, which gave him an opportunity to point out vigorously the danger threatening the country from silver. A be-liever in bimetallism *under international agreement*, he nevertheless saw the futility of the policy now obtaining in the United States. A continuation of this policy would either impair the gold reserve or compel the use of silver for payment of *gold obligations*, thus bringing

Gold reserve threatened.

about the silver standard. The silver funds in the Treasury had increased to $53,000,000. The reduction of tariff and other taxes by the act of March 3, 1883, caused a temporary shrinkage of revenues which presently made it much more difficult to carry a large volume of idle silver.

The annual gold product of the world had now fallen below $100,000,000 and that of silver was over $115,-000,000, the United States furnishing $30,000,000 of the former and $46,000,000 of the latter.

Grover Cleveland had been elected President, and a portion of his party was definitely opposed to silver. Anticipating that he would in his inaugural express himself hostile to silver, 95 Western Democrats early in 1885 addressed a letter requesting him not to do so. He replied (February 24), forcibly declaring his belief that a financial crisis would follow a continuance of the coinage of silver; that the gold reserve was practically already impaired. The silver advocates retorted by pointing out that France with $850,000,000 gold maintained $600,000,000 silver; we had $600,000,000 gold and only $200,000,000 silver, and if the Secretary of the Treasury would only pay out more silver and less gold, the gold reserve would not be endangered.

President Cleveland's views.

The silver advocates persisted in the belief that the Treasury was not only indifferent in getting silver into circulation, but were inclined to the opinion that obstacles were actually placed in the way. In February, 1885, the House passed a resolution asking the Secretary of the Treasury a number of questions on the subject, designed to inform the House as to the action of his department. Secretary McCulloch replied frankly, demonstrating not only that both dollars and certificates were paid out as largely as was possible, but showing that both forms returned to the Treasury in the reve-

McCulloch to Congress.

nues as fast as, and sometimes in greater volume than, he disbursed them ; 40 per cent of the customs revenue was now paid in silver certificates ; the gold currency was preferred, and was very largely withheld in payment of taxes and duties ; the silver issue had reached the saturation point. Yet upon this showing the House refused, in the same month, to suspend the further coinage of dollars, 118 to 152, and again in different form by 90 to 169. So the Treasury was compelled to pay out current money and increase its supply of those forms which were not current. The country barely escaped going upon a silver basis.

President Cleveland and his Secretary of the Treasury, Manning, immediately adopted vigorous measures to prevent a catastrophe. By at once curtailing the issue of small legal tender notes (which was in the discretion of the Secretary), room was made for a larger volume of silver dollars ; by using legal tender notes in disbursements, and avoiding when possible the payment of silver certificates, a smaller proportion of the revenues was received in that form ; and the gold reserve, which in May had fallen to $115,000,000, was increased. Secretary Manning also acquired from the New York banks nearly $6,000,000 in gold in exchange for subsidiary silver coin, of which there was a surplus on hand. By suspending bond purchases the Treasury by December had $148,000,000 gold in its reserve, and also over $76,000,000 of idle silver. These makeshifts served to tide over the interval until the regular session of Congress, to which Secretary Manning, in his report (December, 1885), presented an exhaustive, learned review of the silver question.

Manning's vigorous measures.

He urged a suspension of the coinage of dollars in order that the status of silver might become more definitely determined. The country had now 215,000,000

Suspension of coinage advocated.

of the dollars which could be maintained at parity only by stopping further output; to continue the coinage under existing conditions was merely inviting disaster.

International agreement impossible.

President Cleveland devoted several pages to the subject in his first message. He asserted that the vital part of the act of 1878 was that looking to an international bimetallic agreement; that endeavors in this line had failed, thus leaving the United States alone to battle for silver — a losing contest. An examination of conditions abroad convinced him that no help was to be expected so long as the present policy was persisted in. Indeed, the further accumulation of dollars at the peculiar ratio of 16 to 1, not anywhere else in use, made the chance for an agreement more remote. The supply of dollars now far exceeded the demand. By suspending further coinage, however, these might be ultimately absorbed in the circulation. The plea that the continuation was for the benefit of the "debtor class" implied that this class was dishonest, which he denied; nor would a depreciated dollar help them in the end.

In Europe a marked depression in trade became manifest at this time. In England a commission was appointed to examine the subject, and out of this came eventually a gold and silver commission. In other nations also the question of silver was being considered.

Congress interpellates Manning.

Congress had again called upon the Treasury for a full report as to its action respecting silver, to which Secretary Manning replied (March 3, 1886). The questions embraced the authority for the loan of gold from the New York banks, the amount of free silver in the Treasury, and bonds subject to redemption not paid, implying that the silver could have been used for the payment of debt, and finally asking as to the future policy.

Secretary Manning replied that the loan of gold by

the New York banks was made by placing at their disposal subsidiary silver. He referred to no authority therefor, as the transaction was regarded as an exchange presumably permitted by the act of 1879.

He further stated that there had been no disparagement of any form of money by the Treasury; each citizen was paid his choice of currencies on hand. He had by much labor increased the circulation of silver dollars by $11,500,000. He pointed out that silver certificates, if issued beyond the actual needs, would necessarily flow back into the Treasury, and silver dollars would not circulate if one and two dollar notes were furnished. Interest-bearing debt subject to call amounted to $174,000,000, but to force silver out for this would precipitate the silver basis. On the other hand, there was $346,000,000 of debt in the shape of legal tender notes, the payment of which had been pledged in 1869, but which under the act of May 31, 1878, he was compelled to reissue when paid. These could be replaced by silver certificates.

The country desired to remain bimetallic; free coin- age, or the continuation of the limited coinage, would bring silver monometallism, under which all the surplus silver of Europe would ultimately come here for gold. Discontinuing the coinage was the only thing that would destroy their hopes of doing so. Until the coinage was discontinued it was useless to talk of bimetallism.

The sole action taken by Congress was to authorize the issue of silver certificates of the denominations of $1, $2, and $5, by an amendment tacked to an appropriation act.

Congress endeavored to force Manning to use the accumulating surplus in the purchase of bonds, but he felt that unless he was able to hold a large surplus, he would be hampered by the large silver balance.

In his report for 1886 Manning reviewed the silver question at home and abroad, and again concluded that the only hope lay in the cessation of silver purchases under the act of 1878, thereby causing a change of sentiment in Europe, which was content to look on while we carried the load.

Opinion in Europe was undergoing a change: 243 members of the British Parliament had petitioned that the Gold and Silver Commission inquire into the subject and suggest remedies to be obtained either by sole or concurrent action by the British government. The fall of prices was having its influence.[1]

Small silver certificates.

The issue of small silver certificates had begun, and the $1 and $2 greenbacks were disappearing. There had been a contraction of the currency in circulation this year from $23.02 per capita to $21.82.

President Cleveland in his message for 1886 continued his recommendation to cease purchasing silver, pointing out that as this form of currency was distributed among the people, the duty of protecting it from disaster became greater.

On March 3, 1887, an act was passed (becoming law without the President's signature) to redeem trade dollars, not mutilated, for a period of six months; $7,689,000 were so redeemed and recoined into dollars and smaller pieces.

Fairchild's report.

In 1887 Secretary Fairchild, concluding that the silver acquisition would not be stopped, looked for measures to make it safer. The silver dollars in use had grown to $62,500,000, although in the dull seasons that amount usually shrunk some $7,000,000; the Treasury had only $53,000,000 in its vaults not held for certificates, against nearly $94,000,000 in July, 1886; and the small silver certificate issue had enlarged the total issue to nearly $161,000,000. The bullion value of the

[1] Russell, International Monetary Conferences.

dollar had fallen to 75 cents. The slight increase in the world's gold product was accompanied by a greater increase in the silver product, resulting in a commercial ratio of 21 to 1.

Europe had again been sounded as to international action, but entirely without result. Edward Atkinson, the delegate, returned without the slightest hope of the success of the movement in Europe. President Cleveland had, however, taken strong ground favoring the reduction of tariff taxes to check the growing surplus. This surplus could be used only in redemption of bonds, which meant retiring national bank currency, leaving in turn a "vacuum" for gold or silver. Even if the tariff were lowered, the increased imports of goods would tend to cause exports of gold and the vacuum would have to be filled by silver. Europe did not fail to see this and awaited the issue. No legislation followed, but the discussion served to keep silver in the background, although in the presidential campaign of 1888 silver took a more prominent position than ever before. The Republicans denounced Cleveland's policy as an attempt at silver demonetization. The majority of the Democrats, favorable to silver, were yet unable to dictate the platform, and appreciating the necessity of renominating Cleveland, their declaration was drawn by the eastern wing of the party. It favored both "gold and silver."

Treasury surplus and tariff.

Harrison defeated Cleveland, and his administration was tacitly pledged to "do something for silver."

In 1888 the report of the British Commission appeared.[1] The opinion of the twelve commissioners was unanimous as to the causes of the disturbance of the bimetallic par and the disastrous fall in prices resulting. They said : —

British silver commission report.

"The action of the Latin Union in 1873 broke the link between silver and gold, which had kept the price of the

Cause of fall of silver.

[1] See Senate Misc. Doc., No. 34, 50th Congress, 2d Sess.

former, as measured by the latter, constant at about the legal ratio ; and when this link was broken the silver market was open to the influence of all the factors which go to affect the price of a commodity. These factors happen since 1873 to have operated in the direction of a fall in the gold price of that metal, and the frequent fluctuations in its value are accounted for by the fact that the market has become fully sensitive to the other influences to which we have called attention above,"

viz. the great increase in production of silver and diminution of the gold product, increased use of gold and diminished use of silver, resulting from changes in currency systems, the sale of silver by Germany, the removal of the steadying force of the Latin Union.

The commission's opinion divided.

As to remedies, the commission was evenly divided. One-half headed by Lord Herschell rejected bimetallism and recommended no change in the British system. They said : —

" In our opinion it might be worth while to meet the great commercial nations on any proposal which would lead to a more extended use of silver, and so tend to prevent the apprehended further fall in the value of that metal, and to keep its relation to gold more stable.

*   *   *   *   *   *   *   *   *   *

" Though unable to recommend the adoption of what is commouly known as bimetallism, we desire it to be understood that we are quite alive to the imperfections of standards of value, which not only fluctuate, but fluctuate independently of each other ; and we do not shut our eyes to the possibility of future arrangements between nations which may reduce these fluctuations.

" One uniform standard for all commercial countries would no doubt, like uniformity of coinage or of standards of weight and measure, be a great advantage. But we think that any premature and doubtful step might, in addition to its other dangers and inconveniences, prejudice and retard progress to this end.

*   *   *   *   *   *   *   *   *   *

" Under these circumstances we have felt that the wiser course is to abstain from recommending any fundamental change in a system of currency under which the commerce of Great Britain has attained its present development."

The other half of the commission contended that if the Latin Union's system of bimetallism had steadied the bullion market, as admitted, such a system of free coinage by *all* nations upon an agreed ratio certainly would. They said : —

One-half favored bimetallism.

" Neither metal alone exists in sufficient quantity to serve as a sole standard without causing such a change in the level of prices as to amount to a financial and commercial revolution ; but we cannot doubt that if a sufficiently wide area of agreement between the leading commercial countries can be secured, this most important result may be effectually attained and a great international reform successfully accomplished.

* * * * * * * * * *

"Failing any attempt to reëstablish the connecting link between the two metals, it seems probable that the general tendency of the commercial nations of the world will be towards a single gold standard.

" Any step in that direction would, of course, aggravate all the evils of the existing situation, and could not fail to have a most injurious effect upon the progress of the world.

" A further fall in the value of silver might at any moment give rise to further evils of great and indefinite magnitude in India, while a further rise in the value of gold might produce the most serious consequences at home.

" No settlement of the difficulty is, however, in our opinion, possible without international action.

" The remedy which we suggest is essentially international in its character, and its details must be settled in concert with the other powers concerned.

Remedy suggested.

" It will be sufficient for us to indicate the essential features of the agreement to be arrived at, namely, (1) free coinage of both metals into legal tender money ; and (2) the fixing of a ratio at which the coins of either metal shall be available for the payment of all debts at the option of the debtor.

* * * * * * * * * *

"We therefore submit that the chief commercial nations of the world, such as the United States, Germany, and the States forming the Latin Union, should in the first place be consulted as to their readiness to join with the United Kingdom in a conference, at which India and any of the British colonies which may desire to attend should be represented, with a view to arrive, if possible, at a common agreement on the basis above indicated."

One of the six reporting against bimetallism later came out strongly in favor of it.[1]

The document was a lengthy and scholarly production; its burden was naturally India and her relations to the mother country. Congress ordered it printed for distribution here, and it gave both the international bimetallists and the free coinage advocates much material for study and discussion.

Silver certificates displace bank notes.

By 1888 the national bank circulation had largely made way for silver certificates. Nearly $230,000,000 of the latter were now in existence; about 60,000,000 of the dollars were actually in circulation. The Treasury had only $30,000,000 free. Gratifying as this was from one point of view, Fairchild nevertheless urged action upon his previous recommendations, as a requisite to remove the danger of going to a depreciated silver basis. He still hoped that before a crisis was reached international action would relieve the situation. The feature of the Treasury condition which attracted most attention was the rapid increase of the gold reserve which had during Fairchild's term gone beyond $200,000,000, standing at the end of March, 1888, at almost $219,000,000.

The political status of silver, 1889.

This was the political situation respecting silver: A large majority of the Democrats in both houses of Congress favored free coinage; a sufficient number of Republican senators were also pledged to that policy to

[1] Leonard Courtney.

make it easy to pass a bill through the Senate; in the House the Republican majority was small, and while a large majority of representatives of that party were opposed to free coinage and a lesser number, but still a majority, were opposed to enlarging the use of silver, it was clear that if *nothing were done* a sufficient number of Republicans would join the silver Democrats in passing a free coinage law. The party was at the same time pledged to tariff legislation, and Harrison, as well as McKinley, who was the House leader, deemed the tariff of paramount importance and believed some silver legislation was necessary for the purpose of averting free coinage and preventing the defeat of tariff legislation. The silver Republicans used their power to attain their ends without disguise.

The task of meeting the political exigency fell to Windom, who had been chosen Secretary of the Treasury by Harrison.

Windom's Treasury report for 1889 included a most elaborate review of the silver question. Silver had now fallen so that the ratio was 22 to 1, giving the silver dollar a bullion value of about 72 cents. The world's product of gold was $123,000,000, that of silver $155,000,000. The United States had coined 343,500-000 silver dollars, of which only 60,000,000 were in use, but 277,300,000 were in the Treasury represented by certificates, leaving free in the Treasury only 6,200,000. *Windom's report on silver.*

While the prediction of danger from our financial policy had not been fulfilled, it was due to favorable conditions of trade, large crops, and general prosperity, which served to postpone the crisis. Silver had continued to fall despite the large purchases by the government. Adverse action by the nations of Europe and increased production were the causes.

It had proven impossible to restore bimetallism single-handed. Gold was in fact our standard, and silver circulated only by force. This could not last.

Proposed
solutions
ineffective. The solutions proposed were (1) an international agreement, which it had been urged would be brought about by distress in Europe due to falling prices, and would be accelerated by suspension of purchases by us (he did not favor such a dangerous measure); (2) continuing the present policy of buying the minimum of $2,000,000 worth monthly, which was satisfactory to no one; (3) increasing to the maximum of $4,000,000 monthly as provided in the law of 1878, urged as proper to offset the contraction of currency erroneously supposed to be going on, when in fact it had been expanded nearly $600,000,000, or $4.75 per capita; (this policy would not raise the market price of silver); (4) free coinage (this would surely banish gold, thus causing contraction, and bring the country upon a depreciated standard); (5) coining heavier dollars, "honest dollars" (but this would be impracticable, as the ratio fluctuated too frequently, and would indefinitely postpone international action); (6) issue certificates for bullion at the rate of 412½ grains to the dollar, without limit (which was equivalent to free coinage and hence would be equally disastrous).

Windom therefore proposed the following : —

Windom's
plan. "Issue Treasury notes against deposits of silver bullion at the market price of silver when deposited, payable on demand in such quantities of silver bullion as will equal in value, at the date of presentation, the number of dollars expressed on the face of the notes at the market price of silver, or in gold, at the option of the government; or in silver dollars at the option of the holder. Repeal the compulsory feature of the present coinage act."

The price was not to exceed $1 for 412½ grains of standard metal.

In support of the measure he argued that while satis- Legal tender
silver notes.
fying the demand for the continued use of silver, it pro-
vided a note-issue which could not depreciate, hence
was *sound;* would enhance the value of silver to a point Appreciation
of silver ex-
pected.
where free coinage would be safe; prevented contrac-
tion by supplying the place of bank-notes rapidly being
retired, yet would not cause inordinate or unhealthy expansion; would if successful point a way for other
nations to take. Loss to the government by reason of
depreciation of the bullion was exceedingly remote, but
even if it came to pass, the government having assumed
the duty of providing currency must stand it. Nor
could an opportunity be given for speculation in silver,
the option to redeem in gold being a sufficient check.
No flood of silver need be feared to cause undue inflation, because being taken at the *market price* it would
not pay Europe to surrender her coins. He estimated
the surplus product of silver at 40,000,000 ounces, and
the proposed law, if limited, would at the maximum take
50,000,000 ounces; there was no substantial stock on
hand anywhere. He preferred that there be no limit
on the amount. If any limit were deemed advisable it
should be by excluding foreign silver altogether.

Assuming, as Windom did (for he was impressed by
the Western view), that some action to take care of silver was requisite, this measure was perhaps the least
objectionable.

Harrison in his message declared in favor of some
legislation to increase the use of silver without the
danger of a silver basis. He had not had opportunity
to study the Windom plan, but approved its general
lines.

The measure was introduced in January, 1890, but the The Win-
dom bill in
Congress.
tariff bill had precedence. Congress debated long, and
only by a vote of 120 to 117 was ready to consider it in

June, and then the Committee on Coinage reported a much altered bill. It directed the purchase monthly of $4,500,000 worth of silver with an issue of Treasury notes, which were to be legal tender, with free coinage when silver reached parity (16 to 1). Bland moved to recommit the bill and order the committee to report a free coinage bill, which was defeated 116 to 140.

Materially amended.

The committee's bill passed the House by a majority of 16, no Democrats voting in its favor. In the Senate numerous amendments were proposed. One striking out the legal tender feature of the notes, by Morrill, was defeated 14 to 50 (Carlisle voting for it, Sherman against). One to strike out the free coinage proviso was lost by 16 to 46. Finding themselves strong enough, the silver advocates in the Senate finally substituted a free coinage bill by a vote of 42 to 25, 14 Republicans voting aye and 3 Democrats nay. After a severe contest in the House in which McKinley led the almost solid Republican vote, the Senate free coinage bill was disagreed to, 135 to 152, and the bills went to conference, where, largely under Sherman's lead, the House bill was remodelled into the shape in which it finally passed on July 14, 1890, in the House by 123 to 90 (116 not voting) and in the Senate by 39 to 26; both strict party votes, for it was a purely administration measure.

The "Sherman law" of 1890.

This act, sometimes known as the "Sherman law," provided for a compulsory purchase by means of an issue of legal tender Treasury notes of 4,500,000 ounces of pure silver monthly, at the market price, not to exceed $1 for 371.25 grains of pure silver (equal to $1.29.29 per ounce). Dollars were to be coined for one year, and thereafter only as they were required for redemption of notes, which were made redeemable in gold or silver dollars at the government's option. No greater or less amount of notes was to be outstanding than the cost of the bullion and the dollars coined therefrom in the Treasury, and silver certificates might be issued on the surplus dollars coined (in other words on the "seigniorage"). The act also declared it the purpose of the government to maintain gold and silver at a parity ; the fund of lawful money held for redemption of notes of liquidating or reducing banks was "covered into the Treasury" instead of being held as a trust fund, the notes to be redeemed to be treated as debt of the United States.

The measure as passed was obviously not as safe or conservative as that planned by Windom. But the friends of silver demanded a larger measure of "protection" for the white metal than Windom had accorded it.

Thus "something was done for silver." The tariff bill was also passed, reducing revenues $50,000,000 ; and a pension bill ultimately calling for an additional annual expenditure of $50,000,000 also became law.

The prospect therefore was that the surplus would be annually cut down $100,000,000, and that the inflation of the circulating medium would be at the rate of over $50,000,000 annually, less the reduction in bank-notes. A definite increasing liability against the gold reserve was created without enlarging the reserve. Careful students of the situation calculated that in eighteen months a crash would come, but they had not given full credit to the nation's resources.

The new inflation.

STATISTICAL RÉSUMÉ
(Amounts in millions)
PRODUCTION OF GOLD AND SILVER

| YEAR | WORLD | | | UNITED STATES | | | RATIO | AVERAGE PRICE OF OUNCE OF SILVER |
| | Gold | Silver | | Gold | Silver | | | |
		Commercial Value	Coining Value		Commercial Value	Coining Value		
1879	109	84	96	39	35	41	18.39	$1.124
1880	106	86	97	36	35	39	18.05	1.145
1881	103	90	102	35	38	43	18.25	1.132
1882	102	98	112	33	41	47	18.20	1.136
1883	95	99	115	30	40	46	18.64	1.109
1884	102	91	105	31	42	49	18.61	1.111
1885	108	98	118	32	43	52	19.41	1.065
1886	106	93	121	35	39	51	20.78	.995
1887	106	94	124	33	40	53	21.10	.979
1888	110	102	141	33	43	59	22.00	.940
1889	123	112	155	33	47	65	22.10	.935
1890	119	132	163	33	57	70	19.75	1.046

THE PURCHASE AND COINAGE OF SILVER

FISCAL YEAR	OUNCES FINE	COST	AVERAGE PRICE PER OUNCE	BULLION VALUE OF SILVER DOLLAR	COINAGE OF SILVER DOLLARS	SILVER CERTIFICATES OUT	SILVER DOLLARS OUT	NET SILVER DOLLARS AND BULLION IN TREASURY
1878	11	13	$ 1.2048	$ .9318	22	—	1	15
1879	19	22	1.1218	.8676	28	—	8	33
1880	22	25	1.1440	.8848	27	6	19	44
1881	20	22	1.1328	.8761	28	39	29	27
1882	21	24	1.1351	.8779	28	55	32	36
1883	23	26	1.1174	.8642	28	73	35	44
1884	22	24	1.1120	.8600	28	96	40	43
1885	22	24	1.0897	.8428	29	102	39	68
1886	23	23	1.0334	.7992	31	88	53	96
1887	26	26	.9810	.7587	34	142	56	80
1888	25	24	.9547	.7384	32	200	56	54
1889	26	25	.9338	.7222	35	257	54	33
1890	28	27	.9668	.7477	38	297	56	27

EXPORTS AND IMPORTS OF SPECIE

FISCAL YEAR	GOLD			SILVER		
	Exports	Imports	Excess − Export ÷ Import	Exports	Imports	Excess − Export + Import
1879 . .	5	6	+ 1	20	15	− 5
1880 . .	4	81	+ 77	13	12	− 1
1881 . .	3	100	+ 97	17	11	− 6
1882 . .	33	34	+ 1	17	8	− 9
1883 . .	12	18	+ 6	20	11	− 9
1884 . .	41	23	− 18	26	15	− 11
1885 . .	8	27	+ 19	34	17	− 17
1886 . .	43	21	− 22	30	18	− 12
1887 . .	10	43	+ 33	26	17	− 9
1888 . .	18	44	+ 26	28	15	− 13
1889 . .	60	10	− 50	37	19	− 18
1890 . .	17	13	− 4	35	21	− 14

III. THE NATIONAL BANKING SYSTEM

CHAPTER XIV

1861 TO 1875

BANK currency in the United States in 1861, as has been shown, was issued wholly under state authority and was far from creditable to a nation boasting advanced civilization. In the Eastern states and a few others salutary laws had led to systems which were sound, but in the greater part of the country, owing to lax legislation and want of supervision, bank-notes passed at varying rates of discount and were counterfeited to an extent that was appalling.

Conditions in 1861. The conditions precipitated by the Civil War were therefore favorable to the creation of a national currency, uniform in character and based upon lines of conservatism and safety. The basic principles underlying the National Bank Act and bank legislation in many of the states were evolved by Alexander Hamilton in preparing the charter for the first United States Bank. The laws of several states, especially those of New York, furnished the provisions of the National Bank Act.

The federal government was in pressing need of money. Bonds could not be readily sold for coin, and Secretary Chase would not take bank-notes, even had the subtreasury law of 1846 not forbidden his doing so. A paper issue was indispensable, and Chase recommended a national currency system based upon government bonds. The bill for this purpose, drawn upon the National currency bill. lines suggested by the Secretary, was introduced in Congress by Representative Spaulding (N.Y.) in the winter of 1861–1862. It was necessarily a lengthy measure, and the exigencies of the war devolved great labors upon Congress. It was not believed that the good effects hoped for under this bill could be realized in time to meet the government's necessity, hence the measure went over until the succeeding session, and the result was, as we have seen, the legal tender government note-issue. Chase was persistent, however, urging upon Congress the double advantage of his plan, at once making a market for the bonds and furnishing the people with a safe and uniform currency, permanent in character.

The legal tender issue, owing to its doubtful constitu- A permanent system contemplated. tionality and its dangerous facility of expansion, was regarded as temporary, and no one contemplated its retention as a permanent currency system. Lincoln, in his message, strongly urged the speedy enactment of the proposed law.[1] The act passed both houses of Congress and was approved February 25, 1863, just one year after the approval of the legal tender act. A considerable number of Republicans and practically all the Democrats opposed the measure. The debate showed that the intention was to supplant state bank circulation, and this intensified the opposition. It is also clear that the authors of the measure contemplated that the currency created would ultimately supplant the United States notes. Sherman, in debate, alluding to the latter form of notes, said that they could "be used only during the war. The very moment that peace comes, all this circulation . . . will at once be banished. . . . The issue of government notes can only be a temporary measure."

[1] See page 191.

Spaulding regarded it as "the commencement of a permanent system for providing a national currency."

National
Currency
Act.
The act was known as the National Currency Act and provided for a bureau in the Treasury Department to be in charge of a Comptroller of the Currency under the general direction of the Secretary, to report directly to Congress. This bureau was given supervision of the banks to be established under the act and the currency issued by them. Hugh McCulloch was appointed the first Comptroller. He did not favor the act but learned to appreciate its usefulness.

In order to constrain state banks to nationalize, their notes were by the act of March 30, 1863, taxed two per cent, just double the tax imposed upon national currency. Four hundred banks were immediately organized, but defects in the law were at once discovered, and upon the
Revision of
1864.
recommendation of Treasury officials it was revised by the act of June 3, 1864. The act passed the House by a vote of 80 to 60, no Democrats favoring it and only two Republicans opposing it, in the Senate by 30 to 9, no Democrats favoring and three Republicans opposing. Under its provisions any number of persons not less than five might form a banking association. The minimum capital was fixed at $50,000 for places under 6000 population, $100,000 for places not exceeding 50,000, and $200,000 for larger cities. One-half of the capital was required to be paid in cash before beginning business, the balance in 10 per cent monthly instalments. Shareholders were liable for debts of the bank to an amount equal to the par of their stock. Each
Circulation.
bank was required to deposit with the Treasury, United States bonds bearing not less than 5 per cent interest to the amount of one-third of the capital (but in no case less than $30,000). to be held to secure circulation, which might be issued to the extent of 90 per cent

of the market value of the bonds (not to exceed 90
per cent of par), but not in excess of the bank's capital.
Notes might be in denominations from $1 to $1000 and
were to bear a certificate on their face that bonds of the
United States were held by the Treasury to secure them,
the name of the bank, and signatures of its officers.
They were made redeemable on demand in "lawful
money" (*i.e.* legal tender), receivable for all public
dues except customs and for all payments by the United
States except interest on the public debt and redemption
of national currency. The volume of notes was limited Volume of
notes limited.
to $300,000,000, of which one-sixth might be under $5
until after the resumption of specie payments, when
none under $5 were to be issued. Banks might reduce
their bond deposits to the minimum required by sur-
rendering their notes for cancellation. They were required to receive each other's notes at par and not to
pay out notes of banks failing to redeem on demand.

Seventeen reserve cities were designated by the act.
The banks in these were required to hold a 25 per cent
reserve on circulation and deposits, one-half of which
might be to their credit with an approved reserve agent
in the city of New York, banks in the latter city being
required to keep a 25 per cent cash in bank reserve. Reserves
required.
All other banks were required to keep 15 per cent
reserve on circulation and deposits, three-fifths of which
might be to their credit with a bank approved by the
Comptroller of the Currency in any of the reserve cities.
When reserves were impaired no new loans were to be
made until the same were restored, and if not restored
within thirty days after notice from the Comptroller, a
receiver might, with the approval of the Secretary of
the Treasury, be appointed. A receiver might also be
appointed for failure to redeem notes or provide for
their redemption at the reserve agencies. In case of

receivership the bonds were to be sold by the Comptroller, and the bank's circulation retired with the proceeds. If there were a deficit, the amount thereof was a paramount lien upon all the bank's assets.

General regulation.

The banks might transact a general banking business. Loans in excess of 10 per cent of the capital to any one person or concern were forbidden, bona fide discount or purchase of bills receivable excepted. Interest rates were regulated. Banks were forbidden to acquire real estate other than for their necessary use, unless the same were taken for preëxisting debts. Before dividends were declared, 10 per cent of the profits were required to be passed to a surplus fund until it should equal 20 per cent of the capital. A tax of $\frac{1}{2}$ per cent semiannually was imposed upon circulation, and $\frac{1}{4}$ per cent each upon capital and deposits, in lieu of all other federal taxes. Charters extended for a period of twenty years from date of incorporation, but dissolution might be effected by a two-thirds vote of shareholders, in which case notes were to be advertised for and redeemed. After one year, however, the bank might deposit with the Treasury lawful money to redeem the notes and receive back the bonds held. Periodical examinations, full and verified quarterly reports, and monthly reports of the principal items, were required. The total debts of a bank, aside from its notes and deposits, were not to exceed its capital. Provision was made for the conversion of state banks into the national system. National banks might be designated by the Secretary of the

Public depositories.

Treasury as government depositories for all revenues except customs, such deposits to be secured to the satisfaction of the Secretary "by government bonds and otherwise." Congress reserved the right at any time to amend or repeal the act.

The original act (1863) had a provision under which

state banks could enjoy the privilege of depositing bonds and issuing notes, although remaining under the control of the states. It also provided for an apportionment of circulation among the states according to population and bank facilities, and required a 25 per cent reserve for *all* banks. It omitted the requirement for a surplus fund, for redemption of notes at reserve agencies, and the regulation of discount rates.

By the end of 1864 there were 638 banks, with a capital of over $135,000,000 and circulation of nearly $67,000,000. They owned at that time $176,500,000 government bonds, and had helped to place with the public a much larger amount. The government's deposits with them amounted to nearly $38,000,000.

The state banks experienced little difficulty in redeeming their notes in greenbacks, and constantly maintained a very large volume in circulation. Under the laws of many states bank-notes were issued against the credit or general assets of the banks, and where a deposit of security was required it was easier or more profitable to comply with the state laws than to deposit United States bonds as required by the National Bank Act. The amount of notes which might be issued was less restricted under the state laws and altogether banking under the state systems was more profitable. The currency had not been nationalized, and the national system as a market for bonds had been disappointing. *State banks.*

Therefore, on March 3, 1865, a revenue law imposed a tax of 10 per cent upon state bank-notes paid out by any bank, national or state, and also provided that state banks with branches might come into the national system and retain their branches. In 1866 the 10 per cent tax was extended to state bank-notes used in payment by any one. This legislation very soon caused the disappearance of all such notes and was a powerful factor *Tax on state bank-notes.*

in inducing banks to organize under the national system. At the end of 1865 there were 1582 national banks with over $400,000,000 capital, owning $440,000,000 of bonds, with circulation amounting to $213,000,000. They also had outstanding over $45,000,000 of old notes issued by those which had been state institutions.

The act of March 3, 1865, regulated the proportion of note-issues of largely capitalized banks, diminishing the ratio as the capital increased, and provided that one-half of the maximum circulation ($300,000,000) was to be apportioned among the states according to population, the other half "with due regard to banking capital, resources, and business." This law was the result of a tendency, anticipated in the original currency act, towards a monopolization of the new bank issues by Eastern banks. The Southern states, recently restored to the Union, had now to be provided for. The limit of circulation was soon reached.

State bank-notes.

Let us now turn to the state banks and record the conditions at the period of the disappearance of a system which had existed for thirty years, despite its glaring defects and the want of security, uniformity, and stability of the notes issued thereunder. In the states which formed the Southern Confederacy there were in 1861 about 250 banks, capitalized at $110,000,000, with $68,000,000 of note circulation and $31,000,000 in specie. With some notable exceptions these were the worst of the note-issuing banks of that period. The Civil War served to wipe them out of existence so far as their currency functions were concerned. The system of banks in the remainder of the country at this time was not materially different as to currency and supervision from that existing in the period of 1857–1860 already described. The war gave a wonderful impetus to business. The repeated issue of United States notes, suspension of specie payments, and general inflation of values gave to state banks, with their facility for note expansion, a great opportunity to make money. It was only natural that they should resist the establishment of a national currency system.

The Treasury reports upon the condition of state banks were not continued after 1863. From Secretary Chase's reports it appears that in 1861 there were 1601 state banks, with a capital of $429,600,000; in 1863, 1466 banks, with a capital of $405,000,000. The circulation, which in 1861 was $202,000,000 and in 1862 only $184,000,000, rose to nearly $239,000,000 in 1863, an increase of $55,000,000 coincident with the issue by the government of $400,000,000 legal tender notes. This was the largest amount of state bank-notes ever reported. In the year when the new system was born the old one showed the maximum note-issue, as if to challenge its competitor. With the power of the federal government behind it, however, the national system was rapidly growing. In January, 1864, state bank circulation was estimated at $170,000,000, and on July 1, at $126,000,000. The power of Congress to tax the notes of state banks out of existence was contested and carried to the Supreme Court, which sustained the law (Veazie Bank *vs.* Fenno, 8 Wall. 533).

State bank statistics.

The interest-bearing legal tender notes which were held by the banks in their reserves matured in 1867. It was feared that their retirement and consequent substitution of non-interest-bearing United States notes would occasion a contraction of the currency and interfere with business prosperity. Hence the act of March 2, 1867, authorized the issue of $50,000,000 of 3 per cent temporary loan certificates payable on demand, and the act of July 25, 1868, permitted the use of $25,000,000 more, to take the place of the maturing interest-bearing

Three per cent certificates.

notes in bank reserves.   The maximum issue was about
$60,000,000.

Opposition
to national
banks.
The national currency was absolutely secured by
government bonds and passed at par throughout the
length and breadth of the land.   It presented a strong
contrast to the old system of state bank circulation,
consisting of more or less doubtful promises to pay and
costing the public through discount and losses at its
best about 5 per cent per annum.   But the national bank
circulation was limited to $300,000,000, and notwith-
standing the apportionment act of 1865 the larger portion had been obtained by the Eastern states.   This gave
rise to the cry of monopoly.   The advocates of more
money and cheap money obtained a ready audience,
producing a practical recurrence of the events of 1832.
There arose a substantial party in 1867 which favored
the substitution of legal tender notes for bank-notes,
and in fact the national system suffered a precarious
existence for the next ten years, with strong probabilities
McCulloch's
defence of
the system.
of its abolition.   Secretary McCulloch felt constrained
to defend the system from the attacks of the anti-bank
element, which had the aid of the friends of the old
state banks.   The following summary of his arguments
is interesting.   The national system had been adopted
not to do away with state banks but to supersede a very
defective bank currency with a national one.   The legal
tender notes were only temporary currency, the national
bank-notes were proposed as a permanent currency.
The legal tenders were subject to inflation, depreciation,
and other evils ; the national bank-notes could easily
be regulated and kept from depreciating ; moreover, to
supersede them now would inevitably cause a crisis.
On the other hand, the Nation was bound in honor to
retire the greenbacks, and the policy of contraction of
these notes was the only proper one in view of the

redundancy of paper money and the imperative duty of resuming coin payments at an early date. An increase of greenbacks, such as was contemplated by the anti-bank men, would render resumption much more difficult and cause irretrievable losses. In order to provide the sections inadequately supplied with circulation, he recommended a redistribution by law. He regarded it unwise to increase the volume of notes until after the resumption of coin payments. The circulation per capita at this time was $18.28, against $13.35 for 1860 and $23.80 for 1865.

It is interesting to note the earnestness with which Comptroller Hulburd in 1867, 1868, and 1869 denounced the payments of interest on deposits by New York banks as an element of danger. He argued that interest attracted large deposits of money from the interior when not needed for local purposes, which money to be available must necessarily be loaned to brokers on call; the latter were able to lock up money and raise rates of interest by means of over-certification, resulting in a money stringency and general disturbance when these loans were necessarily called in order to admit of sending the money back to the interior to again serve the local demand. Why brokers as a class should be subjected to the charge of a desire to raise money rates does not appear.

Secretary Boutwell in 1869 strongly indorsed Comptroller Hulburd's recommendations and favored a law absolutely prohibiting the payment of interest on deposits and limiting collateral loans to 10 per cent of a bank's capital. He was also satisfied that the practice of certifying checks, even when funds were in bank to the credit of the drawer, was fraught with evil and should be entirely prohibited. It is indeed strange that so absurd a proposition could emanate from the chief financial officer of the government.

Interest on reserve deposits.

Boutwell on certification of checks.

On February 19, 1869, an act was passed prohibiting making loans either upon legal tender notes or national bank-notes as collateral. This was designed to prevent contraction. On March 3, 1869, a law authorized the Comptroller to fix the dates of reports at his discretion, not less than five each year, and required reports of earnings and dividends semiannually; another prohibited certification of checks in excess of the drawer's balance.

Redistribution of circulation.

The absolute inelasticity of the bank circulation became an important question. The authorized $300,000,000 had been absorbed, and no new banks could be organized except as old ones went out of business. Only fifteen banks had failed, and only fifty-six had gone into voluntary liquidation up to the close of 1869. Moreover, the government was about to retire the 3 per cent reserve certificates, which would cause a greater demand for United States notes for reserve purposes, thereby contracting the currency. In February, 1870, the House of Representatives, by a vote (110 to 73) which was practically sectional rather than partisan, passed a resolution declaring that the country required more money and directed the Banking and Currency Committee to prepare a bill for an increase of $50,000,000. After

Increase by act of 1870.

great labor Congress, on July 12, 1870, passed an act to increase the circulation of national banks $54,000,000. This was to take the place of the 3 per cent reserve certificates about to be retired. The act also provided for a reapportionment of the circulation by taking from banks in states having more than their share, according to wealth and population, and assigning it to banks in states having less. The proportion in the Eastern and Middle states was then some $80,000,000 in excess, the South being entitled to $57,200,000 more than it had. The act also limited the amount of circulation of banks thereafter organized to $500,000 and authorized national gold banks. This latter provision was practically confined to the Pacific slope, where specie payments had not been suspended. The issues of these banks were limited to 80 per cent of the par value of bonds deposited, were redeemable in gold on demand, and gold reserves of 25 per cent were to be maintained; the banks were not required to take the notes of other banks nor to provide for redemption in the East.

During the discussion of this measure propositions were introduced, but defeated, to repeal the 10 per cent tax on state bank-notes, to fix maximum discount rates at 7 per cent, to prohibit the payment of interest on deposits, to pay no interest on bonds while on deposit to secure circulation, and to substitute United States notes for bank-notes.

On June 18, 1872, the Treasury was authorized to receive on deposit legal tender notes (greenbacks) and issue therefor non-interest-bearing currency certificates in denominations of $5000 and $10,000. These certificates were a convenient form of bank reserve, and were especially useful in the settlement of large clearing-house balances. *Currency certificates.*

Statesmen and economists were much in need of some central reservoir of information in regard to all banks and banking institutions, state as well as national. To provide accurate statistical information of such character the act of February 19, 1873, provided that the Comptroller should report the condition of state banks and other financial institutions and private bankers annually. In order to comply with this requirement the Comptroller corresponds with the supervisory departments of the different states, as well as with the various institutions directly, and submits the most accurate data obtainable.

In September, 1873, there occurred a monetary panic in New York, causing a suspension of cash payments *Crisis of 1873.*

for forty days and carrying down many business houses. The unfortunate experience of this trying period greatly emphasized the defects in the currency system. The Treasury aided in relieving the stringency by bond purchases and by the very questionable course of issuing greenbacks "in reserve," that is, greenbacks that had once been redeemed and retired.

The New York banks presently lost $35,000,000 of cash and for relief were compelled to resort to clearinghouse loan certificates, issued upon securities hypothecated, and used in settlement of debit balances at the clearing-house. The maximum amount of this auxiliary currency used was $26,565,000.

Grant on currency.

President Grant, in his message in December, suggested that the crisis may have been a blessing in disguise, and cautioned Congress to heed the lesson and provide against its recurrence. Elasticity of the currency and the prevention of speculative use-of reserves, the prohibition of interest on deposits, the requirement of reserves to be kept at home, the redemption of notes by banks, and "free banking" (*i.e.* removing the limit on circulation and facilitating its retirement) were among the remedies he suggested. The interconvertible bond plan, under which banks could obtain government notes at any time by depositing bonds, returnable when the notes were returned and bearing no interest while on deposit, was also recommended.

The inflation bill.

Congress, regarding the proper remedy an increase of paper money, immediately took up the question, and, after the consideration of numerous propositions, finally passed an act increasing national bank-notes and legal tender notes to $400,000,000 each, prohibiting interest payments on balances held as reserve on circulation, requiring accumulations of coin by banks for redemption of notes, and requiring three-fourths of the reserves to be kept in cash in bank. Grant, after much urging, vetoed the measure, calling attention to the fact that $25,000,000 of bank currency was still subject to reapportionment to states having a deficiency. When that was taken up and specie payments restored, it would be time to consider the demand for "more money."

Congress thereupon passed the act of June 20, 1874, Act of 1874. providing that in lieu of the required reserve (25 and 15 per cent respectively) for redemption of circulation, lawful money to the extent of 5 per cent of the circulation should be deposited and maintained in the Treasury, and the current redemption of notes was thereafter to be made at the Treasury and by the Treasurer instead of by reserve agents. The 5 per cent fund was to be counted as part of the reserve on deposits. This obviously released from reserve requirements a considerable amount of lawful money, estimated by Comptroller Knox in 1874 at over $20,000,000. The act also provided that Provision for retiring notes. banks might deposit lawful money in the Treasury for the reduction or retirement of their circulation and receive back their bonds pro rata. The notes were then to be redeemed out of this fund by the Treasury. The bonds on deposit were not to be reduced below the minimum requirement. Under this provision currency reapportionment was facilitated as banks were by the act compelled to surrender excess circulation. The amount now to be redistributed was $80,000,000. The maximum circulation issuable remained at $354,000,000. A "free Volume of notes increased. banking" provision was presented as an amendment to the bill but defeated, as were also amendments to replace bank-notes with greenbacks, regulate discount rates, and require *all* reserves to be kept in cash in bank. The latter proviso at one stage had passed both houses of Congress but was finally lost. The measure passed by very large majorities.

It appears that all the Comptrollers of the Currency down to and including Knox recommended the prohibition of interest upon deposits by reserve banks, and stringent measures against over-certification of checks, believing that the payment of interest abnormally increased the deposits of interior banks in New York City, while the certification of checks facilitated the use of the same by stock exchange brokers. This money being in use by the brokers when required for crop-moving purposes was what occasioned the annual stringency in money in the fall of the year. Secretary Bristow disapproved the prohibition of interest upon deposits, as a discrimination against national and in favor of state banks, but suggested a tax upon all interest-bearing deposits as a means of discouraging the practice.

Interest on deposits.

The strong position against the payment of interest on deposits by banks, taken by the various Comptrollers of the Currency and Secretaries of the Treasury down to 1874, possesses peculiar interest in view of the fact that Secretary Gage in 1901 and Secretary Shaw in 1902 recommended that surplus funds of the Treasury be deposited with banks and the government receive interest thereon.

The political revolution in 1874, by which the Republicans for the first time since 1859 lost control of the House of Representatives, although primarily due to the conditions after the panic, was also largely caused by the want of public confidence in the dominant party. The halting, hesitating, shuffling, and changing positions which it occupied with reference to the retirement of the greenbacks, the resumption of specie payments, and the question of sound money generally, had, not to use a stronger term, sorely disappointed the public, and it was generally felt that a change might prove beneficial. This feeling was certainly justified by events. Stung by defeat and brought face to face with the political consequences of their insincere and opportunist method of meeting these questions, they strove to regain lost ground and win back the confidence and support of the business interests of the country. In the short session of the old Congress (1874–1875) the Republicans under the lead of Sherman vigorously pushed a specie resumption measure, coupled with free banking, which finally became law January 14, 1875. It repealed all limits on the volume of national bank-notes, thus doing away with the necessity for redistribution. It was passed by a strict party vote, with a small body of extreme sound money Republicans opposing the measure.

Free banking and resumption law.

The passage of the resumption act marks a period in the life of national banks. At this time there were 2027 of these associations, with capital of $496,000,000, circulation $331,000,000, individual deposits $683,000,000, loans $956,000,000, government bonds $413,000,000, specie $22,000,000, legal tenders $116,000,000, and 5 per cent fund with the Treasury $21,000,000. One hundred and seventy-eight banks had gone out of business in the eleven years. Thirty-seven of these failed, twelve of them ultimately paid their debts in full, and the balance generally a very large percentage of their indebtedness. All their notes were paid in full.

Status of banks.

The earnings of the national banks calculated upon capital and surplus had diminished from an average of 11.8 per cent in 1870, the first year this information was reported, to 10.3 per cent in 1874. Dividends averaged in 1870 10.05 per cent, and in 1874 9.9 per cent. A generally higher ratio of earnings prevailed in the West and South.

The incomplete reports of state banks covered only 551, with capital of $69,000,000, deposits $166,000,000, loans $176,000,000, cash $28,000,000. Many of the states still neglected to require reports from banks.

STATISTICAL RÉSUMÉ

(Amounts in millions of dollars)

CONDITION OF NATIONAL BANKS, 1864 TO 1875

(AT DATES NEAREST JANUARY 1)

YEAR	NUMBER	CAPITAL	DEPOSITS	CIRCULA-TION	CASH	LOANS
1864 . .	139	15	19	—	5	11
1865 . .	638	136	221	67	77	166
1866 . .	1582	403	552	213	207	501
1867 . .	1648	420	588	291	207	609
1868 . .	1682	420	562	294	175	617
1869 . .	1628	419	585	294	118	645
1870 . .	1615	426	555	293	136	689
1871 . .	1648	435	517	296	107	726
1872 . .	1790	460	617	318	124	819
1873 . .	1940	483	611	336	134	886
1874 . .	1976	490	553	341	160	857
1875 . .	2027	496	694	331	139	956

CONDITION OF STATE BANKS, 1861 TO 1875, SO FAR AS OBTAINABLE

YEAR	STATE BANKS						SAVINGS BANKS			CLEAR-INGS, NEW YORK
	Number	Capital	De-posits	Circu-lation	Cash	Loans	Deposi-tors (000's)	Depos-its (millions)	Average deposit	
1861	1601	430	257	202	88	697	694	147	$211	5,916
1862	1496	420	297	184	102	648	788	169	215	6,871
1863	1466	405	394	239	101	649	887	206	232	14,868
1864	1089	312	—	163	51	—	976	236	242	24,097
1865	349	71	—	—	—	—	981	243	247	26,032
1866	297	66	—	—	—	—	1067	282	265	28,717
1867	272	65	—	—	—	—	1188	337	284	28,675
1868	247	66	—	—	—	—	1310	393	300	28,484
1869	259	67	—	—	—	—	1467	458	312	37,407
1870	325	87	—	—	—	—	1631	550	337	27,804
1871	452	111	—	—	—	—	1902	651	342	29,301
1872	566	122	—	—	—	—	1993	735	369	33,844
1873	—	43	111	—	11	119	2186	802	367	35,461
1874	—	59	138	—	27	154	2293	865	377	22,856
1875	551	69	166	—	28	176	2360	924	392	25,061

CHAPTER XV

1876 TO 1882

The changes in the National Bank Act in 1875 Continued opposition. broadened the scope and increased the power of national banks with respect to currency by removing all limitation upon the volume, thereby making banking free. This made it possible to organize banks *ad libitum* in the South and West, and tended to relieve in a measure the disadvantages which caused so much just complaint from those sections owing to the inadequacy of currency and credit facilities. Rich in natural, undeveloped resources, these sections needed capital for their development. What they thought they needed was currency, and believing United States notes most likely to meet their wants, the agitation against national banks and in favor of the substitution of greenbacks for bank-notes continued. Although bank organization and the issue of bank currency was now absolutely free, the cry of monopoly was still maintained.

Comptroller Knox in elaborate reports in 1875 and Knox's reports. 1876, in which the history of banking and bank currency in the United States from the beginning of the government was reviewed, demonstrated that the national system was so vastly superior to any that had preceded it that to abrogate it now and return to the former conditions would mean abandonment of a safe and sound currency, a superior banking system, and the substitution of the old state bank systems with all their evils. The cost of domestic exchange which in 1859

averaged 1 per cent had, largely by the national
system, been reduced to a small fraction of that rate.

Against the charge that the national banks made
enormous profits, he showed that, taxation considered,
the earnings were actually less than those of banks outside the system not subjected to the onerous restrictions
of the federal law. The voluntary surrender of over
$50,000,000 of notes by the banks he contended was
proof absolute that the profit on circulation could not be
as large as alleged.

Efforts to repeal the 10 per cent tax on state bank
issues were defeated by decisive majorities.

Receivership.   Congress made several amendments to the bank act
with reference to settling affairs of insolvent banks.
The duties of the Comptroller of the Currency in this
respect are most important. Under the law the
Comptroller appoints receivers for failed national banks,
fixes their compensation, adjusts differences, and approves
compromises in reducing the assets of failed banks to
cash. By means of bank examiners he is fully advised as to conditions. By means of hard and painstaking work he is able to exercise an intelligent judgment and reach a satisfactory conclusion as to the value
and adjustment of claims, thereby effecting compromises,
speedy settlement and payment, avoiding expensive
litigation and delay, realizing a much larger net amount
for the payment of creditors, and securing to them their
dividends in a much shorter space of time. The
Comptroller sustains the same relation to a failed
national bank and the receiver, that the court in any of
our states does to a failed corporation and the receiver
of the same. His powers are parallel and coincident.
The cheapness and celerity and high percentage of
dividends realized in the settlement of failed national
banks compared with the administration of corporate

receiverships in our different states is most gratifying and highly complimentary to the national system as administered by the Comptroller of the Currency.

A very important feature of the national banking system is the supervision exercised by official examiners. The statute provides that the Comptroller, with the approval of the Secretary of the Treasury, shall " appoint a suitable person or persons to make an examination of the affairs of every banking association, who shall have power to make a thorough examination into all the affairs of the association, and, in doing so, to examine any of the officers and agents thereof on oath; and shall make a full and detailed report of the condition of the association to the Comptroller." The above provision is wisely made very general in its terms. There is practically no limit to the power of the examiner so long as he is right. The good the examiners do is largely of a negative character, in preventing wrongs and misman-agement which otherwise might exist. Such work necessarily does not come to the public notice, and the system therefore does not receive the credit it is entitled to. They do not always detect bad management and prevent bank failures, but their restraining and corrective influence is of the greatest value.

Bank exami-nations.

Requiring banks to make and publish five verified re-ports of condition annually upon blanks furnished and in a form prescribed by the Comptroller of the Cur-rency, necessarily compels the banks' bookkeeping to conform to such requirements. It compels system and method in the conduct of each bank's affairs, and in-sures uniformity throughout the nation. This provision is most wholesome and far-reaching in its effect upon the conduct of the bank's business. The data thus ob-tained and collected afford most valuable information as to business and economic conditions. Being subject

Value of reports.

to the verification of the examiner, they are accurate and reliable.

Circulation diminished.

Notwithstanding free banking, the banks did not avail of the opportunity to increase their circulation as had been expected, proving that the demand for "more money" on the part of the South and West simply expressed the need of more capital. Eighteen million dollars of new circulation had been issued under the law of 1875, and hence nearly $14,500,000 of greenbacks had been retired. The privilege of reducing circulation by deposit of "lawful money" was made use of to such an extent that there was a net contraction of national bank circulation of nearly $40,000,000 since the act became operative. Thus the contraction of paper currency was fully $54,000,000. On the other hand, the operation of the changed law with respect to reserve against circulation released $14,000,000 of legal tenders, resulting in a net contraction of $40,000,000. The ability to retire circulation by depositing lawful money and the right to increase at any time, gave to the curreney a measurable degree of flexibility.

During the two years following the enactment of the law of 1874 fully two-thirds of the national bank-notes outstanding were redeemed through the 5 per cent fund and new ones issued, thus furnishing the public a cleanly and wholesome currency.

Greenbacker opposition to banks.

In 1878 a determined effort was made to supplant national bank currency with legal tender notes. The Greenback party favored this movement. Representative Ewing (Dem., O.), one of the chief leaders of the movement, introduced an elaborate bill for the purpose in the House. The measure was defeated by the very close vote of 110 to 114, a dozen Democrats voting against the measure and as many Republicans for it. This vote greatly encouraged the "Greenbackers" to continue their efforts.

In February, 1878, Congress passed the silver purchase and coinage law, under which a new form of paper
currency (silver certificates) was provided, and in May,
1878, another act, under which the further retirement
of greenbacks was prohibited. Both these measures
were intended to operate against the extension of bank-
note issues. Bank circulation had increased during the
year but slightly, and mainly owing to the organization
of new banks.

The national bank system received but indifferent
support from Secretary Sherman, who expressed himself in favor of the continuance of the bank currency at
least until 1883, when the first of the charters were to
expire. The subject could then be discussed, with the
public mind better prepared to consider it. He also opposed the retirement of the greenbacks.

Notwithstanding the continuing warfare made upon
them, the banks worked zealously to aid the government
in meeting the requirements of the resumption law, and
very materially strengthened their gold reserves to bring
their notes to par in specie.

Banks aid resumption.

In 1879, specie payments having been resumed, business materially revived. The circulation of banks
showed a substantial increase, although the capital had
diminished. The issue of the 4 per cent bonds at or
near par helped to make circulation profitable ; on the
other hand, the increased demand for circulating media
was now in considerable measure supplied by gold and
by silver dollars and certificates representing the same.

Comptroller Knox reported (1880) that the banks
held $100,000,000 in specie, and as evidence of an im-
proved condition generally, presented a table showing a
material lessening of prevailing rates of interest in different localities. New York and Philadelphia rates
were from 3 to 5 per cent, Boston and Baltimore, 5 per

Interest rates.

cent, Chicago, 4 to 7 per cent, St. Louis, 5 to 7 per cent, Cleveland and Milwaukee, 6 to 8 per cent, St. Paul, 7 to 10 per cent, Omaha, 10 per cent, Denver, 10 to 15 per cent, and California, 8 to 12 per cent, in the South, 7 to 10 per cent, except in New Orleans, where 4 to 6 per cent prevailed. The increase of circulating media since resumption had been $248,000,000, of which $176,000,000 was gold, $51,000,000 silver, and $20,000,000 bank-notes. Attention was also directed to the average size of loans and discounts by banks — $1082 for all. The Southern and Western states averaged $750, whereas the average of the Bank of France was $188.80, the Imperial Bank of Germany, $402.55. The Bank of France showed over 2,000,000 transactions of less than $100, whereas our national banks showed but 251,000 of such transactions.

Refunding vetoed.Congress passed a refunding measure providing for 3 per cent bonds, which were to be the only bonds available to secure bank circulation. The measure also repealed the provision for reducing circulation by deposit of lawful money, and contained other restrictions and objectionable features. The bill reached President Hayes on the last day of his term, March 3, 1881, and was at once vetoed. In his messages and by his veto power President Hayes proved a strong and firm defender of the national credit and the principles of sound money throughout his administration.

In the absence of a refunding law, Secretary Windom, during the summer of 1881, extended $538,000,000 of 5 and 6 per cent bonds at $3\frac{1}{2}$ per cent interest, redeemable at the pleasure of the government. The banks held about $250,000,000 of these bonds.

Checks used as money.Comptroller Knox obtained and reported data showing the actual amount of cash that entered into the transactions of all national banks on two business days, viz. June 30 and September 17, 1881. The average transactions represented by checks were 95.1 per cent and 94.1 per cent respectively, the balance being in actual money. Of the cash, paper currency represented 4 per cent and 4.36 per cent respectively, coin supplying the balance. Banks outside of reserve cities showed 81.7 per cent of checks on both days.

A curious and interesting controversy arose at this time over the proper construction of the term "lawful money," permitted to be deposited as a part of the 5 per cent redemption fund with which to retire circulating notes, — curious because it shows the tenacity with which the advocates of legal tender notes insisted that they should be used on all occasions. It was paralleled by the fatuous devotion of the advocates of silver later. The statute provided that the Treasury was to redeem bank-notes in "United States notes" and "legal tender notes." The term "lawful money" had become interchangeable, in the minds of legislators, with "legal tender notes," and they insisted that it did not include coin. The Treasury, strange to say, clung to this narrow construction. The banks maintained that gold coin and silver dollars were "lawful money." The Attorney-general, to whom the subject was referred, decided that when a payment was required to be made in promises to pay dollars, the dollars themselves could be used for that purpose.

"Lawful money" interpreted.

A bill to extend the charters of existing banks for a period of twenty years, after a long and determined opposition, became a law on July 12, 1882. The advocates of more money, however, succeeded in incorporating into the act a provision limiting the amount of bank-notes which might be retired to $3,000,000 per month (except when bonds securing the circulation were called for redemption), and banks reducing their circulation were prohibited from again increasing their note-issue

Law of 1882

for the period of six months. Gold certificates were provided for, and these, as well as silver certificates, were to be available for bank reserves.

To prevent alleged discrimination against silver certificates, national banks were prohibited from being members of a clearing-house where such certificates were not taken in payment of balances. This was aimed at the New York clearing-house, which immediately thereafter repealed its rule forbidding the use of silver certificates in the settlement of balances. Provision was made for a 3 per cent bond payable, at the pleasure of the government, to be used in. funding the extended 3½ per cents. The minimum bond deposit with the United States Treasury for banks capitalized at $150,000 or less was fixed at one-quarter of their capital. This allowed a minimum bond deposit of $12,500. Provision was made for retiring the notes of banks whose charters were extended, and all gain by the loss or destruction of bank-notes inured to the benefit of the government. The over-certification of checks was also forbidden under severe penalty.

This legislation was obviously a compromise, although in many respects favorable to the banks. For everything that was obtained by the friends of the banks something had to be yielded. The expansionists succeeded in interfering with the sole provision for flexibility by limiting the power of retiring notes at the pleasure of the banks. An amendment to substitute greenbacks for national bank-notes received only 71 votes, and the votes on other amendments showed that the greenback influence in Congress was on the wane.

This act extending the charters of national banks seemed to mark another period and settle the status of the system. Since then little serious effort has been made to legislate them out of existence or to repeal their power to issue circulating notes, although it has been impossible to obtain any legislation which would give to bank currency greater flexibility and make it responsive to the needs of commerce.

Shortly after the enactment of the law of 1875 bank capital reached a maximum of $505,000,000. It fell to $454,000,000 in October, 1879, recovering to $477,000,-000 July 1, 1882. Circulation (not including that against which lawful money had been deposited) showed a minimum of $298,000,000 and a maximum of $325,000,-000, both in 1881. Individual deposits at the beginning of the period were $683,000,000, at the end $1,067,000,-000, and loans increased from $956,000,000 to $1,209,-000,000. Gauged by their capital the banks could have issued $121,000,000 more notes than they had on July 1, 1882, but the demand for bank-notes was lessened by the existence at this time of $54,500,000 silver certificates which had come into use. The increase in the number of banks was only 212, of which 124 were added in the last year. The losses sustained after the panic of 1873 and the disturbances in 1876–1877 were so large that the aggregate surplus fund was reduced to $114,-000,000 (from $130,000,000). This was recovered during 1880–1882. Earnings receded from 9.7 per cent to 5.1 per cent, recovering to 8.9 per cent. Forty-nine banks failed, 25 of which suspended in 1877–1878. Of the failed banks 21 paid creditors in full, and the balance nearly in full. The tax paid by the banks on circulation in 1864–1882 amounted to $50,700,000, and the tax on capital and deposits to $62,600,000, a total of $113,300,000. In addition, state taxes now averaged more than $8,000,000 annually, so that the rate of taxes paid yearly was equal to 3.7 per cent on the capital.

Despite the utmost freedom given by the act of 1875

Bank statistics.

Failures of banks.

to bank circulation, the Western and Southern states still had only $105,000,000, against $250,000,000 in the Middle and Eastern states.

State banks.   State banks, of which only incomplete reports were available, showed an increase of 121 in number and $23,000,000 in capital. They had increased their surplus from less than $7,000,000 to more than $23,000,000, their deposits by $116,000,000, and their loans by $96,000,000.

The relative supply of banking facilities of the several sections of the country is concisely stated in the following table compiled from the reports of the Comptroller of the Currency. Savings banks are here included, which give the Eastern and Middle states a great preponderance. The savings banks of California in the same manner increase the per capita of the Western section. An almost total absence of such institutions in the Southern states is a remarkable fact in the economic history of that section.

Banking power by sections.

STATES	BANKING POWER (In millions)		PER CAPITA	
	1870	1880	1870	1880
Eastern . . .	637	707	$182.51	$176.37
Middle . . .	1046	1335	107.64	113.50
Southern . .	147	158	11.23	10.36
Central . . .	311	462	27.65	26.86
Western . .	61	140	60.61	73.07
All . . .	2202	2802	57.09	55.88

The increase in banking power in the Southern and Central states did not keep pace with the growth of population, which accounted for the strength there of the "greenback movement."

STATISTICAL RÉSUMÉ

(Amounts in millions of dollars)

CONDITION OF NATIONAL BANKS

(AT DATES NEAREST JANUARY 1)

YEAR	NUMBER	CAPITAL	DEPOSITS	CIRCULA-TION	SPECIE	LEGAL TENDERS	LOANS
1876	2086	505	629	315	17	102	963
1877	2082	497	631	292	33	92	929
1878	2074	477	615	299	33	97	882
1879	2051	462	707	304	41	99	824
1880	2052	454	766	322	79	66	934
1881	2095	459	1018	317	107	65	1071
1882	2164	466	1115	325	114	68	1169

STATE BANKS AND TRUST COMPANIES

YEAR	STATE BANKS[1]					TRUST COMPANIES
	Number	Capital	Deposits	Cash	Loans	Aggregate Resources
1876	633	80	158	30	179	128
1877	592	111	227	37	267	124
1878	475	95	143	32	169	111
1879	616	104	167	39	191	112
1880	620	91	209	55	207	127
1881	652	93	261	41	251	157
1882	672	92	282	42	272	195

[1] This table has little value for comparative purposes; reports from six to twelve states are missing after 1876, but again included in later years.

NEW YORK CLEARING-HOUSE AND SAVINGS BANKS

Year	New York Clearing-house Exchanges	Savings Banks, U. S.			Failures	
	(Millions)	Depositors (000's)	Deposits (Millions)	Average Deposit	Number (000's)	Liabilities (Millions)
1876	21.597	2,369	941	$397	9	191
1877	23.289	2,395	866	361	9	191
1878	22.508	2,401	880	366	10	234
1879	25.178	2,269	802	354	7	98
1880	37.182	2,336	819	351	5	66
1881	48.565	2,529	892	353	6	81
1882	46.552	2,710	967	357	7	102

UNITED STATES BONDS, AND BANK CIRCULATION

Year (June 30)	Total Bonded Debt	Held as Security for Circulation	National Bank Circulation	+ Increase − Decrease	Silver Certificates in Circulation	Price of Bonds[1]	
						High	Low
1865	1110	236	131	+105	——	112⅜	103½
1866	1213	327	268	+137	——	114¾	103¾
1867	1634	341	292	+ 24	——	113¼	106½
1868	2092	341	295	+ 3	——	118⅛	108⅜
1869	2167	343	293	− 2	——	125	111
1870	2051	342	292	− 1	——	118½	112⅜
1871	1953	360	316	+ 24	——	119⅜	110¼
1872	1845	380	327	+ 11	——	113¾	107¾
1873	1760	390	339	+ 12	——	116¼	106¼
1874	1789	391	339	——	——	117	111
1875	1773	376	318	− 21	——	119	113⅝
1876	1761	341	294	− 24	——	119	110⅜
1877	1762	339	290	− 4	——	112⅝	105¼
1878	1845	350	300	+ 10	——	107⅜	103
1879	1952	354	307	+ 7	——	104¼	99
1880	1775	362	318	+ 11	6	113⅝	103
1881	1690	360	312	− 6	39	118⅝	112⅜
1882	1514	358	309	− 3	55	121¾	117¼

[1] 6's of 1881, to 1872; 5's of 1881, to 1878; 4's of 1907 later.

CHAPTER XVI

1883 TO 1890

DURING the period now under discussion the banks were a neglected factor in currency affairs of the country; the government seemingly having assumed the province of furnishing circulating media, no legislation relating to banks was enacted or seriously considered.

Henry W. Cannon became Comptroller of the Currency in 1884, succeeding John Jay Knox. In May of that year a serious financial crisis, produced by conditions in the country generally, but practically limited in its manifestation to New York City, caused numerous suspensions, including two large national banks. The crisis was caused largely by undue expansion of loans induced by speculation in securities. The New York banks again issued clearing-house loan certificates to be used in settling debit balances, the first bearing date May 15, and the maximum amount being $24,915,000. They were practically retired by July 1. The fact that the certificates were promptly issued served to restore confidence in a short time, and prevented more serious consequences.

Crisis of 1884.

The withholding of money from deposit in banks and savings banks, the strengthening of their cash resources by interior banks, which caused a corresponding reduction of their balances in New York, necessarily produced a stringency. Any degree of fear or anxiety which induces the wage-earners employed by our large stores, factories, railroads, and employers of labor gen-

Causes of stringency.

erally, to keep the money received from the pay roll instead of depositing or spending the same, materially and immediately affects the volume of money in circulation. The banks under the rigid currency laws were powerless to afford relief. They could not buy bonds required to be deposited as security for circulation without investing more money in bonds than they would receive circulation in return. Had they borrowed the bonds it would have required about forty-five days after depositing them before the circulation could be prepared for delivery. The banks protected and retained their cash reserves by suspending cash payments as between themselves, and using loan certificates in payment of clearing-house debits. The crisis thus proclaimed undoubtedly drove money into hiding and prevented the banks from strengthening their reserves by the usual receipts of currency.

Clearing-house certificates.

The important and valuable function which clearing-house certificates perform, and the only one which justifies their use, is the temporary inflation of currency which they in a manner produce. A bank may deposit with the clearing-house $1,250,000 of its assets and receive $1,000,000 of loan certificates. It then can loan to its customers $1,000,000 and meet and pay the checks drawn against such loans, in the clearing-house exchanges, with the $1,000,000 loan certificates it has received. It may then deposit the assets taken for said $1,000,000 of loans with the clearing-house and receive $800,000 in loan certificates. It could then in turn loan its customers $800,000 and settle for the same through the clearing-house exchanges with the $800,000 of loan certificates received, and so on. This illustration is given to show the extent to which banks might extend aecommodations to their customers without the use of actual currency. Of course the issuing or withholding of loan certificates rests wholly with the clearing-house authorities, and each particular application is determined by them upon its merits. The beneficial results which these loan certificates have produced rest wholly upon the fact that the banks while maintaining their reserves by retaining their currency have been enabled to extend to the public whatever assistance it may have required. A statement of the several issues of such certificates at New York appears on page 375.

Their charters had been extended by the law of 1882, and the banks were recognized as a permanent part of our monetary system, but many things militated against the increase of their note-issues. As we have seen, the 3 per cent bonds, constituting a large portion of the public debt, were redeemable at the pleasure of the government, and were being rapidly retired with the large Treasury surplus and likely to be called at any time, hence were undesirable as a basis for note-issue, since, in case the bonds were redeemed, a bank would have to purchase and substitute others. All other issues of government bonds commanded high premiums, the 4 per cents standing at 129, which rendered the issue of circulation based upon them unprofitable. *Contraction of bank circulation.*

Another powerful factor in reducing bank circulation was the fact that the government was purchasing silver, coining silver dollars, and issuing certificates, at the minimum rate of $2,000,000 per month, and using all the power of the Treasury to force them into circulation in order to prevent going upon a silver basis. The crusade in favor of free coinage of silver monopolized the attention and sympathy of Congress to such an extent that it continuously refused to permit banks to issue circulation to the par of bonds, retaining the limit at 90 per cent notwithstanding the fact that the bonds commanded a premium of nearly 30 per cent. The entire absence *Influence of silver purchases.*

System
inelastic.
of elasticity, which every bond-secured currency must possess, as well as the growing premium on and lessening volume of United States bonds, induced economists to consider a bank currency without such bonds as security, which would be quite as safe and more responsive to business necessities. Comptroller Henry W. Cannon was the first official to discuss and recommend such a currency issue. He suggested as security a guarantee fund to be accumulated from the tax on circulation, the gain on lost notes, and the interest on the redemption fund in the Treasury.

Cannon's
proposed
remedy.
Examining and analysing the statistics of the 104 national banks that had failed up to that time, with a view to demonstrating the security to note holders under the proposed plan, he said : —

" The experience with these 104 banks shows almost conclusively that if their issues to the amount of 65 per cent of their capital had been secured by a deposit of bonds to an equal amount, the remaining 25 per cent might have been issued without other security than a first lien on the general assets ; and if a safety fund had been in existence it would in the case cited have been drawn upon to the extent of $62,000 only upon a circulation amounting to $5,464,700. For a beginning, therefore, it might be safe to authorize banks to issue circulation amounting to 90 per cent of their capital, 70 per cent to be secured by an equal amount of United States bonds at par value, the remaining 20 per cent being issued without other security than a first lien on such assets. But if the law should provide for the accumulation of a safety fund in the manner suggested, then as such safety fund increased the percentage of circulation unsecured by bonds might be increased as the diminution of the public debt might require and the safety fund warrant."

William L. Trenholm became Comptroller of the Curreney in 1886. In that year Congress authorized banks, by a two-thirds vote, to increase their capital or change their location, and in 1887 prescribed conditions under which Minor changes in law. cities might become reserve and central reserve cities. Chicago and St. Louis became central reserve cities like New York, and three reserve cities were added. At this time a question arose as to the legality of using bonds on which interest had ceased (after being called for redemption), as security for circulation. The Attorney-general decided that under the law such bonds were not available and must be replaced.

Although by 1887 banks had increased largely in number, and their capital had also grown, their circulation was reduced to $167,000,000. A presidential election was at hand, and the trend of public sentiment and political conditions is suggested by the fact that the oft-repeated proposition to substitute greenbacks for national bank-notes was defeated, at this time, by the close vote of 23 to 22 in the Senate.

Secretary Fairchild had endeavored to counteract the Surplus money deposited in banks. absorption of money by the Treasury by depositing surplus revenues with banks. There were 290 bank depositories at this time, and they held $60,000,000 of the Treasury surplus amply secured by government bonds. The Republicans severely criticised this policy in the ensuing campaign as opening the door to political favoritism. They have since paid Mr. Fairchild the compliment of adopting and extending his policy. The number of such depositories, May 1, 1903 (under Secretary Shaw and President Roosevelt), was 257, and the amount of surplus Treasury money on deposit with them was $142,959,727.12.

Benjamin Harrison became President in 1889, and early in his administration Edward S. Lacey was appointed Comptroller of the Currency. The new administration secured no more attention for its recommendations relative to bank currency than its prede-

2 A

cessor. The all-absorbing, crucial question was how to placate the silver advocates and still remain upon a gold basis.

William Windom had succeeded Fairchild as Secretary of the Treasury, and following the logic of the campaign began reducing the Treasury funds in banks. As the surplus locked up in the Treasury was thus increased, the year 1889 closed with an uneasy feeling in the money market, rates for a period ruling from 30 to 40 per cent. Windom's plan for the placation and utilization of silver eventuated in the law of 1890, fully discussed in another chapter.

The enormous Treasury surplus had been made prominent in the presidential campaign, and the relief determined upon was reduction of taxation. The protection influence dominated, and the McKinley act of 1890 retained the duty upon articles produced in this country and removed or reduced the duties upon sugar and other large revenue-yielding commodities not produced to any considerable extent in the United States.

During the summer and early fall of that year the money stringency, which had been foreshadowed by the growing surplus, occurred, and the application of the Treasury funds to bond redemptions amounted to over $100,000,000. Aside from the much criticised policy of depositing money in banks, the only means of counteracting the demoralization of business whenever the government's income exceeds its expenditures under our subtreasury system of withdrawing money from channels of trade, is the "steady by jerks" method of buying bonds, first practised by Secretary Guthrie in 1854, and continued by every Secretary since that day, when the surplus was large. It was the only recourse available to Windom under the circumstances. In the month of September alone over $62,000,000 was disbursed by the Treasury for bonds and anticipated interest payments.

The suspension of Barings in November of this year caused a severe crisis in London and produced scarcely less effect in New York. The Bank of England came to the rescue and eventually restored the Barings to solvency.

The underlying fear that the monetary policy of the government would eventually force the country upon a silver basis rendered the business interests peculiarly sensitive. Credit was easily disturbed and withheld. Under the circumstances the gravity of the situation in London easily precipitated a *quasi* panic in New York, and the banks again resorted to clearing-house loan certificates on November 12. The date of the last issue was December 7, and final retirement occurred February 7, 1891. The total issue was $16,645,000 and the maximum amount outstanding at one time was $15,205,000. Boston and Philadelphia banks adopted the same course to relieve the stringency, the former issuing $5,065,000 and the latter $8,820,000 of such auxiliary currency. No attempt was made by Congress to provide means whereby the banks could afford relief under such circumstances to all sections of the country, instead of leaving relief to clearing-house loan certificates available only in the larger cities, amounting to a partial suspension of currency payments and producing evil results which approximate the amount of good they do.

Clearing-house certificates again.

In 1890 Comptroller Lacey obtained data showing the amount of domestic exchange drawn by the national banks for the year. For the purpose of verification he obtained similar facts in 1891. These data showed the amount in the aggregate to be $13,000,000,000, and he estimated that the state banks drew half as much more, making an aggregate of $19,500,000,000. Sixty per

Domestic exchange statistics.

cent of the total was drawn upon New York. The cost, or charge for exchange, as reported by national banks, varied from 1 cent to 21 cents per $100 and averaged 8½ cents. At the rate of 1½ per cent, prevailing in 1859, the cost to the people of the exchange thus furnished by national banks would approximate $195,000,000, whereas the cost in 1890 was slightly over $11,000,000. This reduction in cost of exchange was not due entirely to the national banking system, but that system contributed largely to bringing about such saving.

The national banking system, designed, as we have seen, to give the people a permanent paper currency, lacked the necessary support even in the ranks of those who had created it. Only by the most strenuous efforts was the system able to survive the political attacks upon the one hand and the untoward conditions of a decreasing volume and enhancing prices of bonds (hence diminution of profits) on the other. Moreover, the introduction of the two forms of silver paper (certificates and Treasury notes of 1890) materially lessened the demand for bank-notes. Nevertheless, as a system of banks of deposit and discount, under the regulation of federal law, it kept pace with the commercial development of the country. Its growth was especially marked in the states from which the principal opposition came. Of the 1545 active banks added to the list since 1882, Texas had contributed 195, Missouri 61, the Dakotas 67, Kansas 134, Nebraska 127, and Iowa 75. Other Southern and Western states also showed substantial increases, although they were still far from adequately provided with banking facilities. The capital of national banks in these states increased from $138,-200,000 to $322,500,000 during the period since 1882. The increase for the entire country included capital

Growth of national system.

$140,000,000, surplus and profits $113,000,000, individual deposits $370,000,000, loans $603,000,000, and cash holdings $78,000,000. The circulation was, however, diminished by $183,000,000. Measured by their capital the banks could under the law have issued $556,000,000 of notes. The amount actually outstanding was $126,000,000, or about 20 per cent of their capital.

The circulation outstanding covered by lawful money deposits (representing the notes of failed, liquidating, and reducing banks) stood at $36,800,000, only slightly in excess of the amount ten years prior; but during the period the amount of such notes had risen to $107,500,000, in 1887, which marked the date of greatest contraction.

The act of July 14, 1890, directed that the funds held in trust in the Treasury for redemption of these notes be turned into the general cash of the Treasury, and the notes assumed as part of the public debt.

The earnings of the banks calculated upon capital and surplus ranged between 6.9 per cent and 8.9 per cent, and dividends, on capital alone, from 8.6 to 7.8 per cent, with a declining tendency. Earnings of banks.

Greater efforts than ever before were made during the period to obtain fuller data relating to state banks, private banks, and trust companies. The report for 1891 showed the following comparison as to state banks: —

YEAR	NUMBER	CAPITAL	DEPOSITS	LOANS	TOTAL RESOURCES
1881 . . .	652	92.9	261.4	250.8	438.8
1891 . . .	2572	208.6	556.6	623.2	906.0

While the increase thus shown was no doubt in part due to the more complete returns in the latter year, it is obvious that these banks more than doubled in number State banks.

and importance during the decade. Examination shows that this was due in great measure to the fact that the national system proved less inviting to capital in the sections showing the greatest growth. The provisions of state laws for small banks, capitalized at $10,000 or even less, accounted for much of this preference.

Trust and loan companies showed increased resources for the same period from $156,500,000 to $536,600,000 and savings banks deposits grew from $891,900,000 to $1,623,500,000.

Banking power by sections.

Appended is a table showing the aggregate banking power of the country, indicating the per capita, and illustrating further the great lack of banking facilities in the sections which continually clamored for measures calculated to result in unsound currency. The two phenomena are unquestionably correlated. The higher interest rates exacted in localities not well supplied with capital and credit facilities — a disparity which is a serious burden upon all productive industry — tends to induce those who suffer therefrom to support any means suggested to remedy the evil, and too often the proposed remedies have been such as would actually render conditions worse.

STATES	BANKING POWER (In millions)		PER CAPITA	
	1880	1890	1880	1890
Eastern . . .	707	1229	$ 176.37	$ 261.86
Middle . . .	1335	2410	113.50	170.92
Central . . .	462	1184	26.86	54.29
Southern . .	158	387	10.36	21.15
Western . .	140	403	73.07	107.15
All	2802	5613	55.88	89.85

STATISTICAL RÉSUMÉ

(Amounts in millions of dollars)

CONDITION OF NATIONAL BANKS

(AT DATES NEAREST JANUARY 1)

YEAR	NUMBER	CAPITAL	DEPOSITS	CIRCULA-TION	SPECIE	LEGAL TENDERS	LOANS
1883 .	2308	485	1080	315	106	77	1230
1884 .	2529	512	1120	305	114	91	1307
1885 .	2664	524	1002	280	140	95	1234
1886 .	2732	529	1126	267	165	79	1344
1887 .	2875	551	1188	202	167	74	1470
1888 .	3070	581	1279	165	159	82	1584
1889 .	3150	594	1382	144	173	92	1677
1890 .	3326	618	1480	126	171	94	1812

UNITED STATES BONDS AND BANK CIRCULATION

YEAR (JUNE 30)	TOTAL BONDED DEBT	HELD AS SECURITY FOR CIRCULATION	NAT'L BANK CIRCULATION	+ IN-CREASE − DE-CREASE	SILVER CERTIFI-CATE CIR-CULATION	+ IN-CREASE − DE-CREASE	PRICE OF BONDS[1]	
							High	Low
1883 .	1389	353	312	+ 3	73	+ 18	$125\frac{1}{8}$	$118\frac{1}{4}$
1884 .	1277	331	295	− 17	96	+ 23	$124\frac{7}{8}$	$118\frac{1}{4}$
1885 .	1247	312	269	− 26	102	+ 6	$124\frac{3}{4}$	$121\frac{5}{8}$
1886 .	1196	276	245	− 24	88	− 14	$129\frac{3}{8}$	123
1887 .	1072	192	167	− 78	142	+ 54	$129\frac{5}{8}$	$124\frac{1}{2}$
1888 .	1001	178	155	− 12	201	+ 59	130	$123\frac{3}{4}$
1889 .	880	148	129	− 26	257	+ 56	$129\frac{7}{8}$	$126\frac{1}{4}$
1890 .	776	145	126	− 3	298	+ 41	$126\frac{1}{2}$	$121\frac{1}{2}$

[1] 4's of 1907.

STATE BANKS, TRUST COMPANIES, PRIVATE BANKS

| YEAR | STATE BANKS | | | | | TRUST COMPANY RE- SOURCES | PRIVATE BANK RE- SOURCES |
	Number	Capital	Deposits	Cash and Cash Items	Loans		
1883 .	754	103	335	78	322	212	394
1884 .	817	110	325	82	331	240	——
1885 .	975	125	344	87	348	248	——
1886 .	849	110	343	91	331	278	——
1887 .	1413	141	447	111	436	319	174
1888 .	1403	155	410	105	432	384	164
1889 .	1671	167	507	133	505	441	143
1890 .	2101	189	553	121	582	504	164

MISCELLANEOUS FINANCIAL

| YEAR | CLEARING-HOUSE EXCHANGES (In millions) | | SAVINGS BANKS | | | FAILURES | |
	New York	United States	Depositors (ooo's)	Deposits (Millions)	Average Deposits	Number (ooo's)	Liabilities (Millions)
1883	40,293	51,731	2876	1025	$356	9	173
1884	34,092	44,200	3015	1073	356	11	226
1885	25,251	41,474	3071	1095	357	11	124
1886	33,375	49,294	3158	1141	361	10	115
1887	34,873	51,147	3418	1235	361	10	168
1888	30,864	49,541	3838	1364	355	11	124
1889	34,796	56,175	4021	1425	354	11	149
1890	37,661	60,624	4258	1525	358	11	190

PART THREE

FROM 1891 TO THE PRESENT DAY

CHAPTER XVII

Silver Contest of 1896

1891 to 1896

THE retention of the national bank system was vir- The currency in 1890. tually settled by the law of 1882 enabling banks to extend their charters for a period of twenty years. Although opposition did not thereafter cease, it very materially subsided. The Supreme Court having decided that Congress had unlimited power to issue legal tender notes at any time, these notes became a settled factor in our currency system, with little hope, in view of popular sentiment, of their retirement. The status of silver was undetermined and in sharp controversy, — free coinage at the ratio of 16 to 1 the contention of one party, the repeal of the existing silver purchase law, the contention of the friends of the gold standard. Gold was the standard of value, but silver was being purchased at the rate of 4,500,000 ounces per month and legal tender coin notes issued in payment therefor. It was only a question of time when the continued purchase of this vast amount of silver, practically redeemable in gold, would exhaust the credit of the government and force it upon a silver basis. The question whether the standard should be gold or silver was paramount, and all forms of our currency were so closely related to the standard that they will be considered together in this and the following chapter.

The financial and monetary conditions of the whole

363

The silver
danger.
commercial world were affected by the position which
this country had assumed respecting silver. By careful
management the gold surplus of the Treasury had been
increased to nearly $219,000,000 in 1888. The estimated
stock of gold in the country at the same time was over
$700,000,000. We had retained all of our gold product,
then averaging more than one-quarter of the world's
output, and had imported more than we exported.

The Baring
crisis.
The embarrassment of Baring Brothers of London,
which culminated in November, 1890, precipitated a
severe stringency in the money market in London which
had its counterpart in New York. The Barings were
financing vast undertakings in South America and elsewhere, which they were unable to carry through. The
Bank of England took charge of their affairs, managed
the same most successfully, and eventually restored the
Barings to solvency and strength. In order to do this
the Bank of England at that time found it convenient to
borrow from the Bank of France $15,000,000 in gold.
The incident was regarded as a warning, and in order to
strengthen their reserves European banks generally
began to make extraordinary efforts to obtain gold from
all points, but mainly from the United States. The
Bank of England, by raising its discount rate and by
raising the price which it will pay for gold bars or
foreign coin, can measurably protect its gold supply.
In addition to these safeguards the Bank of France
goes farther and refuses to pay notes and drafts entirely
in gold, offering a portion in gold, the balance in silver, or
exacts a premium on gold desired for export. The United
States Treasury has no safeguards whatever against withdrawals of gold, and hence ours is the easiest market
from which other nations' necessities may be supplied.

By the end of the fiscal year 1890 over $54,000,000
gold had been exported notwithstanding a favorable

trade balance, showing conclusively a return of American securities from abroad. The inflation resulting from the silver purchase act made money easier, and accelerated the drain of gold. Following the return flow of money to New York after the crops of 1890 were harvested, heavy exports of gold were resumed in January, 1891, the net exports for the fiscal year having been $68,000,000. General business activity and a continuous demand for money in the fiscal year ending June 30, 1892, together with a favorable trade balance resulting largely from bountiful crops in 1891 and a general shortage in Europe, caused heavy importations of gold, so that the net loss in that year was only $500,000. In July, however, large exports again began. The banks finding it impracticable to furnish the gold from their vaults exporters of gold were paid in notes, thus the demand was transferred to the Treasury, and as a consequence its gold reserve steadily diminished. In the seven months following June, 1892, more gold was drawn out of the Treasury in redemption of legal tender notes than in the thirteen years preceding.

Inflation causes gold exports.

The hope that the purchase of silver under the law of 1890 would restore that metal to a parity with gold was not realized. The rise in price to $1.21 per ounce fine ($1.2929 being par) was largely speculative and was followed by a rapid decline. The monometallists experienced the sad satisfaction of having their predictions verified ; the bimetallists saw their arguments against independent action proven by the test of experience. The keen foresight of the business world clearly perceived the impending struggle and realized the baleful effect upon all forms of industry whatever the eventual result might be. New enterprises were abandoned, present business was curtailed, and the more timid proceeded to hide their talent in a napkin.

Price of silver not sustained.

Democratic
victory of
1890.

The party in power was held responsible for unsatisfactory conditions, and the congressional election in 1890 favored the Democrats, giving them the enormous majority of 149 in the House.   This spurred the Republicans in the remaining short session (1890–1891) to endeavor to pass some decisive legislation   A bill was reported in the Senate providing for an increased purchase of silver under the law of 1890 for a period of one year, in order to absorb the surplus in the market, which seemed to keep down the price.   The silver Republicans, however, held the balance of power, and uniting with the silver Democrats passed a measure for free coinage pure and simple by a vote of 39 to 27.   Fifteen Republicans voted for and 18 Democrats against it.   The House voted down all attempts to consider the bill   Windom died, and was succeeded by Charles Foster, of Ohio. The Treasury note-issues continued, and silver fell to 96 cents per ounce.

Harrison's
views.

Harrison, in ·pursuance of authority granted him by Congress, invited the principal nations to join in another conference to consider the question of international bimetallism, but the negotiations were not successful until 1892.   Harrison believed that the scarcity of gold in Europe would incline European nations to favor international bimetallism, and hence urged the accumulation of gold in the Treasury.   He felt satisfied that we could maintain parity, expressed sympathy with the silver producers, and was gratified that the surplus was not large and no longer deposited in banks.

Senate for
free coinage.

Notwithstanding the pendency of this international conference, those favoring independent free coinage persisted in their efforts to force action in both branches of Congress in the session of 1891–1892.   The silver advocates in the Senate were strongly reënforced by members from the recently admitted Rocky Mountain states, and proceeded to pass a bill for free coinage at the ratio of 16 to 1 by a vote of 29 to 25. Seven Democrats, including Carlisle, opposed it. The House rejected the bill by a vote of 136 to 154, the negative including 94 Cleveland Democrats.

In the political campaign of 1892 the Republican plat-form declared for both gold and silver and for interna-tional bimetallism. The Democratic platform, dictated by the Cleveland wing of the party, denounced the silver purchase law as a "cowardly makeshift," demanded that both gold and silver should be used without discrimina-tion, and declared in favor of the repeal of the 10 per cent tax on state bank-notes. An important element, particularly representatives from the South, regarded the restoration of state bank circulation as the best solu-tion of the currency question, and a popular substitute for the silver issue in the campaign. _{Presidential campaign of 1892.}

A new party appeared in the field, composed largely of the old Greenback element. It was called the "Peo-ple's Party," afterward "Populists," and nominated Weaver, of Iowa, for the presidency. The declarations of its state conventions favored various "isms," includ-ing subtreasuries in every important locality for the reception of wheat and other farm products, and the issue of paper money against the same, in a manner similar to the issuing of notes against silver bullion purchased. In the national Populist platform gold monometallism was declared a "vast conspiracy against mankind." A circulation of $50 per capita was demanded. Silver demonetization, it was asserted, added to the purchas-ing power of gold, and the national power to create money had been used to favor the bondholders. The fact that a candidate appealing for public support as the representative of such policies polled 1,041,000 votes, _{Populist party.}

and actually carried four states and received one electoral vote in each of two other states, is a strong commentary upon the vagaries of human nature.

Cleveland was elected over Harrison with a Democratic House of Representatives. The Senate was also Democratic, with a majority in favor of the free coinage of silver.

International conference of 1892.

The international conference on silver called by Harrison, met in Brussels in November following the election. The United States were represented by Senator Allison (Ia.), Senator Jones (Nev.), Representative McCreary (Ky.), ex-Comptroller of the Currency H. W. Cannon, Prof. E. B. Andrews of Brown University, and E. H. Terrell, United States Minister to Belgium. Twenty countries were represented, one of Great Britain's delegates being a member of the banking-house of Rothschild.

The delegates from the United States were instructed to endeavor to secure international bimetallism or, failing in that, action tending to a largely increased monetary use of silver, to arrest depreciation. They soon found the former proposition to be out of the question. The European banks at this time were very strong in gold, that of England alone excepted. On the other hand, the United States had been steadily losing gold, and its Treasury reserve was down to $114,000,000. Our delegates, in their memorandum submitted to the

Propositions considered.

conference, included the proposition for unrestricted coinage by all commercial nations of gold and silver into full legal tender coins at a fixed ratio. They preceded it, however, by two other propositions looking to the increased use of silver upon other plans as more likely of adoption. A sentiment favorable to an increased use of silver was manifest, but no practical method could be agreed upon. Subordinate features, such as the discontinuance of the use of small gold coins and notes of small denominations, were discussed. France would not support any measure which would increase its stock of silver. Great Britain, manifestly concerned chiefly on account of India, seemed anxious that the price of silver be kept steady, but evidently did not intend to change her monetary system. The conference adjourned in January until May, 1893, and again to November, 1893, but never reassembled.

Adjourns without action.

The United States were ably represented at this conference by men schooled in economics and possessed of practical experience as well. The subject was exhaustively discussed and thoroughly considered. Of course their efforts in favor of international bimetallism were largely compromised and nullified by the determined and persistent effort in Congress to force independent action in favor of free coinage at a ratio differing from that obtaining in Europe. The European delegates naturally regarded the formal action of Congress as more representative of public sentiment, and a better indication of probable action on the part of the United States, than any presentation which our delegates were able to make. As negotiators in the interest of silver their power was impaired by the fatuous zeal of silver advocates at home. It should be stated in explanation that the most ardent advocates of free silver regarded the conference as a means devised to postpone the accomplishment of their purpose and enable the party in power to hold the support of the silver Republicans in the pending presidential campaign.

Comments on the conference.

Although barren of affirmative results the conference was productive of the greatest good. It served to concentrate the thought and the study of all nations upon this question, and its failure to reach any agreement convinced

Bimetallism doomed.

2 B

all that the relative value of silver and gold, in the future as in the past, would be determined by the laws of trade and not by international agreement. It demonstrated the impossibility of international bimetallism. The leading European nations were quite satisfied with the gold standard and in no mood for monetary experiments apparently in the interest of commercial rivals. The settled judgment in favor of the single gold standard and the firm determination on the part of the leading European nations to adhere to the same was clearly apparent. That the question of a single gold standard or a single silver standard was the leading issue to be fought out in the United States was equally apparent. With all thinking men bimetallism was impossible. The question was, silver or gold.

Movement for state bank-notes.
In the presidential contest of 1892 the Democratic platform favored the repeal of the prohibitive tax on state bank circulation. The Democrats elected their President, and controlled Congress. Their candidates, and presumably their platform, had been indorsed at the polls. A serious attempt to restore state bank circulation was anticipated. It was known that the incoming administration would exert its influence to secure the repeal of the Silver Purchase Law, and it was feared that the restoration of state bank circulation might be necessary in order to command the support of the representatives from the South. Comptroller Hepburn, in
Hepburn's state bank statistics.
his report, presented the objections to such a policy, and reviewed the history of state banks and state bank circulation in contrast with the existing national system, showing from statistics the saving in exchange, the greater economy, greater safety, and general superiority of the national system. He also urged that greater elasticity be given the national bank currency by removing the limitations upon the retirement and reissue of

circulation. He also elaborated and recommended a plan for the refunding of the presently maturing government bonds into a long-time, low-rate bond. This would result in the saving of interest to the government and at the same time furnish a more desirable basis for note-issues. Such a measure was eventually embodied in the refunding act of March 14, 1900.

The condition of the Treasury upon the eve of the change in administration (March 4, 1893) was far from satisfactory. The cash balance available for current payments was about $24,000,000. The gold reserve was maintained above $100,000,000, which had come to be regarded the danger line, only by extraordinary efforts, the Treasury obtaining gold from the banks in exchange for other forms of currency. The condition of the Treasury which confronted President Cleveland upon resuming office was in sharp contrast with the $196,245,980 gold reserve and $70,158,461 other available cash balance which he left upon retiring from office in March, 1889. His administration was embarrassed for want of funds to meet current expenses without trenching on the gold reserve necessarily maintained to insure the redemption of legal tender notes upon presentation. There was another circumstance which tended still further to reduce the lessening revenues. The Democrats favored a revision of the tariff, a policy to which Cleveland was pledged. Business interests affected by customs laws naturally halted, pending action by Congress. Manufacturing diminished materially, labor was unemployed, consumption was reduced, and the government's income necessarily fell off.

Deplorable condition of Treasury.

Carlisle, who had been an ardent advocate of the free coinage of silver, became Secretary of the Treasury. But for the well-known attitude of President Cleveland

Gold reserve impaired.

on the money question, Carlisle's selection might have occasioned uneasiness. The gold exports continued, and the reserve, for a while maintained by exchanging other funds for gold with the banks, in April fell below the $100,000,000 mark. The administration had not up to this time had occasion to clearly define its policy respecting the Treasury notes of 1890, which were by their terms redeemable *in coin*, and hence, if the government chose, in silver dollars. Considerable alarm had been caused by the reported decision of Carlisle to redeem these notes in silver, hence Cleveland declared his purpose to redeem them in gold and to exercise all the powers of his great office for the maintenance of gold payments. Fear of a silver basis, however, prevailed, especially abroad, owing to the weakness of the Treasury, and every express steamer brought in American securities and took away gold. The net loss during the fiscal year 1893 amounted to $87,500,000.

Crisis of 1893.

The crisis which resulted was severe and its effects enduring. Fear of going upon a silver basis roused the banking and business interests to united action. Within the period of six weeks in midsummer the banks, at great expense, and notwithstanding adverse exchange conditions, imported $50,000,000 of gold. The usual form of transaction was to purchase the gold to arrive, with clearing-house funds, the premium ranging from 1 to 3 per cent.

Extra session of Congress.

President Cleveland convened Congress in extra session in August. In his message the disturbed condition of business was attributed to the silver law of 1890, and its repeal strongly recommended. He pointed out that in three years the Treasury had lost $132,000,000 of gold and gained $147,000,000 of silver. If this continued, all its funds would soon be in silver, and the maintenance of parity between silver and gold impossible. The government had no right to impose upon the people a depreciated currency nor to experiment with currency plans rejected by the leading civilized nations.

He experienced great difficulty in inducing his own party to sustain him. After a long struggle, terminating November 1, with the aid of Republican votes in the Senate, the silver purchasing section of the law of 1890 was repealed. Amendments proposing free coinage at various ratios and the restoration of the act of 1878 were defeated. In the Senate the vote was 43 to 32, only 20 Democrats favoring the repeal and 9 Republicans opposing. In the House the vote stood 239 to 109, only 22 Republicans voting in the affirmative. This repealing act declared it to be the policy of the United States to maintain parity of its gold and silver coins by international agreement or otherwise.

The discontinuance of silver purchases after such a protracted struggle did not restore confidence. It was manifestly not the sole cause of the troubles. Nor did those in Congress, who favored " more money " and were in the majority, desist from urging the free coinage of silver, increased greenback issues, repeal of the tax on state bank-notes, and other measures calculated to unsettle public confidence. A general feeling of uneasiness pervaded the country. Interior banks had over $200,000,000 of reserve deposits in New York. As the Treasury reserve gradually diminished, they became impressed with a desire to strengthen their position at home, and the withdrawal of a large portion of their New York deposits followed. This in turn necessitated curtailing and calling loans, and general liquidation ensued. Reserves of the New York banks fell below the legal requirement. Money on call rose at one time to 74 per cent. Time loans to other than regular customers of the banks were exceedingly difficult to obtain.

Purchase of silver discontinued.

Crisis
conditions.

During the crisis, money was hoarded, and despite the great supply (nearly $24 per capita) a currency "famine" ensued, and premiums as high as 4 per cent were paid for currency of any kind, even silver dollars. The banks in the principal Eastern cities were compelled to curtail cash payments. The use of clearing-house loan certificates in large amounts was resorted to throughout the country as well as various other forms of obligations designed to perform the functions of currency.

Auxiliary
currency.

Shortly after the panic or currency famine of 1893, by means of extensive correspondence with every considerable place in the country, I obtained statistics which justify the estimate that there was issued fully $100,000,000 of clearing-house certificates used in settlement between banks, of certified checks, certificates of deposit, cashier's checks in round amounts (as $1, $5, $10, $20, and $50), due bills from manufacturers and other employers of labor, and clearing-house certificates, in round amounts (in the case of Birmingham, Ala., as small in amount as 25 cents), all designed to take the place of currency in the hands of the public. Clearing-house certificates, issued and used in settling debit balances between banks, were in no wise prohibited, but all of the other above-described evidences of debt which were issued to circulate among the public as money, were clearly subject to the 10 per cent tax enacted for the purpose of getting rid of state bank circulation. This temporary currency, however, performed so valuable a service in such a crucial period, in moving the crops and keeping business machinery in motion, that the government, after due deliberation, wisely forbore to prosecute. In other words, the want of elasticity in our currency system was thus partially supplied. It is worthy of note that no loss resulted from the use of this makeshift currency.

LOAN CERTIFICATES OF THE NEW YORK CLEARING-HOUSE

Year	Date of First Issue	Date of Last Issue	Date of Final Cancellation	Aggregate Issue	Maximum Amount Outstanding	Date	Rate of Interest	Nature of Collaterals
1860	Nov. 23, 1860	Feb. 27, 1861	Mar. 9, 1861	$7,375,000	$6,860,000	Dec. 22, 1860	7%	United States stocks, Treasury notes, stocks of state of New York.
1861	Sept. 19, 1861	Feb. 17, 1862	Apr. 28, 1862	22,585,000	21,960,000	Feb. 7, 1862	6%	Temporary receipts of United States for purchase of government bonds.
1863	Nov. 6, 1863	Jan. 9, 1864	Feb. 1, 1864	11,471,000	9,608,000	Nov. 27 to Dec. 1, 1863	6%	United States or New York State stocks, bonds, etc., or temporary receipts as in 1861.
1864	Mar. 7, 1864	Apr. 25, 1864	June 13, 1864	17,728,000	16,418,000	Apr. 20, 1864	6%	Same as in 1863; committee of that year continued.
1873	Sept. 22, 1873	Nov. 20, 1873	Jan. 14, 1874	26,565,000	22,410,000	Oct. 3, 1873	7%	Bills receivable, stocks, bonds, and other securities.
1884	May 15, 1884	June 6, 1884	Sept. 23, 1886[1]	24,915,000	21,885,000	May 24, 1884	6%	Same as in 1873.
1890	Nov. 12, 1890	Dec. 22, 1890	Feb. 7, 1891	16,645,000	15,205,000	Dec. 12, 1890	6%	Same as in 1873.
1893	June 21, 1893	Sept. 6, 1893	Nov. 1, 1893	41,490,000	38,280,000	Aug. 29 to Sept. 6, 1893	6%	Same as before.

[1] The certificates issued by all banks, except the Metropolitan, were retired by August 25, 1884. The Metropolitan National Bank failed during this stringency, notwithstanding the fact that $7,450,000 of certificates were issued to it. These were retired in the regular course of liquidation of the bank, the last certificate being cancelled September 23, 1886.

Clearing-house certificates.

The Clearing-house Association of New York, in 1893, issued their first certificates June 21, their last September 6. All certificates were finally retired November 1. The total amount issued was $41,490,000. The maximum outstanding at any one time was $38,280,000. The rate of interest paid thereon by the banks to the Clearing-house Association was 6 per cent. The Philadelphia Clearing-house Association issued $11,465,000, and that of Baltimore $1,475,000 in certificates, practically coincident with the New York issue as to time, and similar as to conditions. The Boston banks issued $11,695,000, bearing interest at $7\frac{3}{10}$ per cent; the first issue bore date of June 27, and the final retirement was October 20. The aggregate maximum amount issued in these four cities was $66,125,000. Since this is the last instance of the issue of clearing-house loan certificates in the United States, I think it may be of interest to insert (p. 375) a table giving complete and exact data as to all issues of loan certificates made by the New York Clearing-house.

Increase of currency.

As heretofore stated, this currency famine caused a forced importation of about $50,000,000 of gold in the face of adverse exchange rates and hence at a premium. By means of borrowed bonds national bank circulation was increased. The process, however, was slow, and the worst of the stringency was over before the time required in which to procure notes from the Treasury had elapsed. The scarcity of currency forbade discrimination, and the gold imported found its way largely into the Treasury and served materially to strengthen the reserve.

Failures in 1893.

Commercial agencies reported the suspension of 15,000 individuals and concerns with liabilities aggregating $347,000,000. One hundred and fifty-eight national banks and 425 other banks and trust companies, largely located in the South and West, suspended. Eighty-six of the national banks and many of the others subsequently resumed. Clearing-house exchanges for the year showed a falling off of $13,800,000,000, of which 74 per cent was in the city of New York. Savings bank deposits were reduced $36,000,000, the resources of national banks diminished $350,000,000, and those of state banks $53,000,000.

It had become apparent that the international confer- Fall of silver. ence on silver would not reassemble. The British government had, therefore, closed the mints of India to the free coinage of silver, and endeavored to maintain a fixed par of exchange between the mother country and the dependency. Silver fell to 78 cents per ounce, giving a ratio to gold of $26\frac{1}{2}$ to 1. This further depression of the price of silver added materially to the difficulties and embarrassments of the United States Treasury in its struggle for the maintenance of the gold standard. As marking the trend of thought and events in the world it undoubtedly confirmed and strengthened the advocates of the gold standard.

The usual result followed this money stringency. Currency in hiding came into circulation, business stagnation lessened the demand, and a plethora ensued. The expenditures of the Treasury exceeded its receipts at the rate of $7,000,000 monthly. The Treasury was obliged to use the gold, which it had accumulated as a reserve, to meet its current expenses.

Carlisle, in his report to Congress, asked for authority Treasury deficits. to make temporary loans to cover revenue deficits and also for specific authority to issue bonds for gold for the purpose of increasing the gold reserve. He urged that so long as the Treasury was charged with the functions of a bank of issue, ample provision for the redemption of its notes should be made. Congress disregarded his recommendation. In January, 1894, the gold reserve fell below $66,000,000, and there was but $18,000,000 other available cash. He was therefore compelled to exercise the authority granted by the Resumption Act of 1875, and determined to issue ten-year five per cent bonds, as authorized by the Refunding Act of 1870, to the amount of $50,000,000.

Bonds issued to obtain gold.

He proceeded without consultation with the leading bankers of the country, and especially avoided New York. He endeavored to float the loan by popular subscriptions, and appealed to the country at large for that purpose. The attempt was unsuccessful. He then came to New York, convened the leading bankers at the subtreasury and announced that less than $5,000,000 subscriptions had been received. He said to the bankers present in substance : Unless you take this loan, it will be a failure. Just what effect its failure will have upon the business interests which you represent, you, gentlemen, are better able to judge than I am. What the political effect will be I can perhaps better judge than you. All business interests and all classes of people are suffering,

Carlisle on bond issue.

and have been for many months. The silver purchasing provision of the law of 1890 was denounced as the cause, and its repeal advocated as a remedy. You, gentlemen, joined if you did not lead in this sentiment. The President convened Congress, the law was repealed — not promptly, as it should have been, but it was repealed, nevertheless. The troubles seemed to continue without abatement. Then it was proclaimed that the gold reserve was impaired, hence the credit of the government endangered, and must be restored in order to restore confidence and credit generally, and bonds should be issued for that purpose. Well, we offer you the bonds. If you take them and give the government gold, I think the situation will be relieved. If you refuse, the bond

issue is a failure. In that case, I think an act to coin
the seigniorage in the Treasury or issue silver certificates
against the same will pass both houses of Congress almost immediately. The friends of silver will then say
to the President : " You have tried Wall Street's remedy
twice, and each time it has failed. Now try ours."
Under the circumstances I very much fear that the
President in his poverty will be compelled to sign such
a bill. If this bond issue is taken, the situation will be
relieved, and should a bill to coin the seigniorage reach
the President, he will certainly veto it.

John A. Stewart replied: "Of course we will take the
loan. We have known all along that in the end you
would have to come to us; we have anticipated this in-
terview, and are prepared to take the loan." The loan
was promptly taken. A substantial amount of gold
came into the Treasury from the vaults of the banks.
A portion, however, was furnished by withdrawal
from the Treasury for that purpose by means of greenbacks. This in no wise interfered with the success of
the loan, as the government's stock of cash was so low
that it was obliged to pay out gold for current purposes.

New York
takes the
bonds.

The Secretary's power to issue bonds was questioned
in Congress, and a resolution was introduced to prohibit
the payment of interest on the bonds sold. A labor organization attacked the Secretary's authority in a legal
proceeding in the federal courts, which, however, ruled
in his favor.

Legality of
bond issue
questioned.

Carlisle was severely criticised in some quarters for not
resorting to bond issues at an earlier period, in order to
protect his reserves and prevent a general feeling of
distrust from taking possession of the country. Sentiment or fear is an important element in every financial
crisis, but the success of the Secretary's policy depended
upon public support, and perhaps the delay in issuing

bonds was necessary, in order that the people as a whole might realize the danger so apparent to statesmen and financiers and justify the remedy. The continuance of distrust is amply evidenced by the fact that by the first of September $75,000,000 of gold had been exported, and the gold reserve was down to $55,000,000.

" Coining the seigniorage."

The silver bullion purchased under the act of 1890 had cost $156,000,000. The average cost per ounce was 92.5 cents. This bullion would produce when coined 218,000,000 silver dollars, yielding a seigniorage or profit between cost and coinage value of about $62,000,000. A part of this bullion had already been coined, so that the remainder would produce a seigniorage of about $55,000,000. Congress proposed to anticipate the coinage of this bullion, regard the last-mentioned sum as already coined, and direct the issue of silver certificates to that amount. This ingenious inflation measure is the one alluded to by Carlisle in his interview with the New York bankers. It passed in April, but Cleveland, after some deliberation, during which earnest protests were poured in upon him, vetoed it.

Tariff legislation.

This Congress repealed the law of 1862 and later ones exempting the United States notes and certificates circulating as money from taxation. A law was passed reducing tariff rates generally, but designed to provide for a larger revenue from sugar and other articles. It failed to produce any material increase of revenue immediately, owing, very likely, to the depressed condition of trade and industry. The business troubles were in large part due to the fact that the government's income did not equal its expenditure, and Congress is properly held responsible for failure to give the country a measure that would produce sufficient revenue to meet the ordinary expenditure of government.

In November a further issue of $50,000,000 5 per

cent bonds under the authority of the Resumption Act Carlisle sells more bonds.
became necessary. Carlisle, in his report, urged the
retirement of the greenbacks, and among other things
formulated an elaborate currency scheme, whose principal features were the impounding in the Treasury
of legal tender notes as part security for national bank-
notes and permitting state banks to issue notes under
certain restrictions. The monthly inflation of the curreney by the purchase of silver bullion having ceased,
the time seemed propitious for improving and popu-
larizing the national bank circulation. The American
Bankers' Association, meeting in Baltimore in 1894,
developed a bank-note issue system, afterward known as
the Baltimore plan. It proposed to permit note-issues Baltimore bank-note plan.
under federal supervision to the extent of 50 per cent of
the paid-up, unimpaired capital of banks, subject to $\frac{1}{2}$
per cent taxation, and an additional note-issue equal
to 25 per cent of the capital, subject to a much heavier
tax in order to insure its retirement when the necessity for its issue had disappeared. The notes were to
be a first lien upon the assets of the bank (including
the double liability of shareholders), and a 5 per cent
guarantee fund (in addition to the 5 per cent redemption fund) was to be provided and maintained for the
redemption of notes of failed banks, this fund to be
replenished, if need be, by enforcing the prior lien. The
silver sentiment of the country was so strong, however,
that no currency scheme, however well devised, could
obtain a hearing.

The House of Representatives elected in 1894 was
strongly Republican, and that party also regained control
of the Senate. President Cleveland, who had vigorously Cleveland on legal tenders.
supported the recommendations of Secretary Carlisle on
the subject of the gold reserve and legal tender notes,
sent a special message to Congress on January 9, 1895,

asking for authority to issue a 3 per cent fifty-year gold bond, the proceeds to be used to retire and cancel the legal tender notes. He believed that the time had come when the Treasury should be relieved from the "humiliating process of issuing bonds to procure gold to be immediately drawn for purposes not related to the benefit of the government or our people." Over $300,000,000 notes had been redeemed in gold, yet they were all in existence and mainly in circulation. More than $172,000,000 gold had been paid out by the Treasury in redemption of notes during the year.

More bond sales. One month later, Congress having failed to act, and the continuing exports having reduced the gold reserve to less than $42,000,000, Cleveland informed Congress that, in order to maintain gold payments, he had been compelled to authorize a special contract (with a syndicate) to procure gold under the old law of 1862 (referred to *ante*, p. 189) continued as section 3700 of the Revised Statutes. The contract called for the purchase of gold to the value of $65,116,244, by the sale of $62,315,400 4 per cent, thirty-year *coin* bonds at 104.496. If, however, Congress would authorize a 3 per cent *gold* bond, the same would be taken at par and result in an ultimate saving of over $16,000,000. Inasmuch as the coin bonds would doubtless be paid in gold at maturity, such legislation should be promptly passed, in order that the above-mentioned sum might be saved. Congress refused by a vote of 120 to 167 to grant the authority asked for, and the more expensive course had to be adopted. Four per cent bonds issued in 1877 had but recently been quoted at 129.

The Morgan syndicate. Under this contract the syndicate not only undertook to furnish the gold, but to take none from the Treasury with United States notes, to actually import one-half of the sum contracted for, and to do all in its power to prevent exports of gold during the period of the contract. The importation of so much gold necessarily implied the lapse of a very considerable period of time. Obviously these conditions were of the greatest importance to the Treasury under the circumstances. The syndicate, which included the Rothschilds, was managed by J. P. Morgan. By the establishment of a large credit abroad, and by a combination of all foreign exchange houses on this side, it was able to carry out the undertaking. The syndicate, indeed, furnished over $16,000,000 more gold than their contract called for by exchanging the same with the Treasury for other forms of money.

The action of the administration received the severest criticism in Congress, especially from its own party. A committee was appointed by the Senate to investigate the subject, upon the allegation of irregularities, but the result was unimportant except as it furnished a basis for political speeches. The business interests of the country, on the other hand, applauded the measure as sound and imperatively necessary. The drain of gold ceased at once, and by the end of February the reserve stood at $84,000,000 and in June had increased to $107,500,000. The tide turned, however, and by January 1, 1896, the gold reserve had reached the very low point of $50,000,000.

Carlisle met the situation promptly, and sold in the ordinary way $100,000,000 thirty-year 4 per cent coin bonds. The aggregate bids for the same amounted to over $568,000,000, and the loan was placed at 111⅛. The net loss of gold by export in the fiscal year 1894 was over $4,500,000, in 1895 $31,000,000, and in 1896 $80,500,000. The gold production of the world, especially in the United States, showed a marked increase in 1891, and continued to increase steadily from year

Fourth bond sale.

to year. Coincident therewith the trend of sentiment throughout the world was strongly toward the gold standard. Austria and Russia had adopted this policy and were actively accumulating gold.

In his report for 1895, Carlisle showed a continuing deficit in revenue, but a growing cash balance from the sale of bonds. He ably defended his policy to restore the nation's credit, which had been seriously undermined by long adherence to a false monetary system. He urged Congress (Republican in both branches) to provide for the cancellation of the legal tender notes. He also recommended the authorization of branch banks to supply the smaller towns with facilities not obtainable under the national bank act. Cleveland forcibly urged that the government notes should be funded into bonds, not only to avoid further expense to procure gold, but, much more, to save the cost to the people of periodic crises.

The national banks.

The report of Comptroller Eckels reflected the generally unsatisfactory condition of business throughout the country. The number of national banks had increased only sixty-nine in the two years 1894 and 1895. Their circulation in October, 1895, as in 1893, amounted to $182,000,000. His report of 1894 contained a most valuable abstract of the banking systems under state laws and of foreign countries. In 1895 he presented a report on· the use of credit instruments in retail transactions, and one giving the number of depositors in national banks classified by their average deposits.

The volume of money.

The per capita circulation in July, 1895, was $22.93, and one year later $21.10. The supply, however, was more than equal to the demand. Every bond issue had involved a money stringency of greater or less degree followed by the usual plethora. The change in the tariff law had had an unsettling effect, and the business of the country generally was most unsatisfactory because of the absence of stable conditions which would enable business men to forecast future results with a reasonable degree of certainty. The lessening per capita circulation, lower prices, and hard times produced a condition of mind throughout the country peculiarly favorable for the campaign of the silver propaganda. The movement in favor of free coinage, managed by skilful leaders with ample means at their command, spread rapidly. Pamphlets, books, speeches, and news-papers favoring that policy were distributed plentifully. Every phase of the question was discussed with con-summate ability, and with arguments well calculated to impress the public.

European bimetallists were also exceedingly active. In both Germany and England, where the opposition had been strongest, opinion had apparently altered to such an extent that the outlook for an international agreement was considered favorable. Before adjourn-ing in March, 1895, Congress had appointed three members of each house a delegation to confer with European representatives. The agitation for indepen-dent action by the United States became so strong that the "internationalists" soon became convinced that the question would have to be determined at the polls. Local conventions of the Populists, more numerously attended than ever before, declared unequivocally for independent action and liberation of the people from the alleged slavery to the "money power." The con-duct of the Treasury, the redemption of notes in gold alone when the silver dollar was also full tender, the bond sales to buy gold, and the ranging of the entire banking community against free coinage, were especially de-nounced. Never before was the country roused to such a degree of excitement by an economic question.

Republican conventions in the Western states also

Bimetallism abroad.

Silver issue in politics.

2 C

leaned toward silver, but the national convention opposed free coinage, except under international agreement, and gold was, after much discussion, indorsed as the standard of value. Their candidate, McKinley, was equally cautious and hesitating in the early portion of the campaign.

The Democratic national convention was controlled by the anti-Cleveland wing of the party, which was prepared to coalesce with the Populists. Its platform favored free coinage of silver. The logical nominee, Bland, was passed by because it was feared he could not rally the full support of the radical Populists. Bryan was nominated. The Populists also nominated Bryan, but named a separate candidate for second place.

Bryan's candidacy.

The campaign which followed was, despite the attempt to make the tariff the principal issue, determined mainly on the question of the gold or silver standard. McKinley finally came out unreservedly for gold, and the question was comprehensively discussed.

Non-partisan Sound Money League.

The Republicans desired to hold as large a portion of the silver vote within their organization as possible, and their campaign, especially in certain localities, was more in the nature of an appeal to the advocates of silver than an earnest attempt to show the error of their position and danger to the material interests of the country in case their policy should prevail. The public were therefore dependent upon the independent press and *quasi*-independent element in both political parties for sound money literature and sound money arguments. In this connection most valuable and most effective service was rendered by the National Sound Money League under the leadership of such men as Henry Villard, J. Sterling Morton, John K. Cowen, M. E. Ingalls, George Foster Peabody, Horace White, J. Kennedy Tod, H. P. Robinson, John B. Jackson, James L.

Blair, Louis R. Ehrich, E. V. Smalley, A. B. Hepburn, and many others.

They published in Chicago a paper known as *Sound Money*, which was gratuitously distributed to the press of the country, to public speakers, and to leaders and moulders of thought. In this manner they furnished data and arguments in the interest of right thinking and right voting. They as well as other economists contributed largely to its columns. They raised large sums of money, which were thus expended in a purely academic campaign. The dishonesty of free coinage of silver at the ratio of 16 to 1, when the commercial ratio was more than twice as great, was boldly proclaimed, and logic reënforced by history adduced in demonstration. From the non-partisan character of their organization they were able to reach and command the attention of people who would have rejected similar matter emanating from a political organization.

The contentions of the silver men may be summarized as follows : —

1. Demonetization of silver had deprived the people of one-half the primary money made available by nature.

2. This great contraction of money, increased by the falling off in the production of gold, had caused the steady downward trend in prices since 1873.

3. The consequent enhancement of the purchasing power of gold enormously increased the obligations of the debtors having deferred payments to make.

4. These unsatisfactory conditions would be aggravated by concentrating upon one metal only the measuring of values and debt-paying power; while the alternative existed of paying in either metal, the danger of inordinate enhancement of one was neutralized.

5. The farmer was under the gold standard compelled to compete with producers in other lands (India, etc.), where labor was cheap and the silver basis prevailed.

6. The United States should take the lead by opening the mints to free and unlimited coinage of silver, which would surely bring silver to parity and compel other nations to do likewise.

7. The United States required a larger volume of money, and free coinage was the proper way of increasing it, especially as the country produced so much silver.

The international bimetallists generally agreed with the contentions 1 to 4, but insisted that independent action by the United States would defeat the object in view, place the country on a silver basis, to the lasting detriment of all interests.

Contentions of the opposition.

The gold advocates maintained: —

1. That the volume of money had actually increased in greater ratio than population, and that the growing use of credit instruments had added to the media of exchange.

2. That the fall in prices was due chiefly, and probably wholly, to improved methods of production, and had no relation to the demonetization.

3. That producers were also consumers, and hence had to pay less for commodities, so that relatively they were not injured by the fall in prices.

4. That the theory of having two standards was a delusion. Only one thing could actually be a standard. That in fact gold was the only standard, silver being measured by it.

5. That free coinage meant depreciated money, than which no device was more potent in cheating both the producer and consumer. It would precipitate the country upon a silver basis with gold at a fluctuating premium as in Mexico, not only contracting the volume of money, but causing untold injury to all interests.

6. That Europe would only be too glad to have the United States take up the silver burden alone, enhancing the value of its stock of silver, but would not follow the example.

7. That the volume of money was then greater than the needs of the country, and when greater needs manifested themselves the supply would come from abroad in the shape of gold and from the product of our own mines at home, the output of which was now rapidly increasing.

The silver men appealed to the farmers as producers. The opposition appealed to the workmen, especially in manufacturing lines, and the tariff question was dexterously used to supplement their arguments in favor of an honest dollar. The division of parties was almost sectional. Eastern Democrats refused to follow the leaders of the West and South, and the Central Western states were looked upon as the battle-ground. They generally joined with the East, and Bryan's defeat was regarded as a declaration by the Nation in favor of the gold standard. The popular vote was, McKinley 7,164,000, Bryan 6,562,000. Fortified and encouraged by such a vote, the silver advocates had no idea of abandoning the contest.

The exports of gold, as before stated, continued in large volume during the latter half of the fiscal year, — January to July, 1896. Thereafter imports exceeded exports. During this movement, the withdrawals of gold from the Treasury were in excess of the exports, and continued when exports ceased, showing that the fear of Bryan's election and a silver standard caused hoarding. Fully $50,000,000 was withdrawn from the Treasury because of this fear. The gold reserve, which had risen to $129,000,000 in March, fell to less than $101,000,000 in August. After the election the gold reserve steadily increased.

The average price of silver, which had fallen below $63\frac{1}{2}$ cents per ounce in 1894, recovered to $67\frac{1}{2}$ cents in 1896; but after the election a downward movement set in from which there was no reaction for several years.

Both Carlisle and Cleveland, in their last communica- tions to Congress, elaborated and vigorously argued for the retirement of the legal tender notes. In order to meet their redemption the people had incurred obligations in the form of bonds in excess of $262,000,000, which would require, if held to maturity, a further payment for interest of $379,000,000, making a total cost of $641,000,000 on account of these notes, and the notes were still outstanding and unpaid. This form of currency, designed as a temporary expedient, and retained because of its supposed economy (being a non-interest-bearing loan), had proven most burdensome and costly both in direct taxation and indirect injury to business affairs. Untoward events would again produce similar results unless these notes were finally retired.

Condition of the Treasury. When Cleveland assumed office March 4, 1893, he found a gold reserve of $103,284,219, and other available cash in the Treasury $20,843,869. When he retired from office in March, 1897, he left $148,661,209 gold reserve, and $64,176,047 other available cash, showing an increase of Treasury cash of $88,709,168. The four bond issues placed during his administration netted the Treasury $293,388,061, hence $204,678,893 of the money received from bond sales were used for current expenses. The ordinary expenses of government, by the accepted principles of good administration, should be met by current taxation. The tariff and revenue law passed during the Cleveland administration failed to produce needed revenue, which would unquestionably have averted a very large part of the troubles experienced by the administration and by the public generally. Carlisle was forced to issue bonds under existing authority to replenish the gold reserve. The gold thus received was paid out in redemption of legal tender notes, which had immediately to be used, together with some of the gold, to meet current expenses. Had he possessed other money for current use, and thus been able to impound the redeemed notes, the gold reserve would have been more easily maintained. He was forced to proclaim the weakness of the Treasury and assail the credit of the government with each bond issue, made ostensibly for the purpose of maintaining the gold reserve, but in part as well for the purpose of meeting the ordinary expense of government. Had Congress granted the authority asked to borrow for temporary purposes upon exchequer notes, smaller bond issues would have been required and less trouble and distrust would have been experienced.

Fatal inaction of Congress.

The national banks were constantly growing in importance and usefulness as banks of deposit and discount. Their safe and conservative management had won for them a place in public confidence and favor unsurpassed by the best institutions in any country. The silver controversy had for several years commanded the attention of Congress to the exclusion of legislation affecting bank circulation. The condition and changes sufficiently appear in the statistics following.

STATISTICAL RÉSUMÉ

(Amounts in millions)

NATIONAL FINANCES

Fiscal Year	Revenue			Expenditures			− Deficit + Surplus	Outstanding Debt	+ Increase − Decrease	Price of 4's 1907	
	Customs	Other	Total	Ordinary	Interest	Total				High	Low
1891	220	173	393	318	38	356	+ 37	1006	− 61	122	116
1892	177	178	355	322	23	345	+ 10	968	− 38	118⅛	114
1893	203	183	386	356	27	383	+ 3	961	− 7	115	108
1894	132	166	298	340	28	368	− 70	1017	+ 56	116	112½
1895	152	161	313	325	31	356	− 43	1097	+ 80	113⅝	110
1896	160	167	327	317	35	352	− 25	1223	+126	112½	106

CIRCULATION

July 1st	Gold¹	Silver Dollars	Subsidiary Coin	U. S. Notes	Treasury Notes	National Bank Notes	Total	In Treasury	In Circulation	Population	Per Capita
1891 . .	647	388	78	347	50	168	1678	180	1498	64	$23.41
1892 . .	664	389	77	347	102	173	1752	151	1601	66	24.44
1893 . .	598	391	77	347	147	179	1739	142	1597	67	23.85
1894 . .	627	395	76	347	153	207	1805	144	1661	68	24.28
1895 . .	636	401	77	347	146	212	1819	217	1602	70	22.93
1896 . .	599	422	76	347	130	226	1800	294	1506	71	21.10

¹ Includes certificates.

EXPORTS AND IMPORTS AND GOLD MOVEMENT

Fiscal Year	Merchandise			Silver			Gold			Notes Redeemed in Gold	Gold Reserve
	Exports	Imports	Excess −Exp. +Imp.	Exports	Imports	Excess −Exp. +Imp.	Exports	Imports	Excess −Exp. +Imp.		
1891	884	845	− 39	24	26	+ 2	86	19	−67	6	118
1892	1030	827	−203	34	29	− 5	50	50	—	9	114
1893	848	866	+ 18	42	34	− 8	109	21	−88	102	95
1894	892	655	−237	51	20	−31	77	72	− 5	85	65
1895	808	732	− 76	48	20	−28	67	36	−31	117	108
1896	883	780	−103	61	27	−34	112	34	−78	159	102

PRODUCTION OF GOLD AND SILVER

CALENDAR YEAR	WORLD			UNITED STATES			PRICE OF SILVER	COMMERCIAL RATIO	BULLION VALUE OF DOLLAR
	Gold	*Silver*		Gold	*Silver*				
		Coining Value	Commercial Value		Coining Value	Commercial Value			
1891 . .	131	177	136	33	75	58	$ .98800	20.92	.764
1892 . .	147	198	133	33	82	56	.87145	23.72	.674
1893 . .	157	214	129	36	78	47	.78030	26.49	.604
1894 . .	181	213	104	40	64	31	.63479	32.56	.491
1895 . .	199	217	110	47	72	36	.65406	31.60	.505
1896 . .	202	203	106	53	76	40	.67565	30.59	.522

THE SILVER ACQUISITION

FISCAL YEAR	BULLION PURCHASED			COINAGE OF DOLLARS	STOCK OF DOLLARS	DOLLARS OUT	CERTIFICATES OUT	NET SILVER IN TREASURY	
	Fine Ounces	Cost	Average					Dollars	Bullion
1891[1] . . .	3	3	$1.0901						
1891 . . .	48	51	1.0451	24	391	59	307	22	32
1892 . . .	54	51	.9402	6	397	57	327	5	77
1893 . . .	54	45	.8430	1	398	57	327	7	118
1894 . . .	12	9	.7313	3	401	53	327	16	127
1895 . . .	—	—	—	1	402	52	320	30	124
1896 . . .	—	—	—	20	422	52	331	36	119

[1] Under law of 1878 to August 14, 1890.

NATIONAL BANKS

(AT DATES NEAREST JANUARY I)

YEAR	NUM-BER	CAPITAL	SURPLUS	DE-POSITS	CIRCU-LATION	SPECIE	LEGALS	LOANS
1891 . . .	3573	658	215	1515	123	190	88	1932
1892 . . .	3692	677	228	1620	135	208	103	2001
1893 . . .	3784	690	240	1778	146	210	109	2167
1894 . . .	3787	682	247	1553	180	251	163	1872
1895 . . .	3737	666	245	1719	169	218	157	1992
1896 . . .	3706	657	246	1734	185	207	131	2041

STATE BANKS, ETC.

YEAR	STATE BANKS						TOTAL RESOURCES		
	Number	Capital	Surplus	De-posits	Cash	Loans	Trust Com-panies	Private Banks	Savings Banks
1891 .	2572	209	60	557	108	623	537	152	1855
1892 .	3191	234	67	649	130	700	600	147	1964
1893 .	3579	251	74	707	137	758	727	108	2014
1894 .	3586	244	74	658	145	666	705	105	1981
1895 .	3774	250	74	712	143	693	807	130	2054
1896 .	3708	240	71	696	128	697	855	94	2143

MISCELLANEOUS FINANCIAL

YEAR	CLEARING-HOUSE TRANSACTIONS		SAVINGS BANKS			FAILURES	
	New York	U. S.	Depos-itors (000's)	De-posits (Mill-ions)	Average	Num-ber (000's)	Liabil-ities (Mill-ions)
1891	34,054	57,299	4533	1623	358	12	190
1892	36,280	60,884	4782	1713	358	10	114
1893	34,421	58,881	4831	1785	370	15	347
1894	24,230	45,028	4778	1748	366	14	173
1895	28,264	50,975	4876	1811	371	13	173
1896	29,351	51,936	5065	1907	377	15	226

CHAPTER XVIII

REFORM ACT OF 1900

1897 TO 1902

THE gold standard advocates, who hoped that McKin- ley's election would be accepted as a final declaration in favor of the gold standard and that legislation would be speedily enacted, under the influence of his administration, insuring such result, were doomed to disappointment. McKinley was a safe exponent but not a moulder of public sentiment. His characteristics in this respect earned him the criticism of always "keeping his ear to the ground." The leaders of the Republican party were still influenced by the habit of deference to silver advocates and silver interests, and the very large vote cast for Bryan, under stress of a presidential campaign, was a tangible evidence of strength and a distinct source of inspiration far outweighing any sense of discouragement involved in his defeat. McKinley's congressional record upon the question of the standard justified the silver advocates in expecting no drastic measures at his hands, and the record of other Republican leaders fortified the hope of sufficient Republican assistance to defeat such measures, should they appear. The gold standard had distinctly triumphed, but the lines of battle were still drawn, astute generals were deploying for position on either side, and the struggle was to be finally determined in the presidential contest of 1900.

McKinley was easily persuaded that one more effort to secure international agreement in favor of the enlarged use of silver as money should be made. The troubles of Great Britain in preserving even approximate stability in ratio between the rupee and the pound, among other causes, had precipitated a general discussion of the subject in Europe and perhaps justified this attempt on the part of our government. Senator Wolcott (Colo.), ex-Vice-President Adlai Stevenson, and General Charles J. Paine were sent abroad as commissioners. They visited the different capitals of Europe, were pleasantly received, but elicited no responsive interest. The complete failure of the mission was so generally anticipated in advance that it produced no appreciable effect upon public sentiment at home.

Insufficient revenue.

A deficit in revenue of $18,000,000 was estimated for 1897, although the cash balance including the gold reserve was nearly $213,000,000, resulting from the proceeds of the bond sales in 1894–1896. The fact that Cleveland's struggle to maintain the gold standard was largely caused and greatly intensified by insufficient revenues was fully understood and appreciated. In fact, the most serious criticism upon Cleveland's administration is his failure to influence legislation which would presently produce revenue sufficient for his needs.

McKinley convened Congress in extra session, and an act increasing the tariff generally, including a reimposition of part of the duty on sugar, which had been abolished by the McKinley act of 1890, soon produced sufficient revenue.

Lyman J. Gage, for more than a generation a successful banker in Chicago, had been appointed Secretary of the Treasury. He brought his long experience and study to the work of solving the currency problem, and before the regular session of Congress opened had elaborated a complete plan which was submitted to that body in December, 1897. His purpose was, as he expressed it, to put the country squarely upon a gold basis.

In general the plan was designed to gradually replace the legal tender notes with national bank-notes ; the increase of the gold reserve to $125,000,000 ; the separation of the currency functions of the Treasury by establishing a separate bureau for the purpose; notes once redeemed in gold not to be reissued except for gold ; $200,000,000 notes to be placed in a reserve fund and thus impounded in the Treasury as soon as practicable ; refunding of the debt into 2$\frac{1}{4}$ per cent bonds ; permitting banks to deposit either bonds or government currency to 50 per cent of their capital and receive circulating notes to the par thereof ; notes issued on bonds subject to a tax of $\frac{1}{2}$ per cent annually, those issued on currency free from tax ; the banks so depositing bonds or currency to be permitted to issue circulation in excess of such deposits equal to 25 per cent of their capital, to be secured by first lien upon assets and by a safety fund accumulated by means of a 2 per cent annual tax upon such additional circulation ; the minimum capital of banks to be $25,000 and no bank-notes under $10 to be issued.

Gage's gold standard measure.

Bank-note reform.

In order to show the sufficiency of the 2 per cent fund proposed to guarantee bank-notes, he presented the results of failures of national banks from the beginning of the system, which showed that such a fund would have protected every note holder under the measure proposed. President McKinley only partially indorsed the plan, recommending its careful study by Congress. He heartily concurred in the provision to reissue redeemed notes only for gold, as soon as the revenues exceeded the government's expenses.

The business interests of the country were keenly alive to the necessity for action, and under the leadership of H. H. Hanna delegates from all sections assembled in convention at Indianapolis. The meeting was

Indianapolis monetary convention.

thoroughly representative in character, including some of the ablest men in the country. The present Secretary of the Treasury, Leslie M. Shaw, then governor of Iowa, among others, addressed the convention. A very able commission was created, including Senator George F. Edmunds as chairman, and ex-Secretary Charles S. Fairchild and J. Laurence Laughlin, among its members, to prepare a comprehensive measure or proposed law for currency and coinage reform, together with an academic discussion of the whole subject, for submission to Congress, and to the public generally. Their report, an octavo volume of 600 pages, showed great research, was forceful, lucid, and convincing, and had great influence upon the public mind.

Its currency reform measure.

Their recommendations included the following: declaring the gold dollar the standard of value, but without affecting the legal tender quality of the silver dollar; no further coinage of silver dollars; establishing a separate bureau of issue and redemption, which should hold a 25 per cent gold reserve against both classes of legal tender notes outstanding, and a 5 per cent gold reserve against the total silver dollar coinage, the reserve to be maintained by sales of 3 per cent gold bonds if necessary; silver dollars as well as legal tenders to be redeemed in gold; no silver certificates above $5 to be issued; $50,000,000 of the legal tender notes when redeemed to be cancelled, thereafter such notes to be cancelled equal in amount to the increase of national bank circulation, and after five years the remainder to be cancelled in five equal annual instalments; after ten years the outstanding notes to cease having legal tender power; the silver bullion in the Treasury to be sold for gold to maintain the reserve; no more currency certificates and no legal tender notes under $10 to be issued; certificates of indebtedness (3 per cent five-year gold) authorized to meet any revenue deficiencies; national Abrogation of bond deposit advocated. banks to be permitted to issue circulation equal to their capital less real estate, only 25 per cent of the amount to be secured by bonds deposited with the Treasury, such security to be diminished after five years, one-fifth annually, after ten years no bond security to be required; a 5 per cent gold guaranty fund to be maintained in the Treasury, to be invested in bonds of the United States; bank-notes to be a paramount lien upon all assets of a bank; the notes issued in excess of 60 per cent of capital to be subject to a 2 per cent tax, and notes in excess of 80 per cent to pay 6 per cent tax; a tax of $\frac{1}{4}$ per cent a year on capital, surplus, and profits; no notes under $10 to be issued, the limit on retiring circulation to be removed; small banks ($25,000 capital) and branch banks to be permitted; one-fourth of the required reserves to be held in bank in gold; the 5 per cent current redemption fund to be continued, but no longer to be counted as part of reserves.

A bill embodying these provisions was introduced in Congress, but no action was taken thereon.

Under the portion of the "Sherman Law" of 1890 Treasury notes replaced. which had not been repealed, the Treasury continued to coin silver dollars as "needed to redeem the Treasury notes," and as rapidly as these notes were so redeemed they were cancelled, and when the dollars returned to the Treasury silver certificates were issued, thus substituting the latter form of paper for the Treasury notes and diminishing to that extent the direct burden upon the gold reserve.

The friends of the gold standard became aggressive, and presented to Congress a proposition to redeem silver dollars in gold. This roused the silver leaders who repelled it as an attack upon the legal tender quality of the "dollar of our daddies," and the Senate passed a resolution against the proposition ; the House, however, refused to concur.   The whole trend of the administration toward the establishment of the single gold standard, slow though it was, gave to Bryan and his lieutenants great hope of political success in the ensuing campaign.

The declared issue had theretofore been between the single silver standard, toward which the country had been so rapidly tending prior to the repeal of the silver purchase law, and the bimetallic standard with a strong tendency to the single gold standard.   Aggressive action in favor of the latter was likely to concentrate all other elements in opposition, and the silver advocates scented future victory in the situation.   They were doomed to disappointment.   The Spanish War, which occurred at this time (1898), united the patriotic sentiment of the country in support of the administration.   Republicans no longer entertained any doubt of McKinley's reëlection, and assumed a bolder attitude in favor of the gold standard, as subsequent legislation shows.

Activity of advocates of gold.

An almost continuous rebellion against Spanish rule had existed in Cuba for more than a quarter of a century.   The military occupation of the island necessarily interfered with commercial relations with the United States.   Exorbitant and unusual tariff exactions were imposed, coupled with unexplained and prolonged delay in passing goods, both for export and import, through the custom-houses, producing conditions inimical to successful business ; and these conditions were modified only by the improper use of money with customs officials.   Self-respecting merchants found it difficult to engage in trade with Cuba.   Utter neglect of sanitation in the Cuban ports, excusable or explainable perhaps by the chronic state of war, bred yellow fever without interruption.

Spanish War.

Cuban ports were in close promixity to the Gulf ports
of the United States and easily reached by the smaller
sailing craft, and hence a periodic scourge of the yellow
pest was more or less prevalent in our own country.
The only means of protecting our own people from
this disease seemed to be to compel proper sanitation
in Cuba. These conditions were aggravating, and long
continuance had exasperated people almost to the ex-
plosive point. According to the laws of nations no
provocation of war existed, and yet the happening of
any untoward event was bound to precipitate a conflict.
The blowing up of the battleship *Maine* in Havana
harbor February 15 and the death of a large number
of American sailors produced a crisis, and the conflict
became inevitable.

The recounting of the above events seems justifiable
here for the reason that the Spanish War, resulting as
it did, greatly strengthened McKinley's administration
in the popular mind and nerved the Republican leaders
to firm action in behalf of the gold standard, relieved
as they were from fear of popular defeat. The war
brought other topics to the front, and silver lost its
commanding interest.

To meet the expenses of the war taxes were increased
and a loan of $200,000,000 in 3 per cent bonds was
placed at par. The act authorizing the latter contained a provision which directed a more rapid coinage
of silver dollars. It was, in fact, with difficulty that
the silver majority in the Senate was restrained from
forcing a free silver amendment to this measure, so
imperatively demanded by the exigencies of the war.
In the House, Bland had proposed the further issue of
legal tender notes to cover the cost of the war, instead
of issuing bonds.

After the tariff revision of 1897 was completed, thus

2 D

Effects of tariff revision.

rendering any further change in the near future improbable, the industrial interests rapidly recovered from the depression, and an era of prosperity set in which was materially stimulated by the great demands of the government for war supplies. The world's production of gold steadily increased until disturbed by the South African War, and the United States, with favorable trade balances and a heavy home output, augmented its gold stock at a rate greater than that shown by any other country. Ability to maintain the gold standard was beyond question.

The national banks.

The number of national banks continued to diminish until July, 1898, when there were but 3582 (compared with 3830 in 1893 and 3634 in May, 1897). Their circulation in July, 1898, stood at $190,000,000. The issue of the 3 per cent war loan at par enabled the banks to increase circulation at a profit, and by December, 1899, it had increased to $205,000,000. The number of banks had in the same period increased 20, but their aggregate capital had diminished over $16,000,000. The circulation of the country was now $25.50 per capita. Silver declined to about 60 cents per ounce, making the market ratio to gold 34 to 1 and the bullion value of the silver dollar about 47 cents.

Currency reform determined upon.

The Republican leaders in Congress determined in December (1899) that the time for action on the currency question had arrived. In the House a Republican caucus adopted a bill upon the general lines proposed by the Indianapolis conference, but varying in certain particulars. This bill passed in January by a majority of fifty. The Senate passed a separate measure differing in many respects. The two bills went to conference, an agreement was reached early in March, and on the 14th of that month the conference bill passed and was signed by the President.

The act declared the gold dollar to be the standard The act of 1900. unit of value, and all forms of money issued or coined by the United States were to be maintained at a parity therewith by the Secretary of the Treasury. Both classes of legal tender notes were to be redeemed in such gold coin, the reserve for the purpose to be increased at once to $150,000,000, and maintained, if necessary, by sales of 3 per cent gold bonds. Notes when redeemed were to be reissued only for gold, but if the gold were obtained out of the general Treasury fund, they might be used for any purpose except to meet deficiencies in revenues. The legal tender quality of the silver dollar remained undisturbed by the law. The monetary functions of the Treasury were separated from those of a merely fiscal character by the establishment of a separate division. Treasury notes of 1890 were to be cancelled as received, and silver certificates substituted therefor; the issue of gold certificates to be resumed and continued unless the gold reserve falls below Maintenance of gold reserve. $100,000,000, or the greenbacks and silver certificates in the general fund exceed $60,000,000, and the issue of currency certificates to be discontinued. Denominations of paper are regulated as follows: no gold certificates under $20, but one-fourth at least of the issue to be $50 and under; silver certificates, 90 per cent to be $10 and under, 10 per cent $20, $50, and $100; greenbacks under $10 to be retired as smaller silver certificates are issued, larger greenbacks to be substituted; $5 national banknotes to be issued only to one-third of the amount taken by each bank.

The limit of subsidiary coinage was increased to Refunding bonds. $100,000,000, the silver on hand to be used for this purpose. The new 3 per cent government bonds, the 4 per cents of 1907, and 5 per cents of 1904 outstanding were to be refunded in the discretion of the Secretary into

2 per cent thirty-year gold bonds, upon a $2\frac{1}{4}$ per cent income basis, the premium to be paid in cash. National banks were authorized in smaller towns with $25,000 capital; circulation allowed to the par of bonds, and to the full amount of unimpaired capital, and banks depositing the new 2 per cent United States bonds to be taxed only $\frac{1}{2}$ per cent annually on circulation, whereas the tax on circulation secured by any other issue remained at one per cent.

The provision of the act of 1882 prohibiting banks retiring circulation from again increasing the same for a period of six months was repealed, but the limit of the amount which may be retired in any one month to $3,000,000 remained. The final section disclaims any intention of precluding bimetallism if conditions prove favorable.

Democrat-Populist opposition.

Thus after a struggle covering many years a number of reforms in the monetary system were carried through in a single legislative measure. The opposition at once made itself manifest. The platform of the Democratic-Populist party in Nebraska, which met in convention under the leadership of Bryan five days after the passage of the "gold standard law," declared for free and unlimited coinage of silver and the substitution of greenbacks for national bank-notes. In many of the other states similar declarations were adopted, and although the new issue of "Imperialism," growing out of the war, was for a time prominent in the presidential campaign following, the actual contest was upon the question of the standard of values and opposition to bank-note currency.

"More money" campaign.

All the former arguments for an increased money supply to come from the remonetization of silver, the oppressive effects of the single gold standard, and the inadequacy of the gold supply were rehearsed with little effect as the country was prospering as never before in its history. Prices of agricultural products had risen. The excess of exports over imports had averaged $560,000,000 a year for the preceding three years. The revenues produced a substantial surplus. The world's production of gold was now over $300,000,000 a year, the United States contributing nearly one-fourth, all of which was retained. The money in circulation in the United States had risen to nearly $27 per capita.

Bryan's renomination was a foregone conclusion, and he fatuously insisted upon making the silver question the main issue. The Republicans renominated McKinley, declared for the gold standard and against free coinage of silver, and in favor of legislation looking to an equalization of interest rates by enabling the varying currency needs of the seasons and all sections to be promptly met.

McKinley was reëlected by a largely increased majority, and the country accepted the result as indorsing and confirming the action of Congress in adopting the gold standard by the act of March 14, 1900. Good results flowing from this act were speedily manifest. The refunding of the bonds provided for aggregated $352,000,000, and a large amount of the surplus revenue was paid out for premiums in making the exchange. National banks increased 340 in number, the capital was increased $26,500,000, and circulation nearly $86,000,000 compared with September a year before. Of the new banks 123 were converted state banks and 208 were capitalized at the minimum of $25,000. The bond security for circulation included $270,000,000 of the new 2 per cents.

The issue of gold certificates increased materially, and the changes in the denominations of paper money provided for by the law progressed rapidly, the silver certificates taking the place of the smaller denominations of other issues. With large crops to be moved, the

Gold standard victorious.

Greater volume of money.

country did not suffer from the usual money stringency, owing to the large increase in the gold stock, in bank circulation, and the distribution of the surplus revenue in the process of refunding.

Defects of
law of 1900.
The law of 1900 provided " that the dollar consisting of twenty-five and eight-tenths grains of gold nine-tenths fine, as established by section thirty-five hundred and eleven of the Revised Statutes of the United States, shall be the standard unit of value, and all forms of money issued or coined by the United States shall be maintained at a parity of value with this standard, and it shall be the duty of the Secretary of the Treasury to maintain such parity." It did not, however, provide any method by which this parity should be maintained. Secretary Gage in his report for December, 1900, called attention to this omission, and urged
Gage's plan
for elastic
currency.
that specific power be given. He also renewed his arguments in favor of providing an elastic bank currency. While favoring branch banking, he recognized that public sentiment was averse to such a system, and suggested a federated system or federated bank somewhat analogous to the general government and the states, one of whose principal functions should be the issue of currency. He also recommended that bank-notes be secured, 30 per cent by a deposit of government bonds, 20 per cent by a deposit of legal tenders, the remaining 50 per cent of the issues to be based upon assets and secured by a guaranty fund.

Thus he hoped to accomplish a double reform, the elimination of the greenbacks and an ample paper currency which would not only, as he demonstrated, prove safe to the holder, but would expand and contract as business needs warranted.

The terrible tragedy at Buffalo, which resulted in the death of McKinley and the accession of Roosevelt to

the presidency, engrossed not only Congress but the
public mind generally. Moreover there was a general
feeling that the act of 1900, ratified and confirmed by
the popular vote in the election following, had rendered
our currency and our standard of values safe, and that
further legislation had better be deferred until experience had demonstrated its necessity. The prosperity of
the country was unprecedented. Enterprises requiring ^{removed} Enormous industrial expansion.
enormous and hitherto unheard-of amounts of capital
were undertaken. The growth of banks and trust companies, the underwriting and flotation of securities, the
industrial development, the increase of exports without
a corresponding increase of imports, — all tended to
greatly enlarge the volume of business, and the circulating medium increased in proportion. By 1901 it
reached $28 per capita, and continued to grow. A large
part of this was in gold, the supply of which increased
$429,000,000 from 1897 to 1901. Bank-notes had also
increased more than $120,000,000 in that period, while
silver issues of all classes showed only the slight increase arising from the seigniorage on the coinage.
The character of the increased supply of money in use
was therefore sound, and the entire mass was practically
continuously employed. Notwithstanding this large Money stringency.
volume of money the usual stringency appeared when the
crop season arrived. At its minimum of employment
in the usual channels of trade, the surplus accumulation in the banks was rapidly absorbed by the speculative demand, stimulated no doubt by the large return
of American securities from abroad to pay the enormous
trade balances in our favor. Hence, when the maximum
demand again recurred in the crop-moving season,
stringency manifested itself, aggravated by the accumulation in the subtreasuries of surplus revenues which,
despite the laws reducing taxes after the war had closed,

Treasury relief.

the great consuming power of the Nation continued to pour into the government's coffers.   There were but two means of returning this money to the channels of trade, — the purchase of bonds at high premiums, inaugurated as we have seen by Guthrie in 1854, and the placing of the surplus in depository banks.   Both courses necessarily increased the demand for and the price of government bonds (to be deposited as security for public moneys), which in turn tended to check increase in bank circulation.

The imperfections of the existing laws relating to currency, and the receipt, safe keeping, and payment of the public moneys by means of our subtreasury system, are illustrated in a practical manner with each recurring fall.   These conditions continue, and their solution remains a problem still to be solved.

Shaw's policy.

Leslie M. Shaw succeeded Gage as Secretary of the Treasury, and when in the early fall of the year 1902 the same evils manifested themselves, he endeavored to alleviate the condition by a broader construction of the law governing public deposits, which provides that such deposits shall be secured to the satisfaction of the Secretary by "deposit of government bonds and otherwise." This he rightly construed as authorizing him to accept approved bonds of states and municipalities as part of such security.   By this course an equal amount of government bonds would be released for use to increase the bank circulation.   By this process and by the purchase of bonds and anticipation of interest, Shaw was enabled to render some $40,000,000 of surplus available for use in trade channels and induce an increase of bank-notes to about one-half that sum.

Shaw on asset currency.

In his report for the year, Shaw recommended the issue of notes by banks based upon assets and properly safeguarded, not by making the notes a paramount lien, but by means of a guaranty fund and rigid redemption requirements.   He further recommended a system of public money depositories without the bond security requirement, permitting banks after special examinations to receive such deposits upon their general credit, paying interest thereon at rates subject to the discretion of the Secretary.   He also recommended provision by law for the exchange of gold for silver dollars, the use of the silver bullion on hand for subsidiary coinage, and requiring national banks to redeem their notes in gold. The change of sentiment following the evolution of business is well illustrated by the fact that Secretary Shaw recommended depositing government money with the banks at interest, when so many of his predecessors prior to 1878, as well as comptrollers of the currency, had urged that banks be prohibited by law from paying interest on deposits.

The need of giving our currency elasticity in average conditions is generally recognized, and the necessity of relieving its rigidity so the banks can afford relief and preserve values in time of panic seems to be fully appreciated.   For this reason I have set forth in much detail the principal schemes of currency reform.

As has been stated, the British government adopted a monetary policy for India which prohibited the coinage of silver except on government account, and silver coin was made exchangeable at a fixed ratio, approximately 32 to 1, which corresponded with the commercial ratio, silver having fallen to $64\frac{1}{2}$ cents per ounce.   Japan adopted a similar policy, and minor countries followed these examples, leaving the sole outlets for silver unhampered by law, the Oriental silver standard countries of China, Straits Settlements, and the Philippines.   Since the latter islands have come under the control of the United States, the gold standard with silver coinage on

Policy of India and Japan.

government account has been decreed by the act of Congress March 2, 1903.

Fixed ratio
for silver
countries.
Mexico is a large producer of silver, it constituting her principal export, and is therefore greatly interested in arresting its further depreciation. Her silver piasters have for over a century been the favorite coins of the Orient, and their exportation and further use is threatened by the political and other changes in the Philippines and China. Mexico, for this reason, instituted negotiations for an international agreement, between the countries having colonial possessions where silver is in use, to establish a stable ratio if possible between the two metals. China, the principal silver-using country at this time, joined Mexico, and the United States, having regard for the interests of the Philippines and having important silver-producing interests, has undertaken to aid in this movement; and for this purpose a commission composed of Messrs. H. H. Hanna, C. A. Conant, and J. W. Jenks were sent abroad to confer on the subject with the nations concerned in the hope that a practical solution of this problem of eliminating the violent fluctuations in the price of silver, which upset all exchange calculations, may be arrived at.

DATA RELATING TO BANKS JUNE, 1903

Statistics,
June, 1903.

Number of national banks	4939
Capital	744 millions
Circulation covered by bonds	372 millions
Circulation covered by lawful money	41 millions
Deposits	3348 millions
Loans	3415 millions
Cash	552 millions
Two per cent bonds held to secure notes . . .	367 millions
Other bonds so held	8 millions
Total resources of national banks	6287 millions
Money in circulation	2376 millions
Per capita	$29.39
Public moneys in banks	152 millions

STATISTICAL RÉSUMÉ

(Amounts in millions)

NATIONAL FINANCES

FISCAL YEAR	REVENUE			EXPENDITURES			+SURPLUS −DEFICIT	DEBT		PRICE OF 4%'S OF 1907	
	Customs	Other	Total	Ordinary	Interest	Total		Outstanding	+ Increase − Decrease	High	Low
1897	177	171	348	328	38	366	−18	1227	− 4	115	$111\frac{5}{8}$
1898	150	255	405	406	37	443	−38	1233	+ 6	$114\frac{3}{4}$	108
1899	206	310	516	565	40	605	−89	1437	+204	$115\frac{1}{8}$	112
1900	233	334	567	448	40	488	+79	1413	− 24	$118\frac{1}{8}$	114
1901	239	349	588	478	32	510	+78	1372	− 41	$115\frac{1}{2}$	112
1902	254	308	562	442	29	471	+91	1328	− 44	113	$108\frac{3}{4}$
1903	284	275	559	477	29	506	+53	1309	− 19	——	

CIRCULATION

FISCAL YEAR	GOLD [1]	SILVER [1]	SUBSIDIARY SILVER	U. S. NOTES	TREASURY NOTES	NATIONAL BANK-NOTES	TOTAL	IN TREASURY	IN CIRCULATION	POPULATION	PER CAPITA
1897 .	696	442	76	347	115	230	1906	266	1640	72	$22.87
1898 .	862	460	76	347	101	228	2074	236	1838	73	25.15
1899 .	963	470	75	347	94	241	2190	286	1904	74	25.58
1900 .	1036	491	83	347	75	310	2342	279	2063	76	26.94
1901 .	1125	520	90	347	48	354	2484	306	2178	78	27.98
1902 .	1189	540	97	347	30	356	2559	312	2247	79	28.43
1903 .	1253	554	101	347	19	413	2688	312	2376	80	29.39

[1] Including certificates.

EXPORTS AND IMPORTS AND GOLD MOVEMENT

FISCAL YEAR	MERCHANDISE			SILVER			GOLD			NOTES REDEEMED IN GOLD	NET GOLD
	Exports	Imports	Excess Exports	Exports	Imports	Excess Exports	Exports	Imports	Excess Exports – Imports +		
1897	1051	765	286	63	31	32	40	85	+ 45	78	141
1898	1231	616	615	56	31	25	16	120	+104	25	167
1899	1227	697	530	57	31	26	38	89	+ 51	26	241
1900	1394	850	544	57	35	22	48	45	− 3	36	221
1901	1488	823	665	64	36	28	53	66	+ 13	24	249
1902	1382	903	479	50	28	22	49	52	+ 3	19	254
1903	1420	1026	394	44	24	20	47	45	− 2	36	252

PRODUCTION OF GOLD AND SILVER

YEAR	WORLD			UNITED STATES			PRICE OF SILVER	RATIO	BULLION VALUE OF SILVER DOLLAR
	Gold	Silver		Gold	Silver				
		Commercial Value	Coining Value		Commercial Value	Coining Value			
1897	236	96	207	57	32	70	$.60483	34.20	$.467
1898	287	100	219	64	32	70	.59010	35.03	.456
1899	307	101	217	71	33	71	.60154	34.36	.465
1900	255	107	223	79	36	75	.62007	33.33	.479
1901	263	105	226	79	33	71	.59595	34.68	.461
1902	—	—	—	81	30	76	—	—	—

SILVER STATISTICS

Fiscal Year	Coinage of Silver Dollars	Stock of Dollars	Dollars Out	Silver Certificates Out	Net Silver in the Treasury	
					Dollars	Bullion
1897 . . .	13	442	52	358	32	105
1898 . . .	14	456	58	390	12	98
1899 . . .	15	471	61	402	7	85
1900 . . .	25	496	66	408	16	70
1901 . . .	24	520	67	430	24	48
1902 . . .	23	543	69	447	25	33

NATIONAL BANKS

(AT DATES NEAREST JANUARY I)

Year	Number	Capital	Surplus	Deposits	Circulation	Specie	Legals	Loans
1897	3661	647	247	1655	211	226	156	1901
1898	3607	630	246	1961	194	252	159	2100
1899	3590	621	247	2319	207	329	136	2214
1900	3602	607	250	2461	205	315	115	2480
1901	3942	632	262	2718	299	360	142	2707
1902	4291	665	287	3074	319	370	151	3038
1903	4766	731	351	3308	335	418	153	3351

OTHER BANKS

Year	State Banks						Total Resources		
	Number	Capital	Surplus	Deposits	Cash	Loans	Trust Companies	Private Banks	Savings Banks
1897	3857	229	77	724	145	670	844	78	2199
1898	3965	234	81	912	144	814	943	91	2241
1899	4191	233	77	1164	217	909	1072	88	2401
1900	4369	237	91	1267	202	1030	1380	127	2625
1901	4983	255	104	1611	310	1184	1615	149	2757
1902	5397	277	111	1698	228	1346	1983	160	2893

MISCELLANEOUS FINANCIAL

YEAR	CLEARING-HOUSES		SAVINGS BANKS			FAILURES	
	New York	United States	Depositors (ooo's)	Deposits (Millions)	Average	Number (ooo's)	Liabilities (Millions)
1897	31,338	54,180	5201	1939	373	13	154
1898	39,853	65,925	5386	2066	384	12	131
1899	57,368	88,829	5688	2230	392	9	91
1900	51,965	84,582	6107	2450	401	11	138
1901	77,021	114,190	6359	2597	408	11	113
1902	74,753	116,022	6667	2750	412	12	117

BANKING POWER BY SECTIONS

(Including Capital, Surplus, Undivided Profits and Deposits)

As given in reports of Comptroller of Currency

STATES	BANKING POWER (In millions)			PER CAPITA		
	1890	1900	1902	1890	1900	1902
New England .	1229	1728	2052	$261.86	$312.30	$354.86
Eastern . . .	2410	4281	6233	170.92	251.10	351.37
Middle . . .	1055	1808	3071	54.59	75.00	128.72
Southern . . .	387	552	844	21.15	24.94	36.88
Western . . .	218	306	480	54.83	60.16	89.94
Pacific	315	467	640	139.15	147.01	197.58
All . . .	5614	9142	13,320	89.85	118.73	168.96

In this table the Pacific states are separated from the Western ; but Kansas and Nebraska, heretofore included in Central class, are here included as Western. The designation of sections as employed by the Comptroller has been retained.

The population for 1900 was *estimated* and considerably exceeded the census figures; that for 1902 is estimated on basis of census of 1900, and is more nearly correct. The result is that the per capita for 1900 is less than it should be.

CHAPTER XIX

GENERAL REVIEW

A GENERAL review of the monetary history of the entire period of our national existence shows that each generation had to learn for itself and at its own expense the evils of unsound money. The costly experiences of the preceding generation were generally forgotten, and legislators, following rather than leading the people, failed to correct the evils except after long and disastrous delays. So intolerable were the conditions at times that only the unlimited recuperative powers of our rapidly developing and expanding country prevented the overthrow of that standard of value and honor which is recognized by the world as highest and best.

The problem of furnishing a sound and stable medium for a country of such large area, of such diverse interests, developing at an unprecedented rate, presents unusual difficulties, and no precedent is furnished by any other country with kindred conditions and analogous experience. Principles remain the same, however, and the obstacles could have been overcome and all questions properly solved had not political ambitions and party advantage exercised such a controlling influence. The questions confronting us to-day are in many respects the same that have existed throughout our history, namely, the establishment of a coinage and currency system which will assure stability as to metallic money, security and flexibility to paper currency, to the end

Difficulties of the problem.

that prices may not be subject to ruthless disturbances and interest rates be reasonably uniform and equitable throughout the land.

The coinage. The bimetallic theory, however logical in the days of Hamilton, when the production of precious metals was but small and the greater part of the civilized world preferred silver to gold, has been demonstrated impossible of realization without substantially universal adoption, which has been shown equally impossible. As a practical question bimetallism is for this generation at least a moribund issue. Whether the enormous production of gold shall ultimately impair its desirability as a standard of value or, what is more likely, cause the evolution of entirely novel theories of money, is a question too remote to have any present utility.

Hamilton's writings, his careful study of the subject, with the end always in view of giving his country a just measure of values, show clearly that to-day he would favor a standard resting upon gold alone; nor is it to be doubted that Jefferson would maintain equally sound and conservative views. The statistics presented show that immediately after the adoption of Hamilton's coinage law the production of silver increased largely, dis-
The question of ratio. turbing the commercial ratio between gold and silver. According to Hamilton's theory, this should have been followed by a change in the coinage ratio·as early as 1810. In 1834, when such action was taken, the intelligent opinion of the day was ignored and an extreme ratio adopted which reversed rather than corrected the disparity by undervaluing silver. Within a decade the great increase in gold production had enhanced the relative value of silver, and all coins, fractional silver as well, were exported. To correct this and retain small coins for current use the law of 1853 was passed, reducing the amount of fine silver in fractional coins.

The relatively scant product of the white metal for the following twenty years served to demonstrate the wisdom of the law of 1853. Unfortunately the legislators of that day left the silver dollar unit undisturbed, and when silver was again produced in larger quantities (after 1874) the existence of the law of 1837 gave the advocates of free coinage of silver a precedent and prestige which would not otherwise have existed. The act of 1900 leaves the legal tender power of the dollar of 371.25 grains of pure silver exactly as provided in the acts of 1792 and 1837, except where otherwise expressly provided in the contract.

The silver dollar.

It is only necessary to recapitulate the silver legislation since the beginning of the agitation for remonetization in 1876, in order to appreciate the bearing of the enormous acquisition of silver by the United States and the possible menace which its possession involves. The silver purchased under the laws of 1878 and 1890 amounted to 459,946,701 fine ounces, costing us $464,210,262, an average per ounce of nearly $1.01, parity being $1.2929. The price of silver (December, 1902) was quoted as low as 46 cents per ounce, giving a bullion value to the silver dollar of less than 40 cents. The silver dollars coined amount to $550,000,000, and the bullion still uncoined will produce some $35,500,000 more, giving an ultimate total of $585,500,000. The actual use of silver dollars in circulation will probably never exceed one per capita, now about 80,000,000. The remainder will be represented by silver certificates or remain absolutely idle in the Treasury so far as currency purposes are concerned.

The silver acquisition since 1878.

The entire volume of silver and representative certificates may be utilized for the great and growing retail trade of the country so long as business conditions are prosperous, the labor of the country is employed, and the

Influence of silver on currency system.

consuming power continues unabated ; but the contrary will follow when reaction takes place and business again becomes stagnant. The sole available means, in that event, of avoiding danger from this element in our money supply is the continuation of our large Treasury surplus into which the redundant silver, for which there will be no use as currency, may be absorbed.

Paper currency.

Passing now to the paper representatives of money, we have first to consider the gold and silver certificates which constitute a form of currency not made use of in other countries. While at first gold certificates were permitted to be issued in excess of the gold deposited (law of 1863), the more recent laws governing their issue, as also in the case of silver certificates, require that the full amount of coin shall be held against them. Both forms of certificates are, therefore, merely warehouse receipts, and, although receivable for all public dues and available for bank reserves, they are not legal tenders. Gold certificates as compared with coin save in transportation as well as in abrasion, and cater to a public preference for paper money. The silver certificates serve a similarly useful purpose in floating the silver dollars ; their use has thus unquestionably enabled the advocates of silver to load the currency with an amount of dollars far beyond all needs and perhaps beyond the point of safety.

Legal tenders.

We have seen that the "fathers" intended, without specifically embodying a prohibition to that effect in the Constitution, to prevent the issue of governmental legal tender paper, and a tacit understanding that no such power existed guided legislators for seventy-three years. In the evolution of government the conception of federal power under the Constitution was broadened, and found enlarged expression in legislative, executive, and judicial action. The perils and necessities of the government during the Civil War broke the barriers of the strict constructionists, and the powers which a sovereign government needed to exercise were held to be warranted by the Constitution except where specifically prohibited. Relying upon the opinions expressed in debate, it is safe to assert that Congress believed the legal tender act of 1862 unconstitutional when they voted that it become a law. They were willing to adopt revolutionary means to overcome revolution. The Rubicon once passed, this law furnished a precedent for others to follow. The Supreme Court in its first decision held the law in large part unconstitutional. The second decision reopened the case, and held that Congress had power to issue legal tender notes "for the time being," having reference to the perils of the government in the exigency of war. Upon the third hearing in 1884 the Court held that giving the legal tender quality to paper was a sovereign power, exercisable in time of peace as well as in time of war, in the discretion of Congress.

The Supreme Court decisions.

The right to issue bank-notes was made use of by the few banks existing prior to the adoption of the Constitution as a common law right. The banks in the several states continued to exercise this right after the adoption of the Constitution, under their state charters, whether specifically authorized or not. It was generally admitted that such rights existed, that the states, although prohibited from issuing bills of credit to be used as money, could charter corporations with such powers. This granting to their own creatures powers which the states did not themselves possess was assented to and finally confirmed as constitutional by the Supreme Court. Antecedent thereto Hamilton devised the charter of the first Bank of the United States, and assumed for the federal government a similar power, that of creating a corporation to emit paper to circulate

Apparent basis.

Broad con-
struction.

as money, which it was generally held at that time the government itself could not do under the Constitution. Marshall in his masterly decision on the charter of the second Bank of the United States confirmed the federal power to create such a bank, and enunciated principles in construing the Constitution which became the foundation for the broader assumption of power in the legal tender acts of the Civil War.

Statistics of
legal tenders.

The volume of legal tender notes of the war period continue as they stood in 1878, after the law forbidding their further retirement, at $346,681,016, less such as have been lost or destroyed. Those issued under the act of 1890 are gradually being retired by substitution of silver certificates, only $24,000,000 remaining in existence, December, 1902. Aside from the enormous cost to the people through the depreciation of this currency, the maintenance of coin redemption, since resumption was determined upon, has resulted in bond issues, in order to obtain gold amounting to, 1875-1879, $95,000,000 and, 1894-1896, to $262,300,000, together with the interest thereon.

In order to be able to redeem these notes upon presentation, $357,300,000 of interest-bearing bonds of the government have been issued, which the people have paid or must pay. Compare the amount of these bond issues with the amount of legal tender notes outstanding (greenbacks), $346,681,016, and instead of being a "burdenless debt" and the "best currency ever devised," it would seem pregnant with burden as well as danger. These notes when presented for redemption and paid are not cancelled but reissued, and continue to possess all potentiality of further drain upon the Treasury. Experience in 1893-1896 teaches that continuous deficits in revenue will inevitably render the existence of these notes an element of danger. Congress seems to have realized this and sought to guard against it by establish- ing a gold reserve of $150,000,000. Should the usual banking methods for maintaining the reserve prove unavailing, the act provides : if "said fund shall at any time fall below $100,000,000, then it shall be his (Secretary of the Treasury) duty to restore the same to the maximum sum of $150,000,000 by borrowing money on the credit of the United States," etc. With this power lodged in the hands of the Secretary and this duty imposed upon him, there can be no doubt of the redemption of these notes in gold so long as gold can be borrowed on the credit of the United States. The danger is that still further bonded indebtedness may have to be incurred on account of them.

Ninety per cent of silver certificates are now limited to $10, $5, $2, and $1 issues. Legal tender notes are limited to $10 minimum. Only one-third of the notes issued to a national bank can be of the denomination of $5. All other notes must be $10 and upwards. Silver is by law made the only available currency for the small everyday transactions of the people which are so largely effected by actual money rather than by auxiliary credits. Silver is thus laid under contribution to perform the daily exchanges of the workaday world, and cannot leave its task either directly or indirectly to aid in withdrawing gold from the Treasury. It is chained to the wheels of industry. The volume of currency which may be thus safely impounded by an active commercial people, already numbering 80,000,000 and rapidly increasing, is certainly very large, and since the volume of silver is no longer increasing, it is probable that except under extraordinary conditions the gold standard has little to fear from the present amount of silver currency, and it is believed that whatever danger exists would 'be removed or at least greatly reduced by making silver and gold interchangeable.

Legal
tenders
impounded.

The prejudice or preference of the American people for paper money precludes the use of coin except to a very limited extent. Bank-notes and the gold and silver certificates perform all the essential functions of money, except that they do not possess the debt-paying power — are not legal tenders. Our widely extended country, with many commercial and business centres, requires a considerable volume of legal tender money. The custom which avoids the use of coin makes a continual use for legal tender notes. A very large amount is continually in use for bank reserves. These notes are better than gold certificates, for while they are both redeemable in gold at the Treasury, the notes may be tendered to and forced upon a creditor in satisfaction of his debt. The issue of currency certificates, in denominations of $5000 and $10,000 for legal tender notes deposited, was designed to furnish a currency, convenient in form and size, to enable the banks in large cities to settle their clearing-house balances, which in New York City frequently amount to several

Gold reserve
protected.

millions. They proved an equally convenient instrumentality for withdrawing gold from the Treasury. It was easy to present them and demand notes, and then present the notes and demand gold. Such certificates are no longer issued, Treasury gold certificates and clearing-house gold certificates serving the needs of the banks. It will in future be much more difficult to accumulate legal tenders in large volume as a means of withdrawing gold from the Treasury as they, too, to a very large extent, are kept in constant demand.

The United States was the last stronghold of silver. The gold standard law of 1900, directly in issue in the presidential contest of that year, and hence squarely indorsed and ratified by the people, indeed settled the question in the United States. But our government nursed bimetallism, and sent commissioners abroad to try and interest Europe in the subject, until their courteous reception depended upon the character of the government which sent them rather than the subject which they represented. All the great commercial nations adhered to the gold standard. The consensus of opinion of the civilized world, which in commerce makes law and regulates exchange, adopted the gold standard. This fact, borne in upon the public mind in the United States, found its record in the second defeat of Bryanism, and this fact, more potent than statute law, will preserve the gold standard. Gold standard firmly established.

When the federal revenues increase, the subtreasury system necessarily draws in and locks up a substantial part of the available supply of money, which tends to produce a stringency. As early as 1853 the Treasury was constrained to " come to the relief of the money market " and return the surplus money to the channels of trade by purchasing government bonds. The precedent thus established obtains to-day. The government's obligations have been purchased at premiums ranging up to 28 per cent, in order to counteract the workings of the subtreasury system. Could a more severe arraignment or criticism be made upon the system ? The only other means of preventing the undue absorption of money by the Treasury is to deposit receipts from internal revenue in banks. From 1837 until the establishment of the national banking system (1863), depositing funds with banks was regarded as dangerous. Indeed, the existing system, under which the public deposits are amply secured by government bonds, has been severely criticised, and curiously, most severely by the political party (Republican) which subsequently made the largest use of it. Such deposits are limited to the current internal revenue Influence of the sub-treasury. Depository banks.

receipts. However acute the stringency, customs receipts could not be so deposited, nor money transferred from the Treasury. Under present law customs receipts must be paid directly into the Treasury, and money once in the Treasury can only be gotten out by means of an appropriation by Congress.

In no other civilized country is there such an absurd governmental interference with the currency supply, affecting values, promoting speculation, retarding business, and disturbing the welfare of the people.

The second Bank of the United States had been drawn into the maelstrom of party politics and wrecked. Its continuation and ignominious failure as a state institution shed reflex disgrace upon the original bank, and prevented public sentiment from turning again to a national bank for relief as it did in 1816, during the currency demoralization and financial troubles following the War of 1812. The action of Congress, in creating the subtreasury system in 1846 and seeking safety for its own funds regardless of the public, can be explained but not justified; the continuation of this system of governmental interference with every man's business, a disturbing factor that must be reckoned with in every business forecast, cannot even be intelligently explained.

Remedy proposed.

A law authorizing the Secretary of the Treasury to deposit any and all funds, over and above the reserve maintained against the government's legal tender obligations and his necessary checking balances, in the banks in reserve cities, with due solicitude for safety and prompt repayment whenever required, would free the subtreasury system from its serious defects and relieve business interests from its malinterference. There is much to be said in favor of maintaining the reserve and current checking funds in the government's own coffers.

At the inception of our national existence the genius Hamilton's bank plan. of Hamilton conceived a central bank as the instrumentality through which the fiscal affairs of the government should be conducted. With branches established throughout the country, the standard of banking, the character of currency which this bank established, became the criterion by which all would be judged. Other banks in order to succeed in competition had to be equally sound, their notes equally sure of redemption. His prescience and wisdom were vindicated by the achievements during the period of the first United States Bank (1791–1811). Public and private credit was raised from almost unprecedented chaos to a very high standard.

The deplorable condition of both currency and credit The second bank. following the refusal to renew the bank's charter, coupled with the exigencies of the War of 1812, which resulted in chartering the second United States Bank in 1816 (with the approval of Madison as President and many others who had opposed renewing the charter of the first), may also be noted to the credit of the central bank plan. The second bank was discredited by corruption in its early years, and weakly and most unwisely becoming embroiled in politics in its latter years, suffered party defeat and ceased to exist as a national institution with the expiration of its charter. Its early mistakes were corrected, and for many years its career was most honorable and useful. During this period, the central bank system so regulated the currency that its purchas- Regulation of currency. ing and debt-paying power was practically stable and uniform, with prompt redemption as well as flexibility of volume. It provided safe depositories for public moneys and transferred the same at little or no cost, developed the use of bank credits, greatly diminished the cost of domestic exchange, and by means of its branches and general powers tended to equalize interest and discount rates. When the system was destroyed, all the evils, which had thus been corrected, reappeared and continued until the era of nationalization which the Civil War brought about.

State banks.
It must not, however, be inferred that all of the state bank systems were bad. In theory many were good, although in practice the conservative restraints were not generally observed. In the earlier periods of our history the issuing of currency was regarded the principal function of banks. They generally had limited cash capital and small deposits. Auxiliary currency, checks and drafts, that at the present time perform over 90 per cent of the transactions consummated by the people, were little used. A bank's ability to accommodate the public with loans and discounts depended very largely upon its note-issue. This explains why the people so long tolerated such enormous issues of bank-notes of such uncertain value. In the newer sections the curbing of the power to issue notes was stoutly resented. It was regarded as depriving the locality of the life-blood of its trade notwithstanding the defective character and fluctuating value of such notes. One of the strongest criticisms, and most effective as to public sentiment, against the United States Bank was that it refused to receive the notes of many banks, and promptly presented for redemption such notes as it did receive, instead of paying them out. As the country grew in population and wealth, deposits became a more important factor, and checks and drafts largely superseded currency.

Improved banking system.
The national banking system was planned to make a market for government bonds and secured by such bonds to furnish a currency which should supplant United States notes, and also to create a demand and use

for United States notes in the reserves which the banks were required to hold. Such currency was perfectly safe but not at all responsive to the varying needs of trade. No currency based upon bond security can be elastic. A bank is required to invest as much or more money in the purchase of bonds to secure circulation than the amount of circulation it is permitted to issue. Its ability to extend accommodations to its patrons is thereby limited rather than increased. *Elasticity lacking.*

Bond security is not essential to a perfectly secured circulation. One life insurance company of the city of New York has outstanding 704,567 paid-for policies of insurance amounting to $1,553,628,026. The company is remarkably strong and well managed. All life insurance the world over is based upon mortuary tables, showing the expectation of human life calculated from statistical experience. The business is safe in all particulars. All fire insurance is based upon statistical history of loss by fire and the percentage of probable loss calculated therefrom. The business is safe and prudently and wisely conducted. How much easier to calculate with certainty the mortality among banks and the percentage of probable loss, in view of supervision, examination, and great publicity, and the elaborate data which they are required to furnish! The statistical history of the national banks for thirty-nine years shows that a tax of $\frac{3}{8}$ of 1 per cent levied annually upon outstanding circulation would have produced an amount of money sufficient to have redeemed the outstanding notes of every national bank that has failed, without recourse to bonds held as security or other funds. With business certainty, a safety fund and a guarantee fund involving only a moderate tax can be provided which will make note-issues perfectly safe and sound. *Asset currency*

The experience of other nations furnishes competent

Currency of
Germany.
evidence upon the question of currency. Germany occupies front rank among commercial nations, and her monetary system may be studied with advantage. The Reichsbank (or Imperial Bank) of Germany at the present time is authorized to issue M. 470,000,000 of uncovered or asset currency. These notes are not issued against coin or bullion, nor is any particular asset or security pledged for their redemption, nor is the above limitation inflexible. The bank may issue circulation in excess of its authorized uncovered issue, subject to a tax of 5 per cent upon such excess issue, to be paid into the Imperial Treasury, provided also that a cash reserve exclusive of notes of other banks be maintained equal to one-third of its notes in circulation. In the year 1900 the Reichsbank paid to the Imperial Treasury M. 2,517,853 on account of this 5 per cent tax. Whenever the note-issue exceeds the authorized uncovered circulation, the tax is imposed immediately but collected at the end of the year.

Elasticity of its bank-notes.

In the year 1900 the note circulation of the Imperial Bank was in

		MARKS
January	. . . .	1,099,677,000
March	. . . .	1,309,970,000
May	. . . .	1,090,761,000
June	. . . .	1,309,865,000
August	. . . .	1,096,006,000
September	. . . .	1,343,963,000
November	. . . .	1,166,141,000
December	. . . .	1,409,945,000

The above figures reflect the elasticity and flexibility which a proper currency system should possess. During the year 1900, in March, the excess circulation was M. 238,258,000; April, M. 33,196,000; June, M. 158,645,000. Upon these amounts a 5 per cent tax was paid, the bank rate of interest being 5½ per cent.

Statistical data.

In September the excess circulation was M. 292,527,000; October, M. 138,674,000; November, M. 23,067,000; and December, M. 355,917,000 ($84,708,246). Upon these amounts a tax at the rate of 5 per cent was paid. The bank's interest rate was also 5 per cent; thus the money was loaned at a rate of interest equal to the tax which the bank had to pay. In 1901 the bank paid a 5 per cent tax upon excessive circulation during several months, while the bank's rate of interest was $4\frac{1}{2}$ per cent and 4 per cent. I mention this to show that the bank derived no profit from surplus circulation, rather suffered a loss. It realized its advantage in supplying public needs and averting calamity. In this we have illustrated the successful working of a currency system easily adapting itself to the varying needs of a great commercial nation and especially designed to meet and master any emergency.

Advantage of system.

Dunbar, in his "Theory and History of Banking," states that on more than one occasion the provision for elasticity in the German currency law saved the nation from what would otherwise have been a severe spasm of contraction. It is the consensus of opinion of German financiers that this provision enabled them to pass through the commercial and financial depression during the years 1900 and 1901 with comparative ease, avoiding what otherwise might have entailed serious disaster.

The Dominion of Canada allows its chartered banks to issue circulating notes to the amount of their paid-up capital.[1] The note holders are protected (1) by a prior lien upon the assets of failed banks, including the double liability of stockholders, and (2) by a redemption fund contributed by each bank equal to 5 per cent of its

Canadian bank currency.

[1] In February, 1903, there were in the Dominion 34 banks, with capital of $73,591,500, circulation $55,746,498, and 690 branches.

average circulation and under control of the Minister of Finance. Notes of failed banks draw 5 per cent interest from the time of default until the administrator advertises his readiness to redeem the same. Banks are required to maintain their notes at par throughout the Dominion ; they must redeem the same in the principal cities of each province of the Dominion and in any additional places that may be designated by the Treasury board.

Safety fund.

The safety fund is accumulated by an annual tax of 1 per cent on the average circulation of each bank until the same equals 5 per cent, and is thereafter maintained at that percentage by such annual tax as may be necessary, not exceeding 1 per cent upon the average circulation. This safety fund is invested in Dominion securities drawing 3 per cent interest, which is paid to the respective banks. In case a bank fails, its notes are immediately redeemed from this fund, and the fund is then replenished from the assets of the failed bank before any other claim is paid. There is no pledged security for the redemption of notes. While banks may

Practical results.

issue circulation to the whole amount of their capital, during the year 1902, the circulation at its maximum (October) equalled only 92.68 per cent of the capital ; at its minimum (January) only 71.85 per cent of the capital. The flexible range, the measure of elasticity, was, therefore, 20.83 per cent.

The working of the Canadian system furnishes a valuable object lesson ; expansion and contraction of the currency measured by 20.83 per cent registers the varying needs of commerce in different seasons ; since the maximum currency issue was within the total amount authorized, the needs of commerce and trade must have been fully supplied. There have been but three bank failures in Canada since 1890. Note holders were paid in full, and the redemption fund fully restored from the assets of the failed banks.

The Canadian banking system, unlike ours, requires Other features. no reserve against deposits and no governmental inspection, although elaborate data are required to be furnished by means of verified monthly reports. It has borne the test of experience, and furnishes good evidence that a currency may be both safe and elastic without pledged security for its redemption, while our experience proves that circulation secured by bonds may be perfectly good, but cannot be elastic.

As the government's credit improved after the war Our national banks. and the premium upon bonds increased, it became more profitable to sell bonds and retire circulation, and the banks increased their loanable funds by so doing. For this reason bank circulation decreased at a period when the friends of sound money hoped it would increase and thereby aid in retiring the greenbacks. An opposition to the national banking system existed not unlike that which developed against the two United States banks in intensity and virulence. This opposition championed first the greenbacks and later silver. The system had to struggle for existence, and received little consideration and no indulgence in respect to note-issues. As banks of discount and deposit, the growth of the system is simply marvellous. It is preëminently the best and safest system of local banks which the country has ever possessed, made secure and homogeneous by means of federal supervision and comprehensive publicity. It has Utility of the system. elevated the general credit, very materially reduced the cost of domestic exchange, furnished circulation at par. throughout the country, proved a competent and efficient auxiliary to trade, and paid large tribute to the Treasury for the privilege of so doing.

EXHIBIT OF GROWTH OF NATIONAL BANKS EXPRESSED IN MILLIONS

OCTOBER	NUMBER	CAPITAL	SURPLUS AND PROFITS	LOANS	DEPOSITS	CIRCULA-TION	TOTAL RE-SOURCES
1863 .	66	7	—	5	8	—	17
1873 .	1976	491	175	944	623	339	1831
1883 .	2501	510	203	1309	1049	311	2373
1893 .	3781	679	350	1844	1451	183	3110
1902 .	4601	706	496	3280	3209	317	6113

This exhibit is the most remarkable that the world has to show of financial institutions operating under identical charters and single supervision.

The taxes paid to the United States during the existence of the system amount to $90,419,398. In addition they paid large amounts to the states where located.

The statistics of insolvency show as follows: —

FAILURES OF NATIONAL BANKS

(Amounts in millions)

PERIOD	NUMBER	CAPITAL	CLAIMS PROVED	PAID	PER CENT PAID
1864 to 1873 . .	34	8.2	14.8	10.6	71.6
1874 to 1883 . .	55	11.7	18.9	13.5	71.4
1884 to 1893 . .	161	24.6	54.5	37.6	69.0
1894 to 1902 . .	156	23.2	51.2	35.3	69.0
Total . . .	406	67.7	139.4	97.0	69.6

The circulating notes were of course paid in full upon presentation, and the assets were not entirely distributed.

In short, as a system of *banking* institutions its value cannot be overestimated, and its imperfections are attributable to conditions not inherent in the system, but due to legislative errors of omission or commission. It is wise for those who aim to give the country a model system to endeavor to graft upon this great establishment a note-issuing function which will provide a sound, safe, elastic currency, free from the defects which experience has shown exist.

The establishment of a central or United States bank at the present or in the near future is altogether improbable and perhaps altogether undesirable. The existing national banks, so far as their note-issuing function is concerned, can be sufficiently welded together by uniform law and central supervision to make them practically one institution. Circulation can be made uniform and national in character, good beyond peradventure by means of a redemption fund and a guarantee fund, easily convertible by central redemption, sufficiently elastic to respond to the varying needs of trade by basing the same in whole or in part upon assets or credits, and by graduated taxation the volume may be made to contract, in order to avoid speculative redundancy. In short, it can be made safe, convertible, elastic. All this can be done as well as with a United States bank. In fact, the whole system would amount practically to one bank so far as note-issues are concerned and at the same time by preserving the individuality of the different banks would leave to the various localities the individual enterprise, local pride, and efficiency of management born of local knowledge, which is a consideration of paramount importance in a country of such wide extent and diversified interests as ours.

The labor of the past becomes the experience of the present and the habit of the future. Problems once solved and labor once satisfactorily done, we meet the same questions and the same labor as they recur, and solve them in the same way intuitively and without con-

Probable lines for reform.

Federation not centralization.

2 F

scious mental effort. Guided by knowledge born of experience, the greater portion of our day's doings are mechanical, perfunctory. Were we compelled to fix our mental attention upon each act we perform and ask and answer the question, "How shall this be done and why?" we would experience mental exhaustion before the day was half over. Force of habit is a conservator of strength and a great blessing, even though it too often constrains us to follow the beaten paths rather than make the effort necessary to reach a broader and a better way.

Nations have their habits as well as individuals, and time and custom have fixed existing law with reference to finance with a good degree of firmness. Nevertheless, taught by experience, and prodded by the frequent commercial disturbances resulting therefrom, we may fairly hope that Congress will in the near future modify the subtreasury system and give to our currency a degree of elasticity.

PART FOUR

BIBLIOGRAPHY

BIBLIOGRAPHY

CHAPTER XX

It is proposed in this section to present a categorical list of books and other publications to guide the reader who may desire to consult original records and study the discussions of the several questions at greater length.

The arrangement of the list will enable the reader to determine, without research and additional examination, which of the volumes are requisite for the pursuit of the specific subject upon which further information is desired.

The history of the Colonial and Continental periods is not voluminous, and the official records are not only scant but in many particulars fragmentary; nevertheless, much may be gleaned from the publications named below.

On the subject of COINAGE, the extracts from the Journals and manuscript reports of the Continental Congress appear in : —

> *International Monetary Conference*, 1878, Senate Ex. Doc., No. 58, 45th Cong., 3d Sess. (Washington, 1879).

This also contains Robert Morris's plan for a coinage system, Thomas Jefferson's Notes on the same, the Reports of the Board of Treasury and the Ordinance on Coinage of the Continental Congress, which established the dollar unit.

Unofficial publications are : —

> *History of American Coinage*, David K. Watson, New York, 1899.
>
> *Money and Banking*, Horace White, Boston, 1896; revised 1902.
>
> *The Early Coins of America*, Crosby.
>
> *United States Mint and Coinage*, A. M. Smith, Philadelphia, no date.
>
> *Financial History of the United States*, Albert S. Bolles, New York, 1896. 3 vols.

Consult also the numbers of *Sound Currency*, semimonthly (later quarterly), published by the Reform Club, New York, 1895–1903.

PAPER CURRENCY legislation prior to 1789, from the Journals of Congress, is covered by the books mentioned below, and the data are compiled in the official Treasury publication : —

> *History of the Currency of the Country,* etc., William F. DeKnight, Washington, 1897.
>
> *The Funding System of the United States,* Jonathan Elliot, House Doc., No. 15. 28th Cong., 1st Sess.

Unofficial publications are : —

> *Historical Account of Massachusetts Currency,* J. B. Felt, Boston, 1839.
>
> *History of Bills of Credit of New York,* John H. Hickox, Albany, 1866.
>
> *Short History of Paper Money,* etc., William M. Gouge, Philadelphia, 1833.
>
> *Historical Sketches of the Paper Currency,* etc., Henry Phillips, Jr., 2 vols., Roxbury, 1865–1866.
>
> *Currency and Banking in Massachusetts,* A. McF. Davis, 2 vols., New York, 1900.
>
> *History of American Currency,* William G. Sumner, New York, 1878 ; revised 1884.
>
> *The Financier and the Finances of the American Revolution,* William G. Sumner, 2 vols., New York, 1892.
>
> *Brief Account of Paper Money of the Revolution,* J. W. Schuckers. Philadelphia, 1874.

Short accounts will be found in : —

> *United States Notes,* John Jay Knox. New York, 1888 (3d edition, 1894).
>
> *Money and Banking.* Horace White, Boston, 1895 ; revised 1902.
>
> *Money,* Francis A. Walker. New York. 1891.
>
> *Continental Currency,* Byron W. Holt. *Sound Currency,* Vol. V., No. 7, 1898.

Statistics of the issue of Continental and State currency. during the Revolution, and of its fluctuation. are compiled from various sources in the DeKnight publication. in Phillips's and in Schuckers's mentioned above.

BANKING during the earliest period is discussed in : —

> *History of Banking in the United States.* William G. Sumner (being Vol. I. of the New York *Journal of Commerce* publication, *History of Banking in all Nations,* in 4 vols.), New York, 1896.
>
> *History of Banking in the United States,* John Jay Knox, New York, 1900.

Also the volumes of W. M. Gouge and Horace White noted above, and the *Sound Currency* publications.

The charter of the Bank of North America, the first incorporated bank, may be found in Clarke and Hall, *Legislative and Documentary History of Bank of the United States*, Washington, 1832.

The period from the adoption of the Constitution (1789) to the opening of the Civil War (1861) is in many respects the most important, covering as it does the formative era of the nation ; and respecting the monetary system, the experiments which the people tried and repeated, notwithstanding the many sad experiences, serve as instructive guides to the proper understanding of the subject.

The constitutional provisions will be better understood by consulting : —

Elliot's *Debates of the Constitutional Convention.*

A Plea for the Constitution, etc., George Bancroft, 1884.

The laws will be found in the *Statutes at Large*, but the principal ones have been reprinted, especially in one volume, 1886, and in Senate Report No. 831, 53d Cong., 3d Sess.

The general subject of money is covered in : —

FINANCE REPORTS, being the reports of the Secretaries of the Treasury, including some special reports (many of the latter are, however, to be found elsewhere). These reports are, for the period 1789 to 1849, published in 6 volumes ; thereafter in separate annual volumes, which also contain the reports of subordinate officers of the Treasury.

MESSAGES AND PAPERS OF THE PRESIDENTS, Vols. I. to V., covering this period. In the earlier messages little material is found ; Madison, Jackson, and later presidents devote considerable space to the subject.

Congressional action is recorded officially in *Annals of Congress* (1789-1824), *Register of Debates* (1824-1837), and *Congressional Globe* (1838-1860) ; but for the period from 1789 to 1856 the material is digested in *Abridgment of Debates*, 6 vols., Thomas H. Benton.

Furthermore, Public Documents of Congress, embracing Executive and Miscellaneous Papers, Committee Reports, etc.

Executive action is also recorded in *American State Papers*, 5 vols.

Unofficial publications on the general subject are : —

American Statesmen, Andrew W. Young, 1857.

Statesman's Manual, Edw. Williams, 3 vols., 1858.

Money in Politics, J. K. Upton, Boston, 1884.

Money and Banking, Horace White, Boston, 1902.

Niles's Register, a weekly publication, Baltimore, 1811–1848.

Hunt's Merchant's Magazine, a monthly, New York, 1840–1860.

Consideration on the Currency and Banking System of the United States, Albert Gallatin, Philadelphia. 1831.

Suggestions on Banks and Currency, Albert Gallatin, New York, 1841.

COINAGE is especially considered in Hamilton's *Report on the Establishment of a Mint*, found in *Finance Reports*; Crawford's in 1820, Ingham's in 1830. and Gallatin's paper included in the latter. These and other important documents are reprinted in *International Monetary Conference*, 1878, already referred to. Secretary Corwin's Treasury Reports also contain valuable material. A concise review of the coinage history also appears in the *Report of the Director of the Mint* for 1895.

Congressional action is recorded in the *Annals* and *Debates* and in reports by : —

> *Sanford, Nathan*, Senate Report No. 3, 21st Cong., 2d Sess., 1830.
>
> *White, Campbell P.*, House Reports, 1831, March 1832, June 1832, 1834 ; all of these are reprinted in the last-mentioned Report, No. 278, 23d Cong.. 1st Sess., and are very valuable.
>
> *Hunter, R. M. T.*, Senate Report No. 104, 32d Cong.. 1st Sess.
>
> *Benton's Abridgment of Debates.*

Statistics of the composition of the coins and the volume of coinage from 1792 to date are annually printed in the *Reports of Directors of the Mint*.

Unofficial publications are : —

> *History of Bimetallism in the United States*, J. Laurence Laughlin, 4th edition, 1897.
>
> *Thirty Years' View*, Thomas H. Benton, Boston, 2 vols., 1854–1856.
>
> Watson's *History of Coinage*, and White's *Money and Banking*, already referred to.

On CURRENCY AND BANKING generally the official data for the early portion of the period are exceedingly meagre.

Gallatin's and Crawford's Treasury Reports and the latter's correspondence with State Banks. printed in *American State Papers* ; Crawford's special report of 1820 and Elliot's *Funding System*. contain almost all the information prior to 1833, when Congress directed the Treasury to collect data in State Banks and their Currency.

Knox in *Report Comptroller of Currency*. 1876, compiled the data from the earliest days to 1863, in fairly satisfactory form (statistics in the appendix). This was in large part reprinted in Senate Ex. Doc., No. 38, 52d Cong., 2d Sess.

Hepburn in the same Bureau's Report for 1892 materially enlarged the scope of the information, adding much valuable statistical material in the appendix.

After 1833 the *Finance Reports* contain much important material and the separate annual Treasury *Report on Condition of Banks* gives all the data obtainable at this time. Special mention should be made of the historical compendium on banking embraced in the appendix to Guthrie's Treasury Reports, 1855–1856, and of the reports of the condition of depositary banks, in appendices to the *Finance Reports*, 1835 and thereafter.

Discussions of the operations of State Banks of later date will be found in the *Messages of Presidents*, Jackson, Van Buren, Tyler, and Buchanan, and in the *Finance Reports* of their Secretaries of the Treasury.

The volume of money is discussed by Elliot, Gallatin, and Guthrie.

Unofficial publications of the early period include Gallatin's *Consideration of Currency and Banking System*, wherein a very detailed account of banks is given ; Gouge's *Short History*, which is equally interesting.

The works above referred to of Sumner, Knox, Bolles, and White are valuable, the two former being quite comprehensive. See also *Treatise on Currency and Banking*, Condy Raguet, Philadelphia, 1839.

In *Sound Currency*, monographs treating of the banks and note-issues of the several states are most instructive. See particularly the papers by Horace White, and L. Carroll Root.

Special features are discussed in : —

The Suffolk Bank, D. R. Whitney, Cambridge, Mass., 1878.

The Banks of New York and Panic of 1857, J. S. Gibbons, New York, 1859.

History of the Surplus Revenue of 1837, E. G. Bourne, New York, 1885.

History of the Bank of New York, H. W. Domett, 1886.

TREASURY NOTES, aside from the several *Finance Reports* prior to 1861 are officially and comprehensively treated in DeKnight's volume already mentioned, and in *History of National Loans of the United States*, R. A. Bayley, Washington, 1881. (Also embraced in Vol. VII. of the 10th Census.)

It is also of interest to examine what Madison, Van Buren, and

Tyler in their messages, and Crawford in his special report of 1820, say of the use of these notes as currency.

Unofficial publications include Knox's *United States Notes;* Sumner's several works, and Bolles's *History.*

BANK OF THE UNITED STATES. The most comprehensive publication of official data from 1790 to 1832 is : —

> Clarke and Hall. *Legislative and Documentary History,* embracing Hamilton's original plan; the debates in Congress, opinions of Hamilton and Jefferson on the question of constitutionality, the proposed and adopted charters; the Bank War; Gallatin, Dallas, Madison, Crawford, Webster, Clay, Calhoun, and others on the question generally; Congressional investigations; McDuffie's Reports; and the Supreme Court Decision by Marshall, on the Constitutionality (McCulloch *vs.* Maryland).
>
> *Finance Reports,* contain papers by Hamilton, Gallatin, Dallas, Rush, McLane, Taney, Woodbury. and others on the Bank.
>
> *Messages of Presidents,* Madison, Jackson. Van Buren, Tyler, and Polk.
>
> Benton's *Abridgment of Debates* and his *Thirty Years' View* also cover a great many points.

A concise review may also be found in *Report Comptroller of Currency.* 1876 (Knox). with statistics in the appendix.

Unofficial publications embracing valuable material are the already named Sumner's *History of Banking.* Knox's work of the same name. White's *Money and Banking.* Bolles's *Financial History.* Schouler's *History,* and Gallatin's *Consideration for a Currency System.* Williams's *Statesman's Manual, Niles's Register. Sound Currency.* Vol. IV., Nos. 7, 17, 18. *History of the United States of America,* Henry Adams, N.Y., 1889–1891. 9 vols. *Constitutional and Political History of the United States.* H. E. Von Holst.Chicago, 1877–1892. 7 vols. G. T. Curtis's *Constitutional History of the United States.* 2 vols.

Special features are treated in the works and writings of Hamilton. Jefferson, Madison. Gallatin. Dallas. Clay. Calhoun, Webster, and Woodbury, and in the Essays of Matthew Carey.

In Biographical Works, see Adams and Stevens on Gallatin; Schurz on Clay; Parton and Sumner on Jackson: Lodge, Morse, and Sumner on Hamilton: Shepard on Van Buren.

> See also *Removal of Deposits from Bank of United States,* W. J. Duane. New York. 1838; and on the same topic, Secretary Taney's separate Report in *Finance Report.* 1833.
>
> *General History of Banks,* etc., T. H. Goddard, New York,

1831, contains Cheves's report on the reorganization of the Bank.

THE SUBTREASURY SYSTEM is officially discussed by Van Buren, Tyler, and Polk in their messages, and by Secretaries Woodbury, Ewing, Walker, Guthrie, and Cobb, in the *Finance Reports*. Embraced in some of the later volumes will be found Wm. M. Gouge's reports of examinations of the Subtreasuries ; see especially that of 1854.

The *Abridgment of Debates* covers the Congressional discussion.

Unofficial books on the subject are *Life and Times of Silas Wright*, R. H. Gillette, Albany, 1874.

Also Benton's *Thirty Years' View*; important references are also found in Webster's, Clay's, Woodbury's, and Calhoun's writings, and in the biographical monographs on Clay and Van Buren already referred to.

The Independent Treasury, etc., David Kinley, New York, 1893, is quite a complete treatise.

The period after the Civil War is covered by a multitude of books, pamphlets, reports, etc. ; mention is made here only of the principal ones, giving the reader an opportunity to consult those most effectively presenting the facts and discussions.

The official publications covering the entire field are : —

The *Congressional Globe* to 1873, and *Congressional Record*, 1874 to date, containing the debates in full ; Congressional Documents, of which each house publishes a separate collection, including Executive and Miscellaneous Documents and Committee Reports, presenting the subjects prior to legislative action. A number of these documents are also published separately by the Executive Departments.

Messages and Papers of Presidents, Vols. VI. to X. ; every incumbent of the presidency during the period has had occasion to discuss the money question.

Finance Reports, annually for fiscal years ending June 30, embracing the reports of Secretaries of the Treasury and subordinate officers, of which latter the most important are the *Reports of the Comptrollers of the Currency, Directors of the Mint* and *Treasurers of the United States*, which since about 1870 have also been published separately with exhaustive statistical appendices. The Mint Bureau also publishes, since 1880, annual *Reports on Production of Gold and Silver*, by calendar years. The Bureau of Statistics publishes monthly (formerly also quarterly) and annually *Reports on Commerce and Navigation* ; the monthlies in the later years include besides the statistics of imports and exports, valuable statistical data on monetary subjects, and those statistics are, in digested form, reproduced in the *Statistical Abstracts of the United States*, annually, beginning in 1871.

A *Treasury Circular, No. 113*, in pamphlet form, containing a digest of the laws and statistics of coinage and currency, Washington, 1900. (Previously issued in 1896.)

Unofficial books covering all the subjects generally are: —

> *Money and Banking*, Horace White, Boston, 1895 ; revised 1902.
> *Political History of the Rebellion*, E. McPherson, Washington, 1864.
> *Political History of the Reconstruction*, same author, Washington, 1871.
> *Handbook of Politics*, biennially, 1870-1892, same author.

McPherson's works give the various measures and amendments, the votes on the several propositions, etc., constituting a valuable digest of the actions of Congress.

> *Speeches and Reports in Congress*, John Sherman, New York, 1881.
> *Recollections of Twenty Years*, same author, Chicago, 1895.
> *Twenty Years in Congress*, James G. Blaine, Norwich, Conn., 1884.
> *Financial History of the United States*, Albert S. Bolles.
> *Thirty Years of American Finance*, A. D. Noyes, New York, 1898.
> *Money in Politics*, J. K. Upton, Boston, 1884.
> *Money and Legal Tender*, H. R. Linderman (sometime Director of the Mint), New York, 1877.
> *Reports of Monetary Commission of Indianapolis Convention*. J. Laurence Laughlin, Chicago, 1898. (Covers the entire field of our monetary history and recommends concrete reforms.)
> *The Natural Law of Money*, William Brough, New York, 1894.
> *Open Mints and Free Banking*, same author, New York, 1898.
> *Sound Currency*, published semimonthly (afterwards quarterly) by the Reform Club, New York, 1895-1903.
> *Men and Measures of Half a Century*, Hugh McCulloch, New York, 1889.
> *Monetary Systems of the World*, M. L. Muhleman, New York, 1896 ; a digest of laws and statistics.
> *Money and its Laws*, Henry V. Poor, New York, 1877.
> *Our National Currency and the Money Problem*, Amasa Walker, Boston, 1876.
> *Principles of Money*, J. Laurence Laughlin, Chicago, 1903.

.

Financial History of United States, Davis R. Dewey, New York, 1903.

COINAGE received but little attention during the first decade (1861–1870). The mint reports are almost the sole repositories of information.

International Monetary Conference, 1867, Report of Proceedings, by Samuel B. Ruggles, Senate Ex. Doc., No. 14, 40th Cong., 2d Sess., 1868, also reprinted in *International Monetary Conference*, 1878 (see below).

This conference was called for the purpose of considering the adoption of an international gold coin. The subject was further considered in Senate Reports of the Congress named, and discussed by Sherman in his *Speeches and Reports*.

Early in the second decade of the period, the silver question developed. From the mass of publications which it called forth, the following are especially recommended : —

    History of the Coinage Act of 1873, Senate Misc. Doc.. No. 132, 41st Cong., 2d Sess. In this publication the progressive steps which omitted the silver dollar from the coinage system, improperly denounced as the "Crime of 1873," are fully set forth, refuting the charge. Reprinted in 1900.

    United States Monetary Commission of 1876, Report and Testimony, 2 vols., Senate Report No. 703, 44th Cong., 2d Sess.

    International Monetary Conference, 1878, Report of Proceedings, with appendix containing a mass of valuable material not found elsewhere, compiled by S. Dana Horton, Senate Ex. Doc., No. 58, 45th Cong., 3d Sess., 1879.

    International Monetary Conference, 1881, House Misc. Doc., No. 396, 49th Cong., 1st Sess.

    Bimetallism in Europe, E. Atkinson, Ex. Doc., No. 34, 50th Cong., 1st Sess., 1887, also printed in Consular Report No. 87. Contains translation of A. Soetbeer's remarkable statistical compilation of materials for the study of the coinage question.

    British Gold and Silver Commission, Report of, reprinted as Senate Misc. Doc., No. 34, 50th Cong., 2d Sess., 1889.

    International Monetary Conference, 1892, Senate Ex. Doc., No. 82, 52d Cong., 2d Sess.

Many reports from the Coinage Committee of the House and the Finance Committee of the Senate appear in the Congressional Documents ; among the notable ones are Wickham & Bartine, House

Report No. 3967, 51st Cong., 2d Sess.; Bland's House Report No. 249, 52d Cong., 1st Sess.

Most of the Presidents, beginning with Hayes (whose veto message, in February in 1878, is of special importance), referred to the silver question in their messages. Cleveland's special message in August, 1893, preceding the suspension of silver purchases, is of extraordinary interest. The Secretaries of the Treasury also touch on the subject almost continuously from 1878; the fullest consideration will be found in Manning's report for 1885 and Windom's for 1889. Technical and statistical information, as complete as could be desired, will be found in the reports of the Mint Bureau, that of 1895 containing a review of the coinage question from 1776.

Unofficial publications include : —

> *History of Bimetallism in the United States*, J. Laurence Laughlin, New York, 1892. (Unqualifiedly opposed to bimetallism.)
>
> *History of American Coinage*, David K. Watson, New York, 1899.
>
> *Nomisma or Legal Tender*, Henri Cernuschi, New York, 1877. (A leading exponent of international bimetallism, who published many pamphlets here and abroad.)
>
> *The India Commission Report* (British), reprinted as Senate Misc. Doc. No. 23, 53d Cong., 1st Sess.
>
> *The Berlin Silver Conference* (Germany), reprinted as Senate Misc. Doc. No. 274, 53d Cong., 2d Sess.
>
> *International Bimetallism*, F. A. Walker, New York, 1896.
>
> *The Silver Situation*, Frank W. Taussig, New York, 1876.
>
> *Silver in Europe*, S. Dana Horton, New York, 1890.
>
> *Silver and Gold*, S. Dana Horton, Cincinnati, 1877.

Consult also the numerous pamphlets on Silver in *Sound Currency*.

> *Economic Tracts*, Soc. for Pol. Education, New York, 1884, includes numbers by McCulloch and others.
>
> *International Monetary Conferences*, H. B. Russell, New York, 1898. (A review of all the conferences and connected history.)
>
> *If not Silver, What ?* J. W. Bookwalter, Springfield, O., 1896.
>
> *An Honest Dollar*, E. B. Andrews, New York, 1889.

TREASURY NOTES AND LEGAL TENDER NOTES form the subject of discussion in the *Messages of Presidents* and *Finance Reports* throughout the period, and much space is devoted thereto in the congressional debates. Specially important are the reports of Chase, McCulloch, Sherman, Manning, and Carlisle.

Specie Resumption and Refunding of the Debt, Report by Secretary Sherman, Ex. Doc., No. 9, 46th Cong., 2d Sess., 1880 ; *National Loans of the United States*, R. A. Bayley, Washington, 1880 ; *History of the Currency of the Country*, W. F. DeKnight, Washington, 1897. The two last mentioned give the forms of notes, complete statistics, and brief statements of the legislative provisions.

On the specific questions of LEGAL TENDER, the *Supreme Court Reports*, 8th and 12th Wallace, and 110th U.S.

The unofficial publications besides those already mentioned are : —

United States Notes, John Jay Knox, New York, 1884.

Life of Chase, J. W. Schuckers, New York, 1874.

History of Legal Tender Paper Money, etc., E. G. Spaulding, Buffalo, 1869. (The author of the Greenback Law ; gives abstracts of debates and a succinct historical account.)

A History of the Greenbacks, W. C. Mitchell, Chicago, 1903.

Legal Tender, S. P. Breckinridge, Chicago, 1903.

The legal tender decisions in full also appear in McPherson's *Handbooks*, and a historical discussion in Bancroft's *Plea for the Constitution*, New York, 1884.

Special papers on the legal tenders and their cost, the premium on gold and prices as affected thereby, appear in *Sound Currency*.

The daily premium on gold during suspension of specie payments may be found in Homans's *Merchants' and Bankers' Almanac* (annual) ; also in a small volume published by the New York Gold Exchange (Mersereau). For the *Gold Panic*, 1869, see House Report No. 31, 41st Cong., 2d Sess.

BANKING AND BANK-NOTES. Chase's *Finance Reports*, in which the system is outlined, and the series of *Reports of Comptrollers of the Currency*, 1864–1902, give an adequate survey of the birth and history of the national banking system, with statistics more complete than ever attempted by any country. The original act of 1863 was published as " *The National Currency Act, 1863* " ; the revised act with amendments from time to time appears separately (*National Bank Act*) and most complete in the one of 1900.

Certain of the Reports of Comptrollers contain special features ; Knox in 1875 and 1876 reviews other banking systems, particularly state banks in the latter; Hepburn in 1892 devotes much space to state banks. Knox prepared a special report of the use of credit instruments, 1881 ; and Lacey in 1891, as well as Eckels, 1896, repeated this work. The latter also presented in 1896 a special report on deposits and depositors in banks. A useful digest of legal decisions affecting the banks will be found in each of the reports since 1876.

Congressional documents contain much valuable information, particularly the reports of hearings in the period from 1893 to 1901, when bank-note reform became a burning question, and the many plans suggested are printed in full in these volumes. See on this subject House Reports, No. 1508. 53d Cong., 3d Sess., and No. 1575, 55th Cong., 2d Sess.

Statistics of state banks appear in the *Reports of the Comptrollers of the Currency* since 1874, and in reports in the 90's appear digests of the laws of the states relating to banks.

The most valuable unofficial works are : —

> *History of Banking in the United States*, W. G. Sumner, New York, 1896.
>
> *History of Banking in the United States*, John Jay Knox, New York, 1900.
>
> *History of Modern Banks of Issue*, Charles A. Conant, New York, 1896.
>
> *Theory and History of Banking*, Chas. F. Dunbar, New York, 1894.

ASSET BANKING. branch banking. the Baltimore plan, and other features are specially discussed in a number of the pamphlets in *Sound Currency*, in the two last-named works and in *Report Indianapolis Monetary Commission*.

The reports of the proceedings of the annual meetings of the *American Bankers' Association*, 1875-1902, also contain much valuable material on the subject of banking and currency.

THE CLEARING-HOUSE SYSTEM is discussed in : —

> *The New York Clearing House.* N. Squire, 1888.
>
> *Clearing Houses.* James G. Cannon. New York, 1900.
>
> *Federal Clearing Houses.* Theodore Gilman.

AUXILIARY CURRENCY is well treated in *Sound Currency* by J. D. Warner, Vol. II., No. 6.

Consult also as to the *Subtreasury:* —

> *The Independent Treasury of the United States*, David Kinley, New York, 1893, and White, *Money and Banking*; Sumner, *History of Banking in the United States.*

And on other pertinent topics : —

> *The Canadian Banking System.* R. M. Breckinridge, Toronto, 1894, reprinted in American Economic Association publications.
>
> *The Currency and Banking Law of Canada*, W. C. Cornwell, New York, 1895   .

PRICE, WAGES, etc., in *U. S. Senate* (Aldrich) *Reports*, No. 986, 52d Cong.. 1st Sess. No. 1394, 52d Cong., 2d Sess.

The VOLUME OF MONEY is given in the *Statistical Abstracts* in the *Treasury Circular, No. 113* (1900), and in the *Finance Reports* in recent years. In *Reports of the Treasurer of the United States* will be found monthly statistics since 1878 in detail. Details are discussed also in Muhleman's *Monetary Systems*.

The PANIC OF 1893 and the subsequent years of monetary troubles, and the bond issues, are discussed in the *Messages of the Presidents* and in *Finance Reports* for the years, by White, Noyes, Muhleman, and in numbers of *Sound Currency*.

APPENDIX

I

ACT OF HIS MAJESTY'S PROVINCE OF THE MAS-SACHUSETTS-BAY, IN NEW-ENGLAND

Anno regni Regis Georgii II Vicesimo-tertio

CHAPTER V

AN ACT for ascertaining the Rates at which coined Silver and Gold and English Half-pence and Farthings may pass within this Government.

Whereas in and by an Act made and passed in the twenty-second Year of his present Majesty's Reign, Intituled, An Act for drawing in the Bills of Credit of the several Denominations which have at any Time been issued by this Government and are still outstanding, and for ascertaining the Rate of coin'd Silver in this Province for the future ; *it is enacted in the Words following*, viz. " That all Bargains, and Contracts, Debts and Dues whatsoever which shall be agreed, contracted or made after the thirty-first Day of *March* 1750, shall be understood, and are hereby declared to be in Silver at *six Shillings and eight Pence* per Ounce, and all Spanish mill'd Pieces of Eight of full Weight shall be accounted, taken and paid at the Rate of *six Shillings* per Piece for the discharge of any Contracts or Bargains to be made after the said thirty-first Day of *March* 1750, the Halves, Quarters and other less Pieces of the same Coin to be accounted, received, taken or paid in the same Proportion."

And whereas there is great Reason to apprehend that many and great Inconveniences may arise in Case any coin'd Silver or Gold, or English Half Pence and Farthings should pass at any higher Rate than in a just Proportion to Spanish Pieces of Eight or coin'd Silver at the Rates aforesaid:

Be it therefore enacted by the Lieutenant Governor, Council and House of Representatives, That it shall not be lawful for any Person within this Government from and after the thirty-first Day of *March* One thousand seven Hundred and fifty, to receive, take or pay any of the following Coin at any greater or higher Rate than is allowed by this Act, *viz.* A Guinea at *twenty-eight Shillings ;* An English Crown at *six Shillings and eight Pence :* An half Crown at *three Shillings and four Pence :* An English Shilling at *one Shilling and four Pence :* An English six Pence at *eight Pence :* A double Johannes or Gold Coin of *Portugal* of the Value of *three Pounds twelve Shillings* Sterling, at *four Pounds sixteen Shillings :* A single Johannes of the Value of thirty-six Shillings Sterling at *forty-eight Shillings :* A Moidore at *thirty-six Shillings :* A Pistole of full Weight at *twenty-two Shillings :* Three English Farthings for *one Penny ;* and English Half Pence in greater or less Numbers in Proportion.

And be it further enacted, That if any Person within this Government shall after the thirty-first Day of *March* One thousand seven Hundred and fifty, for the discharge of any Contract or Bargain, account, receive, take or pay any of the several Species of Coins before mentioned at any greater or higher Rate than at which the same is hereby regulated, settled and allowed to be accounted, received, taken or paid, every Person so accounting, receiving, taking or paying the same contrary to the Directions herein contained, shall forfeit the sum of *fifty Pounds* for every such Offence, one Moiety thereof to his Majesty for the Use of this Government, the other Moiety to such Person or Persons as shall sue for the same ; to be recovered with full Costs of Suit by Action of Debt, Bill, Plaint or Information in any of his Majesty's Courts within this Province.

Provided always, and it is hereby declared, That nothing in this Act shall be understood to restrain any Person or Persons from accounting, receiving, taking or paying any of the above mentioned Species or Coins in discharge of any Debts, Contracts or Bargains made before the thirty-first Day of *March* One Thousand seven Hundred and fifty, at the following Rates, *viz.* For any Debt contracted before the said thirty-first Day of *March*, and understood to be payable in Bills of the old Tenor in such Proportion higher or greater than the Rates set at in this Act, as *forty-five Shillings* is to *six Shillings ;* and for any Debt contracted before the said thirty-first Day of *March*, and understood to be payable in Bills of the middle Tenor or Bills of the new Tenor, in such Proportion higher or greater than the Rates set at in this Act, as *eleven Shillings and three Pence* is to *six Shillings :* Any Thing in this Act to the contrary notwithstanding.

II

DIGEST OF LAWS OF THE UNITED STATES RELAT-
ING TO COINAGE, CURRENCY, AND BANKING

THE CONTINENTAL CONGRESS, 1775 TO 1789

Resolutions of June 22, 1775

RESOLVED, That a sum not exceeding two millions of Spanish milled dollars be emitted by the Congress in bills of credit, for the defence of America.

RESOLVED, That the twelve confederated colonies be pledged for the redemption of the bills of credit, now directed to be emitted.

Resolutions of June 23, 1775

RESOLVED, That the form of the bills be as follows:

CONTINENTAL CURRENCY

No. —— —— Dollars.

This bill entitles the bearer to receive —— Spanish milled dollars, or the value thereof in Gold or Silver, according to the resolutions of the Congress, held at Philadelphia, on the 10th day of May, A.D. 1775.

RESOLVED, That Mr. J. Adams, Mr. J. Rutledge, Mr. Duane, doctor Franklin, and Mr. Wilson, be a committee to get proper plates engraved, to provide paper, and to agree with printers to print the above bills.

Resolution of April 19, 1776

RESOLVED, That a committee of seven be appointed to examine and ascertain the value of the several species of Gold and Silver Coins, current in these colonies, and the proportions they ought to bear to Spanish milled dollars.

ARTICLES OF CONFEDERATION OF JULY 9, 1778

ARTICLE 9. . . . The united states in congress assembled shall also have the sole and exclusive right and power of regulating the alloy and value of coin struck by their own authority, or by that of the respective states — fixing the standard of weights and measures throughout the United States. . . .

The united states in congress assembled shall have authority . . . to borrow money or emit bills on the credit of the united states. . . .

Resolutions of July 6, 1785

RESOLVED, That the money unit of the United States of America be one dollar.

RESOLVED, That the smallest coin be of copper, of which 200 shall pass for one dollar.

RESOLVED, That the several pieces shall increase in a decimal ratio.

Resolution of August 8, 1786

RESOLVED, That the Standard of the United States of America for Gold and Silver, shall be Eleven parts fine, and one part alloy.

That the Money Unit of the United States, being by the resolve of Congress of the 6th July, 1785, a dollar, shall contain of fine silver, $375\frac{64}{100}$ grains.

That the money of account, to correspond with the division of coins agreeably to the above resolve, proceed in a decimal ratio agreeably to the forms and manner following, viz. :

Mills: the lowest money of accompt, of which one thousand shall be equal to the federal dollar, or money unit, ... 0.001
Cents: the highest copper piece, of which one hundred shall be equal to the dollar, . . . 0.010
Dismes: the lowest silver coin, ten of which shall be equal to the dollar, ... 0.100
Dollar: the highest silver coin, ... 1.000

That betwixt the dollar and the lowest copper coin, as fixed by the resolve of Congress of the 6th July, 1785, there shall be three silver coins and one copper coin. That the silver coins shall be as follows :

One coin containing $187\frac{82}{100}$ grains of fine silver, to be called a half dollar :

One Coin containing $75\frac{128}{1000}$ grains of fine silver, to be called a double disme :

And one coin containing $37\frac{560}{1000}$ grains of fine silver, to be called a disme.

That the two copper coins shall be as follows : —

One equal to the 100th part of the federal dollar, to be called a cent.

One equal to the 200th part of the federal dollar, to be called a half cent :

That two pounds and a quarter avoirdupois weight of copper, shall constitute one hundred cents.

That there shall be two gold coins : One containing $246\frac{268}{1000}$ grains of fine gold, equal to 10 dollars, and to be stamped with the impression of the American eagle, and to be called an eagle :

One containing $123\frac{134}{1000}$ grains of fine gold, equal to 5 dollars, to be stamped in like manner, and to be called a half eagle.

That the mint price of a pound troy weight of uncoined silver, 11 parts fine and one part alloy, shall be 9 dollars, 9 dismes and 2 cents.[1]

That the mint price of a pound troy weight of uncoined gold, 11 parts fine and one part alloy, shall be 209 dollars, 7 dismes, and 7 cents.

Mint ordinance of October 16, 1786 — *An Ordinance for the establishment of the Mint of the United States of America, and for regulating the value and alloy of coin.*

It is hereby ordained by the United States in Congress assembled, that a mint be established for the coinage of gold, silver and copper Money, agreeably to the resolves of Congress of the 8th August last, under the direction of the following officers, viz.

An Assay-Master, whose duty it shall be to receive gold and silver in bullion, or foreign coin, to assay the same and to give his certificates for the value thereof at the following rates :

For every pound troy weight of uncoined gold or foreign gold coin, 11 parts fine and one part alloy, 209 dollars, 7 dimes and 7 cents, Money of the United States, as established by the resolves of Congress of the 8th of August last, and so in proportion to the fine gold contained in any coined or uncoined gold whatsoever.

For every pound troy weight of uncoined silver, or foreign silver coin, 11 parts fine and one part alloy, 13 dollars, 7 dimes, 7 cents and 7 mills, money of the United States, established as aforesaid ; and so in proportion to the fine silver contained in any coined or uncoined silver whatsoever.

A Master Coiner, whose duty it shall be to receive, from time to time, of the assay-master, the bullion necessary for coinage ; to report to Congress devices and proofs of the proposed pieces of coin, and to procure proper workmen to execute the business of coinage, reporting, from time to time, to the commissioners of the board of treasury of the United

---

[1] Misprint in original. See the ordinance on next page.

States for approbation, and allowance, the occupation, number and pay of the persons so employed.

A Pay-Master, who shall he the treasurer of the United States for the time being, whose duty it shall be to receive and take charge of the coin made under the direction of the master coiner, and to receipt for the same ; to receive and duly enter the certificates for uncoined gold or silver issued by the assay-master, and to pay $\frac{95}{100}$ of the amount thereof in gold or silver, and $\frac{5}{100}$ in the copper coin of the United States.

*   *   *   *   *   *   *   *   *

That the copper coin struck under the authority of the United States in Congress assembled, shall be receivable in all taxes, or payments due to the United States, in the proportion of 5 dollars for every hundred dollars so paid ; but that no other copper coin whatsoever, shall be receivable in any taxes or payments whatsoever to the United States.

And whereas, the great quantities of base copper coin daily imported into, or manufactured within the several states is become so highly injurious to the interest and commerce of the same, as to require the immediate interposition of the powers vested by the confederation in the United States in Congress assembled, of regulating the value of copper, the coin so current as aforesaid :

It is hereby ordained, That no foreign copper coin whatsoever, shall, after the first day of September, 1787, be current within the U. States of America : And that no copper coin struck under the authority of a particular state, shall pass at a greater value than one Federal dollar for two pounds and one quarter of a pound, avoirdupois weight, of such copper coin.

CONSTITUTION OF THE UNITED STATES

ART. 1, SEC. 8, PAR. 5. The Congress shall have power . . . to coin money, regulate the value thereof, and of foreign coin, and fix the standard of weights and measures.

ART. 1, SEC. 10, PAR. 1. No state shall . . . coin money ; emit bills of credit ; make anything but gold and silver coin a tender in payment of debts ; . . .

Act of February 25, 1791 — To incorporate the subscribers to the Bank of the United States

WHEREAS, It is conceived that the establishment of a bank for the United States, upon a foundation sufficiently extensive to answer the purposes intended thereby, and at the same time upon the principles which afford adequate security for an upright and prudent administration thereof, will be very conducive to the successful conducting of the national finances ; will tend to give facility to the obtaining of loans, for the use of the Government, in sudden emergencies ; and will be productive of considerable advantages to trade and industry in general : Therefore,

SEC. 1. *Be it enacted, etc.*, That a Bank of the United States shall be established ; the capital stock whereof shall not exceed $10,000,000, divided into 25,000 shares, each share being $400 ; and that subscriptions towards constituting the said stock, shall, on the first Monday of April next, be opened at the city of Philadelphia, under the superintendence of such persons, not less than three, as shall be appointed for that purpose by the President of the United States (who is hereby empowered to appoint the said persons accordingly) ; which subscriptions shall continue open until the whole of the said stock shall have been subscribed.

SEC. 2. That it shall be lawful for any person, copartnership, or body politic, to subscribe for such or so many shares as he, she or they shall think fit, not exceeding 1,000, except as shall be hereafter directed relatively to the United States ; and that the sums respectively subscribed, except on behalf of the United States, shall be payable one-fourth in gold and silver, and three-fourths in that part of the public debt, which, according to the loan proposed in the fourth and fifteenth sections of the act, entitled "An act making provision for the debt of the United States," shall bear an accruing interest, at the time of payment, of 6 per centum per annum, and shall also be payable in four equal parts, in the aforesaid ratio of specie to debt, at the distance of six calendar months from each other ; the first whereof shall be paid at the time of subscription.

SEC. 3. That all those, who shall become subscribers to the said bank, their successors and assigns, shall be, and are hereby created and made a corporation and body politic, by the name and style of *The President, Directors and Company, of the Bank of the United States ;* and shall so continue, until the fourth day of March, 1811 : and by that name, shall be, and are hereby made able and capable in law, to have, purchase, receive, possess, enjoy, and retain to them and their successors, lands, rents, tenement, hereditaments, goods, chattels and effects of what kind, nature or quality soever, to an amount, not exceeding in the whole fifteen millions of dollars, including the amount of the capital stock aforesaid; and the same to sell, grant, demise, aliene or dispose of; to sue and be sued, plead and be impleaded, answer and be answered, defend and be defended, in courts of record, or any other place whatsoever: and also to make, have, and use a common seal, and the same to break, alter and renew, at their pleasure; and also to ordain, establish, and put in execution, such by-laws, ordinances and regulations, as shall seem necessary and convenient for the government of the said corporation, not being contrary to law, or to the constitution thereof (for which purpose, general meetings of the stockholders shall and may be called by the directors, and in the manner herein after specified), and generally to do and execute all and singular acts, matters and things, which to them it shall or may appertain to do; subject nevertheless to the rules, regulations, restrictions, limitations and provisions herein after prescribed and declared.

SEC. 4. That, for the well ordering of the affairs of the said corporation, there shall be 25 directors; of whom there shall be an election on the first Monday of January in each year, by the stockholders or proprietors of the capital stock of the said corporation, and by plurality of the votes actually given; and those who shall be duly chosen at any election, shall be capable of serving as directors, by virtue of such choice, until the end or expiration of the Monday of January next ensuing the time of such election, and no longer. And the said directors, at their first meeting after each election, shall choose one of their number as president.

SEC. 5. *Provided always*, That, as soon as the sum of $400,000, in gold and silver, shall have been actually received on account of the subscriptions to the said stock, notice thereof shall be given, by the persons under whose superintendence the same shall have been made, in at least two public gazettes printed in the city of Philadelphia; and the said persons shall, at the same time in like manner, notify a time and place within the said city, at the distance of 90 days from the time of such notification, for proceeding to the election of directors; and it shall be lawful for such election to be then and there made; and the persons, who shall then and there be chosen, shall be the first directors, and shall be capable of serving, by virtue of such choice, until the end or expiration of the Monday in January next ensuing the time of making the same, and shall forthwith thereafter commence the operations of the said bank, at the said city of Philadelphia. *And provided further*, That, in case it should at any time happen, that an election of directors should not be made upon any day when pursuant to this act it ought to have been made, the said corporation shall not, for that cause, be deemed to be dissolved; but it shall be lawful, on any other day, to hold and make an election of directors in such manner as shall have been regulated by the laws and ordinances of the said corporation. *And provided lastly,* That, in case of the death, resignation, absence from the United States, or removal of a director by the stockholders, his place may be filled up, by a new choice, for the remainder of the year.

SEC. 6. That the directors for the time being shall have power to appoint such officers, clerks, and servants under them, as shall be necessary for executing the business of the said corporation, and to allow them such compensation, for their services respectively, as shall be reasonable ; and shall be capable of exercising such other powers and authorities, for the well governing and ordering of the affairs of the said corporation, as shall be described, fixed, and determined by the laws, regulations, and ordinances of the same.

SEC. 7. That the following rules, restrictions, limitations and provisions, shall form and be fundamental articles of the constitution of the said corporation, viz.

I. The number of votes to which each stockholder shall be entitled, shall be according to the number of shares he shall hold, in the proportions following : That is to say, for 1 share, and not more than 2 shares, one vote : for every 2 shares above 2, and not exceeding 10, one vote : for every 4 shares above 10, and not exceeding 30, one vote : for every 6 shares above 30, and not exceeding 60, one vote : for every 8 shares above 60, and not exceeding 100, one vote : and for every 10 shares above 100, one vote : — But no person, co-partnership, or body politic shall be entitled to a greater number than 30 votes. And after the first election, no share or shares shall confer a right of suffrage, which shall not have been holden three calendar months previous to the day of election. Stockholders actually resident within the United States, and none other, may vote in elections by proxy.

II. Not more than three fourths of the directors in office, exclusive of the president, shall be eligible for the next succeeding year : but the director, who shall be president at the time of an election, may always be re-elected.

III. None but a stockholder, being a citizen of the United States, shall be eligible as a director.

IV. No director shall be entitled to any emolument unless the same shall have been allowed by the stockholders at a general meeting.   The stockholders shall make such compensation to the president, for his extraordinary attendance at the bank, as shall appear to them reasonable.

V. Not less than seven directors shall constitute a board for the transaction of business, of whom, the president shall always be one, except in case of sickness, or necessary absence ; in which case his place may be supplied by any other director, whom he, by writing under his hand, shall nominate for the purpose.

VI. Any number of stockholders, not less than 60, who, to·gether, shall be proprietors of 200 shares or upwards, shall have power at any time to call a general meeting of the stockholders, for purposes relative to the institution, giving at least ten weeks notice, in two public gazettes of the place where the bank is kept, and specifying, in such notice, the object or objects of such meeting.

VII. Every cashier or treasurer, before he enters upon the duties of his office, shall be required to give bond, with two or more sureties, to the satisfaction of the directors, in a sum not less than $50,000, with condition for his good behavior.

VIII. The lands, tenements and hereditaments which it shall be lawful for the said corporation to hold, shall be only such as shall be requisite for its immediate accommodation in relation to the convenient transacting of its business, and such as shall have been *bona fide* mortgaged to it by way of security, or conveyed to it in satisfaction of debts previously contracted in the course of its dealings, or purchased at sales upon judgments which shall have been obtained for such debts.

IX. The total amount of the debts, which the said corporation shall at any time owe, whether by bond, bill, note, or other contract, shall not exceed the sum of $10,000,000, over and above the monies then actually deposited in the bank for safe keeping, unless the contracting of any greater debt shall have been previously authorized by a law of the United States. In case of excess, the directors, under whose administration it shall happen, shall be liable for the same, in their natural and private capacities ; and an action of debt may, in such case, be brought against them, or any of them, their or any of their heirs, exec·utors or administrators, in any court of record of the United States, or of either of them, by any creditor or creditors of the said corporation, and may be prosecuted to judgment and execution ; any condition, covenant, or agreement to the contrary notwithstanding.   But this shall not be construed to exempt the said corporation, or the lands, tenements, goods or chattels of the same, from being also liable for and chargeable with the said excess. Such of the said directors, who may have been absent when the said excess was contracted or created, or who may have dissented from the resolution or act whereby the same was so contracted or created, may respectively exonerate themselves from being so liable, by forthwith giving notice of the fact, and of their absence or dissent, to the President of the United States, and to the stockholders, at a general meeting, which they shall have power to call for that purpose.

X. The said corporation may sell any part of the public debt whereof its stock shall be composed, but shall not be at liberty to purchase any public debt whatsoever ; nor shall directly or indirectly deal or trade in any thing, except bills of exchange, gold or silver bullion, or in the sale of goods really and truly pledged for money lent and not redeemed in due time; or of goods which shall be the produce of its lands. Neither shall the said corporation take more than at the rate of 6 per centum per annum, for or upon its loans or discounts.

XI. No loan shall be made by the said corporation, for the use or on account of the Government of the United States, to an amount exceeding $100,000, or of any particular State, to an amount exceeding $50,000, or of any foreign prince or state, unless previously authorized by a law of the United States.

XII. The stock of the said corporation shall be assignable and transferable, according to such rules as shall be instituted in that behalf, by the laws and ordinances of the same.

XIII. The bills obligatory and of credit, under the seal of the said corporation, which shall be made to any person or persons, shall be assignable by indorsement thereupon, under the hand or hands of such person or persons, and of his, her, or their assignee or assignees, and so as absolutely to transfer and vest the property thereof in each and every assignee or assignees successively, and to enable such assignee or assignees to bring and maintain an action thereupon in his, her, or their own name or names. And bills or notes, which may be issued by order of the said corporation, signed by the president, and countersigned by the principal cashier or treasurer thereof, promising the payment of money to any person or persons, his, her, or their order, or to bearer, though not under the seal of the said corporation, shall be binding and obligatory upon the same, in the like manner, and with the like force and effect, as upon any private person or persons, if issued by him or them, in his, her, or their private or natural capacity or capacities ; and shall be assignable and negotiable, in like manner, as if they were so issued by such private person or persons — that is to say, those which shall be payable to any person or persons, his, her, or their order, shall be assignable by indorsement, in like manner, and with the like effect, as foreign bills of exchange now are ; and those which are payable to bearer, shall be negotiable and assignable by delivery only.

XIV. Half yearly dividends shall be made of so much of the profits of the bank, as shall appear to the directors advisable ; and once in every three years, the directors shall lay before the stockholders, at a general meeting, for their information, an exact and particular statement of the debts, which shall have remained unpaid after the expiration of the original credit, for a period of treble the term of that credit ; and of the surplus of profit, if any, after deducting losses and dividends. If there shall be a failure in the co-partnership, or body politic, the party failing shall lose the benefit of any dividend, which may have accrued, prior to the time for making such payment, and during the delay of the same.

XV. It shall be lawful for the directors aforesaid, to establish offices wheresoever they shall think fit, within the United States, for the purposes of discount and deposit only, and upon the same terms, and in the same manner, as shall be practised at the bank ; and to commit the management of the said offices, and the making of the said discounts, to such persons, under such agreements, and subject to such regulations as they shall deem proper ; not being contrary to law, or to the constitution of the bank.

XVI. The officer at the head of the Treasury Department of the United States, shall be furnished, from time to time, as often as he may require, not exceeding once a week, with statements of the amount of the capital stock of the said corporation, and of the debts due to the same ; of the monies deposited therein ; of the notes in circulation, and of the cash in hand ; and shall have a right to inspect such general accounts in the books of the bank, as shall relate to the said statements. *Provided*, That this shall not be construed to imply a right of inspecting the account of any private individual or individuals with the bank.

SEC. 8. That if the said corporation, or any person or persons for or to the use of the same, shall deal or trade in buying or selling any goods, wares, merchandise, or commodities whatsoever, contrary to the provisions of this act, all and every person and persons, by whom any order or direction for so dealing or trading shall have been given, and all and every person and persons who shall have been concerned as parties or agents therein, shall forfeit and lose treble the value of the goods, wares, merchandises, and commodities, in which such dealing and trade shall have been ; one-half thereof to the use of the informer, and the other half thereof to the use of the United States, to be recovered with costs of suit.

SEC. 9. That if the said corporation shall advance or lend any sum, for the use or on account of the Government of the United States, to an amount exceeding $100,000 ; or of any particular State to an amount exceeding $50,000 ; or of any foreign prince or state, (unless previously authorized thereto by a law of the United States,) all and every person and persons, by and with whose order, agreement, consent, approbation, or connivance, such unlawful advance or loan shall have been made, upon conviction thereof, shall forfeit and pay, for every such offence, treble the value or amount of the sum or sums which shall have been so unlawfully advanced or lent ; one fifth thereof to the use of the informer, and the residue thereof to the use of the United States ; to be disposed of by law and not otherwise.

SEC. 10. That the bills or notes of the said corporation, originally made payable, or which shall have become payable on demand, in gold and silver coin, shall be receivable in all payments to the United States.[1]

SEC. 11. That it shall be lawful for the President of the United States, at any time or times, within 18 months after the first day of April next, to cause a subscription to be made to the stock of the said corporation, as part of the aforesaid capital stock of $10,000,000, on behalf of the United States, to an amount not exceeding $2,000,000 ; to be paid out of the monies which shall be borrowed by virtue of either of the acts, the one entitled " An act making provision for the debt of the United States ; " and the other entitled " An act making provision for the reduction of the public debt ; " borrowing of the bank an equal sum, to be applied to the purposes for which the said monies shall have been procured ; reimbursable in ten years, by equal annual instalments ; or at any time sooner, or in any greater proportions, that the Government may think fit.

SEC. 12. That no other bank shall be established by any future law of the United States, during the continuance of the corporation hereby created ; for which the faith of the United States is hereby pledged.

Act of April 2, 1792 — Establishing a mint and regulating the Coins of the United States

SECTION 1. *Be it enacted, etc.,* That a mint for the purpose of a national coinage be, and the same is established ; to be

---

[1] This section was repealed March 19, 1812, after the expiration of the charter.

situate and carried on at the seat of the government of the United States, for the time being : And that for the well conducting of the business of the said mint, there shall be the following officers and persons, namely : a Director, an Assayer, a Chief Coiner, an Engraver, a Treasurer.

[SECS. 2 to 8 relate to the duties of the several mint officers, their oaths, bonds, salaries, and accounts, and the establishment and maintenance of the mint.]

SEC. 9. That there shall be from time to time struck and coined at the said mint, coins of gold, silver, and copper, of the following denominations, values and descriptions, viz. Eagles — each to be of the value of 10 dollars or units, and to contain 247¾ grains of pure, or 270 grains of standard gold. Half Eagles — each to be of the value of 5 dollars, and to contain 123⅝ grains of pure, or 135 grains of standard gold. Quarter Eagles — each to be of the value of 2½ dollars, and to contain 61¼ grains of pure, or 67¾ grains of standard gold.[1] Dollars or units — each to be of the value of a Spanish milled dollar as the same is now current, and to contain 371$\frac{4}{16}$ grains of pure, or 416 grains of standard silver. Half Dollars — each to be of half the value of the dollar or unit, and to contain 185$\frac{10}{16}$ grains of pure, or 208 grains of standard silver. Quarter Dollars — each to be of one-fourth the value of the dollar or unit, and to contain 92$\frac{13}{16}$ grains of pure, or 104 grains of standard silver. Dismes — each to be of the value of one-tenth of a dollar or unit, and to contain 37$\frac{2}{16}$ grains of pure, or 41⅗ grains of standard silver. Half Dismes — each to be of the value of one-twentieth of a dollar, and to contain 18$\frac{9}{16}$ grains of pure, or 20⅘ grains of standard silver. Cents — each to be of the value of the one-hundredth part of a dollar, and to contain 11 pennyweights of copper. Half Cents — each to be of the value of half a cent, and to contain 5½ pennyweights of copper.

[SEC. 10 specifies the devices to appear upon the coins authorized.]

SEC. 11. That the proportional value of gold to silver in all coins which shall by law be current as money within the United States, shall be as 15 to 1,[2] according to quantity in weight, of pure gold or pure silver ; that is to say, every 15 pounds weight of pure silver shall be of equal value in all payments, with

---

[1] Act of March 3, 1849, provides for coinage of gold dollars and double eagles. Act of February 21, 1853, provided for $3 piece. Act of September 26, 1890, abolished coinage of $3 and $1 pieces.

[2] For change of coinage ratio, see Act of June 28, 1834, and Act of January 18, 1837, Secs. 8, 9, 10.

1 pound weight of pure gold, and so in proportion as to any greater or less quantities of the respective metals.

SEC. 12. That the standard for all gold coins of the United States shall be 11 parts fine to 1 part alloy; and accordingly that 11 parts in 12 of the entire weight of each of the said coins shall consist of pure gold,[1] and the remaining one-twelfth part of alloy; and the said alloy shall be composed of silver and copper, in such proportions not exceeding one-half silver as shall be found convenient; to be regulated by the director of the mint, for the time being, with the approbation of the President of the United States, until further provision shall be made by law. And to the end that the necessary information may be had in order to the making of such further provision, it shall be the duty of the director of the mint at the expiration of a year after commencing the operations of the said mint to report to Congress the practice thereof during the said year, touching the composition of the alloy of the said gold coins, the reasons for such practice, and the experiments and observations which shall have been made concerning the effects of different proportions of silver and copper in the said alloy.

SEC. 13. That the standard of all silver coins of the United States shall be 1485 parts fine to 179 parts alloy; and accordingly that 1485 parts in 1664 parts of the entire weight of each of the said coins shall consist of pure silver, and the remaining 179 parts of alloy; which alloy shall be wholly of copper.

SEC. 14. That it shall be lawful for any person or persons to bring to the said mint gold and silver bullion, in order to their being coined; and that the bullion so brought shall be there assayed and coined as speedily as may be after the receipt thereof, and that free of expense to the person or persons by whom the same shall have been brought.[2] And as soon as the said bullion shall have been coined, the person or persons by whom the same shall have been delivered, shall upon demand, receive in lieu thereof coins of the same species of bullion which shall have been so delivered, weight for weight, of the pure gold or pure silver therein contained: *Provided nevertheless,* That it shall be at the mutual option of the party or parties bringing such bullion, and of the director of the said mint, to

---

[1] See Act of January 18, 1837, Sec. 8, establishing a uniform standard of fineness of .900.

[2] The retention of sufficient bullion to cover expenses of refining directed by Act of March 3, 1795, Sec. 5; Act of May 27, 1796; and Act of April 24, 1800. The Act of February 12, 1873, fixed a coinage charge on gold of ⅕ of one per cent: this was repealed by Act of January 14, 1875.

2 H

make an immediate exchange of coins for standard bullion, with a deduction of one-half per cent. from the weight of the pure gold, or pure silver contained in the said bullion, as an indemnification to the mint for the time which will necessarily be required for coining the said bullion, and for the advance which shall have been so made in coins. And it shall be the duty of the Secretary of the Treasury to furnish the said mint from time to time whenever the state of the Treasury will admit thereof, with such sums as may be necessary for effecting the said exchanges, to be replaced as speedily as may be out of the coins which shall have been made of the bullion for which the monies so furnished shall have been exchanged ; and the said deduction of one-half per cent. shall constitute a fund towards defraying the expenses of the said mint.

SEC. 15. That the bullion which shall be brought as aforesaid to the mint to be coined, shall be coined, and the equivalent thereof in coins rendered, if demanded, in the order in which the said bullion shall have been brought or delivered, giving priority according to priority of delivery only, and without preference to any person or persons ; and if any preference shall be given contrary to the direction aforesaid, the officer by whom such undue preference shall be given, shall in each case forfeit and pay $1000 ; to be recovered with costs of suit. And to the end that it may be known if such preference shall at any time be given, the assayer or officer to whom the said bullion shall be delivered to be coined, shall give to the person or persons bringing the same, a memorandum in writing under his hand, denoting the weight, fineness and value thereof, together with the day and order of its delivery into the mint.

SEC. 16. That all the gold and silver coins which have been struck at, and issued from the said mint, shall be a lawful tender in all payments whatsoever, those of full weight according to the respective values herein before declared, and those of less than full weight at values proportional to their respective weights.

SEC. 17. That it shall be the duty of the respective officers of the said mint, carefully and faithfully to use their best endeavors that all the gold and silver coins which shall be struck at the said mint shall be, as nearly as may be, conformable to the several standards and weights aforesaid, and that the copper whereof the cents and half cents aforesaid may be composed, shall be of good quality.

SEC. 18. And the better to secure a due conformity of the said gold and silver coins to their respective standards, *Be it further enacted*, That from every separate mass of standard gold or silver, which shall be made into coins at the said Mint, there shall be taken, set apart by the Treasurer and reserved in his custody a certain number of pieces, not less than three, and that once in every year the pieces so set apart and reserved, shall be assayed under the inspection of the Chief Justice of the United States, the Secretary and Comptroller of the Treasury, the Secretary for the Department of State, and the Attorney General of the United States, (who are hereby required to attend for that purpose at the said Mint, on the last Monday in July in each year,) or under the inspection of any three of them, in such manner as they or a majority of them shall direct, and in the presence of the Director, assayer and chief coiner of the said Mint ; and if it shall be found that the gold and silver so assayed, shall not be inferior to their respective standards herein before declared more than 1 part in 144 parts, the officer or officers of the said Mint whom it may concern shall be held excusable ; but if any greater inferiority shall appear, it shall be certified to the President of the United States, and the said officer or officers shall be deemed disqualified to hold their respective offices.

SEC. 19. That if any of the gold or silver coins which shall be struck or coined at the said Mint shall be debased or made worse as to the proportion of fine gold or fine silver therein contained, or shall be of less weight or value than the same ought to be pursuant to the directions of this act, through the default or with the connivance of any of the officers or persons who shall be employed at the said Mint, for the purpose of profit or gain, or otherwise with a fraudulent intent, and if any of the said officers or persons shall embezzle any of the metals which shall at any time be committed to their charge for the purpose of being coined, or any of the coins which shall be struck or coined at the said Mint, every such officer or person who shall commit any or either of the said offences, shall be deemed guilty of felony, and shall suffer death.

SEC. 20. That the money of account of the United States shall be expressed in dollars or units, dismes or tenths, cents or hundredths, and milles or thousandths, a disme being a tenth part of a dollar, a cent the hundredth part of a dollar, a mille the thousandth part of a dollar, and that all accounts in public offices and all proceedings in the courts of the United States shall be kept and had in conformity to this regulation.

NOTE ON MINOR COINS

Act of May 8, 1792 — Provided for the purchase of 150 tons of copper for coinage into cents and half cents, and ordered that six months after the coinage of such pieces to the amount of $50,000, no other copper coins were to be paid or received or pass current as money under penalty of forfeiture and a fine of $10 against both payer and receiver.

Act of January 14, 1793 — Altered weight of cent to 208 grains, half cent to 104 grains.

Act of March 3, 1795 — Authorized the President by proclamation to further reduce these weights; which was done January 26, 1796. The same act provided for the distribution of these coins at public expense.

Act of January 18, 1837, Sec. 8 — Fixes weights of cent and half cent at 168 and 84 grains respectively.

Act of March 3, 1851 — Provides for coinage of 3-cent piece of 12¾ grains, 75 per cent. silver, 25 per cent. copper, to be legal tender up to 30 cents. The fineness was changed to .900 by Act of March 3, 1853.

Act of February 21, 1857 — Reduces weight of cent to 72 grains, 88 per cent. copper, 12 per cent. nickel; coinage of half cents was discontinued.

Act of April 22, 1864 — Substituted for this coin a bronze cent of 48 grains, composed of 95 per cent. copper and 5 per cent. of tin and zinc, and a 2-cent piece of the same composition and of twice the weight. The cent was made a legal tender in any payment to the amount of 10 cents, the 2-cent piece to the amount of 20 cents.

Act of March 3, 1865 — Provided for a 3-cent piece of 30 grains, 75 per cent. copper, 25 per cent. nickel, to be legal tender up to 60 cents, and fixed the legal tender power of 1- and 2-cent pieces at 4 cents.

Act of May 16, 1866 — Provides for a 5-cent piece of 77$\frac{16}{100}$ grains, 75 per cent. copper, 25 per cent. nickel, to be legal tender up to $1, and its redemption in sums of $100 or more.

Act of March 3, 1871 — Authorized redemption of all minor coins in lawful money in sums of not less than $20.

Act of February 12, 1873 — Abolished the coinage of 2-cent pieces, and made minor coin legal tender up to 25 cents.

Act of September 26, 1890 — Abolished the coinage of 3-cent pieces.

Act of February 9, 1793 [1] — *Regulating foreign coins*

SEC. 1. *Be it enacted, etc.*, That from and after the first day of July next, foreign gold and silver coins shall pass current

---

[1] The subsequent legislation upon this subject is as follows:

Act of February 1, 1798 — Suspends section 2 of above act, and continues for three years from January 1, 1798, and until the end of the next session of Congress thereafter, the legal tender quality of foreign gold and silver coins at the same rates as per section 1 of the act of February 9, 1793.

Act of April 30, 1802 — Further suspends section 2 of the act of February 9, 1793. Foreign coins continued as legal tender for three years.

Act of April 10, 1806 — Foreign gold and silver coins to be current and a legal tender in the United States for three years at same rates as by act of February 9, 1793.

Act of April 29, 1816 — Restores legal tender character of foreign coins for three years, at the following rates: Gold coins of Great Britain and Portugal, 100 cents for every 27 grains, or 88⅔ cents per pennyweight; gold coins of France, 100 cents for every 27½ grains, or 87¼ cents per as money within the United States, and be a legal tender for the payment of all debts and demands, at the several and respective rates following, and not otherwise, viz. : The gold coins of Great Britain and Portugal, of their present standard, at the rate of 100 cents for every 27 grains of the actual weight thereof; the gold coins of France, Spain and the

pennyweight; gold coins of Spain, 100 cents for every 28½ grains, or 84 cents per pennyweight; silver crowns of France, 117.6 cents per ounce, or 110 cents for each crown weighing 18 pennyweights 17 grains; 5-franc pieces, 116 cents per ounce, or 93.3 cents for each 5-franc piece weighing 16 pennyweights 2 grains.

Act of March 3, 1819 — Continues in force the legal tender value in the United States of foreign gold coins at the rates of April 29, 1816, until November 1, 1819; "and from and after that day foreign gold coins shall cease to be a tender in the United States for the payment of debts or demands." Part of act of April 29, 1816, relating to silver coins, continued in force until April 29, 1821.

Act of March 3, 1821 — Crown and 5-franc piece of France continued as legal tender until April 29, 1823.

Act of March 3, 1823 — Continues for four years longer the legal tender character of crowns and 5-franc pieces of France.

Act of March 3, 1823 — Gold coins of Great Britain, Portugal, France, and Spain to be received in payment of lands bought from the United States at the rates given in the act of April 29, 1816, but not made legal tender.

Act of June 25, 1834 — Certain silver coins to be of the legal value and to pass by tale, the dollars of Mexico, Peru, Chili, and Central America, of not less weight than 415 grains, and restamped dollars of Brazil of like weight, fineness, not less than 10 ounces 15 pennyweights of pure silver in Troy pound of 12 ounces of standard silver, at 100 cents each; the 5-franc piece of France, weighing not less than 384 grains, at 93 cents.

Act of June 28, 1834 — Regulates the legal tender value of certain gold coins, as follows: Great Britain, Portugal, and Brazil, of not less than 22 carats fine, at 94.8 cents per pennyweight; those of France, $\frac{9}{16}$ fine, 93.1 cents per pennyweight, and those of Spain, Mexico, and Columbia, of 20 carats, 31⅞ grains fine, at 89.9 cents per pennyweight.

Act of March 3, 1843 — Foreign gold coins to pass current " and be receivable, by weight, for the payment of all debts and demands " at the following rates: Those of Great Britain, not less than .915½ fine, 94.6 cents per pennyweight; those of France, of not less than .899 fine, at 92.9 cents per pennyweight.

Silver coins at the following rates: Spanish pillar dollars and dollars of Mexico, Peru, Bolivia, not less than .897 fine and 415 grains in weight, at 100 cents each; 5-franc pieces of France, not less than .900 fine and 384 grains in weight, at 93 cents each.

Act of February 21, 1857 — Spanish and Mexican coins, known as the quarter, eighth, and sixteenth of the Spanish pillar dollar, and Mexican dollar, to be received by the United States, as follows: ¼ of a dollar, or 2 reals, at 20 cents; ⅛ of a dollar, or 1 real, at 10 cents; $\frac{1}{16}$ of a dollar, or ½ real, at 5 cents. Said coins to be recoined when received. Former acts, making foreign coins a legal tender, repealed; assays of foreign coins to be made by the Director of the Mint and annually reported.

dominions of Spain, of their present standard, at the rate of 100 cents for every 27⅗ grains of the actual weight thereof. Spanish milled dollars, at the rate of 100 cents for each dollar, the actual weight whereof shall not be less than 17 pennyweights and 7 grains ; and in proportion for the parts of a dollar. Crowns of France, at the rate of 110 cents for each crown, the actual weight whereof shall be not less than 18 pennyweights and 17 grains, and in proportion for the parts of a crown. But no foreign coin that may have been, or shall be issued subsequent to the first day of January, 1792, shall be a tender, as aforesaid, until samples thereof shall have been found, by assay, at the mint of the United States, to be conformable to the respective standards required, and proclamation thereof shall have been made by the President of the United States.

SEC. 2. *Provided always*, That at the expiration of three years next ensuing the time when the coinage of gold and silver, agreeably to the act, entitled " An act establishing a mint, and regulating the coins of the United States," shall commence at the mint of the United States (which time shall be announced by the proclamation of the President of the United States), all foreign gold coins, and all foreign silver coins, except Spanish milled dollars and parts of such dollars, shall cease to be a legal tender, as aforesaid.

SEC. 3. That all foreign gold and silver coins, (except Spanish milled dollars, and parts of such dollars.) which shall be received in payment for monies due to the United States, after the said time, when the coining of gold and silver coins shall begin at the mint of the United States, shall, previously to their being issued in circulation, be coined anew, in conformity to the act, entitled " An act establishing a mint and regulating the coins of the United States."

[SEC. 4 repeals Sec. 55 of tariff act of July 31, 1789, under which foreign gold and silver coins were received for dues and fees at a different rating.]

[SEC. 5 fixes the time for making annual assays.]

Act of March 3, 1797, authorized the receipt of evidences of public debt in payment for purchases of public lands. This was repealed by the act of April 18, 1806.

Act of June 27, 1798 — [Provides penalties of imprisonment and fine for altering, forging or counterfeiting the bills or notes issued by the Bank of the United States, or any order or check on the cashier or corporation for the payment of money.]

Act of April 21, 1806 — [Provides penalties for counterfeiting coins of the United States, or those of foreign countries made current in the United States ; for importing false or counterfeit coins ; and for impairing, falsifying, etc., the coins of the United States ; not to interfere with the jurisdiction of individual states over offences made punishable by this act.]

Act of June 30, 1812 — *To authorize the issuing of Treasury notes*

Be it enacted, etc., That the President of the United States be, and he is hereby authorized to cause Treasury notes for such sum or sums as he may think expedient, but not exceeding in the whole the sum of $5,000,000 to be prepared, signed and issued in the manner hereinafter provided.

SEC. 2. That the said Treasury notes shall be reimbursed by the United States, at such places, respectively, as may be expressed on the face of the said notes, one year, respectively, after the day on which the same shall have been issued : from which day of issue they shall bear interest, at the rate of $5\frac{2}{5}$ per centum a year, payable to the owner and owners of such notes, at the Treasury, or by the proper commissioner of loans, at the places and times respectively designated on the face of said notes for the payment of principal.

SEC. 3. That the said Treasury notes shall be respectively signed, in behalf of the United States, by persons to be appointed for that purpose by the President of the United States : two of which persons shall sign each note, and shall each receive, as a compensation for that service, at the rate of $1.25 for every 100 notes thus signed by them respectively ; and the said notes shall likewise be countersigned by the commissioner of loans for that State where the notes may respectively be made payable.

SEC. 4. That the Secretary of the Treasury be, and he is hereby authorized, with the approbation of the President of the United States, to cause to be issued such portion of the said Treasury notes as the President may think expedient in payment of supplies, or debts due by the United States, to such public creditors, or other persons, as may choose to receive such notes in payment, as aforesaid, at par : and the Secretary of the Treasury is further authorized, with the approbation of the President of the United States, to borrow, from time to time, not under par, such sums as the President may think expedient, on the credit of such notes. And it shall be a good execution of this provision to pay such notes to such bank or banks as will receive the same at par and give credit to the

Treasurer of the United States for the amount thereof, on the day on which the said notes shall thus be issued and paid to such bank or banks respectively.

SEC. 5. That the said Treasury notes shall be transferable by delivery and assignment endorsed thereon by the person to whose order the same shall, on the face thereof, have been made payable.

SEC. 6. That the said Treasury notes, whenever made payable, shall be everywhere received in payment of all duties and taxes laid by the authority of the United States, and of all public lands sold by the said authority. On every such payment, credit shall be given for the amount of both the principal and the interest which, on the day of such payment, may appear due on the note or notes thus given in payment. And the said interest shall, on such payments, be computed at the rate of one cent and one half a cent per day on every hundred dollars of principal, and each month shall be computed as containing 30 days.

SEC. 7. That any person making payment to the United States in the said Treasury notes into the hands of any collector, receiver of public monies, or other officer or agent, shall, on books kept according to such forms as shall be prescribed by the Secretary of the Treasury, give duplicate certificates of the number and respective amount of principal and interest of each and every Treasury note thus paid by such person ; and every collector, receiver of public monies or other public officer or agent who shall thus receive any of the said Treasury notes in payment, shall, on payment of the same into the Treasury, or into one of the banks where the public monies are or may be deposited, receive credit both for the principal and for the interest, computed as aforesaid, which, on the day of such last-mentioned payment shall appear due on the note or notes thus paid in. And he shall be charged for the interest accrued on such note or notes from the day on which the same shall have been received by him in payment as aforesaid, to the day on which the same shall be paid by him as aforesaid : *Provided always*, That no such charge or deduction shall be made with respect to any bank into which payments as aforesaid may be made to the United States, either by individuals or by collectors, receivers or other public officers or agents, and which shall receive the same as specie, and give credit to the Treasurer of the United States for the amount thereof, including the interest accrued and due on such notes on the day on which the same shall have been thus paid into such bank on account of the United States.

SEC. 8. That the commissioners of the sinking fund be, and they are hereby authorized and directed to cause to be reimbursed and paid the principal and interest of the Treasury notes which may be issued by virtue of this act, at the several time and times when the same, according to the provisions of this act, should be thus reimbursed and paid. And the said commissioners are further authorized to make purchases of the said notes, in the same manner as of other evidences of the public debt, and at a price not exceeding par, for the amount of the principal and interest due at the time of purchase on such notes. So much of the funds constituting the annual appropriation of $8,000,000, for the principal and interest of the public debt of the United States, as may be wanted for that purpose, after satisfying the sums necessary for the payment of the interest and such part of the principal of the said debt as the United States are now pledged annually to pay and reimburse, is hereby pledged and appropriated for the payment of the interest, and for the reimbursement or purchase of the principal of the said notes. And so much of any monies in the Treasury not otherwise appropriated as may be necessary for that purpose, is hereby appropriated for making up any deficiency in the funds thus pledged appropriated for paying the principal and interest as aforesaid.

[SECS. 9 and 10 relate to printing and the punishment for counterfeiting.]

The *Act of February* 25, 1813 and the *Act of March* 4, 1814, authorized further issues of Treasury notes in terms practically identical with the act of 1812.

The *Act of November* 15, 1814 authorized the receipt of certain Treasury notes for loans to be issued by the government.

The *Act of December* 26, 1814 authorized the *Secretary of the Treasury*, with the approval of the President, to issue additional notes.

Act of February 24, 1815 — *To authorize the issuing of Treasury notes for the service of the year* 1815

Be it enacted, etc., That the Secretary of the Treasury, with the approbation of the President of the United States, be, and he is hereby authorized to cause Treasury notes for a sum not exceeding $25,000,000, to be prepared, signed, and issued, at the Treasury of the United States, in the manner hereinafter provided.

[SEC. 2 relates to manner of signing notes.]

SEC. 3. That the said Treasury notes shall be prepared of such denominations as the Secretary of the Treasury, with the approbation of the President of the United States, shall, from time to time, direct ; and such of the said notes as shall be of a denomination less than $100, shall be payable to bearer and be transferable by delivery alone, and shall bear no interest ; and such of the said notes as shall be of the denomination of $100, or upwards, may be made payable to order, and transferable by delivery and assignment, endorsed on the same, and bearing an interest from the day on which they shall be issued, at the rate of $5\frac{2}{5}$ per centum per annum ; or they may be made payable to bearer, and transferable by delivery alone, and bearing no interest, as the Secretary of the Treasury, with the approbation of the President of the United States, shall direct.

SEC. 4. That it shall be lawful for the holders of the aforesaid Treasury notes not bearing an interest and of the Treasury notes bearing an interest at the rate of $5\frac{2}{5}$ per centum per annum, to present them at any time, in sums not less than $100, to the Treasury of the United States, or to any commissioner of loans ; and the holders of the said Treasury notes not bearing an interest, shall be entitled to receive therefor, the amount of the said notes, in a certificate or certificates of funded stock, bearing interest at 7 per centum per annum, and the holders of the aforesaid Treasury notes bearing an interest at the rate of $5\frac{2}{5}$ per centum, shall be entitled to receive therefor the amount of the said notes including the interest due on the same, in a like certificate or certificates of funded stock, bearing an interest of 6 per centum per annum, from the first day of the calendar month next ensuing that in which the said notes shall thus be respectively presented, and payable quarter-yearly, on the same days whereon the interest of the funded debt is now payable. And the stock thus to be issued shall be transferable in the same manner as the other funded stock of [the] United States ; the interest on the same, and its eventual reimbursement, shall be effected out of such fund as has been or shall be established by law for the payment and reimbursement of the funded public debt contracted since the declaration of war against Great Britain. And the faith of the United States is hereby pledged to establish sufficient revenues and to appropriate them as an addition to the said fund, if the same shall, at any time hereafter, become inadequate for effecting the purpose aforesaid : *Provided, however*, That it shall be lawful for the United States to reimburse the stock thus created, at any time after the last day of December, 1824.

SEC. 5. That it shall be lawful for the Secretary of the

Treasury to cause the Treasury notes which, in pursuance of the preceding section, shall be delivered up and exchanged for funded stock, and also the Treasury notes which shall have been paid to the United States for taxes, duties, or demands, in the manner hereinafter provided, to be re-issued, and applied anew, to the same purposes, and in the same manner, as when originally issued.

[Secs. 6 to 11 are similar to the previous provisions.]

Act of April 10, 1816 — To incorporate the subscribers to the Bank of the United States [1]

Be it enacted, etc., That a Bank of the United States of America shall be established, with a capital of $35,000,000, divided into 350,000 shares, of $100 each share. 70,000 shares, amounting to the sum of $7,000,000, part of the capital of the said Bank, shall be subscribed and paid for by the United States, in the manner hereinafter specified ; and 280,000 shares, amounting to the sum of $28,000,000, shall be subscribed and paid for by individuals, companies, or corporations, in the manner hereinafter specified.

[Sec. 2 provides for method of subscribing to shares.]

[Sec. 3 provides for payment for the shares, one-fourth in specie, the remainder in specie or government bonds ; in instalments 30 per cent at once, 35 per cent in six months, 35 per cent in twelve months.]

[Sec. 4 provides regulations for transfer of bonds.]

Sec. 5. That it shall be lawful for the United States to pay and redeem the funded debt subscribed to the capital of the said bank at the rates aforesaid, in such sums, and at such times, as shall be deemed expedient, any thing in any act or acts of Congress to the contrary thereof notwithstanding. And it shall also be lawful for the president, directors, and company, of the said bank, to sell and transfer for gold and silver coin, or bullion, the funded debt subscribed to the capital of the said bank as aforesaid : *Provided always*, That they shall not sell more thereof than the sum of two millions of dollars in any one year ; nor sell any part thereof at any time within the United States, without previously giving notice of their intention to the Secretary of the Treasury, and offering the same to the United States for the period of fifteen days, at least, at the current price, not exceeding the rates aforesaid.

---

[1] The provisions of this act, which merely repeat those of the act of 1791 (*ante*), are not reproduced.

SEC. 6. That at the opening of subscription to the capital stock of the said bank, the Secretary of the Treasury shall subscribe, or cause to be subscribed, on behalf of the United States, the said number of 70,000 shares, amounting to $7,000,000 as aforesaid, to be paid in gold or silver coin, or in stock of the United States, bearing interest at the rate of 5 per centum per annum. . . .

[SEC. 7 limits the life of the charter to March 3, 1836.]

SEC. 8. That for the management of the affairs of the said corporation, there shall be twenty-five directors, five of whom, being stockholders, shall be annually appointed by the President of the United States, by and with the advice and consent of the Senate, not more than three of whom shall be residents of any one State; and twenty of whom shall be annually elected at the banking house in the city of Philadelphia, on the first Monday of January, in each year, by the qualified stockholders of the capital of the said bank, other than the United States. . . .

[SEC. 9 provides for beginning business when $8,400,000 has been paid in on account of subscriptions.]

[SEC. 10 provides for appointment of officers and employees.]

[SEC. 11 contains the "fundamental articles" largely as in the act of 1791, including regulation for voting shares, eligibility of directors, quorum, general meetings of shareholders, dividends, bonds of officers, real estate holdings, general business, issue of notes, branches, examination, etc. The following are important variations from the previous act:]

Eighth — The total amount of debts which the said corporation shall at any time owe, whether by bond, bill, note, or other contract, over and above the debt or debts due for money deposited in the bank, shall not exceed the sum of $35,000,000, unless the contracting of any greater debt shall have been previously authorized by law of the United States.

*　*　*　*　*　*　*　*　*　*

Twelfth — . . . *Provided*, That all bills or notes, so to be issued by said corporation, shall be made payable on demand, other than bills or notes for the payment of a sum not less than $100 each, and payable to the order of some person or persons, which bills or notes it shall be lawful for said corporation to make payable at any time not exceeding 60 days from the date thereof.

*　*　*　*　*　*　*　*　*　*

Seventeenth — No note shall be issued of less amount than $5.

[SECS. 12 and 13 fix penalties for violation of the provisions of the act.]

SEC. 14.[1] That the bills or notes of the said corporation originally made payable, or which shall have become payable on demand, shall be receivable in all payments to the United States, unless otherwise directed by act of Congress.

SEC. 15. That during the continuance of this act, and whenever required by the Secretary of the Treasury, the said corporation shall give the necessary facilities for transferring the public funds from place to place, within the United States, or the territories thereof, and for distributing the same in payment of the public creditors, without charging commissions or claiming allowance on account of difference of exchange, and shall also do and perform the several and respective duties of the commissioners of loans for the several states, or of any one or more of them, whenever required by law.

SEC. 16. That the deposits of the money of the United States, in places in which the said bank and branches thereof may be established, shall be made in said bank or branches thereof, unless the Secretary of the Treasury shall at any time otherwise order and direct; in which case the Secretary of the Treasury shall immediately lay before Congress, if in session, and if not, immediately after the commencement of the next session, the reasons of such order or direction.

SEC. 17. That the said corporation shall not at any time suspend or refuse payment in gold and silver, of any of its notes, bills or obligations; nor of any moneys received upon deposit in said bank, or in any of its offices of discount and deposit. And if the said corporation shall at any time refuse or neglect to pay on demand any bill, note or obligation issued by the corporation, according to the contract, promise or undertaking therein expressed; or shall neglect or refuse to pay on demand any moneys received in said bank, or in any of its offices aforesaid, on deposit, to the person or persons entitled to receive the same, then, and in every such case, the holder of any such note, bill or obligation, or the person or persons entitled to demand and receive such moneys, as aforesaid, shall respectively be entitled to receive and recover interest on the said bills, notes, obligations or moneys, until the same shall be fully paid and satisfied, at the rate of twelve per centum per annum from the time of such demand as aforesaid ; *Provided*, That Congress may at any time hereafter enact laws enforcing and regulating

---

[1] This section was repealed by the Act of June 15, 1836, after the expiration of this charter.

the recovery of the amount of the notes, bills, obligations or other debts, of which payment shall have been refused as aforesaid, with the rate of interest above mentioned, vesting jurisdiction for that purpose in any courts, either of law or equity, of the courts of the United States, or Territories thereof, or of the several States, as they may deem expedient.

[SECS. 18 and 19 provide penalties of imprisonment and fine for forging or counterfeiting the notes or bills of the Bank of the United States, or any order or check on the bank or its cashier.]

SEC. 20. That in consideration of the exclusive privileges and benefits conferred by this act, upon the said bank, the president, directors, and company thereof, shall pay to the United States, out of the corporate funds thereof, the sum of $1,500,000, in three equal payments; that is to say: $500,000 at the expiration of two years; $500,000 at the expiration of three years; and $500,000 at the expiration of four years after the said bank shall be organized, and commence its operations in the manner hereinbefore provided.

SEC. 21. That no other bank shall be established by any future law of the United States during the continuance of the corporation hereby created, for which the faith of the United States is hereby pledged. . . .

[SEC. 22 limits the time within which the bank must begin business.]

SEC. 23. *And be it further enacted*, That it shall, at all times, be lawful, for a committee of either house of Congress, appointed for that purpose, to inspect the books, and to examine into the proceedings of the corporation hereby created, and to report whether the provisions of this charter have been, by the same, violated or not; and whenever any committee, as aforesaid, shall find and report, or the President of the United States shall have reason to believe that the charter has been violated, it may be lawful for Congress to direct, or the President to order a scire facias to be sued out of the circuit court of the district of Pennsylvania, in the name of the United States, (which shall be executed upon the president of the corporation for the time being, at least fifteen days before the commencement of the term of said court,) calling on the said corporation to show cause wherefore the charter hereby granted, shall not be declared forfeited; and it shall be lawful for the said court, upon the return of the said scire facias, to examine into the accounts of the truth of the alleged violation, and if such violation be made appear, then to pronounce and adjudge that the said charter is forfeited and annulled. *Provided, however,* Every issue of fact which may be joined between the United States and the corporation aforesaid, shall be tried by a jury. And it shall be lawful for the court aforesaid to require the production of such of the books of the corporation as it may deem necessary for the ascertainment of the controverted facts : and the final judgment of the court aforesaid, shall be examinable in the Supreme Court of the United States, by writ of error, and may be there reversed or affirmed, according to the usages of law.

Act of March 3, 1817 — Repealed all authority to issue or reissue Treasury notes, and directed cancellation of all notes received or funded.

Act of June 28, 1834 —*Concerning the gold coins of the United States*

Be it enacted, etc., That the gold coins of the United States shall contain the following quantities of metal, that is to say : each eagle shall contain 232 grains of pure gold, and 258 grains of standard gold ; each half eagle 116 grains of pure gold, and 129 grains of standard gold ; each quarter eagle shall contain 58 grains of pure gold, and $64\frac{1}{2}$ grains of standard gold ; every such eagle shall be of the value of $10 ; every such half eagle shall be of the value of $5 ; and every such quarter eagle shall be of the value of 2\frac{1}{2}$; and the said gold coins shall be receivable in all payments, when of full weight, according to their respective values ; and when of less than full weight, at less values, proportioned to their respective actual weights.

Sec. 2. That all standard gold or silver deposited for coinage after the thirty-first of July next, shall be paid for in coin under the direction of the Secretary of the Treasury, within five days from the making of such deposit, deducting from the amount of said deposit of gold and silver one-half of one per centum : *Provided,* That no deduction shall be made unless said advance be required by such depositor within forty days.

Sec. 3. That all gold coins of the United States minted anterior to the thirty-first day of July next, shall be receivable in all payments at the rate of $94\frac{8}{10}$ cents per pennyweight.

[Sec. 4 directs the setting apart of gold coins for assay and makes provision for securing accuracy in fineness and weight.]

Sec. 5. That this act shall be in force from and after the 31st of July, 1834.

Act of June 23, 1836 — To regulate the deposites of the public money. (Repealed 1841)

Be it enacted, etc., That it shall be the duty of the Secretary of the Treasury to select as soon as may be practicable and employ as the depositories of the money of the United States, such of the banks incorporated by the several States, by Congress for the District of Columbia, or by the Legislative Councils of the respective Territories for those Territories, as may be located at, adjacent or convenient to the points or places at which the revenues may be collected, or disbursed, and in those States, Territories or Districts in which there are no banks, or in which no bank can be employed as a deposite bank, and within which the public collections or disbursements require a depository, the said Secretary may make arrangements with a bank or banks, in some other State, Territory or District, to establish an agency or agencies, in the States, Territories or Districts so destitute of banks, as banks of deposite ; and to receive through such agencies such deposites of the public money, as may be directed to be made at the points designated, and to make such disbursements as the public service may require at those points ; the duties and liabilities of every bank thus establishing any such agency to be the same in respect to its agency as are the duties and liabilities of deposite banks generally under the provisions of this act : *Provided,* That at least one such bank shall be selected in each State and Territory, if any can be found in each State and Territory willing to be employed as depositories of the public money, upon the terms and conditions hereinafter prescribed, and continue to conform thereto ; and that the Secretary of the Treasury shall not suffer to remain in any deposite bank, an amount of the public money more than equal to three-fourths of the amount of its capital stock actually paid in, for a longer time than may be necessary to enable him to make the transfers required by the twelfth section of this act ; and that the banks so selected, shall be, in his opinion, safe depositories of the public money, and shall be willing to undertake to do and perform the several duties and services, and to conform to the several conditions prescribed by this act.

SEC. 2. That if, at any point or place at which the public revenue may be collected, there shall be no bank located, which, in the opinion of the Secretary of the Treasury, is in a safe condition, or where all the banks at such point or place shall fail or refuse to be employed as depositories of the public money of the United States, or to comply with the conditions prescribed by this act, or where such banks shall not have sufficient capital to become depositories of the whole amount of moneys collected at such point or place, he shall and may order and direct the public money collected at such point or place to be deposited in a bank or banks in the same State, or in some one or more of the adjacent States upon the terms and conditions hereinafter prescribed : *Provided,* That nothing in this act contained shall be so construed as to prevent Congress at any time from passing any law for the removal of the public money from any of the said banks, or from changing the terms of the deposite, or to prevent the said banks at any time from declining any longer to be the depositories of the public money upon paying over, or tendering to pay, the whole amount of public moneys on hand, according to the terms of its agreement with the said Secretary.

SEC. 3. That no bank shall hereafter be selected and employed by the Secretary of the Treasury as a depository of the public money, until such bank shall have first furnished to the said Secretary a statement of its condition and business, a list of its directors, the current price of its stock ; and also a copy of its charter ; and likewise, such other information as may be necessary to enable him to judge of the safety of its condition.

SEC. 4. That the said banks, before they shall be employed as the depositories of the public money, shall agree to receive the same, upon the following terms and conditions, to wit : *First.* Each bank shall furnish to the Secretary of the Treasury, from time to time, as often as he may require, not exceeding once a week, statements setting forth its condition and business, as prescribed in the foregoing section of this act, except that such statements need not, unless requested by said Secretary, contain a list of the directors, or a copy of the charter. And the said bank shall furnish to the Secretary of the Treasury, and to the Treasurer of the United States, a weekly statement of the condition of his account from their books. And the Secretary of the Treasury shall have the right, by himself, or an agent appointed for that purpose, to inspect such general accounts in the books of the bank, as shall relate to the said statements : *Provided,* That this shall not be construed to imply a right of inspecting the account of any private individual or individuals with the bank.

Secondly. To credit as specie, all sums deposited therein to the credit of the Treasurer of the United States, and to pay all checks, warrants, or drafts, drawn on such deposites in specie if required by the holder thereof.

Thirdly. To give, whenever required by the Secretary of the

21

Treasury, the necessary facilities for transferring the public funds from place to place, within the United States, and the Territories thereof, and for distributing the same in payments of the public creditors, without charging commission or claiming allowance on account of difference of exchange.

Fourthly. To render to the Government of the United States all the duties and services heretofore required by law to be performed by the late Bank of the United States and its several branches or offices.

SEC. 5. That no bank shall be selected or continued as a place of deposite of the public money which shall not redeem its notes and bills on demand in specie ; nor shall any bank be selected or continued as aforesaid, which shall after the fourth of July, in the year 1836, issue or pay out any note or bill of a less denomination than $5 ; nor shall the notes or bills of any bank be received in payment of any debt due to the United States which shall, after the said fourth day of July, in the year 1836, issue any note or bill of a less denomination than $5.

SEC. 6. That the Secretary of the Treasury shall be, and he is hereby authorized, and it shall be his duty, whenever in his judgment the same shall be necessary or proper, to require of any bank so selected and employed as aforesaid, collateral or additional securities for the safe keeping of the public moneys deposited therein, and the faithful performance of the duties required by this act.

SEC. 7. That it shall be lawful for the Secretary of the Treasury to enter into contracts in the name and for and on behalf of the United States, with the said banks so selected or employed, whereby the said banks shall stipulate to do and perform the several duties and services prescribed by this act.

SEC. 8. That no bank which shall be selected or employed as the place of deposite of the public money shall be discontinued as such depository, or the public money withdrawn therefrom except for the causes hereinafter mentioned, that is to say : if at any time, any one of said banks shall fail or refuse to perform any of said duties as prescribed by this act, and stipulated to be performed by its contract ; or, if any of said banks shall at any time refuse to pay its own notes in specie if demanded ; or shall fail to keep in its vaults such an amount of specie as shall be required by the Secretary of the Treasury, and shall be, in his opinion, necessary to render the said bank a safe depository of the public moneys, having due regard to the nature of this business transacted by the bank ; in any and every such case it shall be the duty of the Secretary of the Treasury to discontinue any such bank as a depository, and withdraw from it the public moneys which it may hold on deposite at the time of such discontinuance. And in case of the discontinuance of any of said banks it shall be the duty of the Secretary of the Treasury to report to Congress immediately if in session, and if not in session, then at the commencement of its next session, the facts and reasons which have induced such discontinuance. And in case of the discontinuance of any of said banks as a place of deposite of the public money for any of the causes hereinbefore provided, it shall be lawful for the Secretary of the Treasury to deposite the money thus withdrawn in some other banks of deposite already selected, or to select some other bank as a place of deposite, upon the terms and conditions prescribed by this act. And in default of any bank to receive such deposite, the money thus withdrawn shall be kept by the Treasurer of the United States, according to the laws now in force ; and shall be subject to be disbursed according to law.

SEC. 9. That until the Secretary of the Treasury shall have selected and employed the said banks as places of deposite of the public money, in conformity to the provisions of this act, the several State and District banks at present employed as depositories of the money of the United States, shall continue to be the depositories aforesaid upon the terms and conditions upon which they have been so employed.

SEC. 10. That it shall be the duty of the Secretary of the Treasury to lay before Congress at the commencement of each annual session, a statement of the number and names of the banks employed as depositories of the public money, and of their condition, and the amount of public money deposited in each, as shown by their returns at the Treasury : and if the selection of any bank as a depository of the public money be made by the Secretary of the Treasury, while Congress is in session, he shall immediately report the name and condition of such bank to Congress : and if any such selection shall be made during the recess of Congress, he shall report the same to Congress during the first week of its next session.

SEC. 11. That whenever the amount of public deposites to the credit of the Treasurer of the United States, in any bank shall, for a whole quarter of a year, exceed the one-fourth part of the amount of the capital stock of such bank actually paid in, the banks shall allow and pay to the United States for the use of the excess of the deposites over the one-fourth part of its capital, an interest at the rate of two per centum per annum, to be calculated for each quarter, upon the average excesses of the quarter : and it shall be the duty of the Secretary of the

Treasury at the close of each quarter, to cause the amounts on
deposite in each deposite bank for the quarter, to be examined
and ascertained, and to see that all sums of interest accruing
under the provisions of this section, are, by the banks respectively passed to the credit of the Treasurer of the United
States in his accounts with the respective banks.

SEC. 12. That all warrants or orders for the purpose of
transferring the public funds from the banks in which they now
are, or may hereafter be deposited, to other banks, whether of
deposite or not, for the purpose of accommodating the banks
to which the transfer may be made, or sustain their credit, or
for any other purpose whatever, except it be to facilitate the
public disbursements and to comply with the provision of this
act, be, and the same are hereby, prohibited and declared to
be illegal ; and in cases where transfers shall be required for
purposes of equalization under the provisions of this act, in
consequence of too great an accumulation of deposites in any
bank, such transfers, shall be made to the nearest deposite
banks which are considered safe and secure, and which can receive the moneys to be transferred under the limitations in this
act imposed :   *Provided*, That it may be lawful for the President of the United States to direct transfers of public money
to be made from time to time to the mint and branch mints of
the United States, for supplying metal for coining.

SEC. 13. That the money which shall be in the Treasury of
the United States on the first day of January, 1837, reserving
the sum of $5,000,000, shall be deposited with such of the sev-
eral States, in proportion to their respective representation in
the Senate and House of Representatives of the United States,
as shall, by law, authorize their Treasurers, or other competent
authorities to receive the same on the terms hereinafter specified ; and the Secretary of the Treasury shall deliver the same
to such Treasurers, or other competent authorities, on receiving
certificates of deposite therefor, signed by such competent
authorities, in such form as may be prescribed by the Secretary
aforesaid ; which certificates shall express the usual and legal
obligations, and pledge the faith of the State, for the safe keeping and repayment thereof, and shall pledge the faith of the
States receiving the same, to pay the said moneys and every
part thereof, from time to time, whenever the same shall be
required by the Secretary of the Treasury, for the purpose of
defraying any wants of the public treasury, beyond the amount
of the five millions aforesaid :   *Provided*, That if any State
declines to receive its proportion of the surplus aforesaid, on
the terms before named, the same shall be deposited with the

other States, agreeing to accept the same on deposite in the proportion aforesaid : *and provided further*, That when said money, or any part thereof, shall be wanted by the said Secretary, to meet appropriations by law, the same shall be called for, in ratable proportions, within one year, as nearly as conveniently may be, from the different States, with which the same is deposited, and shall not be called for, in sums exceeding $10,000, from any one State, in any one month, without previous notice of 30 days, for every additional sum of $20,000, which may at any time be required.

SEC. 14. That the said deposites shall be made with the said States in the following proportions, and at the following times, to wit : one quarter part on the first day of January, 1837, or as soon thereafter as may be ; one quarter part on the first day of April, one quarter part on the first day of July and one quarter part on the first day of October, all in the same year.

[SEC. 15 provides for additional clerks, etc.]

The *Act of June* 23, 1836, authorized the Secretary of the Treasury to act as the agent of the United States in all matters relating to their stock in the Bank of the United States.

A *Joint Resolution of March* 3, 1837, authorized the Secretary to receive from the Bank of the United States, under the Pennsylvania charter, payment for the stock of the United States in the late Bank of the United States.

The *Act of July* 7, 1838, was passed " to prevent the issue and circulation of the bills, notes, and other securities of corporations created by acts of Congress which have expired," directed against the late Bank of the United States.

Act of January 18, 1837 — *Supplementary to the act entitled
    " An act establishing a mint, etc."*

[SECS. 1–7, inclusive, relate to the organization of the mint, duties of officers, bonds, salaries, etc.]

SEC. 8. That the standard for both gold and silver coins of the United States shall hereafter be such, that of 1000 parts by weight, 900 shall be of pure metal and 100 of alloy ; and the alloy of the silver coins shall be of copper ; and the alloy of the gold coins shall be of copper and silver, provided that the silver do not exceed one-half of the whole alloy.

SEC. 9. That of the silver coins, the dollar shall be of the weight of $412\frac{1}{2}$ grains ; the half dollar of the weight of $206\frac{1}{4}$ grains ; the quarter dollar of the weight of $103\frac{1}{8}$ grains ; the dime, or tenth part of a dollar, of the weight of 41¼ grains; and the half dime, or a twentieth part of a dollar, of the weight of 20⅝ grains. And that dollars, half dollars, and quarter dollars, dimes and half dimes, shall be legal tenders of payment, according to their nominal value, for any sums whatever.

SEC. 10. That of the gold coins, the weight of the eagle shall be 258 grains; that of the half eagle 129 grains; and that of the quarter eagle 64½ grains. And that for all sums whatever, the eagle shall be a legal tender of payment for 10 dollars; the half eagle for 5 dollars; and the quarter eagle for 2½ dollars.

SEC. 11. That the silver coins heretofore issued at the mint of the United States, and the gold coins issued since the 31st day of July, 1834, shall continue to be legal tenders of payment for their nominal values, on the same terms as if they were of the coinage provided for by this act.

[SEC. 12 relates to copper coins.]

[SEC. 13 provides for the devices upon coins.]

[SECS. 14–24 relate to the deposit of bullion and payment therefor. No charge for coinage is made, except for expense of reducing bullion to standard.]

[SEC. 25 relates to deviations in weights of coins.]

[SECS. 26–38 cover the technique of coinage, organization of the mint, test of coins, delivery of coin in return for bullion, minor coins, etc.]

Treasury Notes were authorized by the *Act of October* 12, 1837, substantially in the same form as acts cited *ante;* the *Act of May* 21, 1838, authorized reissues of such notes.

Additional issues under the provisions of the same act were authorized by the —

> *Act of March* 2, 1839.
> *Act of March* 31, 1840.
> *Act of February* 15, 1841.
> *Act of January* 31, 1842.
> *Act of August* 31, 1842.
> *Act of March* 3, 1843.
> *Act of July* 22, 1846.

The *Act of January* 28, 1847, authorized an issue of notes without reference to the act of 1837, but its terms were practically identical.

The *Act of July* 5, 1838, modified the act June 23, 1836, so as to relieve banks which issued notes under $5 from its operation up to October 1, 1838.

Act of July 7, 1838 — To restrain the circulation of small notes, as a currency, in the District of Columbia, and for other purposes

Be it enacted, etc., That, after the tenth day of April next, it shall be unlawful for any individual, company, or corporation, to issue, pass, or offer to pass, within the District of Columbia, any note, check, draft, bank-bill, or any other paper currency, of a less denomination than $5, and if any person or corporation shall violate the provisions of this section, the persons so offending, or, in case of any corporation so offending, the officers of any such corporation for the time being, shall be liable to indictment by the grand jury of the county within the district where the offence shall have been committed ; and the persons so offending, or the officers of the corporation so offending, shall, on conviction thereof, be fined in a sum not exceeding $50, at the discretion of the court, for every offence ; one-half of said fine shall be paid to the prosecutor, the other half shall be for the use of the county where the offence shall have been committed ; *Provided,* That should the prosecutor offer himself, or be admitted, as a witness for the prosecution, he shall forfeit all claim to any part of the penalty, and the whole shall go to the county, and the court shall give judgment accordingly ; and the person so offending, and the officers of any corporation, shall also be liable to pay the amount of any note, bill, check, draft, or other paper, constituting part of such currency, to any holder thereof, with all costs incident to the protest and legal collection thereof, with 50 per cent. damages for non-payment on demand, to be recovered by action of debt ; and in case of judgment for the plaintiff, execution thereon shall be had forthwith ; and it shall be the duty of the district attorney of the District of Columbia to commence prosecutions against all persons and every corporation offending against this section, of which he shall have knowledge or probable information ; and, in case of corporations, the prosecution shall be against the president or any director or cashier thereof, for the time being ; and it shall be the duty of the grand jurors to present all such offences of which they shall have knowledge or probable information ; and, that no member of the grand jury shall be ignorant of his duty in this particular, it shall be the duty of the court having cognizance of all offences against this section to give the same in charge to the grand juries at the commencement of the term after the passage of this act.

SEC. 2. That from and after the passage of this act, it shall be unlawful for any individual, company, or corporation, to issue, *de novo*, or knowingly to pass, or procure to be issued, passed or circulated, within the District aforesaid, any note, check, bank-bill, or other paper medium, of the denomination aforesaid, evidently intended for common circulation as for and in lieu of small change in gold or silver, or for any other pretense whatever, and which shall be issued and circulated for the first time after the period above limited in this section, under the penalties provided in the foregoing section.

NOTE. — This act related only to the District of Columbia because it was then the opinion that Congress had jurisdiction over this question only in the District (and the Territories) but not in the States.
. The *Act of December* 27, 1854, supplemented this by making the penalties much more severe, even voiding contracts payable in notes under $5.

Act of August 6, 1846 — *To provide for the better organization of the Treasury, and for the collection, safe-keeping, transfer, and disbursement of the public revenue* [1]

Whereas, by the fourth section of the act entitled "An act to establish the Treasury Department," approved September 2, 1789, it was provided that it should be the duty of the Treasurer to receive and keep the moneys of the United States, and to disburse the same upon warrants drawn by the Secretary of the Treasury, countersigned by the Comptroller, and recorded by the Register, and not otherwise ; and whereas it is found necessary to make further provisions to enable the Treasurer the better to carry into effect the intent of the said section in relation to the receiving and disbursing the moneys of the United States : Therefore —

Be it enacted, etc., That the rooms prepared and provided in the new Treasury building at the seat of Government for the use of the Treasurer of the United States, his assistants, and clerks, and occupied by them, and also the fire-proof vaults and safes erected in said rooms for the keeping of the public moneys in the possession and under the immediate control of said Treasurer, and such other apartments as are provided for in this act as places of deposit of the public money, are hereby constituted and declared to be, the Treasury of the United States.   And all moneys paid into the same shall be subject to the draft of the Treasurer, drawn agreeably to appropriations made by law.

[1] The Subtreasury Act of 1840 was so similar to this one (now in force) that it is omitt d.

[SEC. 2 provides that the mints at Philadelphia and New Orleans be places of deposit of public moneys and the treasurers thereof designated assistant treasurers of the United States.]

[SECS. 3 and 4 provide for buildings at New York, Boston, Charleston and St. Louis as places of deposit of public moneys, assistant treasurers to be appointed to take charge thereof.]

SEC. 5. That the President shall nominate, and by and with the advice and consent of the Senate appoint, four officers, to be denominated "assistant treasurers of the United States," which said officers shall hold their respective offices for the term of four years, unless sooner removed therefrom; one of which shall be located at the city of New York, in the State of New York; one other of which shall be located at the city of Boston, in the State of Massachusetts; one other of which shall be located at the city of Charleston, in the State of South Carolina; and one other at St. Louis, in the State of Missouri. And all of which said officers shall give bonds to the United States, with sureties, according to the provisions hereinafter contained, for the faithful discharge of the duties of their respective offices.

SEC. 6. That the Treasurer of the United States, the treasurer of the mint of the United States, the treasurers, and those acting as such, of the various branch mints, all collectors of the customs, all assistant treasurers, all receivers of public moneys at the several land offices, all postmasters, and all public officers of whatsoever character, be and they are hereby required to keep safely, without loaning, using, depositing in banks, or exchanging for other funds than as allowed by this act, all the public money collected by them, or otherwise at any time placed in their possession and custody, till the same is ordered, by the proper Department or officer of the Government, to be transferred or paid out; and, when such orders for transfer or payment are received, faithfully and promptly to make the same as directed, and to do and perform all other duties as fiscal agents of the Government which may be imposed by this or any other acts of Congress, or by any regulation of the Treasury Department made in conformity to law; and also to do and perform all acts and duties required by law, or by direction of any of the Executive Departments of the Government, as agents for paying pensions, or for making any other disbursements which either of the heads of those Departments may be required by law to make, and which are of a character to be made by the depositaries hereby constituted, consistently with the other official duties imposed upon them.

[SECS. 7 and 8 provide for bonding the officers designated in the act.]

SEC. 9. That all collectors and receivers of public money, of every character and description, within the District of Columbia, shall, as frequently as they may be directed by the Secretary of the Treasury, or the Postmaster General so to do, pay over to the Treasurer of the United States, at the Treasury, all public moneys collected by them, or in their hands ; that all such collectors and receivers of public moneys within the cities of Philadelphia and New Orleans shall, upon the same direction, pay over to the treasurers of the mints in their respective cities, at the said mints, all public moneys collected by them, or in their hands ; and that all such collectors and receivers of public moneys within the cities of New York, Boston, Charleston, and St. Louis, shall, upon the same direction, pay over to the assistant treasurers in their respective cities, at their offices, respectively, all the public moneys, collected by them, or in their hands, to be safely kept by the said respective depositaries until otherwise disposed of according to law ; and it shall be the duty of the said Secretary and Postmaster General respectively to direct such payments by the said collectors and receivers at all the said places, at least as often as once in each week, and as much more frequently, in all cases, as they in their discretion may think proper.

SEC. 10. That it shall be lawful for the Secretary of the Treasury to transfer the moneys in the hands of any depositary hereby constituted to the Treasury of the United States, to be there safely kept, to the credit of the Treasurer of the United States, according to the provisions of this act; and also to transfer moneys in the hands of any one depositary constituted by this act to any other depositary constituted by the same, at his discretion, and as the safety of the public moneys, and the convenience of the public service shall seem to him to require ; which authority to transfer the moneys belonging to the Post Office Department is also conferred upon the Postmaster General, so far as its exercise by him may be consistent with the provisions of existing laws; and every depositary constituted by this act shall keep his account of the money paid to or deposited by him, belonging to the Post Office Department, separate and distinct from the account kept by him of other public moneys so paid or deposited. And for the purpose of payments on the public account, it shall be lawful for the Treasurer of the United States to draw upon any of the said depositaries, as he may think most conducive to the public interest, or to the convenience of the public creditors, or both.

And each depositary so drawn upon shall make returns to the Treasury and Post Office Departments of all moneys received and paid by him, at such times and in such form as shall be directed by the Secretary of the Treasury or the Postmaster General.

SEC. 11. That the Secretary of the Treasury shall be and he is hereby authorized to cause examinations to be made of the books, accounts, and money on hand of the several depositaries constituted by this act ; and for that purpose to appoint special agents, as occasion may require, with such compensation, not exceeding six dollars per day and travelling expenses, as he may think reasonable, to be fixed and declared at the time of each appointment. The agents selected to make these examinations shall be instructed to examine as well the books, accounts, and returns of the officer, as the money on hand, and the manner of its being kept, to the end that uniformity and accuracy in the accounts, as well as safety to the public moneys, may be secured thereby.

SEC. 12. That, in addition to the examinations provided for in the last preceding section, and as a further guard over the public moneys, it shall be the duty of each naval officer and surveyor, as a check upon the assistant treasurers, or the collectors of the customs, of their respective districts ; of each register of a land office, as a check upon the receiver of his land office ; and of the director and superintendent of each mint and branch mint, when separate officers, as a check upon the treasurers, respectively, of the said mints, or the persons acting as such, at the close of each quarter of the year, and as much more frequently as they shall be directed by the Secretary of the Treasury to do so, to examine the books, accounts, returns, and money on hand, of the assistant treasurers, collectors, receivers of land offices, treasurers of the mint, and each branch mint, and persons acting as such, and to make a full, accurate, and faithful return to the Treasury Department of their condition.

[SEC. 13 makes provision for clerks, etc., for these offices.]

SEC. 14. That the Secretary of the Treasury may, at his discretion, transfer the balances remaining with any of the present depositories, as he may deem the safety of the public money or the public convenience may require : *Provided*, That nothing in this act shall be so construed as to authorize the Secretary of the Treasury to transfer the balances remaining with any of the present depositories to the depositories constituted by this act before the first day of January next : *And, provided*, That, for the purpose of payments on public account, out of balances remaining with the present depositories, it shall be lawful for the Treasurer of the United States to draw upon any of the said depositories as he may think most conducive to the public interests, or to the convenience of the public creditors, or both.

[SEC. 15 provides that all officers and others having money to pay to the United States may do so at the sub-treasuries established.]

SEC. 16. That all officers and other persons, charged by this act, or any other act, with the safe-keeping, transfer, and disbursement of the public moneys, other than those connected with the Post Office Department, are hereby required to keep an accurate entry of each sum received, and of each payment or transfer ; and that if any one of the said officers, or of those connected with the Post Office Department, shall convert to his own use, in any way whatever, or shall use, by way of investment in any kind of property or merchandise, or shall loan, with or without interest, or shall deposite in any bank, or shall exchange for other funds, except as allowed by this act, any portion of the public moneys intrusted to him for safe-keeping, disbursement, transfer, or for any other purpose, every such act shall be deemed and adjudged to be an embezzlement of so much of the said moneys as shall be thus taken, converted, invested, used, loaned, deposited, or exchanged, which is hereby declared to be a felony ; and any failure to pay over or to produce the public moneys intrusted to such person shall be held and taken to be *prima facie* evidence of such embezzlement ; and if any officer charged with the disbursements of public moneys shall accept or receive, or transmit to the Treasury Department to be allowed in his favor, any receipt or voucher from a creditor of the United States, without having paid to such creditor, in such funds as the said officer may have received for disbursement, or such other funds as he may be authorized by this act to take in exchange, the full amount specified in such receipt or voucher, every such act shall be deemed to be a conversion by such officer to his own use of the amount specified in such receipt or voucher ; and any officer or agent of the United States, and all persons advising or participating in such act, being convicted thereof before any court of the United States of competent jurisdiction, shall be sentenced to imprisonment for a term of not less than six months nor more than ten years, and to a fine equal to the amount of the money embezzled. And upon the trial of any indictment against any person for embezzling public money under the provisions of this act, it shall be sufficient evidence, for the purpose of showing a balance against such person, to produce a transcript from the books and proceedings of the Treasury, as required in civil cases, under the provisions of the act entitled " An act to provide more effectually for the settlement of accounts between the United States and receivers of public money," approved March 3, 1797 ; and the provisions of this act shall be so construed as to apply to all persons charged with the safe-keeping, transfer, or disbursement of the public money, whether such persons be indicted as receivers or depositaries of the same ; and the refusal of such person, whether in or out of office, to pay any draft, order, or warrant which may be drawn upon him by the proper officer of the Treasury Department, for any public money in his hands belonging to the United States, no matter in what capacity the same may have been received or may be held, or to transfer or disburse any such money promptly, upon the legal requirement of any authorized officer of the United States, shall be deemed and taken, upon the trial of any indict-ment against such person for embezzlement, as *prima facie* evidence of such embezzlement.

[SEC. 17 provides that until proper offices are fitted up, tem-porary ones shall be furnished.]

And whereas, by the thirtieth section of the act entitled " An act to regulate the collection of duties imposed by law on the tonnage of ships or vessels, and on goods, wares, and merchan-dises imported into the United States," approved July 31, 1789, it was provided that all fees and dues collected by virtue of that act should be received in gold and silver coin only ; and whereas, also, by the fifth section of the act approved May 10, 1800, en-titled " An act to amend the act entitled ' An act providing for the sale of the lands of the United States in the territory north-west of the Ohio, and above the mouth of Kentucky river,' " it was provided that payment for the said lands shall be made by all purchasers in specie, or in evidence of the public debt; and whereas, experience has proved that said provisions ought to be revived and enforced, according to the true and wise in-tent of the Constitution of the United States —

SEC. 18. That on the first day of January, 1847, and there-after, all duties, taxes, sales of public lands, debts, and sums of money accruing or becoming due to the United States, and also all sums due for postages or otherwise, to the General Post Office Department, shall be paid in gold and silver coin only, or in Treasury notes issued under the authority of the United States : *Provided,* That the Secretary of the Treasury shall publish, monthly, in two newspapers at the city of Washington, the amount of specie at the several places of deposite, the amount of Treasury notes or drafts issued, and the amount outstanding on the last day of each month.

SEC. 19. That on the first day of April, 1847, and thereafter, every officer or agent engaged in making disbursements on account of the United States, or of the General Post Office, shall make all payments in gold and silver coin, or in Treasury notes, if the creditor agree to receive said notes in payment; and any receiving or disbursing officer or agent who shall neglect, evade, or violate the provisions of this and the last preceding section of this act, shall, by the Secretary of the Treasury, be immediately reported to the President of the United States, with the facts of such neglect, evasion, or violation; and also to Congress, if in session; and if not in session, at the commencement of its session next after the violation takes place.

SEC. 20. That no exchange of funds shall be made by any disbursing officers or agents of the Government, of any grade or denominations whatsoever, or connected with any branch of the public service, other than on exchange for gold and silver; and every such disbursing officer, when the means for his disbursements are furnished to him in gold and silver, shall make his payments in the money so furnished; or when those means are furnished to him in drafts, shall cause those drafts to be presented at their place of payment, and properly paid according to the law, and shall make his payments in the money so received for the drafts furnished, unless, in either case, he can exchange the means in his hands for gold and silver at par. And it shall be and is hereby made the duty of the head of the proper Department immediately to suspend from duty any disbursing officer who shall violate the provisions of this section, and forthwith to report the name of the officer or agent to the President, with the fact of the violation, and all the circumstances accompanying the same and within the knowledge of the said Secretary, to the end that such officer or agent may be promptly removed from office, or restored to his trust and the performance of his duties. as to the President may seem just and proper: *Provided, however,* That those disbursing officers, having at present credits in the banks, shall, until the first day of January next, be allowed to check on the same, allowing the public creditors to receive their pay from the banks either in specie or bank notes.

SEC. 21. That it shall be the duty of the Secretary of the Treasury to issue and publish regulations to enforce the speedy presentation of all Government drafts for payment at the places where payable, and to prescribe the time, according to the different distances of the depositaries from the seat of

Government, within which all drafts upon them, respectively, shall be presented for payment; and, in default of such presentation, to direct any other mode and place of payment which he may deem proper; but, in all these regulations and directions, it shall be the duty of the Secretary of the Treasury to guard, as far as may be, against those drafts being used or thrown into circulation as a paper currency or medium of exchange. And no officer of the United States shall, either directly or indirectly, sell or dispose of to any person or persons, or corporations, whatsoever, for a premium, any Treasury note, draft, warrant, or other public security, not his private property, or sell or dispose of the avails or proceeds of such note, draft, warrant, or security in his hands for disbursement, without making return of such premium, and accounting therefor by charging the same in his accounts to the credit of the United States; and any officer violating this section shall be forthwith dismissed from office.

[SECS. 22 and 23 make provision for salaries and expenses of the offices; prohibit assistant treasurers from receiving commissions for services.]

[SEC. 24 repeals laws in conflict herewith.]

NOTE. — In appropriation and other acts, Congress authorized the establishment of other sub-treasuries, and a class of designated depositaries (individuals) at selected points. All of the latter were discontinued,—finally in 1879. Sub-treasuries now existing under the laws are located at Boston, New York, Philadelphia, Baltimore, Cincinnati, Chicago, St. Louis, New Orleans, and San Francisco. There is no longer any official connection with the mint offices as was originally the case.

Act of February 21, 1853 — *Amendatory of existing laws relative to the half dollar, quarter dollar, dime, and half dime*

Be it enacted, etc., That from and after the first day of June, 1853,[1] the weight of the half dollar, or piece of 50 cents, shall be 192 grains, and the quarter dollar, dime, and half dime, shall be, respectively, one-half, one-fifth, and one-tenth of the weight of said half dollar.

SEC. 2. That the silver coins issued in conformity with the above section, shall be legal tenders in payment of debts for all sums not exceeding $5.

SEC. 3. That in order to procure bullion for the requisite coinage of the subdivisions of the dollar authorized by this act, the Treasurer of the Mint shall, with the approval of

[1] By Sec. 7 of an Act of March 3, 1853, this act was made to take effect on April 1, 1853.

the Director, purchase such bullion with the bullion fund of the mint. He shall charge himself with the gain arising from the coinage of such bullion into coins of a nominal value exceeding the intrinsic value thereof, and shall be credited with the difference between such intrinsic value and the price paid for said bullion, and with the expense of distributing said coins as hereinafter provided. The balances to his credit, or the profit of said coinage, shall be, from time to time, on a warrant of the Director of the mint, transferred to the account of the Treasury of the United States.

SEC. 4. That such coins shall be paid out at the mint, in exchange for gold coins at par, in sums not less than $100; and it shall be lawful, also, to transmit parcels of the same, from time to time, to the assistant treasurers, depositaries, and other officers of the United States, under general regulations, proposed by the Director of the Mint, and approved by the Secretary of the Treasury: *Provided, however*, That the amount coined into quarter dollars, dimes, and half dimes, shall be regulated by the Secretary of the Treasury.

SEC. 5. That no deposits for coinage into the half dollar, quarter dollar, dime, and half dime, shall hereafter be received, other than those made by the Treasurer of the Mint, as herein authorized, and upon account of the United States.

[SEC. 6 provides for casting bars for depositors of bullion.]

[SEC. 7 provides for a $3 piece.]

SEC. 8. That this act shall be in force from and after the first day of June next.

Act of March 3, 1853 — [*Establishing assay office in New York City*]

*   *   *   *   *   *   *   *   *   *

SEC. 10. That the Secretary of the Treasury is hereby authorized and required to establish in the City of New York an office for the receipt and for the melting, refining, parting, and assaying of gold and silver bullion and foreign coin, and for casting the same into bars, ingots or disks. . . .

SEC. 11. That the owner or owners of any gold or silver bullion, in dust or otherwise, or of any foreign coin, shall be entitled to deposit the same in said office, and the treasurer thereof shall give a receipt, stating the weight and description thereof, in the manner and under the regulations that are or may be provided in like cases or deposits at the Mint of the United States with the treasurer thereof. And such bullion shall, without delay, be melted, parted, refined, and assayed, and the net value thereof, and of all foreign coins deposited in said office, shall be ascertained ; and the treasurer shall thereupon forthwith issue his certificate of the net value thereof, payable in coins of the same metal as that deposited, either at the office of the Assistant Treasurer of the United States, in New York, or at the Mint of the United States, at the option of the depositor, to be expressed in the certificate, which certificates shall be receivable at any time within sixty days from the date thereof in payment of all debts due to the United States at the port of New York for the full sum therein certified. . . .

Act of February 21, 1857 — *Relating to foreign coins, and to the coinage of cents*

Be it enacted, etc., That the pieces commonly known as the quarter, eighth, and sixteenth of the Spanish pillar dollar, and of the Mexican dollar, shall be receivable at the Treasury of the United States, and its several offices, and at the several post-offices, and land-offices, at the rates of valuation following, — that is to say, the fourth of a dollar, or piece of two reals, at 20 cents ; the eighth of a dollar, or piece of one real, at 10 cents ; and the sixteenth of a dollar, or half real, at 5 cents.

SEC. 2. That the said coins, when so received, shall not again be paid out, or put in circulation, but shall be recoined at the Mint. And it shall be the duty of the Director of the Mint, with the approval of the Secretary of the Treasury, to prescribe such regulations as may be necessary and proper, to secure their transmission to the Mint for recoinage, and the return or distribution of the proceeds thereof, when deemed expedient, and to prescribe such forms of account as may be appropriate and applicable to the circumstances : *Provided*, that the expenses incident to such transmission or distribution, and of recoinage, shall be charged against the account of silver profit and loss, and the net profits, if any, shall be paid from time to time into the Treasury of the United States.

SEC. 3. That all former acts authorizing the currency of foreign gold or silver coins, and declaring the same a legal tender in payment for debts, are hereby repealed ; but it shall be the duty of the director of the mint to cause assays to be made, from time to time, of such foreign coins as may be known to our commerce, to determine their average weight, fineness, and value, and to embrace in his annual report a statement of the results thereof.

[SECS. 4 to 7 relate to minor coins, etc.]

2 K

The *Act of December* 23, 1857, authorized issues of treasury notes for one year only, and for their reissue when received into the Treasury. The act contained no provisions not already in previous acts except to limit denominations to $100 and over.

Act of March 3, 1859 and

Act of June 22, 1860, extended the time limit of the issue.

The *Act of December* 17, 1860, practically re-enacted the provisions of the act of 1857, authorizing notes as low as $50.

Acts of February 8, 1861, and *March* 2, 1861, provided for bond issues to retire Treasury notes.

Act of July 17, 1861 — *To authorize a national loan, and for other purposes*

Be it enacted, etc. [Authorizes a loan of $250,000,000, in twenty-year bonds at 7 per cent. interest, or three-year treasury notes of denominations not less than $50, at 7.3 per cent. interest.] And the Secretary of the Treasury may also issue in exchange for coin, and as part of the above loan, or may pay for salaries or other dues from the United States, treasury notes of a less denomination than $50, not bearing interest, but payable on demand by the Assistant Treasurers of the United States at Philadelphia, New York, or Boston, or treasury notes bearing interest at the rate of 3.65 per centum, payable in one year from date, and exchangeable at any time for treasury notes for $50 and upwards, issuable under the authority of this act, and bearing interest as specified above : *Provided,* That no exchange of such notes in any less amount than $100 shall be made at any one time : *And provided further,* That no treasury notes shall be issued of a less denomination than $10,[1] and that the whole amount of treasury notes, not bearing interest, issued under the authority of this act, shall not exceed $50,000,000.

* * * * * * * * * *

SEC. 6. That whenever any treasury notes of a denomination less than $50, authorized to be issued by this act, shall have been redeemed, the Secretary of the Treasury may reissue the same, or may cancel them and issue new notes to an equal amount : *Provided,* That the aggregate amount of bonds and treasury notes issued under the foregoing provisions of this act shall never exceed the full amount authorized by the first section of this act ; and the power to issue or reissue such notes shall cease and determine after the 31st of December, 1862.

[1] Changed to $5 by Act of August 5, 1861, Sec. 3.

SEC. 7. That the Secretary of the Treasury is hereby authorized, whenever he shall deem it expedient, to issue in exchange for coin, or in payment for public debts, treasury notes of any of the denominations hereinbefore specified, bearing interest not exceeding 6 per centum per annum, and payable at any time not exceeding 12 months from date, provided that the amount of notes so issued, or paid, shall at no time exceed $20,000,000.

* * * * * * * * * *

Act of August 5, 1861 — [Amending the preceding act]

Be it enacted, etc., . . . any part of the Treasury notes payable on demand, authorized by said act [of July 17, 1861], may be made payable by the Assistant Treasurer at St. Louis, or by the depositary at Cincinnati.

[SEC. 2. How Treasury notes shall be signed.]

SEC. 3. That so much of the act to which this is supplementary as limits the denomination of a portion of the Treasury notes authorized by said act at not less than $10, be and is so modified as to authorize the Secretary of the Treasury to fix the denomination of said notes at not less than $5.

[SEC. 4. Appropriation of $100,000 for expenses.]

SEC. 5. That the Treasury notes authorized by the act to which this is supplementary, of a less denomination than $50, payable on demand without interest, and not exceeding in amount the sum of $50,000,000, shall be receivable in payment of public dues.

SEC. 6. That the provisions of the act entitled " An act to provide for the better organization of the Treasury, etc.," passed August 6, 1846, be and the same are hereby suspended, so far as to allow the Secretary of the Treasury to deposit any of the moneys obtained on any of the loans now authorized by law, to the credit of the Treasurer of the United States, in such solvent specie-paying banks as he may select ; and the said moneys, so deposited, may be withdrawn from such deposit for deposit with the regular authorized depositaries, or for the payment of public dues, or paid in redemption of the notes authorized to be issued under this act or the act to which this is supplementary, payable on demand, as may seem expedient to, or be directed by, the Secretary of the Treasury.

[SEC. 7. May sell bonds under Act of July 17, 1861, bearing not more than 6 per centum at rate not less than equivalent to 7 per centum bonds at par.]

Act of February 12, 1862 — Authorized an additional issue of $10,000,000 demand notes.

Act of February 25, 1862 — *To authorize the issue of United States notes, and for the redemption or funding thereof and for funding the floating debt of the United States*

Be it enacted, etc., That the Secretary of the Treasury is hereby authorized to issue, on the credit of the United States, $150,000,000 of United States notes, not bearing interest, payable to bearer, at the Treasury of the United States, and of such denominations as he may deem expedient, not less than $5 each : *Provided, however,* That fifty millions of said notes shall be in lieu of the demand Treasury notes authorized to be issued by the act of July 17, 1861 ; which said demand notes shall be taken up as rapidly as practicable, and the notes herein provided for substituted for them : *And provided further,* That the amount of the two kinds of notes together shall at no time exceed the sum of $150,000,000, and such notes herein authorized shall be receivable in payment of all taxes, internal duties, excises, debts, and demands of every kind due to the United States, except duties on imports, and of all claims and demands against the United States of every kind whatsoever, except for interest upon bonds and notes, which shall be paid in coin, and shall also be lawful money and a legal tender in payment of all debts, public and private, within the United States, except duties on imports and interest as aforesaid. And any holders of said United States notes depositing any sum not less than $50 or some multiple of $50, with the Treasurer of the United States, or either of the Assistant Treasurers, shall receive in exchange therefor duplicate certificates of deposit, one of which may be transmitted to the Secretary of the Treasury, who shall thereupon issue to the holder an equal amount of bonds of the United States, coupon or registered, as may by said holder be desired, bearing interest at the rate of 6 per centum per annum, payable semi-annually, and redeemable at the pleasure of the United States after 5 years, and payable 20 years from the date thereof. And such United States notes shall be received the same as coin, at their par value, in payment for any loans that may be hereafter sold or negotiated by the Secretary of the Treasury, and may be reissued from time to time as the exigencies of the public interest shall require.

SEC. 2. That, to enable the Secretary of the Treasury to fund the Treasury notes and floating debt of the United States, he is hereby authorized to issue, on the credit of the United States, coupon bonds or registered bonds, to an amount not exceeding $500,000,000, redeemable at the pleasure of the United States after 5 years, and payable 20 years from date, and bearing interest at the rate of 6 per centum per annum, payable semi-annually. And the bonds herein authorized shall be of such denominations, not less than $50, as may be determined upon by the Secretary of the Treasury. And the Secretary of the Treasury may dispose of such bonds at any time, at the market value thereof, for the coin of the United States, or for any of the Treasury notes that have been or may hereafter be issued under any former act of Congress, or for United States notes that may be issued under the provisions of this act ; and all stocks, bonds, and other securities of the United States held by individuals, corporations, or associations, within the United States, shall be exempt from taxation by or under State authority.

[SEC. 3. Form of bond ; how signed, etc. ; appropriation for expenses.]

SEC. 4. That the Secretary of the Treasury may receive from any person or persons, or any corporation, United States notes on deposit for not less than 30 days, in sums of not less than $100, with any of the Assistant Treasurers or designated depositaries of the United States authorized by the Secretary of the Treasury to receive them, who shall issue therefor certificates of deposit made in such form as the Secretary of the Treasury shall prescribe, and said certificates of deposit shall bear interest at the rate of 5 per centum per annum ; and any amount of United States notes so deposited may be withdrawn from deposit at any time after 10 days' notice on the return of said certificates : *Provided,* That the interest on all such deposits shall cease and determine at the pleasure of the Secretary of the Treasury : *And provided further,* That the aggregate of such deposit shall at no time exceed the amount of $25,000,000.[1]

SEC. 5. That all duties on imported goods shall be paid in coin, or in notes payable on demand heretofore authorized to be issued and by law receivable in payment of public dues, and the coin so paid shall be set apart as a special fund, and shall be applied as follows :

First. To the payment in coin of the interest on the bonds and notes of the United States.

---

[1] See increase to $50,000,000 by Act of March 17, 1862, Sec. 2, **and by** Act of July 11, 1862, Sec. 3, to $100,000,000.

Second. To the purchase or payment of one per centum of the entire debt of the United States, to be made within each fiscal year after the first day of July, 1862, which is to be set apart as a sinking fund, and the interest of which shall in like manner be applied to the purchase or payment of the public debt as the Secretary of the Treasury shall from time to time direct.

Third. The residue thereof to be paid into the Treasury of the United States.

[SECS. 6 and 7 prohibit, and provide penalties for, all counterfeiting, forging, etc.]

Act of March 1, 1862 — To authorize the Secretary of the Treasury to issue certificates of indebtedness to public creditors

Be it enacted, etc., That the Secretary of the Treasury be, and he is hereby authorized, to cause to be issued to any public creditor who may be desirous to receive the same, upon requisition of the head of the proper department, in satisfaction of audited and settled demands against the United States, certificates for the whole amount due, or parts thereof not less than $1000, signed by the Treasurer of the United States, and countersigned as may be directed by the Secretary of the Treasury; which certificates shall be payable in one year from date or earlier, at the option of the Government, and shall bear interest at the rate of 6 per centum per annum.

Act of March 17, 1862 — To authorize the purchase of coin, and for other purposes

Be it enacted, etc., That the Secretary of the Treasury may purchase coin with any of the bonds or notes of the United States, authorized by law, at such rates and upon such terms as he may deem most advantageous to the public interest ; and may issue, under such rules and regulations as he may prescribe, certificates of indebtedness, such as are authorized by an act entitled "An act to authorize the Secretary of the Treasury to issue certificates of indebtedness to public creditors," approved March 1st, 1862, to such creditors as may desire to receive the same, in discharge of checks drawn by disbursing-officers upon sums placed to their credit on the books of the Treasurer, upon requisitions of the proper departments, as well as in discharge of audited and settled accounts, as provided by said act.

SEC. 2. That the demand notes authorized by the act of

July 17, 1861, and the act of February 12, 1862, shall, in addition to being receivable in payment of duties on imports, be receivable, and shall be lawful money and a legal tender, in like manner, and for the same purposes, and to the same extent, as the notes authorized by an act entitled " An act to authorize the issue of United States notes," etc., approved February 25, 1862.

[SEC. 3 authorizes temporary deposits to an amount not exceeding $50,000,000, rates of interest prescribed by the Secretary of the Treasury not exceeding the annual rate of 5 per centum.]

SEC. 4. That, in all cases where the Secretary of the Treasury is authorized by law to reissue notes, he may replace such as are so mutilated or otherwise injured as to be unfit for use with others of the same character and amount ; and such mutilated notes, and all others which by law are required to be taken up and not reissued, shall, when so replaced, or taken up, be destroyed in such manner and under such regulations as the Secretary of the Treasury may prescribe.

Act of July 11, 1862 — *To authorize an additional issue of United States notes, and for other purposes*

Be it enacted, etc., That the Secretary of the Treasury is hereby authorized to issue, in addition to the amounts heretofore authorized, on the credit of the United States, $150,000,000 of United States notes, not bearing interest, payable to bearer at the treasury of the United States, and of such denominations as he may deem expedient: *Provided*, that no note shall be issued for the fractional part of a dollar, and not more than $35,000,000 shall be of lower denominations than $5 ; and such notes shall be receivable in payment of all loans made to the United States, and of all taxes, internal duties, excises, debts, and demands of every kind due to the United States, except duties on imports and interest, and of all claims and demands against the United States, except for interest upon bonds, notes, and certificates of debt or deposit ; and shall also be lawful money and a legal tender in payment of all debts, public and private, within the United States, except duties on imports and interest, as aforesaid. And any holder of said United States notes depositing any sum not less than $50, or some multiple of $50, with the Treasurer of the United States or either of the assistant treasurers, shall receive in exchange therefor duplicate certificates of deposit, one of which may be transmitted to the Secretary of the Treasury, who shall thereupon issue to the holder an equal amount of bonds of the United States, coupon or registered, as may by said holder be desired, bearing interest at the rate of 5 per centum per annum, payable semi-annually, and redeemable at the pleasure of the United States after 5 years, and payable 20 years from the date thereof : *Provided, however*, that any notes issued under this act may be paid in coin, instead of being received in exchange for certificates of deposit as above specified, at the direction of the Secretary of the Treasury. And the Secretary of the Treasury may exchange for such notes, on such terms as he shall think most beneficial to the public interest, any bonds of the United States bearing 6 per centum interest, and redeemable after 5 and payable in 20 years, which have been or may be lawfully issued under the provisions of any existing act ; may reissue the notes so received in exchange ; may receive and cancel any notes heretofore lawfully issued under any act of Congress, and in lieu thereof, issue an equal amount in notes such as are authorized by this act ; and, may purchase, at rates not exceeding that of the current market, and cost of purchase not exceeding one-eighth of one per centum, any bonds or certificates of debt of the United States as he may deem advisable.

[Sec. 2 relates to the printing and engraving of United States notes.]

Sec. 3. That the limitation upon temporary deposits of United States notes with any assistant treasurer, or designated depositary authorized by the Secretary of the Treasury to receive such deposits, to $50,000,000 be, and is hereby, repealed ; and the Secretary of the Treasury is authorized to receive such deposits, under such regulations as he may prescribe, to such amount as he may deem expedient, not exceeding $100,000,000, for not less than 30 days, in sums not less than $100, at a rate of interest not exceeding 5 per centum per annum ; and any amount so deposited may be withdrawn from deposit, at any time after 10 days' notice on the return of the certificate of deposit. And of the amount of United States notes authorized by this act, not less than $50,000,000 shall be reserved for the purpose of securing prompt payment of such deposits when demanded, and shall be issued and used only when, in the judgment of the Secretary of the Treasury, the same, or any part thereof may be needed for that purpose. And certificates of deposit and of indebtedness issued under this or former acts, may be received on the same terms as United States notes in payment for bonds redeemable after 5 and payable in 20 years.

[Sec. 4 relates to loans.]
[Sec. 5 makes appropriations for detecting counterfeiting.]

Act of July 17, 1862 — *To authorize payments in stamps, and to prohibit circulation of notes of less denomination than one dollar*

Be it enacted, etc., That the Secretary of the Treasury be, and he is hereby directed to furnish to the Assistant Treasurers, and such designated depositaries of the United States as may be by him selected, in such sums as he may deem expedient, the postage and other stamps of the United States to be exchanged by them, on application, for United States notes ; and from and after the first day of August next, such stamps shall be receivable in payment of all dues to the United States less than $5, and shall be received in exchange for United States notes when presented to any Assistant Treasurer or any designated depositary selected as aforesaid, in sums not less than $5.

SEC. 2. That from and after the first day of August, 1862, no private corporation, banking association, firm, or individual, shall make, issue, circulate, or pay any note, check, memorandum, token, or other obligation, for a less sum than $1, intended to circulate as money or to be received or used in lieu of lawful money of the United States ; and every person so offending shall, on conviction thereof, in any district or circuit court of the United States, be punished by fine not exceeding $500, or by imprisonment not exceeding six months, or by both, at the option of the court.

Joint Resolution of January 17, 1863 — *To provide for the immediate payment of the Army and Navy of the United States*

Whereas it is deemed expedient to make immediate provision for the payment of the army and navy ; therefore, *Be it resolved, etc.*, That the Secretary of the Treasury be, and he is hereby, authorized, if required by the exigencies of the public service, to issue on the credit of the United States the sum of $100,000,000 of United States notes, in such form as he may deem expedient, not bearing interest, payable to bearer, on demand, and of such denominations not less than $1, as he may prescribe, which notes so issued shall be lawful money and a legal tender, like the similar notes heretofore authorized in payment of all debts, public and private, within the United States, except for duties on imports and interest on the public debt ; and the notes so issued shall be part of the amount provided for in any bill now pending for the issue of Treasury notes, or that may be passed hereafter by this Congress.

Act of February 25, 1863 — To provide a national currency, secured by a pledge of United States stocks, and to provide for the circulation and redemption thereof

[NOTE. — This act was superseded by the act of June 3, 1864, the provisions of which were largely the same. The most important differences from the latter were the following:]

*   *   *   *   *   *   *   *   *   *

SEC. 17. That the entire amount of circulating notes to be issued under this act shall not exceed $300,000,000. $150,000,000 of which sum shall be apportioned to associations in the States, in the District of Columbia, and in the Territories, according to representative population, and the remainder shall be apportioned by the Secretary of the Treasury among associations formed in the several States, in the District of Columbia, and in the Territories, having due regard to the existing banking capital, resources, and business, of such States, District, and Territories.

*   *   *   *   *   *   *   *   *   *

SEC. 62. That any bank or banking association, authorized by any State law to engage in the business of banking, and duly organized under such State law at the time of the passage of this act, and which shall be the holder and owner of United States bonds to the amount of 50 per centum of its capital stock, may transfer and deliver to the Treasurer of the United States such bonds, or any part thereof, in the manner provided by this act; and upon making such transfer and delivery, such bank or banking association shall be entitled to receive from the Comptroller of the Currency, circulating notes, as herein provided, equal in amount to 80 per centum of the amount of the bonds so transferred and delivered.

SEC. 63. That upon the failure of any such State bank or banking association, to redeem any of its circulating notes issued under the provisions of the preceding section, the Comptroller of the Currency shall, when satisfied that such default has been made, and within thirty days after notice of such default, proceed to declare the bonds transferred and delivered to the treasurer, forfeited to the United States, and the same shall thereupon be forfeited accordingly. And thereupon the circulating notes which have been issued by such bank or banking association shall be redeemed and paid at the treasury of the United States in the same manner as other circulating notes issued under the provisions of this act are redeemed and paid.

SEC. 64. That the bonds forfeited, as provided in the last

preceding section, may be cancelled to an amount equal to the circulating notes redeemed and paid, or such bonds may be sold, under the direction of the Secretary of the Treasury, and after retaining out of the proceeds a sum sufficient to pay the whole amount of circulating notes for the redemption of which such bonds are held, the surplus, if any remains, shall be paid to the bank or banking association from which such bonds were received.

* * * * * * * * * *

Act of March 3, 1863 — To provide ways and means for the support of the Government

Be it enacted, etc. [Secretary authorized to borrow not more than $300,000,000 in fiscal year 1863, and $600,000,000 in fiscal year 1864, on ten-forty bonds at not more than 6 per cent. interest.] And all the bonds and Treasury notes or United States notes issued under the provisions of this act shall be exempt from taxation by or under State or municipal authority : *Provided*, That there shall be outstanding of bonds, treasury notes, and United States notes, at any time, issued under the provisions of this act, no greater amount altogether than the sum of $900,000,000.

SEC. 2. That the Secretary of the Treasury be, and he is hereby, authorized to issue, on the credit of the United States, $400,000,000 in treasury notes, payable at the pleasure of the United States, or at any such time or times not exceeding three years from date, as may be found most beneficial to the public interests, and bearing interest at a rate not exceeding 6 per centum per annum, payable at periods expressed on the face of said treasury notes ; and the interest on the said treasury notes and on certificates of indebtedness and deposit hereafter issued, shall be paid in lawful money. The treasury notes thus issued shall be of such denomination as the Secretary may direct, not less than $10, and may be disposed of on the best terms that can be obtained, or may be paid to any creditor of the United States willing to receive the same at par. And said treasury notes may be made a legal tender to the same extent as United States notes, for their face value, excluding interest ; or they may be made exchangeable under regulations prescribed by the Secretary of the Treasury, by the holder thereof, at the Treasury in the City of Washington, or at the office of any assistant treasurer or depositary designated for that purpose, for United States notes equal in amount to the Treasury notes offered for exchange, together with the interest accrued and due thereon at the date of interest payment next preceding such exchange. And in lieu of any amount of said treasury notes thus exchanged, or redeemed or paid at maturity, the Secretary may issue an equal amount of other treasury notes ; and the treasury notes so exchanged, redeemed, or paid, shall be cancelled and destroyed as the Secretary may direct. In order to secure certain and prompt exchanges of United States notes for Treasury notes, when required, as above provided, the Secretary shall have power to issue United States notes to the amount of $150,000,000, which may be used if necessary for such exchanges ; but no part of the United States notes authorized by this section shall be issued for or applied to any other purposes than said exchanges ; and whenever any amount shall have been so issued and applied, the same shall be replaced as soon as practicable from the sales of Treasury notes for United States notes.

SEC. 3. That the Secretary of the Treasury be, and he is hereby, authorized, if required by the exigencies of the public service, for the payment of the army and navy, and other creditors of the Government, to issue on the credit of the United States the sum of $150,000,000 of United States notes, including the amount of such notes heretofore authorized by the joint resolution approved January 17, 1863, in such form as he may deem expedient, not bearing interest, payable to bearer, and of such denominations, not less than $1, as he may prescribe, which notes so issued shall be lawful money and a legal tender in payment of all debts, public and private, within the United States, except for duties on imports and interest on the public debt ; and any of the said notes, when returned to the treasury, may be reissued from time to time as the exigencies of the public service may require. And in lieu of any of said notes, or any other United States notes, returned to the treasury, and cancelled or destroyed, there may be issued equal amounts of United States notes, such as are authorized by this act. And so much of the act to authorize the issue of United States notes, and for other purposes, approved February 25, 1862, and of the act to authorize an additional issue of United States notes, and for other purposes, approved July 11, 1862, as restricts the negotiation of bonds to market value, is hereby repealed. And the holders of United States notes, issued under and by virtue of said acts, shall present the same for the purpose of exchanging the same for bonds, as therein provided, on or before the first day of July, 1863, and thereafter the right so to exchange the same shall cease and determine.

SEC. 4. That in lieu of postage and revenue stamps for fractional currency, and of fractional notes, commonly called postage currency, issued or to be issued, the Secretary of the Treasury may issue fractional notes of like amounts in such form as he may deem expedient, and may provide for the engraving, preparation, and issue thereof in the treasury department building. And all such notes issued shall be exchangeable by the assistant-treasurers and designated depositaries for United States notes, in sums not less than $3, and shall be receivable for postage and revenue stamps, and also in payment of any dues to the United States less than $5, except duties on imports, and shall be redeemed on presentation at the treasury of the United States in such sums and under such regulations as the Secretary of the Treasury shall prescribe : *Provided,* That the whole amount of fractional currency issued, including postage and revenue stamps issued as currency, shall not exceed $50,000,000.

SEC. 5. That the Secretary of the Treasury is hereby authorized to receive deposits of gold coin and bullion with the treasurer or any assistant-treasurer of the United States, in sums not less than $20, and to issue certificates therefor, in denominations of not less than $20 each, corresponding with the denominations of the United States notes. The coin and bullion deposited for or representing the certificates of deposit shall be retained in the treasury for the payment of the same on demand. And certificates representing coin in the treasury may be issued in payment of interest on the public debt, which certificates, together with those issued for coin and bullion deposited, shall not at any time exceed 20 per centum beyond the amount of coin and bullion in the treasury ; and the certificates for coin or bullion in the Treasury shall be received at par in payments for duties on imports.

[SEC. 6. Form of bond and notes ; signatures, etc.]

SEC. 7. That all banks, associations, corporations, or individuals, issuing notes or bills for circulation as currency, shall be subject to and pay a duty of 1 per centum each half year from and after April 1, 1863, upon the average amount of circulation of notes or bills as currency issued beyond the amount hereinafter named, that is to say : banks, associations, corporations, or individuals, having a capital of not over $100,000, ninety per centum thereof; over $100,000 and not over $200,000, eighty per centum thereof; over $200,000 and not over $300,000, seventy per centum thereof; over $300,000 and not over $500,000, sixty per centum thereof; over $500,000 and not over $1,000,000, fifty per centum thereof; over $1,000,000 and not over $1,500,000, forty per centum thereof; over $1,500,000 and not over $2,000,000, thirty per centum

thereof; over $2,000,000, twenty-five per centum thereof. In
the case of banks with branches, the duty herein provided for
shall be imposed upon the circulation of the notes or bills of
such branches severally, and not upon the aggregate circulation
of all; and the amount of capital of each branch shall be considered to be the amount allotted to or used by such branch;
and all such banks, associations, corporations, and individuals
shall also be subject to and pay a duty of one half of one per
centum each half year from and after April 1, 1863, upon the
average amount of notes or bills not otherwise herein taxed and
outstanding as currency during the six months next preceding
the return hereinafter provided for; and the rates of tax or duty
imposed on the circulation of associations which may be organized under the act " to provide a national currency, secured by
a pledge of United States stocks, and to provide for the circulation and redemption thereof," approved Feb. 25, 1863,
shall be the same as that hereby imposed on the circulation
and deposits of all banks, associations, corporations, or individuals, but shall be assessed and collected as required by said
act; all banks, associations, or corporations, and individuals
issuing or reissuing notes or bills for circulation as currency
after April 1, 1863, in sums representing any fractional part of
a dollar, shall be subject to and pay a duty of five per centum
each half year thereafter upon the amount of such fractional
notes or bills so issued. And all banks, associations, corporations, and individuals receiving deposits of money subject to
payment on check or draft, except savings institutions, shall be
subject to a duty of one-eighth of one per centum each half
year from and after April 1, 1863, upon the average amount of
such deposits beyond the average amount of their circulating
notes or bills lawfully issued and outstanding as currency.

[The remainder of the section provides for forms of reports
and for penalties for non-compliance with the law.]

* * * * * * * * * *

*Act of June 3, 1864 — To provide a national currency, secured
by a pledge of United States bonds, and to provide for the
circulation and redemption thereof*

Be it enacted, etc., That there shall be established in the
Treasury Department a separate Bureau, which shall be charged
with the execution of this and all other laws that may be
passed by Congress respecting the issue and regulation of a
national currency secured by United States bonds. The chief

officer of the said Bureau shall be denominated the Comptroller of the Currency, and shall be under the general direction
of the Secretary of the Treasury. He shall be appointed by
the President, on the recommendation of the Secretary of the
Treasury, by and with the advice and consent of the Senate,
and shall hold his office for the term of 5 years unless sooner
removed by the President, upon reasons to be communicated
by him to the Senate ; he shall receive an annual salary of five
thousand dollars ; he shall have a competent deputy, appointed
by the Secretary, whose salary shall be $2,500,[1] and who shall
possess the power and perform the duties attached by law to
the office of Comptroller during a vacancy in such office and
during his absence or inability ; he shall employ, from time to
time, the necessary clerks to discharge such duties as he shall
direct, which clerks shall be appointed and classified by the
Secretary of the Treasury in the manner now provided by law.
Within 15 days from the time of notice of his appointment
the Comptroller shall take and subscribe the oath of office
prescribed by the Constitution and laws of the United States ;
and he shall give to the United States a bond in the penalty of
$100,000, with not less than two responsible sureties, to be
approved by the Secretary of the Treasury, conditioned for the
faithful discharge of the duties of his office. The deputy
comptroller so appointed shall also take the oath of office
prescribed by the Constitution and laws of the United States,
and shall give a like bond in the penalty of $50,000. The
Comptroller and deputy-comptroller shall not, either directly
or indirectly, be interested in any association issuing national
currency under the provisions of this act.

[SEC. 2 provides for a seal of office.]

[SEC. 3 provides for rooms for office in Treasury building.]

SEC. 4. That the term " United States bonds," as used in
this act, shall be construed to mean all registered bonds now
issued, or that may hereafter be issued, on the faith of the United
States by the Secretary of the Treasury in pursuance of law.

SEC. 5. That associations for carrying on the business of
banking may be formed by any number of persons, not less in
any case than 5, who shall enter into articles of association,
which shall specify in general terms the object for which the
association is formed, and may contain any other provisions,
not inconsistent with the provisions of this act, which the
association may see fit to adopt for the regulation of the business of the association and the conduct of its affairs, which

---

[1] Subsequently increased to $2,800.

said articles shall be signed by the persons uniting to form the association, and a copy of them forwarded to the Comptroller of the Currency, to be filed and preserved in his office.

SEC. 6. That the persons uniting to form such an association shall, under their hands, make an organization certificate, which shall specify —

I. The name assumed by such association, which name shall be subject to the approval of the Comptroller.

II. The place where its operations of discount and deposit are to be carried on, designating the State, Territory, or District, and also the particular county and city, town, or village.

III. The amount of its capital stock, and the number of shares into which the same shall be divided.

IV. The names and places of residence of the shareholders, and the number of shares held by each of them.

V. A declaration that said certificate is made to enable such persons to avail themselves of the advantages of this act.

The said certificate shall be acknowledged before a judge of some court of record or a notary public, and such certificate, with the acknowledgment thereof authenticated by the seal of such court or notary, shall be transmitted to the Comptroller of the Currency, who shall record and carefully preserve the same in his office. Copies of such certificate, duly certified by the Comptroller, and authenticated by his seal of office, shall be legal and sufficient evidence in all courts and places within the United States, or the jurisdiction of the Government thereof, of the existence of such association, and of every other matter or thing which could be proved by the production of the original certificate.

SEC. 7. That no association shall be organized under this act, with a less capital than $100,000, nor in a city whose population exceeds 50,000 persons, with a less capital than $200,000: *Provided,* That banks with a capital of not less than $50,000 may, with the approval of the Secretary of the Treasury, be organized in any place the population of which does not exceed 6000 inhabitants. [Amended March 14, 1900.]

SEC. 8. That every association formed pursuant to the provisions of this act shall, from the date of the execution of its organization certificate, be a body corporate, but shall transact no business except such as may be incidental to its organization and necessarily preliminary, until authorized by the Comptroller of the Currency to commence the business of banking. Such association shall have power to adopt a corporate seal, and shall have succession by the name designated in its organization certificate, for the period of 20 years from its organization, unless sooner dissolved according to the provisions of its articles of association, or by the act of its shareholders owning two thirds of its stock, or unless the franchise shall be forfeited by a violation of this act; by such name it may make contracts, sue and be sued, complain and defend, in any court of law and equity as fully as natural persons; it may elect or appoint directors, and by its board of directors appoint a president, vice-president, cashier, and other officers, define their duties, require bonds of them and fix the penalty thereof, dismiss said officers or any of them at pleasure, and appoint others to fill their places, and exercise under this act all such incidental powers as shall be necessary to carry on the business of banking by discounting and negotiating promissory notes, drafts, bills of exchange, and other evidences of debt; by receiving deposits; by buying and selling exchange, coin, and bullion; by loaning money on personal security; by obtaining, issuing, and circulating notes according to the provisions of this act; and its board of directors shall also have power to define and regulate by by-laws, not inconsistent with the provisions of this act, the manner in which its stock shall be transferred, its directors elected or appointed, its officers appointed, its property transferred, its general business conducted, and all the privileges granted by this act to associations organized under it shall be exercised and enjoyed; and its usual business shall be transacted at an office or banking house located in the place specified in its organization certificate.

Sec. 9. That the affairs of every association shall be managed by not less than 5 directors, one of whom shall be the president. Every director shall, during his whole term of service, be a citizen of the United States; and at least three fourths of the directors shall have resided in the State, Territory, or District in which such association is located one year next preceding their election as directors, and be residents of the same during their continuance in office. Each director shall own, in his own right, at least ten shares of the capital stock of the association of which he is a director. Each director, when appointed or elected, shall take an oath that he will, so far as the duty devolves on him, diligently and honestly administer the affairs of such association, and will not knowingly violate, or willingly permit to be violated, any of the provisions of this act, and that he is the bona fide owner, in his own right, of the number of shares of stock required by this act, subscribed by him, or standing in his name on the books of the association, and that the same is not hypothecated, or in any way pledged, as security for any loan or debt; which oath, subscribed by

2 L

himself, and certified by the officer before whom it is taken, shall be immediately transmitted to the Comptroller of the Currency, and by him filed and preserved in his office.

Sec. 10. That the directors of any association first elected or appointed shall hold their places until their successors shall be elected and qualified. All subsequent elections shall be held annually on such day in the month of January as may be specified in the articles of association; and the directors so elected shall hold their places for one year, and until their successors are elected and qualified. But any director ceasing to be the owner of the requisite amount of stock, or having in any other manner become disqualified, shall thereby vacate his place. Any vacancy in the board shall be filled by appointment by the remaining directors, and any director so appointed shall hold his place until the next election. If from any cause an election of directors shall not be made at the time appointed, the association shall not for that cause be dissolved, but an election may be held on any subsequent day, 30 days' notice thereof in all cases having been given in a newspaper published in the city, town, or county in which the association is located; and if no newspaper is published in such city, town, or county, such notice shall be published in a newspaper published nearest thereto. If the articles of association do not fix the day on which the election shall be held, or if the election should not be held on the day fixed, the day for the election shall be designated by the board of directors in their by-laws, or otherwise: *Provided*, That if the directors fail to fix the day, as aforesaid, shareholders representing two thirds of the shares may.

Sec. 11. That in all elections of directors, and in deciding all questions at meetings of shareholders, each shareholder shall be entitled to one vote on each share of stock held by him. Shareholders may vote by proxies duly authorized in writing; but no officer, clerk, teller, or book-keeper of such association shall act as proxy; and no shareholder whose liability is past due and unpaid shall be allowed to vote.

Sec. 12. That the capital stock of any association formed under this act shall be divided into shares of $100 each, and be deemed personal property and transferable on the books of the association in such manner as may be prescribed in the by-laws or articles of association; and every person becoming a shareholder by such transfer shall, in proportion to his shares, succeed to all the rights and liabilities of the prior holder of such shares, and no change shall be made in the articles of association by which the rights, remedies, or security of the existing creditors of the association shall be impaired. The shareholders of each association formed under the provisions of this act, and of each existing bank or banking association that may accept the provisions of this act, shall be held individually responsible, equally and ratably, and not one for another, for all contracts, debts, and engagements of such association to the extent of the amount of their stock therein at the par value thereof, in addition to the amount invested in such shares ; except that shareholders of any banking association now existing under State laws, having not less than $5,000,000 of capital actually paid in, and a surplus of 20 per centum on hand, both to be determined by the Comptroller of the Currency, shall be liable only to the amount invested in their shares ; and such surplus of 20 per centum shall be kept undiminished, and be in addition to the surplus provided for in this act ; and if at any time there shall be a deficiency in said surplus of 20 per centum, the said banking association shall not pay any dividends to its shareholders until such deficiency shall be made good ; and in case of such deficiency, the Comptroller of the Currency may compel said banking association to close its business and wind up its affairs under the provisions of this act. And the Comptroller shall have authority to withhold from an association his certificate authorizing the commencement of business, whenever he shall have reason to suppose that the shareholders thereof have formed the same for any other than the legitimate objects contemplated by this act.

SEC. 13. That it shall be lawful for any association formed under this act, by its articles of association, to provide for an increase of its capital from time to time, as may be deemed expedient, subject to the limitations of this act : *Provided,* That the maximum of such increase in the articles of association shall be determined by the Comptroller of the Currency ; and no increase of capital shall be valid until the whole amount of such increase shall be paid in, and notice thereof shall have been transmitted to the Comptroller of the Currency, and his certificate obtained specifying the amount of such increase of capital stock, with his approval thereof, and that it has been duly paid in as part of the capital of such association.[1] And every association shall have power, by the vote of shareholders owning two thirds of its capital stock, to reduce the capital of such association to any sum not below the amount required by this act, in the formation of associations : *Provided,* That by no such reduction shall its capi-

[1] Sec. 1 of the Act of May 1, 1886, amended the provision of this section to permit an increase of capital to any amount by a vote of two thirds of the stockholders and upon the approval of the Comptroller, regardless of the limit fixed in the original articles of association.

tal be brought below the amount required by this act for its outstanding circulation, nor shall any such reduction be made until
the amount of the proposed reduction has been reported to the
Comptroller of the Currency and his approval thereof obtained.

SEC. 14. That at least 50 per centum of the capital stock of
every association shall be paid in before it shall be authorized
to commence business ; and the remainder of the capital stock
of such association shall be paid in instalments of at least 10
per centum each on the whole amount of the capital as frequently as one instalment at the end of each succeeding month
from the time it shall be authorized by the Comptroller to commence business ; and the payment of each instalment shall be
certified to the Comptroller, under oath, by the president or
cashier of the association.

SEC. 15. That if any shareholder or his assignee, shall fail to
pay any instalment on the stock when the same is required by
the foregoing section to be paid, the directors of such association may sell the stock of such delinquent shareholder at public
auction, having given three weeks' previous notice thereof in a
newspaper published and of general circulation in the city or
county where the association is located, and if no newspaper is
published in said city or county, then in a newspaper published
nearest thereto, to any person who will pay the highest price
therefor, and not less than the amount then due thereon, with
the expenses of advertisement and sale ; and the excess, if any,
shall be paid to the delinquent shareholder. If no bidder can
be found who will pay for such stock the amount due thereon
to the association, and the cost of advertisement and sale, the
amount previously paid shall be forfeited to the association, and
such stock shall be sold as the directors may order, within 6
months from the time of such forfeiture, and if not sold it shall
be cancelled and deducted from the capital stock of the association ; and if such cancellation and reduction shall reduce the
capital of the association below the minimum of capital required
by this act, the capital stock shall, within 30 days from the
date of such cancellation, be increased to the requirements of
the act ; in default of which a receiver may be appointed to
close up the business of the association according to the provisions of the 50th section of this act.

SEC. 16. That every association, after having complied with
the provisions of this act, preliminary to the commencement of
banking business under its provisions, and before it shall be
authorized to commence business, shall transfer and deliver to
the Treasurer of the United States any United States registered
bonds bearing interest to an amount not less than $30,000 nor

less than one third of the capital stock paid in, which bonds shall be deposited with the Treasurer of the United States and by him safely kept in his office until the same shall be otherwise disposed of, in pursuance of the provisions of this act; and the Secretary of the Treasury is hereby authorized to receive and cancel any United States coupon bonds, and to issue in lieu thereof registered bonds of like amount, bearing a like rate of interest, and having the same time to run; and the deposit of bonds shall be, by every association, increased as its capital may be paid up or increased, so that every association shall at all times have on deposit with the Treasurer registered United States bonds to the amount of at least one third of its capital stock actually paid in: *Provided*, That nothing in this section shall prevent an association that may desire to reduce its capital or to close up its business and dissolve its organization from taking up its bonds upon returning to the Comptroller its circulating notes in the proportion hereinafter named in this act, nor from taking up any excess of bonds beyond one third of its capital stock and upon which no circulating notes have been delivered.[1]

Sec. 17. That whenever a certificate shall have been transmitted to the Comptroller of the Currency, as provided in this act, and the association transmitting the same shall notify the Comptroller that at least 50 per centum of its capital stock has been paid in as aforesaid, and that such association has complied with all the provisions of this act as required to be complied with before such association shall be authorized to commence the business of banking, the Comptroller shall examine into the condition of such association, ascertain especially the amount of money paid in on account of its capital, the name and place of residence of each of the directors of such association, and the amount of the capital stock of which each is the bona fide owner, and generally whether such association has complied with all the requirements of this act to entitle it to engage in the business of banking; and shall cause to be made and attested by the oaths of a majority of the directors and by the president or cashier of such association, a statement of all the facts necessary to enable the Comptroller to determine whether such association is lawfully entitled to commence the business of banking under this act.

Sec. 18. That if, upon a careful examination of the facts so reported, and of any other facts which may come to the knowledge of the Comptroller, whether by means of a special com-

[1] Amended by Acts of June 20, 1874, July 12, 1882, and March 14, 1900.

mission appointed by him for the purpose of inquiring into
the condition of such association, or otherwise, it shall appear
that such association is lawfully entitled to commence the business of banking, the Comptroller shall give to such association
a certificate, under his hand and official seal, that such association has complied with all the provisions of this act required
to be complied with before being entitled to commence the
business of banking under it, and that such association is
authorized to commence said business accordingly; and it
shall be the duty of the association to cause said certificate to
be published in some newspaper published in the city or
county where the association is located for at least 60 days
next after the issuing thereof : *Provided*, That if no newspaper is
published in such city or county the certificate shall be published in a newspaper published nearest thereto.

[SECS. 19 and 20 provide for method of transferring and
recording bonds.]

SEC. 21. That upon the transfer and delivery of bonds to
the Treasurer, as provided in the foregoing section, the association making the same shall be entitled to receive from the
Comptroller of the Currency circulating notes of different denominations, in blank, registered, and countersigned as hereinafter provided, equal in amount to 90 per centum of the
current market value of the United States bonds so transferred
and delivered, but not exceeding 90 per centum of the amount
of said bonds at the par value thereof, if bearing interest at a
rate not less than 5 per centum per annum [1]; and at no time
shall the total amounts of such notes, issued to any such association, exceed the amount at such time actually paid in of its
capital stock.

SEC. 22. That the entire amount of notes for circulation to
be issued under this act shall not exceed $300,000,000.[2] In
order to furnish suitable notes for circulation, the Comptroller
of the Currency is hereby authorized and required, under the
direction of the Secretary of the Treasury, to cause plates and
dies to be engraved, in the best manner to guard against counterfeiting and fraudulent alterations, and to have printed therefrom, and numbered, such quantity of circulating notes, in
blank, of the denominations of $1, $2, $3, $5, $10, $20, $50,
$100, $500, and $1000, as may be required to supply, under
this act, the associations entitled to receive the same ; which
notes shall express upon their face that they are secured by

[1] Amended by Acts of July 12, 1882, and March 14, 1900.
[2] See Acts of March 3, 1865, July 12, 1870, June 20, 1874, and January
14, 1875.

United States bonds, deposited with the Treasurer of the United States by the written or engraved signatures of the Treasurer and Register, and by the imprint of the seal of the Treasury ; and shall also express upon their face the promise of the association receiving the same to pay on demand, attested by the signatures of the president or vice-president and cashier. And the said notes shall bear such devices and such other statements, and shall be in such form, as the Secretary of the Treasury shall, by regulation, direct : *Provided,* That not more than one sixth part of the notes furnished to an association shall be of a less denomination than $5, and that after specie payments shall be resumed no association shall be furnished with notes of less denomination than $5. [Amended by Act of March 14, 1900.]

SEC. 23. That after any such association shall have caused its promise to pay such notes on demand to be signed by the president or vice-president and cashier thereof, in such manner as to make them obligatory promissory notes, payable on demand, at its place of business, such association is hereby authorized to issue and circulate the same as money ; and the same shall be received at par in all parts of the United States in payment of taxes, excises, public lands, and all other dues to the United States, except for duties on imports ; and also for all salaries and other debts and demands owing by the United States to individuals, corporations, and associations within the United States, except interest on the public debt, and in redemption of the national currency. And no such association shall issue post notes or any other notes to circulate as money than such as are authorized by the foregoing provisions of this act.

SEC. 24. That it shall be the duty of the Comptroller of the Currency to receive worn-out or mutilated circulating notes issued by any such banking association, and also, on due proof of the destruction of any such circulating notes, to deliver in place thereof to such association other blank circulating notes to an equal amount. And such worn-out or mutilated notes, after a memorandum shall have been entered in the proper books, in accordance with such regulations as may be established by the Comptroller, as well as all circulating notes which shall have been paid or surrendered to be cancelled, shall be burned to ashes in presence of four persons, one to be appointed by the Secretary of the Treasury, one by the Comptroller of the Currency, one by the Treasurer of the United States, and one by the association, under such regulations as the Secretary of the Treasury may prescribe. And a certificate of such burning, signed by the parties so appointed, shall be made in the books of the Comptroller, and a duplicate thereof forwarded to the association whose notes are thus cancelled.   [Amended by Acts of June 20 and June 23, 1874.]

SEC. 25.   That it shall be the duty of every banking association having bonds deposited in the office of the Treasurer of the United States, once or oftener in each fiscal year, and at such time or times during the ordinary business hours as said officer or officers may select, to examine and compare the bonds so pledged with the books of the Comptroller and the accounts of the association, and, if found correct, to execute to the said Treasurer a certificate setting forth the different kinds and the amounts thereof, and that the same are in the possession and custody of the Treasurer at the date of such certificate.   Such examination may be made by an officer or agent of such association, duly appointed in writing for that purpose, whose certificate before mentioned shall be of like force and validity as if executed by such president or cashier; and a duplicate signed by the Treasurer shall be retained by the association.

SEC. 26.   That the bonds transferred to and deposited with the Treasurer of the United States, as hereinbefore provided, by any banking association for the security of its circulating notes, shall be held exclusively for that purpose, until such notes shall be redeemed, except as provided in this act; but the Comptroller of the Currency shall give to any such banking association powers of attorney to receive and appropriate to its own use the interest on the bonds which it shall have so transferred to the Treasurer; but such powers shall become inoperative whenever such banking association shall fail to redeem its circulating notes as aforesaid.   Whenever the market or cash value of any bonds deposited with the Treasurer of the United States, as aforesaid, shall be reduced below the amount of the circulation issued for the same, the Comptroller of the Currency is hereby authorized to demand and receive the amount of such depreciation in other United States bonds at cash value, or in money, from the association receiving said bills, to be deposited with the Treasurer of the United States as long as such depreciation continues.   And said Comptroller, upon the terms prescribed by the Secretary of the Treasury, may permit an exchange to be made of any of the bonds deposited with the Treasurer by an association for other bonds of the United States authorized by this act to be received as security for circulating notes, if he shall be of opinion that such an exchange can be made without prejudice to the United States, and he may direct the return of any of said bonds to the banking association which transferred the same, in sums of not less than $1000, upon the surrender to him and the cancellation of a proportionate amount of such circulating notes [1] : *Provided,* That the remaining bonds which shall have been transferred by the banking association offering to surrender circulating notes shall be equal to the amount required for the circulating notes not surrendered by such banking association, and that the amount of bonds in the hands of the Treasurer shall not be diminished below the amount required to be kept on deposit with him by this act : *And provided,* That there shall have been no failure by such association to redeem its circulating notes, and no other violation by such association of the provisions of this act, and that the market or cash value of the remaining bonds shall not be below the amount required for the circulation issued for the same.

SEC. 27. That it shall be unlawful for any officer acting under the provisions of this act to countersign or deliver to any association, or to any other company or person, any circulating notes contemplated by this act, except as hereinbefore provided, and in accordance with the true intent and meaning of this act. And any officer who shall violate the provisions of this section shall be deemed guilty of a high misdemeanor, and on conviction thereof shall be punished by fine not exceeding double the amount so countersigned and delivered, and imprisonment not less than one year and not exceeding 15 years, at the discretion of the court in which he shall be tried.

SEC. 28. That it shall be lawful for any such association to purchase, hold, and convey real estate as follows :

I. Such as shall be necessary for its immediate accommodation in the transaction of its business.

II. Such as shall be mortgaged to it in good faith by way of security for debts previously contracted.

III. Such as shall be conveyed to it in satisfaction of debts previously contracted in the course of its dealings.

IV. Such as it shall purchase at sales under judgments, decrees, or mortgages held by such association, or shall purchase to secure debts due to said association.

Such association shall not purchase or hold real estate in any other case or for any other purpose than as specified in this section. Nor shall it hold the possession of any real estate under mortgage, or hold the title and possession of any real estate purchased to secure any debts due to it for a longer period than five years.

SEC. 29. That the total liabilities to any association, of any person, or of any company, corporation, or firm for money borrowed, including in the liabilities of a company or firm the

[1] See Acts of June 20, 1874; and July 12, 1882.

liabilities of the several members thereof, shall at no time exceed one tenth part of the amount of the capital stock of such association actually paid in : *Provided*, That the discount of bona fide bills of exchange drawn against actually existing values, and the discount of commercial or business paper actually owned by the person or persons, corporation, or firm negotiating the same shall not be considered as money borrowed.

SEC. 30. That every association may take, receive, reserve, and charge on any loan or discount made, or upon any note, bill of exchange, or other evidences of debt, interest at the rate allowed by the laws of the State or Territory where the bank is located, and no more, except that where by the laws of any State a different rate is limited for banks of issue organized under State laws, the rate so limited shall be allowed for associations organized in any such State under this act. And when no rate is fixed by the laws of the State or Territory, the bank may take, receive, reserve, or charge a rate not exceeding 7 per centum, and such interest may be taken in advance, reckoning the days for which the note, bill, or other evidence of debt has to run. And the knowingly taking, receiving, reserving, or charging a rate of interest greater than aforesaid shall be held and adjudged a forfeiture of the entire interest which the note, bill, or other evidence of debt carries with it, or which has been agreed to be paid thereon. And in case a greater rate of interest has been paid, the person or persons paying the same, or their legal representatives may recover back, in any action of debt, twice the amount of the interest thus paid from the association taking or receiving the same : *Provided*, That such action is commenced within two years from the time the usurious transaction occurred. But the purchase, discount, or sale of a bona fide bill of exchange, payable at another place than the place of such purchase, discount, or sale, at not more than the current rate of exchange for sight drafts in addition to the interest, shall not be considered as taking or receiving a greater rate of interest.

SEC. 31. That every association in the cities hereinafter named shall, at all times, have on hand, in lawful money of the United States, an amount equal to at least 25 per centum of the aggregate amount of its notes in circulation and its deposits ; and every other association shall, at all times, have on hand, in lawful money of the United States, an amount equal to at least 15 per centum of the aggregate amount of its notes in circulation, and of its deposits.[1]   And whenever the

---

[1] Amended by Act of June 20, 1874. See also Act of March 2, 1867.

lawful money of any association in any of the cities hereinafter named shall be below the amount of 25 per centum of its circulation and deposits, and whenever the lawful money of any other association shall be below 15 per centum of its circulation and deposits, such association shall not increase its liabilities by making any new loans or discounts otherwise than by discounting or purchasing bills of exchange payable at sight, nor make any dividend of its profits until the required proportion between the aggregate amount of its outstanding notes of circulation and deposits and its lawful money of the United States shall be restored : *Provided,* That three fifths of said 15 per centum may consist of balances due to an association available for the redemption of its circulating notes from associations approved by the Comptroller of the Currency, organized under this act, in the cities of Saint Louis, Louisville, Chicago, Detroit, Milwaukee, New Orleans, Cincinnati, Cleveland, Pittsburg, Baltimore, Philadelphia, Boston, New York, Albany, Leavenworth, San Francisco, and Washington City : [1] *Provided, also,* That clearing-house certificates representing specie or lawful money specially deposited for the purpose of any clearing-house association, shall be deemed to be lawful money in the possession of any association belonging to such clearing-house holding and owning such certificate, and shall be considered to be a part of the lawful money which such association is required to have under the foregoing provisions of this section : *Provided,* That the cities of Charleston and Richmond may be added to the list of cities in the national associations of which other associations may keep three fifths of their lawful money, whenever, in the opinion of the Comptroller of the Currency, the condition of the Southern States will warrant it. And it shall be competent for the Comptroller of the Currency to notify any association, whose lawful money reserve as aforesaid shall be below the amount to be kept on hand as aforesaid, to make good such reserve ; and if such association shall fail for 30 days thereafter so to make good its reserve of lawful money of the United States, the Comptroller may, with the concurrence of the Secretary of the Treasury, appoint a receiver to wind up the business of such association, as provided in this act.

Sec. 32. That each association organized in any of the cities named in the foregoing section shall select, subject to the approval of the Comptroller of the Currency, an association in the city of New York, at which it will redeem its circulating notes

---

[1] Reserve cities increased by Act of March 3, 1887.

at par.[1] And each of such associations may keep one half of its lawful money reserve in cash deposits in the city of New York. And each association not organized within the cities named in the preceding section shall select, subject to the approval of the Comptroller of the Currency, an association in either of the cities named in the preceding section at which it will redeem its circulating notes at par, and the Comptroller shall give public notice of the names of the associations so selected at which redemptions are to be made by the respective associations, and of any change that may be made of the association at which the notes of any association are redeemed.   If any association shall fail either to make the selection or to redeem its notes as aforesaid, the Comptroller of the Currency may, upon receiving satisfactory evidence thereof, appoint a receiver, in the manner provided for in this act, to wind up its affairs : *Provided,* That nothing in this section shall relieve any association from its liability to redeem its circulating notes at its own counter, at par, in lawful money, on demand : *And provided, further,* That every association formed or existing under the provisions of this act shall take and receive at par, for any debt or liability to said association, any and all notes or bills issued by any association existing under and by virtue of this act.

SEC. 33. That the directors of any association may, semi-annually, each year, declare a dividend of so much of the nett profits of the association as they shall judge expedient ; but each association shall, before the declaration of a dividend, carry one tenth part of its nett profits of the preceding half year to its surplus fund until the same shall amount to 20 per centum of its capital stock.

SEC. 34. That every association shall make to the Comptroller of the Currency a report, according to the form which may be prescribed by him, verified by the oath or affirmation of the president or cashier of such association ; which report shall exhibit in detail, and under appropriate heads, the resources and liabilities of the association before the commencement of business on the morning of the first Monday of the months of January, April, July, and October of each year, and shall transmit the same to the Comptroller within 5 days thereafter. And any bank failing to make and transmit such report shall be subject to a penalty of $100 for each day after 5 days that such report is delayed beyond that time. And the Comptroller shall publish abstracts of said reports in a newspaper to be designated

[1] Amended by Act of June 20, 1874. Changed under operation of Act of March 3, 1887 ; Chicago and St. Louis added.

by him for that purpose in the city of Washington, and the separate report of each association shall be published in a newspaper in the place where such association is established, or if there be no newspaper at such place, then in a newspaper published at the nearest place thereto, at the expense of the association making such report. In addition to the quarterly reports required by this section, every association shall, on the first Tuesday of each month, make to the Comptroller of the Currency a statement, under the oath of the president or cashier, showing the condition of the association making such statement, on the morning of the day next preceding the date of such statement, in respect to the following items and particulars, to wit : average amount of loans and discounts, specie, and other lawful money belonging to the association, deposits, and circulation. And associations in other places than those cities named in the 31st section of this act shall also return the amount due them available for the redemption of their circulation.[1]

SEC. 35. That no association shall make any loan or discount on the security of the shares of its own capital stock, nor be the purchaser or holder of any such shares, unless such security or purchase shall be necessary to prevent loss upon a debt previously contracted in good faith ; and stock so purchased or acquired shall, within 6 months from the time of its purchase, be sold or disposed of at public or private sale, in default of which a receiver may be appointed to close up the business of the association, according to the provisions of this act.

SEC. 36. That no association shall at any time be indebted, or in any way liable, to an amount exceeding the amount of its capital stock at such time actually paid in and remaining undiminished by losses or otherwise, except on the following accounts, that is to say : —

I. On account of its notes of circulation.

II. On account of moneys deposited with, or collected by, such association.

III. On accounts of bills of exchange or drafts drawn against money actually on deposit to the credit of such association, or due thereto.

IV. On account of liabilities to its stockholders for dividends and reserved profits.

SEC. 37. That no association shall, either directly or indirectly, pledge or hypothecate any of its notes of circulation, for the purpose of procuring money to be paid in on its capital stock,

---

[1] Act of March 3, 1869, amends form of and manner of making reports.

or to be used in its banking operations, or otherwise ; nor shall any association use its circulating notes, or any part thereof, in any manner or form, to create or increase its capital stock.

SEC. 38. That no association, or any member thereof, shall, during the time it shall continue its banking operations, withdraw, or permit to be withdrawn, either in form of dividends or otherwise, any portion of its capital. And if losses shall at any time have been sustained by any such association equal to or exceeding its undivided profits then on hand, no dividend shall be made ; and no dividend shall ever be made by any association, while it shall continue its banking operations, to an amount greater than its nett profits then on hand, deducting therefrom its losses and bad debts. And all debts due to any association, on which interest is past due and unpaid for a period of 6 months, unless the same shall be well secured, and shall be in process of collection, shall be considered bad debts within the meaning of this act : *Provided*, That nothing in this section shall prevent the reduction of the capital stock of the association under the 13th section of this act.

SEC. 39. That no association shall at any time pay out on loans or discounts, or in purchasing drafts or bills of exchange, or in payment of deposits, or in any other mode pay or put in circulation the notes of any bank or banking association which shall not, at any such time, be receivable, at par, on deposit and in payment of debts by the association so paying out or circulating such notes ; nor shall it knowingly pay out or put in circulation any notes issued by any bank or banking association which at the time of such paying out or putting in circulation is not redeeming its circulating notes in lawful money of the United States.

SEC. 40. That the president and cashier of every such association shall cause to be kept at all times a full and correct list of the names and residences of all the shareholders in the association, and the number of shares held by each, in the office where its business is transacted ; and such list shall be subject to the inspection of all the shareholders and creditors of the association, and the officers authorized to assess taxes under State authority, during business hours of each day in which business may be legally transacted ; and a copy of such list, on the first Monday of July in each year, verified by the oath of such president or cashier, shall be transmitted to the Comptroller of the Currency.

SEC. 41. That the plates and special dies to be procured by the Comptroller of the Currency for the printing of such circulating notes shall remain under his control and direction, and the expenses necessarily incurred in executing the provisions of this act respecting the procuring of such notes, and all other expenses of the Bureau, shall be paid out of the proceeds of the taxes on duties now or hereafter to be assessed on the circulation, and collected from associations organized under this act. And in lieu of all existing taxes, every association shall pay to the Treasurer of the United States, in the months of January and July, a duty of one half of one per centum each half year from and after the 1st of January, 1864, upon the average amount of its notes in circulation, and a duty of one-quarter of one per centum each half year upon the average amount of its deposits, and a duty of one-quarter of one per centum each half year, as aforesaid, on the average amount of its capital stock beyond the amount invested in United States bonds; [1] and in case of default in the payment thereof of any association, the duties aforesaid may be collected in the manner provided for the collection of United States duties of other corporations, or the Treasurer may reserve the amount of said duties out of the interest, as it may become due, on the bonds deposited with him by such defaulting association. And it shall be the duty of each association, within 10 days from the first days of January and July of each year, to make a return, under the oath of its president or cashier, to the Treasurer of the United States, in such form as he may prescribe, of the average amount of its notes in circulation, and of the average amount of its deposits, and of the average amount of its capital stock, beyond the amount invested in United States bonds, for the 6 months next preceding said first days of January and July as aforesaid, and in default of such return, and for each default thereof, each defaulting association shall forfeit and pay to the United States the sum of $200, to be collected either out of the interest as it may become due such association on the bonds deposited with the Treasurer, or, at his option, in the manner in which penalties are to be collected of other corporations under the laws of the United States ; and in case of such default the amount of the duties to be paid by such association shall be assessed upon the amount of notes delivered to such association by the Comptroller of the Currency, and upon the highest amount of its deposits and capital stock, to be ascertained in such other manner as the Treasurer may deem best : *Provided*, That nothing in this act shall be construed to prevent all the shares in any of the said associations, held by any per-

---

[1] Amended by Acts of March 3, 1883, and March 14, 1900.

son or body corporate, from being included in the valuation of
the personal property of such person or corporation in the assessment of taxes imposed by or under State authority at the place
where such bank is located, and not elsewhere, but not at a
greater rate than is assessed upon other moneyed capital in the
hands of individual citizens of such State : *Provided, further,*
That the tax so imposed under the laws of any State upon the
shares of any of the associations authorized by this act shall not
exceed the rate imposed upon the shares in any of the banks
organized under authority of the State where such association
is located : *Provided, also,* That nothing in this act shall exempt
the real estate of associations from either State, county, or
municipal taxes to the same extent, according to its value, as
other real estate is taxed.

SEC. 42. That any association may go into liquidation and
be closed by the vote of its shareholders owning two thirds of
its stock.[1]   And whenever such vote shall be taken it shall be
the duty of the board of directors to cause notice of this fact
to be certified, under the seal of the association, by its president
or cashier, to the Comptroller of the Currency, and publication
thereof to be made for a period of two months in a newspaper
published in the city of New York, and also in a newspaper
published in a city or town in which the association is located,
and if no newspaper be there published, then in the newspaper
published nearest thereto, that said association is closing up its
affairs, and notifying the holders of its notes and other creditors
to present the notes and other claims against the association for
payment.   And at any time after the expiration of one year from
the time of the publication of such notice as aforesaid, the said
association may pay over to the Treasurer of the United States
the amount of its outstanding notes in the lawful money of the
United States, and take up the bonds which said association has
on deposit with the Treasurer for the security of its circulating
notes ;[2] which bonds shall be assigned to the bank in the manner
specified in the 19th section of this act, and from that time the
outstanding notes of said association shall be redeemed at the
Treasury of the United States, and the said association and
the shareholders thereof shall be discharged from all liabilities
therefor.

SEC. 43. That the Treasurer, on receiving from an association lawful money for the payment and redemption of its
outstanding notes, as provided for in the preceding section of
this act, shall execute duplicate receipts therefor, one to the

[1] See Act of July 14, 1870.
[2] See Act of July 12, 1882.

association and the other to the Comptroller of the Currency, stating the amount received by him, and the purpose for which it has been received, which amount shall be paid into the Treasury of the United States, and placed to the credit of such association upon redemption account. And it shall be the duty of the Treasurer, whenever he shall redeem any of the notes of said association, to cause the same to be mutilated, and charged to the redemption account of said association; and all notes so redeemed by the Treasurer shall, every three months, be certified to and burned in the manner prescribed in the twenty-fourth section of this act.[1]

SEC. 44. That any bank incorporated by special law, or any banking institution organized under a general law of any State, may, by authority of this act, become a national association under its provisions, by the name prescribed in its organization certificate ; and in such case the articles of association and the organization certificate required by this act may be executed by a majority of the directors of the bank or banking institution ; and said certificate shall declare that the owners of two-thirds of the capital stock have authorized the directors to make such certificate and to change and convert the said bank or banking institution into a national association under this act. And a majority of the directors, after executing said articles of association and organization certificate, shall have power to execute all other papers, and to do whatever may be required to make its organization perfect and complete as a national association.[2] The shares of any such bank may continue to be for the same amount each as they were before said conversion, and the directors aforesaid may be the directors of the association until others are elected or appointed in accordance with the provisions of this act; and any state bank which is a stockholder in any other bank, by authority of state laws, may continue to hold its stock, although either bank, or both, may be organized under and have accepted the provisions of this act. When the comptroller shall give to such association a certificate, under his hand and official seal, that the provisions of this act have been complied with, and that it is authorized to commence the business of banking under it, the association shall have the same powers and privileges, and shall be subject to the same duties, responsibilities, and rules, in all respects as are prescribed in this act for other associations organized under it, and shall be held and regarded as an association under this act : *Provided,*

---

[1] Maceration in lieu of burning provided for June 23, 1874.
[2] See Act of March 3, 1865, as to banks with branches.

2 M

however, That no such association shall have a less capital than the amount prescribed for banking associations under this act.

SEC. 45. That all associations under this act, when designated for that purpose by the Secretary of the Treasury, shall be depositaries of public money, except receipts from customs, under such regulations as may be prescribed by the Secretary; and they may also be employed as financial agents of the Government; and they shall perform all such reasonable duties, as depositaries of public moneys and financial agents of the Government, as may be required of them. And the Secretary of the Treasury shall require of the associations thus designated satisfactory security, by the deposit of United States bonds and otherwise, for the safe-keeping and prompt payment of the public money deposited with them, and for the faithful performance of their duties as financial agents of the Government: *Provided*, That every association which shall be selected and designated as receiver or depositary of the public money shall take and receive at par all of the national currency bills, by whatever association issued, which have been paid into the Government for internal revenue, or for loans or stocks.

SEC. 46. That if any such association shall at any time fail to redeem, in the lawful money of the United States, any of its circulating notes, when payment thereof shall be lawfully demanded, during the usual hours of business, at the office of such association, or at its place of redemption aforesaid, the holder may cause the same to be protested, in one package, by a notary-public, unless the president or cashier of the association whose notes are presented for payment, or the president or cashier of the association at the place at which they are redeemable, shall offer to waive demand and notice of the protest, and shall, in pursuance of such offer, make, sign, and deliver to the party making such demand an admission in writing, stating the time of the demand, the amount demanded, and the fact of the non-payment thereof; and such notary-public, on making such protest, or upon receiving such admission, shall forthwith forward such admission or notice of protest to the Comptroller of the Currency, retaining a copy thereof. And after such default, on examination of the facts by the Comptroller, and notice by him to the association, it shall not be lawful for the association suffering the same to pay out any of its notes, discount any notes or bills, or otherwise prosecute the business of banking, except to receive and safely keep money belonging to it, and to deliver special deposits: *Provided*, That if satisfactory proof be produced to such notary-public that the payment of any such notes is restrained by order of any court of competent jurisdiction, such notary-public shall not protest the same ; and when the holder of such notes shall cause more than one note or package to be protested on the same day, he shall not receive pay for more than one protest.

SEC. 47. That on receiving notice that any such association has failed to redeem any of its circulating notes, as specified in the next preceding section, the Comptroller of the Currency, with the concurrence of the Secretary of the Treasury, may appoint a special agent (of whose appointment immediate notice shall be given to such association) who shall immediately proceed to ascertain whether such association has refused to pay its circulating notes in the lawful money of the United States, when demanded as aforesaid, and report to the Comptroller the fact so ascertained ; and if, from such protest or the report so made, the Comptroller shall be satisfied that such association has refused to pay its circulating notes as aforesaid and is in default, he shall, within 30 days after he shall have received notice of such failure, declare the United States bonds and securities pledged by such association forfeited to the United States, and the same shall thereupon be forfeited accordingly. And thereupon the Comptroller shall immediately give notice in such manner as the Secretary of the Treasury shall, by general rules or otherwise, direct, to the holders of the circulating notes of such association to present them for payment at the Treasury of the United States, and the same shall be paid as presented in lawful money of the United States ; whereupon said Comptroller may, in his discretion, cancel an amount of bonds pledged by such association equal at current market rates, not exceeding par, to the notes paid. And it shall be lawful for the Secretary of the Treasury, from time to time, to make such regulations respecting the disposition to be made of such circulating notes after presentation thereof for payment as aforesaid, and respecting the perpetuation of the evidence of the payment thereof as may seem to him proper ; but all such notes, on being paid, shall be cancelled. And for any deficiency in the proceeds of the bonds pledged by such association, when disposed of as hereinafter specified, to reimburse to the United States the amount so expended in paying the circulating notes of such association, the United States shall have a first and paramount lien upon all the assets of such association ; and such deficiency shall be made good out of such assets in preference to any and all other claims whatsoever, except the necessary costs and expenses of administering the same.

SEC. 48. That whenever the Comptroller shall become satisfied, as in the last preceding section specified, that any association has refused to pay its circulating notes as therein mentioned, he may, instead of cancelling the United States bonds pledged by such association, as provided in the next preceding section, cause so much of them as may be necessary to redeem the outstanding circulating notes of such association to be sold at public auction in the city of New York, after giving 30 days' notice of such sale to such association.

SEC. 49. That the Comptroller of the Currency may, if he shall be of opinion that the interests of the United States will be best promoted thereby, sell at private sale any of the bonds pledged by such association, and receive therefor either money or the circulating notes of such failing association : *Provided*, That no such bonds shall be sold by private sale for less than par, nor less than the market value thereof at the time of sale : *And provided, further*, That no sales of any such bonds, either public or private, shall be complete until the transfer thereof shall have been made with the formalities prescribed in this act.

SEC. 50. That on becoming satisfied, as specified in this act, that any association has refused to pay its circulating notes as therein mentioned, and is in default, the Comptroller of the Currency may forthwith appoint a receiver, and require of him such bond and security as he shall deem proper, who, under the direction of the Comptroller, shall take possession of the books, records, and assets of every description of such association, collect all debts, dues, and claims belonging to such association, and, upon the order of a court of record of competent jurisdiction, may sell or compound all bad or doubtful debts, and, on a like order, sell all the real and personal property of such association, on such terms as the court shall direct ; and may, if necessary to pay the debts of such association, enforce the individual liability of the stockholders provided for by the 12th section of this act ; and such receiver shall pay over all money so made to the Treasurer of the United States, subject to the order of the Comptroller of the Currency, and also make report to the Comptroller of the Currency of all his acts and proceedings. The Comptroller shall thereupon cause notice to be given, by advertisement in such newspapers as he may direct, for three consecutive months, calling on all persons who may have claims against such association to present the same, and to make legal proof thereof. And from time to time the Comptroller, after full provision shall have been first made for refunding to the United States any such deficiency in redeeming the notes of such association as is mentioned in this act, shall make a ratable dividend of the money so paid over to him by such receiver on all such claims as may have been proved to his satisfaction or adjudicated in a court of competent jurisdiction ; and from time to time, as the proceeds of the assets of such association shall be paid over to him, he shall make further dividends, as aforesaid, on all claims previously proved or adjudicated ; and the remainder of such proceeds, if any, shall be paid over to the shareholders of such association, or their legal representatives, in proportion to the stock by them respectively held : *Provided, however,* That if such association against which proceedings have been so instituted, on account of any alleged refusal to redeem its circulating notes as aforesaid, shall deny having failed to do so, such association may, at any time within ten days after such association shall have been notified of the appointment of an agent, as provided in this act, apply to the nearest circuit, or district, or Territorial court of the United States, to enjoin further proceedings in the premises ; and such court, after citing the Comptroller of the Currency to show cause why further pro-ceedings should not be enjoined, and after the decision of the court or finding of a jury that such association has not refused to redeem its circulating notes, when legally presented, in the lawful money of the United States, shall make an order enjoin-ing the Comptroller, and any receiver acting under his direction, from all further proceedings on account of such alleged refusal.

SEC. 51. That all fees for protesting the notes issued by any such banking association shall be paid by the person procuring the protest to be made, and such banking association shall be liable therefor ; but no part of the bonds pledged by such banking association, as aforesaid, shall be applied to the pay-ment of such fees. And all expenses of any preliminary or other examinations into the condition of any association shall be paid by such association ; and all expenses of any receiver-ship shall be paid out of the assets of such association before distribution of the proceeds thereof.

SEC. 52. That all transfer of the notes, bonds, bills of exchange, and other evidences of debt owing to any associa-tion, or of deposits to its credit ; all assignments of mortgages, sureties on real estate, or of judgments or decrees in its favor ; all deposits of money, bullion, or other valuable thing for its use ; or for the use of any of its shareholders or creditors ; and all payments of money to either, made after the commis-sion of an act of insolvency, or in contemplation thereof, with a view to prevent the application of its assets in the manner prescribed by this act, or with a view to the preference of one creditor to another, except in payment of its circulating notes, shall be utterly null and void.

SEC. 53. That if the directors of any association shall knowingly violate, or knowingly permit any of the officers, agents, or servants of the association to violate any of the provisions of this act, all the rights, privileges, and franchises of the association derived from this act shall be thereby forfeited. Such violation shall, however, be determined and adjudged by a proper circuit, district, or Territorial court of the United States, in a suit brought for that purpose by the Comptroller of the Currency, in his own name, before the association shall be declared dissolved. And in cases of such violation, every director who participated in or assented to the same shall be held liable in his personal and individual capacity for all damages which the association, its shareholders, or any other person, shall have sustained in consequence of such violation.

SEC. 54. That the Comptroller of the Currency, with the approbation of the Secretary of the Treasury, as often as shall be deemed necessary or proper, shall appoint a suitable person or persons to make an examination of the affairs of every banking association, which person shall not be a director or other officer in any association whose affairs he shall be appointed to examine, and who shall have power to make a thorough examination into all the affairs of the association, and, in doing so, to examine any of the officers and agents thereof on oath; and shall make a full and detailed report of the condition of the association to the Comptroller. And the association shall not be subject to any other visitorial powers than such as are authorized by this act, except such as are vested in the several courts of law and chancery. And every person appointed to make such examination shall receive for his services at the rate of $5 for each day by him employed in such examination, and $2 for every 25 miles he shall necessarily travel in the performance of his duty, which shall be paid by the association by him examined.

SEC. 55. That every president, director, cashier, teller, clerk, or agent of any association, who shall embezzle, abstract, or willfully misapply any of the moneys, funds, or credits of the association, or shall, without authority from the directors, issue or put in circulation any of the notes of the association, or shall, without such authority, issue or put forth any certificate of deposit, draw any order or bill of exchange, make any acceptance, assign any note, bond, draft, bill of exchange, mortgage, judgment, or decree, or shall make any false entry in any book, report, or statement of the association, with intent, in either case, to injure or defraud the association or any other company, body politic or corporate, or any individual person or to deceive any officer of the association, or any agent appointed to examine the affairs of any such association, shall be deemed guilty of a misdemeanor, and upon conviction thereof shall be punished by imprisonment not less than 5 nor more than 10 years.

SEC. 56. That all suits and proceedings arising out of the provisions of this act, in which the United States or its officers or agents shall be parties, shall be conducted by the district attorneys of the several districts, under the direction and supervision of the Solicitor of the Treasury.

SEC. 57. That suits, actions, and proceedings, against any association under this act, may be had in any circuit, district, or Territorial court of the United States held within the district in which such association may be established; or in any State, county, or municipal court in the county or city in which said association is located, having jurisdiction in similar cases: *Provided, however,* That all proceedings to enjoin the Comptroller under this act shall be had in a circuit, district, or Territorial court of the United States, held in the district in which the association is located.

SEC. 58. That every person who shall mutilate, cut, deface, disfigure, or perforate with holes, or shall unite or cement together, or do any other thing to any bank bill, draft, note, or other evidence of debt, issued by any such association, or shall cause or procure the same to be done, with intent to render such bank bill, draft, note, or other evidence of debt unfit to be reissued by said association, shall, upon conviction, forfeit $50 to the association who shall be injured thereby, to be recovered by action in any court having jurisdiction.

SEC. 59. That if any person shall falsely make, forge, or counterfeit, or cause or procure to be made, forged or counterfeited, or willingly aid or assist in falsely making, forging, or counterfeiting, any note in imitation of, or purporting to be in imitation of, the circulating notes issued under the provisions of this act, or shall pass, utter, or publish, or attempt to pass, utter, or publish, any false, forged, or counterfeited note, purporting to be issued by any association doing a banking business under the provisions of this act, knowing the same to be falsely made, forged, or counterfeited, or shall falsely alter, or cause or procure to be falsely altered, or willingly aid or assist in falsely altering, any such circulating notes, issued as aforesaid, or shall pass, utter, or publish, or attempt to pass, utter, or publish, as true, any falsely altered or spurious circulating note issued, or purporting to have been issued, as aforesaid, knowing the same to be falsely altered or spurious, every such person shall be deemed and adjudged guilty of felony, and being thereof convicted by due course of law shall be sentenced to be imprisoned and kept at hard labor for a period of not less than 5 years, nor more than 15 years, and fined in a sum not exceeding $1,000.

SEC. 60. That if any person shall make or engrave, or cause or procure to be made or engraved, or shall have in his custody or possession any plate, die, or block after the similitude of any plate, die, or block from which any circulating notes issued as aforesaid shall have been prepared or printed, with intent to use such plate, die, or block, or cause or suffer the same to be used, in forging or counterfeiting any of the notes issued as aforesaid, or shall have in his custody or possession any blank note or notes engraved and printed after the similitude of any notes issued as aforesaid, with intent to use such blanks, or cause or suffer the same to be used, in forging or counterfeiting any of the notes issued as aforesaid, or shall have in his custody or possession any paper adapted to the making of such notes, and similar to the paper upon which any such notes shall have been issued, with intent to use such paper, or cause or suffer the same to be used, in forging or counterfeiting any of the notes issued as aforesaid, every such person, being thereof convicted by due course of law, shall be sentenced to be imprisoned and kept to hard labor for a term not less than 5 or more than 15 years, and fined in a sum not exceeding $1,000.

SEC. 61. That it shall be the duty of the Comptroller of the Currency to report annually to Congress at the commencement of its session —

I. A summary of the state and condition of every association from whom reports have been received the preceding year, at the several dates to which such reports refer, with an abstract of the whole amount of banking capital returned by them, of the whole amount of their debts and liabilities, the amount of circulating notes outstanding, and the total amount of means and resources, specifying the amount of lawful money held by them at the times of their several returns, and such other information in relation to said associations as, in his judgment, may be useful.

II. A statement of the associations whose business has been closed during the year, with the amount of their circulation redeemed and the amount outstanding.

III. Any amendment to the laws relative to banking by

which the system may be improved, and the security of the holders of its notes and other creditors may be increased.

IV. The names and compensation of the clerks employed by him, and the whole amount of the expenses of the banking department during the year. And such report shall be made by or before the 1st day of December in each year, and the usual number of copies for the use of the Senate and House, and 1,000 copies for the use of the department, shall be printed by the Public Printer and in readiness for distribution at the first meeting of Congress.[1]

[SEC. 62 provides for the repeal of the Act of 1863 and the legalization of all proceedings taken under it by banks, etc.]

SEC. 63. That persons holding stock as executors, administrators, guardians, and trustees, shall not be personally subject to any liabilities as stockholders; but the estates and funds in their hands shall be liable in like manner and to the same extent as the testator, intestate, ward, or person interested in said trust-funds would be if they were respectively living and competent to act and hold the stock in their own names.

SEC. 64. That Congress may at any time amend, alter, or repeal this act.

Act of June 30, 1864 — *To provide ways and means for the support of the Government, and for other purposes*

Be it enacted, etc. [SEC. 1 authorizes the Secretary of the Treasury to issue $400,000,000 of bonds.]

SEC. 2. That the Secretary of the Treasury may issue on the credit of the United States, and in lieu of an equal amount of bonds authorized by the preceding section, and as a part of said loan, not exceeding $200,000,000, in treasury notes of any denomination not less than $10, payable at any time not exceeding 3 years from date, or, if thought more expedient, redeemable at any time after 3 years from date, and bearing interest not exceeding the rate of $7\frac{3}{10}$ per centum, payable in lawful money at maturity, or, at the discretion of the Secretary, semi-annually. And the said treasury notes may be disposed of by the Secretary of the Treasury, on the best terms that can be obtained, for lawful money; and such of them as shall be made payable, principal and interest, at maturity, shall be a legal tender to the same extent as United States notes for their face value, excluding interest, and may be paid to any creditor of the United States at their face value, excluding interest, or to any

[1] In 1873 he was also required to collect statistics of state banks, etc., and report thereon.

creditor willing to receive them at par, including interest; and any treasury notes issued under the authority of this act may be made convertible, at the discretion of the Secretary of the Treasury, into any bonds issued under the authority of this act. And the Secretary of the Treasury may redeem and cause to be cancelled and destroyed any treasury notes or United States notes heretofore issued under authority of previous acts of Congress, and substitute, in lieu thereof, an equal amount of treasury notes such as are authorized by this act, or of other United States notes : *Provided,* That the total amount of bonds and treasury notes authorized by the first and second sections of this act shall not exceed $400,000,000, in addition to the amounts heretofore issued ; nor shall the total amount of United States notes, issued or to be issued, ever exceed $400,000,000, and such additional sum, not exceeding $50,000,000, as may be temporarily required for the redemption of temporary loan ; nor shall any treasury note bearing interest, issued under this act, be a legal tender in payment or redemption of any notes issued by any bank, banking association, or banker, calculated or intended to circulate as money.

[SEC. 3. Bonds may be issued in exchange for the 7–30 treasury notes ; interest on notes to cease in 3 months after notice of redemption. Limitation of loan of March 3, 1864, to current fiscal year repealed. Authority to issue bonds under Act of March 3, 1863, repealed except as to $75,000,000 already advertised.]

SEC. 4. That the Secretary of the Treasury may authorize the receipt, as a temporary loan, of United States notes or the notes of national banking associations on deposit for not less than 30 days, in sums of not less than $50, by any of the assistant treasurers of the United States, or depositaries designated for that purpose, other than national banking associations, who shall issue certificates of deposit in such form as the Secretary of the Treasury shall prescribe, bearing interest not exceeding 6 per centum annually, and payable at any time after the term of deposit, and after 10 days' subsequent notice, unless time and notice be waived by the Secretary of the Treasury ; and the Secretary of the Treasury may increase the interest on deposits at less than 6 per centum to that rate, or, on 10 days' notice to depositors, may diminish the rate of interest as the public interest may require ; but the aggregate of such deposits shall not exceed $150,000,000 ; and the Secretary of the Treasury may issue, and shall hold in reserve for payment of such deposits, United States notes not exceeding $50,000,000, including the amount already applied in such payment ; and the United

States notes, so held in reserve, shall be used only when needed, in his judgment, for the prompt payment of such deposits on demand, and shall be withdrawn and placed again in reserve as the amount of deposits shall again increase.

SEC. 5. That the Secretary of the Treasury may issue notes of the fractions of a dollar as now used for currency, in such form, with such inscriptions, and with such safeguards against counterfeiting, as he may judge best,[1] and provide for the engraving and preparation, and for the issue of the same, as well as of all other notes and bonds, and other obligations, and shall make such regulations for the redemption of said fractional notes and other notes when mutilated or defaced, and for the receipt of said fractional notes in payment of debts to the United States, except for customs, in such sums, not over $5, as may appear to him expedient ; and it is hereby declared that all laws and parts of laws applicable to the fractional notes engraved and issued as herein authorized, apply equally and with like force to all the fractional notes heretofore authorized, whether known as postage currency or otherwise, and to postage stamps issued as currency ; but the whole amount of all descriptions of notes or stamps less than $1 issued as currency, shall not exceed $50,000,000.

[SECS. 6–13. Form of bonds and notes ; issue of registered bonds for coupon ; instructions to receivers of public moneys ; necessary expenses not to exceed one per cent. of amount of notes and bonds issued ; penalties against counterfeiting, etc.]

Act of January 28, 1865 — Amending the preceding act of June 30, 1864

Be it enacted, etc., That in lieu of any bonds authorized to be issued by the first section of the act entitled " An act to provide ways and means for the support of the Government," approved June 30, 1864, that may remain unsold at the date of this act, the Secretary of the Treasury may issue, under the authority of said act, treasury notes of the description and character authorized by the second section of said act : *Provided,* That the whole amount of bonds authorized as aforesaid, and Treasury notes issued and to be issued in lieu thereof, shall not exceed the sum of $400,000,000 ; and such treasury notes may be disposed of for lawful money, or for any other treasury notes

---

[1] By the Act of March 3, 1865, authorizing the coinage of three-cent pieces and for other purposes, the issue of fractional notes of less denomination than five cents was forbidden, and by the Act of May 16, 1866, the issue of such notes of less denomination than ten cents was forbidden.

or certificates of indebtedness or certificates of deposit issued under any previous act of Congress; and such notes shall be exempt from taxation by or under State or municipal authority.

SEC. 2. [Unsold 5-20 bonds, not exceeding $4,000,000, may be sold by the Secretary in Europe or in the United States, on such terms as he may deem most advisable.] *Provided,* That this act shall not be so construed as to give any authority for the issue of any legal tender notes, in any form, beyond the balance unissued of the amount authorized by the second section of the act to which this is an amendment.

Act of March 3, 1865 — To provide ways and means for the support of the Government

Be it enacted, etc., That the Secretary of the Treasury be, and he is hereby, authorized to borrow from time to time, on the credit of the United States, in addition to the amounts heretofore authorized, any sums not exceeding in the aggregate $600,000,000, and to issue therefor bonds or Treasury notes of the United States, in such form as he may prescribe; and so much thereof as may be issued in bonds shall be of denominations not less than $50, and may be made payable at any period not more than 40 years from date of issue, or may be made redeemable, at the pleasure of the Government, at or after any period not less than 5 years nor more than 40 years from date, or may be made redeemable and payable as aforesaid, as may be expressed upon their face; and so much thereof as may be issued in Treasury notes may be made convertible into any bonds authorized by this act, and may be of such denominations — not less than $50 — and bear such dates and be made redeemable or payable at such periods as in the opinion of the Secretary of the Treasury may be deemed expedient. And the interest on such bonds shall be payable semi-annually; and on Treasury notes authorized by this act the interest may be made payable semi-annually, or annually, or at maturity thereof; and the principal, or interest, or both, may be made payable in coin or in other lawful money: *Provided,* That the rate of interest on any such bonds or Treasury notes, when payable in coin shall not exceed 6 per centum per annum; and when not payable in coin shall not exceed $7\frac{3}{10}$ per centum per annum; and the rate and character of interest shall be expressed on all such bonds or Treasury notes: *And provided further,* That the act entitled "An act to provide ways and means for the support of the Government, and for other purposes," approved June 30, 1864, shall be so construed as to authorize the issue of bonds of any description authorized by this act. And any Treasury notes or other obligations bearing interest, issued under any act of Congress, may, at the discretion of the Secretary of the Treasury, and with the consent of the holder, be converted into any description of bonds authorized by this act ; and no bonds so authorized shall be considered a part of the amount of $600,000,000 hereinbefore authorized.

SEC. 2. That the Secretary of the Treasury may dispose of any of the bonds or other obligations issued under this act, either in the United States or elsewhere, in such manner, and at such rates and under such conditions, as he may think advisable, for coin, or for other lawful money of the United States, or for any Treasury notes, certificates of indebtedness, or certificates of deposit, or other representatives of value, which have been or may be issued under any act of Congress ; and may, at his discretion, issue bonds or Treasury notes authorized by this act, in payment for any requisitions for materials or supplies which shall have been made by the appropriate Department or offices upon the Treasury of the United States, on receiving notice in writing, through the Department or office making the requisition, that the owner of the claim for which the requisition is issued desires to subscribe for an amount of loan that will cover said requisition, or any part thereof ; and all bonds or other obligations issued under this act shall be exempt from taxation by or under State or municipal authority.

SEC. 3. . . . That nothing herein contained shall be construed as authorizing the issue of legal tender notes in any form ; . . .

Act of March 3, 1865 — [*Tax on state bank-notes and conversion of state banks*]

＊　＊　＊　＊　＊　＊　＊　＊　＊

SEC. 6. That every national banking association, state bank, or state banking association shall pay a tax of 10 per centum on the amount of notes of any state bank or state banking association paid out by them after the first day of July, 1866.

SEC. 7. That any existing bank organized under the laws of any State, having a paid-up capital of not less than $75,000, which shall apply before the first day of July next for authority to become a national bank under the act entitled " An act to provide a national currency," etc., approved June 3, 1864, and shall comply with all the requirements of said act, shall, if

---

[1] See Acts of July 13, 1866, March 3, 1867, and February 8, 1875.

such bank be found by the Comptroller of the Currency to be in good standing and credit, receive such authority in preference to new associations applying for the same : *Provided,* That it shall be lawful for any banking association organized under State laws, and having branches, the capital being joint and assigned to and used by the mother bank and branches in definite proportions, to become a national banking association in conformity with existing laws, and to retain and keep in operation its branches, or such one or more of them as it may elect to retain ; the amount of the circulation redeemable at the mother bank and each branch to be regulated by the amount of capital assigned to and used by each.

Act of March 3, 1865 — Amending " An act to provide a national currency," etc.

Be it enacted, etc., That section 21 of said act be so amended that said section shall read as follows :

Sec. 21. That upon the transfer and delivery of bonds to the Treasurer, as provided in the foregoing section, the association making the same shall be entitled to receive from the Comptroller of the Currency circulating notes of different denominations, in blank, registered and countersigned as hereinafter provided, equal in amount to 90 per centum of the current market value of the United States bonds so transferred and delivered, but not exceeding 90 per centum of the amount of said bonds at the par value thereof, if bearing interest at a rate not less than 5 per centum per annum ; and the amount of said circulating notes to be furnished to each association shall be in proportion to its paid-up capital as follows, and no more : To each association whose capital shall not exceed $500,000, 90 per centum of such capital ; to each association whose capital exceeds $500,000, but does not exceed $1,000,000, 80 per centum of such capital ; to each association whose capital exceeds $1,000,000, but does not exceed $3,000,000, 75 per centum of such capital ; to each association whose capital exceeds $3,000,000, 60 per cent. of such capital. And that $150,000,000 of the entire amount of circulating notes authorized to be issued shall be apportioned to associations in the States, in the District of Columbia, and in the Territories, according to representative population, and the remainder shall be apportioned by the Secretary of the Treasury among associations formed in the several States, in the District of Columbia, and in the Territories, having due regard to the existing banking capital, resources, and business of such States, District, and Territories.

Act of April 12, 1866 — To amend an act entitled " An act to provide ways and means to support the Government," approved March 3, 1865

Be it enacted, etc., That the act entitled " An act to provide ways and means to support the Government," approved March 3, 1865, shall be extended and construed to authorize the Secretary of the Treasury, at his discretion, to receive any Treasury notes or other obligations issued under any act of Congress, whether bearing interest or not, in exchange for any description of bonds authorized by the act to which this is an amendment; and also to dispose of any description of bonds authorized by said act, either in the United States or elsewhere, to such an amount, in such manner, and at such rates as he may think advisable, for lawful money of the United States, or for any Treasury notes, certificates of indebtedness, or certificates of deposit, or other representatives of value, which have been or which may be issued under any act of Congress, the proceeds thereof to be used only for retiring Treasury notes or other obligations issued under any act of Congress; but nothing herein contained shall be construed to authorize any increase of the public debt: *Provided,* That of United States notes not more than $10,000,000 may be retired and cancelled within 6 months from the passage of this act, and thereafter not more than $4,000,000 in any one month:[1] *And provided further,* That the act to which this is an amendment shall continue in full force in all its provisions, except as modified by this act.

Act of July 13, 1866 — [Tax on state bank-notes]

SEC. 9. [Amends section 6 of the Act of March 3, 1865 (*ante*), to read] : That every national banking association, state bank, or state banking association, shall pay a tax of 10 per centum on the amount of notes of any person, state bank, or state banking association, used for circulation and paid out by them after the first day of August, 1866, and such tax shall be assessed and paid in such a manner as shall be prescribed by the commissioner of internal revenue.

[1] See Act of February 4, 1868.

Act of March 2, 1867 — [*Provides for temporary loan certificates*]

Be it enacted, etc., That for the purpose of redeeming and re-tiring any compound-interest notes outstanding, the Secretary of the Treasury is hereby authorized and directed to issue tem-porary loan certificates in the manner prescribed by section four of the act entitled " An act to authorize the issue of United States notes, etc.," approved February 25, 1862, bearing interest at a rate not exceeding 3 per centum per annum, principal and interest payable in lawful money on demand ; and said certifi-cates of temporary loan may constitute and be held, by any national bank holding or owning the same, as a part of the re-serve provided for in sections 31 and 32 of the act entitled "An act to provide a national currency, etc.," approved June 3, 1864 : *Provided*, That not less than two-fifths of the entire re-serve of such bank shall consist of lawful money of the United States : *And provided further*, That the amount of such tem-porary certificates at any time outstanding shall not exceed $50,000,000.

Act of March 26, 1867 — [*Tax on state bank-notes, etc.*]

SEC. 2. That every national banking association, state bank or banker, or association, shall pay a tax of 10 per centum on the amount of notes of any town, city, or municipal corporation, paid out by them after the first day of May, A.D. 1867, to be collected in the mode and manner in which the tax on the notes of state banks is collected.

Act of February 4, 1868 — *To suspend further reduction of the currency*

Be it enacted, etc., That, from and after the passage of this act, the authority of the Secretary of the Treasury to make any reduction of the currency, by retiring or cancelling United States notes, shall be, and is hereby, suspended ; but nothing herein contained shall prevent the cancellation and destruction of mutilated United States notes, and the replacing of the same with notes of the same character and amount.

[Became a law without the President's signature.]

Act of July 25, 1868 — *To provide for a further issue of temporary loan certificates, etc.*

Be it enacted, etc., That for the sole purpose of redeeming and retiring the remainder of the compound interest notes out-

standing, the Secretary of the Treasury is hereby authorized
and directed to issue an additional amount of temporary loan
certificates, not exceeding $25,000,000 ; said certificates to bear
interest at the rate of 3 per centum per annum, principal and
interest payable in lawful money on demand, and to be similar
in all respects to the certificates authorized by the act . . .
approved March 2, 1867 ; and the said certificates may constitute and be held by any national bank holding or owning the
same as a part of the reserve, in accordance with the provisions
of the above mentioned act of March 2, 1867.

Act of February 19, 1869 — *To prevent loaning money upon United States notes*

Be it enacted, etc., That no national banking association shall
hereafter offer or receive United States notes or national bank
notes as security or as collateral security for any loan of money,
or for a consideration shall agree to withhold the same from
use, or shall offer to receive the custody or promise of custody
of such notes as security, or as a collateral security, or consideration for any loan of money ; and any national banking association offending against the provisions of this act shall be
deemed guilty of a misdemeanor, and upon conviction thereof
in any United States court having jurisdiction shall be punished
by a fine not exceeding $1000, and by a further sum equal to
one-third of the money so loaned ; and the officer or officers of
said bank who shall make such loan or loans shall be liable for
a further sum equal to one-quarter of the money so loaned ; and
the prosecution of such offenders shall be commenced and conducted as provided for the punishment of offences in an act to
provide a national currency, approved June 3, 1864, and the
fine or penalty so recovered shall be for the benefit of the party
bringing such suit.

Act of March 3, 1869 — *Regulating the reports of national bank-ing associations*

Be it enacted, etc., That in lieu of all reports required by section 34 of the national currency act, every association shall
make to the Comptroller of the Currency, not less than five reports during each and every year, according to the form which
may be prescribed by him, verified by the oath or affirmation
of the president or cashier of such association, and attested by
the signature of at least three of the directors ; which report
shall exhibit, in detail and under appropriate heads, the resources

2 N

and liabilities of the association at the close of business on any past day to be by him specified, and shall transmit such report to the Comptroller within five days after the receipt of a request or requisition therefor from him; and the report of each association above required, in the same form in which it is made to the Comptroller, shall be published in a newspaper published in the place where such association is established, or if there be no newspaper in the place, then in the one published nearest thereto in the same county, at the expense of the association; and such proof of publication shall be furnished as may be required by the Comptroller. And the Comptroller shall have power to call for special reports from any particular association whenever in his judgment the same shall be necessary in order to a full and complete knowledge of its condition. Any association failing to make and transmit any such report shall be subject to a penalty of one hundred dollars for each day after five days that such bank shall delay to make and transmit any report as aforesaid; and in case any association shall delay or refuse to pay the penalty herein imposed when the same shall be assessed by the Comptroller of the Currency, the amount of such penalty may be retained by the Treasurer of the United States, upon the order of the Comptroller of the Currency, out of the interest, as it may become due to the association, on the bonds deposited with him to secure circulation; and all sums of money collected for penalties under this section shall be paid into the Treasury of the United States.

SEC. 2. That, in addition to said reports, each national banking association shall report to the Comptroller of the Currency the amount of each dividend declared by said association, and the amount of net earnings in excess of said dividends, which report shall be made within ten days after the declaration of each dividend, and attested by the oath of the president or cashier of said association, and a failure to comply with the provisions of this section shall subject such association to the penalties provided in the foregoing section.

Act of March 3, 1869 — *In reference to certifying checks by national banks*

Be it enacted, etc., That it shall be unlawful for any officer, clerk, or agent of any national bank to certify any check drawn upon said bank unless the person or company drawing said check shall have on deposit in said bank at the time such check is certified an amount of money equal to the amount specified in such check; and any check so certified by duly authorized officers shall be a good and valid obligation against such bank ; and any officer, clerk, or agent of any national bank violating the provisions of this act shall subject such bank to the liabilities and proceedings on the part of the Comptroller as provided for in section 50 of the national banking law, approved June 3, 1864.

Act of March 18, 1869 — *To strengthen the public credit*

Be it enacted, etc., That in order to remove any doubt as to the purpose of the government to discharge all just obligations to the public creditors, and to settle conflicting questions and interpretations of the laws by virtue of which such obligations have been contracted, it is hereby provided and declared that the faith of the United States is solemnly pledged to the payment in coin or its equivalent of all the obligations of the United States not bearing interest, known as United States notes, and of all the interest-bearing obligations of the United States, except in cases where the law authorizing the issue of any such obligation has expressly provided that the same may be paid in lawful money or other currency than gold and silver. But none of said interest-bearing obligations not already due shall be redeemed or paid before maturity unless at such time United States notes shall be convertible into coin at the option of the holder, or unless at such time bonds of the United States bearing a lower rate of interest than the bonds to be redeemed can be sold at par in coin. And the United States also solemnly pledges its faith to make provision at the earliest practicable period for the redemption of the United States notes in coin.

Act of July 12, 1870 — *To provide for the redemption of the three per cent. temporary loan certificates, and for an increase of national bank notes*

Be it enacted, etc., That $54,000,000 in notes for circulation may be issued to national banking associations, in addition to the $300,000,000 authorized by the 22d section of the "Act to provide a national currency, etc.," approved June 3, 1864 ; and the amount of notes so provided shall be furnished to banking associations organized, or to be organized, in those states and territories having less than their proportion under the apportionment contemplated by the provisions of the "Act to amend an act to provide a national currency, etc.," approved March 3, 1865, and the bonds deposited with the Treasurer of the United States, to secure the additional circulating notes herein authorized, shall be of any description of bonds of the United States bearing interest in coin ; but a new apportionment of the increased circulation herein provided for shall be made as soon as practicable, based upon the census of 1870 : *Provided,* That if applications for the circulation herein authorized shall not be made within one year after the passage of this act by banking associations organized, or to be organized, in States having less than their proportion, it shall be lawful for the Comptroller of the Currency to issue such circulation to banking associations applying for the same in other states or territories having less than their proportion, giving the preference to such as have the greatest deficiency :[1] *And provided further,* That no banking association hereafter organized shall have a circulation in excess of $500,000.[2]

SEC. 2. That at the end of each month after the passage of this act, it shall be the duty of the Comptroller of the Currency to report to the Secretary of the Treasury the amount of circulating notes issued, under the provisions of the preceding section, to national banking associations, during the previous month ; whereupon the Secretary of the Treasury shall redeem and cancel an amount of three per centum temporary loan certificates issued under the acts of March 2, 1867, and July 25, 1868, not less than the amount of circulating notes so reported, and may, if necessary, in order to procure the presentation of such temporary loan certificates for redemption, give notice to the holders thereof, by publication or otherwise, that certain of said certificates (which shall be designated by number, date, and amount) shall cease to bear interest from and after a day to be designated in such notice ; and that the certificates so designated shall no longer be available as any portion of the lawful money reserve in possession of any national banking association ; and, after the day designated in such notice, no interest shall be paid on such certificates, and they shall not thereafter be counted as a part of the reserve of any banking association.

SEC. 3. That upon the deposit of any United States bonds, bearing interest payable in gold, with the treasurer of the United States, in the manner prescribed in the 19th and 20th sections of the national currency act, it shall be lawful for the comptroller of the currency to issue to the association making the same, circulating notes of different denominations, not less than $5, not exceeding in amount 80 per centum of the par

[1] All these regulations for the distribution of bank currency were repealed by the Act of January 14, 1875, which see.
[2] Repealed by Act of July 12, 1882, Sec. 10.

value of the bonds deposited, which notes shall bear upon their
face the promise of the association to which they are issued to
pay them, upon presentation at the office of the association, in
gold coin of the United States,[1] and shall be redeemable upon
such presentation in such coin : *Provided*, That no banking
association organized under this section shall have a circulation
in excess of $1,000,000.

SEC. 4. That every national banking association formed under
the provisions of the preceding section of this act shall at all
times keep on hand not less than 25 per centum of its outstanding circulation in gold or silver coin of the United States,
and shall receive at par in the payment of debts the gold notes
of every other such banking association which at the time of
such payments shall be redeeming its circulating notes in gold
coin of the United States.

SEC. 5. That every association organized for the purpose of
issuing gold notes as provided in this act shall be subject to all
the requirements and provisions of the national currency act,
except the first clause of section 22, which limits the circulation
of national banking associations to $300,000,000 ; the first clause
of section 32, which, taken in connection with the preceding
section, would require national banking associations organized
in the city of San Francisco to redeem their circulating notes
at par in the city of New York ; and the last clause of section
32, which requires every national banking association to receive
in payment of debts the notes of every other national banking
association at par : *Provided*, That in applying the provisions
and requirements of said acts to the banking associations herein
provided for, the terms " lawful money," and " lawful money of
the United States," shall be held and construed to mean gold
or silver coin of the United States.

SEC. 6. That to secure a more equitable distribution of the
national banking currency there may be issued circulating notes
to banking associations organized in States and Territories
having less than their proportion as herein set forth. And the
amount of circulation in this section authorized shall, under the
direction of the Secretary of the Treasury, as it may be required
for this purpose, be withdrawn, as herein provided, from banking associations organized in States having a circulation exceeding that provided for by the act entitled " An act to amend an
act entitled ' An act to provide for a national banking currency,

---

[1] The provisions of this act for national gold banks were modified by
the Act of January 19, 1875, and practically repealed by the Act of February 14, 1880, resumption of specie payments having obviated the need for
a distinction.

etc.,'" approved March 3, 1865, but the amount so withdrawn shall not exceed $25,000,000. The comptroller of the currency shall, under the direction of the Secretary of the Treasury, make a statement showing the amount of circulation in each State and Territory, and the amount to be retired by each banking association in accordance with this section, and shall, when such redistribution of circulation is required, make a requisition for such amount upon such banks, commencing with the banks having a circulation exceeding $1,000,000 in States having an excess of circulation, and withdrawing their circulation in excess of $1,000,000, and then proceeding pro-rata with other banks having a circulation of $300,000 in States having the largest excess of circulation, and reducing the circulation of such banks in States having the greatest proportion in excess, leaving undisturbed the banks in States having a smaller proportion, until those in greater excess have been reduced to the same grade, and continuing thus to make the reduction provided for by this act until the full amount of $25,000,000, herein provided for, shall be withdrawn ; and the circulation so withdrawn shall be distributed along the States and Territories having less than their proportion, so as to equalize the same. And it shall be the duty of the comptroller of the currency, under the direction of the Secretary of the Treasury, forthwith to make a requisition for the amount thereof upon the banks above indicated as herein prescribed. And upon failure of such associations, or any of them, to return the amount so required within one year, it shall be the duty of the comptroller of the currency to sell at public auction, having given twenty days' notice thereof in one daily newspaper printed in Washington and one in New York city, an amount of bonds deposited by said association, as security for said circulation, equal to the circulation to be withdrawn from said association and not returned in compliance with such requisition ; and the comptroller of the currency shall with the proceeds redeem so many of the notes of said banking association, as they come into the treasury, as will equal the amount required and not so returned, and shall pay the balance, if any, to such banking association : *Provided*, That no circulation shall be withdrawn under the provisions of this section until after the $54,000,000 granted in the first section shall have been taken up.

SEC. 7. That after the expiration of six months from the passage of this act any banking association located in any State having more than its proportion of circulation, may be removed to any State having less than its proportion of circulation, under such rules and regulations as the comptroller of the currency, with the approval of the Secretary of the Treasury, may require :

Provided, That the amount of the issue of said banks shall not be deducted from the amount of new issue provided for in this issue.

Act of July 14, 1870 — *To require national banks going into liquidation to retire their circulating notes*

Be it enacted, etc., That every bank that has heretofore gone into liquidation under the provisions of section 42 of the national currency act, shall be required to deposit lawful money of the United States for its outstanding circulation within 60 days from the date of the passage of this act. And every bank that may hereafter go into liquidation shall be required to deposit lawful money of the United States for its outstanding circulation within 6 months from the date of the vote to go into liquidation; whereupon the bonds pledged as security for such circulation shall be surrendered to the association making such deposit. And if any bank shall fail to make the deposit and take up its bonds for 30 days after the expiration of the time specified, the Comptroller of the Currency shall have power to sell the bonds pledged for the circulation of said bank at public auction in New York City, and after providing for the redemption and cancellation of said circulation, and the necessary expenses of the sale, to pay over any balance remaining from the proceeds to the bank, or its legal representative : *Provided,* That banks which are winding up in good faith for the purpose of consolidating with other banks shall be exempt from the provisions of this act : *And provided further,* That the assets and liabilities of banks so in liquidation shall be reported by the banks with which they are in process of consolidation.

Act of July 14, 1870 — *To authorize the refunding of the national debt*

Be it enacted, etc., That the Secretary of the Treasury is hereby authorized to issue, in a sum or sums not exceeding in the aggregate $200,000,000, coupon or registered bonds of the United States, in such form as he may prescribe, and of denominations of $50, or some multiple of that sum, redeemable in coin of the present standard value, at the pleasure of the United States, after 10 years from the date of their issue, and bearing interest, payable semi-annually in such coin, at the rate of 5 per cent. per annum ; also a sum or sums not exceeding in the aggregate $300,000,000 of like bonds, the same in all respects, but payable at the pleasure of the United States, after 15 years from the date of their issue, and bearing interest at the rate of 4½ per cent. per annum ; also a sum or sums not exceeding in the aggregate $1,000,000,000 of like bonds, the same in all respects, but payable at the pleasure of the United States, after 30 years from the date of their issue, and bearing interest at the rate of 4 per cent. per annum ; all of which said several classes of bonds and the interest thereon shall be exempt from the payment of all taxes or duties of the United States, as well as from taxation in any form by or under State, municipal, or local authority ; and the said bonds shall have set forth and expressed upon their. face the above specified conditions, and shall, with their coupons, be made payable at the Treasury of the United States.   But nothing in this act, or in any other law now in force, shall be construed to authorize any increase whatever of the bonded debt of the United States.

*   *   *   *   *   *   *   *   *

Act of June 8, 1872 — For the better security of bank reserves, and to facilitate bank clearing-house exchanges

Be it enacted, etc., That the Secretary of the Treasury is hereby authorized to receive United States notes on deposit, without interest, from national banking associations, in sums not less than $10,000, and to issue certificates therefor in such form as the Secretary may prescribe, in denominations of not less than $5000 ; which certificates shall be payable on demand in United States notes, at the place where the deposits were made.

SEC. 2. That the United States notes so deposited in the Treasury of the United States shall not be counted as part of the legal reserve ; but the certificates issued therefor may be held and counted by national banks as part of their legal reserve, and may be accepted in the settlement of clearing-house balances at the places where the deposits therefor were made.

SEC. 3. That nothing contained in this act shall be construed to authorize any expansion or contraction of the currency and the United States notes for which such certificates are issued, or other United States notes of like amount, shall be held as special deposits in the Treasury, and used only for the redemption of such certificates.

Act of February 12, 1873 — Revising and amending the laws relative to the Mints, assay-offices, and coinage of the United States

[This act contains 67 sections. Those omitted refer to the organization and the technical operation of the mint service, to minor coin, counterfeiting, etc.]

SEC. 13. That the standard for both gold and silver coins of the United States shall be such that of 1000 parts by weight 900 shall be of pure metal and 100 of alloy; and the alloy of the silver coins shall be of copper, and the alloy of the gold coins shall be of copper, or of copper and silver; but the silver shall in no case exceed one-tenth of the whole alloy.

SEC. 14. That the gold coins of the United States shall be a $1 piece, which, at the standard weight of $25\frac{8}{10}$ grains, shall be the unit of value; a quarter-eagle, or $2\frac{1}{2}$ piece; a $3 piece; a half-eagle, or $5 piece; an eagle, or $10 piece; and a double-eagle, or $20 piece. And the standard weight of the gold dollar shall be $25\frac{8}{10}$ grains; of the quarter-eagle, or $2\frac{1}{2}$ piece, $64\frac{1}{2}$ grains; of the $3 piece, $77\frac{4}{10}$ grains; of the half-eagle, or $5 piece, 129 grains; of the eagle, or $10 piece, 258 grains; of the double-eagle, or $20 piece, 516 grains; which coins shall be a legal tender in all payments at their nominal value when not below the standard weight and limit of tolerance provided in this act for the single piece, and when reduced in weight, below said standard and tolerance, shall be a legal tender at valuation in proportion to their actual weight; and any gold coin of the United States, if reduced in weight by natural abrasion not more than one-half of one per centum below the standard weight prescribed by law, after a circulation of 20 years, as shown by its date of coinage, and at a ratable proportion for any period less than 20 years, shall be received at their nominal value by the United States Treasury and its offices, under such regulations as the Secretary of the Treasury may prescribe for the protection of the Government against fraudulent abrasion or other praetices; and any gold coins in the Treasury of the United States reduced in weight below this limit of abrasion shall be recoined.

SEC. 15. That the silver coins of the United States shall be a trade-dollar, a half-dollar, or 50-cent piece, a quarter-dollar, or 25-cent piece, a dime, or 10-cent piece; and the weight of the trade-dollar shall be 420 grains troy; the weight of the half-dollar shall be $12\frac{1}{2}$ grams (grammes); the quarter-dollar and the dime shall be, respectively, one-half and one-fifth of the weight of said half-dollar; and said coins shall be a legal tender at their nominal value for any amount not exceeding $5 in any one payment.[1]

SEC. 17. That no coins, either of gold, silver, or minor coinage, shall hereafter be issued from the mint other than those of the denominations, standards, and weights herein set forth.

SEC. 20. That any owner of gold bullion may deposit the same at any mint, to be formed into coin or bars for his benefit:

[1] Changed to $10 by the Act of June 9, 1879.

but it shall be lawful to refuse any deposit of less value than $100, or any bullion so base as to be unsuitable for the operations of the mint; and when gold and silver are combined, if either metal be in such small proportion that it cannot be separated advantageously, no allowance shall be made to the depositor for its value.

SEC. 21. That any owner of silver bullion may deposit the same at any mint, to be formed into bars, or into dollars of the weight of 420 grains, troy, designated in this act as trade-dollars, and no deposit of silver for other coinage shall be received; but silver bullion contained in gold deposits, and separated therefrom, may be paid for in silver coin, at such valuation as may be, from time to time, established by the Director of the Mint.

[SEC. 25 fixes a charge of $\frac{1}{5}$ of one per cent. for gold coinage. This was abrogated by the act of January 14, 1875.]

Act of March 3, 1873 — To establish the custom-house value of the sovereign or pound sterling of Great Britain, and to fix the par of exchange

Be it enacted, etc., That the value of foreign coin as expressed in the money of account of the United States shall be that of the pure metal of such coin of standard value; and the values of the standard coins in circulation of the various nations of the world shall be estimated annually by the Director of the Mint, and be proclaimed on the first day of January by the Secretary of the Treasury.

SEC. 2. That in all payments by or to the Treasury, whether made here or in foreign countries, where it becomes necessary to compute the value of the sovereign or pound sterling, it shall be deemed equal to $4.8665, and the same rule shall be applied in appraising merchandise imported where the value is, by the invoice, in sovereigns or pounds sterling, and in the construction of contracts payable in sovereigns or pounds sterling; and this valuation shall be the par of exchange between Great Britain and the United States; and all contracts made after the first day of January, 1874, based on an assumed par of exchange with Great Britain of 54 pence to the dollar, or 4.44\frac{4}{9}$ to the sovereign or pound sterling, shall be null and void.

Act of March 3, 1873 — To require national banks to restore their capital when impaired, and to amend the national-currency act

Be it enacted, etc., That all national banks which shall have failed to pay up their capital stock, as required by law, and all national banks whose capital stock shall have become impaired by losses or otherwise, shall, within 3 months after receiving notice thereof from the Comptroller of the Currency, be required to pay the deficiency in the capital stock by assessment upon the shareholders, pro rata, for the amount of capital stock held by each and the Treasurer of the United States shall withhold the interest upon all bonds held by him in trust for such association, upon notification from the Comptroller of the Currency, until otherwise notified by him ; and if such banks shall fail to pay up their capital stock, and shall refuse to go into liquidation, as provided by law, for 3 months after receiving notice from the Comptroller, a receiver may be appointed to close up the business of the association, according to the provisions of the 50th section of the national-currency act.

SEC. 2. That section 57 of said act be amended by adding thereto the following : "*And provided further*, That no attachment, injunction, or execution shall be issued against such association, or its property, before final judgment in any such suit, action, or proceeding in any State, county, or municipal court."

SEC. 3. That all banks not organized, and transacting business under the national-currency act, and all persons, companies or corporations doing the business of bankers, brokers, or savings institutions, except saving-banks, authorized by Congress to use the word "national" as a part of their corporate names are prohibited from using the word "national" as a portion of the name or title of such bank, corporation, firm, or partnership ; and every such bank, corporation, or firm, which shall use the word "national" as a portion of their corporate title or partnership name 6 months after the passage of this act, shall be subject to a penalty of $50 for each day thereafter in which said word shall be employed as aforesaid as part of such corporate name or title, such penalty to be recovered by action in any court having jurisdiction.

SEC. 4. That it shall be the duty of the Comptroller of the Currency to cause to be examined each year the plates, dies, but-pieces, and other material from which the national-bank circulation is printed in whole or in part, and file in his office annually a correct list of the same ; and such material as shall have been used in the printing of the notes of national banks which are in liquidation, or have closed business, shall be destroyed under such regulations as shall be prescribed by the Comptroller of the Currency, and approved by the Secretary of the Treasury ; and the expense of such examination and destruction shall be paid out of any appropriation made by

Congress for the special examination of national banks and bank plates.

Act of June 20, 1874 — Fixing the amount of United States notes, providing for a redistribution of the national-bank currency, and for other purposes

Be it enacted, etc., That the act entitled " An act to provide a national currency, etc.," approved June 3d, 1864, shall hereafter be known as " The national-bank act."

SEC. 2. That section 31 of " The national-bank act " be so amended that the several associations therein provided for shall not hereafter be required to keep on hand any amount of money whatever, by reason of the amount of their respective circulations ; but the moneys required by said section to be kept at all times on hand shall be determined by the amount of deposits in all respects, as provided for in the said section.

SEC. 3. That every association organized, or to be organized, under the provisions of the said act, and of the several acts amendatory thereof, shall at all times keep and have on deposit in the Treasury of the United States, in lawful money of the United States, a sum equal to 5 per centum of its circulation, to be held and used for the redemption of such circulation ; which sum shall be counted as part of its lawful reserve, as provided in section 2 of this act ; and when the circulating notes of any such associations, assorted or unassorted, shall be presented for redemption, in sums of $1,000 or any multiple thereof, to the Treasurer of the United States, the same shall be redeemed in United States notes. All notes so redeemed shall be charged by the Treasurer of the United States to the respective associations issuing the same, and he shall notify them severally, on the first day of each month, or oftener, at his discretion, of the amount of such redemptions ; and whenever such redemptions for any association shall amount to the sum of $500, such association so notified shall forthwith deposit with the Treasurer of the United States a sum in United States notes equal to the amount of its circulating notes so redeemed. And all notes of national banks worn, defaced, mutilated, or otherwise unfit for circulation, shall, when received by any assistant treasurer, or at any designated depository of the United States, be forwarded to the Treasurer of the United States for redemption as provided herein. And when such redemptions have been so re-imbursed, the circulating-notes so redeemed shall be forwarded to the respective associations by which they were issued ; but if any of such notes are worn, mutilated, defaced, or rendered otherwise unfit for use, they shall be forwarded to the Comptroller of the Currency and destroyed and replaced as now provided by law : *Provided*, That each of said associations shall re-imburse to the Treasury the charges for transportation,[1] and the cost for assorting such notes ; and the associations hereafter organized shall also severally re-imburse to the Treasury the cost of engraving such plates as shall be ordered by each association respectively ; and the amount assessed upon each association shall be in proportion to the circulation redeemed, and be charged to the fund on deposit with the Treasurer : *And provided further*, That so much of section 32 of said national bank act requiring or permitting the redemption of its circulating notes elsewhere than at its own counter except as provided for in this section, is hereby repealed.

SEC. 4. That any association organized under this act, or any of the acts of which this is an amendment, desiring to withdraw its circulating notes,[2] in whole or in part, may, upon the deposit of lawful money with the Treasurer of the United States in sums of not less than $9,000, take up the bonds which said association has on deposit with the Treasurer for the security of such circulating notes ; which bonds shall be assigned to the bank in the manner specified in the nineteenth section of the national-bank act ; and the outstanding notes of said association, to an amount equal to the legal-tender notes deposited, shall be redeemed at the Treasury of the United States, and destroyed as now provided by law : *Provided*, That the amount of the bonds on deposit for circulation shall not be reduced below $50,000.

SEC. 5. That the Comptroller of the Currency shall, under such rules and regulations as the Secretary of the Treasury may prescribe, cause the charter-numbers of the associations to be printed upon all national-bank notes which may be hereafter issued by him.

SEC. 6. That the amount of United States notes outstanding and to be used as a part of the circulating-medium shall not exceed the sum of $382,000,000, which said sum shall appear in each monthly statement of the public debt, and no part thereof shall be held or used as a reserve.

SEC. 7. That so much of the act entitled "An act to provide for the redemption of the 3 per centum temporary loan certificates, and for an increase of national-bank notes," as provides that no circulation shall be withdrawn under the provisions of section 6 of said act, until after the $54,000,000

[1] See Act of July 12, 1882, Sec. 8.
[2] See Act of July 12, 1882, Sec. 9.

granted in section 1 of said act shall have been taken up, is hereby repealed ; and it shall be the duty of the Comptroller of the Currency, under the direction of the Secretary of the Treasury, to proceed forthwith, and he is hereby authorized and required, from time to time, as applications shall be duly made therefor, and until the full amount of $55,000,000 shall be withdrawn, to make requisitions upon each of the national banks described in said section, and in the manner therein provided, organized in States having an excess of circulation, to withdraw and return so much of their circulation as by said act may be apportioned to be withdrawn from them, or, in lieu thereof, to deposit in the Treasury of the United States lawful money sufficient to redeem such circulation, and upon the return of the circulation required, or the deposit of lawful money, as herein provided, a proportionate amount of the bonds held to secure the circulation of such association as shall make such return or deposit shall be surrendered to it.

SEC. 8. That upon the failure of the national banks upon which requisition for circulation shall be made, or of any of them, to return the amount required, or to deposit in the Treasury lawful money to redeem the circulation required, within 30 days, the Comptroller of the Currency shall at once sell, as provided in section 49 of the national currency act, approved June 3, 1864, bonds held to secure the redemption of the circulation of the association or associations which shall so fail, to an amount sufficient to redeem the circulation required of such association or associations, and with the proceeds, which shall be deposited in the Treasury of the United States, so much of the circulation of such association or associations shall be redeemed as will equal the amount required and not returned and if there be any excess of proceeds over the amount required for such redemption, it shall be returned to the association or associations whose bonds shall have been sold. And it shall be the duty of the Treasurer, assistant treasurers, designated depositaries, and national bank depositaries of the United States, who shall be kept informed by the Comptroller of the Currency of such associations as shall fail to return circulation as required, to assort and return to the Treasury for redemption the notes of such associations as shall come into their hands until the amount required shall be redeemed, and in like manner to assort and return to the Treasury, for redemption, the notes of such national banks as have failed, or gone into voluntary liquidation for the purpose of winding up their affairs, and of such as shall hereafter so fail or go into liquidation.

SEC. 9. That from and after the passage of this act it shall be lawful for the Comptroller of the Currency, and he is hereby required, to issue circulating-notes without delay, as applications therefor are made, not to exceed the sum of $55,000,000, to associations organized, or to be organized, in those States and Territories having less than their proportion of circulation, under an apportionment made on the basis of population and of wealth, as shown by the returns of the census of 1870 ; and every association hereafter organized shall be subject to, and be governed by, the rules, restrictions, and limitations, and possess the rights, privileges, and franchises, now or hereafter to be prescribed by law as to national banking associations, with the same power to amend, alter, and repeal provided by " the national bank act " : *Provided*, That the whole amount of circulation withdrawn and redeemed from banks transacting business shall not exceed $55,000,000, and that such circulation shall be withdrawn and redeemed as it shall be necessary to supply the circulation previously issued to the banks in those States having less than their apportionment : *And provided further*, That not more than $30,000,000 shall be withdrawn and redeemed as herein contemplated during the fiscal year ending June 30, 1875.[1]

Act of June 23, 1874. — [*Sundry civil appropriation Law.*]

For the maceration of national-bank notes, United States notes, and other obligations of the United States authorized to be destroyed, $10,000 ; and that all such issues hereafter destroyed may be destroyed by maceration instead of burning to ashes, as now provided by law ; and that so much of sections 24 and 43 of the national currency act as requires national-bank notes to be burned to ashes is hereby repealed.

Act of January 14, 1875 — *To provide for the resumption of specie payments*

Be it enacted, etc., That the Secretary of the Treasury is hereby authorized and required, as rapidly as practicable, to cause to be coined, at the mints of the United States, silver coins of the denominations of 10, 25, and 50 cents, of standard value, and to issue them in redemption of an equal number and amount of fractional currency of similar denominations, or, at his discretion, he may issue such silver coins through the

[1] Superseded by the Act of January 14, 1875.

mints, the sub-treasuries, public depositaries, and post-offices of the United States ; and, upon such issue, he is hereby authorized and required to redeem an equal amount of such fractional currency, until the whole amount of such fractional currency outstanding shall be redeemed.[1]

SEC. 2. That so much of section 3524 of the Revised Statutes[2] of the United States as provides for a charge of one-fifth of one per centum for converting standard gold bullion into coin is hereby repealed, and hereafter no charge shall be made for that service.

SEC. 3. That section 5177 of the Revised Statutes of the United States, limiting the aggregate amount of circulating-notes of national-banking associations be, and is hereby, repealed; and each existing banking-association may increase its circulating-notes in accordance with existing law without respect to said aggregate limit; and new banking-associations may be organized in accordance with existing law without respect to said aggregate limit; and the provisions of law for the withdrawal and redistribution of national-bank currency among the several States and Territories are hereby repealed. And whenever, and so often, as circulating-notes shall be issued to any such banking-association, so increasing its capital or circulating-notes, or so newly organized as aforesaid, it shall be the duty of the Secretary of the Treasury to redeem the legal-tender United States notes in excess only of $300,000,000, to the amount of 80 per centum of the sum of national bank-notes so issued to any such banking-association as aforesaid and to continue such redemption as such circulating-notes are issued until there shall be outstanding the sum of $300,000,000 of such legal-tender United States notes,[3] and no more. And on and after the first day of January, anno Domini, 1879, the Secretary of the Treasury shall redeem, in coin,[4] the United States legal-tender notes then outstanding, on their presentation for redemption, at the office of the assistant treasurer of the United States in the city of New York,[5] in sums not less than $50. And to enable the Secretary of the Treasury to prepare and provide for the redemption in this act author-

---

[1] See the Act of April 17, 1876, making further provision for issue of silver coin in lieu of fractional currency.

[2] Act of February 12, 1873.

[3] Subsequent Act of May 31, 1878, forbade further retirement of legal-tender notes, and fixed the limit at amount then outstanding, $346,681,016.

[4] See Sec. 2 of the Act of March 14, 1900, making these notes redeemable in gold.

[5] San Francisco added by Sec. 3 of Act of March 3, 1887.

ized or required, he is authorized to use any surplus revenues, from time to time, in the Treasury not otherwise appropriated, and to issue, sell, and dispose of, at not less than par, in coin, either of the descriptions of bonds of the United States described in the act of Congress approved July 14, 1870, entitled " An act to authorize the refunding of the national debt," with like qualities, privileges, and exemptions, to the extent necessary to carry this act into full effect, and to use the proceeds thereof for the purposes aforesaid. And all provisions of law inconsistent with the provisions of this act are hereby repealed.

Act of February 8, 1875 — *To amend existing customs and internal-revenue laws, and for other purposes*

SEC. 19. That every person, firm, association other than national bank associations, and every corporation, State bank, or State banking association, shall pay a tax of 10 per centum on the amount of their own notes used for circulation and paid out by them.

SEC. 20. That every such person, firm, association, corporation, State bank, or State banking association, and also every national banking association, shall pay a like tax of 10 per centum on the amount of notes of any person, firm, association other than a national banking association, or of any corporation, State bank, or State banking association, or of any town, city, or municipal corporation, used for circulation and paid out by them.

SEC. 21. That the amount of such circulating notes, and of the tax due thereon, shall be returned, and the tax paid at the same time, and in the same manner, and with like penalties for failure to return and pay the same, as provided by law for the return and payment of taxes on deposits, capital, and circulation, imposed by the existing provisions of internal revenue law.

[*Act of February* 19, 1875, fixes the compensation of examiners of national banks.]

Act of March 3, 1875. [*Legislative, executive, and judicial appropriations.*]

* * * * * * * * * *

Provided, That the national bank notes shall be printed under the direction of the Secretary of the Treasury, and

20

upon the distinctive or special paper which has been, or may hereafter be, adopted by him for printing United States notes.

* * * * * * * * * *

[*Act of March* 3, 1875 — Provides for the issue of a silver coin of the denomination of 20 cents, weight 5 grams, legal tender for an amount not exceeding $5 in any one payment.[1]]

Act of April 17, 1876 — *To provide for a deficiency in the Printing and Engraving Bureau of the Treasury Department, and for the issue of silver coin of the United States in place of fractional currency*

SEC. 2. That the Secretary of the Treasury is hereby directed to issue silver coins of the United States of the denomination of 10, 20, 25, and 50 cents of standard value, in redemption of an equal amount of fractional currency, whether the same be now in the Treasury awaiting redemption, or whenever it may be presented for redemption;[2] and the Secretary of the Treasury may, under regulations of the Treasury Department, provide for such redemption and issue by substitution at the regular sub-treasuries and public depositories of the United States until the whole amount of fractional currency outstanding shall be redeemed. And the fractional currency redeemed under this act shall be held to be a part of the sinking-fund provided for by existing law, the interest to be computed thereon, as in the case of bonds redeemed under the act relating to the sinking-fund.

[*Act of June* 30, 1876, amends national bank act respecting receiverships.]

Joint Resolution of July 22, 1876 — *For the issue of silver coin*

Resolved, etc., That the Secretary of the Treasury, under such limits and regulations as will best secure a just and fair distribution of the same through the country, may issue the silver coin at any time in the Treasury to an amount not exceeding $10,000,000, in exchange for an equal amount of legal-tender notes; and the notes so received in exchange

[1] Coinage prohibited by Act of May 2, 1878.
[2] See provisions of the Resumption Act of January 14, 1875.

shall be kept as a special fund[1] separate and apart from all other money in the Treasury, and be reissued only upon the retirement and destruction of a like sum of fractional currency received at the Treasury in payment of dues to the United States; and said fractional currency, when so substituted, shall be destroyed and held as part of the sinking fund, as provided in the act approved April 17, 1876.

SEC. 2. That the trade dollar shall not hereafter be a legal tender, and the Secretary of the Treasury is hereby authorized to limit from time to time, the coinage thereof to such an amount as he may deem sufficient to meet the export demand for the same.

SEC. 3. That in addition to the amount of subsidiary silver coin authorized by law to be issued in redemption of the fractional currency it shall be lawful to manufacture at the several mints, and issue through the Treasury and its several offices, such coin to an amount, that, including the amount of subsidiary silver coin and of fractional currency outstanding, shall, in the aggregate, not exceed, at any time, $50,000,000.

SEC. 4. That the silver bullion required for the purposes of this resolution shall be purchased, from time to time, at market rate, by the Secretary of the Treasury, with any money in the Treasury not otherwise appropriated; but no purchase of bullion shall be made under this resolution when the market rate for the same shall be such as will not admit of the coinage and issue, as herein provided, without loss to the Treasury; and any gain or seigniorage arising from this coinage shall be accounted for and paid into the Treasury, as provided under existing laws relative to the subsidiary coinage : *Provided,* That the amount of money at any one time invested in such silver bullion, exclusive of such resulting coin, shall not exceed $200,000.

Act of February 28, 1878 — To authorize the coinage of the standard silver dollar, and to restore its legal-tender character[2]

Be it enacted, etc., That there shall be coined at the several mints of the United States, silver dollars of the weight of 412½ grains Troy of standard silver, as provided in the act of January

---

[1] Under Sec. 3 of the legislative, executive and judicial appropriations Act of June 21, 1879 (21 Statutes at Large, p. 23), the Secretary of the Treasury is directed to issue immediately, in payment of arrearages of pensions, the legal-tender notes held as a special fund under above authority, and it is further provided that " fractional currency presented for redemption shall be redeemed in any moneys in the Treasury not otherwise appropriated."

[2] Vetoed by the President. Became a law on February 28, 1878, on passing each house by a two-thirds vote.

18, 1837, on which shall be the devices and superscriptions provided by said act ; which coins, together with all silver dollars heretofore coined by the United States, of like weight and fineness, shall be a legal tender, at their nominal value, for all debts and dues public and private, except where otherwise expressly stipulated in the contract.   And the Secretary of the Treasury is authorized and directed to purchase, from time to time, silver bullion, at the market price thereof, not less than $2,000,000 worth per month, nor more than $4,000,000 worth per month, and cause the same to be coined monthly, as fast as so purchased, into such dollars ; and a sum sufficient to carry out the foregoing provision of this act is hereby appropriated out of any money in the Treasury not otherwise appropriated.   And any gain or seigniorage arising from this coinage shall be accounted for and paid into the Treasury, as provided under existing laws relative to the subsidiary coinage : *Provided*, That the amount of money at any one time invested in such silver bullion, exclusive of such resulting coin, shall not exceed $5,000,000 ; *And provided further*, That nothing in this act shall be construed to authorize the payment in silver of certificates of deposit issued under the provisions of section 254 of the Revised Statutes.[1]

SEC. 2. That immediately after the passage of this act, the President shall invite the governments of the countries composing the Latin Union, so-called, and of such other European nations as he may deem advisable, to join the United States in a conference to adopt a common ratio between gold and silver, for the purpose of establishing, internationally, the use of bi-metallic money, and securing fixity of relative value between those metals ; such conference to be held at such place, in Europe or in the United States, at such times within 6 months, as may be mutually agreed upon by the executives of the governments joining in the same, whenever the governments so invited, or any three of them, shall have signified their willingness to unite in the same.

. The President shall, by and with the advice and consent of the Senate, appoint three commissioners, who shall attend such conference on behalf of the United States, and shall report the doings thereof to the President, who shall transmit the same to Congress.

Said commissioners shall each receive the sum of $2500 and their reasonable expenses, to be approved by the Secretary of State ; and the amount necessary to pay such compensation and expenses is hereby appropriated out of any money in the Treasury not otherwise appropriated.

---

[1] Refers to gold certificates.

Sec. 3. That any holder of the coin authorized by this act may deposit the same with the Treasurer or any assistant treasurer of the United States, in sums not less than $10, and receive therefor certificates of not less than $10 each, corresponding with the denominations of the United States notes. The coin deposited for or representing the certificates shall be retained in the Treasury for the payment of the same on demand. Said certificates shall be receivable for customs, taxes, and all public dues, and, when so received, may be re-issued.

Sec. 4. All acts and parts of acts inconsistent with the provisions of this act are hereby repealed.

Act of May 31, 1878 — *To forbid the further retirement of United States legal-tender notes*

Be it enacted, etc., That from and after the passage of this act it shall not be lawful for the Secretary of the Treasury or other officer under him to cancel or retire any more of the United States legal-tender notes. And when any of said notes may be redeemed or be received into the Treasury under any law from any source whatever, and shall belong to the United States, they shall not be retired, cancelled, or destroyed, but they shall be reissued and paid out again and kept in circulation :[1] *Provided,* That nothing herein shall prohibit the cancellation and destruction of mutilated notes and the issue of other notes of like denomination in their stead, as now provided by law.

Act of June 9, 1879 — *To provide for the exchange of subsidiary coins for lawful money of the United States, etc.*

Be it enacted, etc., That the holder of any of the silver coins of the United States of smaller denominations than $1, may, on presentation of the same in sums of $20, or any multiple thereof at the office of the Treasurer or any assistant treasurer of the United States, receive therefor lawful money of the United States.

Sec. 2. The Treasurer or any assistant treasurer of the United States who may receive any coins under the provision of this act shall exchange the same in sums of $20, or any multiple thereof, for lawful money of the United States, on demand of any holder thereof.

Sec. 3. That the present silver coins of the United States of smaller denominations than $1 shall hereafter be a legal tender in all sums not exceeding $10 in full payment of all dues public and private.

[1] See Act of March 14, 1900.

SEC. 4. That all laws or parts of laws in conflict with this act be, and the same are hereby, repealed.

[*Act of February* 14, 1880 — Authorizes the conversion of national gold banks into ordinary national banks, specie payments having been resumed.]

Act of May 26, 1882 — To authorize the receipt of United States gold coin in exchange for gold bars [1]

Be it enacted, etc., That the superintendents of the coinage mints, and of the United States assay office at New York, are hereby authorized to receive United States gold coin from any holder thereof in sums not less than $5000, and to pay and deliver in exchange therefor gold bars in value equaling such coin so received.

Act of July 12, 1882 — To enable national banking associations to extend their corporate existence, and for other purposes

Be it enacted, etc., That any national banking association organized under the acts of February 25th, 1863, June 3d, 1864, and February 14th, 1880, or under sections 5133, 5134, 5135, 5136, and 5154 of the Revised Statutes of the United States,[2] may, at any time within the 2 years next previous to the date of the expiration of its corporate existence under present law, and with the approval of the Comptroller of the Currency, to be granted, as hereinafter provided, extend its period of succession by amending its articles of association for a term of not more than 20 years from the expiration of the period of succession named in said articles of association, and shall have succession for such extended period, unless sooner dissolved by the act of shareholders owning two-thirds of its stock, or unless its franchise becomes forfeited by some violation of law, or unless hereafter modified or repealed.

[SECS. 3 to 5 inclusive regulate the details of procedure.]

SEC. 6. That the circulating notes of any association so extending the period of its succession which shall have been issued to it prior to such extension shall be redeemed at the Treasury of the United States, as provided in section 3 of the act of June 20th, 1874, entitled " An act fixing the amount of United States notes, etc.," and such notes when redeemed shall be forwarded to the Comptroller of the Currency, and destroyed as now provided by law ; and at the end of 3 years from the

---

[1] See Act of March 3, 1891, amending this Act.
[2] Secs. 5, 6, 8 and 36 of Act of June 3, 1864.

date of the extension of the corporate existence of each bank the association so extended shall deposit lawful money with the Treasurer of the United States sufficient to redeem the remainder of the circulation which was outstanding at the date of its extension, as provided in sections 5222, 5224, and 5225 of the Revised Statutes ;[1] and any gain that may arise from the failure to present such circulating notes for redemption shall inure to the benefit of the United States ; and from time to time, as such notes are redeemed or lawful money deposited therefor as provided herein, new circulating notes shall be issued as provided by this act, bearing such devices, to be approved by the Secretary of the Treasury, as shall make them readily distinguishable from the circulating notes heretofore issued : *Provided, however*, That each banking association which shall obtain the benefit of this act shall reimburse to the Treasury the cost of preparing the plate or plates for such new circulating notes as shall be issued to it.

[SEC. 7 relates to winding up banks which do not extend charters.]

SEC. 8. That national banks now organized or hereafter organized having a capital of $150,000 or less, shall not be required to keep on deposit or deposit with the Treasurer of the United States United States bonds in excess of one-fourth of their capital stock as security for their circulating notes ; but such banks shall keep on deposit or deposit with the Treasurer of the United States the amount of bonds as herein required. And such of those banks having on deposit bonds in excess of that amount are authorized to reduce their circulation by the deposit of lawful money as provided by law : *Provided*, That the amount of such circulating notes shall not in any case exceed 90 per centum of the par value of the bonds deposited as herein provided : *Provided, further*, That the national banks which shall hereafter make deposits of lawful money for the retirement in full of their circulation shall, at the time of their deposit, be assessed for the cost of transporting and redeeming their notes then outstanding, a sum equal to the average cost of the redemption of national-bank notes during the preceding year, and shall thereupon pay such assessment. And all national banks which have heretofore made or shall hereafter make deposits of lawful money for the reduction of their circulation, shall be assessed, and shall pay an assessment in the manner specified in section 3 of the act approved June 20th, 1874, for the cost of transporting and redeeming their notes redeemed from such deposits subsequently to June 30th, 1881.

---

[1] Act of July 14, 1870.

SEC. 9. That any national banking association now organized, or hereafter organized, desiring to withdraw its circulating notes, upon a deposit of lawful money with the Treasurer of the United States, as provided in section 4 of the act of June 20th, 1874, entitled " An act fixing the amount of United States notes, etc.," or as provided in this act, is authorized to deposit lawful money and withdraw a proportionate amount of the bonds held as security for its circulating notes in the order of such deposits ; and no national bank which makes any deposit of lawful money in order to withdraw its circulating notes shall be entitled to receive any increase of its circulation for the period of 6 months from the time it made such deposit of lawful money for the purpose aforesaid : [1] *Provided*, That not more than $3,000,000 of lawful money shall be deposited during any calendar month for this purpose : *And provided further*, That the provisions of this section shall not apply to bonds called for redemption by the Secretary of the Treasury, nor to the withdrawal of circulating notes in consequence thereof.

SEC. 10. That upon a deposit of bonds as described by sections 5159 and 5160,[2] except as modified by section 4 of an act entitled "An act fixing the amount of United States notes, etc.," approved June 20th, 1874, and as modified by section 8 of this act, the association making the same shall be entitled to receive from the Comptroller of the Currency circulating notes of different denominations, in blank, registered and countersigned as provided by law, equal in amount to 90 per centum of the current market value, not exceeding par, of the United States bonds so transferred and delivered, and at no time shall the total amount of such notes issued to any such association exceed 90 per centum of the amount at such time actually paid in of its capital stock ; [3] and the provisions of sections 5171[4] and 5176 of the Revised Statutes [5] are hereby repealed.

[SEC. 11 provides for an issue of 3 per cent bonds.]

SEC. 12. That the Secretary of the Treasury is authorized and directed to receive deposits of gold coin with the Treasurer or assistant treasurers of the United States, in sums not less than $20, and to issue certificates therefor in denominations of not less than $20 each, corresponding with the denominations of United States notes. The coin deposited for or representing the certificates of deposit shall be retained in the

---

[1] See Act of March 14, 1900.
[2] Secs. 30 and 31, Act of June 3, 1864.
[3] See Act of March 14, 1900.
[4] Act of March 3, 1865.
[5] Act of July 12, 1870.

Treasury for the payment of the same on demand. Said certificates shall be receivable for customs, taxes, and all public dues, and when so received may be reissued ; and such certificates, as also silver certificates, when held by any national-banking association, shall be counted as part of its lawful reserve ; and no national-banking association shall be a member of any clearing-house in which such certificates shall not be receivable in the settlement of clearing-house balances : *Provided,* That the Secretary of the Treasury shall suspend the issue of such gold certificates whenever the amount of gold coin and gold bullion in the Treasury reserved for the redemption of United States notes falls below $100,000,000 ; and the provisions of section 5207 of the Revised Statutes shall be applicable to the certificates herein authorized and directed to be issued.[1]

SEC. 13. That any officer, clerk, or agent of any national-banking association who shall willfully violate the provisions of an act entitled "An act in reference to certifying checks by national banks," approved March 3, 1869 (being section 5208 of the Revised Statutes of the United States), or who shall resort to any device, or receive any fictitious obligation, direct or collateral, in order to evade the provisions thereof, or who shall certify checks before the amount thereof shall have been regularly entered to the credit of the dealer upon the books of the banking association, shall be deemed guilty of a misdemeanor, and shall, on conviction thereof in any circuit or distriet court of the United States, be fined not more than five thousand dollars, or shall be imprisoned not more than five years, or both, in the discretion of the court.

Act of August 7, 1882 — Making appropriations for sundry civil expenses of the government for the fiscal year ending June 30, 1883, etc.

*　　*　　*　　*　　*　　*　　*　　*　　*　　*

For the transportation of silver coins : That the Secretary of the Treasury be, and he is hereby, authorized and directed to transport, free of charge, silver coins when requested to do so : *Provided,* That an equal amount in coin or currency shall have been deposited in the Treasury by the applicant or applicants ; and that there is hereby appropriated $10,000, or so much thereof as may be necessary, for that purpose, and that the same be available from and after the passage of this act. . . .

---

[1] See Sec. 6, Act of March 14, 1900, now governing the issue of gold certificates.

Act of March 3, 1883, *to reduce internal revenue* repeals tax on deposits and capital of national banks, and stamp tax on bank-checks.

Act of August 4, 1886 — *Making appropriations for sundry civil expenses of the Government for the fiscal year ending June* 30th, 1887, *etc.*

Be it enacted, etc., . . . For labor and expenses of engraving and printing . . . : *Provided,* That no portion of this sum shall be expended for printing United States notes of large denomination in lieu of notes of small denomination cancelled or retired.[1]

And the Secretary of the Treasury is hereby authorized and required to issue silver certificates in denominations of 1, 2, and 5 dollars, and the silver certificates herein authorized shall be receivable, redeemable, and payable in like manner and for like purposes as is provided for silver certificates by the act of February 28th, 1878, entitled "An act to authorize the coinage of the standard silver dollar, and to restore its legal-tender character," and denominations of 1, 2, and 5 dollars may be issued in lieu of silver certificates of larger denominations in the Treasury or in exchange therefor upon presentation by the holder and to that extent said certificates of larger denominations shall be cancelled and destroyed.[2]

* * * * * * * * * *

Act of March 29, 1886, applies to receiverships of national banks.

Act of May 1, 1886, provides general procedure for increasing capital and changing name or location of national banks.

Act of March 3, 1887 — [*To amend national bank act relative to reserve cities*]

Be it enacted, etc., That whenever three-fourths in number of the national banks located in any city of the United States having a population of 50,000 people shall make application to the Comptroller of the Currency, in writing, asking that the name of the city in which such banks are located shall be added to the cities named in sections 5191 and 5192 of the Revised Statutes,[3] the Comptroller shall have authority to grant such request, and every bank located in such city shall at all

---

[1] The same provision is in the appropriation acts for succeeding years slightly altered in verbiage.

[2] See Sec. 7 of the Act of March 14, 1900.

[3] Secs. 31 and 32, Act of June 3, 1864.

times thereafter have on hand, in lawful money of the United States, an amount equal to at least 25 per centum of its deposits, as provided in sections 5191 and 5195 of the Revised Statutes.

Sec. 2. That whenever three-fourths in number of the national banks located in any city of the United States having a population of 200,000 people shall make application to the Comptroller of the Currency, in writing, asking that such city may be a central reserve city, like the city of New York, in which one-half of the lawful-money reserve of the national banks located in other reserve cities may be deposited, as provided in section 5195[1] of the Revised Statutes, the Comptroller shall have authority, with the approval of the Secretary of the Treasury, to grant such request, and every bank located in such city shall at all times thereafter have on hand, in lawful money of the United States, 25 per centum of its deposits, as provided in section 5191 of the Revised Statutes.

Sec. 3. That section 3 of the act of January 14, 1875, entitled "An act to provide for the resumption of specie payments," be, and the same is, hereby, amended by adding after the words "New York" the words "and the city of San Francisco, California."

Act of March 3, 1887 — For the retirement and recoinage of the trade dollar [2]

Be it enacted, etc., That for a period of six months after the passage of this act, United States trade-dollars, if not defaced, mutilated or stamped, shall be received at the office of the Treasurer, or any assistant treasurer of the United States, in exchange for a like amount, dollar for dollar, of standard silver dollars, or of subsidiary coins of the United States.

Sec. 2. That the trade-dollars received by, paid to, or deposited with the Treasurer or any assistant treasurer or national depositary of the United States shall not be paid out or in any other manner issued, but, at the expense of the United States, shall be transmitted to the coinage mints and recoined into standard silver dollars or subsidiary coin, at the discretion of the Secretary of the Treasury: *Provided,* that the trade-dollars recoined under this act shall not be counted as part of the silver bullion required to be purchased and coined into standard dollars as required by the act of February 28, 1878.

---

[1] Sec. 32, Act of June 3, 1864.
[2] Received by the President, February 19, 1887. Became a law without his signature on March 3, 1887.

SEC. 3. That all laws and parts of laws authorizing the coinage and issuance of United States trade-dollars are hereby repealed.

Act of July 14, 1890 — Directing the purchase of silver bullion and the issue of Treasury notes thereon, and for other purposes

Be it enacted, etc., That the Secretary of the Treasury is hereby directed to purchase, from time to time, silver bullion to the aggregate amount of 4,500,000 ounces, or so much thereof as may be offered in each month, at the market price thereof, not exceeding one dollar for 371 and $\frac{25}{100}$ grains of pure silver, and to issue in payment for such purchases of silver bullion Treasury notes of the United States to be prepared by the Secretary of the Treasury, in such form and of such denominations, not less than $1 nor more than $1,000, as he may prescribe, and a sum sufficient to carry into effect the provisions of this act is hereby appropriated out of any money in the Treasury not otherwise appropriated.[1]

SEC. 2. That the Treasury notes issued in accordance with the provisions of this act shall be redeemable on demand, in coin,[2] at the Treasury of the United States, or at the office of any assistant treasurer of the United States, and when so redeemed may be reissued; but no greater or less amount of such notes shall be outstanding at any time than the cost of the silver bullion and the standard silver dollars coined therefrom, then held in the Treasury purchased by such notes; and such Treasury notes shall be a legal tender in payment of all debts, public and private, except where otherwise expressly stipulated in the contract, and shall be receivable for customs, taxes, and all public dues, and when so received may be reissued; and such notes, when held by any national banking association, may be counted as a part of its lawful reserve. That upon demand of the holder of any of the Treasury notes herein provided for the Secretary of the Treasury shall, under such regulations as he may prescribe, redeem such notes in gold or silver coin, at his discretion, it being the established policy of the United States to maintain the two metals on a parity with each other upon the present legal ratio, or such ratio as may be provided by law.[3]

[1] Repealed by Act of November 1, 1893.

[2] See Sec. 2 of the Act of March 14, 1900, making these notes redeemable in gold.

[3] See Act of March 14, 1900, providing for cancellation and retirement of Treasury notes as rapidly as they reach the Treasury, and substitution of silver certificates therefor.

SEC. 3. That the Secretary of the Treasury shall each month coin 2,000,000 ounces of the silver bullion purchased under the provisions of this act into standard silver dollars until the first day of July, 1891, and after that time he shall coin of the silver bullion purchased under the provisions of this act as much as may be necessary to provide for the redemption of the Treasury notes herein provided for, and any gain or seigniorage arising from such coinage shall be accounted for and paid into the Treasury.[1]

SEC. 4. That the silver bullion purchased under the provisions of this act shall be subject to the requirements of existing law and the regulations of the mint service governing the methods of determining the amount of pure silver contained, and the amount of charges or deductions, if any, to be made.

SEC. 5. That so much of the act of February 28, 1878, entitled "An act to authorize the coinage of the standard silver dollar and to restore its legal-tender character," as requires the monthly purchase and coinage of the same into silver dollars of not less than $2,000,000, nor more than $4,000,000 worth of silver bullion, is hereby repealed.

SEC. 6. That upon the passage of this act the balances standing with the Treasurer of the United States to the respective credits of national banks for deposits made to redeem the circulating notes of such banks, and all deposits thereafter received for like purpose, shall be covered into the Treasury as a miscellaneous receipt, and the Treasury of the United States shall redeem from the general cash in the Treasury the circulating notes of said banks which may come into his possession subject to redemption.

And upon the certificate of the Comptroller of the Currency that such notes have been received by him and that they have been destroyed and that no new notes shall be issued in their place, reimbursement of their amount shall be made to the Treasurer, under such regulations as the Secretary of the Treasury may prescribe, from an appropriation hereby created, to be known as "National bank notes: Redemption account," but the provisions of this act shall not apply to the deposits received under section 3 of the act of June 20th, 1874, requiring every national bank to keep in lawful money with the Treasurer of the United States a sum equal to 5 per centum of its circulation, to be held and used for the redemption of its circulating notes; and the balance remaining of the deposits so covered shall, at the close of each month, be reported on the

---

[1] See Sec. 34 of the Act of June 13, 1898; also Act of March 14, 1900.

monthly public debt statement as debt of the United States bearing no interest.

SEC. 7. That this act shall take effect 30 days from and after its passage.

Act of October 1, 1890 — *To reduce the revenue and equalize duties on imports, and for other purposes*

Be it enacted, etc.

*   *   *   *   *   *   *   *   *   *

SEC. 52. That the value of foreign coin as expressed in the money of account of the United States shall be that of the pure metal of such coin of standard value ; and the values of the standard coins in circulation of the various nations of the world shall be estimated quarterly by the Director of the Mint, and be proclaimed by the Secretary of the Treasury immediately after the passage of this act, and thereafter quarterly on the first day of January, April, July and October in each year.

*   *   *   *   *   *   *   *   *   *

Act of March 3, 1891 — [*Legislative, executive, and judicial appropriations Act*]

SEC. 3. That an act to authorize the receipt of United States gold coin in exchange for gold bars, approved May 26th, 1882, be amended to read as follows :

" That the superintendents of the coinage mints and of the United States assay office at New York may, with the approval of the Secretary of the Treasury, but not otherwise, receive United States gold coin from any holder thereof in sums of not less than $5000, and pay and deliver in exchange therefor gold bars in value equaling such coin so received : *Provided,* That the Secretary of the Treasury may impose for such exchange a charge which, in his judgment, shall equal the cost of manufacturing the bars."

*   *   *   *   *   *   *   *   *   *

Act of March 3, 1891 — *Making appropriations for sundry civil expenses of the Government for the fiscal year ending June* 30, 1892, *etc.*

. . . For recoinage of the uncurrent fractional silver coins abraded below the limit of tolerance in the Treasury, to be expended under the direction of the Secretary of the Treasury,

$150,000: *Provided,* That the Secretary of the Treasury shall, as soon as practicable, coin into standard silver dollars the trade-dollar bullion and trade dollars now in the Treasury, the expense thereof to be charged to the silver profit fund. . . .

Act of July 28, 1892 — To amend the National Bank Act in providing for the redemption of national bank notes stolen from or lost by banks of issue

Be it enacted, etc., That the provisions of the Revised Statutes of the United States, providing for the redemption of national bank notes, shall apply to all national bank notes that have been or may be issued to, or received by, any national bank, notwithstanding such notes may have been lost by, or stolen from, the bank and put in circulation without the signature or upon the forged signature of the president or vice-president and cashier.

Act of August 3, 1892, relates to appointment of receivers of national banks.

Act of August 5, 1892, provides for coinage of half-dollars for World's Fair, making them legal tender.

Act of August 5, 1892 — Making appropriations for sundry civil expenses of the Government, etc.

Be it enacted, etc.

*　　*　　*　　*　　*　　*　　*　　*　　*　　*

The President of the United States is hereby authorized to appoint five commissioners to an international conference, to be held at a place to be hereafter designated, with a view to secure, internationally, a fixity of relative value between gold and silver, as money, by means of a common ratio between those metals, with free mintage at such ratio, and for compensation of said commissioners, and for all reasonable expenses connected therewith, to be approved by the Secretary of State, including the proportion to be paid by the United States of the joint expenses of such conference, $80,000, or so much thereof as may be necessary.

Act of March 3, 1893, provided for coinage of quarter dollars for World's Fair.

Act of November 1, 1893 — *To repeal a part of an act approved July* 14th, 1890, *entitled "An Act directing the purchase of silver bullion and the issue of Treasury notes thereon, and for other purposes"*

Be it enacted, etc., That so much of the act approved July 14th, 1890, entitled " An act directing the purchase of silver bullion and issue of Treasury notes thereon, and for other purposes," as directs the Secretary of the Treasury to purchase from time to time silver bullion to the aggregate amount of 4,500,000 ounces, or so much thereof as may be offered in each month at the market price thereof, not exceeding $1 for 371 and $\frac{25}{100}$ grains of pure silver, and to issue in payment for such purchases Treasury notes of the United States, be, and the same is hereby, repealed. And it is hereby declared to be the policy of the United States to continue the use of both gold and silver as standard money, and to coin both gold and silver into money of equal intrinsic and exchangeable value, such equality to be secured through international agreement, or by such safeguards of legislation as will insure the maintenance of the parity in value of the coins of the two metals, and the equal power of every dollar at all times in the markets and in the payment of debts. And it is hereby further declared that the efforts of the Government should be steadily directed to the establishment of such a safe system of bimetallism as will maintain at all times the equal power of every dollar coined or issued by the United States, in the markets and in the payment of debts.

Act of August 13, 1894 — *To subject to State taxation national-bank notes and United States Treasury notes*

Be it enacted, etc., That circulating notes of national banking associations and United States legal-tender notes and other notes and certificates of the United States payable on demand and circulating or intended to circulate as currency and gold, silver or other coin shall be subject to taxation as money on hand or on deposit under the laws of any State or territory : *Provided,* That any such taxation shall be exercised in the same manner and at the same rate that any such State or Territory shall tax money or currency circulating as money within its jurisdiction.

SEC. 2. That the provisions of this act shall not be deemed or held to change existing laws in respect of the taxation of national banking associations.

Act of June 13, 1898 — *To provide ways and means to meet war expenditures and for other purposes*

Be it enactĕd, etc., . . .

*   *   *   *   *   *   *   *   *   *

SEC. 34. That the Secretary of the Treasury is hereby authorized and directed to coin into standard silver dollars, as rapidly as the public interests may require, to an amount, however, of not less than $1,500,000 in each month, all of the silver bullion now in the Treasury purchased in accordance with the provisions of the Act approved July 14, 1890, entitled, "An act directing the purchase of silver bullion and the issue of Treasury notes thereon, and for other purposes," and said dollars, when so coined, shall be used and applied in the manner and for the purposes named in said Act.

Act of March 14, 1900 — *To define and fix the standard of value, to maintain the parity of all forms of money issued or coined by the United States, to refund the public debt, and for other purposes*

Be it enacted, etc., That the dollar consisting of $25\frac{8}{10}$ grains of gold, nine-tenths fine, as established by section 3511 of the Revised Statutes of the United States,[1] shall be the standard unit of value, and all forms of money issued or coined by the United States shall be maintained at a parity of value with this standard, and it shall be the duty of the Secretary of the Treasury to maintain such parity.

SEC. 2. That United States notes, and Treasury notes issued under the Act of July 14, 1890, when presented to the Treasury for redemption, shall be redeemed in gold coin of the standard fixed in the first section of this Act, and in order to secure the prompt and certain redemption of such notes as herein provided it shall be the duty of the Secretary of the Treasury to set apart in the Treasury a reserve fund of $150,000,000 in gold coin and bullion, which fund shall be used for such redemption purposes only, and whenever and as often as any of said notes shall be redeemed from said fund it shall be the duty of the Secretary of the Treasury to use said notes so redeemed to restore and maintain such reserve fund in the manner following, to wit:

1. By exchanging the notes so redeemed for any gold coin in the general fund of the Treasury;

[1] Act of February 12, 1873, Sec. 14.

2. By accepting deposits of gold coin at the Treasury or at any sub-treasury in exchange for the United States notes so redeemed ;

3. By procuring gold coin by the use of said notes, in accordance with the provisions of section 3700 of the Revised Statutes of the United States.[1]

If the Secretary of the Treasury is unable to restore and maintain the gold coin in the reserve fund by the foregoing methods, and the amount of such gold coin and bullion in said fund shall at any time fall below $100,000,000, then it shall be his duty to restore the same to the maximum sum of $150,000,000 by borrowing money on the credit of the United States, and for the debt thus incurred to issue and sell coupon or registered bonds of the United States, in such form as he may prescribe, in denominations of $50 or any multiple thereof, bearing interest at the rate of not exceeding 3 per centum per annum, payable quarterly, such bonds to be payable at the pleasure of the United States after one year from the date of their issue, and to be payable, principal and interest, in gold coin of the present standard value, and to be exempt from the payment of all taxes or duties of the United States, as well as from taxation in any form by or under state, municipal, or local authority ; and the gold coin received from the sale of said bonds shall first be covered into the general fund of the Treasury and then exchanged, in the manner hereinbefore provided, for an equal amount of the notes redeemed and held for exchange, and the Secretary of the Treasury may, in his discretion, use said notes in exchange for gold, or to purchase or redeem any bonds of the United States, or for any other lawful purpose the public interests may require, except that they shall not be used to meet deficiencies in the current revenues. That United States notes when redeemed in accordance with the provisions of this section shall be reissued, but shall be held in the reserve fund until exchanged for gold, as herein provided ; and the gold coin and bullion in the reserve fund, together with the redeemed notes held for use as provided in this section, shall at no time exceed the maximum sum of $150,000,000.

Sec. 3. That nothing contained in this act shall be construed to affect the legal tender quality as now provided by law of the silver dollar, or of any other money coined or issued by the United States.

Sec. 4. That there shall be established in the Treasury Department, as a part of the office of the Treasurer of the United

[1] Act of March 17, 1862.

States, divisions to be designated and known as the division
of issue and the division of redemption, to which shall be assigned, respectively, under such regulations as the Secretary of
the Treasury may approve, all records and accounts relating to
the issue and redemption of United States notes, gold certificates, silver certificates, and currency certificates. There shall
be transferred from the account of the general fund of the
Treasury of the United States, and taken up on the books of said
divisions, respectively, accounts relating to the reserve fund for
the redemption of United States notes and Treasury notes, the
gold coin held against outstanding gold certificates, the United
States notes held against outstanding currency certificates, and
the silver dollars held against outstanding silver certificates, and
each of the funds represented by these accounts shall be used
for the redemption of the notes and certificates for which they
are respectively pledged, and shall be used for no other purpose, the same being held as trust funds.

SEC. 5. That it shall be the duty of the Secretary of the
Treasury, as fast as standard silver dollars are coined under the
provisions of the Acts of July 14, 1890, and June 13, 1898,
from bullion purchased under the Act of July 14, 1890, to retire
and cancel an equal amount of Treasury notes whenever received
into the Treasury, either by exchange in accordance with the provisions of this Act or in the ordinary course of business, and
upon the cancellation of Treasury notes silver certificates shall
be·issued against the silver dollars so coined.

SEC. 6. That the Secretary of the Treasury is hereby authorized and directed to receive deposits of gold coin with the
Treasurer or any assistant treasurer of the United States in sums
of not less than $20, and to issue gold certificates therefor in
denominations of not less than $20, and the coin so deposited
shall be retained in the Treasury and held for the payment of
such certificates on demand, and used for no other purpose.
Such certificates shall be receivable for customs, taxes, and all
public dues, and when so received may be reissued, and when
held by any national banking association may be counted as a
part of its lawful reserve : *Provided*, That whenever and so long
as the gold coin held in the reserve fund in the Treasury for the
redemption of United States notes and Treasury notes shall fall
and remain below $100,000,000, the authority to issue certifi-
cates as herein provided shall be suspended : *And provided further*, That whenever and so long as the aggregate amount of
United States notes and silver certificates in the general fund
of the Treasury shall exceed $60,000,000 the Secretary of the
Treasury may, in his discretion, suspend the issue of the certifi-

cates herein provided for : *And provided further*, That of the amount of such outstanding certificates one-fourth at least shall be in denominations of $50 or less : *And provided further*, That the Secretary of the Treasury may, in his discretion, issue such certificates in denominations of $10,000, payable to order. And section 5193 of the Revised Statutes of the United States[1] is hereby repealed.

SEC. 7. That hereafter silver certificates shall be issued only of denominations of $10 and under, except that not exceeding in the aggregate 10 per centum of the total volume of said certificates, in the discretion of the Secretary of the Treasury, may be issued in denominations of $20, $50, and $100 ; and silver certificates of higher denomination than $10, except as herein provided, shall, whenever received at the Treasury or redeemed, be retired and canceled, and certificates of denominations of $10 or less shall be substituted therefor, and after such substitution, in whole or in part, a like volume of United States notes of less denomination than $10 shall from time to time be retired and canceled, and notes of denominations of $10 and upward shall be reissued in substitution therefor, with like qualities and restrictions as those retired and canceled.

SEC. 8. That the Secretary of the Treasury is hereby authorized to use, at his discretion, any silver bullion in the Treasury of the United States purchased under the Act of July 14, 1890, for coinage into such denominations of subsidiary silver coin as may be necessary to meet the public requirements for such coin : *Provided*, That the amount of subsidiary silver coin outstanding shall not at any time exceed in the aggregate $100,-000,000. Whenever any silver bullion purchased under the Act of July 14, 1890, shall be used in the coinage of subsidiary silver coin an amount of Treasury notes issued under said Act equal to the cost of the bullion contained in such coin shall be canceled and not reissued.

SEC. 9. That the Secretary of the Treasury is hereby authorized and directed to cause all worn and uncurrent subsidiary silver coin of the United States now in the Treasury, and hereafter received to be recoined, and to reimburse the Treasurer of the United States for the difference between the nominal or face value of such coin and the amount the same will produce in new coin from any moneys in the Treasury not otherwise appropriated.

SEC. 10. That section 5138 of the Revised Statutes[2] is hereby amended so as to read as follows :

[1] Act of June 8, 1872.
[2] Sec. 7, Act of June 3, 1864.

"Section 5138. No association shall be organized with a less capital than $100,000, except that banks with a capital of not less than $50,000 may, with the approval of the Secretary of the Treasury, be organized in any place the population of which does not exceed 6,000 inhabitants, and except that banks with a capital of not less than $25,000 may, with the sanction of the Secretary of the Treasury, be organized in any place the population of which does not exceed 3,000 inhabitants. No association shall be organized in a city the population of which exceeds 50,000 persons with a capital of less than $200,000."

SEC. 11. That the Secretary of the Treasury is hereby authorized to receive at the Treasury any of the outstanding bonds of the United States bearing interest at 5 per centum per annum, payable February 1, 1904, and any bonds of the United States bearing interest at 4 per centum per annum, payable July 1, 1907, and any bonds of the United States bearing interest at 3 per cent. per annum, payable August 1, 1908, and to issue in exchange therefor an equal amount of coupon or registered bonds of the United States, in such form as he may prescribe, in denominations of $50 or any multiple thereof, bearing interest at the rate of 2 per centum per annum, payable quarterly, such bonds to be payable at the pleasure of the United States after thirty years from the date of their issue, and said bonds to be payable, principal and interest, in gold coin of the present standard value, and to be exempt from the payment of all taxes or duties of the United States, as well as from taxation in any form by or under state, municipal, or local authority : *Provided*, That such outstanding bonds may be received in exchange at a valuation not greater than their present worth to yield an income of $2\frac{1}{4}$ per centum per annum ; and in consideration of the reduction in interest effected, the Secretary of the Treasury is authorized to pay to the holders of the outstanding bonds surrendered for exchange, out of any money in the Treasury not otherwise appropriated, a sum not greater than the difference between their present worth, computed as aforesaid, and their par value, and the payments to be made hereunder shall be held to be payments on account of the sinking fund created by section 3694 of the Revised Statutes.[1] *And provided further*, That the 2 per centum bonds to be issued under the provisions of this Act shall be issued at not less than par, and they·shall be numbered consecutively in the order of their issue, and when

[1] Act of February 25, 1862.

payment is made the last numbers issued shall be first paid, and this order shall be followed until all the bonds are paid, and whenever any of the outstanding bonds are called for payment, interest thereon shall cease three months after such call ; and there is hereby appropriated out of any money in the Treasury not otherwise appropriated, to effect the exchanges of bonds provided for in this Act, a sum not exceeding one-fifteenth of 1 per centum of the face value of said bonds, to pay the expense of preparing and issuing the same, and other expenses incident thereto.

SEC. 12. That upon the deposit with the Treasurer of the United States, by any national banking association, of any bonds of the United States in the manner provided by existing law, such association shall be entitled to receive from the Comptroller of the Currency circulating notes in blank, registered, and countersigned as provided by law, equal in amount to the par value of the bonds so deposited ; and any national banking association now having bonds on deposit for the security of circulating notes, and upon which an amount of circulating notes has been issued less than the par value of the bonds, shall be entitled, upon due application to the Comptroller of the Currency, to receive additional circulating notes in blank to an amount which will increase the circulating notes held by such association to the par value of the bonds deposited, such additional notes to be held and treated in the same way as circulating notes of national banking associations heretofore issued, and subject to all the provisions of law affecting such notes : *Provided,* That nothing herein contained shall be construed to modify or repeal the provisions of section 5167 of the Revised Statutes of the United States,[1] authorizing the Comptroller of the Currency to require additional deposits of bonds or of lawful money in case the market value of the bonds held to secure the circulating notes shall fall below the par value of the circulating notes outstanding for which such bonds may be deposited as security : *And provided further,* That the circulating notes furnished to national banking associations under the provisions of this act shall be of the denominations prescribed by law, except that no national banking association shall, after the passage of this act, be entitled to receive from the Comptroller of the Currency, or to issue or reissue or place in circulation, more than one-third in amount of its circulating notes of the denomination of $5 : *And provided further,* That the total amount of such notes issued to any such association may equal at any time but shall not ex-

[1] Sec. 26, Act of June 3, 1864.

ceed the amount at such time of its capital stock actually paid in : *And provided further*, That under regulations to be prescribed by the Secretary of the Treasury, any national banking association may substitute the 2 per centum bonds issued under the provisions of this act for any of the bonds deposited with the Treasurer to secure circulation or to secure deposits of public money ; and so much of an Act entitled " An Act to enable national banking associations to extend their corporate existence, and for other purposes," approved July 12, 1882, as prohibits any national bank which makes any deposit of lawful money in order to withdraw its circulating notes from receiving any increase of its circulation for the period of 6 months from the time it made such deposit of lawful money for the purpose aforesaid, is hereby repealed, and all other Acts or parts of Acts inconsistent with the provisions of this section are hereby repealed.

SEC. 13. That every national banking association having on deposit, as provided by law, bonds of the United States bearing interest at the rate of 2 per centum per annum, issued under the provision of this Act, to secure its circulating notes, shall pay to the Treasurer of the United States, in the months of January and July, a tax of one-fourth of 1 per centum each half year upon the average amount of such of its notes in circulation as are based upon the deposit of said 2 per centum bonds ; and such taxes shall be in lieu of existing taxes on its notes in circulation imposed by section 5214 of the Revised Statutes.[1]

SEC. 14. That the provisions of this Act are not intended to preclude the accomplishment of international bimetallism whenever conditions shall make it expedient and practicable to secure the same by concurrent action of the leading commercial nations of the world, and at a ratio which shall insure permanence of relative value between gold and silver.

The *Act of April* 12, 1902, authorized the further extension of charters of national banks for a period of 20 years.

III. DOCUMENTS

THOMAS JEFFERSON'S NOTES ON THE ESTABLISHMENT OF A MONEY UNIT AND OF A COINAGE FOR THE UNITED STATES

1782

In fixing the unit of money these circumstances are of principal importance.

[1] Sec. 41, Act of June 3, 1864.

1. That it be of a convenient size to be applied as a measure to the common money transactions of life.

2. That its parts and multiples be in an easy proportion to each other so as to facilitate the Money Arithmetic.

3. That the Unit and its parts or divisions be so nearly of the value of some of the known coins as that they may be of easy adoption for the people.

The Spanish Dollar seems to fulfill all these conditions.

1. Taking into our view all money transactions great and small, I question if a common measure of more convenient size than the dollar could be proposed. The value of 100. 1,000. 10,000 dollars is well estimated by the mind; so is that of the 10th or the hundredth of a dollar. Few transactions are above or below these limits. The expediency of attending to the size of the money Unit will be evident to any one who will consider how inconvenient it would be to a manufacturer or merchant, if instead of the yard for measuring cloth, either the inch or the mill had been made the unit of measure.

2. The most easy ratio of multiplication and division is that by ten. Every one knows the facility of decimal arithmetic. Every one remembers that when learning money arithmetic, he used to be puzzled with adding the farthings, taking out the fours and carrying them on, adding the pence, taking out the twelves and carrying them on; adding the shillings, taking out the twenties and carrying them on; but when he came to the pounds, when he had only tens to carry forward, it was easy & free from error.

The bulk of mankind are school-boys thro' life. These little perplexities are always great to them. And even mathematical heads feel the relief of an easier substituted for a more difficult process. Foreigners, too who have trade or who travel among us will find a great facility in understanding our coins and accounts from this ratio of subdivision. Those who have had occasion to convert the livres, sols and deniers of the French, the Gilders Stivers and penings of the Dutch, the pounds, shillings, pence and farthings of these several states into each other can judge how much they would have been aided had their several subdivisions been in a decimal ratio. Certainly in all cases where we are free to chuse between easy and difficult modes of operation, it is most rational to chuse the easy. The financier[1] therefore in his report well proposes that our coins should be in decimal proportions to one another. If we adopt the dollar for our unit, we should strike four coins, one of gold, two of silver and one of copper viz

[1] Robert Morris.

1. A Golden piece equal in value to 10 dollars.
2. The unit or dollar itself, of silver.
3. The tenth of a dollar, of silver also.
4. The hundredth of a dollar of copper.

Compare the arithmetical operations on the same sum of money expressed in this form, & expressed in the pound sterling and its divisions :

ADDITION.		SUBTRACTION.	
£ s. d. [Dollars.]		£ s. d. [Dollars.]	
8 13 11½ = 38.65		8 13 11½ = 38.65	
4 12 8¾ = 20.61		4 12 8¾ = 20.61	
13 6 8¼ = 59.26		4 1 2¾ = 18.04	

MULTIPLICATION BY 8.   DIVISION BY 8.

[£ s. d. qrs. Dollars.]   [£ s. d. qrs. Dollars.]
   8 13 11¼ = 38.65   8 13 11¼ = 38.65
  20   8   20   8)———
                                                      4.83
  ———   ———   ———
  173   309.2 D   173
   12   12

  ———   ———
  2087 or   8 13.11½   2087
     4   8   4

  ———   ———   ———
  8350   69 11 8   8)8350
     8   ———
                                           4)1043⅞
  ———   ———
  66800   12)260¾
                                           ———
  ———   20)21.8
¼ 16700   ———
                                           [£]1.1.8¾
  ———
¹⁄₁₂ 1391 8

  ———
¹⁄₂₀ [£]69 11 8

A bare inspection of the above operation will evince the labour which is occasioned by subdividing the unit into 20ths 240ths and 960ths as the English do and as we have done ; and the case of subdivisions in a decimal ratio. The same difference arises in making payment. An Englishman to pay £8. 13. 11½ must find by calculation what combination of the coins of His country will pay this sum. But an American having the same sum to pay thus expressed 38.65 will know by inspection only that three golden pieces 8 units or dollars 6 tenths and 5 coppers pay it precisely.

3 The third condition required is that the unit, its multiples and subdivisions coincide in value with some of the known coin so nearly, that the people may by a quick reference in the mind

estimate their value. If this be not attended to, they will be very long in adopting the innovation, if ever they adopt it. Let us examine in this point of view each of the four coins proposed.
1. The golden piece will be $\frac{1}{5}$ more than a half Joe [1] and $\frac{1}{15}$ more than a double guinea. It will be readily estimated then by reference to either of them but more readily and accurately as equal to 10 dollars.

2 The unit or dollar is a known coin and the most familiar of all to the mind, of the people. It is already adopted from South to North, has identified our currency and therefore happily offers itself as an Unit already introduced. Our public debt, our requisitions and their apportionments have given it actual and long possession of the place of Unit. The course of our commerce too will bring us more of this than of any other foreign coin, and therefore renders it more worthy of attention. I know of no Unit which can be proposed in competition with the dollar, but the pound : But what is the pound ? 1547 grains of fine silver in Georgia : 1289 grains in Virginia, Connecticut, Rhode Island, Massachusetts and New Hampshire ; 1031¼ grains in Maryland, Delaware Pennsylvania and New Jersey ; 966¾ grains in North Carolina and New York.

Which of these shall we adopt ? To which State give that pre-eminence of which all are so jealous ? And on which impose the difficulties of a new estimate for their coin, their cattle and other commodities? Or shall we hang the pound sterling as a common badge about all their necks ? This contains 1718¾ grains of pure silver. It is difficult to familiarise a new coin to a people. It is more difficult to familiarise them to a new coin with an old name. Happily the Dollar is familiar to them all, and is already as much referred to for a measure of value as their respective State [provincial] pounds.

3. The tenth will be precisely the Spanish bit or half pistreen in some of the States, and in others will differ from it but a very small fraction. This is a coin perfectly familiar to us all. When we shall make a new coin then equal in value to this, it will be of ready estimate with the people.

4. The hundredth or copper will be very nearly the penny or copper of New York and North Carolina, this being $\frac{1}{96}$ of a dollar, and will not be very different from the penny or copper of New Jersey, Pennsylvania, Delaware, and Maryland, which is $\frac{1}{90}$ of a dollar. It will be about the medium between the old and the new coppers of these States and therefore will soon be

---

[1] The " Half-Joe," or piece of 6400 rees was a Portuguese coin 22 carats fine weighing one-half ounce of Portugal equal to about 221 grains Troy.

substituted for them both. In Virginia coppers have never been in use. It will be as easy therefore to introduce them there of one value as of another. The copper coin proposed will be nearly equal to three-fourths of their penny which is the same with the penny lawful of the Eastern States. A great deal of small change is useful in a State, and tends to reduce the prices of small articles. Perhaps it would not be amiss, coin three more pieces of silver, one of the value of five-tenths or half a dollar, one of the value of two tenths, which would be equal to the Spanish pistreen, and one of the value of 5 coppers, which would be equal to the Spanish half bit. We should then have four silver coin viz :

1. The Unit or Dollar
2. The half dollar or .five tenths
3. The double tenth, equal to 2 [tenths] or $\frac{1}{5}$ of a dollar [or] to a pistreen.
4. The tenth, equal to a Spanish bit
5. The five copper piece equal to 05 or $\frac{1}{20}$ of a dollar or to the half bit.

The plan reported by the financier is worthy of his sound judgment. It admits however of objection in the size of the unit. He proposes that this shall be the 1440th part of a dollar; so that it will require 1440 of his units to make them the one before proposed. He was led to adopt this by a mathematical attention to our old currencies, all of which this unit will measure without leaving a fraction. But as our object is to get rid of those currencies, the advantage derived from this coincidence will soon be past. Whereas the inconveniences of this unit will forever remain, if they do not altogether prevent its introduction. It is defective in two of the three requisites of a money Unit.

1. It is inconvenient in its application to the ordinary money transactions. 10.000 dollars will require 8 figures to express them, to wit, 14,400,000. A horse or bullock of 80 dollars value will require a notation of six figures to wit 115,200 units. As a money of account this will be laborious even when facilitated by the aid of decimal arithmetic. As a common measure of the value of property it will be too minute to be comprehended by the people. The French are subjected to very laborions calculations, the livre being their ordinary money of account, and this but between the $\frac{1}{5}$ & $\frac{1}{6}$ of a dollar. But what will be our labours should our money of account be $\frac{1}{1440}$ of a dollar only ?

2. It is neither equal nor near to any of the known coins in value.

If we determine that a dollar shall be our Unit, we must then say with precision what a dollar is. This coin as struck at different times, of different weights and fineness is of different values. Sir Isaac Newton's Assay and representation to the lords of the treasury in 1717 of those which he examined make their values, as follows

	dwt grs	grains
The Seville piece of eight . .	17. 12	containing 387 of pure silver.
The Mexico piece of eight . .	17. 10⅝	containing 385½ of pure silver.
The Pillar piece of eight . . .	17. 9	containing 385¾ of pure silver.
The new Seville piece of eight .	14.	containing 308$\frac{7}{10}$ of pure silver.

The financier states the old dollar as containing 376 grains of fine silver and the new 365 grains. If the dollars circulating among us be of every date equally, we should examine the quantity of pure metal in each and from them form an average for our Unit. This is a work proper to be committed to Mathematicians as well as merchants and which should be decided on actual and accurate experiment.

The quantum of alloy is also to be decided. Some is necessary to prevent the coin from wearing too fast. Too much fills our pockets with coppers instead of silver. The silver coins assayed by Sir Isaac Newton varied from 1½ to 76 pennyweight alloy in the pound troy of mixed metal. The British standard has 18 dwt. The Spanish coins assayed by Sir Isaac Newton have from 18 to 19½ dwt. The new French crown has in fact 19½, though by edict it should have 20 dwt, that is $\frac{1}{12}$. The taste of our countrymen will require that the [their] furniture plate should be as good as the British standard. Taste cannot be controuled by law. Let it then give the law in a point, which is indifferent to a certain degree. Let the Legislatures fix the alloy of furniture plate at 18 dwt. the British standard, and Congress that of their coin at one ounce in the pound, the French standard. This proportion has been found convenient for the alloy of gold coin and it will simplify the system of our mint to alloy both metals in the same degree. [The coin too being the least pure will be less easily melted into plate.] These reasons are light indeed and of course will only weigh, if no heavier ones can be opposed to them.

The proportion between the values of gold and silver is a mercantile problem altogether. It would be inaccurate to fix it by the popular exchanges of a half Joe for eight dollars, a Louis for 4 French crowns or five Louis for 23 dollars. The first of these would be to adopt the Spanish proportion between gold and silver; the second the French, the third a mere popular barter, wherein convenience is consulted more than accuracy. The legal proportion in Spain is 16 for 1. in England 15⅕ for 1. in France 15 for 1. The Spaniards and English are found in experience to retain an over proportion of gold coins and to lose their silver. The French have a greater proportion of silver. The difference at market has been on the decrease. The financier states it at present at 14½ for 1.

Just principles will lead us to disregard legal proportions altogether; to enquire into the market price of gold in the several countries with which we shall principally be connected in commerce, and to take an average from them. Perhaps we might with safety lean to a proportion somewhat above par for gold, considering our neighbourhood and commerce with the sources of the coins and the tendency which the high price of gold in Spain has to draw thither all that of their mines, leaving silver principally for our and other markets. It is not impossible that 15 for 1 may be found an eligible proportion. I state it however as conjectural only.

As to the alloy for gold coin, the British is an ounce in the pound; the French, Spanish and Portugese differ from that only from ¼ of a grain [to a grain] and a half. I should therefore prefer the British, merely because its fraction stands in a more simple form and facilitates the calculations into which it enters.

Should the unit be fixed at 365 grains of pure silver gold at 15 for 1, and the alloy of both be one-twelfth, the weight of the coins will be as follows.

	Grains.	Grains.	Dwt. Grs.
The gold piece cont'g	243⅓ pure metal,	22.12 of alloy will weigh	11: 145
The unit, or dollar	365 pure metal,	33.18 of alloy will weigh	16: 14.18
The half doll., or 5-tenths . . .	182½ pure metal,	16.59 of alloy will weigh	8: 7.09
The fifth, or pistreen	73 pure metal,	6.63 of alloy will weigh	3: 7.63
The tenth, or bit	36½ pure metal,	3.318 of alloy will weigh	1: 15.818
The twentieth, or half-bit . . .	18¼ pure metal,	1.659 of alloy will weigh	19.9

The quantity of fine silver, which shall constitute the unit being settled and the proportion of the value of gold to that of silver; a table should be formed from the assay before suggested, classing the several foreign coins according to their fineness, declaring the worth of a pennyweight or grain in each class and that they shall be lawful tender at those rates if not clipped or otherwise diminished, and where diminished offering their value for them at the mint, deducting the expence of recoinage. Here the legislatures should co-operate with Congress in providing that no money be received or paid at their treasuries or by any of their officers or any bank but on actual weight; in making it criminal in a high degree to diminish their own coins and in some smaller degree to offer them in payment when diminished.

That this subject may be properly prepared and in readiness for Congress to take up at their meeting in November, something must now be done. The present session drawing to a close they probably would not choose to enter far into this undertaking themselves. The Committee of the States however, during the recess, will have time to digest it thoroughly, if Congress will fix some general principles for their government.

Suppose then they be instructed —

To appoint proper persons to assay and examine with the utmost accuracy practicable the Spanish milled dollars of different dates in circulation with us.

To assay and examine in like manner the fineness of all the other coins which may be found in circulation within these states.

To receive and lay before Congress the reports on the result of these assays.

To appoint also proper persons to enquire what are the proportions between the values of fine gold and fine silver at the markets, of the several countries with which we are or probably may be connected in commerce and what would be the proper proportion here, having regard to the average of their values at those markets and to other circumstances, and to report the same to the Committee to be by them laid before Congress.

To prepare an Ordinance for establishing the Unit of money within these states ; for subdividing it and for striking coins of gold, silver and copper on the following principles

That the money unit of these States shall be equal in value to a Spanish milled dollar containing so much fine silver as the assay before directed shall show to be contained, on an average in dollars of the several dates circulating with us.

That this Unit shall be divided into tenths and hundredths,

That there shall be a coin of silver of the value of an Unit. One other of the same metal of the value of one-tenth of an unit. One other of copper of the value of the hundredth of an unit. That there shall be a coin of gold of the value of ten Units, according to the report before directed and the judgment of the Committee thereon.

That the alloy of the said coins of gold and silver shall be equal in weight to one eleventh part of the fine metal.

That there be proper devices for these coins.

That measures be proposed for preventing their diminution and also their currency and that of any others when diminished.

That the several foreign coins be described and classed in
the said ordinance, the fineness of each class stated and its
value by weight estimated in Units and decimal parts of an
Unit, and that the said draught of an Ordinance be reported
to Congress at their next meeting for their consideration and
determination.

REPORT OF ALEXANDER HAMILTON ON THE ESTABLISH-
MENT OF A MINT, TO THE HOUSE OF REPRESENTA-
TIVES OF THE UNITED STATES, MAY 5, 1791

*The Secretary of the Treasury having attentively considered the
subject referred to him by the order of the House of Representatives, of the fifteenth day of April last, relative to
the establishment of a Mint, most respectfully submits the
result of his inquiries and reflections : —*

A plan for an establishment of this nature, involves a great
variety of considerations, intricate, nice, and important.   The
general state of debtor and creditor ; all the relations and consequences of price ; the essential interests of trade and industry ; the value of all property ; the whole income, both of the
State and of individuals, are liable to be sensibly influenced,
beneficially or otherwise, by the judicious or injudicious regulation of this interesting object.

It is one, likewise, not more necessary than difficult to be
rightly adjusted ; one which has frequently occupied the reflections and researches of politicians, without having harmonized
their opinions on some of the most important of the principles
which enter into its discussion.   Accordingly, different systems
continue to be advocated, and the systems of different nations,
after much investigation, continue to differ from each other.

But if a right adjustment of the matter be truly of such
nicety and difficulty, a question naturally arises, whether it may
not be most advisable to leave things in this respect, in the
state in which they are ? Why, might it be asked, since they
have so long proceeded in a train which has caused no general
sensation of inconvenience, should alterations be attempted,
the precise effect of which cannot with certainty be calculated?

The answer to this question is not perplexing.   The immense
disorder which actually reigns in so delicate and important a
concern, and the still greater disorder which is every moment
possible, call loudly for a reform.   The dollar originally con-

templated in the money transactions of this country, by successive diminutions of its weight and fineness, has sustained a depreciation of five per cent.; and yet the new dollar has a currency, in all payments in place of the old, with scarcely any attention to the difference between them. The operation of this in depreciating the value of property depending upon past contracts, and (as far as inattention to the alteration in the coin may be supposed to leave prices stationary) of all other property, is apparent. Nor can it require argument to prove that a nation ought not to suffer the value of the property of its citizens to fluctuate with the fluctuations of a foreign mint, and to change with the changes in the regulations of a foreign sovereign. This, nevertheless, is the condition of one which, having no coins of its own, adopts with implicit confidence those of other countries.

The unequal values allowed, in different parts of the Union, to coins of the same intrinsic worth; the defective species of them which embarrass the circulation of some of the States; and the dissimilarity in their several moneys of account, are inconveniences which, if not to be ascribed to the want of a national coinage, will at least be most effectually remedied by the establishment of one: a measure that will, at the same time, give additional security against impositions by counterfeit as well as by base currencies.

It was with great reason, therefore, that the attention of Congress, under the late confederation, was repeatedly drawn to the establishment of a mint; and it is with equal reason that the subject has been resumed, now that the favorable change which has taken place in the situation of public affairs admits of its being carried into execution.

But, though the difficulty of devising a proper establishment ought not to deter from undertaking so necessary a work, yet it cannot but inspire diffidence in one, whose duty it is made to propose a plan for the purpose, and may perhaps be permitted to be relied upon as some excuse for any errors which may be chargeable upon it, or for any deviations from sounder principles which may have been suggested by others, or even in part acted upon by the former Government of the United States.

In order to a right judgment of what ought to be done, the following particulars require to be discussed:

1st. What ought to be the nature of the money unit of the United States?

2d. What the proportion between gold and silver, if coins of both metals are to be established?

3d. What the proportion and composition of alloy in each kind?

4th. Whether the expense of coinage shall be defrayed by the Government, or out of the material itself?

5th. What shall be the number, denominations, sizes, and devices of the coins?

6th. Whether foreign coins shall be permitted to be current or not; if the former, at what rate, and for what period?

A prerequisite to determining with propriety what ought to be the money unit of the United States, is to endeavor to form as accurate an idea as the nature of the case will admit of what it actually is. The pound, though of various value, is the unit in the money of account of all the States. But it is not equally easy to pronounce what is to be considered as the unit in the coins. There being no formal regulation on the point, (the resolutions of Congress of the 6th of July, 1785, and 8th of August, 1786, having never yet been carried into operation,) it can only be inferred from usage or practice. The manner of adjusting foreign exchanges, would seem to indicate the dollar as best entitled to that character. In these, the old piaster of Spain, or old Seville piece of eight *rials*, of the value of four shillings and six-pence sterling, is evidently contemplated. The computed par between Great Britain and Pennsylvania, will serve as an example. According to that, one hundred pounds sterling is equal to one hundred and sixty-six pounds and two-thirds of a pound, Pennsylvania currency; which corresponds with the proportion between 4*s.* 6*d.* sterling, and 7*s.* 6*d.* the current value of the dollar in that State, by invariable usage. And, as far as the information of the Secretary goes, the same comparison holds in the other States.

But this circumstance in favor of the dollar, loses much of its weight from two considerations. That species of coin has never had any settled or standard value, according to weight or fineness, but has been permitted to circulate by tale, without regard to either, very much as a mere money of convenience, while gold has had a fixed price by weight, and with an eye to its fineness. This greater stability of value of the gold coins, is an argument of force for regarding the money unit as having been hitherto virtually attached to gold, rather than to silver.

Twenty-four grains and six-eighths of a grain of fine gold, have corresponded with the nominal value of the dollar in the several States, without regard to the successive diminutions of its intrinsic worth.

But, if the dollar should, notwithstanding, be supposed to have the best title to being considered as the present unit in

2 Q

the coins, it would remain to determine what kind of dollar ought to be understood ; or, in other words, what precise quantity of fine silver.

The old piaster of Spain, which appears to have regulated our foreign exchanges, weighed 17 dwt. 12 grains, and contained 386 grains and 15 mites of fine silver. But this piece has been long since out of circulation. The dollars now in common currency, are of recent date, and much inferior to that, both in weight and fineness. The average weight of them, upon different trials, in large masses, has been found to be 17 dwt. 8 grains. Their fineness is less precisely ascertained ; the results of various assays made by different persons, under the direction of the late Superintendent of the Finances, and of the Secretary, being as various as the assays themselves. The difference between their extremes is not less than 24 grains in a dollar of the same weight and age ; which is too much for any probable differences in the pieces. It is rather to be presumed, that a degree of inaccuracy has been occasioned by the want of proper apparatus, and, in general, of practice. The experiment which appears to have the best pretensions to exactness, would make the new dollar to contain 370 grains and 933 thousandth parts of a grain of pure silver.

According to an authority on which the Secretary places reliance, the standard of Spain for its silver coin in the year 1761, was 261 parts fine, and 27 parts alloy ; at which proportion, a dollar of 17 dwt. 8 grains, would consist of 377 grains of fine silver, and 39 grains of alloy. But there is no question that this standard has been since altered considerably for the worse : to what precise point, is not as well ascertained as could be wished ; but, from a computation of the value of dollars in the markets both of Amsterdam and London, (a criterion which cannot materially mislead,) the new dollar appears to contain about 368 grains of fine silver and that which immediately preceded it about 374 grains.

In this state of things, there is some difficulty in defining the dollar, which is to be understood as constituting the present money unit, on the supposition of its being most applicable to that species of coin. The old Seville piece of 386 grains and 15 mites fine, comports best with the computations of foreign exchanges, and with the more ancient contracts respecting landed property ; but far the greater number of contracts still in operation concerning that kind of property, and all those of a merely personal nature, now in force, must be referred to a dollar of a different kind. The actual dollar at the time of contracting, is the only one which can be supposed to have been intended; and it has been seen that, as long ago as the year 1761, there had been a material degradation of the standard. And even in regard to the more ancient contracts, no person has ever had any idea of a scruple about receiving the dollar of the day as a full equivalent for the nominal sum which the dollar originally imported.

A recurrence, therefore, to the ancient dollar, would be in the greatest number of cases an innovation *in fact*, and, in all, an innovation in respect to opinion. The actual dollar in common circulation has evidently a much better claim to be regarded as the actual money unit.

The mean intrinsic value of the different kinds of known dollars has been intimated as affording the proper criterion. But, when it is recollected that the more ancient and more valuable ones are not now to be met with at all in circulation, and that the mass of those generally current is composed of the newest and most inferior kinds, it will be perceived that even an equation of that nature would be a considerable innovation upon the real present state of things; which it will certainly be prudent to approach, as far as may be consistent with the permanent order designed to be introduced.

An additional reason for considering the prevailing dollar as the standard of the present money unit, rather than the ancient one, is, that it will not only be conformable to the true existing porportion between the two metals in this country, but will be more conformable to that which obtains in the commercial world generally.

The difference established by custom in the United States between coined gold and coined silver has been stated, upon another occasion, to be nearly as 1 to 15.6. This, if truly the case, would imply that gold was extremely overvalued in the United States; for the highest *actual proportion*, in any part of Europe, very little, if at all, exceeds 1 to 15; and the average proportion throughout Europe is probably not more than about 1 to 14.8. But that statement has proceeded upon the idea of the ancient dollar. One pennyweight of gold of twenty-two carats fine, at 6*s*. 8*d*., and the old Seville piece of 386 grains and 15 mites of pure silver, at 7*s*. 6*d*., furnish the exact ratio of 1 to 15.6262. But this does not coincide with the real difference between the metals in our market, or, which is with us the same thing, in our currency. To determine this, the quantity of fine silver in the general mass of the dollars now in circulation must afford the rule. Taking the rate of the late dollar of 374 grains, the proportion would be as 1 to 15.11. Taking the rate of the newest dollar, the proportion would then be as 1 to 14.87. The mean of the two would give the proportion of 1 to 15, very nearly; less than the legal proportion in the coins of Great Britain, which is as 1 to 15.2; but somewhat more than the actual or market proportion, which is not quite 1 to 15.

The preceding view of the subject does not indeed afford a precise or certain definition of the present unit in the coins, but it furnishes data which will serve as guides in the progress of the investigation. It ascertains, at least, that the sum in the money of account of each State, corresponding with the nominal value of the dollar in such State, corresponds also with 24 grains and $\frac{8}{8}$ of a grain of fine gold; and with something between 368 and 374 grains of fine silver.

The next inquiry towards a right determination of what ought to be the future money unit of the United States, turns upon these questions: Whether it ought to be peculiarly attached to either of the metals, in preference to the other or not? and, if to either, to which of them?

The suggestions and proceedings hitherto have had for their object the annexing of it emphatically to the silver dollar. A resolution of Congress of the 6th of July, 1785, declares that the money unit of the United States shall be a dollar; and another resolution of the 8th of August, 1786, fixes that dollar at 375 grains and 64 hundredths of a grain of fine silver. The same resolution, however, determines that there shall also be two gold coins: one of 246 grains and 268 parts of a grain of pure gold, equal to ten dollars; and the other, of half that quantity of pure gold, equal to five dollars. And it is not explained whether either of the two species of coins, of gold or silver, shall have any greater legality in payments than the other. Yet it would seem that a preference in this particular is necessary to execute the idea of attaching the unit exclusively to one kind. If each of them be as valid as the other, in payments to any amount, it is not obvious in what effectual sense either of them can be deemed the money unit, rather than the other.

If the general declaration, that the dollar shall be the money unit of the United States, could be understood to give it a superior legality in payments, the institution of coins of gold, and the declaration that each of them shall be *equal* to a certain number of dollars, would appear to destroy that inference. And the circumstance of making the dollar the unit in the money of account, seems to be rather matter of form than of substance.

Contrary to the ideas which have hitherto prevailed, in the suggestions concerning a coinage for the United States, though not without much hesitation, arising from a deference for those ideas, the Secretary is, upon the whole, strongly inclined to the opinion, that a preference ought to be given to neither of the metals for the money unit. Perhaps, if either were to be preferred, it ought to be gold rather than silver.

The reasons are these : —

The inducement to such a preference is, to render the unit as little variable as possible ; because on this depends the steady value of all contracts, and, in a certain sense, of all other property. And it is truly observed, that if the unit belong indiscriminately to both the metals, it is subject to all the fluctuations that happen in the relative value which they bear to each other. But the same reason would lead to annexing it to that particular one, which is itself the least liable to variation ; if there be, in this respect, any discernible difference between the two.

Gold may, perhaps, in certain senses, be said to have greater stability than silver ; as, being of superior value, less liberties have been taken with it, in the regulations of different countries. Its standard has remained more uniform, and it has, in other respects, undergone fewer changes ; as, being not so much an article of merchandise, owing to the use made of silver in the trade with the East Indies and China, it is less likely to be influenced by circumstances of commercial demand. And if, reasoning by analogy, it could be affirmed, that there is a physical probability of greater proportional increase in the quantity of silver than in that of gold, it would afford an additional reason for calculating on greater steadiness in the value of the latter.

As long as gold, either from its intrinsic superiority as a metal, from its greater rarity, or from the prejudices of mankind, retains so considerable a preëminence in value over silver, as it has hitherto had, a natural consequence of this seems to be that its condition will be more stationary. The revolutions, therefore, which may take place in the comparative value of gold and silver, will be changes in the state of the latter, rather than in that of the former.

If there should be an appearance of too much abstraction in any of these ideas, it may be remarked, that the first and most simple impressions do not naturally incline to giving a preference to the inferior or least valuable of the two metals.

It is sometimes observed, that silver ought to be encouraged rather than gold, as being more conducive to the extension of bank circulation, from the greater difficulty and inconvenience which its greater bulk, compared with its value, occasions in the transportation of it. But bank circulation is desirable, rather as *an auxiliary to*, than as *a substitute for* that of the precious metals, and ought to be left to its natural course. Artificial expedients to extend it, by opposing obstacles to the other, are at least not recommended by any very obvious advantages. And, in general, it is the safest rule to regulate every particular institution or object, according to the principles which, in relation to itself, appear the most sound. In addition to this, it may be observed, that the inconvenience of transporting either of the metals, is sufficiently great to induce a preference of bank paper, whenever it can be made to answer the purpose equally well.

But, upon the whole, it seems to be most advisable, as has been observed, not to attach the unit exclusively to either of the metals ; because this cannot be done effectually, without destroying the office and character of one of them as money, and reducing it to the situation of a mere merchandise ; which, accordingly, at different times, has been proposed from different and very respectable quarters ; but which would probably be a greater evil than occasional variations in the unit, from the fluctuations in the relative value of the metals ; especially if care be taken to regulate the proportion between them, with an eye to their average commercial value.

To annul the use of either of the metals, as money, is to abridge the quantity of circulating medium ; and is liable to all the objections which arise from a comparison of the benefits of a full, with the evils of a scanty circulation.

It is not a satisfactory answer to say, that none but the favored metal would in this case find its way into the country, as in that all balances must be paid. The practicability of this would, in some measure, depend on the abundance or scarcity of it in the country paying. Where there was but little, it either would not be procurable at all, or it would cost a premium to obtain it ; which, in every case of a competition with others, in a branch of trade, would constitute a deduction from the profits of the party receiving. Perhaps, too, the embarrassments which such a circumstance might sometimes create, in the pecuniary liquidation of balances, might lead to additional efforts to find a substitute in commodities, and might so far impede the introduction of the metals. Neither could the exclusion of either of them be deemed, in other respects, favorable to commerce. It is often, in the course of trade, as desirable to possess the kind of money, as the kind of commodities best adapted to a foreign market.

It seems, however, most probable, that the chief, if not the sole, effect of such a regulation, would be to diminish the utility of one of the metals. It could hardly prove an obstacle to the introduction of that which was excluded in the natural course of trade, because it would always command a ready sale for the purpose of exportation to foreign markets. But such an effect, if the only one, is not to be regarded as a trivial inconvenience.

If, then, the unit ought not to be attached exclusively to either of the metals, the proportion which ought to subsist between them, in the coins, becomes a preliminary inquiry, in order to its proper adjustment. This proportion appears to be, in several views, of no inconsiderable moment.

One consequence of overvaluing either metal, in respect to the other, is the banishment of that which is undervalued. If two countries are supposed, in one of which the proportion of gold to silver is as 1 to 16, in the other as 1 to 15, gold being worth more, silver less, in one than in the other, it is manifest that, in their reciprocal payments, each will select that species which it values least, to pay to the other where it is valued most. Besides this, the dealers in money will, from the same cause, often find a profitable traffic in an exchange of the metals between the two countries. And hence it would come to pass, if other things were equal, that the greatest part of the gold would be collected in one, and the greatest part of the silver in the other. The course of trade might in some degree counteract the tendency of the difference in the legal proportions by the market value; but this is so far and so often influenced by the legal rates, that it does not prevent their producing the effect which is inferred. Facts, too, verify the inference. In Spain and England, where gold is rated higher than in other parts of Europe, there is a scarcity of silver; while it is found to abound in France and Holland, where it is rated higher in proportion to gold than in the neighboring nations. And it is continually flowing from Europe to China and the East Indies, owing to the comparative cheapness of it in the former, and dearness of it in the latter.

This consequence is deemed by some not very material; and there are even persons who, from a fanciful predilection to gold, are willing to invite it, even by a higher price. But general utility will best be promoted by a due proportion of both metals. If gold be most convenient in large payments, silver is best adapted to the more minute and ordinary circulation.

But it is to be suspected that there is another consequence, more serious than the one which has been mentioned. This is the diminution of the total quantity of specie which a country would naturally possess.

It is evident that as often as a country, which overrates either of the metals, receives a payment in that metal, it gets a less actual quantity than it ought to do, or than it would do if the rate were a just one.

It is also equally evident, that there will be a continual effort to make payment to it in that species to which it has annexed an exaggerated estimation, wherever it is current at a less proportional value. And it would seem to be a very natural effect of these two causes, not only that the mass of the precious metals in the country in question would consist chiefly of that kind to which it had given an extraordinary *value*, but that it would be absolutely less than if they had been duly proportioned to each other.

A conclusion of this sort, however, is to be drawn with great caution. In such matters, there are always some local and many other particular circumstances, which qualify and vary the operation of general principles, even where they are just ; and there are endless combinations, very difficult to be analyzed, which often render principles, that have the most plausible pretensions, unsound and delusive.

There ought, for instance, according to those which have been stated to have been formerly a greater quantity of gold in proportion to silver in the United States, than there has been ; because the actual value of gold in this country, compared with silver, was perhaps higher than in any other. But our situation in regard to the West India islands, into some of which there is a large influx of silver directly from the mines of South America, occasions an extraordinary supply of that metal, and consequently a greater proportion of it in our circulation than might have been expected from its relative value.

What influence the proportion under consideration may have upon the state of prices, and how far this may counteract its tendency to increase or lessen the quantity of the metals, are points not easy to be developed ; and yet they are very necessary to an accurate judgment of the true operation of the thing.

But however impossible it may be to pronounce with certainty, that the possession of a less quantity of specie is a consequence of overvaluing either of the metals, there is enough of probability in the considerations which seem to indicate it, to form an argument of weight against such overvaluation.

A third ill consequence resulting from it is, a greater and more frequent disturbance of the state of the money unit, by a greater and more frequent diversity between the legal and market proportions of the metals. This has not hitherto been experienced in the United States, but it has been experienced elsewhere ; and from its not having been felt by us hitherto, it does not follow that this will not be the case hereafter, when our commerce shall have attained a maturity, which will place it under the influence of more fixed principles.

In establishing a proportion between the metals, there seems to be an option of one of two things —

To approach, as nearly as it can be ascertained, the mean or average proportion, in what may be called the commercial world ; or,

To retain that which now exists in the United States. As far as these happen to coincide, they will render the course to be pursued more plain and more certain.

To ascertain the first, with precision, would require better materials than are possessed, or than could be obtained, without an inconvenient delay.

Sir Isaac Newton, in a representation to the Treasury of Great Britain, in the year 1717, after stating the particular proportions in the different countries of Europe, concludes thus : — " By the course of trade and exchange between nation and nation, in all Europe, fine gold is to fine silver as $14\frac{4}{5}$, or 15 to 1."

But however accurate and decisive this authority may be deemed, in relation to the period to which it applies, it cannot be taken, at the distance of more than seventy years, as a rule for determining the existing proportion. Alterations have been since made in the regulations of their coins by several nations ; which, as well as the course of trade, have an influence upon the market values. Nevertheless, there is reason to believe, that the state of the matter, as represented by Sir Isaac Newton, is not very remote from its actual state.

In Holland, the greatest *money* market of Europe, gold was to silver, in December, 1789, as 1 to 14.88 ; and in that of London it has been, for some time past, but little different, approaching perhaps something nearer 1 to 15.

It has been seen that the existing proportion between the two metals in this country is about as 1 to 15.

It is fortunate, in this respect, that the innovations of the Spanish mint have imperceptibly introduced a proportion so analogous as this is to that which prevails among the principal commercial nations, as it greatly facilitates a proper regulation of the matter.

This proportion of 1 to 15 is recommended by the particular situation of our trade, as being very nearly that which obtains in the market of Great Britain ; to which nation our specie is principally exported. A lower rate for either of the metals, in our market, than in hers, might not only afford a motive the more, in certain cases, to remit in specie rather than in commodities; but it might, in some others, cause us to pay a greater quantity of it for a given sum than we should otherwise do. If the effect should rather be to occasion a premium to be given for the metal which was underrated, this would obviate those disadvantages; but it would involve another, a customary difference between the market and legal proportions, which would amount to a species of disorder in the national coinage.

Looking forward to the payments of interest hereafter to be made to Holland, the same proportion does not appear ineligible. The present legal proportion in the coins of Holland is stated at 1 to $14\frac{9}{10}$. That of the market varies somewhat at different times, but seldom very widely from this point.

There can hardly be a better rule in any country, for the legal, than the market proportion, if this can be supposed to have been produced by the free and steady course of commercial principles. The presumption in such case is, that each metal finds its true level, according to its intrinsic utility, in the general system of money operations.

But it must be admitted that this argument in favor of continuing the existing proportion is not applicable to the state of the coins with us. There have been too many artificial and heterogeneous ingredients — too much want of order in the pecuniary transactions of this country — to authorize the attributing the effects which have appeared to the regular operations of commerce. A proof of this is to be drawn from the alterations which have happened in the proportion between the metals merely by the successive degradations of the dollar, in consequence of the mutability of a foreign mint. The value of gold to silver appears to have declined, wholly from this cause, from $15\frac{6}{10}$ to about 15 to 1 ; yet, as this last proportion, however produced, coincides so nearly with what may be deemed the commercial average, it may be supposed to furnish as good a rule as can be pursued.

The only question seems to be, whether the value of gold ought not to be a little lowered, to bring it to a more exact level with the two markets which have been mentioned ; but, as the ratio of 1 to 15 is so nearly conformable to the state of those markets, and best agrees with that of our own, it will probably be found the most eligible. If the market of Spain continues to give a higher value to gold (as it has done in time past) than that which is recommended, there may be some advantage in a middle station.

A further preliminary to the adjustment of the future money unit is, to determine what shall be the proportion and compositiou of alloy in each species of the coins.

The first, by the resolution of the 8th of August, 1786, before referred to, is regulated at one-twelfth, or in other words, at 1 part alloy to 11 parts fine, whether gold or silver ; which appears to be a convenient rule ; unless there should be some collateral consideration which may dictate a departure from it. Its correspondency, in regard to both metals, is a recommendation of it, because a difference could answer no purpose of pecuniary or commercial utility, and uniformity is favorable to order.

This ratio, as it regards gold, coincides with the proportion, real or professed, in the coins of Portugal, England, France and Spain. In those of the two former, it is real; in those of the two latter, there is a deduction for what is called *remedy of weight and alloy*, which is in the nature of an allowance to the master of the mint for errors and imperfections in the process ; rendering the coin either lighter or baser than it ought to be. The same thing is known in the theory of the English mint, where $\frac{1}{6}$ of a carat is allowed. But the difference seems to be, that *there*, it is merely an occasional indemnity within a certain limit, for real and unavoidable errors and imperfections ; whereas, in the practice of the mints of France and Spain, it appears to amount to a stated and regular deviation from the nominal standard. Accordingly, the real standards of France and Spain are something worse than 22 carats, or 11 parts in 12 fine.

The principal gold coins in Germany, Holland, Sweden, Denmark, Poland, and Italy, are finer than those of England and Portugal, in different degrees, from 1 carat and $\frac{1}{4}$ to 1 carat and $\frac{7}{8}$, which last is within $\frac{1}{8}$ of a carat of pure gold.

There are similar diversities in the standards of the silver coins of the different countries of Europe. That of Great Britain is 222 parts fine, to 18 alloy ; those of the other European nations vary from that of Great Britain as widely as from about 17 of the same parts better, to 75 worse.

The principal reasons assigned for the use of alloy, are the saving of expense in the refining of the metals, (which in their natural state are usually mixed with a portion of the coarser kinds,) and the rendering of them harder as a security against too great waste by friction or wearing. The first reason, drawn from the original composition of the metals, is strengthened at present by the practice of alloying their coins, which has obtained among so many nations. The reality of the effect to which the last reason is applicable, has been denied, and experience has been appealed to as proving that the more alloyed coins wear faster than the purer. The true state of this matter may be worthy of future investigation, though first appearances are in favor of alloy. In the mean time, the saving of trouble and expense are sufficient inducements to following those examples which suppose its expediency. And the same considerations lead to taking as our models those nations with whom we have most intercourse, and whose coins are most prevalent in our circulation. These are Spain, Portugal, England, and France. The relation which the proposed proportion bears to their gold coins, has been explained. In respect to their silver coins, it will not be very remote from the mean of their several standards.

The component ingredients of the alloy in each metal, will also require to be regulated. In silver, copper is the only kind in use, and it is doubtless the only proper one. In gold, there is a mixture of silver and copper; in the English coins consisting of equal parts, in the coins of some other countries varying from $\frac{1}{6}$ to $\frac{2}{5}$ silver.

The reason of this union of silver with copper is this : The silver counteracts the tendency of the copper to injure the color or beauty of the coin, by giving it too much redness, or rather a coppery hue, which a small quantity will produce ; and the copper prevents the too great whiteness which silver alone would confer. It is apprehended that there are considerations which may render it prudent to establish, by law, that the proportion of silver to copper in the gold coins of the United States shall not be more than $\frac{1}{2}$, nor less than $\frac{1}{3}$; vesting a discretion in some proper place to regulate the matter within those limits, as experience in the execution may recommend.

A third point remains to be discussed, as a prerequisite to the determination of the money unit, which is, whether the expense of coining shall be defrayed by the public, or out of the material itself ; or, as it is sometimes stated, whether coinage shall be free, or shall be subject to a duty or imposition ? This forms perhaps, one of the nicest questions in the doctrine of money.

The practice of different nations is dissimilar in this particular. In England, coinage is said to be entirely free ; the mint price of the metals in bullion being the same with the value of them in coin. In France, there is a duty, which has been, if it is not now, eight per cent. In Holland, there is a difference between the mint price and the value in the coins, which has been computed at .96 or something less than one per cent. upon gold ; at 1.48, or something less than one and a half per cent. upon silver. The resolution of the 8th of August, 1786, proceeds upon the idea of a deduction of a half per cent. from gold, and of two per cent. from silver, as an indemnification for the expense of coining. This is inferred from a report of the late board of treasury, upon which that resolution appears to have been founded.

Upon the supposition that the expense of coinage ought to be defrayed out of the metals, there are two ways in which it may be effected : one, by a reduction of the quantity of fine gold and silver in the coins ; the other, by establishing a difference between the value of those metals in the coins, and the mint price of them in bullion.

The first method appears to the Secretary inadmissible. He is unable to distinguish an operation of this sort from that of raising the denomination of the coin ; a measure which has been disapproved by the wisest men of the nations in which it has been practised, and condemned by the rest of the world. To declare that a less weight of gold or silver shall pass for the same sum, which before represented a greater weight ; or to ordain that the same weight shall pass for a greater sum, are things substantially of one nature. The consequence of either of them, if the change can be realized, is to degrade the money unit; obliging creditors to receive less than their just dues, and depreciating property of every kind ; for it is manifest that every thing would, in this case, be represented by a less quantity of gold and silver than before.

It is sometimes observed, on this head, that though any article of property might, in fact, be represented by a less actual quantity of pure metal, it would nevertheless be represented by something of the same intrinsic value. Every fabric, it is remarked, is worth intrinsically the price of the raw material and the expense of fabrication ; a truth not less applicable to a piece of coin than to a yard of cloth.

This position, well founded in itself, is here misapplied. It supposes that the coins now in circulation are to be considered as bullion, or, in other words, as a raw material ; but the fact is, that the adoption of them as money, has caused them to become the fabric; it has invested them with the character and office of coins, and has given them a sanction and efficacy, equivalent to that of the stamp of the sovereign. The prices of all our commodities, at home and abroad, and of all foreign commodities in our markets, have found their level in conformity to this principle. The foreign coins may be *divested* of the privilege they have hitherto been permitted to enjoy, and may of course be *left* to find their value in the market as a raw material. But the quantity of gold and silver in the national coins, corresponding with a given sum, cannot be made less than heretofore, without disturbing the balance of intrinsic value, and making every acre of land, as well as every bushel of wheat, of less actual worth than in time past. If the United States were isolated, and cut off from all intercourse with the rest of mankind, this reasoning would not be equally conclusive. But it appears decisive, when considered with a view to the relations which commerce has created between us and other countries.

It is, however, not improbable, that the effect meditated would be defeated by a rise of prices proportioned to the diminution of the intrinsic value of the coins. This might be looked for in every enlightened commercial country; but perhaps in none with greater certainty than in this, because in none are men less liable to be the dupes of sounds; in none has authority so little resource for substituting names for things.

A general revolution in prices, though only nominally, and in appearance, could not fail to distract the ideas of the community; and would be apt to breed discontents as well among those who live on the income of their money, as among the poorer classes of the people, to whom the necessaries of life would seem to have become dearer. In the confusion of such a state of things, ideas of value would not improbably adhere to the old coins, which, from that circumstance, instead of feeling the effect of the loss of their privilege as money, would perhaps bear a price in the market relatively to the new ones, in exact proportion to weight. The frequency of the demand for the metals to pay foreign balances, would contribute to this effect.

Among the evils attendant on such an operation, are these: creditors, both of the public and of individuals, would lose a part of their property; public and private credit would receive a wound; the effective revenues of the government would be diminished. There is scarcely any point in the economy of national affairs, of greater moment than the uniform preservation of the intrinsic value of the money unit. On this the security and steady value of property essentially depend.

The second method, therefore, of defraying the expense of the coinage out of the metals, is greatly to be preferred to the other. This is to let the same sum of money continue to represent in the new coins exactly the same quantity of gold and silver as it does in those now current; to allow at the mint such a price only for those metals as will admit of profit just sufficient to satisfy the expense of coinage; to abolish the legal currency of the foreign coins, both in public and private payments; and of course to leave the superior utility of the national coins for domestic purposes, to operate the difference of market value, which is necessary to induce the bringing of bullion to the mint. In this case, all property and labor will still be represented by the same quantity of gold and silver as formerly ; and the only change which will be wrought, will consist in annexing the office of money exclusively to the national coins ; consequently, withdrawing it from those of foreign countries, and suffering them to become, as they ought to be, mere articles of merchandise.

The arguments in favor of a regulation of this kind are : First. That the want of it is a cause of extra expense : there being then no motive of individual interest to distinguish between the national coins and bullion, they are, it is alleged, indiscriminately melted down for domestic manufactures, and exported for the purposes of foreign trade ; and it is added, that when the coins become light by wearing, the same quantity of fine gold or silver bears a higher price in bullion than in the coins ; in which state of things, the melting down of the coins to be sold as bullion is attended with profit ; and from both causes, the expense of the mint, or, in other words, the expense of maintaining the specie capital of the nation, is materially augmented.

Secondly. That the existence of such a regulation promotes a favorable course of exchange, and benefits trade ; not only by that circumstance, but by obliging foreigners, in certain cases, to pay dearer for domestic commodities, and to sell their own cheaper.

As far as relates to the tendency of a free coinage to produce an increase of expense in different ways that have been stated, the argument must be allowed to have foundation, both in reason and in experience. It describes what has been exemplified in Great Britain.

The effect of giving an artificial value to bullion, is not at first sight obvious ; but it actually happened at the period immediately preceding the late reformation in the gold coin of the country just named. A pound troy in gold bullion, of standard fineness, was then from 19*s.* 6*d.* to 25*s.* sterling dearer than an equal weight of guineas, as delivered at the mint. The phenomenon is thus accounted for — the old guineas were more than two per cent. lighter than their *standard weight.* This *weight,* therefore, in bullion, was truly worth two per cent. more than those guineas. It consequently had, in respect to them, a correspondent rise in the market.

And as guineas were then current by *tale,* the new ones, as they issued from the mint, were confounded in circulation with the old ones ; and, by the association, were depreciated below their intrinsic value, in comparison with bullion. It became, of course, a profitable traffic to sell bullion for coin, to select the light pieces, and re-issue them in currency, and to melt down the heavy ones, and sell them again as bullion. This practice, besides other inconveniences, cost the Government large sums in the renewal of the coins.

But the remainder of the argument stands upon ground far more questionable. It depends upon very numerous and very complex combinations, in which there is infinite latitude for fallacy and error.

The most plausible part of it is that which relates to the course of exchange. Experience in France has shown that the market price of bullion has been influenced by the mint difference between that and coin — sometimes to the full extent of the difference; and it would seem to be a clear inference, that whenever that difference materially exceeded the charges of remitting bullion from the country where it existed, to another in which coinage was free, exchange would be in favor of the former.

If, for instance, the balance of trade between France and England were at any time equal, their merchants would naturally have reciprocal payments to make to an equal amount, which, as usual, would be liquidated by means of bills of exchange. If, in this situation, the difference between coin and bullion should be in the market, as at the mint of France, eight per cent.; if, also, the charges of transporting money from France to England should not be above two per cent.; and if exchange should be at par, it is evident that a profit of six per cent. might be made, by sending bullion from France to England, and drawing bills for the amount. One hundred louis d'ors in coin, would purchase the weight of one hundred and eight in bullion; one hundred of which, remitted to England, would suffice to pay a debt of an equal amount; and two being paid for the charges of insurance and transportation there would remain six for the benefit of the person who should manage the negotiation. But as so large a profit could not fail to produce competition, the bills, in consequence of this, would decrease in price, till the profit was reduced to the *minimum* of an adequate recompense for the trouble and risk. And, as the amount of one hundred louis d'ors in England, might be afforded for ninety-six in France, with a profit of more than one and a half per cent., bills upon England, might fall in France to four per cent. below par; one per cent. being a sufficient profit to the exchanger or broker for the management of the business.

But it is *admitted* that this advantage is lost, when the balance of trade is against the nation which imposes the duty in question;

because, by increasing the demand for bullion, it brings this to a par with the coins; and it is to be *suspected*, that where commercial principles have their free scope, and are well understood, the market difference between the metals in coin and bullion, will seldom approximate to that of the mint, if the latter be considerable. It must be not a little difficult to keep the money of the world, which can be employed to an equal purpose in the commerce of the world, in a state of degradation, in comparison with the money of a particular country.

This alone would seem sufficient to prevent it: whenever the price of coin to bullion, in the market, materially exceeded the par of the metals, it would become an object to send the bullion abroad, if not to pay a foreign balance, to be invested in some other way in foreign countries, where it bore a superior value; an operation by which immense fortunes might be amassed, if it were not that the exportation of the bullion would of itself restore the intrinsic par. But, as it would naturally have this effect, the advantage supposed would contain in itself the principle of its own destruction. As long, however, as the exportation of bullion could be made with profit, which is as long as exchange could remain below par, there would be a drain of the gold and silver of the country.

If anything can maintain, for a length of time, a material difference between the value of the metals in coin and in bullion, it must be a constant and considerable balance of trade in favor of the country in which it is maintained. In one situated like the United States, it would in all probability be a hopeless attempt. The frequent demand for gold and silver, to pay balances to foreigners, would tend powerfully to preserve the equilibrium of intrinsic value.

The prospect is, that it would occasion foreign coins to circulate by common consent, nearly at par with the national.

To say, that as far as the effect of lowering exchange is produced, though it be only occasional and momentary, there is a benefit the more thrown into the scale of public prosperity, is not satisfactory. It has been seen, that it may be productive of one evil, the investment of a part of the national capital in foreign countries; which can hardly be beneficial but in a situation like that of the United Netherlands, where an immense capital, and a decrease of internal demand, render it necessary to find employment for money in the wants of other nations; and, perhaps on a close examination, other evils may be descried.

One allied to that which has been mentioned, is this — taking France, for the sake of more concise illustration, as the scene.

2 R

Whenever it happens that French louis-d'ors are sent abroad, from whatever cause, if there be a considerable difference between coin and bullion in the market of France, it will constitute an advantageous traffic to send back these louis-d'ors, and bring away bullion in lieu of them ; upon all which exchanges, France must sustain an actual loss of a part of its gold and silver.

Again : such a difference between coin and bullion may tend to counteract a favorable balance of trade. Whenever a foreign merchant is the carrier of his own commodities to France for sale, he has a strong inducement to bring back specie, instead of French commodities ; because a return in the latter may afford no profit, may even be attended with loss ; in the former, it will afford a certain profit. The same principle must be supposed to operate in the general course of remittances from France to other countries. The principal question with a merchant naturally is, in what manner can I realize a given sum, with most advantage, where I wish to place it ? And, in cases in which other commodities are not likely to produce equal profit with bullion, it may be expected that this will be preferred ; to which, the greater certainty attending the operation must be an additional incitement. There can hardly be imagined a circumstance less friendly to trade, than the existence of an extra inducement arising from the possibility of a profitable speculation upon the articles themselves, to export from a country its gold and silver, rather than the products of its land and labor.

The other advantages supposed, of obliging foreigners to pay dearer for domestic commodities, and to sell their own cheaper, are applied to a situation which includes a favorable balance of trade. It is understood in this sense : the prices of domestic commodities, (such, at least, as are peculiar to the country,) remain attached to the denominations of the coins. When a favorable balance of trade realizes in the market the mint difference between coin and bullion, foreigners, who must pay in the latter, are obliged to give more of it for such commodities than they otherwise would do. Again : the bullion, which is now obtained at a cheaper rate in the home market, will procure the same quantity of goods in the foreign market as before, which is said to render foreign commodities cheaper. In this reasoning, much fallacy is to be suspected. If it be true that foreigners pay more for domestic commodities, it must be equally true that they get more for their own when they bring them themselves to market. If peculiar, or other domestic commodities adhere to the denominations of the coins, no reason occurs why foreign commodities of a like character should not do the same thing ;

and in this case, the foreigner, though he receive only the same value in coin for his merchandise as formerly, can convert it into a greater quantity of bullion. Whence the nation is liable to lose more of its gold and silver than if their intrinsic value in relation to the coins were preserved. And whether the gain or the loss will, on the whole, preponderate, would appear to depend on the comparative proportion of active commerce of the one country with the other.

It is evident, also, that the nation must pay as much gold and silver as before, for the commodities which it procures *abroad;* and whether it obtains this gold and silver cheaper, or not, turns upon the solution of the question just intimated, respecting the relative proportion of active commerce between the two countries.

Besides these considerations, it is admitted in the reasoning, that the advantages supposed, which depend on a favorable balance of trade, have a tendency to affect that balance disadvantageously. Foreigners, it is allowed, will in this case seek some other vent for their commodities, and some other market where they can supply their wants at an easier rate. A tendency of this kind, if real, would be a sufficient objection to the regulation. Nothing which contributes to change a beneficial current of trade, can well compensate, by particular advantages, for so injurious an effect. It is far more easy to transfer trade from a less to a more favorable channel, than, when once transferred, to bring it back to its old one. Every source of artificial interruption to an advantageous current, is, therefore, cautiously to be avoided.

It merits attention, that the able minister, who lately and so long presided over the finances of France, does not attribute to the duty of coinage in that country, any particular advantages in relation to exchange and trade. Though he rather appears an advocate for it, it is on the sole ground of the revenue it affords, which he represents as in the nature of a very moderate duty on the general mass of exportation.

And it is not improbable that, to the singular felicity of situation of that kingdom, is to be attributed its not having been sensible of the evils which seem incident to the regulation. There is, perhaps, no part of Europe which has so little need of other countries as France. Comprehending a variety of soils and climates, an immense population, its agriculture in a state of mature improvement, it possesses within its own bosom, most, if not all, the productions of the earth, which any of its most favored neighbors can boast. The variety, abundance, and excellence of its wines, constitute a peculiar advantage in its favor. Arts and manufactures are there also in a very advanced state; some of them, of considerable importance, in higher perfection than elsewhere. Its contiguity to Spain; the intimate nature of its connexion with that country; a country with few fabrics of its own, consequently numerous wants, and the principal receptacle of the treasures of the new world: These circumstances concur, in securing to France so uniform and so considerable a balance of trade, as in a great measure to counteract the natural tendency of any errors which may exist in the system of her mint; and to render inferences from the operation of that system there, in reference to this country, more liable to mislead than to instruct. Nor ought it to pass unnoticed, that, with all these advantages, the government of France has found it necessary, on some occasions, to employ very violent methods to compel the bringing of bullion to the mint; a circumstance which affords a strong presumption of the inexpediency of the regulation, and of the impracticability of executing it in the United States.

This point has been the longer dwelt upon, not only because there is a diversity of opinion among speculative men concerning it, and a diversity in the practice of the most considerable commercial nations, but because the acts of our own government, under the confederation, have not only admitted the expediency of defraying the expense of coinage out of the metals themselves, but upon this idea have both made a deduction from the weight of the coins, and established a difference between their regulated value and the mint price of bullion, greater than would result from that deduction. This double operation in favor of a principle so questionable in itself, has made a more particular investigation of it a duty.

The intention, however, of the preceding remarks, is rather to show that the expectation of commercial advantages ought not to decide in favor of a duty of coinage, and that, if it should be adopted, it ought not to be in the form of a deduction from the intrinsic value of the coins, than absolutely to exclude the idea of any difference whatever between the value of the metals in coin and in bullion. It is not clearly discerned that a small difference between the mint price of bullion, and the regulated value of the coins, would be pernicious, or that it might not even be advisable, in the first instance, by way of experiment, merely as a preventive to the melting down and exportation of the coins. This will now be somewhat more particularly considered.

The arguments for a coinage entirely free, are, that it

preserves the intrinsic value of the metals ; that it makes the expense of fabrication a general instead of a partial tax ; and that it tends to promote the abundance of gold and silver, which, it is alleged, will flow to that place where they find the best price, and from that place where they are in any degree undervalued.

The first consideration has not much weight, as an objection to a plan which, without diminishing the quantity of metals in the coins, merely allows a less price for them in bullion at the national factory or mint. No rule of intrinsic value is violated, by considering the raw material as worth less than the fabric, in proportion to the expense of fabrication. And by divesting foreign coins of the privilege of circulating as money, they become the raw material.

The second consideration has perhaps greater weight. But it may not amount to an objection, if it be the best method of preventing disorders in the coins, which it is in a particular manner the interest of those on whom the tax would fall to prevent. The practice of taking gold by weight, which has of late years obtained in Great Britain, has been found, in some degree, a remedy ; but this is inconvenient, and may on that account fall into disuse. Another circumstance has had a remedial operation. This is the delays of the mint. It appears to be the practice there, not to make payment for the bullion which is brought to be exchanged for coin, till it either has in fact, or is pretended to have, undergone the process of recoining.

The necessity of fulfilling prior engagements is a cause or pretext for postponing the delivery of the coin in lieu of the bullion. And this delay creates a difference in the market price of the two things. Accordingly, for some years past, an ounce of standard gold, which is worth in coin £3 17s. 10½d. sterling, has been in the market of London, in bullion, only £3 17s. 6d., which is within a small fraction of one-half per cent. less. Whether this be management in the mint, to accommodate the bank in the purchase of bullion, or to effect indirectly something equivalent to a formal difference of price, or whether it be the natural course of the business, is open to conjecture.

It at the same time indicates that if the mint were to make prompt payment, at about half per cent. less than it does at present, the state of bullion, in respect to coin, would be precisely the same as it now is. And it would be then certain that the Government would save expense in the coinage of gold ; since it is not probable that the time actually lost in the course of the year, in converting bullion into coin, can be an equivalent to half per cent. on the advance, and there will generally be at the command of the Treasury a considerable sum of money waiting for some periodical disbursement, which, without hazard, might be applied to that advance.

In what sense a free coinage can be said to promote the abundance of gold and silver, may be inferred from the instances which have been given of the tendency of a contrary system to promote their exportation. It is, however, not probable, that a very small difference of value between coin and bullion can have any effect which ought to enter into calculation. There can be no inducement of positive profit, to export the bullion, as long as the difference of price is exceeded by the expense of transportation. And the prospect of smaller loss upon the metals than upon commodities, when the difference is very minute, will be frequently overbalanced by the possibility of doing better with the latter, from a rise of markets. It is, at any rate, certain, that it can be of no consequence in this view, whether the superiority of coin to bullion in the market, be produced, as in England, by the delay of the mint, or by a formal discrimination in the regulated values.

Under an impression that a *small* difference between the value of the coin and the mint price of bullion, is the least exceptionable expedient for restraining the melting down, or exportation of the former, and not perceiving that, if it be a very moderate one, it can be hurtful in other respects — the Secretary is inclined to an experiment of one half per cent. on each of the metals. The fact which has been mentioned, with regard to the price of gold bullion in the English market, seems to demonstrate that such a difference may safely be made. In this case, there must be immediate payment for the gold and silver offered to the mint. How far one half per cent. will go towards defraying the expense of the coinage, cannot be determined beforehand with accuracy. It is presumed that, on an economical plan, it will suffice in relation to gold. But it is not expected that the same rate on silver will be sufficient to defray the expense attending that metal. Some additional provision may therefore be found necessary, if this limit be adopted.

It does not seem to be advisable to make any greater difference in regard to silver than to gold ; because it is desirable that the proportion between the two metals in the market, should correspond with that in the coins, which would not be the case if the mint price of one was comparatively lower than that of the other ; and because, also, silver being proposed to be rated in respect to gold, somewhat below its general commercial value, if there should be a disparity to its disadvantage in the mint prices of the two metals, it would obstruct too much the bringing of it to be coined, and would add an inducement to export it. Nor does it appear to the Secretary safe to make a greater difference between the value of coin and bullion, than has been mentioned. It will be better to have to increase it hereafter, if this shall be found expedient, than to have to recede from too considerable a difference, in consequence of evils which shall have been experienced.

It is sometimes mentioned, as an expedient, which, consistently with a free coinage, may serve to prevent the evils desired to be avoided, to incorporate in the coins a greater proportion of alloy than is usual; regulating their value, nevertheless, according to the quantity of pure metal they contain. This, it is supposed, by adding to the difficulty of refining them, would cause bullion to be preferred both for manufacture and exportation.

But strong objections lie against this scheme : — an augmentation of expense ; an actual depreciation of the coin ; a danger of still greater depreciation in the public opinion ; the facilitating of counterfeits; while it is questionable whether it would have the effect expected from it.

The alloy being esteemed of no value, an increase of it is evidently an increase of expense. This, in relation to the gold coins, particularly, is a matter of moment. It has been noted, that the alloy in them consists partly of silver. If, to avoid expense, the addition should be of copper only, this would spoil the appearance of the coin, and give it a base countenance. Its beauty would, indeed, be injured, though in a less degree, even if the usual proportions of silver and copper should be maintained in the increased quantity of alloy.

And however inconsiderable an additional expenditure of copper in the coinage of a year may be deemed, in a series of years it would become of consequence. In regulations which contemplate the lapse and operation of ages, a very small item of expense acquires importance.

The actual depreciation of the coin by an increase of alloy, results from the very circumstance which is the motive to it — the greater difficulty of refining. In England, it is customary for those concerned in manufactures of gold to make a deduction in the price of four pence sterling per ounce, of fine gold, for every carat which the mass containing it is below the legal standard. Taking this as a rule, an inferiority of a single carat, or one twenty-fourth part in the gold coins of the United States,

compared with the English standard, would cause the *same
quantity* of pure gold in them to be worth nearly four-tenths per
cent. less than in the coins of Great Britain. This circumstance
would be likely, in process of time, to be felt in the market of
the United States.

A still greater depreciation, in the public opinion, would be
to be apprehended from the *apparent* debasement of the coin.
The effects of imagination and prejudice cannot safely be disregarded in anything that relates to money. If the beauty of
the coin be impaired, it may be found difficult to satisfy the
generality of the community that what appears worst is not
really less valuable ; and it is not altogether certain that an impression of its being so may not occasion an unnatural augmentation of prices.

Greater danger of imposition, by counterfeits, is also to be
apprehended from the injury which will be done to the appearance of the coin. It is a just observation, that " the perfection
of the coins is a great safeguard against counterfeits." And it
is evident that the color, as well as the excellence of the work-
manship, is an ingredient in that perfection. The intermixture
of too much alloy, particularly of copper, in the gold coins at
least, must materially lessen the facility of distinguishing,
by the eye, the purer from the baser kind, the genuine from
the counterfeit.

The inefficacy of the arrangement to the purpose intended
to be answered by it, is rendered probable by different considerations. If the standard of plate in the United States should
be regulated according to that of the national coins, it is to be
expected that the goldsmith would prefer these to the foreign
coins, because he would find them prepared to his hand, in the
state which he desires ; whereas he would have to *expend* an
additional quantity of alloy to bring the foreign coins to that
state. If the standard of plate, by law or usage, should be
superior to that of the national coins, there would be a possibility of the foreign coins bearing a higher price in the market ;
and this would not only obstruct their being brought to the
mint, but might occasion the exportation of the national coin
in preference. It is not understood that the practice of making
an abatement of price for the inferiority of standard is applicable to the English mint ; and if it be not, this would also contribute to frustrating the expected effect from the increase of
alloy. For, in this case, a given quantity of pure metal, in our
standard, would be worth as much there as in bullion of the
English or any other standard.

Considering, therefore, the uncertainty of the success of the expedient, and the inconveniences which seem incident to it, it would appear preferable to submit to those of a free coinage. It is observable, that additional expense, which is one of the principal of these, is also applicable to the proposed remedy.

It is now proper to resume and finish the answer to the first question, in order to which the three succeeding ones have necessarily been anticipated. The conclusion to be drawn from the observations which have been made on the subject, is this : That the unit, in the coins of the United States, ought to correspond with 24 grains and $\frac{3}{4}$ of a grain of pure gold, and with 371 grains and $\frac{1}{4}$ of a grain of pure silver, each answering to a dollar in the money of account. The former is exactly agreeable to the present value of gold, and the latter is within a small fraction of the mean of the two last emissions of dollars — the only ones which are now found in common circulation, and of which the newest is in the greatest abundance. The alloy in each case to be one-twelfth of the total weight, which will make the unit 27 grains of standard gold, and 405 grains of standard silver.

Each of these, it has been remarked, will answer to a dollar in the money of account. It is conceived that nothing better can be done in relation to this, than to pursue the track marked out by the resolution of the 8th of August, 1786. This has been approved abroad, as well as at home, and it is certain that nothing can be more simple or convenient, than the decimal subdivisions. There is every reason to expect that the method will speedily grow into general use, when it shall be seconded by corresponding coins. On this plan, the unit in the money of account will continue to be, as established by that resolution, a dollar ; and its multiples, dimes, cents, and mills, or tenths, hundredths, and thousandths.

With regard to the number of different pieces which shall compose the coins of the United States, two things are to be consulted — convenience of circulation, and cheapness of the coinage. The first ought not to be sacrificed to the last ; but as far as they can be reconciled to each other, it is desirable to do it. Numerous and small (if not too minute) subdivisions assist circulation ; but the multiplication of the smaller kinds increases expense ; the same process being necessary to a small as to a large piece.

As it is easy to add, it will be most adviseable to begin with a small number, till experience shall decide whether any other kinds are necessary. The following, it is conceived, will be sufficient in the commencement :

One gold piece, equal in weight and value to ten units or dollars.

One gold piece, equal to a tenth part of the former, and which shall be a unit or dollar.

One silver piece, which shall also be a unit or dollar.

One silver piece, which shall be, in weight and value, a tenth part of the silver unit or dollar.

One copper piece, which shall be of the value of a hundredth part of a dollar.

One other copper piece, which shall be half the value of the former.

It is not proposed that the lightest of the two gold coins should be numerous, as, in large payments, the larger the pieces the shorter the process of counting, the less risk of mistake, and, consequently, the greater the safety and the convenience; and, in small payments, it is not perceived that any inconvenience can accrue from an entire dependence on the silver and copper coins. The chief inducement to the establishment of the small gold piece, is to have a sensible object in that metal, as well as in silver, to express the unit. Fifty thousand at a time in circulation may suffice for this purpose.

The tenth part of a dollar is but a small piece, and, with the aid of the copper coins, will probably suffice for all the more minute uses of circulation. It is less than the least of the silver coins now in general currency in England.

The largest copper piece will nearly answer to the half-penny sterling, and the smallest, of course, to the farthing. Pieces of very small value are a great accommodation, and the means of a beneficial economy to the poor, by enabling them to purchase, in small portions, and at a more reasonable rate, the necessaries of which they stand in need. If there are only cents, the lowest price for any portion of a vendible commodity, however inconsiderable in quantity, will be a cent; if there are half cents, it will be a half-cent; and, in a great number of cases, exactly the same things will be sold for a half-cent which, if there were none, would cost a cent. But a half-cent is low enough for the *minimum* of price. Excessive minuteness would defeat its object. To enable the poorer classes to procure necessaries cheap, is to enable them, with more comfort to themselves, to labor for less; the advantages of which need no comment.

The denominations of the silver coins contained in the resolution of the 8th of August, 1786, are conceived to be significant and proper. The dollar is recommended by its correspondency with the present coin of that name, for which it is designed to be a substitute, which will facilitate its ready adoption as such in the minds of the citizens. The dime, or tenth, the cent, or hundredth, the mill, or thousandth, are proper, because they express the proportions which they are intended to designate. It is only to be regretted that the meaning of these terms will not be familiar to those who are not acquainted with the language from which they are borrowed. It were to be wished that the length, and, in some degree, the clumsiness, of some of the corresponding terms in English did not discourage from preferring them. It is useful to have names which signify the things to which they belong; and, in respect to objects of general use, in a manner intelligible to all. Perhaps it might be an improvement to let the dollar have the appellation either of dollar or unit, (which last will be the most significant,) and to substitute " tenth " for dime. In time, the unit may succeed to the dollar. The word " cent," being in use in various transactions and instruments, will, without much difficulty, be understood as the hundredth; and the half-cent, of course, as the two hundredth part.

The eagle is not a very expressive or apt appellation for the largest gold piece; but nothing better occurs. The smallest of the two gold coins may be called the dollar or unit, in common with the silver piece, with which it coincides.

The volume or size of each piece is a matter of more consequence than its denomination. It is evident that the more superficies or surface, the more the piece will be liable to be injured by friction; or, in other words, the faster it will wear. For this reason, it is desirable to render the thickness as great, in proportion to the breadth, as may consist with neatness and good appearance. Hence, the form of the double guinea, or double louis-d'or, is preferable to that of the half johannes for the large gold piece. The small one cannot well be of any other size than the Portuguese piece of eight, of the same metal.

As it is of consequence to fortify the idea of the identity of the dollar, it may be best to let the form and size of the new one, as far as the quantity of matter (the alloy being less) permits, agree with the form and size of the present. The diameter may be the same.

The tenths may be in a mean between the Spanish $\frac{1}{8}$ and $\frac{1}{16}$ of a dollar.

The copper coins may be formed merely with a view to good appearance, as any difference in the wearing that can result from difference of form, can be of little consequence in reference to that metal.

It is conceived that the weight of the cent may be eleven pennyweight; which will about correspond with the value of

the copper and the expense of coinage. This will be to conform to the rule of intrinsic value, as far as regard to the convenient size of the coins will permit ; and the deduction of the
expense of coinage in this case will be the more proper, as the
copper coins, which have been current hitherto, have passed
till lately for much more than their intrinsic value. Taking
the weight as has been suggested, the size of the cent may
be nearly that of the piece herewith transmitted, which weighs
10dwt. 11grs. 10m. Two-thirds of the diameter of the cent
will suffice for the diameter of the half cent.

It may, perhaps, be thought expedient, according to general
practice, to make the copper coinage an object of profit ; but
where this is done to any considerable extent, it is hardly possible to have effectual security against counterfeits. This consideration, concurring with the soundness of the principle of
preserving the intrinsic value of the money of a country, seems
to outweigh the consideration of profit.

The foregoing suggestions, respecting the sizes of the several
coins, are made on the supposition that the legislature may
think fit to regulate this matter. Perhaps, however, it may be
judged not unadviseable to leave it to executive discretion.

With regard to the proposed size of the cent, it is to be confessed, that it is rather greater than might be wished, if it could
with propriety and safety be made less : and should the value
of copper continue to decline, as it has done for some time
past, it is very questionable whether it will long remain alone a
fit metal for money. This has led to a consideration of the expediency of uniting a small proportion of silver with the copper,
in order to be able to lessen the bulk of the inferior coins. For
this, there are precedents in several parts of Europe. In
France, the composition which is called billion, has consisted
of one part silver and four parts copper ; according to which
proportion, a cent might contain 17 grains, defraying out
of the material the expense of coinage. The conveniency of
size is a recommendation of such a species of coin ; but the
Secretary is deterred from proposing it, by the apprehension of
counterfeits. The effect of so small a quantity of silver, in comparatively so large a quantity of copper, could easily be imitated
by a mixture of other metals of little value, and the temptation
to doing it would not be inconsiderable.

The devices of the coins are far from being matters of indifference, as they may be made the vehicles of useful impressions.
They ought, therefore, to be emblematical, but without losing
sight of simplicity. The fewer sharp points and angles there
are, the less will be the loss by wearing. The Secretary thinks

it best, on this head, to confine himself to these concise and general remarks.

The last point to be discussed, respects the currency of foreign coins.

The abolition of this, in proper season, is a necessary part of the system contemplated for the national coinage. But this it will be expedient to defer, till some considerable progress has been made in preparing substitutes for them. A gradation may, therefore, be found most convenient.

The foreign coins may be suffered to circulate, precisely upon their present footing, for one year after the mint shall have commenced its operations. The privilege may then be continned for another year, to the gold coins of Portugal, England, and France, and to the silver coins of Spain. And these may still be permitted to be current for one year more, at the rates allowed to be given for them at the mint; after the expiration of which, the circulation of all foreign coins to cease.

The moneys which will be paid into the Treasury during the first year, being re-coined before they are issued anew, will afford a partial substitute, before any interruption is given to the pre-existing supplies of circulation. The revenues of the succeeding year, and the coins which will be brought to the mint, in consequence of the discontinuance of their currency, will materially extend the substitute in the course of that year; and its extension will be so far increased, during the third year, by the facility of procuring the remaining species to be re-coined, which will arise from the diminution of their current values, as probably to enable the dispensing wholly with the circulation of the foreign coins after that period. The progress which the currency of bank bills will be likely to have made, during the same time, will also afford a substitute of another kind.

This arrangement, besides avoiding a sudden stagnation of circulation, will cause a considerable proportion of whatever loss may be incident to the establishment, in the first instance, to fall, as it ought to do, upon the Government, and will probably tend to distribute the remainder of it more equally among the community.

It may, nevertheless, be advisable, in addition to the precautions here suggested, to repose a discretionary authority in the President of the United States to continue the currency of the Spanish dollar, at a value corresponding with the quantity of fine silver contained in it, beyond the period above mentioned, for the cessation of the circulation of the foreign coins. It is possible that an exception in favor of this particular species of coin may be found expedient; and it may tend to obviate inconveniences, if there be a power to make the exception, in a capacity to be exerted when the period shall arrive.

The Secretary for the Department of State, in his report to the House of Representatives, on the subject of establishing a uniformity in the weights, measures, and coins of the United States, has proposed that the weight of the dollar should correspond with the unit of weight. This was done on the supposition that it would require but a very small addition to the quantity of metal which the dollar, independently of the object he had in view, ought to contain; in which he was guided by the resolution of the 8th of August, 1786, fixing the dollar at 375 grains and 64 hundredths of a grain.

Taking this as the proper standard of the dollar, a small alteration, for the sake of incorporating so systematic an idea, would appear desirable. But, if the principles which have been reasoned from, in this report, are just, the execution of that idea becomes more difficult. It would certainly not be advisable to make, on that account, so considerable a change in the money unit, as would be produced by the addition of 5 grains of silver to the proper weight of the dollar, without a proportional augmentation of its relative value; and to make such an augmentation would be to abandon the advantage of preserving the identity of the dollar, or to speak more accurately, of having the proposed one received and considered as a mere substitute for the present.

The end may, however, be obtained, without either of these inconveniences, by increasing the proportion of alloy in the silver coins. But this would destroy the uniformity, in that respect, between the gold and silver coins. It remains, therefore, to elect which of the two systematic ideas shall be pursued or relinquished; and it may he remarked, that it will be more easy to convert the present silver coins into the proposed ones, if these last have the same, or nearly the same proportion of alloy, than if they have less.

The organization of the Mint, yet remains to be considered.

This relates to the persons to be employed, and to the services which they are respectively to perform. It is conceived that there ought to be —

A Director of the Mint; to have the general superintendence of the business.

An Assay Master, or Assayer; to receive the metals brought to the Mint, ascertain their fineness, and deliver them to be coined.

A Master Coiner; to conduct the making of the coins.

A Cashier; to receive and pay them out.

An Auditor ; to keep and adjust the accounts of the Mint.

Clerks ; as many as the Directors of the Mint shall deem necessary, to assist the different officers.

Workmen ; as many as may be found requisite.

A Porter.

In several of the European Mints, there are various other officers, but the foregoing are those only who appear to be indispensable. Persons in the capacity of clerks, will suffice instead of the others, with the advantage of greater economy.

The number of workmen is left indefinite, because, at certain times, it is requisite to have more than at others. They will, however, never be numerous. The expense of the establishment, in an ordinary year, will probably be from fifteen to twenty thousand dollars.

The remedy for errors in the weight and alloy of the coins, must necessarily form a part, in the system of a mint ; and the manner of applying it will require to be regulated. The following account is given of the practice in England, in this particular :

A certain number of pieces are taken promiscuously out of every fifteen pounds of gold, coined at the Mint, which are deposited, for safe keeping, in a strong box, called the pix. This box, from time to time, is opened in the presence of the Lord Chancellor, the officers of the Treasury, and others, and portions are selected from the pieces of each coinage, which are melted together, and the mass assayed by a jury of the Company of Goldsmiths. If the imperfection and deficiency, both in fineness and weight, fall short of a sixth of a carat, or 40 grains of pure gold, upon a pound of standard, the master of the Mint is held excusable ; because, it is supposed, that no workman can reasonably be answerable for greater exactness. The expediency of some similar regulation seems to be manifest.

All which is humbly submitted.

ALEXANDER HAMILTON,
Secretary of the Treasury.

Mr. Jefferson to Col. Hamilton [1]

FEBRUARY — 1792.

DEAR SIR : I return you the report on the mint, which I have read over with a great deal of satisfaction. I concur with you in thinking that the unit must stand on both metals, that the alloy should be the same in both, also in the proportion you establish between the value of the two metals. As to the ques-

[1] From Jefferson's Works, Vol. III., p. 330.

tion on whom the expense of coinage is to fall, I have been so little able to make up an opinion satisfactory to myself as to be ready to concur in either decision. With respect to the dollar, it must be admitted by all the world, that there is great incertainty in the meaning of the term, and therefore all the world will have justified Congress for their first act of removing the incertainty by declaring what they understand by the term, but the incertainty once removed, exists no longer, and I very much doubt a right now to change the value and especially to lessen it. It would lead to so easy a mode of paying off their debts. Besides, the parties injured by this reduction of the value would have so much matter to urge in support of the first point of fixation. Should it be thought, however, that Congress may reduce the value of the dollar, I should be for adopting for our unit, instead of the dollar, either one ounce of pure silver, or one ounce of standard silver, so as to keep the unit of money a part of the system of measures, weights and coins. I hazard these thoughts to you extempore, and am, dear sir, respectfully and affectionately.

REPORT OF ALEXANDER HAMILTON WHILE SECRETARY OF THE TREASURY ON THE SUBJECT OF A NATIONAL BANK

Read in the House of Representatives, Dec. 13, 1790

In obedience to the order of the House of Representatives, of the ninth day of August last, requiring the Secretary of the Treasury to prepare and report, on this day, such further provision as may, in his opinion, be necessary for establishing the Public Credit, the said Secretary further respectfully reports : —

That, from a conviction (as suggested in his report No. 1, herewith presented) that a National Bank is an institution of primary importance to the prosperous administration of the finances, and would be of the greatest utility in the operations connected with the support of the public credit; his attention has been drawn to devising the plan of such an institution upon a scale which will entitle it to the confidence, and be likely to render it equal to the exigencies, of the public.

Previously to entering upon the detail of this plan, he entreats the indulgence of the House towards some preliminary reflections naturally arising out of the subject, which he hopes will be deemed neither useless nor out of place. Public opinion being the ultimate arbiter of every measure of Government, it can scarcely appear improper, in deference to that, to accompany the origination of any new proposition with explanations, which the superior information of those to whom it is immediately addressed would render superfluous.

It is a fact, well understood, that public banks have found admission and patronage among the principal and most enlightened commercial nations. They have successively obtained in Italy, Germany, Holland, England and France, as well as in the United States. And it is a circumstance which cannot but have considerable weight, in a candid estimate of their tendency, that, after an experience of centuries, there exists not a question about their utility in the countries in which they have been so long established. Theorists and men of business unite in the acknowledgment of it.

Trade and industry, wherever they have been tried, have been indebted to them for important aid ; and Government has been repeatedly under the greatest obligations to them in dangerous and distressing emergencies. That of the United States, as well in some of the most critical conjunctures of the late war, as since the peace, has received assistance from those established among us, with which it could not have dispensed.

With this two-fold evidence before us, it might be expected that there would be a perfect union of opinions in their favor. Yet doubts have been entertained ; jealousies and prejudices have circulated ; and though the experiment is every day dissipating them, within the spheres in which effects are best known, yet there are still persons by whom they have not been entirely renounced. To give a full and accurate view of the subject would be to make a treatise of a report ; but there are certain aspects in which it may be cursorily exhibited, which may perhaps conduce to a just impression of its merits. These will involve a comparison of the advantages with the disadvantages, real or supposed, of such institutions.

The following are among the principal advantages of a bank : —

First. The augmentation of the active or productive capital of a country. Gold and silver, where they are employed merely as the instruments of exchange and alienation, have been not improperly denominated dead stock ; but when deposited in banks, to become the basis of a paper circulation, which takes their character and place, as the signs or representatives of value, they then acquire life, or, in other words,

2 S

an active and productive quality. This idea, which appears rather subtile and abstract, in a general form, may be made obvious and palpable, by entering into a few particulars. It is evident, for instance, that the money which a merchant keeps in his chest, waiting for a favorable opportunity to employ it, produces nothing till that opportunity arrives. But if, instead of locking it up in this manner, he either deposits it in a bank, or invests it in the stock of a bank, it yields a profit during the interval, in which he partakes, or not, according to the choice he may have made of being a depositor, or a proprietor; and when any advantageous speculation offers, in order to be able to embrace it, he has only to withdraw his money, if a depositor, or, if a proprietor, to obtain a loan from the bank, or to dispose of his stock; an alternative seldom or never attended with difficulty, when the affairs of the institution are in a prosperous train. His money, thus deposited or invested, is a fund upon which himself and others can borrow to a much larger amount. It is a well established fact, that banks in good credit can circulate a far greater sum than the actual quantum of their capital in gold and silver. The extent of the possible excess seems indeterminate; though it has been conjecturally stated at the proportions of two and three to one. This faculty is produced in various ways. First: A great proportion of the notes which are issued and pass current as cash, are indefinitely suspended in circulation, from the confidence which each holder has, that he can at any moment turn them into gold and silver. Secondly: Every loan which a bank makes, is, in its first shape, a credit given to the borrower on its books, the amount of which it stands ready to pay, either in its own notes, or in gold or silver, at his option. But, in a great number of cases, no actual payment is made in either. The borrower frequently, by a check or order, transfers his credit to some other person, to whom he has a payment to make; who, in his turn, is as often content with a similar credit, because he is satisfied that he can, whenever he pleases, either convert it into cash, or pass it to some other hand, as equivalent for it. And in this manner the credit keeps circulating, performing in every stage the office of money, till it is extinguished by a discount with some person who has a payment to make to the bank, to an equal or greater amount. Thus large sums are lent and paid, frequently through a variety of hands, without the intervention of a single piece of coin. Thirdly: There is always a large quantity of gold and silver in the repositories of the bank, besides its own stock, which is placed there with a view partly to its safe keeping, and partly to the accommodation of an institution which is itself a source of general accommodation. These deposits are of immense consequence in the operations of a bank. Though liable to be redrawn at any moment, experience proves that the money so much oftener changes proprietors than place, and that what is drawn out is generally so speedily replaced as to authorize the counting upon the sums deposited as an *effective fund;* which, concurring with the stock of the bank, enables it to extend its loans and to answer all the demands for coin, whether in consequence of those loans, or arising from the occasional return of its notes.

These different circumstances explain the manner in which the ability of a bank to circulate a greater sum than its actual capital in coin is acquired. This, however, must be gradual, and must be preceded by a firm establishment of confidence ; a confidence which may be bestowed on the most rational grounds, since the excess in question will always be bottomed on good security of one kind or another. This, every well conducted bank carefully requires, before it will consent to advance either its money or its credit ; and where there is an auxiliary capital, (as will be the case in the plan hereafter submitted,) which, together with the capital in coin, define the boundary that shall not be exceeded by the engagements of the bank, the security may, consistently with all the maxims of a reasonable circumspection, be regarded as complete.

The same circumstances illustrate the truth of the position that it is one of the properties of banks to increase the active capital of a country. This, in other words, is the sum of them : The money of one individual, while he is waiting for an opportunity to employ it, by being either deposited in the bank for safe keeping, or invested in its stock, is in a good condition to administer to the wants of others, without being put out of his own reach when occasion presents. This yields an extra profit, arising from what is paid for the use of his money by others, when he could not himself make use of it, and keeps the money itself in a state of incessant activity. In the almost infinite vicissitudes and competitions of mercantile enterprise, there never can be danger of an intermission of demand, or that the money will remain for a moment idle in the vaults of the bank. This additional employment given to money, and the faculty of a bank to lend and circulate a greater sum than the amount of its stock in coin, are, to all the purposes of trade and industry, an absolute increase of capital. Purchases and undertakings, in general, can be carried on by any given sum of bank paper or credit, as effectually as by an equal sum of gold and silver. And thus, by contributing to enlarge the mass of industrious and commercial enterprise, banks become nurseries of national wealth; a consequence as satisfactorily verified by experience, as it is clearly deducible in theory.

Secondly. Greater facility to the Government in obtaining pecuniary aids, especially in sudden emergencies. This is another, and an undisputed advantage of public banks; one which, as already remarked, has been realized in signal instances among ourselves. The reason is obvious: the capitals of a great number of individuals are, by this operation, collected to a point and placed under one direction. The mass formed by this union, is, in a certain sense, magnified by the credit attached to it; and while this mass is always ready, and can at once be put in motion in aid of the Government, the interest of the bank to afford that aid, independent of regard to the public safety and welfare, is a sure pledge for its disposition to go as far in its compliances as can in prudence be desired. There is, in the nature of things, as will be more particularly noticed in another place, an intimate connection of interest between the Government and the bank of a nation.

Thirdly. The facilitating of the payment of taxes. This advantage is produced in two ways. Those who are in a situation to have access to the bank, can have the assistance of loans, to answer, with punctuality, the public calls upon them. This accommodation has been sensibly felt in the payment of the duties heretofore laid, by those who reside where establishments of this nature exist. This, however, though an extensive, is not a universal benefit. The other way in which the effect here contemplated is produced, and in which the benefit is general, is the increasing of the quantity of circulating medium, and the quickening of circulation. The manner in which the first happens has already been traced. The last may require some illustration. When payments are to be made between different places having an intercourse of business with each other, if there happen to be no private bills at market, and there are no bank notes which have a currency in both, the consequence is, that coin must be remitted; this is attended with trouble, delay, expense and risk. If, on the contrary, there are bank notes current in both places, the transmission of these by the post, or any other speedy or convenient conveyance, answers the purpose; and these again, in the alternations of demand, are frequently returned very soon after to the place from whence they were first sent: whence the transportation and retransportation of the metals are obviated, and a more convenient and more expeditious medium of payment is substituted. Nor is this all : the metals, instead of being suspended from their usual functions, during this process of vibration from place to place, continue in activity and administer still to the ordinary circulation, which, of course, is prevented from suffering either diminution or stagnation. These circumstances are additional causes of what, in a practical sense, or to the purposes of business, may be called greater plenty of money. And it is evident, that whatever enhances the quantity of circulating money, adds to the ease with which every industrious member of the community may acquire that portion of it of which he stands in need, and enables him the better to pay his taxes as well, as to supply his other wants. Even where the circulation of the bank paper is not general, it must still have the same effect, though in a less degree ; for, whatever furnishes additional supplies to the channels of circulation in one quarter, naturally contributes to keep the streams fuller elsewhere. This last view of the subject serves both to illustrate the position that banks tend to facilitate the payment of taxes, and to exemplify their utility to business of every kind in which money is an agent.

It would be to intrude too much on the patience of the house to prolong the details of the advantages of banks ; especially as all those which might still be particularized, are readily to be inferred from those which have been enumerated. Their disadvantages, real or supposed, are now to be reviewed. The most serious of the charges which have been brought against them are :

That they serve to increase usury ;

That they tend to prevent other kinds of lending ;

That they furnish temptations to overtrading ;

That they afford aid to ignorant adventurers, who disturb the natural and beneficial course of trade ;

That they give to bankrupt and fraudulent traders a fictitious credit, which enables them to maintain false appearances, and to extend their impositions ; and, lastly,

That they have a tendency to banish gold and silver from the country.

There is great reason to believe that, on a close and candid survey, it will be discovered that these charges are either without foundation, or that, as far as the evils they suggest have been found to exist, they have proceeded from other, or partial, or temporary causes ; are not inherent in the nature and permanent tendency of such institutions ; or are more than counterbalanced by opposite advantages. This survey shall be had, in the order in which the charges have been stated. The first of them is—

That banks serve to increase usury.

It is a truth, which ought not to be denied, that the method of conducting business, which is essential to bank operations, has, among us, in particular instances, given occasion to usurious transactions. The punctuality in payments, which they necessarily exact, has sometimes obliged those who have adventured beyond both their capital and *credit*, to procure money at any price, and, consequently, to resort to usurers for aid.

But experience and practice gradually bring a cure to this evil. A general habit of punctuality among traders is the natural consequence of the necessity of observing it with the bank ; a circumstance which, itself, more than compensates for any occasional ill which may have sprung from that necessity, in the particular under consideration. As far, therefore, as traders depend on each other for pecuniary supplies, they can calculate their expectations with greater certainty ; and are in proportionably less danger of disappointments, which might compel them to have recourse to so pernicious an expedient as that of borrowing at usury ; the mischiefs of which, after a few examples, naturally inspire great care in all but men of desperate circumstances, to avoid the possibility of being subjected to them. One, and not the least of the evils incident to the use of that expedient, if the fact be known, or even strongly suspected, is loss of credit with the bank itself.

The directors of a bank, too, though in order to extend its business and its popularity in the infancy of an institution, they may be tempted to go further in accommodation than the strict rules of prudence will warrant, grow more circumspect, of course, as its affairs become better established, and as the evils of too great facility are experimentally demonstrated. They become more attentive to the situation and conduct of those with whom they deal : they observe more narrowly their operations and pursuits ; they economize the credit they give to those of suspicious solidity ; they refuse it to those whose career is more manifestly hazardous. In a word, in the course of practice, from the very nature of things, the *interest* will make it the *policy* of a bank to succor the wary and industrious ; to discredit the rash and unthrifty ; to discountenance both the usurious lenders and the usurious borrowers.

There is a leading view in which the tendency of banks will be seen to be to abridge rather than to promote usury. This relates to their property of increasing the quantity and quickening the circulation of money. If it be evident that usury will prevail or diminish, according to the proportion which the demand for borrowing bears to the quantity of money at market to be lent — whatever has the property just mentioned, whether it be in the shape of paper or coin, by contributing to render the supply more equal to the demand, must tend to counteract the progress of usury.

But bank lending, it is pretended, is an impediment to other kinds of lending ; which, by confining the resource of borrowing to a particular class, leaves the rest of the community more destitute, and therefore more exposed to the extortions of usurers. As the profits of bank stock exceed the legal rate of interest, the possessors of money, it is argued, prefer investing it in that article to lending it at this rate ; to which there are the additional motives of a more prompt command of the capital and of more frequent and exact returns, without trouble or perplexity in the collection. This constitutes the second charge which has been enumerated.

The fact on which this charge rests, is not to be admitted without several qualifications, particularly in reference to the state of things in this country. *First.* The great bulk of the stock of a bank will consist of the funds of men in trade, among ourselves, and moneyed foreigners ; the former of whom could not spare their capitals out of their reach, to be invested in loans for long periods, on mortgages or personal security ; and the latter of whom would not be willing to be subjected to the casualties, delays and embarrassments of such a disposition of their money in a distant country. *Secondly.* There will always be a considerable proportion of those who are properly the money lenders of a country, who, from that spirit of caution which usually characterizes this description of men, will incline rather to vest their funds in mortgages on real estate than in the stock of a bank, which they are apt to consider as a more precarious security.

These considerations serve, in a material degree, to narrow the foundation of the objection, as to the point of fact. But there is a more satisfactory answer to it. The effect supposed, as far as it has existence, is temporary. The reverse of it takes place in the general and permanent operation of the thing.

The capital of every public bank will, of course, be restricted within a certain defined limit. It is the province of legislative prudence so to adjust this limit, that while it will not be too contracted for the demand which the course of business may create, and for the security which the public ought to have for the solidity of the paper which may be issued by the bank, it will still be within the compass of the pecuniary resources of the community ; so that there may be an easy practicability of completing the subscriptions to it. When this is once done, the supposed effect of necessity ceases.   There is then no longer room for the investment of any additional capital. Stock may indeed change hands, by one person selling and another buying; but the money which the buyer takes out of the common mass to purchase the stock, the seller receives and restores to it.   Hence the future surpluses which may accumulate, must take their natural course and lending at interest must go on as if there were no such institution.

It must, indeed, flow in a more copious stream.   The bank furnishes an extraordinary supply for borrowers, within its immediate sphere.   A larger supply consequently remains for borrowers elsewhere.   In proportion as the circulation of the bank is extended, there is an augmentation of the aggregate mass of money for answering the aggregate mass of demand. Hence greater facility in obtaining it for every purpose.

It ought not to escape without a remark, that, as far as the citizens of other countries become adventurers in the bank, there is a positive increase of the gold and silver of the country. It is true that from this a half yearly rent is drawn back, accruing from the dividends upon the stock.   But as this rent arises from the employment of the capital by our own citizens, it is probable that it is more than replaced by the profits of that employment.   It is also likely that a part of it is, in the course of trade, converted into the products of our country.   And it may even prove an incentive, in some cases, to emigration to a country in which the character of citizen is as easy to be acquired, as it is estimable and important.   This view of the subject furnishes an answer to an objection which has been deduced from the circumstance here taken notice of, namely, the income resulting to foreigners from the part of the stock owned by them, which has been represented as tending to drain the country of its specie.   In this objection, the original investment of the capital, and the constant use of it afterwards, seem both to have been overlooked.

That banks furnish temptations to overtrading, is the third of the enumerated objections.   This must mean that, by affording additional aids to mercantile enterprise, they induce the merchant sometimes to adventure beyond the prudent or salutary point.   But the very statement of the thing shows that the subject of the charge is an occasional ill, incident to a general good. Credit of every kind (as a species of which only can bank lending have the effect supposed) must be, in different degrees, chargeable with the same inconvenience.   It is even applicable to gold and silver, when they abound in circulation.   But would it be wise on this account to decry the precious metals, to root out credit, or to proscribe the means of that enterprise which is the mainspring of trade and a principal source of national wealth, because it now and then runs into excesses, of which overtrading is one ?

If the abuses of a beneficial thing are to determine its condemnation, there is scarcely a source of public prosperity which will not speedily be closed. In every case, the evil is to be compared with the good ; and in the present case, such a comparison will issue in this, that the new and increased energies derived to commercial enterprise from the aid of banks, are a source of general profit and advantage, which greatly outweigh the partial ills of the overtrading of a few individuals at particular times, or of numbers in particular conjunctures.

The fourth and fifth charges may be considered together. These relate to the aid which is sometimes afforded by banks to unskilful adventurers and fraudulent traders. These charges also have some degree of foundation, though far less than has been pretended ; and they add to the instances of partial ills connected with more extensive and overbalancing benefits.

The practice of giving fictitious credit to improper persons, is one of those evils which experience, guided by interest, speedily corrects. The bank itself is in so much jeopardy of being a sufferer by it that it has the strongest of all inducements to be on its guard. It may not only be injured immediately by the delinquencies of the persons to whom such credit is given, but eventually by the incapacities of others, whom their impositions or failures may have ruined.

Nor is there much danger of a bank's being betrayed into this error from want of information. The directors themselves, being, for the most part, selected from the class of traders, are to be expected to possess individually an accurate knowledge of the characters and situations of those who come within that description. And they have, in addition to this, the course of dealing of the persons themselves with the bank, to assist their judgment, which is in most cases a good index of the state in which those persons are. The artifices and shifts which those in desperate or declining circumstances are obliged to employ, to keep up the countenance which the rules of the bank require, and the train of their connections, are so many prognostics not difficult to be interpreted, of the fate which awaits them. Hence it not unfrequently happens that banks are the first to discover the unsoundness of such characters, and, by withholding credit, to announce to the public that they are not entitled to it.

If banks, in spite of every precaution, are sometimes betrayed into giving a false credit to the persons described, they more frequently enable honest and industrious men of small or perhaps of no capital, to undertake and prosecute business with advantage to themselves and to the community; and assist merchants of both capital and credit, who meet with fortuitous and unforeseen shocks which might, without such helps, prove fatal to them and to others, to make head against their misfortunes and finally to retrieve their affairs; circumstances which form no inconsiderable encomium on the utility of banks.

But the last and heaviest charge is still to be examined: this is, that banks tend to banish the gold and silver of the country.

The force of this objection rests upon their being an engine of paper credit, which, by furnishing a substitute for the metals, is supposed to promote their exportation. It is an objection which, if it has any foundation, lies not against banks peculiarly but against every species of paper credit.

The most common answer given to it is that the thing supposed is of little or no consequence; that it is immaterial what serves the purpose of money, whether paper or gold or silver; that the effect of both upon industry is the same; and that the intrinsic wealth of a nation is to be measured not by the abundance of the precious metals contained in it, but by the quantity of the productions of its labor and industry.

This answer is not destitute of solidity, though not entirely satisfactory. It is certain that the vivification of industry, by a full circulation, with the aid of a proper and well regulated paper credit, may more than compensate for the loss of a part of the gold and silver of a nation, if the consequence of avoiding that loss should be a scanty or defective circulation.

But the positive and permanent increase or decrease of the precious metals in a country can hardly ever be a matter of indifference. As the commodity taken in lieu of every other, it is a species of the most effective wealth; and as the money of the world, it is of great concern to the State that it possess a sufficiency of it to face any demands which the protection of its external interests may create.

The objection seems to admit of another and more conclusive answer, which controverts the fact itself. A nation that has no mines of its own must derive the precious metals from others, generally speaking, in exchange for the products of its labor and industry. The quantity it will possess will, therefore, in the ordinary course of things, be regulated by the favorable or unfavorable balance of its trade; that is, by the proportion between its abilities to supply foreigners and its wants of them; between the amount of its exportations and that of its importations. Hence, the state of its agriculture and manufactures, the quantity and quality of its labor and industry must, in the main, influence and determine the increase or decrease of its gold and silver. If this be true, the inference seems to be, that well constituted banks favor the increase of the precious metals. It has been shown that they augment, in different ways, the active capital of a country. This it is which generates employment; which animates and expands labor and industry. Every addition which is made to it, by contributing to put in motion a greater quantity of both, tends to create a greater quantity of the products of both; and, by furnishing more materials for exportation, conduces to a favorable balance of trade and consequently, to the introduction and increase of gold and silver. This conclusion appears to be drawn from solid premises. There are, however, objections to be made to it.

It may be said, that, as bank paper affords a substitute for specie, it serves to counteract that rigorous necessity for the metals, as a medium of circulation, which, in the case of a wrong balance, might restrain, in some degree, their exportation; and it may be added that, from the same cause, in the same case, it would retard those economical and parsimonious reforms in the manner of living, which the scarcity of money is calculated to produce, and which might be necessary to rectify such wrong balance.

There is, perhaps, some truth in both these observations; but they appear to be of a nature rather to form exceptions to the generality of the conclusion, than to overthrow it. The state of things in which the *absolute exigencies* of circulation can be supposed to resist, with any effect, the urgent demands for specie which a wrong balance of trade may occasion, presents an *extreme case*. And a situation in which a too expensive manner of living of a community, compared with its means, can stand in need of a corrective, from distress or necessity, is one which, perhaps, rarely results but from extraordinary and adventitious causes: such, for example, as a national revolution, which unsettles all the established habits of a people, and inflames the appetite for extravagance, by the illusions of an ideal wealth, engendered by the continual multiplication of a depreciating currency, or some similar cause. There is good reason to believe that, where the laws are wise and well executed, and the inviolability of property and contracts maintained, the economy of a people will, in the general course of things, correspond with its means.

The support of industry is, probably, in every case, of more consequence towards correcting a wrong balance of trade than any practicable retrenchment in the expenses of families or individuals ; and the stagnation of it would be likely to have more effect in prolonging, than any such savings in shortening, its continuance.   That stagnation is a natural consequence of an inadequate medium, which, without the aid of bank circulation, would, in the cases supposed, be severely felt.

It also deserves notice that, as the circulation of a bank is always in a compound ratio to the fund upon which it depends, and to the demand for it, and as that fund is itself affected by the exportation of the metals, there is no danger of its being overstocked, as in the case of paper issued at the pleasure of the Government, or of its preventing the consequences of any unfavorable balance from being sufficiently felt to produce the reforms alluded to, as far as circumstances may require and admit.

Nothing can be more fallible than the comparisons which have been made between different countries to illustrate the truth of the position under consideration.   The comparative quantity of gold and silver in different countries depends upon an infinite variety of facts and combinations, all of which ought to be known in order to judge whether the existence or non-existence of paper currencies has any share in the relative proportions they contain.   The *mass* and *value* of the productions of the labor and industry of each, compared with its wants ; the nature of its establishments abroad ; the kind of wars in which it is usually engaged ; the relations it bears to the countries which are the original possessors of those metals ; the privileges it enjoys in their trade ; these, and a number of other circumstances, are all to be taken into the account, and render the investigation too complex to justify any reliance on the vague and general surmises which have been hitherto hazarded on the point.

In the foregoing discussion, the objection has been considered as applying to the permanent expulsion and diminution of the metals.   Their temporary exportation, for particular purposes, has not been contemplated.   This, it must be confessed, is facilitated by banks, from the faculty banks possess of supplying their place.   But their utility is in nothing more conspicuous than in these very cases.   They enable the government to pay its foreign debts, and to answer any exigencies which the external concern of the community may have produced.   They enable the merchant to support his credit, (on which the prosperity of trade depends,) when special circumstances prevent remittances in other modes.   They enable him also to prosecute enterprises which ultimately tend to an augmentation of the species of wealth in question.   It is evident that gold and silver may often be employed in procuring commodities abroad, which, in a circuitous commerce, replace the original fund, with considerable addition. But it is not to be inferred, from this facility given to temporary exportation, that banks, which are so friendly to trade and industry, are, in their general tendency inimical to the increase of the precious metals.

These several views of the subject appear sufficient to impress a full conviction of the utility of banks, and to demonstrate that they are of great importance, not only in relation to the administration of the finances, but in the general system of the political economy.

The judgment of many concerning them has, no doubt, been perplexed by the misinterpretation of appearances which were to be ascribed to other causes. The general devastation of personal property, occasioned by the late war, naturally produced, on the one hand, a great demand for money, and, on the other, a great deficiency of it to answer the demand. Some injudicious laws, which grew out of the public distresses, by impairing confidence, and causing a part of the inadequate sum in the country to be locked up, aggravated the evil. The dissipated habits contracted by many individuals during the war, which, after the peace, plunged them into expenses beyond their incomes ; the number of adventurers without capital, and, in many instances, without information, who at that epoch rushed into trade, and were obliged to make any sacrifices to support a transient credit ; the employment of considerable sums in speculations upon the public debt, which, from its unsettled state, was incapable of becoming itself a substitute ; all these circumstances concurring, necessarily led to usurious borrowing, produced most of the inconveniences, and were the true cause of most of the appearances, which, where banks were established, have been by some erroneously placed to their account : a mistake which they might easily have avoided by turning their eyes towards places where there were none, and where, nevertheless, the same evils would have been perceived to exist, even in a greater degree than where those institutions had obtained.

These evils have either ceased or been greatly mitigated. Their more complete extinction may be looked for from that additional security to property which the constitution of the United States happily gives ; (a circumstance of prodigious moment in the scale, both of public and private prosperity ;) from the attraction of foreign capital, under the auspices of that security, to be employed upon objects, and in enterprises, for which the state of this country opens a wide and inviting field ; from the consistency and stability which the public debt is fast acquiring, as well in the public opinion at home and abroad, as, in fact, from the augmentation of capital which that circumstance and the quarter-yearly payment of interest will afford; and from the more copious circulation which will be likely to be created by a well constituted national bank.

The establishment of banks in this country seems to be recommended by reasons of a peculiar nature. Previously to the Revolution, circulation was in a great measure carried on by paper emitted by the several local governments. In Pennsylvania alone, the quantity of it was near a million and a half of dollars. This auxiliary may be said to be now at an end. And it is generally supposed that there has been, for some time past, a deficiency of circulating medium. How far that deficiency is to be considered as real or imaginary, is not susceptible of demonstration; but there are circumstances and appearances, which, in relation to the country at large, countenance the supposition of its reality.

The circumstances are, besides the fact just mentioned respecting paper emissions, the vast tracts of waste land, and the little advanced state of manufactures. The progressive settlement of the former, while it promises ample retribution in the generation of future resources, diminishes or obstructs, in the mean time, the *active* wealth of the country. It not only draws off a part of the circulating money, and places it in a more passive state, but it diverts, into its own channels, a portion of that species of labor and industry which would otherwise be employed in furnishing materials for foreign trade, and which, by contributing to a favorable balance, would assist the introduction of specie. In the early periods of new settlements, the settlers not only furnish no surplus for exportation, but they consume a part of that which is produced by the labor of others. The same thing is a cause that manufactures do not advance, or advance slowly. And notwithstanding some hypotheses to the contrary, there are many things to induce a suspicion that the precious metals will not abound in any country which has not mines, or variety of manufactures. They have been sometimes acquired by the sword; but the modern system of war has expelled this resource, and it is one upon which it is to be hoped the United States will never be inclined to rely.

The appearances alluded to, are, greater prevalency of direct barter in the more interior districts of the country — which, however, has been for some time past gradually lessening; and greater difficulty, generally, in the advantageous alienation of improved real estate; which, also, has of late diminished, but is still seriously felt in different parts of the Union. The difficulty of getting money, which has been a general complaint, is not added to the number; because it is the complaint of all times, and one in which imagination must ever have too great scope to permit an appeal to it.

If the supposition of such a deficiency be in any degree founded, and some aid to circulation be desirable, it remains to inquire what ought to be the nature of that aid.

The emitting of paper money by the authority of Government is wisely prohibited to the individual States by the national constitution ; and the spirit of that prohibition ought not to be disregarded by the Government of the United States. Though paper emissions, under a general authority, might have some advantages not applicable, and be free from some disadvantages which are applicable, to the like emissions by the States, separately, yet they are of a nature so liable to abuse — and, it may even be affirmed, so certain of being abused — that the wisdom of the Government, will be shown in never trusting itself with the use of so seducing and dangerous an expedient. In times of tranquillity, it might have no ill consequence ; it might even perhaps be managed in a way to be productive of good : but in great and trying emergencies, there is almost a moral certainty of its becoming mischievous. The stamping of paper is an operation so much easier than the laying of taxes, that a Government, in the practice of paper emissions, would rarely fail, in any such emergency, to indulge itself too far in the employment of that resource, to avoid as much as possible one less auspicious to present popularity. If it should not even be carried so far as to be rendered an absolute bubble, it would at least be likely to be extended to a degree which would occasion an inflated and artificial state of things, incompatible with the regular and prosperous course of the political economy.

Among other material differences between a paper currency, issued by the mere authority of Government, and one issued by a bank, payable in coin, is this : that, in the first case, there is no standard to which an appeal can be made, as to the quantity which will only satisfy, or which will surcharge, the circulation ; in the last, that standard results from the demand. If more should be issued than is necessary, it will return upon the bank. Its emissions, as elsewhere intimated, must always be in a compound ratio to the fund and the demand : whence it is evident, that there is a limitation in the nature of the thing ; while the discretion of the Government is the only measure of the extent of the emissions by its own authority.

This consideration further illustrates the danger of emissions of that sort, and the preference which is due to bank paper.

The payment of the interest of the public debt at thirteen different places, is a weighty reason, peculiar to our immediate situation, for desiring a bank circulation. Without a paper, in general currency, equivalent to gold and silver, a considerable proportion of the specie of the country must always be suspended from circulation, and left to accumulate, preparatorily to each day of payment; and as often as one approaches, there must be in several cases an actual transportation of the metals, at both expense and risk, from their natural and proper reservoirs, to distant places. This necessity will be felt very injuriously to the trade of some of the States; and will embarrass, not a little, the operations of the Treasury in those States. It will also obstruct those negotiations between different parts of the Union, by the instrumentality of Treasury bills, which have already afforded valuable accommodations to trade in general.

Assuming it, then, as a consequence, from what has been said, that a national bank is a desirable institution, two inquiries emerge: Is there no such institution, already in being, which has a claim to that character, and which supersedes the propriety or necessity of another? If there be none, what are the principles upon which one ought to be established?

There are at present three banks in the United States: That of North America, established in the City of Philadelphia; that of New York, established in the City of New York; that of Massachusetts, established in the town of Boston. Of these three, the first is the only one which has at any time had a direct relation to the Government of the United States.

The Bank of North America originated in a resolution of Congress of the 26th of May, 1781, founded upon a proposition of the Superintendent of Finance, which was afterwards carried into execution by an Ordinance of the 31st of December following, entitled "An Ordinance to Incorporate the subscribers to the Bank of North America."

The aid afforded to the United States by this institution, during the remaining period of the war, was of essential consequence; and its conduct towards them, since the peace, has not weakened its title to their patronage and favor. So far, its pretensions to the character in question are respectable; but there are circumstances which militate against them and considerations which indicate the propriety of an establishment on different principles.

The directors of this bank, on behalf of their constituents, have since *accepted* and *acted* on the new charter from the State of Pennsylvania, materially variant from their original one, and which so narrows the foundation of the institution, as to render it an incompetent basis for the extensive purposes of a national bank.

The limit assigned by the ordinance of Congress to the stock of the bank, is ten millions of dollars. The last charter of Pennsylvania confines it to two millions. Questions naturally arise, whether there be not a direct repugnancy between two charters so differently circumstanced? And whether the acceptance of the one, is not to be deemed a virtual surrender of the other? But perhaps it is neither advisable nor necessary to attempt a solution of them.

There is nothing in the acts of Congress, which imply an exclusive right in the institution to which they relate, except during the term of war. There is, therefore, nothing, if the public good require it, which prevents the establishment of another. It may, however, be incidentally remarked, that in the general opinion of the citizens of the United States, the Bank of North America has taken the station of a bank of Pennsylvania only. This is a strong argument for a new institution, or for a renovation of the old, to restore it to the situation in which it originally stood in the view of the United States.

But, though the ordinance of Congress contains no grant of exclusive privileges, there may be room to allege that the Government of the United States ought not, in point of candor and equity, to establish any rival or interfering institution, in prejudice of the one already established ; especially as this has, from services rendered, well-founded claims to protection and regard.

The justice of such an observation ought, within proper bounds, to be admitted. A new establishment of the sort ought not to be made without cogent and sincere reasons of public good. And, in the manner of doing it, every facility should be given to a consolidation of the old with the new, upon terms not injurious to the parties concerned. But there is no ground to maintain, that, in a case in which the Government has made no condition restricting its authority, it ought voluntarily to restrict it, through regard to the interests of a particular institution, when those of the States dictate a different course ; especially, too, after such circumstances have intervened, as characterise the actual situation of the Bank of North America.

The inducements to a new disposition of the thing are now to be considered. The first of them which occurs, is, the at least ambiguous situation in which the Bank of North America has placed itself, by the acceptance of its last charter. If this

2 T

has rendered it the mere bank of a particular state, liable to dissolution at the expiration of fourteen years, (to which term the act of that state has restricted its duration,) it would be neither fit nor expedient to accept it as an equivalent for a Bank of the United States.

The restriction of its capital also, which, according to the same supposition, cannot be extended beyond two millions of dollars, is a conclusive reason for a different establishment. So small a capital promises neither the requisite aid to Government, nor the requisite security to the community. It may answer very well the purposes of local accommodation, but is an inadequate foundation for a circulation co-extensive with the United States, embracing the whole of their revenues, and affecting every individual into whose hands the paper may come.

And, inadequate as such a capital would be to the essential ends of a national bank, it is liable to be rendered still more so, by that principle of the constitution of the Bank of North America, contained equally in its old and in its new charter, which leaves the increase of the *actual* capital at any time (now far short of the allowed extent) to the discretion of the directors or stockholders. It is naturally to be expected that the allurements of an advanced price of stock, and of large dividends, may disincline those who are interested to an extension of capital, from which they will be apt to fear a diminution of profits. And from this circumstance, the interest and aecommodation of the public, as well individually as collectively, are made more subordinate to the interest, real or imagined, of the stockholders, than they ought to be. It is true that, unless the latter be consulted, there can be no bank, (in the sense at least in which institutions of this kind, worthy of confidence, can be established in this country;) but it does not follow that this is alone to be consulted, or that it even ought to be paramount. Public utility is more truly the object of public banks, than private profit. And it is the business of Government to constitute them on such principles, that while the latter will result in a sufficient degree to afford competent motives to engage in them, the former be not made subservient to it. To effect this, a principal object of attention ought to be to give free scope to the creation of an ample capital; and with this view, fixing the bounds which are deemed safe and convenient, to leave no discretion either to stop short of them, or to overpass them. The want of this precaution, in the establishment of the Bank of North America, is a further and an important reason for desiring one differently constituted.

There may be room at first sight for a supposition, that, as the profits of a bank will bear a proportion to the extent of its operations, and as for this reason the interest of the stockholders will not be disadvantageously affected by any necessary augmentations of capital, there is no cause to apprehend that they will be indisposed to such augmentations. But most men, in matters of this nature, prefer the certainties they enjoy to probabilities depending on untried experiments; especially when these promise rather that they will not be injured, than that they will be benefited.

From the influence of this principle, and a desire of enhancing its profits, the directors of a bank will be more apt to overstrain its faculties, in an attempt to face the additional demands which the course of business may create, than to set on foot new subscriptions which may hazard a diminution of the profits, and even a temporary reduction of the price of stock.

Banks are among the best expedients for lowering the rate of interest in a country; but, to have this effect, their capitals must be completely equal to all the demands of business, and such as will tend to remove the idea that the accommodations they afford are in any degree favors; an idea very apt to accompany the parsimonious dispensation of contracted funds. In this, as in every other case, the plenty of the commodity ought to beget a moderation of the price.

The want of a principle of rotation in the constitution of the Bank of North America, is another argument for a variation of the establishment. Scarcely one of the reasons which militate against this principle in the constitution of a country, is applicable to that of a bank; while there are strong reasons in favor of it, in relation to the one, which do not apply to the other. The knowledge to be derived from experience is the only circumstance common to both, which pleads against rotation in the directing officers of a bank.

But the objects of the government of a nation, and those of the government of a bank, are so widely different, as greatly to weaken the force of that consideration in reference to the latter. Almost every important case of legislation requires, towards a right decision, a general and accurate acquaintance with the affairs of the State, and habits of thinking seldom acquired but from a familiarity with public concerns. The administration of a bank, on the contrary, is regulated by a few simple fixed maxims, the application of which is not difficult to any man of judgment, especially if instructed in the principles of trade. It is, in general, a constant succession of the same details.

But, though this be the case, the idea of the advantages of

experience is not to be slighted.   Room ought to be left for the
regular transmission of official information ; and for this purpose,
the head of the direction ought to be excepted from the principle of rotation.   With this exception, and with the aid of the
information of the subordinate officers, there can be no danger
of any ill effects from want of experience or knowledge ; especially as the periodical exclusion ought not to reach the whole
of the directors at one time.

The argument in favor of the principle of rotation is this :
that, by lessening the danger of combinations among the directors, to make the institution subservient to party views, or to the
accommodation, preferably, of any particular set of men, it will
render the public confidence more firm, stable, and unqualified.

When it is considered that the directors of a bank are not
elected by the great body of the community, in which a diversity of views will naturally prevail at different conjunctures, but
by a small and select class of men, among whom it is far more
easy to cultivate a steady adherence to the same persons and
objects, and that those directors have it in their power so immediately to conciliate, by obliging the most influential of this
class, it is easy to perceive that, without the principle of rotation, changes in that body can rarely happen, but as a conces-
sion which they may themselves think it expedient to make to
public opinion.

The continual administration of an institution of this kind,
by the same persons, will never fail, with or without cause,
from their conduct, to excite distrust and discontent.   The
necessary secrecy of their transactions gives unlimited scope to
imagination to infer that something is or may be wrong   And
this *inevitable* mystery is a solid reason for inserting in the
constitution of a bank the necessity of a change of men.   As
neither the mass of the parties interested, nor the public in
general, can be permitted to be witnesses of the interior
management of the directors, it is reasonable that both should
have that check upon their conduct, and that security against
the prevalency of a partial or pernicious system, which will be
produced by the certainty of periodical changes.   Such, too,
is the delicacy of the credit of a bank, that everything which
can fortify confidence and repel suspicion, without injuring its
operations, ought carefully to be sought after in its formation.

A further consideration in favor of a change, is the improper
rule by which the right of voting for directors is regulated in
the plan upon which the Bank of North America was originally
constituted, namely, a vote for each share, and the want of a
rule in the last charter ; unless the silence of it, on that point,

may signify that every stockholder is to have an equal and a single vote, which would be a rule in a different extreme not less erroneous. It is of importance that a rule should be established on this head, as it is one of those things which ought not to be left to discretion ; and it is, consequently, of equal importance that the rule should be a proper one.

A vote for each share renders a combination between a few principal stockholders, to monopolize the power and benefits of the bank, too easy. An equal vote to each stockholder, however great or small his interest in the institution, allows not that degree of weight to large stockholders which it is reasonable they should have, and which, perhaps, their security, and that of the bank require. A prudent mean is to be preferred. A conviction of this has produced a by-law of the corporation of the Bank of North America, which evidently aims at such a mean. But a reflection arises here, that a like majority with that which enacted this law, may, at any moment, repeal it.

The last inducement which shall be mentioned is the want of precautions to guard against a foreign influence insinuating itself into the direction of the bank. It seems scarcely reconcilable with a due caution, to permit that any but citizens should be eligible as directors of a national bank, or that non-resident foreigners should be able to influence the appointment of directors by the votes of their proxies. In the event, however, of an incorporation of the Bank of North America, in the plan it may be necessary to qualify this principle, so as to leave the right of foreigners, who now hold shares of its stock, unimpaired ; but without the power of transmitting the privileges in question to foreign alienees.

It is to be considered that such a bank is not a mere matter of private property, but a political machine of the greatest importance to the state.

There are other variations from the constitution of the Bank of North America, not of inconsiderable moment, which appear desirable, but which are not of magnitude enough to claim a preliminary discussion. These will be seen in the plan which will be submitted in the sequel.

If the objections which have been stated to the constitution of the Bank of North America are admitted to be well founded, they will, nevertheless, not derogate from the merit of the main design, or of the services which that bank has rendered, or of the benefits which it has produced. The creation of such an institution, at the time it took place, was a measure dictated by wisdom. Its utility has been amply evinced by its fruits — American independence owes much to it. And it is very conceivable, that reasons of the moment may have rendered those features in it inexpedient, which a revision, with a permanent view, suggests as desirable.

The order of the subject leads next to an inquiry into the principles upon which a national bank ought to be organized.

The situation of the United States naturally inspires a wish that the form of the institution could admit of a plurality of branches. But various considerations discourage from pursuing this idea. The complexity of such a plan would be apt to inspire doubts, which might deter from adventuring in it. And the practicability of a safe and orderly administration, though not to be abandoned as desperate, cannot be made so manifest in perspective, as to promise the removal of those doubts, or to justify the government in adopting the idea as an original experiment. The most that would seem advisable, on this point, is, to insert a provision which may lead to it hereafter, if experience shall more clearly demonstrate its utility, and satisfy those who may have the direction that it may be adopted with safety. It is certain that it would have some advantages, both peculiar and important. Besides more general accommodation, it would lessen the danger of a run upon the bank.

The argument against it is, that each branch must be under a distinct, though subordinate direction, to which a considerable latitude of discretion must of necessity be intrusted. And as the property of the whole institution would be liable for the engagements of each part, that and its credit would be at stake upon the prudence of the directors of every part. The mismanagement of either branch might hazard serious disorder in the whole.

Another wish, dictated by the particular situation of the country, is, that the bank could be so constituted as to be made an immediate instrument of loans to the proprietors of land ; but this wish also yields to the difficulty of accomplishing it. Land is alone an unfit fund for a bank circulation. If the notes issued upon it were not to be payable in coin, on demand, or at a short date, this would amount to nothing more than a repetition of the paper emissions, which are now exploded by the general voice. If the notes are to be payable in coin, the land must first be converted into it by sale or mortgage. The difficulty of effecting the latter, is the very thing which begets the desire of finding another resource ; and the former would not be practicable on a sudden emergency, but with sacrifices which would make the cure worse than the disease. Neither is the idea of constituting the fund partly of coin and partly of land, free from impediments. These two species of property do not, for the most part, unite in the same hands. Will the moneyed man consent to enter into a partnership with the landholder, by which *the latter* will share in the profits *which will be made by the money of the former?* The money, it is evident, will be the agent or efficient cause of the profits; the land can only be regarded as an additional security. It is not difficult to foresee that a union, on such terms, will not readily be formed. If the landholders are to procure the money by sale or mortgage of a part of their lands, this they can as well do when the stock consists wholly of money, as if it were to be compounded of money and land.

To procure for the landholders the assistance of loans, is the great desideratum. Supposing other difficulties surmounted, and a fund created, composed partly of coin and partly of land, yet the benefit contemplated could only then be obtained by the bank's advancing them its notes for the whole, or part, of the value of the lands they had subscribed to the stock. If this advance was small, the relief aimed at would not be given; if it was large, the quantity of notes issued would be a cause of *distrust*, and, if received at all, they would be likely to return speedily upon the bank for payment; which, after exhausting its coin, might be under the necessity of turning its lands into money, at any price that could be obtained for them, to the irreparable prejudice of the proprietors.

Considerations of public advantage suggest a further wish, which is, that the bank could be established upon principles that would cause the profits of it to redound to the immediate benefit of the State. This is contemplated by many who speak of a national bank, but the idea seems liable to insuperable objections. To attach full confidence to an institution of this nature, it appears to be an essential ingredient in its structure that it shall be under a *private*, not a *public* direction; under the guidance of *individual interest*, not of *public policy*, which would be supposed to be, and, in certain emergencies, under a feeble or too sanguine administration, would really be, liable to being too much influenced by *public necessity.* The suspleion of this would most probably be a canker that would continually corrode the vitals of the credit of the bank, and would be most likely to prove fatal in those situations in which the public good would require that they should be most sound and vigorous. It would, indeed, be little less than a miracle, should the credit of the bank be at the disposal of the government, if, in a long series of time, there was not experienced a calamitous abuse of it. It is true, that it would be the real interest of the government not to abuse it; its genuine policy to husband and cherish it with the most guarded circumspection, as an inestimable treasure. But what government ever uniformly consulted its true interests in opposition to the temptations of momentary exigencies? What nation was ever blessed with a constant succession of upright and wise administrators?

The keen, steady, and, as it were, magnetic sense of their own interest as proprietors, in the directors of a bank, pointing invariably to its true pole, the prosperity of the institution, is the only security that can always be relied upon for a careful and prudent administration. It is, therefore, the only basis on which an enlightened, unqualified, and permanent confidence can be expected to be erected and maintained.

The precedents of the banks established in several cities of Europe, (Amsterdam, Hamburgh and others,) may seem to militate against this position. Without a precise knowledge of all the peculiarities of their respective constitutions, it is difficult to pronounce how far this may be the case. That of Amsterdam, however, which we best know, is rather under a municipal than a governmental direction. Particular magistrates of the city, not officers of the republic, have the management of it. It is also a bank of deposite, not of loan or circulation; consequently, less liable to abuse, as well as less useful. Its general business consists in receiving money for safe keeping, which, if not called for within a certain time, becomes a part of its stock, and irreclaimable; but a credit is given for it on the books of the bank, which being transferable, answers all the purposes of money.

The directors being magistrates of the city, and the stockholders, in general, its most influential citizens, it is evident that the principle of private interest must be prevalent in the management of the bank. And it is equally evident that, from the nature of its operations, that principle is less essential to it than to an institution constituted with a view to the accommodation of the public and individuals, by direct loans and a paper circulation.

As far as may concern the aid of the bank, within the proper limits, a good Government has nothing more to wish for than it will always possess, though the management be in the hands of private individuals. As the institution, if rightly constituted, must depend for its renovation, from time to time, on the pleasure of the Government, it will not be likely to feel a disposition to render itself, by its conduct, unworthy of public patronage. The Government, too, in the administration of its finances, has it in its power to reciprocate benefits to the bank, of not less importance than those which the bank affords to the Government, and which, besides, are never unattended with an immediate and adequate compensation. Independent of these more particular considerations, the natural weight and influence of a good Government will always go far towards procuring a compliance with its desires ; and as the directors will usually be composed of some of the most discreet, respectable, and well-informed citizens, it can hardly ever be difficult to make them sensible of the force of the inducements which ought to stimulate their exertions.

It will not follow, from what has been said, that the State may not be the holder of a part of the stock of a bank, and, consequently, a sharer in the profits of it. It will only follow that it ought not to desire any participation in the direction of it, therefore, ought not to own the whole, or a principal part of the stock ; for, if the mass of the property should belong to the public, and if the direction of it should be in private hands, this would be to commit the interests of the State to persons not interested, or not enough interested in their proper management.

There is one thing, however, which the Government owes to itself and the community — at least to all that part of it who are not stockholders — which is, to reserve to itself a right of ascertaining, as often as may be necessary, the state of the bank ; excluding, however, all pretension to control. This right forms an article in the primitive constitution of the bank of North America; and its propriety stands upon the clearest reasons. If the paper of a bank is to be permitted to insinuate itself into all the revenues and receipts of a country ; if it is even to be tolerated as the substitute for gold and silver in all the transactions of business, it becomes, in either view, a national concern of the first magnitude. As such, the ordinary rules of prudence require that the Government should possess the means of ascertaining, whenever it thinks fit, that so delicate a trust is executed with fidelity and care. A right of this nature is not only desirable, as it respects the Government, but it ought to be equally so to all those concerned in the institution, as an additional title to public and private confidence, and as a thing which can only be formidable to practices that imply mismanagement. The presumption must always be, that the characters who would be intrusted with the exercise of this right on behalf of the Government, will not be deficient in the discretion which it may require ; at least, the admitting of this presumption cannot be deemed too great a return of confidence for that very large portion of it which the Government is required to place in the bank.

Abandoning, therefore, ideas which, however agreeable or desirable, are neither practicable nor safe, the following plan, for the constitution of a national bank, is respectfully submitted to the consideration of the house.

1. The capital stock of the bank shall not exceed ten millions of dollars, divided into twenty-five thousand shares, each share being four hundred dollars; to raise which sum subscriptions shall be opened on the first Monday of April next, and shall continue open until the whole shall be subscribed. Bodies politic as well as individuals may subscribe.

2. The amount of each share shall be payable, one fourth in gold and silver coin, and three fourths in that part of the public debt which, according to the loan proposed by the act making provision for the debt of the United States, shall bear an accruing interest at the time of payment of six per centum per annum.

3. The respective sums subscribed shall be payable in four equal parts, as well specie as debt, in succession, and at the distance of six calendar months from each other; the first payment to be made at the time of subscription. If there shall be a failure in any subsequent payment, the party failing shall lose the benefit of any dividend which may have accrued prior to the time for making such payment, and during the delay of the same.

4. The subscribers to the bank, and their successors, shall be incorporated, and shall so continue until the final redemption of that part of its stock which shall consist of the public debt.

5. The capacity of the corporation to hold real and personal estate shall be limited to fifteen million of dollars, including the amount of its capital or original stock. The lands and tenements which it shall be permitted to hold, shall be only such as shall be requisite for the immediate accommodation of the institution; and such as shall have been bona fide mortgaged to it by way of security, or conveyed to it in satisfaction of debts previously contracted, in the usual course of its dealings, or purchased at sales upon judgments which shall have been obtained for such debts.

6. The totality of the debts of the company, whether by bond, bill, note, or other contract, (credits for deposits excepted,) shall never exceed the amount of its capital stock. In case of excess, the directors, under whose administration it shall happen, shall be liable for it in their private or separate capacities. Those who may have dissented may excuse themselves from this responsibility by immediately giving notice of the fact and their dissent to the President of the United

States, and to the stockholders, at a general meeting, to be called by the president of the bank, at their request.

7. The Company may sell or demise its lands and tenements, or may sell the whole or any part of the public debt, whereof its stock shall consist; but shall *trade* in nothing, except bills of exchange, gold and silver bullion, or in the sale of goods pledged for money lent; nor shall take more than at the rate of six per centum per annum, upon its loans or discounts.

8. No loans shall be made by the bank for the use or on account of the government of the United States, or of either of them, to an amount exceeding fifty thousand dollars, or of any foreign prince or state, unless previously authorized by a law of the United States.

9. The stock of the bank shall be transferable, according to such rules as shall be instituted by the company in that behalf.

10. The affairs of the bank shall be under the management of twenty-five directors, one of whom shall be the president; and there shall be, on the first Monday in January, in each year, a choice of directors, by a plurality of suffrages of the stockholders, to serve for a year. The directors, at their first meeting after each election, shall choose one of their number as president.

11. The number of votes to which each stockholder shall be entitled shall be according to the number of shares he shall hold, in the proportions following — that is to say: For one share, and not more than two shares, one vote; for every two shares above two, and not exceeding ten, one vote; for every four shares above ten, and not exceeding thirty, one vote; for every six shares above thirty, and not exceeding sixty, one vote; for every eight shares above sixty and not exceeding one hundred, one vote; and for every ten shares above one hundred, one vote; but no person, copartnership, or body politic, shall be entitled to a greater number than thirty votes. And, after the first election, no share or shares shall confer a right of suffrage, which shall not have been holden three calendar months previous to the day of election. Stockholders actually resident within the United States, and none other, may vote in elections by proxy.

12. Not more than three fourths of the directors in office, exclusive of the president, shall be eligible for the next succeeding year. But the director who shall be president at the time of an election, may be always re-elected.

13. None but a stockholder, being a citizen of the United States shall be eligible as a director.

14. Any number of stockholders not less than sixty, who together shall be proprietors of two hundred shares or upwards, shall have power at any time to call a general meeting of the stockholders, for purposes relative to the institution; giving at least six weeks' notice in two public gazettes of the place where the bank is kept, and specifying in such notice the object of the meeting.

15. In case of the death, resignation, absence from the United States, or removal of a director by the stockholders, his place may be filled by a new choice for the remainder of the year.

16. No director shall be entitled to any emolument, unless the same shall have been allowed by the stockholders at a general meeting. The stockholders shall make such compensation to the president, for his extraordinary attendance at the bank, as shall appear to them reasonable.

17. Not less than seven directors shall constitute a board for the transaction of business.

18. Every cashier or treasurer, before he enters on the duties of his office, shall be required to give bond, with two or more sureties, to the satisfaction of the directors, in a sum not less than twenty thousand dollars, with conditions for his good behavior.

19. Half yearly dividends shall be made of so much of the profits of the bank, as shall appear to the directors advisable. And once in every three years, the directors shall lay before the stockholders, at a general meeting, for their information, an exact and particular statement of the debts which shall have remained unpaid, after the expiration of the original credit, for a period of treble the term of that credit, and of the surplus of profit, if any, after deducting losses and dividends.

20. The bills and notes of the bank originally made payable, or which shall have become payable on demand in gold and silver coin, shall be receivable in all payments to the United States.

21. The officer at the head of the treasury department of the United States shall be furnished, from time to time, as often as he may require, not exceeding once a week, with statements of the amount of the capital stock of the bank, and of the debts due to the same, of the moneys deposited therein, of the notes in circulation, and of the cash in hand; and shall have a right to inspect such general accounts in the books of the bank as shall relate to the said statements; provided that this shall not be construed to imply a right of inspecting the account of any private individual or individuals with the bank.

22. No similar institution shall be established by any future act of the United States, during the continuance of the one hereby proposed to be established.

23. It shall be lawful for the directors of the bank to establish offices wheresoever they shall think fit, within the United States, for the purpose of discount and deposit only, and upon the same terms, and in the same manner, as shall be practiced at the bank, and to commit the management of the said offices, and the making of the said discounts, either to agents specially appointed by them, or to such persons as may be chosen by the stockholders residing at the place where any such office shall be, under such agreements, and subject to such regulations, as they shall deem proper, not being contrary to law, or to the constitution of the bank.

24. And, lastly, The President of the United States shall be authorized to cause a subscription to be made to the stock of the said company, on behalf of the United States, to an amount not exceeding two millions of dollars, to be paid out of the moneys which shall be borrowed by virtue of either of the acts, the one entitled " An Act making provision for the debt of the United States," and the other, entitled " An Act making provision for the reduction of the public debt," borrowing of the bank an equal sum, to be applied to the purposes for which the said moneys shall have been procured, reimbursable in ten years by equal annual instalments ; or at any time sooner, or in any greater proportions, that the Government may think fit.

The reasons for the several provisions, contained in the foregoing plan, have been so far anticipated, and will for the most part be so readily suggested by the nature of those provisions, that any comments which need further be made will be both few and concise.

The combination of a portion of the public debt, in the formation of the capital, is the principal thing of which an explanation is requisite. The chief object of this is to enable the creation of a capital sufficiently large to be the basis of an extensive circulation, and an adequate security for it. As has been elsewhere remarked, the original plan of the Bank of North America contemplated a capital of ten millions of dollars which is certainly not too broad a foundation for the extensive operations to which a national bank is destined. But to collect such a sum in this country in gold and silver into one depository, may, without hesitation, be pronounced impracticable. Hence the necessity of an auxiliary, which the public debt at once presents.

This part of the fund will be always ready to come in aid of the specie; it will more and more command a ready sale, and can therefore expeditiously be turned into coin, if an exigency of the bank should at any time require it. This quality of prompt convertibility into coin renders it an equivalent for the necessary agent of bank circulation, and distinguishes it from a fund in land, of which the sale would generally be far less compendious, and at great disadvantage. The quarter-yearly receipts of interest will also be an actual addition to the specie fund, during the intervals between them and the half-yearly dividends of profits. The objection to combining land with specie, resulting from their not being generally in possession of the same persons, does not apply to the debt, which will always be found in considerable quantity among the moneyed and trading people.

The debt composing part of the capital, besides its collateral effect in enabling the bank to extend its operations, and consequently to enlarge its profits, will produce a direct annual revenue of six per centum from the Government, which will enter into the half-yearly dividends received by the stockholders.

When the present price of the public debt is considered, and the effect which its conversion into bank stock, incorporated with a specie fund, would in all probability have to accelerate its rise to the proper point, it will easily be discovered that the operation presents, in its outset, a very considerable advantage to those who may become subscribers; and from the influence which that rise would have on the general mass of the debt, a proportional benefit to all the public creditors, and, in a sense which has been more than once adverted to, to the community at large.

There is an important fact which exemplifies the fitness of the public debt for a bank fund, and which may serve to remove doubts in some minds on this point: it is this, that the Bank of England, in its first erection, rested wholly on that foundation. The subscribers to a loan to government of one million two hundred thousand pounds sterling, were incorporated as a bank, of which the debt created by the loan, and the interest upon it, were the sole fund. The subsequent augmentations of its capital, which now amounts to between eleven and twelve millions of pounds sterling, have been of the same nature.

The confining of the right of the bank to contract debts to the amount of its capital, is an important precaution, which is not to be found in the constitution of the Bank of North America, and which, while the fund consists wholly of coin, would be a restriction attended with inconveniences; but would be free from any, if the composition of it should be such as is now proposed. The restriction exists in the establishment of the Bank of England, and, as a source of security, is worthy of imitation. The consequence of exceeding the limit there, is, that each stockholder is liable for the excess, in proportion to his interest in the bank. When it is considered that the directors owe their appointment to the choice of the stockholders, a responsibility of this kind on the part of the latter does not appear unreasonable ; but, on the other hand, it may be deemed a hardship upon those who may have dissented from the choice ; and there are many among us, whom it might perhaps discourage from becoming concerned in the institution. These reasons have induced the placing of the responsibility upon the directors by whom the limit prescribed should be transgressed.

The interdiction of loans on account of the United States, or of any particular State, beyond the moderate sum specified, or of any foreign power, will serve as a barrier to executive encroachments, and to combinations inauspicious to the safety, or contrary to the policy of the Union.

The limitation of the rate of interest is dictated by the consideration, that different rates prevail in different parts of the Union; and as the operations of the bank may extend through the whole, some rule seems to be necessary. There is room for a question, whether the limitation ought not rather to be five than six per cent., as proposed. It may with safety be taken for granted, that the former rate would yield an ample dividend, perhaps as much as the latter, by the extension which it would give to business. The natural effect of low interest is to increase trade and industry ; because undertakings of every kind can be prosecuted with greater advantage. This is a truth generally admitted ; but it is requisite to have analyzed the subject in all its relations, to be able to form a just conception of the extent of that effect. Such an analysis cannot but satisfy an intelligent mind, that the difference of one per cent. in the rate at which money may be had, is often capable of making an essential change for the better in the situation of any country or place.

Everything, therefore, which tends to lower the rate of interest, is peculiarly worthy of the cares of legislators. And though laws which violently sink the legal rate of interest greatly below the market level are not to be commended, because they are not calculated to answer their aim ; yet whatever has a tendency to effect a reduction, without violence to the natural course of things, ought to be attended to and pur-

sued.   Banks are among the means most proper to accomplish
this end ; and the moderation of the rate at which their discounts are made, is a material ingredient towards it ; with
which their own interest, viewed on an enlarged and permanent
scale, does not appear to clash.

But, as the most obvious ideas are apt to have greater force
than those which depend on complex and remote combinations,
there would be danger that the persons whose funds must
constitute the stock of the bank, would be diffident of the
sufficiency of the profits to be expected, if the rate of loans and
discounts were to be placed below the point to which they have
been accustomed ; and might, on this account, be indisposed
to embarking in the plan.   There is, it is true, one reflection,
which, in regard to men actually engaged in trade, ought to be
a security against this danger ; it is this — that the accommodations which they might derive in the way of their business, at a
low rate, would more than indemnify them for any difference in
the dividend; supposing even that some diminution of it were
to be the consequence.   But, upon the whole, the hazard of
contrary reasoning among the mass of moneyed men is a
powerful argument against the experiment.   The institutions of
the kind already existing add to the difficulty of making it.
Mature reflection, and a large capital, may, of themselves, lead
to the desired end.

The last thing which requires any explanatory remark is,
the authority proposed to be given to the President to subscribe to the amount of two millions of dollars on account of
the public.   The main design of this is to enlarge the specie
fund of the bank, and to enable it to give a more early extension to its operations.   Though it is proposed to borrow with
one hand what is lent with the other, yet the disbursement of
what is borrowed will be progressive, and bank notes may be
thrown into circulation instead of the gold and silver.   Besides,
there is to be an annual reimbursement of a part of the sum
borrowed, which will finally operate as an actual investment
of so much specie.   In addition to the inducements to this
measure, which result from the general interest of the Government to enlarge the sphere of the utility of the bank, there is
this more particular consideration, to wit : that, as far as the
dividend on the stock shall exceed the interest paid on the loan,
there is a positive profit.

The Secretary begs leave to conclude with this general observation : that if the Bank of North America shall come forward
with any propositions which have for their object the ingrafting
upon that institution the characteristics which shall appear to

the legislature necessary to the due extent and safety of a national bank, there are, in his judgment, weighty inducements to giving every reasonable facility to the measure. Not only the pretensions of that institution, from its original relation to the Government of the United States, and from the services it has rendered, are such as to claim a disposition favorable to it, if those who are interested in it are willing, on their part, to place it on a footing satisfactory to the Government, and equal to the purposes of a Bank of the United States, but its co-operation would materially accelerate the accomplishment of the great object ; and the collision, which might otherwise arise, might, in a variety of ways, prove equally disagreeable and injurious. The incorporation or union here contemplated may be effected in different modes, under the auspices of an act of the United States, if it shall be desired by the Bank of North America, upon terms which shall appear expedient to the Government.

All which is humbly submitted.

ALEXANDER HAMILTON,
Secretary of the Treasury.

TREASURY DEPARTMENT,
December 13, 1790.

INDEX

The Citizen's Library of Economics, Politics, and Sociology

Colonial Government. By Paul S. Reinsch, Ph.D., LL.B., Assistant Professor of Political Science in the University of Wisconsin. Cloth, 12mo. *Now ready.* $1.25 net.

The main divisions of the book are as follows: 1. The Extant and Component Parts of Existing Colonial Empires. 2. Motives and Methods of Colonization. 3. Forms of Colonial Government. 4. Relations between the Mother Country and the Colonies. 5. Internal Government of the Colonies. 6. The Ethical Element in Colonial Politics. 7. The Special Colonial Problems of the United States.

Democracy and Social Ethics. By Jane Addams, head of "Hull House," Chicago; joint author of "Philanthropy and Social Progress." Cloth, 12mo. *Now ready.* $1.25 net.

Miss Addams's work as head of "Hull House" is known to all persons who are interested in social amelioration, and her writings in the best periodical literature have produced the impression that they proceed from a personality equally strong and gracious. This work will show the profound insight into social conditions and the practical wisdom which we all expect from Miss Addams. As the title implies, it will be occupied with the reciprocal relations of ethical progress and the growth of democratic thought, sentiment, and institutions.

Municipal Engineering and Sanitation. By M. N. Baker, Ph.B., Associate Editor of *Engineering News;* Editor of *A Manual of American Water Works.* Cloth, 12mo. $1.25 net.

[*Now ready.*]

This work will discuss in a general introduction the city and its needs, and the plan of the city, and then pass on to such practical questions as ways and means of communication, municipal supplies, collection and disposal of wastes, recreation and art, administration, finance, and public policy. Mr. Baker's work on the *Engineering News* and the annual *Manual of American Water Works* has made him known as one of the leading authorities on all questions of municipal policy. He has the important advantage of combining the technical knowledge of the engineer with long familiarity with economic discussions; and it is expected that this volume will appeal to all classes in any way concerned in municipal affairs.

American Municipal Progress. By Charles Zueblin, B.D., Associate Professor of Sociology in the University of Chicago. Cloth, 12mo. *Now ready.* $1.25 net.

Professor Zueblin is well known as one of the most successful University extension lecturers of the country, and his favorite theme in recent years has been municipal progress. In the preparation of this work, he has repeatedly conducted personal investigations into the social life of the leading cities of Europe, especially England, and the United States. This work combines thoroughness with a popular and pleasing style. It takes up the problem of the so-called public utilities, public schools, libraries, children's playgrounds, public baths, public gymnasiums, etc. All these questions are discussed from the standpoint of public welfare.

Irrigation Institutions : A Discussion of the Economic and Legal Questions created by the Growth of Irrigated Agriculture in the West. By Elwood Mead, C.E., M.S., Chief of Irrigation Investigations, Department of Agriculture; Professor of Institutions and Practice of Irrigation in the University of California, and Special Lecturer on Irrigation Engineering in Harvard University. Cloth, 12mo. $1.25, *net. Ready.*

This book is based on twenty years' experience in the development of irrigated agriculture in the arid West. This experience brought the author in contact with farmers, ditch builders, investors in irrigation securities, legislatures and jurists, who were shaping the legal principles which are to control the distribution and use of Western water supplies, and the social and economic fabric under which unnumbered millions of people must dwell. All phases of the subject have been dealt with. Irrigation laws are so ambiguous or contradictory that their meaning is not easy to interpret, and the water rights which govern the value of farms have many forms and are acquired by many methods.

THE MACMILLAN COMPANY
66 FIFTH AVENUE, NEW YORK